MW00807647

# The New Orleans of Fiction

*A Resource Guide*

James A. Kaser

ROWMAN & LITTLEFIELD
*Lanham • Boulder • New York • London*

Published by Rowman & Littlefield
A wholly owned subsidary of The Rowman & Littlefield Publishing Group, Inc.
4501 Forbes Boulevard, Suite 200, Lanham, Maryland 20706
www.rowman.com

16 Carlisle Street, London W1D 3 BT, United Kingdom

British Library Cataloguing in Publication Information Available

**Library of Congress Cataloging-in-Publication Data**
Kaser, James A., 1960–
   The New Orleans of fiction : a resource guide / James A. Kaser.
      pages cm.
   Includes bibliographical references and index.
   ISBN 978-0-8108-9199-9 (cloth : alk. paper) – ISBN 978-0-8108-9204-0 (ebook)  1.
New Orleans (La.)–In literature–Bio-bibliography. 2.  American fiction–20th century–
Bio-bibliography. 3.  American fiction–19th century–Bio-bibliography 4.  Authors,
American–20th century–Biography–Dictionaries. 5.  Authors, American–19th century–
Biography–Dictionaries.  I. Title.
   Z1290.N4K37 2014
   [PS374.N427]
   016.813009'35876335–dc23
   [B]                                         2014016036

⊖™ The paper used in this publication meets the minimum requirements of American
National Standard for Information Sciences—Permanence of Paper for Printed Library
Materials, ANSI/NISO Z39.48-1992.

Printed in the United States of America

To friends and family who were patient over the years as I engaged in solitary research, often excluding their company.

# Contents

# Preface

Prior to the 1980s, catalogers rarely gave subject designations for works of fiction. Not until 2000 did the American Library Association issue cataloging guidelines for including geographic descriptors. So, although bibliographic databases are available to scholars, these tools are of little use in locating works of fiction set in New Orleans published before the 1970s. This book guides scholars to novels and short story collections with New Orleans settings, provides extensive annotations for works published before 1981, and was created by consulting libraries with collections of New Orleans fiction, as well as online and published bibliographies that offered a subject approach to fiction.

# Acknowledgments

Research for this work was funded in part by grants from the Professional Staff Congress of the City University of New York. Further support was obtained from the College of Staten Island/CUNY in the form of reassignment leave used for extended periods of research.

I am also grateful for the encouragement and assistance I received from a number of people. The enthusiasm and advice of my department chair, Prof. Wilma Jones, Chief Librarian, College of Staten Island, kept me focused and productive over years of research and writing. Sally Milner's skilled proofreading aided me in seeing that to which I was blinded by authorial propinquity. My research assistants, including Roman Yevchenko and, most notably, Jeffrey Coogan, diligently tracked down bibliographical and biographical citations. Finally, I thank the libraries and librarians without which my research would not have been possible: The Louisiana Research Collection at the Howard-Tilton Memorial Library of Tulane University, particularly public services librarian, Sean Benjamin; the Louisiana and Lower Mississippi Valley Collection of the Louisiana State University Libraries; The Williams Research Center of The Historic New Orleans Collection; The Louisiana Division of the New Orleans Public Library, especially Head, Irene Wainwright; The Library of Congress; and The Library of the College of Staten Island, particularly the interlibrary loan office.

# Introduction

This book includes works of fiction set in New Orleans; specifically, novels and collections of short stories eighty pages or more in length written for juveniles and adults (dramatic works are not included). Only short story collections whose works are wholly or mostly set in New Orleans are included. Detailed annotations are provided for works dating from 1828 through 1980; bibliographic information for works dating from 1981 through 2013 is included in an appendix. While attempting to be as inclusive as possible, some works have been excluded. Such books might have only a few pages, or even a chapter, or more, set in New Orleans, but few references to the city. On the other hand, works that are mostly or wholly set in the city, but have little overt New Orleans content, are included. Furthermore, works that have as little as a chapter set in New Orleans were sometimes included if the use of the city was significant. In these works, New Orleans usually has a strong symbolic role throughout the book. For instance, through the majority of a book a man might live on a plantation but consider New Orleans the focus of his business and social life. Although, as a reader, I was fascinated by what the novels revealed about changing understandings of New Orleans and what the city symbolizes, my role in this book is to identify the materials that future researchers will use to analyze the novels and their interrelationships.

Although the supplemental material and extent of the annotations in the current work distinguish it from all other efforts, I take this opportunity to acknowledge earlier bibliographies and lists that include New Orleans fiction. Most such works are usually more broadly focused on Louisiana and do not distinguish between authors using Louisiana as a setting or merely residing in the state. One example is Thomas Payne Thompson's *Louisiana Writers Native and Resident, Including Others Whose Books Belong to a Bibliography of that State, to Which Is Added a List of Artists*. (New Orleans: Louisiana State Commission, 1904) published for the Louisiana Purchase Exposition. Other, more recent works, such as Barbara C. Ewell's essay "Louisiana Literature" (*KnowLA Encyclopedia of Louisiana*, Louisiana Endowment for the Humanities, http://www.knowla.org/ category/6/Literature/&view=overview /, accessed 24 March 2014) provide a descriptive overview and do not attempt a comprehensive bibliography.

The most comprehensive previously published bibliography is Charles B Wordell's two-part article in the *Louisiana Library Bulletin* (Charles B. Wordell, "Tales of the Town of Dreamy Dreams. A Bibliography of Fiction Set in New Orleans," Part I, Louisiana Library Association Bulletin, vol. 61, no. 1, 1998, 16-32; Part II, Louisiana Library Association Bulletin, vol. 61, no. 2, 1998, 72-90. Wordell makes a siginificant contribution, but does not include annotations and some of the books he included did not meet my criteria.

Because of the obscurity of so many authors of pre-1980s books, biographical information is provided in a section that also serves as an author index. The reader who wishes to browse this section will discover the wide range of people who were motivated to write about New Orleans, including journalists, politicians, society women, and freelance writers of genre fiction. As in any group of people randomly gathered, there are also some remarkable lives worthy of further exploration.

The decision not to annotate works published after 1980 responds to book cataloging and marketing phenomena. As library catalogs became electronic and publishers began providing information electronically, more summary content about fiction, including geographic designators, became easily available and was incorporated into catalog records. More recently as catalogs have become Web based, images of book jackets, jacket text, and review excerpts can be found in catalogs. This cataloging trend is one factor that led to the creation of an official geographic descriptor for fiction works in cataloging rules published in 2000. In addition, internet-based book marketers provide researchers the opportunity of keyword searching an extensive bibliographic database and increasingly provide the option of full-text searching for phrases or words (such as New Orleans). In such an environment, researchers have many ways of identifying recent New Orleans fiction and reviewing abstracts of book contents.

Appendix A provides a bibliography of works published from 1980 through 2013; Appendix B presents citations for the pre-1980s fiction in a chronological arrangement so that themes common to a specific era can be easily discovered.

Readers are cautioned that I have often used culturally sensitive words in the same manner as the authors whose works I annotated. While I frequently point out ethnocentrism and racism, I have also relied upon readers to understand the cultural and historical limitations of some authors when applying terms such as, "Acadian," "Cajun," "Creole," and any number of designations in talking about race.

# Annotated Bibliography, 1828–1980

1. Abaunza, Virginia. *Sundays from Two to Six*. Indianapolis: Bobbs-Merrill, 1956. 222pp.

Although this domestic novel's household is in New Orleans, the book has few direct references to the city. Sixteen-year-old Clotilde "Cody" Benson chronicles family life in the months after her mother and father decide to divorce. Cody's brothers, nine-year-old Peter and seven-year-old Francis "Pancho" (sic) Benson, dominate the household that includes, in addition to Mrs. Benson, a maid/cook named Martha. The children play elaborate games and keep everyone alert with pranks that sometimes go awry. Amongst her siblings, Cody has the most difficult time adjusting to the divorce, even though the millionaire parents of her friend Jane Colt divorced and were not stigmatized by Cody's upper-class circle. By the end of the novel Cody realizes that the loss of social status was not her main concern, but the unassailable feeling of paternal rejection. Once she sees the divorce from her parents' viewpoint, she is able to appreciate how important it is for them to be able to choose new, happier lives. In the final chapter, the Benson house has been sold and Cody and her brothers are headed to separate boarding schools, but anticipate reunions in their mother's new apartment. Cody's life revolves around family and school girlfriends. She presents extended descriptions of her grandmothers, contrasting the values of her maternal, farm-dwelling grandmother who focuses on cooking and baking for family and neighbors, and her paternal grandmother for whom urban society life is a priority and keeps her in constant motion from one social event to another. Cody does step outside her family circle once in the novel when she has her first dinner date at the Blue Room of the Roosevelt Hotel. The novel includes many descriptions of social situations and households that convey a sense of 1950s upper-class family life.

2. Ackland, William Hayes. *Sterope: The Veiled Pleiad*. Washington, D.C.: Gibson Brothers, 1892. 300pp.

At the center of this antebellum novel is the human toll of the De Bienville family's fervid attachment to Cypresmort Plantation. The current owner, Marigny De Bienville, although possessing wealth and social prominence, inherited a heavily mortgaged Cypresmort. His second marriage to Anna Adair, his daughter Helene's Ursuline Convent school friend, enabled him to pay off most of the debts with her inheritance. However, Anna was never fully accepted by the extended Bienville family since she was the granddaughter of James Adair, a "Kaintuck" (Kentuckian) who accumulated his fortune by operating a Mississippi freight barge. Orphaned early in life and raised by nuns, Anna is a devout Roman Catholic whose spiritual life insulates her from social slights. When she dies in childbirth her own daughter gets a very different upbringing. Delivered by an astronomer who frequents the Bienville household, Anna Tranchepain De Bienville is known from infancy as Sterope because she was born with a veil of tissue over her face, a phenomenon that reminded the astronomer of the star "Sterope" in the Pleiades constellation noted for nebulae of cosmic debris. Sterope De Bienville is primarily raised in the New Orleans household of Anna's childhood friend and sister-in-law, Helene (née De Bienville) Detrelan, the wife of a wealthy banker and commission merchant. Although Sterope attends Ursuline Convent and exhibits rare intellectual gifts, Marigny has destined her to become the belle of Cypresmort Plantation. Her Aunt Helene is most concerned about Sterope's social advancement and fills her days with dancing school and evenings with social events. By the time Sterope graduates, Marigny has gone into debt rejuvenating Cypresmort with a view toward Sterope reigning from there as a society belle.

Helene hosts Sterope's debutante season at her mansion on New Orleans' Esplanade Street and immediately afterwards Marigny takes Sterope to Saratoga Springs, New York, to escape a yellow fever epidemic. Although she continues to socialize with fellow Southerners sojourning in the North, she also is in the company of Northerners and hears abolitionists for the first time; her family and friends refer to them as "negropholists." In fact she falls in love with a negropholist, Ernest Wright, an impoverished artist whose father's abolitionist views ruined his business in New Orleans. When Sterope returns to the South she is pursued by Wright, and also by Robert Macomb, a calculating adventurer with his eye on Cypresmort Plantation. During the New Orleans social season, Désiré Boisbriant, a distant cousin, joins Wright and Macomb in jockeying for Sterope's favor. Marigny had already rejected Boisbriant as a suitor on the grounds of improvidence. Macomb endears himself to Marigny through skillful intrigue, and even though he has no money, convinces the debtor that he is wealthy. Knowing his own suit is lost, Boisbriant witnesses the love between Sterope and Wright and becomes the artist's advocate, finding portrait commissions for him in New Orleans. When Boisbriant discovers that Macomb has mistreated young women in the past he informs a disbelieving Marigny, and later pleads with Marigny to let his creditors seize Cypresmort to free Sterope from Macomb's designs. As Marigny and Helene begin to pursue a wedding contract with Macomb, Boisbriant duels Macomb, and is mortally wounded in an underhanded way. The desperate Wright and Sterope elope, but they perish when the Bienville family slave Ptolemy, whose daughter had been unfairly punished by Marigny, destroys their steamboat just offshore in an act of arson. The action of the latter half of the novel is set against a New Orleans social season involving balls, the opera, and frequent visits to the Orleans Club and the St. Charles Hotel. Throughout the novel slaves, slavery, and race are openly discussed with the conclusion that true African slaves are appropriately slaves, but mixed-race people like Ptolemy are monsters of nature and a corrupting influence on the institution of slavery.

3. Algren, Nelson. *A Walk on the Wild Side.* New York: Farrar, Straus, and Cudahy, 1956. 346pp.
    The street-life and places frequented by the disenfranchised in Depression-era New Orleans form the backdrop for this novel. Protagonist Dove Linkhorn grew up in the single-parent household of his father Fitz in an oil region near the Rio Grande in Arroyo, Texas. By the time he was sixteen he had endured several years of Dust Bowl conditions and a lifetime of poverty, silently witnessing the incessant wrangling of his father, a self-proclaimed Christian prophet, and Dove's older brother Byron, ill with tuberculosis that Fitz credits to God's vengeance for his addiction to marijuana. Dove begins a relationship with thirty-year-old Terasina Vidavirri, a Mexican woman who operates a Tex-Mex diner out of an abandoned hotel. He successfully attracts Vidavirri by working odd jobs at the diner and seduces the socially isolated woman. Later, when she rejects Linkhorn's advances due to their age difference, he becomes enraged and rapes her. He flees into a hobo life he had learned about by talking to the drifters who passed through Arroyo and after several adventures, one again involving force against a woman, arrives in New Orleans in 1931. After quickly running through stolen money on visits to brothels, Linkhorn allies himself to Luther "Fort" Myers and a young accomplice, helping them work door-to-door scams and living with them in a single room near the intersection of Canal and Tchoupitoulas Streets. Myers lost a fortune earned as a Florida real estate man and although he generates ideas for various flimflams his bitterness over his losses at times incapacitates him. As time passes, Linkhorn gets involved with Oliver Finnerty, a pimp famous for transporting his girls to brothels around Louisiana in his own single-prop plane. Through Finnerty, Linkhorn also works for a scandalous ex-gynecologist, appropriately named Gross, who performs abortions and supervises a sweatshop condom-making operation in his residence. Linkhorn finally establishes some financial security for himself by working for Finnerty in a sex show in a Perdido Street brothel, but soon is in prison for violating Prohibition. After his release in 1932, he returns to Perdido Street and is blinded and beaten almost to death by a double-amputee who had lost his wife in part to Linkhorn's womanizing. Linkhorn returns to Arroyo to find Vidavirri, assuming that she will take him in. At several points in

the novel, Algren summarizes the life trajectories of people who have ended up in squalid circumstances in New Orleans. He does this for the prostitutes of Perdido Street, the patrons of a bar, and Linkhorn's prison cellmates. Such encapsulations of human misery, added to his vignettes of daily life on New Orleans streets, convincingly portray what the city was like during the Depression. Although racism is not a major theme in the novel, Algren depicts the great divide that separates races in the city, perpetuated by whites for economic and social reasons and by blacks out of self-preservation.

4. Allen, Hervey. *Anthony Adverse*. New York: Farrar and Rinehart, 1933. 1224pp.

Adverse, the adventurous and entrepreneurial sea-faring merchant, travels to France, Italy, Cuba, Argentine, England and Spain through the course of this novel set in the late eighteenth and early nineteenth centuries, before arriving in New Orleans in 1802. As the principal partner in an international banking house, Adverse settles in the city after realizing the settlement's potential to be a worldwide port. Over the ten years he is in New Orleans he dramatically increases his wealth, establishes a residence, marries and has children. The narrative details business and political conditions in the rapidly growing town and presents a number of historical personages, including Edward Livingston (1764–1836) and Governor Claiborne (c.1772/75–1817). The novel emphasizes the diverse culture of New Orleans, as well as the port's commercial significance.

5. Altsheler, Joseph A(lexander). *The Free Rangers: A Story of Early Days Along the Mississippi*. New York: Appleton, 1909. 364pp.

When five young men on the Kentucky frontier learn of Spanish nobleman Don Francisco Alvarez's plot to wrest control of the Louisiana Territory from Governor Bernardo Galvez, they set out to warn Galvez. The Kentuckians, Henry Ware, Tom Ross, Jim Hart, Paul Cotter, and "Shif'less Sol," know that Alvarez plans to set Indian tribes upon the Kentucky settlements, supplemented by Spanish troops under his control. Although their primary goal is to avoid bloodshed and forestall Alvarez's designs on the Mississippi River, they are also concerned that after Alvarez is in control he will ally himself with the British in the American Revolution. Soon after beginning their trip the quintet realizes Alvarez is in pursuit and his men later capture and imprison them. However, they escape, and on a stolen boat, arrive in New Orleans a short time before Alvarez. They are fortunate in almost immediately befriending merchant Oliver Pollock. Pollock realizes how economically disastrous Spanish control of the river would be for the American cause. They also find an ally in one of the governor's lieutenants, Diego Bernal. When the governor must imprison the Kentuckians as boat thieves and is unable to accept the accusations against Alvarez without hard evidence, Pollock and Bernal work clandestinely and help the boys to obtain damning evidence against Alvarez. Approximately eighty pages of the novel are set in New Orleans (pp. 230–311); the narrative conveys a sense of the multi-cultural nature of the city while making clear the strength of control the Spanish had on the city and surrounding territory.

6. Altsheler, Joseph A(lexander). *A Herald of the West: An American Story of 1811–1815*. New York: D. Appleton, 1898. 359pp.

Philip Ten Broeck is a Kentuckian whose father fought in the Continental Army during the Revolution and against the Indians in the Northwest Territory at the famous battles of Blue Licks and Fallen Timbers. Ten Broeck is in Washington working as a clerk for Albert Gallatin, secretary of the Treasury, and living in one of the Six Buildings in Georgetown. He is in love with Marian, daughter of Cyrus Pendleton, a major Kentucky landholder, whose ideas of American aristocracy prevent him from seeing Ten Broeck as an appropriate suitor. Philip's cousin, Gilbert Northcote, whose family remained loyal to Britain during the Revolution, is also in town. By contrasting the viewpoints of Philip with those of his cousin and acquaintances in Washington, Altsheler articulates many perspectives on the future direction of the United States. Philip sees himself and other Westerners as new beings with distinctive accents, manners, clothing, and physiques. A number of people in Washington still ape European fashions and customs, and, for some of these, like North-cote, the unfinished Federal City is clear evidence of why the United States should reunite with Britain. To Philip, the city's incompleteness and discomforts are temporary inconveniences in a place that will soon be notable. After he turns evidence over to Gallatin that his cousin Gilbert is a British spy, Gallatin commissions him to travel to Philadelphia, Boston, and New York to assess public opinion concerning the seemingly inevitable war with Britain. This provides Altsheler with a chance to describe travel and conditions in East Coast cities in 1811 and, through his adventures, presents examples of dueling, impressments, and the British Blockade. When he returns to Washington, he fights in the Battle of Bladensburg and witnesses the burning of the Capitol. In the last sixty pages of the novel Ten Broeck fights in the Battle of New Orleans. For the last time he confronts his cousin Major Northcote, who imprisons him for being a spy since he appears behind British lines in civilian clothing. However, Northcote relents and allows Philip to escape the night before he is to face a firing squad. Ten Broeck describes New Orleans as the most distinctive American city, both for its architecture and lively populace, composed of excitable Latin peoples (Spanish, French, and amalgamations). On the lines during the decisive battle, he sees the bravest British regiments flee from the deadly accuracy of Tennessee and Kentucky marksmen, with the exception of his cousin, who stands his ground and quickly dies from numerous gunshot wounds. Altsheler ends his account with a note on the importance of the battle as the last time that a foreign power threatened the United States and the significance of the victory for the principles on which the United States was founded, as well as a triumph for the Anglo Saxon race and Manifest Destiny. After this peroration, Altsheler's hero travels west to find Marian Pendleton, the woman he intends to marry.

7. Amoss, Berthe. *The Chalk Cross.* New York: Seabury, 1976. 150pp.

In this Gothic tale for teenagers, when Stephanie Martin enrolls at an historic New Orleans art school, l'Académie aux Bois, Collège des Beaux Arts de la Nouvelle Orléans, her first assignment brings the past alive for her in an unexpected way. The orphaned Stephanie has been living unhappily with her Aunt Kate, who treats her in the manner of a Dickensian orphan, by telling her she is unattractive and giving her ill-fitting, hand-me-down clothing. Spartan conditions are imposed by the nuns at the art school (students live in unadorned cells and must wear a school uniform), but for the first time in her life Stephanie feels valued. For her first sketching assignment she is drawn to nearby St. Anne's Street where she begins investigating the history of an 1830s house. She finds that Marie Laveau (c. 1801–1881) lived in the dwelling with her daughters Sidonie, Dédé, and infant son Denaud. Before long Stephanie is channeling Sidonie's spirit and time-traveling to witness events through Sidonie's eyes. Her explorations lead her to contemplate the nature of Voodoo, religion, and spirituality. She is also exposed to the evils of slavery when she befriends two plantation slaves who are in love and will be separated when they are sold. The book conveys some of the history of 1830s New Orleans, and presents a sense of what it would have been like to live in the city during a yellow fever outbreak.

8. Amoss, Berthe. *Secret Lives.* Boston: Little, Brown, 1979. 180pp.

Set in 1937 in New Orleans' Garden District at 320 Audubon Avenue and the neighboring houses, this novel for young adults explores issues of maturity and mortality. Orphaned years before, Adelaide "Addie" Aspasie lives with two elderly aunts, but also has aunts and uncles on neighboring properties and a cousin, Sandra Lee, who is nearly her age and lives next door. Addie loves her relatives, but is also becoming frustrated with her lack of freedom. Believing that she is plain, and ruing the contrast between herself and the blonde beauty of her mother, as depicted in an oil portrait, Addie resents her Cousin Sandra's physical attractiveness. The very fact that she knows so little about her mother also upsets Addie and she is puzzled why she married a much older man, fearing she was attracted by his wealth. All Addie knows is that her mother perished in a hurricane near the banana plantation Addie's father managed. Her father died soon afterwards from malaria. By the end of the novel, Addie learns that her mother was not the perfect woman portrayed in the portrait. She had flaws, but was still loved by her family and she had in fact married Addie's father out of love, not calculation. When Addie finally learns her mother's story, she begins to be more tolerant of the character flaws of others and, after the deaths of her aunts, becomes resigned to the flawed nature of human existence and starts to develop the mature serenity that her aunts possessed. Addie's life is narrowly confined to her neighborhood, but she does go to dancing school, catechism classes (she is Roman Catholic), and public school. The novel captures 1930s life in the Garden District and in that context devotes considerable attention to burial customs. Addie's Uncle Ben had died six months before the start of the novel and was placed in a wooden coffin in the family crypt in St. Louis Cemetery, No. 2. When Addie's oldest aunt dies, she cannot be interred in the crypt because too much of Ben is still present in the coffin for his remains to be burned and his ashes and bones raked through the grate and into the pit containing the remnants of previous generations. From the standpoint of cultural history, it is interesting to note that Addie is not the only orphan among her immediate acquaintances. Furthermore, her best friend is an African-American girl, the granddaughter of her aunts' cook.

9. Anonymous. *Fashion and Consequence, as Now Found in High Places and Low Places.* Louisville, Ky.: Author, 1855. 329pp.

This extended social commentary by a Christian minister is included here mostly because other bibliographies describe the work as fiction. To make his point about the corruption he sees among young people, the author does create the characters of Kate and James, whose shortcomings he describes in a few chapters, in the midst of many sections of commentary. The author disdains at length: novel reading, the idolatry of money, naked arms and necks, lap dogs, intemperance in food and drink, card playing, cosmetics, idleness, and irreligiosity. He uses New Orleans as an example of his despised world of fashion, describing the opera, masked balls, and Creoles at great length.

10. Anonymous. *James Wellard, Companion of John A. Murrell, the Great Western Land-Pirate.* Cincinnati, Ohio: The Author, 1855. 95pp.

Two young men meet two beautiful women in New Orleans during Mardi Gras, become their rescuers, and eventually marry them. Charles Edgar and his friend Kit are both in their mid-twenties and arrive in New Orleans just as Mardi Gras begins, although they are there to recover slaves stolen from Edgar's plantation. On their way to a ball they save Eveline and Emma, who are trapped in a runaway carriage. When they meet them later the same evening, they discover that Eveline has been betrothed by her uncle, James Wellard, to a man that she has never met, but she fears for his control over her uncle. Edgar and Kit pledge to aid Eveline before knowing that her evil fiancé is John A. Murrell, a notorious criminal. Murrell and his gang are involved in large-scale criminality, including the theft and resale of slaves. His gang had, in fact, stolen the slaves Edgar and Kit are seeking. After the resolution of several subplots, including one involving the crimes of a man who murdered his own mother, the heroes arrive at Murrell's stronghold on the grounds of Wellard's Lake Pontchartrain residence and free Eveline and Emma. Although the novel is mostly set in New Orleans, little description of the place is provided beyond the Mardi Gras scenes.

11. Anonymous. *The Sisters of Orleans.* New York: G.P. Putnam and Sons, 1871. 341pp.

In this novel dealing with the treatment of mixed-race people in the antebellum South, educated slaves possess information that they use to redress injustices. Phillip Grandaville, the father of Ruy Grandaville, made an arranged marriage for his son with Isabella Castello through her father, Ferdinand Castello, when both were children. Now that Isabella is eighteen and Ruy twenty the wedding is at hand, even though Phillip is dead and Ruy does not love his intended. Isabella is an additional impediment to the marriage since she despises slavery. Unfortunately, a friend of her father's bequeathed her a fortune in slaves with the proviso that she does not come into full owner-ship until she reaches the age of twenty-four. Isabella wants to free the slaves and tries to put off Ruy so that he will not gain control of the slaves before she does. Ruy concocts a ruse with lawyer Seabry (sic) Anthony that convinces Isabella that he has presented her with a legal document ex-empting her slaves from becoming his property upon their marriage. Anthony's slave Tully, treated as part of his master's office furniture, knows the truth. He is a friend of Aunt Esther, the African-American manager of Ferdinand Castello's household, and reports to her because Isabella is actually her daughter by Ferdinand Castello. Castello also had a legitimate daughter around the same time with identical features and Esther switched the two. To Esther's surprise, even though her Isabella does not know her true identity, she taught English to African-Americans at a contra-band school in New Orleans. There she fell in love with Charles Brown, a Northern teacher. When a mob, partly incited by Ruy Grandaville, broke in and gravely injured Brown, the African-American students carried him to Esther, who nursed him in secret. In his delirium he had called for Isabella and when he was fully rational Esther asked whether he could ever imagine marrying Isabella if he found out that she was of mixed race. When Esther hears that he has no qualms she lays a plot for the salvation of her Isabella. Ferdinand Castello's legitimate daughter (who he thought was Esther's offspring) was sent abroad to be educated, but when Castello fell into finan-cial difficulties he sent the girl to Grandaville's plantation for protection, not realizing that Ruy would make her his bed slave. The legitimate Isabella had been on the point of escaping with Ed-mond Sorlogne, a friend of Ruy's, but he discovered them and killed Sorlogne, more deeply hard-ening Isabella's hatred for him. Esther is able to convince Ferdinand to free her with the impend-ing nuptials as an excuse. At the wedding of Ruy and Isabella, Esther dramatically reveals that the bride is her daughter and her slave (such was the law). Ruy, who has realized he is in love with the true Isabella, his bed slave, hurries back to her. However, during his absence she incited a slave rebellion by claiming that Ruy would sell off all the slaves after his wedding. The slaves burn down his mansion with him inside. Although a portion of the book is set in the countryside and on plantations, most of the novel is set in New Orleans and illustrates the ease with which mobs could be gathered and incited in the years immediately before the Civil War.

12. Ansell, Jack. *Jelly.* New York: Arbor House, 1971. 221pp.

In this novel about the culture-clash between traditional religious faith and the 1970s celeb-ration of the unconstrained id, Jacob Weiss makes the long journey from rabbi to New Orleans jazz musician. As the son of a successful Jewish businessman who owns a chain of delicatessens in Dallas, Jacob Weiss had always lived among observant Jews and gravitated into rabbinical studies as a natural result. Soon after graduation from Hebrew Union College, he wed Miriam Zimmerman, the plain, but devout daughter of a rabbi and began a career as a Reform rabbi, suc-cessively working for wealthier and larger congregations. His life does not change appreciably until he is a thirty-three-year-old living in Mannerville, Louisiana. One Friday evening, Jo Ellen "Jelly" Johnson, the nineteen-year-old blonde daughter of the local Baptist minister, remains after service claiming she has a private trouble best discussed at her house. Once there, she serves Weiss a drugged beverage and he wakes to find himself in the middle of coitus with her. Initially, he is shocked, but as he awakens sexually he cannot resist further encounters that unsettle the foundations of his life. Although he tries to escape Jelly by accepting a rabbinate with a New Orleans congregation, she follows him and he is eventually forced to separate from his wife and leave the rabbinate. He becomes the main act at a Bourbon street club where he sings pop tunes, changes his name to Jake White, and lives openly with Jelly in the heart of the French Quarter in a building where other apartments are occupied by counter-cultural young people, bohemians, gays, and lesbians. Weiss' brother tries several times to get him to return to Dallas, but only when Mir-iam reveals that she is pregnant does Jacob leave Jelly. However, the baby is stillborn, and Miriam commits suicide six months later. Weiss moves back to the French Quarter and is eventually reu-nited with Jelly, although her enraged interim lover beats him so badly that his survival is, for a time, in doubt. After recovering, Weiss begins playing the Sazerac Room at the Roosevelt Hotel and finally convinces Jelly to marry him after the birth of their son. By the end of the novel, however, their relationship is once again imperiled by Jelly's waywardness. The book depicts a 1970s New Orleans on the cutting edge of the youth movement, filled with drug users, alcoholics, iconoclasts, and pansexual men and women who are open to any form of stimulation.

13. Antrobus (Robinson), Suzanne. *The King's Messenger.* New York: Harper and Brothers, 1901. 347pp.

In this historical romance novel a female is entrusted with great responsibilities and acts with surprising independence. Jeanne Poché, the wife of high-ranking soldier Emile Poché and the daughter of Comte d'Antin, a courtier to King Louis XV, arrives in New Orleans in 1728 as the king's messenger. Poché was forced to marry at seventeen to secure her father's social status. Jeanne arrives in New Orleans with a sealed royal dispatch which she suspects will condemn Julian Laville, an outspoken critic of both the India Company that controls New Orleans, and of Governor Périer, a toady of the company. Laville has also been agitating for the reappointment of Jean-Baptiste Le Moyne, Sieur de Bienville (1680–1767) as governor. When she falls in love with Laville, she conceals the dispatch and when confronted she claims that she is not the king's messenger. However, chief of police Rossart, one of Jeanne's spurned courtiers, discovers the romance and engineers Laville's transfer to Fort Rosalie. He later puts plot in motion that leads to an accusation of treason against Laville and to a duel with Emile Poché that leaves Jeanne a widow. Shortly afterwards she is forced to admit she was the royal courier and the dispatch is unsealed. However, the contents have nothing to do with Laville, but accuse Rossart and Emile Poché of treason. By the end of the novel, Bienville has been reappointed governor and Laville, as his ally, has secured his power in the colony. Two years later Jeanne and Laville finally marry. The novel introduces some historical personages and presents some actual events but the work is primarily a romance novel. Although it is not clear how seriously the reader is to take Jeanne's arguments for love as a moral imperative above matters of state, they do constitute an underlying philosophical current in the book and touch on the issue of women's status in society.

14. Arguedas, Janet Wogan [Anne Labranche, pseud.]. *The Last Days of Oak Lane Plantation.* Illustrated by Warren J. Guthrie. New Orleans: Laborde and Sons, 1962. 136pp.

Set in Monte Carlo, Paris, Rome, St. James Parish, and New Orleans in the 1820s, this novel focuses on the third generation of the Fernandez family. The first Fernandez arrived in New Orleans in 1768 from Andalusia, Spain and, after fighting against the British under Bernardo de Galvez, received a substantial land grant in St. James Parish. Three generations later, Ernesto Fernandez enters the final stage of his life, moves into his New Orleans house on Toulouse Street with his wife, turns his plantation operations over to a manager, and looks forward to the marriage of his son Pablo to the daughter of his friend Antonio Rodriguez. However, during his engagement, Pablo travels to Paris and after trying to study art and write poetry, sees Maria Francini, a seventeen-year-old Italian dancer, perform. Immediately smitten, the two soon move into an apartment together and marry after Maria becomes pregnant. The rest of the novel traces their frivolous pleasure-seeking approach to life. Ernesto Fernandez gives his son a chance to redeem himself by returning an abandoned sugar plantation to profitability. However, Pablo spends little time on the plantation before making arrangements to live in New Orleans, where Maria gives birth and then quickly devotes herself to enjoying New Orleans social life with a childhood friend whose father has become the Italian consul. The two lovers meet an early end when they perish in a shipwreck while returning from the French Riviera. Although this poorly written morality tale is mostly concerned with displaying the petulant behavior of Pablo and Maria, some sense of established social life in New Orleans is conveyed.

15. Arguedas, Janet Wogan [Anne Labranche, pseud.]. *The Vow: Romance of Old New Orleans.* New Orleans: Laborde and Sons, 1964. 338pp.

Harvard-educated lawyer Pierre de la Tour begins violating his Creole family's expectations while he is still a very young man in legal practice with a friend in 1857. He has Northern views in his opposition to slavery and refuses to marry Carmelite de Monteil, the girl chosen for him by his mother. He insists upon marrying Yvonne Marie Marchand, who is not a Creole but is the daughter of an Irish immigrant who has made his fortune as a riverboat captain. His mother, upon graduation from Ursuline Academy, formally vowed to her best school friend, Hortense de Monteil, that if their first-born children were of opposite sexes (as they were) their offspring would marry each other. Pierre's father, Louis Philippe Aristide de la Tour, is more forward thinking than his mother. He believes that Americans, particularly those connected to Northern business interests, represent the future of New Orleans. So, he sent Pierre to Harvard rather than to a Parisian university, as was traditional in Creole society. Louis is also pleased that Pierre is in a law firm formed by Northerners and has been invited to join the Northerners' Mardi Gras krewe, Comus. Despite his progressive views, Louis is as insistent as his wife that Pierre marry Carmelite, for the young woman will have a large dowry from her wealthy father, and is the sole heiress to the tract of land being developed into the suburb of Gentilly. In what he refers to as a traditional Creole approach, Louis separates love from family responsibility and indicates that Carmelite will understand if Pierre engages in love affairs outside marriage. Rejecting his father's understanding of love and his respect for the slave-based wealth of the de Monteil family, Pierre asks Captain Marchand directly for his daughter's hand and is surprised when he is told that it would be unfair for him to marry Yvonne until his family will accept her. Frustrated with the older generation, Pierre plans to elope with Yvonne, but gets caught in a storm and is seriously injured while rescuing a baby from a shack endangered by flooding. Afterwards, his mother speaks privately with Yvonne, convincing her that the accident happened because of Pierre's intention to break the vow, and persuades the girl that should she and Pierre marry, Pierre will fall ill and die. As a result, Yvonne refuses to see Pierre and goes into a depression, causing anxiety in everyone from Pierre's father and aunts to Captain Marchand and his family. When the reason behind her emotional state is revealed, this evidence of the depth of her love removes all opposition to the wedding, (except for that of Pierre's mother). The novel provides a great deal of information about Creole daily life and traditions, as well as the history of New Orleans, and includes vividly clownish, racist portrayals of African-American slaves.

16. Aswell, James (Benjamin), (Jr.). *The Midsummer Fires: A Long Fiction.* New York: William Morrow, 1948. 311pp.

In this novel about the travails of reaching middle age, forty-one-year-old Gael Ring experiences a career crisis that leads to bankruptcy and the end of his marriage. For decades he had lived in New York City and enjoyed an affluence won from his success as a commercial artist, creating air-brushed women that titillated male fantasies and establishing a type: "Ring Girls." He was even fortunate enough to marry a model upon whom he had based his most successful Ring Girl. However, overnight she ceased to inspire his art and shortly afterwards, he realized she was not even inspiring his erections (although later he determines that his impotence is a more general condition). At the peak of his success, he and Anne had moved to Rivermark, a beautiful Mississippi river town, and small enough that he could become the center of social life. As his income slipped, however, he continued to spend and acknowledged his imminent bankruptcy too late. His only chance at a paycheck is a portrait commission in New Orleans that also holds out the chance of meeting a woman who will inspire a new Ring Girl. Although some flashbacks intervene, approximately half of the novel is set in New Orleans, where Ring experiences the nadir of his crisis, as well as an emotional peak that foretells a return to fortune's favor. To escape an unpleasant situation on his journey to New Orleans, Ring jumps off the train just short of the city. In the darkness and confusion of a protest by farmers over milk prices, he is mistaken for a photojournalist and badly beaten. Fortunately, "Gibbie" Gibberoux, an alcoholic New Orleans cab driver is sleeping off a binge nearby and rescues Ring, letting him clean up at his apartment before going to meet his clients, General Ted Dorning and his mother Carlotta Morro Dorning, in their historic St. Charles Avenue mansion. In the remainder of the novel, Ring is on a wild orbit between the upper-class respectability of the Dornings, where he is an honored houseguest, and the dive bars and squalid apartment of Gibbie in the French Quarter, where he sees a future of alcoholism, peder-asty, and early death. Fortunately, Carlotta Dorning is a well-connected patron of art and engineers the sale of one of Ring's portraits, which foreshadows his entrance into a whole new arena of commercial art, using beautiful images of elderly people to sell products they need. Ring is able to return to Rivermark and face down his creditors, knowing he has the cash to pay all of his debts. Whether he is any more mature for his experiences is left to the reader to judge. The novel pre-sents a convincing image of the tawdry life of the French Quarter in 1941, just before the huge naval buildup of World War II will transform the city.

17. Aswell, James (Benjamin), (Jr.). *The Young and Hungry-Hearted.* New York: New American Library, 1955. 127pp.

Most of the stories in this collection are set outside of New Orleans, in Rivermark. However, two—"Nocturne Creole" and "The Bright Look" evoke the mysteries of the city. In the first story, nineteen-year-old Maryse Ducros has married Private Hank Smith in the midst of World War II during Mardi Gras. The couple had met several years before in New York City where the or-phaned Ducros was supporting herself working in a nightclub. She had always been intrigued by talk of an aunt and uncle in New Orleans and had been puzzled when her parents had stopped mentioning them. When Smith proposes, Ducros suggests a New Orleans wedding. The romantic city seems to justify her choice of venue until, after a day of drinking, her new husband refers to her as a Creole mongrel. She storms out of the hotel room intending never to return. Fortunately, Renne, one of her friends from New York City, had married the owner of the Gargling Pelican bar and offers her a job there. She then decides to find 222 ½ Esplanade, the return address on the let-ters her mother received from New Orleans. To her shock she discovers that her aunt and uncle, Rive and Cecile de Riviere, are still alive but have never gotten over the shock of her mother's marriage to a Northerner. In fact, they are stuck in a time twenty years earlier, before her mother eloped and believe that Maryse is her mother when she appears. In the course of the evening, she considers staying with them and working at the nightclub. However, when Hank shows up the Rivieres believe he is Arbaud Blanchissard, the suitor they considered appropriate for Ducros' mother. At this point, Ducros is happy to leave with Hank, eager to escape the fusty prejudices of New Orleans for the social freedom of New York City. In the second story, another young woman, Joanna Bayes, also must make the decision whether to live in a shadowy past or leave the Esplan-ade household of her father for a frightening life in the larger world. As a ten-year-old, Bayes had watched her mother, a daredevil performer, plunge to her death during what was to be her last show as the Blonde Bullet. Her father, Arthur Bayes, had inherited his aunt's house on Esplanade and had taken a job as an oil company accountant. The day after the Blonde Bullet's performance the little family was to settle into their new life. The traumatized Bayes becomes a reclusive stamp dealer instead and tries to protect his daughter from the influence of the seedy neighborhood sur-rounding them. As an eighteen-year-old, Joanna meets Johnny Rosario for the first time even though he had always lived only a few blocks away. The two immediately fall in love and marry secretly, since Rosario had served time in federal prison, and Joanna is uncertain of her father's acceptance. On the first evening she spends outside of Bayes' Esplanade house she is so frightened that she retreats to her childhood room. Only remembering the words her mother mouthed as she stood on the platform before her death . . ."Dive, when you must Joanna, darling, dive!" motivates her to return to her new life. The New Orleans in this work is a place under a debilitating enchant-ment with the past.

18. Augustin, George. *The Haunted Bridal Chamber, a Romance of Old-Time New Orleans.* New Orleans: The Author, 1902. 249pp.

The narratives in this short story collection mostly consist of the amorous adventures of mainly upper class young men who socialize through the Cercle des Sans Souci and the Cercle des Artistes, and drink absinthe and vermouth at the Old Absinthe House. With the exception of an 1890 event that serves as an epilogue, the action transpires between 1826 and 1831. Although New Orleans is part of the United States at this point, the author portrays characters whose lives are lived entirely within a French cultural enclave. The story of Lucien Dumont, one of the wealthiest of the young men, frames the other tales. Dumont is engaged to heiress Madeline de St. Croix, a childhood friend of his sister, when he meets milliner's assistant Lollotte on the street and is immediately smitten with her. Although Lollotte immediately announces that she is engaged to mechanic Pierre Latour, who she plans to marry when he is promoted to foreman in his foundry, Dumont does not mention his own engagement. Even though Lollotte knows that Dumont is keeping his friendship with her a secret, she eventually throws over Latour, believing that Dumont will marry her. Their story is not the only one of cross-class romance. Eminent portrait painter Maxime Milliston falls in love with Minette, who lives on the streets and supports herself by dancing at Mère Jiguette's disreputable club. At first Minette seems too attached to her friends from the streets to be reformed into a gentlewoman. However Milliston is able to take her to Paris to visit his elderly, wealthy aunt. With a made up genealogy for Minette and the fortune Milliston inherits when his aunt dies, they return to New Orleans as an affluent and socially respectable young couple. Lawyer and journalist Guoneuille has a much different experience when he falls in love with a waif. Called to the notorious Blue Light Saloon on St. Philip Street to get the facts surrounding the murder of a young woman, he discovers a girl named Marianne begging for food. Over time he visits her at her mother's boarding house room and tries to help the two with his meager salary. When the mother dies, he places Marianne in the Ursuline Convent. As she grows older, the two begin to acknowledge their love for each other. However, soon after Marianne leaves the convent as a sixteen-year-old, Guoneuille discovers her true identity as the missing granddaughter of an elderly, eccentric, wealthy couple who then establish her in their large plantation home. Although Guoneuille's romantic letters thrill Marianne, it is clear that her newfound family will never entertain a marriage proposal from the impoverished and disreputable lawyer. The romance between Lollotte and Dumont follows yet another course. Refusing all money and gifts from Dumont in anticipation of marrying him, Lollotte eventually hears the banns read for Dumont and Madeline's wedding to be held one year hence. On her way back from visiting a swamp-dwelling Voodoo priestess, to get what she believes is a love potion that will win her Dumont's sole attention, Lollotte freezes to death in a doorway during New Orleans' historic blizzard of November 26, 1830. Dumont makes a great show of giving her an expensive funeral and earns the acclaim of New Orleaneans for his superior sentiments. A second tragedy strikes Dumont more directly when on his wedding night he responds to screams to find both his wife and sister murdered in the Dumont mansion. Although he falls into madness for a while, he recovers in time to be tried and found guilty of murder, in part on the evidence of mechanic Pierre Latour, who claims to have heard Dumont arguing with a woman on the night of the murder. Lapsing again into madness, Dumont dies soon afterwards in an insane asylum. Years later, in 1890, the elderly Pierre Latour confesses on his deathbed that he had committed the murders and also committed perjury to revenge the death of Lollotte. Whether exaggerated, or not, according to the narrator, the stories in this self-published work are loosely based on scandalous past events in New Orleans and the common theme of romances across social classes may touch on a predominant cultural issue.

19. Augustin, George. *Romances of New Orleans*. New Orleans: L. Graham and Son, 1891. 214pp.

This collection of the author's work includes short stories and poems previously published in magazines and newspapers, with the bulk of the work (pp. 1–196) consisting of short stories. The longest work, "Yetta the Nun" (pp. 1–82) relates the story of a tragic, youthful love affair between two cousins that ends in an accidental death and suicide in the courtyard of a convent. In "Irreconcilable" (pp. 101–119) a father declares his daughter dead to him after she elopes. When she returns several years later to present a granddaughter to her parents, she finds her mother dead and father still adamant about their estrangement. Even when her husband's fortune collapses and he dies from a fever after working as a waterfront laborer, she gets no recognition from her father. When she falls ill and goes with her starving baby to her father's house he still rejects her, although after her death he kills himself in remorse. The stories tend to be melodramatic and describe characters under the sway of emotions that overrule reason. New Orleans gets no general descriptions, although the context of the stories provides information about the importance of religious orders and the nature of several industries, including pharmacies and cigar manufacturers.

20. Baker, Julie Keim Wetherill. *The Wandering Joy*. New York: Broadway, 1910. 172pp.

The anonymous narrator's father dies of yellow fever while she is still an infant and the timid child is sent to live with her paternal uncle and aunt in the North. Her aunt believes she should be strengthened physically and be outgoing and boisterous like her own children. The narrator finds the environment harsh. She feels unloved and her only friend and confidante is her cousin Jane, who is of a similar age. After Jane dies she is completely alone. By the time she is in her twenties, the narrator lives with a paid companion, Mrs. Manners, and the two take up residence in the French Quarter of New Orleans, renting from a quadroon woman. The novel includes extensive descriptions of household life and of quadroon society. Today's readers will probably find the author's great interest in intermarriage and the ascription of personality traits to racial identity as racist. As a woman with no emotional connections beyond her companion, the narrator spends her days observing children, cats, and street life in the French Quarter. She observes architecture, describes the market, and churches, and reflects with sentimental religiosity on her life and relative sanity. Eventually committed to a hospital for a physical or mental affliction, she resigns herself to death, until she is sent outside of the city, finds a nurse who inspires her with her vigor, rejects the role of lifelong invalid she was on the verge of adopting, and forms a romantic relationship with her physician. The book has strong descriptions of daily life in the French Quarter around the turn of the twentieth century.

21. Banks, (Algernon) Polan. *Black Ivory*. New York: A.L. Burt, 1926. 305pp.

In this historical romance dealing with Jean Lafitte (c.1776–c.1823) and the redeeming power of a woman's love, Polan's Lafitte is a businessman in the twentieth-century mold who understands transportation networks and the power to be gained through organizing competing interests into a corporate structure. After a random bullet from a dueling opponent's gun kills his first love, Lizette Fondac, Lafitte pledges revenge. He and his brother Pierre soon have their own ship, named the Lizette, and get their revenge on the duelist in Caribbean waters. Lafitte dedicates himself to gaining economic hegemony over a vast region of the South by establishing a port in Barataria that would eclipse New Orleans in importance. The economy of this piratical entrepreneur will focus on auctioning slaves from captured ships, taking advantage of a market demand exacerbated by the 1808 U.S. ban on the importation of new slaves. Within ten years, Lafitte has created docks, warehouses, slave pens, and auction floors. His business skills and presumed wealth mean that he is treated as a member of Creole society, though Northerners, like Governor Claiborne (c.1772/75–1817), who oppose piracy and the slave trade, consider him a criminal. In this account the second transformative moment in Lafitte's life is when he meets Virginia, the daughter of district attorney John Randolph Grymes (c.1746–1854). Not only does he begin to realize that his youthful romance with Lizette Fondac was mere infatuation compared with his feelings for Virginia, but she inspires him with her vision of the future might of the United States and of the wrongheadedness of slavery. Although he does not consent to her pleas that he give up his outlaw existence, during the War of 1812 he rejects the British offer of gold and military rank to support the United States, even though he correctly suspects the British fleet will destroy his port. Virginia Grymes is also crucial in getting her father to successfully intercede with Andrew Jackson on Lafitte's behalf. After fighting bravely and being gravely wounded (in this account his brother dies of battle wounds), President Madison issues a pardon for Lafitte and the Baratarians who fought to defend New Orleans. By the close of the novel, Jean's heroic patriotism has made it possible for Virginia to reciprocate his love. This novel is filled with ethnocentrism and racism as a whole range of characteristics are attributed to country of origin or race. Although the book opposes slavery, African-Americans are described in uniformly negative terms, except for the author's breathless fascination with their glistening, muscled bodies.

22. Banks, (Algernon) Polan. *Carriage Entrance*. New York: G.P. Putnam's Sons, 1947. 280pp.

This historical romance novel set in the 1890s is preoccupied with the power of female sexuality. The orphaned Barbara Beauravel was raised by her aunt Eulalie Beauravel, a fixture in Creole society. After learning that her mother was a Basin Street madam, Barbara harshly imposed on herself her aunt's ascetic code, which eschewed even the mildest sensuality and distrusted men. By her debutante year she had earned for herself the sobriquet, "marble maiden." Her cousin, the tradition-obsessed Paul Beauravel, carefully orchestrates her society debut at New Orleans' French Opera House, down to making certain that each of her suitors—Pierre Lestrade, New Orleans' wealthiest banker, and wealthy society man Claiborne Villermont—have equal time with her. The unexpected happens, however, when Barbara's eyes lock with those of a slim-hipped, aquiline-nosed man in his thirties who she eventually meets and comes to know as Dr. Quentin Cushing, a Yankee doctor working on cures for infectious tropical diseases at Tulane University. The immediate romantic attraction and intellectual sympathy Barbara experiences with Cushing overcomes much of her reticence, but even after they are secretly engaged and he is about to go on a four-month research trip to South America, she refuses to kiss him. On shipboard, Cushing meets Corinne Ware. Corinne is an openly sexual blonde, wearing dresses that accentuate her "pointed breasts." Having repressed his sexuality up until then, Cushing, a man in his early thirties, is easily manipulated by Corinne and soon marries her. The jilted Barbara vows revenge and fate literally gives her the means, when she inherits the fortune of a distant relative who died intestate. She buys a famous plantation in Bayou St. John and when Cushing returns she hosts an elaborate dinner for him and his wife, demonstrating her ostensible magnanimity and subtly presenting him with an image of what could have been his. Barbara realizes that Corinne's social inferiority is markedly apparent and introduces her in society as widely as possible while secretly plotting with her cousin Paul. She will give him the money he wants for a business opportunity if he will romance Corinne and make a cuckold of Cushing. On the night the affair is to be consummated, Corinne falls and hits her head, dying instantly. Paul flees just as Cushing arrives. The police, believing a murder has been committed, have no concrete evidence of a crime of passion, but the grand jury returns a finding of "No Bill" that leaves Cushing a perpetual suspect, ruining his career. When Cushing learns that Barbara, who witnessed the accident, has come forward, jeopardizing her social status, he seeks her out and pledges his undying love. This romance novel provides information about many traditions within Creole society and describes a number of social events, including balls, dinners, holiday parties, opera attendance, and visiting flower-decorated graves on All Saints Day. The result is a convincing portrait of life for a segment of New Orleaneans in the 1890s. In this book, women can have a powerful role in society by becoming arbiters of manners and fashion, although they usually must have wealthy husbands. African-Americans in the novel are a constant, silent presence, but are necessary accoutrements to a wealthy household.

The book was made into a film under the title *My Forbidden Past* (RKO, 1951), starring Robert Mitchum and Ava Gardner.

23. Barker, Lillian. *Cabaret Love*. New York: Grosset and Dunlap, 1933. 278pp.

In this jazz age romance novel, New Orleans is a national center for musical performance that attracts orphaned Jeanne Dupré from Baton Rouge to employ her talents to support her aunt and cousin. Marie quickly attracts interest at the Moulin Rouge Cabaret for her singing, while her beauty wins the attention of Randolph Churchill, the son of one of the city's wealthiest lawyers, home on spring break from college. Within a few days he wins Dupré's heart and proposes marriage, although he knows his family will be opposed, and tells Dupré that she must keep the betrothal a secret until he graduates and reaches his majority. Their secrecy is destroyed when Dupré wins a contest sponsored by a local shoe store and she is acclaimed for having the most beautiful feet in New Orleans. Unfortunately, wealthy Sylvia McCormick, Churchill's childhood sweetheart, who his parents and Sylvia both assumed he would marry, had also entered the contest, as well and in a rage to discover who had beat her, surprises Churchill and Dupré in an intimate conversation that reveals their love for each other. She and Churchill's parents get him out of town and have an engagement announcement published in New Orleans newspapers so he will be obligated to marry McCormick out of a sense of honor. Dupré never learns the truth and accepts the offer of wealthy Hugh van Suydenham to pay for her to study in Paris in preparation for a career in opera. Dupré has several opportunities to marry before her studies in Paris come to fruition, but realizes that she will always be in love with Churchill. He finally arrives after she has triumphed in the role of Manon Lescaut and reveals the plot that was enacted against them. Freed of McCormick, he proposes to Dupré. Approximately half of the novel is set in New Orleans, but the book is so focused on parallels between Paris and the city that it does little to establish a sense of the American city.

24. Barron, Ann Forman [Annabel Erwin, pseud.]. *Aurielle*. New York: Warner, 1979. 461pp.

This historical romance is set in New Orleans during the years 1812 to 1814 and tells the story of an orphaned girl's discoveries about her parentage, her inner strengths, and her ability to love. Aurielle Stuart was orphaned as a child in England, with her only inheritance and clue to her parentage a jeweled dagger. In 1812 when she is twelve-years-old, a kindly, educated sailor helps her sail to New Orleans where she will be sold as an indentured servant to redeem the cost of her passage. Captain Quentin Kincannon, one of Lafitte's pirates, captures the ship before reaching the city and she is taken to Grand Terre. Fortunately Rôdeur Cheviot becomes her protector when he recognizes her dagger as that of his compatriot John Bayard Smith, with whom he was involved in a plot to restore the French monarchy. Taken into Cheviot's household, she is informally adopted by Antoinette Desmottes, his housekeeper. On her first trip to New Orleans she meets beautiful Ondine Chaille and dreams of moving to the city under Chaille's protection. Soon afterwards she and Desmottes, along with Roxanne Deveret, are forced to flee Grand Terre when Cheviot is killed in the aftermath of the Lafittes' arrest. In New Orleans, Desmottes agrees to present Deveret and Aurielle as her nieces. The bulk of the novel is devoted to depicting New Orleans society during this time period as Desmottes teaches the tempestuous young women how to behave and win the hearts of men. Just as Aurielle is poised to marry a wealthy Creole, she decides instead to depart for the Texas frontier with the returned Kincannon. The novel is of interest for yet another portrayal of the Baratarian pirates, the Battle of New Orleans, and New Orleans society.

25. Bartlett, Napier. *Clarimonde: A Tale of New Orleans Life, and of the Present War*. Richmond, Va.: M.A. Malsby, 1863. 79pp.

In this tale of thwarted love, Oscar St. Arment first becomes acquainted with Clarimonde as a child, when they attend the same primary school near his family's rural plantation. They are separated before St. Arment even knows the girl's last name, when St. Arment's high-living parents move into New Orleans, where their life of dissipation soon leaves him an orphan. The heir to a distinguished name and depleted estate, St. Arment is taken in by Father Grivot, who makes him a chorister so that he is able to get an education. The novel briefly describes such a life and the schoolboy pastimes of such youths. Before too long, St. Arment is discovered by his maternal uncle, a man of great wealth, who has been living in Paris. His uncle at first hopes St. Arment can be formed in his own mold, as an effete sybarite, devoted to his tailor and gourmandizing. St. Arment fails at being merely ornamental and his uncle, losing interest, simply gives the young man an allowance and permission to see after himself. St. Arment befriends Henri D'Armas, who introduces him to racing and womanizing. When he is reintroduced to Clarimonde, she is on the verge of her debutante season and D'Armas becomes his rival for her attentions. The rivals eventually duel when D'Armas behaves badly and Arment leaves the field thinking he has killed D'Armas. When he later meets D'Armas in New Orleans, the man has already married Clarimonde. The novel ends with a poignant Civil War battlefield scene in which the three are reunited. The novel is of interest for the descriptions of St. Arment's uncle, the focus on emotion-laden male friendships, and descriptions of the pastimes of affluent young men. However, the treatment of New Orleans remains cursory.

26. Bartlett, Napier. *Stories of the Crescent City.* New Orleans: Steel, 1869. 100pp.

These fifteen stories are all principally set in New Orleans. Primarily concerned with the activities of young men, they focus on evening entertainments such as balls and opera house performances. Plots focus on defending one's honor and avoiding marriage to the wrong woman. Although some discussions of wealth are present, no one engages in a profession (except for a famous restaurateur) or is a university student. There are several mentions of Civil War service, but none of African-Americans or Creoles. With the exception of a faithful wife, responsible for her husband's success, the women in the novels have often suffered unjust disgraces to their honor for which they have no recourse except suicide. In general, the stories follow popular images of New Orleans as a place of duels, lavish entertainments, and ancient houses and families, now in decay. A number of characters, even though impoverished, make arrangements for their own funerals.

27. Basso, (Joseph) Hamilton. *Cinnamon Seed.* New York: Charles Scribner's Sons, 1934. 379pp.

In a novel that contrasts the Old South with the industrializing New South of the 1920s, the Blackheath family, prominent in Louisiana for two hundred years, is helpless before political demagogues. These are Harry Brand, the grandson of Blackheath's former Wildwood Plantation manager, and local bootlegger Tard Sturkins, an offspring of one of the poorest families in the neighborhood of their plantation. Protagonist Dekker Blackheath, orphaned at an early age by his father's suicide, was forced to leave the plantation and live in New Orleans with his uncle Carter Blackheath, his father's brother and business partner. However, Dekker, like his father, is typical of earlier generations of the family in his connection to the land and never fits into the household of Carter, an unsuccessful lawyer, whose wife Elizabeth, a prudish Yankee, is incessantly critical of Dekker's behavior. She is preoccupied with social position and horrified that Dekker embraces the street life of New Orleans and is friendly with immigrant shopkeepers and their children, as well as sailors and ship's captains. She makes certain her son John attends private schools and later Harvard, while Dekker is sent to public school. Dekker returns to Wildwood to try to make it profitable, but is drawn back to New Orleans by John, who has entered the advertising profession and married a Creole society beauty. For a brief time Dekker tries to fit in with society women and businessmen, but, in the end cannot embrace their values. He finds Harry Brand particularly repugnant. Brand came back into contact with the Blackheaths as an attention-getting lawyer who takes Dekker's father's place in the Blackheath family law firm. Both Carter and Elizabeth find his origins distasteful, but Carter realizes his financial value, a value that increases dramatically when Brand is elected governor. Other Blackheaths of Carter's generation are not so ready to forget

Brand's background, for his grandfather was responsible for bringing public shame to Robert and Emily Blackheath, the Civil War owners of Wildwood. By the close of the novel, a highway construction project touted by Governor Brand is edging onto the Wildwood plantation and is on track to demolish the Blackheath ancestral home. Although the novel is only partially set in New Orleans, the city is a constant presence, as younger generations of the family live there, with the city symbolizing an ethos that places money above all else, a value system in stark contrast to that of Dekker and older generations of Blackheaths.

28. Basso, (Joseph) Hamilton. *Days before Lent*. New York: Charles Scribner's Sons, 1939. 371pp.

The day before and day of Mardi Gras form the backdrop for Peter Kent's increasingly agonized reflections on his future. A thirty-year-old bacteriologist, Kent must decide whether to accept his mentor Dr. Hunt's offer to go to India to continue the research on infectious diseases that he began in the bayous south of New Orleans. For Kent, accepting Hunt's offer would mean breaking off his romance with Susanna Fuller and his connection to New Orleans. Kent's mother died when he was a child and his father, a physician with a very modest practice in the French Quarter, raised him. Living above an Italian grocery, the elder Dr. Kent became a mentor to Joe Piavi, the son of the grocery owners, teaching him how to box and helping him find a trainer. Piavi won a name for himself, but the effects of boxing hit him hard in middle age, and his impaired reflexes have ended his career, while his general mental confusion and black-outs, heightened by alcoholism, have prevented him from holding onto a job. Kent senior's recent death (a suicide as his stomach cancer worsened) has left Peter Kent feeling responsible for Piavi, a major presence in his life since childhood. Piavi has become increasingly erratic, and is on a collision path with organized crime figure, Nick Weinstein, his former manager, over Weinstein's claim that Piavi owes him money. As Mardi Gras begins, Kent's love interest, Susanna, a peripatetic woman of wealth who travels from resort to resort with her social circle, arrives to participate in society balls held in conjunction with Mardi Gras. Her socializing thwarts Kent's attempts to have a serious discussion with her about the future. Then, via newspaper headlines, Kent learns that Piavi has murdered Weinstein, and he begins a frantic search for his friend, trying to find him before the police. Through his reminiscences about his father, whose adult life in the Quarter began in the 1880s, and his own reflections on the importance of his friendships, the author conveys a sense of the Quarter as a close-knit working-class neighborhood of Irish and Italian immigrant families. The French Quarter is only beginning to change as wealthy people like Susanna's friends, the Mansons, begin to acquire and renovate properties. The novel records daily life in some detail, mentioning restaurants and food and describing street life, presenting a nostalgic paean to a neighborhood hard-hit by the Depression and beginning to undergo a dramatic transformation from working-class/immigrant slum to an upper-middle-class fantasy land.

29. Basso, (Joseph) Hamilton. *Relics and Angels*. New York: Macaulay, 1929. 286pp.

Anthony "Tony" Clezak had gone to Rome with his grandfather, Antoine Clezak, and had begun a purposeful life assisting in Dr. Hugo Mullendorf's yellow fever research. When his grandfather dies, however, he is called back to New Orleans to work in his family's business, the Forward Shoe Company that his grandfather had founded. To his regret, Mullendorf encourages Tony to take the job since an unmarried sister and great-aunt are dependent on him, while research pays little. His return to the city as a twenty-five-year-old, after many years abroad, prompts extended internal reminiscences about his orphaned childhood, living with his sister Laurine. They lived in the Clezak ancestral home, to which he returns, a place still filled with art and antiques that make a physical connection between the family and the history of New Orleans, dating back to Governor Bienville. At the shoe factory Epstein is now controlling partner. A Russian immigrant who had escaped the pogroms, Epstein began making shoes, but worked his way up through the company, slowly purchasing stock and suffering the prejudice of Anthony's grandfather Antoine. His admiration for Antoine Clezak, if misplaced, was persistent, and he transfers the same veneration to Anthony, who he makes a second vice-president of the firm. Anthony resents his job and is pre-occupied by his obsession with a college sweetheart, Helen, who has married Bill Montross, a man who had bullied Anthony when they were boys. Montross is now a yacht-sailing man of wealth and, although Helen allows herself a physical encounter with Anthony, she is mortified when Anthony begins to insist that she should leave Bill for him, and forbids him to have further contact. Shortly afterward, Anthony quits his job and, after his great-aunt dies and his sister announces her engagement to a member of the affluent country club circle he despises, makes plans to return to Rome. However, a dramatic revelation changes the course of his life. The novel evokes aspects of social class in the New Orleans of the 1920s and describes households and entertainments of working-class, as well as upper-class citizens. Issues of race emerge through descriptions of family servants.

30. Basso, (Joseph) Hamilton. *Sun in Capricorn.* New York: C. Scribner's Sons, 1942. 266pp.

While Hazzard (never given a first name) was still an infant, his mother died, and several years later his father succumbed to heartbreak. His maternal aunt and Uncle Thomas, in rural northern Louisiana, raised him. His uncle, a lawyer from an old family, has a large but financially modest practice and Hazzard joins the firm. An honorable man in politics during the Coolidge era, Hazzard's uncle decides to oppose Gilgo Slade for U.S. Senator, outraged over the man's political demagoguery. Hazzard travels to New Orleans on firm business before his uncle has announced his campaign and there meets his nemesis, Fritz Cowan, a boyhood friend, who courted and married Hazzard's girlfriend while he was away at law school. Cowan shows off his connections by taking Hazzard to Gilgo Slade's private suite in the hotel he owns. Hazzard is sickened there as he watches the brazen awarding of state contracts in return for promises of political support and is shocked as Slade announces that he will conduct his campaign as part of an actual circus (the fat woman and dwarf are present) that will travel around the state. He believes this demonstrates his knowledge of the electorate. Soon after leaving the hotel, news comes of his uncle's entrance into the race and Cowan, in the belief that Hazzard was spying on the opposition, has him followed. Unfortunately, over a few days in New Orleans, Hazzard meets and falls in love with the attractive Erin, who recently moved to New Orleans and is working as a music store clerk. Photographs are taken of the two that the Slade campaign uses to make their activities seem like an illicit liaison and a warrant is sworn for the arrest of Erin on a morals violation. Hazzard is able to get Erin out of town and almost gets home himself before he is arrested near a Slade campaign rally. Slade's campaign is brought to an alarming end before Hazzard can suffer repercussions. Although a family tragedy ensues, Hazzard and Erin seem about to spend a happy life together. New Orleans in the novel is both the romantically charming place that forms a backdrop for Hazzard and Erin's romance and the seat of the basest political corruption.

31. Bay, Gabriel. *A Lord in His Fool-castle: A Novel; and Molly Anathema: A Tale.* New Orleans: Erstwhil (sic), 1902. 89pp.

In this social satire society people are lampooned for their misalliances. Mrs. Beltinore, née Pappen has made Commodore Beltinore something of a laughingstock for many years because of her pretensions, despite the unsavoriness of the Pappen family, many of whom are impoverished and several of whom have been committed to lunatic asylums. The Beltinores have two daughters, Yvonne, who conscientiously fulfills social expectations and Caro, who likes to thwart them. Mrs. Beltinore particularly disapproves of Caro's romance with Gayoso Leroy and during a garden party at the Beltinore summerhouse, Beltinoria, she accuses Leroy of having African-American ancestry. He flees to New Orleans, living in a boarding house operated by Mrs. Bridgetta O'Brien in the Irish Channel (near Adele and St. Thomas Streets). He earns money as an artist's model, and met Caro while posing in the nude in the guise of Narcissus for a group of society ladies. When she receives a telegram informing her that her father has received a serious wound and summoning her to Beltinoria, he comforts her and accompanies her. When Caro and Leroy arrive, they hear a true society lady denounce Mrs. Beltinore for a plot to kill the Commodore and marry her own first cousin. She also attacks Mrs. Beltinore for besmirching Leroy. It is explained that, although the young man's father initially married a quadroon, his second wife was entirely Caucasian and Leroy is the product of that second union. On his deathbed the Commodore denounces his wife's plot against his life and reveals he has altered his will so that Caro and Yvonne share the entire estate, to the exclusion of Mrs. Beltinore. Although much of the work is set at a seaside summerhouse, it does reveal the seriousness with which mixed-race parentage was taken in some New Orleans circles at the turn of the twentieth century.

32. Beach, Rex (Ellingwood). *The Crimson Gardenia and Other Tales of Adventure.* Illustrated by Anton Otto Fischer and Charles Sarka. New York: Harper and Brothers, 1916. 377pp.

The sixty-five page title story in this collection is the only one set in New Orleans. However, the author clearly considered the work the most prominent in the volume since the cover illustration is of New Orleans and, in a book that includes stories set in Haiti, the Caribbean, and Cuba, New Orleans is treated as the most exotic of all. Wealthy, young New York society man Roland Van Dam has been traveling with his fiancée, Eleanor Banniman, her parents, and some family friends on board the Banniman family yacht. At Van Dam's suggestion they have come from Palm Beach to experience Mardi Gras. When Van Dam goes into the streets disguised in a domino mask, he is mistaken for another man and ends up aiding a beautiful young woman; eluding the henchman of the notorious gangster, Black Wolf; and thwarting a safe-breaking. Although Van Dam narrowly escapes death at the hands of criminals and arrest by the police, he is far from eager to return to the tedious company of his fiancée's family and their friends and the reader cannot help thinking that he has been forever unsettled by his Mardi Gras adventure in New Orleans.

33. Beach, Rex (Ellingwood). *The Net.* New York: Harper and Brothers, 1912. 332pp.

In this racist, anti-immigrant novel, Norvin Blake, the young heir to a Louisiana cotton plantation and a New Orleans resident, gets drawn into searching for a Mafia leader when he witnesses his friend's execution by Mafia gangsters. While residing in Paris as a young man, before taking up his responsibilities in New Orleans, Blake befriends Italian nobleman Count Martel Savigno, an art student. When Savigno returns to his family estate in Palermo, Sicily in 1866 to marry Countess Margherita Ginini, Blake makes the trip although he considers Italy a place too primitive to afford much in the way of enjoyment or comfort. During his short visit he is shocked to learn how the Mafia controls economic, political and social life. Savigno, whose estate includes large orange groves, has been waging a struggle against Mafia control of his family business. On the night before the wedding, Blake is with Savigno and his estate agent when they are murdered. The estate manager's daughter, Olivetta Ferara (sic), and Countess Margherita, realize that the Sicilian police will never bring the murderers to justice and pursue the killers to the United States, where Blake loses track of them. Returning to New Orleans, he takes up life as a New Orleans businessman and president of the Cotton Exchange. He also serves as his parish sheriff, "dealing with unruly niggers." In this role he gets to know New Orleans Police Chief Donnelly and in 1890, when Donnelly begins getting anonymous tips regarding the local Mafia leader, Blake is privy to their contents. When Donnelly is murdered he searches for the killers and realizes they are the men who killed Savigno. He also discovers that the anonymous informants are Olivetta and Margherita. Although Blake gathers compelling evidence and witnesses, the Mafia control is so strong, that the trial turns into a farcical miscarriage of justice and the murderers are declared not guilty. Since the trial received national coverage, long-standing New Orleans citizens take to the streets, feeling that their city has been disgraced. While Blake, inspired by Margherita's stand against vigilantism, tries to reason with the mob they nonetheless break into the prison. The Mafia leaders and conspirators are killed in a series of violent acts (one criminal is beaten by the crowd and literally pulled to pieces). Throughout the novel Italians, particularly immigrants to the United States, are portrayed negatively and the underlying stance of the novel is that the "white" race must be defended against the "human trash" washing up on American shores and settling into its cities, forming noisome, crime-ridden neighborhoods, like the Italian district in New Orleans. This book presents a version of events surrounding the 1891 anti-Italian riots described in other novels in this bibliography.

34. Beach, Rex (Ellingwood). *Woman in Ambush.* New York: G.P. Putnam's Sons, 1951. 280pp.

This record of youthful rebellion has various settings, but after a visit to New Orleans, protagonist Dick Banning's life is threatened by gangsters and his psyche is deeply affected by an act of sexual aggression. A wunderkind, seventeen-year-old Banning, son of a well-known physician, has already finished college and been admitted to Oxford with a one year deferral due to his youth. Banning's father was distant and preoccupied and only his mother provided emotional support but died when he was six. After years of isolating study, Banning tries to establish a social life. Oddly, he makes his first real friendship in prison, where he was remanded after he tossed a brick through the window of a florist's shop where he believed he had been cheated. Banning serves four weeks under the assumed name of Ronald LeGrand, with a cell mate named Jim "Jimmy the Lark" Larkin, a grifter and card shark who offers Banning the chance to become his buddy and traveling companion. Banning returns home after his release only long enough to declare his independence from parental control. His physician father sees the rebellion as an expression of "juvenile sex impulses," but is unable to raise the subject due to the formality of their relationship. Larkin and Banning head for New Orleans, the city Larkin, who has traveled widely, praises most highly. Through a successful card counting scam, Banning is able to repeatedly cheat the savviest of con men, Tom McPhee, the owner of New Orleans largest casino, who hires him as a dealer. He soon attracts Madame Angela Rondo's attention. Rondo, a forty-year-old woman, is proud of her descent from the casket girls brought from France to marry New Orleans' pioneers in the eighteenth century. She has become a wealthy woman through illicit businesses and under-the-table deals with local politicians. Banning, who has never been interested in women, ignores Jimmy's warnings that Rondo is treating him like a lover. To the naïve Banning, the cigar-smoking, older woman with her faint moustache is just a powerful friend. However, after he saves her from disfigurement during an accident involving café brûlot, she invites him to her glorified brothel of a home and gives him a "love potion." When he flees in horror back to Jimmy, the grifter realizes that they must run for their lives now that Banning has humiliated Rondo. Most of the remainder of the novel records their adventures eluding Rondo and her henchmen. These include managing a circus and a partnership in a ranch on the Western frontier. Banning's many opportunities with women are spoiled by a neurotic repulsion instilled by his experience with Madame Rondo. Through periodic, analytic conversations with his father, Dr. Banning, the troubled young man eventually realizes that only writing will free him from his horrors. Under an assumed name he authors a novel that he turns into a successful play that is performed throughout a theater chain owned by Madame Rondo. When she insists on meeting the author, Banning is freed from his dark obsession when he sees that she has become a crippled, old woman. The section of the novel set in New Orleans focuses on gambling houses and the political and economic power of illicit activities like prostitution. The focus on sexual psychology may reveal more about the author than the culture of the time.

35. Bedford-Jones, Henry. *The Mardi Gras Mystery.* Garden City, N.Y.: Doubleday, Page, 1921. 313pp.

Mysteries abound in this novel in which most of the action transpires at Mardi Gras balls. During the week leading up to the celebration, the balls, hosted by some of the city's wealthiest individuals and prominent krewes, have been victimized by an elegant thief, the self-denominated "Midnight Masquer" who appears in a leather aviator costume, complete with goggles, and steals jewelry and cash at gunpoint from revelers. Because of his costume and the sound of an engine that accompanies his arrival and departure, he is thought to pilot an airplane to and from his thefts, a technically mysterious undertaking given the French Quarter location of some of his crimes. We soon learn that Henry Gramont, a French nobleman who has given up his title to become an American citizen, is the Midnight Masquer and has not been stealing for his own benefit, but as a way to surreptitiously gain access to the safe of Joseph Maillard, one of the ball hosts. Maillard had been legal guardian and financial advisor to Lucie Ledanois, after the early deaths of her parents. Gramont, who had met Ledanois in Paris, knew that her inheritance had been sadly depleted by Maillard's poor decisions and believes he may find evidence of malfeasance amongst Maillard's papers. Instead, he realizes, Maillard's son Bob, with whom Gramont had invested money to form an oil company whose activities are focused on bayous near New Orleans, has been enriching himself through a series of deceptions. Through the rest of the novel, Gramont tries to extricate himself from the younger Maillard's business venture and establish a fortune for Ledanois based on the remaining lands she owns in the bayou. In the course of his investigations, he discovers that Jachin Fell is the mastermind behind an illegal, interstate lottery and an automobile-stealing ring. Fell, a second father to Ledanois, is a mysterious figure in New Orleans society and politics. The final scion of an old family, Fell is a trained lawyer who has never worked, presumably living off family wealth, and is said to occupy an old Spanish mansion in the Quarter. He never entertains, supposedly because of the ill-health of his mother, with whom he lives, but is invited everywhere in society and is influential with politicians at every level of government from the mayor, to the governor, to a senator who may be elected president. In a final showdown between Gramont and Fell, each man learns important information about the other that reverses expectations the author has carefully fostered in the reader. Although the novel is almost exclusively set in New Orleans with the exception of a few scenes in Bayou Terrebonne, physical description is limited to society events and upper-class interiors, including that of the Chess and Checkers Club, where the novel begins and ends. However, descriptions of Mardi Gras events convey a sense of social life. The narrative captures aspects of larger cultural life in the early 1920s including the continuing impact of World War I on veterans, paternalistic attitudes toward women, and dramatic changes brought by Louisiana oil fields.

36. Bell, Sallie Lee. *The Hidden Treasure*. Grand Rapids, Mich.: Zondervan, 1960. 159pp.
    In this Christian romance novel, the impoverished, twenty-year-old Pamela Gilbert arrives in New Orleans to work as a paid companion for the bedridden Mrs. Rachel Marcy, who resides in a splendid mansion in Bayou St. John, attended by servants. From early in her employment Gilbert and Mrs. Marcy develop a deep bond based on their shared Christian faith. However, she must also deal with Mrs. Marcy's family, all of whom she has given up on with the exception of her youngest son Garth, who is kind and has Christian values. Mrs. Marcy's daughter, the divorced Mildred Lacey and her children, Amelia, Helen, and Johnnie, are all driven by greed and lust, as is Norman Ludlow, Lacey's son from an earlier marriage. Lacey resents Gilbert's presence and creates difficulties for her with the servants. Gilbert is surprised when she falls in love with Ludlow, but is unsuccessful in converting him to Christianity. A crisis comes when Ludlow secretly kills his grandmother to get his inheritance and he and his mother begin tearing the house apart to find the treasure to which Mrs. Marcy often referred. They are disgusted when the treasure chest contains a Bible. The despairing Ludlow rushes away from the house and is involved in an automobile crash. On his deathbed he confesses to the murder but he does not repent. Pamela inherits the house and an income, which Lacey at first resents, but her emotions soften when she learns of Pamela's love for Ludlow. By the end of the novel, Garth, who had been in love with Pamela, is united with her.

37. Bell, Sallie Lee. *The Last Surrender*. Grand Rapids, Mich.: Zondervan, 1959. 183pp.
    This Christian romance novel, intended to be released to coincide with Civil War Centennial observations, addresses the pathos of a divided country by introducing into New Orleans society a

man with Northern sympathies. This is Keith Roland, who had been born in New Orleans, was educated in the North and graduated from West Point. When he returns to the South with his family they occupy the plantation next to that owned by Roger Wilborn. Wilborn has two daughters, Diana and Angela, who have just entered society and engage in a steady round of social activities. Equal in beauty, the girls are very different in temperament; Angela seeks true love, Diana takes pleasure in romantic conquests. Wartime suffering, including the battlefield deaths and maiming of friends, the indignities inflicted during the occupation of Benjamin Butler's forces, and the new legal status of African-Americans reform Diana and prepare Angela to see that her true love is Keith Roland, who is part of the Union occupation force and is billeted with the Wilborns in their Esplanade Avenue mansion. Bell researched the Civil War and is conscientious in her attempts to incorporate historical details into this romance novel.

38. Bell, Sallie Lee. *The Long Search*. Grand Rapids, Mich.: Zondervan, 1958. 194pp.

James Thornton travels by bus from his Arizona hometown to New Orleans to revenge himself on Thomas Martin. To gain control of the business they co-owned, Martin framed Thornton's father for a crime that he did not commit. Thornton's father died in prison and his mother has died more recently of tuberculosis, exacerbated by emotional stress. Although Thornton is on a mission, he is distracted when twenty-year-old Faith Ransom awkwardly boards the bus, since she is so helpless and out of place. He learns that Ransom's mother recently died and she is traveling to New Orleans to live with her aunt. After he helps her find the address, they discover the aunt is dead and Ransom has nowhere to go. They find rooms in a Garden District mansion converted to a rooming house. Soon after Thornton begins the job he had arranged for himself, Ransom gets a job in a Royal Street antiques shop. Although Thornton begins tracking down every New Orleans possessor of the common name, "Thomas Martin," he keeps getting distracted by Ransom's problems and his feelings for her. By the time she is falsely accused of stealing valuable jewelry, he is prepared to marry her. Although Ransom is convicted and begins her prison sentence, she is eventually acquitted through the efforts of Martin, a sympathetic lawyer and an insurance investigator who uncovers the fraudulent activities of the antiques shop owner for whom Ransom worked. Prison was too hard on Ransom, and she is brought back to New Orleans in an ambulance and taken to a hospital for treatment of tuberculosis. While there she fulfills her dead mother's wish that she embrace Christianity, after evangelist Linda Martinez begins visiting her. Martinez also befriends Thornton and after Ransom's death, he confesses his controlling passion for vengeance and is eventually converted to Christianity. When he finally discovers Martin, he realizes the truth of the biblical text, "Vengeance is mine, saith the Lord" and is freed from his obsession with revenge. Even though this novel is almost entirely set in New Orleans, little is specific to the city except for general descriptions of the Garden District and French Quarter that establish the setting.

39. Bell, Sallie Lee. *Marcel Armand: A Romance of Old Louisiana.* Illustrated by Harold Cue. Boston: L.C. Page, 1935. 343pp.

This historical romance novel is another retelling of events surrounding the Battle of New Orleans. In this account, Jean Lafitte's (c.1776–c.1823) second-in-command is Marcel Armand. The British offer Lafitte and his men lucrative commissions in the British Navy and tracts of land in return for the pirates allowing the British fleet to use the Bay of Barataria as their base of operations. Armand convinces Lafitte to use information about the bribe to barter for the freedom of Pierre Lafitte, who is being held in U.S. government custody. On his way to Governor Claiborne, Armand encounters Elbee Rochelle, the daughter of Paul Rochelle, a wealthy New Orleanean, and he falls in love. He still completes his mission by successfully negotiating with Claiborne, who agrees to release Pierre and end any criminal action against Lafitte and his men so long as Armand gives him the British plans and Lafitte and his men give up piracy. Elbee's suitor, Andrew Fournier, hears of Claiborne's deal with Armand and rues his involvement with the British for he was the one who led them to Barataria. Most of the rest of the novel is dedicated to the alliance between Andrew Jackson (1767–1845) and Lafitte to defeat the British and the rivalry between Fournier and Armand for the hand of Elbee. In a bizarre plot twist, Elbee is also a friend of Armand's sister Mathilde who resides in New Orleans. Near the novel's dramatic conclusion we learn that Fournier had an affair with Mathilde that resulted in a pregnancy and miscarriage. In the aftermath of the miscarriage, she kills Fournier and then commits suicide. Descriptions include a governor's ball, a Voodoo ceremony, a duel, and general New Orleans street scenes. The book is mostly concerned with the Lafittes and the British threat.

40. Bell, Sallie Lee. *The Promise.* Grand Rapids, Mich.: Zondervan, 1966. 147pp.

In this Christian romance novel, a young man, Dick James, is disappointed in his romance with Nancy Crawford, a new girl in town, when she reveals that she could never take his attentions seriously because he is not a Christian. Dick's life has been filled with losses and he cannot see God's loving design in them. He was born a twin into the impoverished household of a loving couple. The intense emotional relationship with his parents and twin came to an end when he was just a child. A drunken driver ran down his mother while she was on her way to catch a bus to the hospital where Dick's father had been taken with appendicitis, from which he died. The twins were adopted by different families who quickly lost touch with each other after the James family moved to New Orleans. Dick's adoptive parents are devoutly Christian but he never converts. A popular football hero, he is a high school senior when Nancy Crawford moves to town, and he dates her by introducing her to New Orleans. As a result the novel is filled with history and information about famous sites and restaurants. Although Nancy likes Dick, she admires Brad Forrest and is drawn into his church group. Dick's thwarted love affair is followed by the deaths of his adoptive father and mother. He begins a joyless post-school existence, distracting himself by working very hard at his new job (which happens to be at the same company for which Brad works). Brad consistently tries to convert Dick, but has no success. However, when he saves Dick's life after a fire on the work site, Brad sees a distinctive scar on Brad's body and realizes he has been reunited with his twin. He converts and Nancy reveals she never stopped loving him. While primarily a tool for proselytization, the novel includes a surprising amount of information on New Orleans distilled from history books and tourist guides.

41. Bell, Sallie Lee. *The Silver Cord.* Grand Rapids, Mich.: Zondervan, 1958. 216pp.

Childhood sweethearts Gwen and Sonny grow up in Christian homes in New Orleans but have difficulty following God's plan for them as they make difficult choices for which they are unprepared. Not long after the death of her parents Gwen is at a revival with Sonny when he responds to an altar call that leads to a scholarship at a Christian school in Georgia. Gwen is embittered by the separation, but Sonny remains faithful to their engagement and saves all the money he makes from touring with the school's gospel quartet in order to visit her in New Orleans. In the hope of rapidly saving enough money to marry Gwen, he accepts a position with a secular radio station, but Gwen believes he is going against God's will by using his voice for non-religious purposes and breaks with him. When Sonny meets the talented Lora they begin a professional partnership that leads to television work and romance. However, Sonny's television career and relationship with Lora ends in disaster when he succumbs to the temptations of drink while socializing with other entertainers. No longer able to support himself as a singer, he enlists as a soldier, is sent to Korea and is reunited there with Gwen, who is engaged in missionary work, with both once again seeing the plan God has for their lives. Although New Orleans is a backdrop for much of the novel (that includes descriptions of Mardi Gras) the city is mostly a malign presence as the home of the music industry that almost destroys Sonny.

42. Bell, Sallie Lee. *Torchbearer.* Grand Rapids, Mich.: Zondervan, 1956. 185pp.

Although much of this novel is set small Southern towns, the most dramatic sequence of events transpires in New Orleans and the city has an important symbolic role in the book. Barry

Carter and David Gardner, friends since childhood, are about to graduate from the college where they were roommates. However, their plans for the future have taken newly divergent paths that trouble Carter. While he was ill with influenza, Gardner attended a series of revival meetings and realized his vocation as a Christian minister. So, instead of following the career path he and Carter had planned, of graduating law school and starting a shared practice, Gardner will attend seminary. This is the first time that Gardner, always the quieter, physically slight, weaker one, has not followed Carter's leadership and Carter is resentful. When the two return to their hometown for the summer, Carter is also angry that his former girlfriend, Cicily (sic), is dating Roy Farlan, a rich boy, who Carter knows to be a psychologically damaged sadist. He wins back Cicily and is engaged to marry her, but at his bachelor's party, he breaks his promise to Gardner not to drink and, while driving drunk, causes an accident that kills Gardner. Seriously injured and recovering in a hospital bed, Carter receives visits from Gardner's girlfriend Dale, whose subtle influence sets him on the course to a Christian conversion experience. Furthermore, he becomes convinced that he should carry out Gardner's vocation. When he announces to Cicily his plans to become a Christian minister, she rejects him and marries Roy Farlan for a life of material ease. Soon afterwards, Farlan has an automobile accident that leaves him dependent on a wheelchair, as well as embittered and vicious. Sometime later, when Farlan discovers Cicily had clipped a newspaper announcement of Carter's appointment to a New Orleans pastorate, he formulates a plan for revenge. Farlan rents a furnished house in the Garden District, complete with servants, for several months. Arriving the week before Mardi Gras, he insists that they attend Carter's church. Then on a day when he announces he will be out of the city on business, Cicily behaves as he surmises and invites Carter to their house to vent her unhappiness. Farlan surprises them in an innocent kiss, announces he has a brain tumor that will kill him in six months, and tells them he will kill one or both of them without fear of punishment. Cicily gains control of the gun and shoots him, but he lives long enough to tell a maid that Gardner shot him. To protect Cicily, Gardner does not resist arrest and trial, but is deeply disappointed when Cicily perjures herself. Fortunately, a New Orleans man Carter had converted is a lawyer who wins him a light sentence based on a self-defense argument and engineers Carter's release after he helps prison officials thwart an escape attempt. Later he also helps him get a job as a factory foreman far away from New Orleans. Carter eventually earns social redemption when he helps prevent a violent strike and is recalled to his church when Cicily, in her dying breath, confesses her crime. In the novel New Orleans represents urban life with all of its opportunities and threats.

43. Best, Allena Champlin [Erick Berry, pseud.]. *Homespun.* Illustrated by Harold Von Schmidt. New York: Junior Literary Guild and Lothrop, Lee and Shepard, 1937. 308pp.

Yankee thrift, industry and business genius is celebrated in this paean to American industry, published as the United States was emerging from the Depression and when corporate America and an enlarged federal government were being touted as the country's saviors. The Greenman family lives on a farm outside the village of Friendship, New York, in a frontier area close enough to the recently completed Erie Canal to benefit from trade opportunities with distant places. After years of saving to raise capital, one of the seven Greenman children, Mark, is about to set off for Santa Fe with his new wife to transport bolts of New England calico fabric in return for a share of the profits. They travel to St. Louis with Mark's brother Stephen, who is off to work in the office of his maternal uncle, Nathan Stillman, who buys and sells indigo, molasses, and cotton. Stillman's office is on Toulouse Street and he resides in Faubourg St. Marie in a house that replicates the Rhode Island Stillman family houses. His wife Persis keeps house exactly as she would have done in New England, without slaves, or even servants. This adherence to origins does not mean that Stillman has isolated himself from New Orleans culture. He knows that business is built on personal relationships and he encourages Stephen's friendship with Enrique Roldan, the son of a wealthy Creole, just back from Paris. Through Roldan, Stephen is introduced to upper-class Creole life and horse culture, eventually getting to ride a horse from the Roldan stables in the St.

Mary's Day race. Horses are also the basis for his first meeting with Alexandrine Foucher, when he rescues her from an ill-behaved mount. Foucher's father owns a large plantation and has cotton contracts with Stillman. When Stephen treats Foucher with fairness by canceling a contract that could have ruined the plantation owner, Foucher gives Stephen a slave, Musa, with whom Stephen has bonded over Musa's knowledge of horses. Soon Musa, the prince to an African kingdom, is headed back to Africa on a journey funded by Stephen. New Orleans is the setting for only seventy-six pages (pp. 137–213), yet the author makes vivid use of the backdrop and touches on the mixed allegiances of New Orleaneans, slavery, the relationship between cotton and slavery, and the importance of the city's location as a hub for extensive transportation networks.

44. Biery, William. *The House on Esplanade*. New York: Mason and Lipscomb, 1973. 216pp.

After graduating from Loyola University and rejecting his father's plan that he work for his employer, the railroad, Mark Dennick returns to New Orleans in February 1957 as a hitchhiker, having failed to establish himself elsewhere. When he reconnects with his former girlfriend, Michelle DeJoie, he discovers she is pregnant with his child and he is suddenly eager to settle down and follow his father's footsteps, no matter how mind-numbing the work. However, when he impulsively takes Michelle to get a marriage license, Miss Pearl Marie LeCroix, Deputy Registrar, who maintains a personal file of mixed-race individuals, in which Michelle is listed, personally denies their application. The novel explores the anti-miscegenation law, the unfair power the law gave bureaucrats such as LeCroix, and the human costs (Michelle attempts suicide and later abortion from which she nearly dies). A few people in the novel—a priest and a physician—have begun fighting the law and win a small victory in getting LeCroix dismissed from her job. Even so, Mark and Michelle cannot marry in New Orleans and she refuses to move elsewhere, which would entail leaving her job as a librarian at Tulane University and her family, who through decades of hard labor have raised themselves from poverty in Treme to middle-class respectability in the Garden District. By the end of the novel, through an entry level job at Jax Brewery in the advertising department, Mark has discovered his gift for public relations and is about to start the city's first public relations office, even though the dark views he held of New Orleans as a corrupt, troubled city have been deepened by his experiences since his return to the city. Written from the perspective of the 1970s, the 1950s New Orleans of the novel has few redeeming qualities. Mardi Gras celebrations are denigrated, the French Quarter consists of bars and decaying housing, and family life is a quagmire of dangerous mendacity.

45. Blake, Christopher Stanislas. *The Fair Fair Ladies of Chartres Street*. New Orleans: Beale, 1965. 189pp.

All of the short stories in this volume are set in New Orleans and evoke life on Chartres Street in the 1960s. After years of neglect and decline, historic preservation efforts have made the French Quarter and Chartres Street in particular an attractive place to live. The women in the book all share a love for the French Quarter, but only a few of them work for pay and these are among the few who are native to New Orleans. Liva Hautcourt embarrasses her prominent Garden District family by operating an antiques shop out of a house on Chartres Street, which she chose since it was less expensive than the same place would be on Royal Street, the typical location for such a business. As the story develops, we learn the importance even modest amounts of money have for Hautcourt. She destroys her opportunity to marry a wealthy, attractive man when she refuses to spend the five hundred dollars he gave her to pay for a grand engagement party, and from her twisted perspective is happier to hold onto the money than she would have been to hold onto the man. Manuela O'Brien is the proprietor of a restaurant patronized by locals who appreciate her execution of simple dishes like red beans and rice and also respect the piety she expresses to a doll effigy of Saint Anthony of Padua that never leaves her arms. Her fiancé is less understanding and meets a terrible end after physically separating O'Brien from her saint. Another eccentric, Psyche Dearborne, the daughter of a wealthy New Orleans family who has dressed in antebellum clothes since her youth, is intent on spending her fortune on renovating one house after another in the district, and when the man she is forced to marry through social pressure resents her life work and destroys an antique, she responds with violence. Other women who work or have a vocation include a kept woman and a nun. In general, though, the women in the stories move to New Orleans from New England, the Northwest, or the Midwest to walk into the historic settings they so admire and create lives for themselves as poets, society hostesses, artists, or women of leisure devoted to their hobbies. Their physical settings bring happiness to few of them, while they struggle against manipulative men who deceive and take advantage of them. The book presents many cultural attitudes toward the French Quarter and conveys a sense of social life in the neighborhood while touching on the plight of middle-aged women in a sexist society. Written by a man, in many of these stories the women find redress through violence.

46. Blake, Gladys. *Belinda in Old New Orleans*. New York: D. Appleton, 1932. 295pp.

Belinda Morton's mother died when Belinda was only four-years-old and although well-provided for by her affluent, physician father, Morton received little affection from her emotionally distant parent. As a fourteen-year-old, when she learns that her father is going to remarry, she reminds him that he had promised her mother that, should he wed again, he would send Morton to live with her maternal aunt, the widowed Madame Pauline de Chanterelle, in New Orleans. Fascinated by her mother's Creole origins and eager to connect with female relatives (her aunt has two daughters, fifteen-year-old Ismanie and eleven-year-old Suzette) Morton does not realize that her father is secretly hurt by her eagerness to leave him. Consigned to the care of an Alexandria merchant and his wife, she sets off in the spring of 1814 on a trip by private carriage and steamboat. When the steamboat boiler explodes, Simon "Sim" Kent, a sixteen-year-old boy from the Kentucky frontier saves Morton's life. He is traveling to New Orleans to deliver a letter to Monsieur Henri de Chanterelle, Morton's aunt's father-in-law, with whom she lives. So, he also delivers Morton to her aunt. Initially, Morton's relatives are shocked by Kent and his frontier manners, contrasting him negatively with Auguste St. Elmo, the young man who Monsieur de Chanterelle intends to make his heir, since both of his sons are dead. Outer appearances deceive the Chanterelles however, for the orphaned Kent was mentored by a judge, through whom he became acquainted with both Andrew Jackson (1767–1845) and Governor Claiborne (c.1772/75–1817). While in New Orleans, he takes on secret missions for Claiborne to ferret out spies and, with the aid of Morton and her cousins, gathers evidence against Auguste St. Elmo, saving Andrew Jackson's life when Elmo attempts to assassinate him. The novel relates an outline history of New Orleans and the War of 1812. Morton crosses paths with all of the major historical figures, including Jean Lafitte (c.1776–c.1823). Morton's father, concerned for her safety, arrives in New Orleans, redeeming himself in her eyes. After Henri de Chanterelle reveals that the letter Sim delivered indicated that Sim was the son of Chanterelle's estranged son, now deceased (a claim Chanterelle investigated and found to be true) Morton's father privately advises him to return to Kentucky and the lawyer training he had planned, to make his own way in the world, rather than depending upon his inheritance. The novel treats Auguste St. Elmo as the typical product of a corrupt New Orleans society reliant upon slave labor and adhering to anti-republican views in which social status is dependent upon inherited wealth and lineage.

47. Blassingame, Wyatt. *John Smith Hears Death Walking*. New York: Bartholomew House, 1944. 190pp.

In the title work of this volume of detective mystery novellas and short stories, John Smith and his savvy reporter wife, Marion, battle a seemingly all-powerful blackmailer, "The Master of Murder." Lured by odd messages to a house on Lake Pontchartrain, each of them separately witnesses the murder of Judge Bowden Harker from potassium cyanide, while in the presence of his daughter. Harker had been blackmailed for years and forced to throw cases appearing before him. He dies just as he is about to hand Smith evidence of blackmailing. When Marion and Smith return to their St. Charles Avenue home, their servant, Bushelmouth Johnson, admits a newspaper publisher and crime reporter on an urgent mission. The pair warns Smith that they have received incontrovertible evidence that he murdered the judge out of jealousy since his wife frequented the man's Lake Pontchartrain house and give him twenty-four hours to try to prove his innocence. After putting Marion in hiding on a Bayou St. John houseboat, Smith follows leads around New Orleans, mostly in the French Quarter and the Central Business District. The novella ends inconclusively, but Nathan Holcomb, a steamship executive, is suspected of being the mastermind with a Japanese servant of the police commissioner, Glen Duval, his henchman. While several instances of harsh racism are vented against Johnson, his heroism saves Marion. However, throughout this World War II era novel, Japanese people are portrayed as treacherous. A second novella featuring the detective and his wife deals with a man seemingly threatened by a ghost. The ghost appears to be Claude Lorraine, who had died thirty-five years before, murdered by the brother of Philip De Gault, the man hearing the threatening ghost. De Gault knew his brother Maximilian had murdered Lorraine, but never informed the police. They may have suspected, but the De Gaults were a prominent family. Maximilian's motive for murder was that Lorraine had discovered an illegitimate son to whom he had decided to leave his fortune, cutting out the De Gault brothers. In solving the crime, Smith draws upon the historical knowledge of a cemetery caretaker who has become obsessed with the life stories of the skeletons in his charge. The book includes several other novellas in which Smith solves murders, all of them set at least in part in New Orleans. The novellas often feature a well-kept secret revolving around some past event, eerie abandoned houses, cemeteries, and boats on swampy waterways just outside New Orleans.

48. Bontemps, Arna(ud) Wendell. *God Sends Sunday.* New York: Harcourt, Brace, 1931. 199pp.

Augie, the African-American protagonist of this novel, was born on a plantation where his family had been enslaved and where his sister still lives and works. Although Augie begins working when still a child he is too slight-of-build to be given very difficult tasks and spends his time day-dreaming, a tendency that fits his compatriots' understanding that he has a connection to the spirit world, since he was born with a caul over his face. Not yet a teenager, he stows away on a steamboat bound for New Orleans. Within hours of arriving in the city he has a place to stay and a job, after befriending the elderly African-American manager of Horace Woodbine's extensive stables. Augie's sensitivity gives him a way with horses that makes him an excellent stable hand, and his small stature eventually earns him the chance to become a jockey. Soon he is wearing the flashy clothing and jewelry of a racetrack habitué and pursuing women as an entitlement of his new status. Among these women, however, Florence Dessau stands out as all that Augie most desires in a female, starting with the "yellow" skin tone that reveals she is of mixed race. Augie actively courts Florence even though Woodbine has made her his mistress, establishing her in her own house with a maid, carriage, and driver. Fortunately, the racetrack circuit takes Augie away from New Orleans for extended periods so that he can try to forget Florence in the company of other "yellow" women. He spends extended time in St. Louis because of the active racing scene there and the extensive red-light district, where he finds Della Green. Thwarted by Green's pimp, Bigelow Brown, in forming an exclusive relationship, the two have a public showdown during the cakewalk at the Cotton Flower Ball. With little provocation, Augie shoots Brown to death. Although he is tried the legal system is said to pay little attention to black on black crime in the red-light district and he is released with a warning to avoid such rough characters as Brown. When he returns to New Orleans he is at the apogee of his rise in wealth and social acclaim until he seeks out Florence and the two begin openly living together (Woodbine stopped seeing her after the success of Augie's earlier attentions became public). This is a violation, however, of the social mores of the time and the constant public censure drives Florence out of the house Woodbine had given her and to a shack by the rail yards. Woodbine gets his revenge on Augie by giving him the worst mounts, and he experiences loss after loss. No longer earning any money he takes up gambling and further destroys his reputation for luck. With his fortune gone he seeks out his sister who has moved to the Watts section of Los Angeles and the rest of the novel is set on the West Coast. Although the book is only partly set in New Orleans the African-American community, racing community, and some aspects of race politics are illuminated. Readers will find the violence against women that is presented as an expected part of sexual relations, particularly disturbing.

49. Bouchon, Henry L. *Beyond Indecency: A Novel.* New Orleans: Roy L. Wilson Printing, 1974. 197pp.

In the sexually liberated 1970s, eighteen-year-old Helen Braud, the granddaughter of an insurance agency owner, who lost her mother as a youngster, arrives in New Orleans to visit her grandparents, although secretly she hopes to explore her sexuality. Helen's remarried father is the stepbrother of Randolph Braud, a Tulane University graduate who is in his late twenties, lives on Canal Street, works as an apprentice draftsman in an architectural firm, and aspires to be a novelist. Randolph sets up a double date with his office colleague Harvey Foster. He escorts his girlfriend, twenty-one-year-old Patricia Naquin. The evening begins at the Monteleone Hotel and includes a walk along Bourbon Street, a steak dinner at Arnaud's, and excursion to Lake Pontchartrain. The evening ends with Helen's offer to type the manuscript for a draft of Randolph's novel. Her time is quickly occupied by her work for Randolph and by being shown off by her grandmother at New Orleans society events, mostly in private homes, but also in the dining rooms of St. Charles Avenue apartment hotels. Randolph becomes increasingly enamored of her and competes with Foster to take Helen out for titillating evening entertainments, including riverboat excursions, visits to City Park, drinks at the Roosevelt Hotel's Blue Room, an excursion to Covington, a movie at the Loews State, a burlesque show on Bourbon Street, and drinks at the Dollhouse Lounge, where Randolph knows the proprietress and is acquainted with the romantic life of a number of the waitresses and entertainers, some of whom are having affairs with married men, and others of whom are outright call girls. Although Helen and Randolph eventually have sex, she is too unsophisticated to realize that she has the power to displace Randolph's girlfriend, Patricia. So, when Donald Mead invites her on a date she accepts. They go to a cocktail party at J.C. Yates' mansion (in addition to a large swimming pool it has three elevators). There is also a yachting party on Yates' yacht (he is married but lives apart from his wife who resides on the Riviera) and Mead turns out to be procurer for Yates, who will pay him two hundred and fifty dollars if Helen will have sex with him, causing her to flee. Not long afterwards, Helen realizes she is pregnant with Randolph's baby, but is disturbed by his reaction when she breaks the news, and achieves an abortion through homely methods. Wanting to show her independence from him she increasingly explores dive bars, slumming with a girlfriend at a gay bar named Gay Power and a lesbian bar named Off Limits. When they go to a gangster hangout, the Hot Spot, Helen is given a drug and is about to be raped by two gangsters when Randolph shows up to rescue her. They escape to Algiers and Randolph proposes. Although Helen gets the opportunity to explore a sexually liberal New Orleans (in addition to wealthy roués, gays, and lesbians, sexually carefree hippies are discussed), by the end of the experience she is eager to settle down into a traditional marriage with an older man.

50. Bouvet, Marguerite. *Clotilde.* Illustrated by Maginel Wright Enright. Chicago: A.C. McClurg, 1908. 216pp.

Clotilde is the daughter of Chevalier de la Motte Leroix, a French nobleman who had fled France during the Revolution. Arriving in New Orleans as a fifty-year-old man with few resources, in sixteen years he has amassed a fortune even greater than the one he had inherited and lost. He also married the most beautiful woman in his social circle, even though she was forty years his junior. His sisters were alarmed for Clotilde, the daughter of the union, and undertook her education in France. Madame Leroix quickly forgot about Clotilde, particularly after the Chevalier dies and she gets control of his estate. As a young woman Clotilde returns from France and is shocked by her mother's behavior. She is introduced to New Orleans by servants and a governess and falls in love with the city and its culture. She also finds one person in Madame Leroix's circle whom she comes to respect, the Spanish Captain de Sabla. Unable to overcome her repugnance for her mother's loose living she goes into a convent. After several trials, she realizes she is not called to become a nun. When she is reunited with her mother, she finds a chastened woman who has lost her youth, her beauty, and most of the money that Clotilde should have inherited. Fortunately, Clotilde's frugal aunts saved and invested the money the Chevalier sent them for Clotilde's education and care and, upon their death, a legacy comes to Clotilde. When she is reunited with Captain de Sabla they plan for their marriage and a life together in the house the Chevalier constructed, which they will restore together. The novel is set during the period when New Orleans is ruled by France and describes the city during this era and the astonishment citizens' experience as the territory is sold to the United States.

51. Bowden, Jean [Barbara Annandale, pseud.]. *The French Lady's Lover.* New York: Coward, McCann and Geoghegan, 1978. 288pp.

Around the turn of the nineteenth century, when nineteen-year-old Will Napier learns from his mother that his long dead father was an American who served with Captain John Paul Jones, he is inspired to leave the house of his stepfather, a Scottish laird, and to travel to the United States. He arrives in Philadelphia in time to briefly meet and become intrigued by thirteen-year-old Jacqueline de L'Ebenoit, who is commencing a voyage to Paris with her wealthy, New Orleans father. As Napier follows leads to track down his father's friends and acquaintances, he is informed that one of his business partners recently died, leaving Napier the sole owner of the Newfoundland and Ocean Shipping Company, a rapidly growing concern. Furthermore, Benjamin Franklin's daughter Sarah (1743–1808) and her husband, Richard Bache (1737–1811), are eager to aid Napier because of his father's friendship with the now deceased Franklin. They introduce him into Philadelphia society and Bache mentors him in business. Before long, Napier is on his way to Paris to gather inside information on Napoleon Bonaparte (1769–1821) for Vice-President Thomas Jefferson (another of his father's acquaintances). While in France, Napier re-encounters the young Jacqueline, but his romantic interests focus on Josephine Bonaparte. When he saves the life of Jacqueline and her father at the battle of Marengo, a jealous Josephine soon arranges for him to be convicted of a crime he did not commit and to be sent to the Devil's Island penal colony. Only Jacqueline's efforts back in the United States eventually win his release. However, the traditional romantic ending, a wedding, is still years away, for Jacqueline's powerful father is adamantly opposed to having an American in the family. When Napier follows Jacqueline to New Orleans, much of the plot revolves around the surprising importance of the code duello, the uneasy relationship between New Orleans social leaders and the United States in the years after the Louisiana Purchase, and shifting allegiances after the fall of Bonaparte, and during the War of 1812. Although Jacqueline's father insists she marry an impoverished and unattractive French nobleman who has been living in Canadian exile, the marriage is never consummated, and after Will Napier helps nurse Jacqueline back from a nearly fatal accident, the couple begins living together as lovers while Jacqueline's father is stranded in Martinique and her husband is living in Pensacola. A number of figures important to New Orleans history appear in the novel, including, most prominently, Jean Lafitte (c.1776–c.1823), whose closeness to Jacqueline and Will eventually inspires the pirate to take sides with the Americans against the British.

52. Braddon, M(ary) E(lizabeth). *The Octoroon, or, The Lily of Louisiana.* New York: R.M. DeWitt, 1869. 116pp.

This work concerned with racial injustice is substantially set in New Orleans, but physical description is insubstantial. Not surprisingly, considering the book's origins in serial format, the novel is filled with incident and characters. One plot line follows the household of Don Juan Moraquitos, who appeared in 1840s New Orleans with a fortune rumored to have been won through piracy and other violent misdeeds. He built a lavish mansion for his beautiful wife,

Olympia, who promptly died leaving an infant daughter, Camilla. Shortly afterwards, Tomaso Crivelli, Moraquitos' brother-in-law, died on a business trip to New Orleans just after willing his fortune to Moraquitos. He left behind a boy, Paul Lisimons, who becomes a part of Moraquitos' household. In another plot line, Cora Leslie, who has been educated in Switzerland and England by her wealthy father, Gerald Leslie, is spotted at a ball by New Orleanean Mortimer Percy, who is familiar with her background. He warns various people that Cora is of mixed race, including his relative Adelaide Horton, who had been Leslie's dear friend. Cora's father had come to England to celebrate the completion of her schooling and, secretly, to resettle there with his daughter. He had sold all of his properties and investments and given the cash to his friend Philip Treverton to transmit to Silas Craig for investment. When the body of the man presumed to be Treverton is found without any cash, Craig insists he never received the money. Without resources, the Leslies are unable to relocate and Cora must return to New Orleans. Before her arrival, rumor has spread that Leslie had educated his illegitimate, mixed-race daughter and thus he had broken the law and could be prosecuted. Furthermore, because of his recent impoverishment, Cora could be seized and sold as an asset by his creditors. A number of characters, including young Gilbert Margrave, are not only ready to accept Cora, but celebrate her as a jewel of her race. However, corrupt people employ the law for selfish ends and Cora is soon on the auction block. In the meantime, Camilla Moraquitos returns from her education abroad and love blossoms between her and Paul Lisimons. It is a thwarted love, for although Moraquitos has raised him as a son, the Don knows that Lisimons is the mixed-race offspring of Tomaso Crivelli and will not permit any romance. By the end of the novel at least one death, and one resurrection (that of Philip Treverton, who was not actually dead), bring about justice for Lisimons, who gets access to his father's wealth by marrying Camilla after her father's death, and for the Leslies when Gerald forces Silas Craig to give back the money he had stolen from Treverton. All of the lovers and honorable characters leave the United States for Europe and for societies that do not suppress mixed-race people through legal strictures. The corruption of New Orleans is expressed in scenes of the auction block and the crooked gambling house owned by Silas Craig.

53. Bradford, Roark. *John Henry*. Illustrated by J.J. Lankes. New York: Harper and Brothers, 1931. 225pp.

Although John Henry is a "ramblin'" man, significant sections of this ode to his life are set in New Orleans. Born in the depths of the Mississippi Delta's Black River country, African-American John Henry is remarkable for his strength and ability to work, which he demonstrates in the cotton field, on the levee toting cotton bales onto steamboats, and, later, on the railroad. His work on the levee finances his travel as far North as Natchez, as does his work supplying coal to a railroad fireman. The only place he returns to repeatedly is New Orleans. When he first arrives there he is immediately marked as a man from a rural area by his clothes and way of speaking. However, when he outwits a con man and proves he is no one's fool, he integrates into local culture with the help of a bevy of admiring women and begins to dress like an urbanite in a Stetson hat and colorful clothing. Before long he falls in love with Julie Ann, although other women, like Ruby, never give up on winning him back. Just as John Henry is about to leave New Orleans, the police round him up with many of the African-Americans he knows, and they are unfairly sentenced to sixty days of labor on the roads. The novel makes plain that city road construction progresses through such practices. Although John Henry needs the stimulation of travel and opportunities to show his prowess for hard labor, he loves Julie Ann and keeps returning to her in New Orleans. Unfortunately, she is unfaithful, claiming that the loneliness of his absence is unbearable. The consolations of gin and cocaine do not salve his emotional pain, and he converts to Christianity as a source of sustenance. He tries living with Julie Ann in New Orleans while she supports them by taking in laundry, but eventually rejects this life to resume his labor on the levees. When he gets there, however, he finds that a steam powered winch system has been put in place and the roustabouts like him are out of work. While trying to prove that he can outwork the machine, he collapses. At his funeral we learn that Julie Ann died in sympathy after witnessing his death. Written as a prose ballad with excerpts of verse, this book captures vernacular speech and presents some aspects of life for African-Americans in New Orleans' Back-of-Town neighborhood.

54. Bradford, Roark. *Let the Band Play Dixie.* New York: Harper and Brothers, 1934. 320pp.

The short stories in this collection are more concerned with characterization, colorful stories, and rhythms of speech than place, but New Orleans does serve as a setting. The characters tend to be field hands and roustabouts under the sway of often-violent sexual passions, while settings include jazz bars, Bienville Street landing, and Back-of-Town (historically New Orleans was divided into Uptown, Downtown, and Back of Town—less developed swampy land).

55. Brandon, Winnie. *Dixiana: A Romance of New Orleans.* New York: A.L. Burt, 1930. 253pp.

A novelization of the screenplay by Luther Trent for the film of the same name by RKO Radio Pictures, this book was released in the same year. Although Dixiana Lee, the star performer with the Cayetano Circus, might be assumed worldly, Ginger and Peewee, clowns from her act, have sheltered her from the world. However, as she enters adulthood she has become headstrong and even though the clowns warn her against riverboat gambler Montagne (sic), she begins accepting his attention. Montagne has an unwilling ally in Señor Cayetano, the former owner of the circus, who still manages the enterprise at Montagne's pleasure after losing the business to him during a riverboat poker game. Plantation owner and New Orleans businessman Philip Van Horne had witnessed the gambling and realizing that Montagne was cheating. He subsequently challenged the card shark to a duel, since he owned the building Montagne has been renting for use as a gambling hall and felt implicated in Montagne's regular practice of cheating customers. Montagne's underling, Blondell, tampers with the dueling pistols and Van Horne is mortally wounded. Montagne's plans to possess Dixiana are thwarted by the arrival in New Orleans of Carl Van Horne, the nephew and heir of the deceased. He and Dixiana are immediately smitten with each other and, seething with jealousy, Montagne forces Cayetano to void Dixiana's circus contract. She goes to work singing and dancing in his gambling parlor. Determined to marry Dixiana, Carl appears at the gambling parlor, but is tricked into getting drunk and joining a poker game with Montagne. Dixiana saves him from losing his plantation when she knocks cards out of Montagne's sleeves, but in his confused state Carl thinks she is the gambler's accomplice. Carl's trusted New Orleans lawyer, Colonel Porter, convinces him of Dixiana's loyalty and reveals that he has found evidence that Dixiana is his own granddaughter, the child of his estranged daughter. However, a duel, prison escape, and two kidnappings of Dixiana intervene before the novel's happy ending. The evils of slavery and a foreshadowing of the tragedy of the Civil War are touched on in a perfunctory fashion in the novel, and New Orleans appears as a colorful backdrop for a melodramatic story with little physical description specific to the city except for Mardi Gras street scenes.

56. Braun, Matthew. *The Stuart Women.* New York: Putnam, 1980. 362pp.

Although this novel is not exclusively set in New Orleans, significant sections take place there and the city plays an important role in establishing one of the major themes: the novelty of American social class. The plot centers on Tom Stuart's efforts to establish a Rio Grande shipping company in the late 1840s. A twenty-four-year-old Irish immigrant, Stuart had worked as a riverboat pilot under a contract with the Army Quartermaster and in this capacity had earned the trust of General Zachary Taylor. As the Mexican-American War came to a close, Stuart realized that American settlement along the Rio Grande would create demand for steamboat transportation to and from New Orleans. He designs a new steamboat to enable navigation in water too shallow for traditional steamboats. His banker is the Creole gentleman Jacques Lescaut and through Lescaut he is introduced to the widowed man's adopted family: Jovette St. Vrain and her brother Henri, the youngest generation of the St. Vrain family. Jovette and Stuart fall in love at first sight, but Jovette is betrothed to the unpleasant Etienne Blanque in an arranged marriage, even though

Jovette feels no love for him. Fortunately, Henri befriends Stuart since, unlike many Creoles, he is an admirer of Americans. Through a series of Creole social events, Stuart realizes the strict social hierarchies Creoles observe and hopes Jovette has a more American view of social mobility. Before she can fully explore her feelings, Stuart is forced into a duel with Blanque, whom he kills. Although the St. Vrain family would have managed the potential for scandal by a long trip to France, Stuart passionately sweeps her to the altar and the two wed in St. Louis Cathedral before a huge crowd of curious Creoles. The couple departs for Brownsville, Texas to avoid the vengeful friends of Blanque and the remainder of the novel, dealing with a violent rivalry between Stuart and another steamboat company owner, is set there. In the frontier settlement of Brownsville, Jovette, who had been at the pinnacle of New Orleans society, is disdained for exactly the same reserved behavior that was admired in Creole society. Throughout the book the impulsive, energetic Stuart is portrayed as an American type to be admired and celebrated over people such as the St. Vrains who hold too tightly to European notions of behavior and social class.

57. Breslin, Howard. *Concert Grand.* New York: Dodd, Mead, 1963. 307pp.

Breslin's fictional biography of Louis Moreau Gottschalk commences in 1848 when he is already in Paris, and the book is only briefly set in New Orleans (pp. 119–150). In February 1853, Gottschalk returns to his native New Orleans, the place where he was first acclaimed. Taking long walks in the city, Gottschalk observes changes and takes pleasure in buildings he remembers from his youth. When he is feted at dinners, he is reintroduced to Creole cuisine. However, he is also introduced to new aspects of the city from which he was excluded as a boy, including roulette at St. Cyr's, drinking at The Gem, and an octoroon ball where he meets the sophisticated Zenaida Cadiz, an orphan who was educated in a French convent and who had heard Gottschalk perform in Paris. Her character is used to illustrate Gottschalk's opposition to racial discrimination and help explain his Union stance during the Civil War.

58. Bristow, Gwen. *This Side of Glory.* New York: Thomas Y. Crowell, 1940. 400pp.

Transpiring between 1912 and 1918, this romance novel is mostly set on Ardeith Plantation, but New Orleans plays an important role as the urban center for plantation owners in need of society, supplies, and financing. In novels from earlier eras, plantation owners spent seasons in New Orleans. By the era of this novel, the ease of transportation by automobile and train has made the city more accessible and strengthens the connectedness of plantation and town life. Eleanor Upjohn is representative of the town; the daughter of an engineer who owns and operates a company that builds levees, she grew up in New Orleans and has internalized the frugal, hard-working ethos of her parents, each of whom had to make his/her way in the world. Her mother was an orphan who worked in a department store as a young woman and her father was the illegitimate son of a Reconstruction tax collector and a prostitute, who worked his way up from the bottom in the world of levee construction. The couple built an affluent upper-middle-class life for themselves in New Orleans. By contrast, Kester Larne is the offspring of generations of plantation owners. Not only has he never worked; he has been accustomed to living on bank credit tendered against the next cotton crop. He meets Eleanor while she is working as her father's secretary on a levee project near the Larne family's Ardeith Plantation. They fall in love immediately, but each of their families opposes the match. The Upjohns are concerned for the financial well-being of their daughter if she marries a man who has never worked and lives on a bankrupt plantation (even if the place does total more than two-thousand acres). The Larnes suffered during the Civil War and Reconstruction as their finances crumbled and they were frequently at the mercy of "common" people, and fear that no matter how stellar Eleanor's qualities may seem on the surface, when subjected to personal trials her commonness will emerge. Both Kester and Eleanor are strong willed, however, and marry over their parents' objections. Eleanor quickly learns that Ardeith Plantation is owned by the bank and forces Kester to realize his true financial situation. Although she motivates him to transform aspects of plantation operations, he begins to resent her seriousness just as Isabel Valcour, a beautiful, carefree society belle from his youth, returns to New Orleans. An affair follows, as does Kester's prolonged absence during World War I. By the time he returns, Eleanor has paid off the plantation's debts and transformed production on the property; but she has also become older and plainer and more serious. After a crisis over the health of one of their children, the two must decide where their priorities lie and whether they can build a life together. Throughout the novel Eleanor visits New Orleans to socialize with her family and meet with bankers and financial advisors. Furthermore, the novel makes frequent contrasts between the becalmed life on the plantation and a New Orleans that was transformed by successive waves of immigrants and Northern businessmen. Eleanor points out that Kester is a Southerner and she is an American and, perhaps surprisingly for some readers, New Orleans, that symbol for aspects of Southern life is here treated as an American city, characterized by immigrant assimilation and industry.

59. Bristow, Gwen and Bruce Manning. *The Gutenberg Murders.* New York: Mystery League, 1931. 286pp.

The plot of this murder mystery revolves around the private Sheldon Library, pages from a Gutenberg Bible stolen from the library that may or may not have been authentic, and the library staff and their tangled romantic attachments. When the Bible pages go missing, District attorney Dan Farrell, a plainspoken man with more street smarts than formal education, teams up with Wade (no last name given), a reporter for *The Morning Creole,* who is intelligent and learned but is described as ugly in appearance and off-putting in manner. Quentin Ulman, assistant librarian, is the main suspect in the theft until he is found dead near the library's bindery located between Algiers and Harvey, his features incinerated beyond recognition. Later, Winifred, the wife of Alfredo Gonzales, a professor and library trustee, is also murdered. The solution of the case, in part stems from a study of the complicated will that established the library. Michael Sheldon had made a fortune in sugar in Cuba, married a Cuban woman, and had one daughter, Muriel. When Sheldon returned to New Orleans with his family, two scholars, Dr. Prentiss, and Alfredo Gonzales courted Muriel. Initially, Prentiss was engaged to Muriel, but while on a research trip to Europe, Prentiss was displaced in Muriel's affections by Gonzales. However, in 1911, before the two could marry, Muriel committed suicide. Sheldon and his wife died within the year leaving a nephew, the sculptor Terry Sheldon, as their closest relative. When the Sheldon will was opened it proved a complicated document that established the Muriel Sheldon Library, which was to be directed by whichever of her lovers remained unmarried, Gonzalez or Prentiss. By this point, Gonzalez was engaged, so Prentiss became the director, although Gonzalez was given power through the will by his appointment as trustee over the endowment that funded the library. By the time of the novel, the two have fought with each other for almost twenty years. While Prentiss had been outspoken in his theory that Ulman had stolen the Gutenberg pages, he also referenced the open knowledge that Ulman had been having an affair with Gonzalez' wealthy spouse, Winifred. When Winifred is murdered, the police are quick to conclude that Gonzalez killed her, just as he had killed her lover. Wade and Farrell have a more sophisticated view of the case that is confirmed when they prematurely get legal permission to open a codicil to the Sheldon will. Settings include newsrooms, police stations, elegant St. Charles Avenue residences, a Pontalba Buildings apartment, a ball at a private club, and a trip to Isle Bonne. One of the characters has made a caricature out of himself through extreme anglophilia, and racist generalizations are made about Cubans and Chinese. Although primarily an action novel, the book includes some atmospheric descriptions of New Orleans, particularly of the French Quarter.

60. Bristow, Gwen and Bruce Manning. *The Invisible Host.* New York: The Mystery League, 1930. 286pp.

All the action of this locked door murder mystery transpires in an Art Deco penthouse apartment, decorated in black and silver and sitting atop a twenty-one story building on Carondelet

Street. As eight prominent New Orleaneans receive identical telegrams inviting them to a party in their honor, the reader cannot resist beginning to assess their individual characters through their own explanations for why they were invited. For example, a social arbiter believes she is being honored for her success in excluding the daughter of a newly prominent politician from Society. Academic administrator Dr. Murray Chambers Reid thinks he is being recognized for getting a young instructor quietly dismissed for espousing communist views. A female lawyer credits her invitation to the slightly shady approach she took to proving that an opponent of her candidate for mayor was not eligible to run for the office. Other invitees, an actress recently back from appearing in Hollywood films, a writer returning from seeing a dramatization of his book on Broadway, and an artist with a newly won painting prize, each seem to have less objectionable characters. Each guest learns during the course of the evening that their host believes they have committed offenses against the public good of New Orleans. As they gather in the penthouse (set in a roof garden), they engage in lively debate over who sent the telegrams. Through a voice broadcast on a radio they learn that they have been invited to compete with their invisible host in an intellectual challenge that may leave all of them dead. They are trapped by electrified door handles and the butler and staff who served them drinks and dinner have been drugged into a narcotic sleep from which they will not awake until the following day. Imprisoned with each other in the apartment and filled with suspicions that are, in some cases, egged on by the voice over the radio, the guests begin dying one by one, mostly from poisons ingeniously administered. When two of the guests finally realize who the murderer is they are able to escape with their lives. Although the novel includes no general physical description of New Orleans, the transgressions of the guests reveal aspects of cultural, political, and social life in the city. The novel features several women who have achieved prominence in New Orleans life and reflect on gender inequality in the time period.

61. Bristow, Gwen and Bruce Manning. *The Mardi Gras Murders.* New York: Mystery League, 1932. 286pp.

During Mardi Gras season, a photojournalist, a features writer, and a maid help police solve a murder. Some of the main characters in this novel are the same as in the authors' earlier work, *The Gutenberg Murders*, including Wade, the journalist with *The Daily Creole*, District Attorney Dan Farrell, and Police Detective Dennis Murphy. When Anthony Wiggins, photojournalist for *The Daily Creole* is sent to the French Quarter house of Cynthia Fortenay to take photographs of the alternative Mardi Gras krewe known as Dis, he finds much to intrigue him. With the exception of Fortenay, the identity of the fifty krewe members is a well-guarded mystery. They are assumed to be bohemian French Quarter denizens and signal through their name their "discontent, disappointment, disenchantment, and dismay" with society, even though they sponsor a parade and crown a king and queen in a public ceremony. To maintain their secrecy, they dress uniformly in devil costumes. Although the Dis krewe members are fairly drunk, they readily pose for the photograph Wiggins has been invited to take and he spends most of his time chatting up Fortenay's beautiful, red-headed maid, Lucy Lake, partly to discover if she knows who Fortenay's fourth husband will be, but mostly to get a date with her. Later, when Roger Parnell, the most attractive man in New Orleans, is found murdered the two are drawn together in their pursuit of the culprit. Before the end of the novel three more people are murdered, two of them in a dramatically public fashion during Mardi Gras events. After determining that the murderer must be a counterfeiter, one of the prime suspects is a U.S. Treasury Department agent. While counterfeiting connects a number of suspects and victims, other main characters are connected through The Red Cat nightclub. Parnell secretly owned the club, but could only operate it with the cooperation of Fritz Valdon, who extorts protection money from clubs throughout New Orleans. The money used for the club purchase was Fortenay's and Parnell had gotten the cash by threatening to reveal that he and Fortenay had been married when she was sixteen (the union had later been annulled). Gambling debts of some thousands of dollars, a surprisingly large amount considering the Great Depression time period, link other characters. In addition to descriptions of affluent households, the novel describes Mardi Gras celebrations and, in a particularly evocative few pages, police officers struggle through streets filled with revelers, whose costumes and behavior are detailed. The novel's dialogue incorporates extensive examples of slang of the time period.

62. Bromfield, Louis. *Wild is the River.* New York: Harper and Brothers, 1941. 326pp.

In depicting New Orleans during the Union occupation, Bromfield illustrates the degrading effects of military rule, while celebrating the city's gentility and sophistication, even as he acknowledges the sensuality of the residents. Bromfield's romance novel is mainly populated by members of a Boston mercantile family named Wicks. The family is involved in the Civil War on many levels. Patriarch Ethan Wicks, a textile manufacturer and capitalist, is a war profiteer, selling shoddy blankets and paper-soled shoes to the army. His brother, General Wicks, is the commanding officer of occupied New Orleans. An economic opportunist in the same vein as his brother, Wicks confiscates the private property of New Orleans' Confederate families for himself, using subterfuges orchestrated by a cabal of Northern businesses he has called to the city to help in the plunder. His wife, the romantically thwarted and sexually frustrated Louisa, throws her passions into accumulating capital. However her husband's aide-de-camp, Tom Bedloe, becomes a distraction for her, even though he is the fiancé of her niece, nineteen-year-old Agnes Wicks. Although Bedloe leads Louisa on, knowing that her favor will gain him a bigger cut of the General's pilfering, Bedloe's true focus is his sexual affair with Félice "La Lionne" Duchêsne, owner and manager of the Café Imperial, a bar patronized by Yankee soldiers and carpetbaggers. Whether they gamble, drink, or make love to the mixed-race women in residence, La Lionne collects money from them, accumulating a heavy percentage of their misbegotten wealth. Accustomed to controlling men, La Lionne falls under the influence of Bedloe, infatuated with his curly black hair and muscular body, and employees a Voodoo priestess to compound a powerful love potion to make Bedloe hers alone. Her competition, in addition to Agnes and Louisa Wicks, includes Madame Èliane de Lèche, the widow and sole heiress of a French Baron whose family has historically owned large plantations and prominent New Orleans houses. Although Bedloe is billeted in the de Lèche mansion, he only gets glimpses of Madame Èliane, but when members of a gang plotting the overthrow of General Wicks capture him, she aids him in his captivity. Eventually, she helps him escape and the two begin an intense affair. Madame de Lèche has also obtained a love potion from a Voodoo priestess, not to bind Bedloe to her, but to captivate Hector MacTavish, the heir to the plantation next to that of the de Lèche family. From Bedloe, Madame de Lèche wants only enough devotion to persuade General Wicks to release her inherited gold from the Planters Bank where it is impounded as contraband. While Bedloe is occupied with graft and womanizing, his fiancée Agnes is slowly making her way South with her maiden Aunt Tam to surprise him and end their long engagement with matrimony. She is fortunate to be journeying with her strong-willed and independent aunt, a friend of Emerson and other Transcendentalists. She draws upon an inner strength that preserves her and her niece through a hurricane, through passage as the only women on a Spanish ship with a rebellious crew, through a cholera epidemic on the same vessel, and on a journey across the swamps to New Orleans protected only by a freed slave. When Agnes finally arrives in New Orleans, she is still a virgin, but has experienced a mental and emotional liberation that gives her the sophistication to accept the changes New Orleans has wrought upon her circle. Her brother, twenty-year-old David Wicks, an aide to his uncle along with Bedloe, has gone from being an effeminate poet to the swaggering lover of La Lionne's most beautiful quadroon, Clélie. When Agnes discovers Bedloe's affair with Madame de Lèche, she maturely approaches him about the matter and then meets the young heiress face-to-face to cede her fiancé, realizing that although she loves Bedloe and can tolerate his womanizing, she finds the unmarried life of her Aunt Tam more desirable. The novel ends, not in New Orleans, but in the bayous, where Aunt Tam and Agnes are under the protection of a French priest and Agnes has started a school to teach English to all the local children no matter their race or ethnic origins. Hector MacTavish, who has rejected Latin-influenced culture, represented most vividly by de Lèche, in favor of the logical clear-headedness of his Scots ancestors, ends up by Agnes' side. While several novels treat the Civil War occupation of the city, this book is the only one to look at the impact of the city's sexually-charged climate on Northerners, some of whom succumb, and some of whom reject a life of sensuality for one of intellectual endeavor and service.

63. Brown, Beth. *For Men Only*. New York: Claude Kendall, 1930. 288pp.

The madam of the most exclusive brothel in New Orleans, and the entire South, is thirty-year-old Lily Love. The focus of this novel deals with her past, the life of the brothel, and the major conflicts with which she copes. When her daughter Viola, who knows her as Aunt Kate, returns from France after finishing school, Love feels threatened by the new district attorney Jim Swift's campaign to close New Orleans' brothels. Furthermore, for one of the first times in her adult life, Love is between lovers, even though she is being courted by Tuxedo Jim, a powerful figure in horse racing and gambling circles. Amongst her former lovers are a U.S. senator, a sugar millionaire, a millionaire fruit importer, and, most recently, the chief of the New Orleans police department, who was shot dead in a brawl. Love's current focus, in addition to tending her bank account and shopping in the city's most exclusive shops, is the magnificent cemetery monument being created for her by an expert stone carver. To her surprise, Viola's return has less impact than the arrival of a new girl, Tessie Christmas. Love sees something of herself in Christmas, who had worked for a famous Washington, D.C. madam after an unscrupulous man got her pregnant and abandoned her, forcing her into prostitution. During the frivolity of a brewers' convention, William Scanlon, the man who had ruined Christmas, inveigles himself into Love's mansion and unwittingly asks for the new girl. Christmas stabs him to death and when the police eventually arrest her, Love tells Christmas' story to D.A. Swift. The other girls at the Mansion learn that Christmas is pregnant, make certain no witnesses come forward, and she is acquitted. However, when Christmas miscarries, she poisons herself. Love pays for an elaborate funeral and has Christmas interred under her own monument. This tragedy is followed by a more personal tribulation when she discovers her daughter Viola in the arms of Tuxedo Jim and the girl declares her love for him. However, throughout the novel Jim Swift has gone from an adversary to an understanding friend and when he resigns his position, Love realizes how close they have become and by the end of the novel they have become lovers. Although the novel's focus on the social injustice experienced by nineteenth-century women and the life of prostitutes is not specific to the New Orleans, the novel is set there, a place notorious Storyville, and one section describes the plight of Storyville prostitutes who are far less fortunate than Love.

64. Brown, Joe David. *Addie Pray*. New York: Simon and Schuster, 1971. 308pp.

Up to the time she is twelve-years-old, Addie Pray is constantly on the move with her grifter father, Long Boy, who works his scams up and down the South. However, during the Great Depression, the era in which much of the novel is set, the two are mostly in Alabama. Written from Addie's perspective, much of the novel is an account of Long Boy's mostly small-scale swindles. His golden opportunity comes when a fellow grifter proposes Addie masquerade as the granddaughter of Amelia Sass, a fabulously wealthy New Orleans woman. Sass's estranged daughter and son-in-law (the cause of the estrangement) were killed in a hurricane, but they had supposedly placed their infant daughter in the hands of distant friends, although Sass was never able to discover their identity. Aided by Sass's despicable nephew, Beau Goldsborough, who will be the major beneficiary of the swindle, Addie is soon accepted into Sass's household. Sass lives in a grand St. Charles Avenue mansion in the Garden District with Mayflower, a lifelong female servant. Soon genuinely attached to Sass, Addie is determined to help the woman when she learns from Mayflower that Sass's great fortune is gone, through the embezzlement and mismanagement of a man who committed suicide in 1929. Long Boy and his accomplices get involved when they become irritated by Goldsborough's greed. They put into place a legal way of conning a significant amount of money from Goldsborough once he thinks he has been formally named Sass's heir, as he still believes her to be wealthy. Approximately one hundred pages of this novel are set in New Orleans. Although some locations (like Audubon Park) are directly referenced, the book is mostly set in Sass's mansion. The novel was adapted as a motion picture, entitled *Paper Moon*, directed by Peter Bogdanovich and starring Ryan and Tatum O'Neal (Paramount, 1973).

65. Bryan, Jack Yeaman. *Come to the Bower*. New York: Viking, 1963. 496pp.

The author uses his story, set in 1835 and 1836 in New Orleans and on the Texas frontier, as a platform to espouse his views on the nature of democracy and the role of U.S. Manifest Destiny, while asserting that both Southern slave culture and capitalism are antithetical to the democratic principles of the founding fathers. Still in her early twenties, Camilla Palmer is the widow of Robert Palmer, her much older, affluent husband. Her father, Major Cedric Burleigh, a Virginian, had fought with Andrew Jackson (1767–1845) and moved to Louisiana hoping to establish himself. Instead, a financial reversal forced him to work his land directly along with his wife and children, including Camilla. Their next-door neighbor, Palmer, pitied the fifteen-year-old beautiful Camilla and saw to it that she was rescued from the fields and educated for a few years in Philadelphia. Flattered by the attention of the much older man, she accepted his marriage proposal when she came of age, only to be widowed soon afterwards when he was found murdered in the bed of a French Quarter quadroon. His death revealed one aspect of his character, and the debts he left behind another. Ostensibly the prosperous mistress of a plantation and of a New Orleans townhouse, she owes so many creditors that she really owns very little. Soon Edmond Beaufait, a thirty-nine-year-old banker, starts to take an interest in her and by the time he is finished she owns even less. By this time, Major Burleigh is the publisher of *The New Orleans Commentator* and suspects Beaufait's intentions, knowing him to be a man who likes to own people and who sees Camilla as an attractive social ornament. Burleigh finds an appropriate suitor for Camilla in twenty-two-year-old lawyer Perry Allan who understands that she is headstrong and must figure her life out on her own. One of the properties to which Camilla still retains clear title is in Texas. Allan heads to the frontier out of his political convictions to fight against Mexico, but also as Camilla's representative to inspect her land. Impressed by its potential, Allan is able to establish a claim on an adjoining tract before commencing his militia service. While he is away from New Orleans, a fire (that Burleigh suspects is arson) destroys major buildings on Camilla's plantation and the recently harvested cotton crop. In the aftermath, Beaufait restructures her debts so that he controls all of them. Before realizing her true situation, Camilla is thankful to Beaufait and agrees to marry him. After Allan returns to New Orleans, she realizes how much she loves him, even though his visit ends in an argument. She is also is forced to realize that Beaufait has purchased her, as surely as one would a slave, by acquiring her debts. Along with her father she strikes out for Texas, hoping to create her own future by taming her land and eventually reconciling with Allan. After experiencing frontier hardships while Allan is absent fighting with the militia, she is eventually reunited with him and it seems clear that the two will establish themselves in Texas. Although New Orleans social events are described, more description is devoted to slave pen auctions, the insidious nature of New Orleans bankers, and corrupt plantation owners. New Orleans in the novel epitomizes the evils of a capitalist system in which most men work their whole lives under debt to capitalists. Texas provides the only opportunity the protagonists have to own their own means of production and live in freedom.

66. Buckner, Alice Morris. *Towards the Gulf: A Romance of Louisiana*. New York: Harper and Brothers, 1887. 315pp.

In this extended apologia for anti-miscegenation theory, the experiences of the Morant family figure predominantly. French Huguenots, the Morants were early settlers of Louisiana and established a large, successful cotton plantation. Prior to the Civil War, the revered grandmother of the current generation built a townhouse in the French Quarter, expressive of the most refined and fashionable antebellum taste, as well as demonstrating a savvy understanding of real estate. Wartime deaths and economic reversals, including some unfortunate speculation, have reduced the family to the barest remnant and the town house has become the primary residence of Major Morant, his son John, daughter Isabel, and John's "mammy," Celine, an elderly former slave who has held onto her role as trusted family servant. Although Major Morant owns the family plantation, he no longer has enough money to operate it. His poverty has seriously impacted his children's lives. He could not afford a coming-out year for Isabel and has been unable to assemble a dowry for her. John has essentially left traditional society by getting a job in a cotton exchange office and he eventually moves to Uptown with the nouveaux riches and petite bourgeoisie. Furthermore, he marries outside his former social circle, selecting Alabama Muir for his bride. Although she is a lively beauty, her parentage is obscure. Her father, Alfred Muir, is the son of a Liverpool merchant who has achieved some wealth. He met Alabama's long-deceased mother in antebellum New Orleans while traveling as a commercial agent for his father. While Muir educated Alabama in Europe and made certain she traveled extensively on the Continent, as she was coming of age, he retired from business and relocated with her to New Orleans in order to help her experience the country her mother loved so much. John Morant fell in love with Alabama when he first saw her in the Muirs' Garden District mansion. He overcomes his father's concerns about the girl's ancestry by relaying Muir's account that Alabama's mother was an orphan adopted by one of the antebellum South's wealthiest and most politically powerful families. Only Celine remains opposed to the match, although she only hints that Alabama is not who she seems to be. After an extended bridal tour, John takes his new bride to the Morant plantation that he hopes to rehabilitate. There, he begins to connect Alabama with whispered family stories about Billy Bush, the man who owned the plantation adjacent to the Morants and who destroyed himself and his family through drink and his attachment to one of his octoroon slaves. John soon has evidence that Alabama's mother was the daughter of Bush and the octoroon. Puzzled by John's tortured emotional state, Alabama seeks out Celine and learns about her mother. A short time later she commits suicide with self-administered chloroform after giving birth to John's son. Fortunately, Isabel is happy to add the infant to her household. Reclusive in her youth, she came alive socially during the period of John's betrothal and marriage, and eventually marries. Rejecting beaus her own age, since none of them shared her attachment to antebellum manners and fashion, she chose one of her father's wealthy, bachelor friends for her husband. Although Isabel establishes a happy household around John's son, John only visits to observe his son as the object of research on the dangers of racial blending, and thinks he sees disturbing, racially-determined, character flaws in the child. Though just a preschooler, John's son is disturbed by his father's scrutiny and unloving attitude. While visiting the Morant plantation, the boy throws himself into a cotton gin so that he can go join his mother in heaven. In addition to rehearsing all of the supposed evils of interracial sexual relations, the book takes great steps to demonstrate that characters we would think of today as racist are spiritually and emotionally refined. The novel makes a number of concerned asides about the people who are moving into New Orleans in the 1880s (African-Americans, people of mixed race, and Northerners), changing the city's culture. However, even in the novel the influx seems to have a beneficial influence on the French Quarter in terms of the restoration of houses and rejuvenation of shops.

67. Burroughs, William S(eward) [William Lee, pseud.]. *Junkie.* New York: Ace Books, 1953. 149pp.

Approximately one-third of this seminal work of American fiction is set in New Orleans. Burroughs' protagonist, his alter ego William Lee, forthrightly details how his life comes to be focused on drug use. Unlike many stories of addiction the protagonist has no regrets about addiction, claiming that narcotics have been good for him physically, keeping him young and teaching him "facts of general validity," primarily focused on his great truth that, "all pleasure is relief." Born in 1914 and rebelling against a Midwestern life of comfort funded by his father's lumber industry, Lee nonetheless gets through college and military service before trying narcotics for the first time in New York City. Living on trust fund payments, Lee soon finds that his entire life becomes focused on acquiring narcotics and quickly realizes that dealing drugs is the surest means of guaranteeing access. Eventually, fearful of arrest, he departs for Cincinnati, but soon finds himself in Lexington, Kentucky where he completes a drug treatment program. He then leaves for Texas, where he remains sober for four months, before relocating to New Orleans. As Lee explores the French Quarter and begins spending time in bars, he soon backslides into a drug habit that he supports by drug dealing. The city is described from the drug addict's perspective, noting which blocks are safe for buying drugs and which bars dealers and addicts frequent. Although Lee resides in Algiers with a common-law wife, he engages in homosexual liaisons, even though he is derisive in his descriptions of the city's gay bars and their patrons. Within five or six weeks of Lee's arrival in New Orleans he is charged with a series of crimes, most of which are connected to his drug addiction. The informant network is portrayed as particularly effective in New Orleans and practices of entrapment and harsh jail conditions are commonplace. Lee skips bail and takes up residence in Mexico to avoid serving time in Louisiana. The novel goes into great detail about the ways in which addicts prey upon Bourbon Street drunks to fund their drug purchases.

68. Butterworth, W(illiam) E(dmund), (III). *M\*A\*S\*H Goes to New Orleans.* Based on characters developed by W(ilfred) C(harles Heinz and Richard Hornberger under the joint pseudonym Richard Hooker. New York: Pocket Books, 1975. 189pp.

New Orleans is the shallow backdrop for this book in a series of titles that capitalized on the popularity of the television program *M\*A\*S\*H.* Benjamin Franklin Pierce, M.D. has finally settled down with his own medical practice in Spruce Harbor, Maine, happily married and the father of three children. However, his buddies from Korea resent the fact that he never attends conventions or meetings through which they might relive their friendship. So, when his wife Mary asks help in getting him out of town during the week that she is to deliver their fourth child (since she cannot stand the prospect of having him in the delivery room), his former MASH unit kidnaps him and flies him to New Orleans where they all rendezvous. New Orleans' reputation as a convention city for a wide assortment of organizations takes center place in this tale of drinking and shenanigans that mostly transpires in hotels and bars.

69. Cable, George Washington. *Bonaventure: A Prose Pastoral of Acadian Louisiana.* New York: Charles Scribner's Sons, 1888. 314pp.

A paean to Acadian people and culture, the book is divided into three novella-length sections, the last of which, "Au Large," is significantly set in New Orleans. While the rest of book was set in a rural environment, in the final section George W. Tarbox, an Anglo-American bookseller, who had visited the school that the selfless Bonaventure started in Acadia, takes Bonaventure's star pupil, Claude St. Pierre, to New Orleans. St. Pierre is searching for economic opportunity and a means of continuing to see Marguerite Beausolcil, who had moved to New Orleans for an extended visit to enjoy the art and culture. Marguerite's mother Josephine soon realizes that Marguerite will never happily return to her rural hometown and takes up residence with her in rooms above the Women's Exchange restaurant on Bourbon Street in 1884. Although St. Pierre first experiences the prejudice of Anglo-Americans and Creoles against Acadians in the city, he does settle down to work on inventions in a work/studio space on Carondelet Street, occasionally escaping to the cottage and orange grove of his father at the end of the Company Canal. Tarbox helps St. Pierre's father sell produce and aids Claude St. Pierre in marketing his inventions. Most of the narrative, however, is concerned with the course of the romances between Tarbox and the reluctant Josephine, and the awkward, shy Claude St. Pierre and the receptive Marguerite. A double wedding brings closure to the novel. In addition to illustrating prejudices against Acadians, the book reveals the depth of the continuing divide between the American Uptown section and the French Quarter.

70. Cable, George Washington. *Creoles and Cajuns: Stories of Old Louisiana.* Edited by Arlin Turner. Garden City, N.Y.: Doubleday, 1959. 432pp.

Incorporating chapters from novels and short stories previously published in periodicals and collections, this book emphasizes Cable's interest in New Orleans' most historic places, people from Francophone cultures and, African-Americans. Since Cable published his novels serially, printing chapters from novels here does not entirely violate the author's intent. Readers of Cable will not be surprised to find some of his most beloved characters here, such as 'Sieur George, Bras-Coupe, 'Tite Poulette, Jean-ah Poquelin, Posson Jone' and Madame Delphine. The editor also includes several non-fiction works describing dancing in Congo Square and a discussion of slave songs with examples.

71. Cable George Washington. *Dr. Sevier.* Boston: J.R. Osgood, 1884. 473pp.

Unlike the works that presented a romanticized, exotic New Orleans and established Cable's popularity as a writer, the focus here is on realistically portraying the plight of the poor through the title character's interactions with Mr. and Mrs. John Richling in the period 1856 to 1865. When Sevier first meets the couple, newcomers from Milwaukee, Mary Richling is ill and John spends most of his time looking for work. With no profession and no letters of reference, he tries for bookkeeping jobs. The fact that he is new to the city prejudices employers against him, as does his partial deafness. Dr. Sevier, a pragmatic man, is impatient with the couple's unrealistic optimism and encourages them to return to Milwaukee as he becomes a witness of their distressing decline in fortunes, as they move from a modest house on St. Mary Street near Prytania, to shared accommodations on an alley off Prieur between Conti and St. Louis. The doctor takes a special interest in Mary because she reminds him of his own wife Alice. The couple eventually lives with a young widow, Kate Riley, whose engineer husband was killed in an accident just before she had his baby. The couple also become acquainted with Raphael Ristofalo, a Sicilian immigrant who also arrived in the city with nothing, but has the skill of making money, creating a job for himself by buying odd lots of fruits and vegetables, discarding rotten ones, cleaning up the remainder and selling to owners of produce stands. Even with his example Richling cannot make enough money to feed himself and his wife and at a time when they have gone without food for several days, he accidentally falls asleep under the steps of the St. Charles Hotel while waiting for Sevier. When he is awakened by the kick of a foot he responds impulsively before realizing that the prodding is from a police officer. Arrested, he is soon sentenced to prison, where he contracts the lung disease that will eventually kill him. In the meantime, Sevier convinces the pregnant Mary to return to the North to get aid from relatives. While she is gone the Civil War breaks out and by the time she makes her circuitous return through enemy lines, New Orleans has fallen, but her husband has died. As Richling is on his deathbed, he tells Sevier that he is actually from a wealthy Kentucky family who had trained him to be a master and never to engage in work. He was disowned for marrying poor Mary, a Northerner, but thought he could make it on his own. He claims his story is one of patient resignation to his fate. Sevier had repeatedly cautioned him to make connections to the rest of humanity rather than standing aloof, with the example of the striving immigrant Ristofalo ever before him. During the course of the novel, the Sicilian builds a wholesale produce business, fights in the Civil War, rises to the rank of colonel, and marries Kate Riley. The novel gives a good sense of the challenges of daily life in New Orleans for the poor, contrasts the American and French neighborhoods and their inhabitants, and touches on the many public health issues in the city.

72. Cable, George Washington. *The Flower of the Chapdelaines.* New York: Charles Scribner's Sons, 1918. 339pp.

This romance novel is set in the French Quarter in 1915 as the St. Louis Hotel, is being torn down and war rages in Europe. Geoffry (sic) Chester, a young, newly-arrived lawyer, is taken in by a circle of French Quarter artisans and property owners whose families have lived in the Vieux

Carré and known each other for generations. Chester comes to their attention through Ovide Landry, a former slave who operates a bookstore where Chester buys old New Orleans maps and books. The circle of family friends includes Marcel Castanado, a costumier and mask maker; Seraphine Alexandre, an embroiderer; Scipion Beloiseau, a metalworker; and Placide La Porte, a perfumer. Although they appreciate Chester's interest in history, they also are concerned about a young lady in their circle, for whom they are eager to find an appropriate suitor. Aline Chapdelaine was orphaned as a child and lives with two maternal aunts, Yvonne and Corinne, in an ancient house in the Quarter that is increasingly threatened with destruction as the area becomes "Italianized" due to an influx of immigrants who cater to the tourist trade, rather than engage in the traditional industries practiced by members of the circle. Aline's grandfather and father operated a large store that specialized in French goods, the family having maintained a connection to their country of origin for generations after fleeing the Revolution. However, after the business was destroyed by the Civil War and certain other properties were lost, Aline's father supported his family on a salary earned as an inspector on the docks, but died young, leaving his family in genteel poverty. Aline's only asset is a family manuscript concerning the dramatic escape of a family of slaves. The family was connected to slavery through Aline's grandfather, who bought slaves at the St. Louis Hotel and had them trained in the crafts of the various members of his circle so that the slaves could earn money to buy their freedom and practice a trade. A significant portion of the novel sets down the contents of a manuscript Chester received from an uncle that, by astounding coincidence, deals with the same slaves and their successful efforts to recover one family member who had been recaptured. The surprising revelation that some of their ancestors knew each other, adds to the attraction Chester and Aline feel for each other. However, when Chester finally proposes, after inheriting some money and becoming a partner in a law firm, Aline at first rejects him, concerned by the fact that he is not Catholic. Through many complications, the romance is helped along by the Vieux Carré artisans and by the end of the novel the couple has married and lives in one of the Quarter's historic houses.

73. Cable, George Washington. *The Grandissimes: A Story of Creole Life.* New York: Charles Scribner's Sons, 1880. 448pp.

Set in the first decade of the nineteenth century, Cable's tale of family conflict also presents the author's observations about racial hatred in his own time. The foil for Cable's tale is Joseph Frowenfeld, a Northerner with German heritage who moves with his family to New Orleans and develops a close friendship with Honoré Grandissime. When fever kills his entire family, he continues to live on his own in the city developing a pharmacy business. To Grandissime, Frowenfeld is one of the few people he knows who is not a New Orleans Creole, and is the ideal sounding board as he retells family secrets and tries to embolden himself to take action to correct old wrongs. In keeping with a common cultural practice, Honoré's father had a quadroon mistress with whom he had a child, also known as Honoré. Grandissime wants to acknowledge his mixed-race brother and even have him share in the family business. His desire for justice is also compelling him to find a way to aid Aurora Nancanou and her daughter Clotilde, who are living in comparative poverty after Grandissime's father killed Aurora's husband in a duel and cheated Aurora of money in a business deal. The only path for Grandissime is marriage to Aurora. He knows that his close-knit, status-conscious family would not tolerate his open acknowledgement of his father's wrongfulness and to do so would alienate him from the only social world he knows and could even lead to his death. Supported only by his cousin Raoul, who is too young to carry any weight, Grandissime's friendship with Frowenfeld is crucial to acting on his much-contemplated impulses. Known for his sociological approach to his subjects, this is one of Cable's most open accounts of racism in Southern culture.

74. Cable, George Washington. *Kincaid's Battery*. Illustrated by Alonzo Kimball. New York: Charles Scribner's Sons, 1908. 396pp.

As the Civil War approaches, a circle of relatives and friends gather in New Orleans, with their romances and rivalries, set against the backdrop of the war, occupying the remainder of the novel. The elderly bachelor, General Brodnax, is quite rightly thinking of the disposition of his large estate as he prepares to take up his commission in the Confederate Army. His chosen successor is his nephew Hilary Kincaid, but when he tells Kincaid that the inheritance is dependent on Kincaid marrying Anna Callender, the young man defies him and makes clear that he will choose his own bride. He has his eyes on Flora Valcour. Kincaid has been educated at a Northern military academy and spent a year abroad. He is knowledgeable about metal casting and when Brodnax raised money for a battery of guns from Anna and her wealthy stepmother, the young widow Miranda Callender, Kincaid was commissioned to cast them. Almost the entire first half of the novel is concerned with social events in New Orleans as the city entertains the troops, preparing for deployment, and the regiments parade through the streets as they leave for various fronts. All around New Orleans beautiful young women allow officers to express admiration and bestow tokens for them carry to the battlefront. Anna Callender makes a flag for Kincaid's battery and as Kincaid becomes more acquainted with her she wins his heart. Her Northern friend Fred Greenleaf has also fallen in love with her. Even though Greenleaf departs for the Union Army, Northerner Flora Valcour, who had been told by the confused Brodnax that Kincaid was still interested in her, remains to pursue a rivalry with Callender. Once Kincaid's battery is posted to Mobile, he makes risky trips to see Callender and they eventually marry. His disappearance and presumed death help bring the seriousness of war to the ladies on the home front, as does the return on furlough of the traumatized Charles Valcour, Flora's nineteen-year-old brother. Although the fall of New Orleans is described with high-flown sentiment, the narrative avoids portraying the Union occupiers in too negative a light and after the departure of General Butler, Fred Greenleaf appears as a Union officer to intercede on behalf of several of the main characters. Before the end of the novel there are charges of treason, aiding and abetting, and for a time the returned Kincaid is held in a Union prison in New Orleans. By the end of the novel, Brodnax's concern about protecting his wealth seems pathetic in light of the collapse of the Southern economy. Kincaid eventually returns to New Orleans but with no prospect of inheriting wealth, and begins determining his own future by re-establishing his forge.

75. Cable, George Washington. *Lovers of Louisiana (To-Day)*. New York: Charles Scribner's Sons, 1918. 351pp.

While ostensibly a story of star-crossed lovers, Cable's main concern is to present views on Louisiana political issues. Philip Castleton, the great-grandson of a Confederate general, was raised by his maiden aunt and grandfather, a judge, on Prytania Street, in what was historically known as the American part of the city. Castleton was educated at Princeton, and at twenty-six has begun an academic career at Tulane University, lecturing on politics. While he is staunch in his support of Louisiana and the South, he is open in his critiques of the state, calling for an end to cronyism and second-class citizenship for African-Americans. One of his examples of injustice is Ovide Landry who, for a brief period during Reconstruction, held elected office and earned respect for his education and political skills. When politics as usual came back after Reconstruction, he was reduced to shop keeping. Through hard work he came to own and operate one of New Orleans' most respected bookstores, but this was hardly in keeping with his skills and willingness for public service. Traveling in the North for the summer with his family in 1914, Castleton falls into company with a Scot who is particularly critical of race issues and who presses him on Southern politics. The Castletons also become acquainted with a New Orleans family, the Durels, who are remarkably similar, but entirely different from the Castletons for they are Creoles with a long history in the French Quarter. Madame Durel, née Ducatel, comes from a family as long-settled in New Orleans as that of her husband. Mr. Durel is a banker whose personal dignity echoes that of Judge Castleton. The Durels and Castletons meet through the chance encounter of Philip with the Durels' twenty-one-year-old daughter Rosalie on the Atlantic City boardwalk, where both families briefly vacation. While Philip and Rosalie seem to fall immediately in love, even the first days of their acquaintanceship are rocky. Though from the same region the two quickly learn that their political views are dramatically divergent (Ovide Landry was the slave of Madame Durel's father, and his sister continues to work as a domestic for the Durels). When the families return to New Orleans, Philip and Rosalie continue to meet at social events, but Rosalie becomes increasingly disenchanted with Philip's politics, especially after he makes a speech at Landry's bookstore. When Philip approaches Alphonse Durel to ask permission to court Rosalie according to Creole custom, Alphonse refuses and tells Philip the story of his own attempted courtship of the woman who would become Philip's mother, failing due to Castleton family opposition mounted by Philip's aunt. In the rest of the novel Philip continues his attempts to pursue the courtship, frequently needing to restrain his temper, especially when he hears the Ku Klux Klan defended. A great change in the relationship among the Castletons and Durels comes when a secret scandal at the bank calls the Durels to question their own sense of honor when Ovide Landry becomes one of their saviors, thus preparing the way for matrimony. Concerns with articulating multiple positions on race and the New South through dialogue limit other content in this novel, but references to places, restaurants, private clubs, and social events convey some sense of New Orleans in the early twentieth century.

76. Cable, George Washington. *Madame Delphine*. New York: Charles Scribner's Sons, 1881. 125pp.

In this novella Cable uses the noble sacrifice of a mother for her daughter to question race laws and illustrate the redemptive power of love. Having grown up in the New Orleans of the early nineteenth century, Madame Delphine Carraze had known a culture more accepting of mixed-race people like herself and had been a celebrated beauty at quadroon balls attended by men from the highest social circles. One of these men fell in love with her and established her in a Royal Street residence. The daughter they had together, named Olive, was from all appearances Caucasian, and in her infancy they sent her to be raised by the man's mother and sisters on the family plantation. After his death and the death of his mother in 1821, Madame Delphine became concerned for the safety of Olive, and went to retrieve her after sixteen years of separation. Pirates captured their boat but the brigand's captain, Ursin Lemaitre, spared the passengers when he fell in love with the beautiful Olive. Lemaitre returns to New Orleans under the protection of friends, including a Roman Catholic priest, Father Jerome. The holy man also becomes the confidant to Madame Delphine. Through him Lemaitre gives up his life of smuggling to open a banking house under the name of Vignevielle. He helps people with the money he had stolen and Father Jerome sees to it the Madame Delphine goes to him when she needs to protect money earned in the sale of some land. When Ursin and Olive meet again and become engaged, the protectors of the former pirate are outraged by the prospect of a mixed-race marriage and threaten Madame Delphine. She convincingly denies her motherhood and the marriage goes ahead. Father Jerome has the privilege of granting absolution to Madame Delphine for her lie immediately before her death. Throughout the novel, Cable introduces a note of cultural relativism surprising for the time period, using French society as an example of one that grants full legal rights to mixed-race persons.

77. Cable, George Washington. *Old Creole Days*. New York: Charles Scribner's Sons, 1879. 229pp.

Cable's collection of short stories fall within the local color movement of the time period and evoke picturesque qualities of New Orleans while focusing on all that makes the city exotic compared to other areas of the country. The first story "Madame Delphine Carraze" is set in the first quarter of the nineteenth century and elucidates the culture of the "quadroon caste." Cable returned to these characters in his novel, *Madame Delphine* above. In addition to the exoticism of a former pirate (Lemaitre), and mixed-race people, the story includes descriptions of St. Louis Cathedral and of the dooryards and gardens of middle-class houses where owners, their families, and their servants gather in the evenings. In "Café des Exiles," Galahad Shaughnessy forms a burial society for Hispanics so that their ashes will be sent back to their beloved islands (Barbados, Martinique, and Cuba). However, the great secrecy in which the society meets makes more sense when it is revealed that the coffins sent on the eve of the war with Mexico were filled with muskets. In "Belle Demoiselles Plantation," the Creole De Charleu family may be in its last generation as there are only seven daughters. Even so, the elderly De Charleu who owns Belle Demoiselles refuses to sell the plantation and soon afterwards the house and land is inundated by the Mississippi, rendering them worthless. The story includes extended description of a bullfight at Congo Plains and a charivari. Several stories address the issue of miscegenation as mothers encourage their children not to acknowledge that they have black ancestry. One story deals with the influx of new ethnicities (Irish, Italian, German) when New Orleans is first under U.S. control.

78. Cable, George Washington. *"Posson Jone" and Père Raphaël.* Illustrated by Stanley M. Arthurs. New York: Charles Scribner's Sons, 1909. 162pp.

   Although previously published in magazines, these novellas were presented together in this single volume because many of their important scenes occurred around the same blocks, near Royale and Conti, now occupied by the Louisiana Supreme Court Building which was under construction when Cable published the book (as he notes in his preface). In the first novella, Parson Jones of Smyrna Church in West Florida is on his way back from Mobile when he passes through New Orleans with his slave, Colossus of Rhodes, and meets the twenty-two-year-old Jules St.-Ange, who retrieves the hat that had toppled from Jones' head and points out to him the exposed state of the roll of cash that he had concealed there. Jules, a Creole and the son a sugar plantation owner, is accompanied by his mulatto servant Baptiste and fits Jones' notion of a gentleman. As the two fall into companionship, most of their conversation centers on Jones' assertion of religious proscriptions since it is a Sunday. He is so unaccustomed to urbane settings and pastimes that he never realizes that St.-Ange surreptitiously gets him drunk, borrows his money, and uses it to gamble while Jones runs amok at Cayetano's Circus on Congo Square. St.-Ange bails Jones out of jail and eventually sees that he gets all of his money back. The accompanying story, "Père Raphaël," tells the same story from the perspective of Jules' father, René de Blanc St.-Ange. Upset by his son's profligacy, René says that Jules cannot return to the household or ask for the hand of Florestine, the orphan of the judge's law partner who lives in the household, until he pays his debts. Without anyone's knowledge, Florestine has arranged with Dmitry Davezac for him to pawn items from the household which he will use to gamble. Both of them are confident that Davezac will pay Jules' debts with his winnings and redeem the household goods from the pawnbroker before they are missed. When the plan goes awry all of the principal characters end up on the dueling ground before the matter gets straightened out. As in the earlier story, Creole gentlemen are presented as gamblers prone to dueling.

79. Cable, George Washington. *Strange True Stories of Louisiana.* New York: Charles Scribner's Sons, 1889. 350pp.

   Cable's stories in this volume are based on memoirs, court cases, or correspondence and most are at least in part set in New Orleans. Several have to do with early French and German immigrants, fleeing revolution and other terrifying conditions in their countries of origin. One of these stories focuses on a German immigrant who had been forced into slavery by an unscrupulous man who claimed she was of mixed race. Another story has to do with a woman who is actually of mixed race and the complications she faces by having debtors who are white. One of the longest stories in the book recounts the history of a house on Royal Street and its most famous former inhabitant, Madame LaLaurie (1775–1842), the notorious slave torturer.

80. Cable, George Washington. *Strong Hearts.* New York: Charles Scribner's Sons, 1899. 214pp.

A foreword to these three short stories claims they illustrate the "indivisible twinship" of poetry and religion. In "The Solitary" a Civil War veteran returns from his harsh battlefield experiences still feeling his natural response to life is weakness rather than courage. After losing the girl he loves when he is too reserved to speak out and she marries another, he accidentally runs a charter vessel aground on a deserted island. His survival gives him the courage to make the island his home and start a cattle operation on the land. The "Taxidermist" explores the character of Manouvrier, a Creole with a shop on St Peter Street. Fascinated by the way in which the taxidermist achieves artistry in his dedication to his craft, the narrator is curious about what transformation Manouvrier and his hard-working wife will experience when they win a lottery prize of seventy five thousand dollars. They build a new house but, reluctant to change their life, let a relative reside in it rather than making their home there. The final story, "The Entomologist" tells a romantic story about a young woman who loves flowers and her much older husband who studies insects (to which she sacrifices her flowers). The stories convey the intimacy among upper-middle-class residents of New Orleans who are neighbors.

81. Cain, James M(allahan). *Mignon.* New York: Dial, 1962. 246pp.

Written by the author of noir works such as *The Postman Rings Twice*, this book is a period romance, but despite Cain's historical research the book's characters behave in ways more appropriate to the 1960s. In 1864 when twenty-eight-year-old Bill Cresap arrives in New Orleans during Mardi Gras, he has been recently discharged from the Union Army with a battlefield wound and is ready to resume civilian life by starting a construction firm with surplus government goods. Before he arrives in the city to meet his incumbent partner Sandy Gregg, who had gone ahead, Gregg's telegrams announce the hopelessness of carrying out their plan unless they have ten times their current capital. As Cresap prepares to leave the Crescent City shortly after his arrival, he is accosted by Mrs. Mignon Fournet, née Landry, a Confederate widow acquainted with Gregg, who seeks Cresap's help in freeing her father Adolphe Landry, who is being held on trumped up charges in a Union jail. Landry had been in partnership with Frank Burke in an elaborate scam that could result in the sale of a warehouse of cotton for one hundred thousand dollars. To cut Landry out, Burke gets his partner arrested. Cresap is able to gather evidence that gets Landry released and documents Burke's bribery of Union officers. However, the bribes are so well placed that Cresap's charges do not lead to prosecution and Burke soon leaves town to recover the cotton, closely followed by the Landrys. Cresap follows them all for a variety of reasons, including the opportunity to woo the alluring Mignon. The New Orleans section of the novel names actual places, describes buildings and locales, and evokes the Union-occupied city.

82. Caldwell, Barry. *Carnival Is for Lovers.* New York: Godwin, 1936. 291pp.

In this romance novel, Mardi Gras transforms lives and unites lovers in unexpected ways. Brad Lemare and Lois Bellon grew up together as childhood sweethearts in the Louisiana countryside. After graduating from Tulane, Lemare established a successful insurance business in New Orleans, but Bellon resisted his marriage proposals, as she was concerned about leaving the household of her mother, who has a heart condition. When Lemare is finally successful in getting Bellon to elope, her mother continues to have a strong hold over her, repeatedly calling her back to nurse her, even though Lois' brother and sister-in-law have re-shaped their lives to take care of Mrs. Bellon. Two years pass and when Lois, just before Mardi Gras, receives a telegram from Mrs. Bellon, she rushes off once again. This is in spite of the fact that she will be leaving her husband alone with important business client Parke Winter and his wife Isobel, who had made a play for Lemare in the past. At Lois' suggestion, Lemare gets her friend, bohemian artist Joan Winslow, to pretend to be her. She must think this a safe choice since Winslow has steadfastly claimed she has no interest in men, as she needs to focus on becoming a successful commercial artist. Lemare is well-connected and socially obligated to attend weeks of Mardi Gras balls and the two get in the habit of playing the role of a couple. From the beginning they have feelings toward each other that they probably would have been able to resist had they not had to publicly act out interest in each other to protect Lemare from Isobel Winter's advances. At the same time, alcoholic journalist Harry Rawlins is romantically pursuing Winters. As Mardi Gras reaches a climax everyone's emotions run higher and Winslow and Lemare become intimate. Eventually, Lemare must confess his new love to Lois, but he does so with the plea that she devotes herself to him alone and let her brother take care of her mother. When she refuses, he is free to pursue a relationship with Winslow. In addition to describing Mardi Gras and New Orleans and contrasting Lemare's Garden District life with Winslow's bohemian life in the French Quarter, the novel touches on issues of gender roles.

83. Carb, David. *Sunrise in the West.* New York: Brewer, Warren, and Putnam, 1931. 384pp.

This novel about the immigrant experience is unusual for being told from the viewpoint of a Jewish woman, Babette Rosenbaum. Despite her French first name, Rosenbaum grew up in mid-nineteenth-century Karlsruhe, in the German-speaking Rhineland. The implications of her family's poverty were made clear to her when, as an adolescent, she lived for a time with her Uncle David in Paris, and realized that with no dowry from her family she would never have a chance to marry. When she learned that dowries were not expected in the United States, she began to strategize about emigration. Returning to Karlsruhe, she formed a plan with her sisters Sarah and Hannah to secretly earn money sewing for a seamstress. As she and her sisters approach their goal, their father discovers their scheme and mounts a vehement opposition, seizing their money, until their mother shames him into its return. They eventually run away to Paris and from there sail to New Orleans. Although they are free to work in the city, initially they earn only room and board and must vigilantly protect their virginity. Furthermore, they find young Jewish men are very rare in the city. Hannah marries one of the few, Moses Hollander, a cobbler. Eventually, Babette meets Simeon Joseph, a Jewish man who owns a small farm in Hillsboro, Mississippi. After a hurried courtship the two wed and Babette moves to his farm where she must cope with the fact that he owns a slave couple. Babette transforms the woman, Maggie, into a friend, over Simeon's objections. By the time the Civil War breaks out, Babette and Simeon have three children and one on the way, but Simeon enlists anyway, thinking that the two slaves and a nearby neighbor will be support enough for Babette. However, after marauding soldiers appear on the farm, Babette flees back to New Orleans, making an arduous trip by oxcart. With help from her brother-in-law, she opens a small shop on Baronne Street, where she is eventually aided by Maggie, who fled the plantation and is now officially free, but still wants to be Babette's servant. When Babette finally receives word that Simeon has returned to Hillsboro, she also learns that he has been wounded. She makes the difficult journey to retrieve him and brings him to New Orleans where doctors confirm that he will never fully recover. The family, which eventually includes six children, continues to struggle until the oldest son Isadore, strikes out to Texas, eventually marrying and establishing himself in Fort Worth. He is never a great success, but by the time Simeon dies and some of Babette's other children have begun lives of their own, he is able to offer Babette and her under-age children a new home. The novel is of interest for presenting the reasons why New Orleans, rather than New York, made sense for some immigrants, and illustrating how a struggling immigrant might get a start there.

84. Carpenter, Edward Childs. *The Code of Victor Jallot: A Romance of Old New Orleans.* Philadelphia: G.W. Jacobs, 1907. 334pp.

In 1806, around the time that Louisiana is being transferred to the United States, French immigrant barber Victor Jallot aids in the capture of conspirators who were plotting to establish an independent Louisiana Territory under the protection of France and Spain. At twenty-seven, Jallot may have a lowly occupation, but he is in command of a wealth of talents. In addition to being a skilled fencing master and dance instructor, he is a poet and playwright of merit. He has also built a financially secure life for himself and has been so skilled with investments and handling money that he will soon reach his goal of living off his investments and devoting himself full-time to writing. All would be well if he could make any progress in his courtship of Antoinette, the adopted daughter of Ludwig Froebel. Neither Froebel, a German immigrant who owns a large plantation and an investment firm, nor Antoinette, who was educated in Paris and is a member of New Orleans highest social circles, consider a barber an appropriate suitor. Circumstances change dramatically when Luiz Delicado returns to New Orleans. Before he left on an overseas trip Delicado entrusted Froebel with the management of his estate and care of Antoinette. Then, word came that Delicado was dead and after the appropriate period of time the Spaniard's estate became Froebel's. Over the past decade Froebel has made a series of investments and wise management decisions and built a large portfolio. With the return of Delicado, Froebel must liquidate assets for cash and take huge losses to repay the value of the estate, forcing him into bankruptcy. At the same time, Delicado publicly announces that Antoinette is an octoroon who was intended to be a household slave. When he declares he will auction her off, a room full of gentlemen, not all with good intentions, bid higher and higher until Jallot has pledged almost all of his assets to purchase her. In the meantime he is secretly gathering evidence on the plot of Delicado and his associates to establish sovereignty for Louisiana. After turning his evidence over to authorities, Jallot has time to take his revenge on Delicado. Shortly after revealing that he is the son of a well-known French soldier, he presents evidence that Antoinette was a redemptioner, not a slave, and is, in fact, the Princess Marguerite Yolande de Guich. Although still his social superior, Antoinette has repeatedly witnessed Jallot's heroism and his respect for her and finally accepts his marriage proposal. Although the book references New Orleans landmarks, historical events, and people, it is mostly concerned with romance and courtly love more associated with a European country than the democratic New World.

85. Carr, John Dickson. *Deadly Hall.* New York: Harper and Row, 1971. 251pp.

The settlement of Harald (sic) Hobart's estate brings back to New Orleans Jeff Caldwell with his friends David and Serena Hobart. In an odd coincidence, on the same steam wheeler down the Mississippi, are two New Orleans policemen who have been assigned to re-investigate the death of Thad Peters, whose death in the Hobart mansion had been ruled an accident seventeen years ago. The Hobart mansion in which David and Serena live was built by Commodore Fitzhugh Hobart who made the family fortune in the nineteenth century by recovering gold bullion from sunken eighteenth-century Spanish treasure ships. In 1883 he purchased a brick English manor house, Delys Hall, and arranged for its entire removal and reassembly seventeen miles up the River Road from New Orleans. Caldwell learns from his uncle, Gilbert Bethune, New Orleans' prosecuting attorney, that Thad Peters' death in the house is being investigated, due to a series of anonymous letters claiming murder. Caldwell has also been informed by lawyer Ira Rutledge that Harald Hobart's will mysteriously indicates that should neither David nor Serena Hobart survive until Halloween, Caldwell will become principal beneficiary of the estate. He is already wealthy from his family's tobacco company and is concerned for the Hobarts, particularly when he discovers that the estate has been depleted and they are being forced to sell Delys Hall. Then, Serena is found murdered and a short time later David is assaulted and a whole series of suspects must be eliminated. In this novel, as in an earlier book by Carr, the solution rests on one of the character's ability to create an elaborate disguise. New Orleans receives some atmospheric description and is mostly represented by the French Quarter, especially through Prohibition Era nightclubs.

86. Carr, John Dickson. *The Ghosts' High Noon.* New York: Harper and Row, 1969. 255pp.

In this detective novel, the year is 1912 and Jim Blake is on assignment for *Harper's Weekly* to write a profile of similarly-named New Orleans politician James Claiborne "Clay" Blake, who is running for Congress. Thirty-five-year-old Jim lives in elegant bachelor quarters, funded in part by proceeds from his successful novels and his trip South features deluxe accommodations paid for by *Harper's* publisher, Colonel George Harvey. Leo Shepley, a flamboyant wealthy college friend, serves as Jim's guide to New Orleans. Jim stays at the St. Charles Hotel and during most of his stay interacts with journalists, writers, and policemen. Just as Jim discovers that Clay has received blackmail letters threatening to expose his patronage of under-age prostitutes provided by exclusive madam Flossie Yates, Leo Shepley is murdered. Jim tries to find the criminal, who may be also be the blackmailer. The novel is filled with people using assumed names and concealing aspects of their identities, including secret marriages. Mansions on Esplanade Avenue, in the Garden District, and in Bayou St. John are described, as well as the Cave dining room in the Grunewald Hotel (now the Roosevelt Hotel).

87. Carr, John Dickson. *Papa Lá-Bas.* New York: Harper and Row, 1968. 277pp.

This murder mystery, set in New Orleans in 1858, references a number of historical figures, including slave torturer Delphine LaLaurie (1775–1842). Isabelle de Sancerre comes to British Consul Richard Macrae and U.S. Senator Judah P. Benjamin (1811–1884) for help in freeing her daughter Margot from her obsession over Delphine LaLaurie, that has made the girl melancholy and unwilling to finalize marriage plans. Margot's friend, Ursula Ede, believes that Margot's preoccupation has something to do with Voodoo and Marie Laveau (c. 1801–1881) is a minor character. As the two men investigate, they attend a quadroon ball, at which they witness the murder of Judge Horace Benjamin, a murder that seems connected to Margot's odd behavior. Carr has clearly done considerable research into New Orleans history and presents convincing physical and social descriptions of the city as it was shortly before the Civil War. Some readers may be concerned that his presentation of slavery from a Southern viewpoint seems to justify the institution. The book's title is taken from a name for Satan used by Voodoo practitioners.

88. Carter, John Henton. *Mississippi Argonauts: A Tale of the South.* Illustrated by L. Berneker. New York: Dawn, 1903. 291pp.

The summer after Charles Faulkner graduates from Washington University he takes a job assisting his Uncle, Captain Delaney, in managing a new steamboat, the *Belle Creole* as it travels with passengers and freight down the Mississippi River to New Orleans. Among the passengers are Sir William Hamilton and his family, who are touring the United States and are much taken with Faulkner, from whom they learn about American history and culture. When the party arrives in New Orleans, they stay at the St. Charles Hotel, tour the city, and they (and the reader) learn about the history of the place and its character during the antebellum period. Delaney absents himself from the party to visit Blanche Dole, a young woman with whom he had become acquainted on earlier trips. She lives in a modest room on Rue Bienville. A refined lady, she has been reduced to taking in sewing, but when Delaney, a wealthy man and the owner of a plantation in addition to his boat, proposes marriage, she refuses since she had pledged to take care of her younger siblings. Delaney begins an investigation into her family and traces her German family's connections, and, with the help of a lawyer, discovers a legacy to which she and her siblings are entitled. Freed from her responsibilities, she agrees to marry Delaney, even though she expresses reservations about the fact that he owns slaves on his plantation. In the meantime, Faulkner receives a half share ownership in the *Belle Creole* from his uncle and deliberates over marrying Sir Hamilton's daughter, or a Kentucky girl, only to eventually marry Blanche after the death of Captain Delaney. The novel conveys a great deal of touristic information about New Orleans and touches on aspects of slavery. Written long after the Civil War, it strikes an elegiac tone toward antebellum culture and an apologist stance toward slavery.

89. Cash, Charles E. *The Great Oriental and Trans-Continental Railroad.* Vicksburg, Miss.: Commercial Herald, 1896. 171pp.

This political satire tells of the 1894 through 1914 construction and operation of a railroad that spans the Bering Strait to connect New Orleans to St. Petersburg, Paris and London. Given the nature of the work, the physical setting is not important. However the author clearly thought New Orleans' waterways and manufacturing made it an important transportation hub. While relating the history of the railroad, the author airs his opinions on economics, local and regional politics (noting corruption), race, ethnicity, and gender equality. There are many references to current events, including the debate over the gold standard and Coxey's Army, as well as actual historical figures like Eugene V. Debs, Grover Cleveland, and William McKinley. Near the end of the novel the author begins to address gender equality by discussing the implementation of a plan to hire and train female railroad conductors. The project literally derails when the women cause an accident by wearing bloomers. They are tried in New Orleans and locales in the city are mentioned. The novel is of interest for placing New Orleans at the center of an international transportation network and also for characterizing the city as politically corrupt.

90. Catling, Patrick Skene. *Jazz, Jazz, Jazz: A Novel.* London: Blond and Briggs, 1980. 320pp.

Roughly half of this fictionalized history of jazz is set in New Orleans. The protagonist, Alan Chesley Poindexter IV, is the white son of a cotton broker who is expected to follow his father into the successful family business that has provided the Poindexters with wealth and political power. Instead, by 1913 when he is thirteen, Alan idolizes an African-American boy, Moses Decatur, an illegitimate, abandoned fourteen-year-old, living as the adopted son of the Poindexter's cook and chauffeur. Alan's father, A. Chesley Poindexter, III, is irritated by the boys' friendship and their shared interest in jazz and is pleased when Moses is sent to the Colored Waif's Home. In the aftermath of the separation, Alan's time gets absorbed in his study of classical piano at the local conservatory. As a sixteen-year-old, however, he is distracted by classmate Louise Mercier and begins dating. When his father investigates the Merciers and finds they may have some mixed-race ancestors he sends Alan to a Northern military academy. After a long period of hazing he begins to fit in with the other boys, but he runs away when he is forbidden access to a piano. Taking the name Alan Dexter, he returns to New Orleans and gets a job playing piano at The Alhambra, one of Storyville's most glamorous brothels. With a job and savings in place, he proposes to Louise. She is shocked by his disreputable employment and when she realizes she will be unsuccessful in getting him to return to his family, she abandons him. He, in turn, becomes the lover of Madame Robichaux, the notorious owner of The Alhambra. When his father finally locates Alan, he uses his political power to prevent his employment and a short time later, in 1922, reformers close down Storyville. Alan and the other jazz musicians relocate to Chicago, but are later able to return to New Orleans. The novel portrays New Orleans and Storyville in the period 1913 to 1922 and the author has done enough research to name the principal jazz performers, clubs and brothels active in the city. He also captures aspects of race relations and the dangers of drug abuse and alcoholism for musicians.

91. Chapman, John Stanton Higham and Mary Ilsley Chapman [Maristan Chapman, joint pseud.]. *Tennessee Hazard.* Philadelphia: J.B. Lippincott, 1953. 367pp.

This historical romance elucidates frontier issues during the Federal Period. Spain had agreed to recognize American independence only in return for control of Mississippi trade. As American settlement spread west of the Mississippi, Spain rescinded the American right to bring goods into New Orleans. This novel begins in 1788 as Tennessee Hazard travels from the American frontier to New Orleans in an attempt to intercept a letter from John Sevier to the Spanish governor, accepting terms of agreement for Spanish control of frontier areas. Hazard thinks that by intercepting the letter, he will delay the negotiations long enough for the U.S. Constitution to be ratified and the frontier will become part of the United States. Hazard arrives in a New Orleans only partially rebuilt after a devastating fire the previous year. However, the Mississippi River trade is bustling despite river pirates and crooked Spanish tax collectors. Hazard's local ally is Captain George Farragut, who had come to America in 1776 and settled on the Tennessee frontier. With his Spanish origins, Farragut has connections to prominent men in New Orleans, even though he is a Federalist. Although the book is preoccupied with the political issues of Spanish control and presents historical figures on both sides, social events are described in some detail as Hazard pursues his romance with Annette Gaillard. She is also from Tennessee, but her uncle, John Sevier, intends her to marry Don d'Alcacer Salcedo to further strengthen his ties with Spain. Approximately one hundred and thirty pages of the novel are set in New Orleans with the remainder set in frontier settlements in Tennessee and North Carolina. The book presents a good deal of information about the incident, based in New Orleans, that has come to be known as the Spanish Conspiracy.

92. Charnley, Mitchell V. *The Buccaneer: The Story of Jean Lafitte; originally published as, Jean Lafitte, Gentleman Smuggler.* New York: Grosset and Dunlap, 1934. 240pp.

This fictionalized account of Jean Lafitte's (c.1776–c.1823) biography differs from many other accounts. To begin with, the book portrays Lafitte as thoroughly integrated into New Orleans society, with a house in the city and a blacksmith shop on St. Anne's Street frequented by prominent men. In addition, it openly asserts that Lafitte's great success came through smuggling slaves and that this trade was what so agitated Governor Claiborne. While other accounts note the role New Orleans' district attorney John Randolph Grymes (c.1746–1854) played in defending Lafitte, this book devotes a great deal of attention to the friendship between the two men, portraying Grymes as somewhat notorious. As in other fictionalized accounts of Lafitte, here, too, he redeems himself by proving his patriotism during the Battle of New Orleans. However, this book is also different in that it provides a lengthy account of Lafitte's life after 1814, hypothesizing that he did not give up piracy. Forced out of Louisiana and later Haiti, he experienced a period of recovered fortunes while preying upon Spanish ships from his base in Galveston, until a hurricane destroyed the settlement in 1818. Increasing demands for prosecution eventually drove him to Latin America by 1820 and, after dying of fever, he was buried in an unmarked grave in 1826. The book provides some different perspectives on Lafitte and his impact on the New Orleans of his era.

93. Chastain, Madye Lee. *Steamboat South.* New York: Harcourt, Brace, 1951. 233pp.

Orphaned Amy Travis is relieved when her Texas aunt, Agnes, sends her money for travel from Wellsburg, West Virginia to the Red River Valley, saving her from working as Miss Evelina Purdy's servant. She travels with the Beazey family, taking care of their six children, but is also looked after by an English paleontologist. This book for children includes much description of steamboat travel. New Orleans is the final destination of many of the passengers and they describe the city. Amy's trip down the Mississippi was to end before New Orleans, but one of her wards gets lost at a landing. Just as she finds him on a flatboat the vessel makes its way into the middle of the river and the steamboat goes off in another direction. She eventually gets passage to New Orleans and sells family heirlooms (small pieces of silver) to continue her journey. Approximately twenty pages are set in the city, including descriptions of the French Quarter, market, and levee. However the accounts of New Orleans by Amy's fellow travelers make the place a prominent component of this young-adult novel.

94. Chaze, (Lewis) Elliott. *The Golden Tag: A Novel.* New York: Simon and Schuster, 1950. 279pp.

When Steve Monaghan gets a job with the International Wire Service in New Orleans, he moves his pregnant wife Sally and young son Tim to the city and begins a long period of learning about modern journalism and New Orleans. Most of Steve's life centers on his work, although he also he socializes with his colleagues in Canal Street bars and on trips to cover stories out of town (including travel to the state penitentiary to witness the electrocution of a female convict). One of Monaghan's closest colleagues is Jewish, but unthinking anti-Semitism is rampant in his office. While Monaghan adjusts to life in the city, his wife Sally does not. She hates the way New

Orleaneans speak and hates many aspects of her neighborhood. One issue she has is that there is only one grocery store that is a long walk away on oyster shell paving overhung by crape myrtles and patrolled by free-roving dogs. She also dislikes their modern apartment building that contrasts dramatically with the historic buildings of the French Quarter. Finally, she hates her neighbors, Captain Bear of the police force, and his wife and son. Monaghan and Bear have little in common except for Mrs. Barclay, a flirtatious, frequently intoxicated neighbor, whose husband is often away on business. In this 1950s novel, New Orleans appears as a gritty modern city, with none of the moonlit romantic charm usually associated with it in fiction. The book includes extended descriptions of streetcar commuting, segregation, Mardi Gras, summer heat, and a hurricane.

95. Chesnutt, Charles W(addell). *Paul Marchand.* Jackson, Miss.: Univ. Press of Mississippi, 1998. 144pp. (Completed in 1921, but unpublished in the author's lifetime).
   By 1821 Paul Marchand has lived the life of a quadroon for twenty five years. Born in Louisiana, he lived as an orphan with an income provided by a trust administered by New Orleans lawyer Jules Renard. Although the money enabled a middle-class life and paid for his education in Paris, his benefactor and patrimony remained secret, denying him any chance at social status. While in Paris he met and married a woman in a similar situation. Unlike Marchand, his wife's father acknowledged her and in the absence of other heirs, she inherited his sizable estate. Since Marchand could pass as white, he could have returned to New Orleans and lived a privileged life, had he not married a woman whose non-white race was obvious. As a quadroon, Marchand was oppressed by a system of laws and suffered humiliating slights, many at the hands of members of the Beaurepas family, several of whom were members of an association of New Orleans citizens determined to oppress people of mixed race. The patriarch of the family, Pierre Beaurepas, possesses most of the accumulated wealth of the family and has no children. Upon his death, his lawyer, Jules Renard, announces that Paul Marchand is his son, exclusive heir, and is not of mixed race, but the product of a secret marriage. Subsequently Marchand reclaims his honor and wins a series of duels with Beaurepas men. In the end, however, he rejects the bequest and turns the property and money over to a Beaurepas cousin. He leaves Louisiana for France where mixed-race persons enjoy full legal status as citizens. Chesnutt's parable is set at a time when mixed-race people who had been treated equitably in French Louisiana were adjusting to living with the same restricted social and legal status as African-Americans. His work draws a clear picture of oppression in daily life and provides, in expository fashion, information about the legal status of mixed-race people in New Orleans.

96. Chidsey, Donald Barr. *Pistols in the Morning.* New York: Day, 1930. 282pp.
   Felix St. Blake, a gardener's son, had worked with his father at the house of Judge Joseph Bartlett on Esplanade Avenue until his father died. Orphaned and with few prospects, his life is transformed when he disarms and wounds Réné Lavigne with his own gun, while the drunken Lavigne is terrorizing some African-American stevedores on the New Orleans waterfront. Blake is celebrated for punishing a riverfront bully. Staked to a game of roulette, he is soon making his living as a riverboat gambler. His fame increases when he challenges notorious gambler and famed duelist, Major Meserole, to a duel and kills him. Judge Bartlett and his nineteen-year-old daughter, Eugenie, witnessed the slight that prompted the challenge. When he kills Meserole, his reputation on the river is established. A short time later Bartlett and his daughter are returning to New Orleans when Bartlett decides to spend a night on his own in Natchez-Under-the-Hill and insists on a poker game while drunk. To protect him, Blake joins in when two New Yorkers offer him a game. Blake soon realizes the Northerners are cheating. He controls the game in favor of Bartlett, but the Judge thinks Blake has been in on the cheating. After he storms out, Blake kills the New Yorkers, enhancing his reputation as an honest riverboat gambler. When he tries to give the Judge his winnings, the man is irate and tells Blake to throw it in the river. When he does, pandemonium breaks out in Natchez, advancing Blake's notoreity. He returns to New Orleans and

opens his own gambling parlor, having nothing to do with the Bartletts, until Eugenie asks him to deny a challenge her cousin Harold Saintsbury will make after being thrown out of Blake's establishment for being drunk. His refusal of the challenge is complicated by the second in the affair, Captain de Villeray, who is affianced to Eugenie in an arranged marriage. A Parisian, de Villeray continues to demand satisfaction, but Blake maintains his promise and is essentially driven from New Orleans for what is interpreted as a failure of nerve. Settled in Vicksburg with attractive income from money invested in gambling parlors, Blake is bored and depressed and contemplating suicide until he receives a letter from Eugenie begging him to save her from a marriage to de Villeray. He makes a dramatic entrance at the New Orleans wedding and with a gang of associates takes off with the bride. By the end of the book they have been married on board a ship bound for Mexico. Major topics in the book include codes of honor, dueling, gambling houses, and gender roles.

97. Child, Lydia Maria. *A Romance of the Republic.* Boston: Ticknor and Fields, 1867. 442pp.

This novel concerned with racism focuses on New Orleans to show the injustices suffered by people of mixed race. Alfred Royal had come to the city from the North and experienced business success, but had difficulties establishing himself socially as a Northerner. Gonzalez, one of Royal's business associates, a man from St. Augustine, Florida had been in a loving relationship with a mixed-race woman who had died. Pursued by creditors as a bankrupt, his daughter Eulalie could be seized as an asset and sold as a slave. Royal fell in love with Eulalie and had two daughters by her, but never married her, because the marriage would not be recognized in New Orleans. Oddly, he never manumitted her. She predeceased him, but by the time he died, he had also not manumitted her daughters by him, Floracita and Rosabella. Unfortunately, he has numerous creditors at the time of his sudden death and the girls are subject to sale. Fortunately, their music teacher, Signor Papanti and their sewing instructor Madame Guirlande hide them and make plans to get them to Boston. Unfortunately, the girls trust Gerald Fitzgerald, a man who had frequented their father's house and shown an interest in Rosabella. He buys the girls and pretends to marry Rosabella, but keeps her in a remote house on his plantation. By the time she finds out that he is already married to a society woman who resides in the plantation house, she is carrying his child. She steals his white son and flees with her slave Tulipa and her own son. They get to New Orleans before she realizes she will only be able to get herself to Boston. From there, she will make a plan to retrieve the children. The Civil War intervenes and, by the time she returns, Tulipa and the boys are gone. The rest of the novel is devoted to finding the missing children. The book includes little general description of New Orleans and is devoted to repeatedly and melodramatically stating the plight of mixed-race people.

98. Chipman, William Pendleton. *The Boy Spies at the Battle of New Orleans: A Boys Story of the Greatest Battle of the War of 1812.* New York: A.L. Burt, 1910. 276pp.

When Governor Claiborne (c.1772/75–1817) travels to New Orleans to meet with General Andrew Jackson (1767–1845), he takes his son William Claiborne, Jr. and Louis Villere, son of General Villere, commander in chief of the state militia. Once they arrive, the boys meet up with their friend Robert Livingston, son of the Louisiana State Attorney General. Although Governor Claiborne is confident that the British General Nicholls will be defeated at Mobile, Jackson thinks the British are getting reinforcements in Bermuda and will make a surprise attack on New Orleans through inland waterways and lakes. Since the boys are familiar with the route (as they just traveled it), they are commissioned to be pickets and lookouts for British troops, to keep Jackson informed. Although the events of the novel are important to the history of New Orleans, not a great deal of the action occurs there. Most of the book is devoted to the boys' adventures in their race to return to New Orleans after they realize the British are coming. Later they aid in the defense of the city. An epilogue summarizes the real life history of 1814.

99. Chopin, Kate. *The Awakening.* New York: H.S. Stone, 1899. 303pp.

Chopin's novel has been much read and analyzed in recent decades as an early account of the social constraints under which women were forced to live. Edna Pelletier accompanies her husband Léonce and two young boys to escape New Orleans' summer heat in Grand Isle. As usual, her friend Adèle Ratignolle is staying nearby with her family. Unlike other summers, Edna becomes acquainted with a local, Robert LeBrun, the son of the owner of the resort where the Pelletiers are staying. Friendship turns into love and, to end the heated situation, Robert leaves, claiming business in Mexico. With summer over Edna returns to New Orleans, but she begins to make choices based not on social obligations, as in the past, but on her own happiness. She starts to draw and paint and wants an atelier. She also spends more time with her new friend, Madame Reisz, a pianist who lives apart from society. As she cultivates her own development, Edna stops directly supervising household staff and Léonce begins to complain about the quality of the food. More dramatically, Edna ends her "at homes," the hours when she has made herself available to receive callers. Léonce is alarmed since this will have an impact on their social position. Although he tries to get a physician to confirm his own diagnosis that his wife has become mentally unstable, the doctor refuses. However, Léonce does not take Edna along on a business trip to New York City and sends their sons to live with his mother. On her own in New Orleans, Edna moves into a bungalow and eventually has an affair with womanizer Alcee Arobin who is known for being something of a womanizer. The relationship is unsatisfactory and then, through Madame Reisz, she learns that Robert is still interested in her. He arrives in New Orleans and after a period of feigning aloofness, confesses his love. Before matters can progress, Edna is called to help Adèle in childbirth. When she returns, she finds Robert's note saying he has gone away never to return. As a New Orleans novel the book is of interest for so clearly showing what the life of a married upper-class woman was like and the specificity of social responsibilities, some of which would have been common to other American cities, but some of which are distinctive to a woman living in New Orleans.

100. Chopin, Kate. *A Night in Acadie.* Chicago: Way and Williams, 1897. 416pp.

A significant number of short stories in this collection are set in New Orleans. When Athénaïse (in the eponymous story), in a fit of pique, takes a vacation from her husband Cazeau, her brother helps her leave the bayou country for New Orleans and arranges for her to stay in a respectable boarding house on Dauphine Street. With no friends in the city, Athénaïse passes the time strolling the French Quarter and shopping, until she befriends her fellow boarder, Monsieur Gouvernail, a scholarly journalist who takes her on short excursions in New Orleans and out to dine. Her idyll ends when she realizes she is pregnant and returns to her husband, resigning herself to married life. In "A Matter of Prejudice," life in a family house in the French Quarter is the focus. The haughty, elderly Madame Carambeau deigns to allow her widowed daughter, Madame Lelonde, to live with her. The household is governed by the prejudiced older woman, who disdains the intrusion of any element that is not part of French Culture. On one day of the year violations are permitted during the children's birthday party Madame Lelonde hosts for her son Gustave. By coincidence, a sick little American girl is brought to Madame Carambeau to be nursed, completely winning her over. When she later learns that the child is her own granddaughter by her son Henri, estranged because he married an American woman from Prytania Street, Madame Carambeau decides that divine providence is leading her to accept her daughter-in-law and the American community in New Orleans. In "Nég Créol," seventy-five-year-old, Mamzelle Aglaé, is prostrated in prayer every time Chicot, an impoverished French Market fishmonger, visits her top floor room in her squalid French Quarter boarding house. Although she complains to Chicot of her rheumatism and what she must endure from her many downstairs neighbors, on the whole she pretends to ignore him and the scraps of food he brings from the market to keep her alive. The bond between the two is based on her family identity as a Boisduré, even though she was disinherited when she became an actress. For Chicot had been a servant in the Boisduré family and in his current life, tries to establish social status by his tie to a family he believes is prominent in New Orleans, only to discover upon her death that no one even remembers her family. The "Sentimental Soul" is the story of Mamzelle Fleurette, an unmarried woman past middle age who operates a small store and falls in love with Lacodie, the locksmith, who regularly purchases his newspaper there and often lingers to air his political views with other frequent customers. Fleurette knows that he is married and never carries on a conversation with him. However, she believes she is living in sin because of her feelings for him and tires her priest with her confessions. When Lacodie dies of a fever, the priest denies her wish to attend the funeral, but when Lacodie's widow remarries a short time later, Fleurette takes secret pleasure in becoming Lacodie's chief mourner and tending his grave. The eponymous Cavanelle in a story of that name is a dry goods merchant who devotes all of his time and money to his sister Mathilde, in the conviction that she has great talent as a singer and needs voice and music lessons to become a performer. Unfortunately, she has no voice. The narrator of the tale learns Mathilde has died and expresses that Cavanelle, now free of his burdensome delusion, has begun to enjoy life. The story ends with Cavanelle taking in his Aunt Èlicie, a woman wrongfully impoverished by the war who is in need frequent medical care. As a whole the stories capture the intimacy of life in the French Quarter among people of the lower social classes.

101. Churchill, Winston. *The Crossing*. New York: Macmillan, 1904. 598pp.
      In the form of an autobiography by fictional protagonist David Ritchie, Churchill explores the history of settlement in Kentucky and Tennessee from 1774 through 1800. David is living alone on the frontier with his father, Alec Ritchie, when Alec volunteers for a military campaign against Cherokee Indians. Alexander Cameron, an enemy of Alec Ritchie's from his native Scotland, has been inciting the Indians to support the British. Alec leaves David in Charleston with his mother's family, the wealthy Temples. Although David finds a comrade in Nicholas Temple, he despises Temple's Tory parents and returns to Kentucky after Alec's death to join the household of Tom and Polly McChesney. Through Tom he becomes a drummer boy in George Rogers Clark's campaign against the Indians in the Northwest Territory. He later studies law in Virginia and when he returns to Kentucky at twenty-one he is reunited with Nicholas Temple. The two of them are tasked with a secret mission to New Orleans to gather evidence of General James Wilkinson's treasonous agreement with Spanish Governor Rodriguez Miro to give Kentucky a trading monopoly on the Mississippi River. Wilkinson had taken an oath to the Spanish king and accepted land and a pension in return for trying to get Kentucky to reject the U.S. Constitution and become part of Spain's Louisiana Territory. Ritchie's New Orleans adventure is described over the course of the culminating one-hundred and fifty pages of the book, which are mostly concerned with Nick Temple's romance with a French woman of noble heritage. Arriving in 1789, one year after fire destroyed many of the city's buildings, Ritchie generally interacts with members of the large, well-established French population who resent Spanish rule. The narrative presents aspects of political and economic history and vignettes of some of the important New Orleans residents of the time period, including Daniel Clark, uncle of the man of the same name who was to become a wealthy and influential figure in the later development of New Orleans. The novel explores aspects of the relationship between Kentucky, New Orleans, and westward expansion of the frontier.

102. Clack, Marie Louise. *Our Refugee Household*. New York: Blelock, 1866. 226pp.
      This novel is presented as a first-hand account of refugee life during the Civil War, as a small group of gentlewomen, their servants and a few children use an abandoned house for shelter. Although the book includes an extended account of a Christmas celebration and some descriptions of hospital service and aiding convalescent soldiers, the bulk of the volume is devoted to recording stories the women tell each other to pass the time. While not exclusively set in New Orleans, the tales illustrate the centrality of the city in Southern social life since most of the narratives transpire

there. In "Pet's Story; or, The Marble Slab," a newlywed murders his beautiful, socially brilliant wife within a few weeks of the wedding, in their honeymoon suite at the St. Louis Hotel. "Queen's Story; or, Mrs. Desborough's Secret," tells of a young woman who stays in the house of a wealthy relative, forty-year-old Mrs. Desborough, who lives in mysterious seclusion with only one servant in a huge French Quarter mansion. She even has a local restaurant prepare all of her food so that she does not need to have a cook on the premises. Eventually Desborough's young visitor witnesses a jeweled woman playing the harp and singing before a portrait in a wing of the house that is usually kept locked up. As a result, Desborough is forced to explain that her younger sister, thirty-eight-year-old Aglaie, lost her mind after her young husband never returned from a business trip to Cuba, and for twenty years has had only enough lucidity to sing his favorite song each evening, as she promised to do upon his return. Desborough keeps her sister a secret out of fear that her daughter's marriage chances will be negatively impacted by a case of lunacy in the family. In "Sister Maddie's Story; or, Leoline and Rosaline," The tragic tale of the Marchmont twins, Leoline and Rosaline, tale begins with the death of their insolvent father when they are fifteen. The two of them and their nineteen-year-old brother George have no recourse but to move into the household of a wealthy relative, the widow Mrs. Monson, whose plantation is on the Red River. Soon after their arrival, the austerity of the household begins to burden their lively spirits and George sets off to try to make a fortune to free them. In the meantime, life with Mrs. Monson takes a hostile tone when she forbids the girls to practice their Roman Catholic faith. Rosaline soon runs away, but the circumstances are such that she is presumed dead. Shortly afterwards George comes to the rescue of the grief-stricken Leoline, taking her to New Orleans where she eventually marries the well-to-do Clarence Fortescue and begins the decorous social life of a young matron. Eventually, Rosaline appears in the guise of the widow Mrs. Brunswick, whose dissipated life is funded by the estate of an Italian nobleman she loved and outlived after separating from Clarence Fortescue, whom she had married several years before he met Leoline. The twins are horrified and Leoline enters a convent.

103. Clark, Ellery H(arding). *The Strength of the Hills*. New York: Crowell, 1929. 350pp.
This work of historical fiction presents the life of Andrew Jackson (1767–1845), with the last fifty pages being set in New Orleans. Protagonist David Trevor, born in 1760, spends much of his youth in the frontier region that would become Tennessee. He befriends Jackson as a compatriot of his generation and the novel covers Jackson's career through David's eyes. In the New Orleans section of the book, Trevor fights alongside Jackson. As in other fictionalized accounts of the action leading up to Battle of New Orleans, Jean Lafitte (c.1776–c.1823) plays a role, but this book provides less description of the city to focus more on military strategy and the historical significance of the battle.

104. Cleaver, Anastasia N. [Natasha Peters, pseud.]. *Savage Surrender*. New York: Ace Books, 1977. 600pp.
In early nineteenth-century France, Elise Lesconflair, an orphaned French noblewoman, is married off to a Bavarian Baron by her uncle to settle the gambling debts of her brother Honoré (her uncle thought it a point of honor to pay them). The daughter of a famous general, her uncle is an impoverished Count and she is the goddaughter of Napoleon Bonaparte (1769–1821), but as a woman even she is unprotected when she is set upon and raped in the forest surrounding her uncle's chateau. When her brothers discover that her attacker, a man they believe to be the Marquis de Pellissier, is one of the guests at the feast on the evening before her wedding to the baron, they force him to marry her with the aid of a senile Cardinal Soon afterwards, the seventeen-year-old Elise discovers her new husband is not actually the Marquis, but an American spy named Garth McClelland whose only escape from France is by pre-arranged transport on the slave ship, the Charleston Belle. Even he has difficulty protecting her in such a setting when she begins to rail against the captain for the behavior of the crew. When sailors from a British navy

ship board the Charleston Belle and impress a number of sailors, including Garth, the captain and his crew turn Elise into their whore. She is finally rescued when the pirate Jean Lafitte (c.1776–c.1823) captures the ship. After a long period of recovery, Lafitte begins to romance Elise and, in 1812, presents her to New Orleans society from his house on Dumaine Street, using her real name and socially respectable lineage. She is entirely unprepared when Garth McClelland appears at a masked ball and uses the growing controversy between Governor Claiborne and Lafitte as an excuse to persuade the pirate to return to Barataria. However, Garth follows the couple and reveals his status as husband to the pirate. Lafitte is willing to let Elise go when he realizes that she is in love with him. However, Garth only wants a ship that Lafitte has captured and tries to use Elise to strike a bargain. So begins a lengthy story in which Garth and Elise alternately come together in love and rush apart in hatred, all set against the dramatic historical events of the War of 1812. Their lasting reunion as husband and wife only comes at the end of the novel after Elise has been the victim of a plot in which she was falsely accused of murder. The intermittent New Orleans setting includes historical details and fictionalized historical figures as the city comes to symbolize the American character, as does the fearless Elise, who would never return to the life of a European aristocrat after experiencing the social freedoms (no matter how incomplete) of the American woman. By the end of the novel, Garth and Elise are headed to the Texas frontier.

105. Clevely, Hugh [Tod Claymore, pseud.]. *Appointment in New Orleans.* Baltimore, Md.: Penguin Books, 1955. 215pp.

Tod Claymore is asked to New Orleans by his old friend Louis Curel, who arranges for transportation on one of his freighter ships sailing from Rotterdam. Around a dozen other passengers are on board, including a beautiful Finnish woman, Taimi Lanner. When Claymore arrives in New Orleans Mrs. Curel, Louis' mother, explains that Claymore was summoned to investigate Taimi Lanner, who claims that she married the Curel's son Paul after the end of World War II. If true, she stands to inherit his fortune should he die from the wounds he received from an airplane crash that paralyzed him ten months earlier. A childhood friend of Paul's, who was stationed with him and has since returned to New Orleans, claims Lanner's story is true. While Claymore investigates, he engages in house party activities and explores New Orleans Mardi Gras parades and attends krewe balls with the rest of the household. He also goes to bars, nightclub shows, and boxing gyms. Not long after, Louis Curel is shot to death, Claymore and Lanner are kidnapped, and left in a shack in Bayou St. Christophe. Once the perpetrator, who was motivated by the fear of losing their inheritance, is caught, Claymore accompanies Lanner to the bedside of Paul Curel, who is sure to recover under her care. Descriptions of New Orleans in the novel are shallow and touristic, but warmly appreciative.

106. Cline, C(harles) Terry, Jr. *Cross Current.* Garden City, N.Y.: Doubleday, 1979. 299pp.

Although much of this novel is set in New Orleans, the book provides little description of the city. When Josh McDavid, an Episcopal priest in his early thirties who serves a church in Mobile, Alabama, begins having seizures, his bishop sends him to Dr. Judith Borland, a world-famous New Orleans neurologist, requesting both physical and psychological evaluation. As Borland explores McDavid's condition, knowledge of his family background becomes crucial to his well-being and McDavid's live-in girlfriend, Madelyn Neely, carries out an investigation that takes her back to his orphanage outside Atlanta, to London and, finally to Israel. She discovers that generation after generation of McDavid's male ancestors experienced seizures in their early thirties and soon committed suicide. When she arrives in Israel, she finds that the McDavid genealogy can be traced all the way back to 1 A.D., for he is directly descended from one of the centurions who crucified Jesus of Nazareth. For McDavid and Neely, this knowledge provides an interpretive framework for the vivid images connected with the convulsions. However, Dr. Borland performs an operation to which she attributes his cure. The book portrays New Orleans as an internationally important center for medical research and the city is mostly viewed as a skyline from medical buildings more than ten stories high. Gender roles, extramarital sex, and prejudice against epileptics are all major themes.

107. Cobb, Joseph B(eckham) *The Creole, or, Siege of New Orleans. An Historical Romance: Founded on the Events of 1814–15.* Philadelphia: A. Hart, 1850. 131pp.

Evil fathers, tragic love affairs, concealed identities, and remarkable coincidences abound in this novel, which is primarily set in the weeks before and during the Battle of New Orleans. In this account, the pirate Lafitte has no brother and has the first name Antoine. His second in command is Hector Diable, a.k.a. Henry La Sasuriere, a.k.a. Henri Paget, a man Lafitte rescued as a boy from a burning ship. Fifteen years before, Lafitte also rescued Violante, the seventeen-year-old daughter of a Martinique sugar planter, with whom he had fallen in love and took away from her evil, violently opposed father. The couple's son, Antoine, went missing in the violent scuffle of Violante's departure, only to be secretly cared for by her faithful slave Amri, an Obi-woman, who took the child to Port Royal, where he benefited from the patronage of a wealthy man who paid for his schooling. Later, he was reunited with his grandfather, who had become a Roman Catholic priest named Father Spinelli, in order to make amends for his former life. Spinelli brought Antoine to New Orleans, but the young man was never to know that Violante was his mother since he was the bastard son of the notorious pirate Lafitte. To conceal her relationship with the pirate, Violante lives in New Orleans as the sister of Henri Paget and has established herself in the upper echelons of New Orleans society under this false identity. One of her best friends is Adele Lavaret, the daughter of a mean-spirited, but wealthy banker. Over time Lavaret and Henri Paget fall in love. These details are sketched out in lengthy flashbacks during late 1813, after Lafitte and his men have been accepted for military service to defend New Orleans. These Baratarians and their supporters believe that the military conflict is their chance to redeem their reputations and live more openly. Unlike other accounts of Lafitte and the defense of New Orleans, the focus here is not on the effort to convince Governor Claiborne and General Jackson to accept the aid of the pirates, instead, the focus is on complex personal relationships and the vindication of honor. The novel takes the position that Lafitte and his men were not like other pirates since they never attacked American vessels and treated their captives honorably, never distressing women, resorting to torture, or disturbing the personal property of passengers. In addition, the novel asserts that Lafitte and his men had legitimately claimed Barataria as their territory when the region was under no political control; therefore, Barataria was not part of the Louisiana Territory and had been illegally ceded to the United States. The book never really explains why the pirates then decide to aid the United States. However, their reputations are positively benefited by their service. Lafitte is considered a hero of the battle, although he experiences serious personal losses. His son is killed and Violante dies immediately from shock and grief. Hector Diable serves so brilliantly that Commodore Patterson singles him out for praise. However, this holds no merit in the eyes of Adele Lavaret's father, who still considers him a pirate. Fortunately, Father Spinelli is convinced that Diable is actually a relative of his, named Henry Barriere, and the legitimate heir to a French marquisate. Spinelli assists him in returning to France where he serves the king after Napoleon's escape from Elba and, based on this and his commendation by Commodore Patterson, is granted his inheritance, despite his former life as a pirate. Unfortunately, he is too late to be united with Lavaret, whose father has forced her to marry another man. The two lovers see each other only briefly before Lavaret succumbs to disease and death. The book depicts Orleaneans as consumed with European notions of courtliness, honor, and genealogy.

108. Cohen, Alfred J. [Alan Dale, pseud.]. *Ned Bachman: The New Orleans Detective.* New York: J.S. Ogilvie, 1886. 134pp.

Two orphans find love and domestic security after repeated aggression by a criminal gang, in this New Orleans novel published as pulp fiction by a Manhattan department store. When the father of Hero Carnsea (later referred to as Miss Dalton) dies, she learns he was not a successful merchant but a debtor. Raised as a lady, she has no means of earning her keep except by fancy embroidery work. Just as she realizes the direness of her situation, Eugene Barton, a wealthy young man with a passion for her that she does not reciprocate, tries to abduct her. She is rescued by Ned Bachman, who takes her to his paternal Uncle George's mansion on the outskirts of New Orleans. Ned's father Robert Bachman had disappeared years before to avoid some unnamed disgrace after the death of Ned's mother, and George, who has no heirs, has made Ned his heir. Ned is astounded when one member of a gang of robbers who breaks into his uncle's mansion claims to be his father and does bear a striking resemblance to his Uncle George. The band is driven off, but Ned visits taverns in the city until he finds Robert, who goes by the name Captain Lavern (sic) and is the leader of the Black Band. Ned offers to give up his life with George and go abroad with Robert, if Robert will give up his life of crime. Robert claims to need money enough to support them and insists that Ned assist him in stealing a large amount of gold from George's premises, inviting Ned to think the matter over and meet him at the Black Band hideout. In a subplot, Ned's, girlfriend Hortense de Noir, who is actually the lover of the married Eugene Barton, is also forcing him into a commitment. When Ned begins to fall in love with Hero, he tries to break off with Hortense, but she and Barton lay a plot to force Ned to propose. Not only is Ned unaware of their affair, he also does not realize that Hortense is the hostess for her father Antoine's gambling parlor. When Ned visits the Black Band's hideout, Hero follows him in secret, concerned that Robert is an imposter. In serial fashion each of them are held captive and escape several times. Ned is aided by Hortense, who truly loves him, while Miss Dalton is aided by a dwarf, Mansauel (sic), who claims to love her, and must resist the advances of Antoine de Noir once she is imprisoned in his household. After chases through secret passages and Ned's rescue of Miss Dalton with the aid of secret police hired by George, Captain Lavern is mortally wounded and confesses that he is actually the illegitimate half-brother of Robert and George. When Robert left New Orleans, Lavern followed him to France and assumed his identity when Robert died. With certain knowledge that his father is dead, Ned's attachment to his uncle is even deeper and he is free to marry Hero since he has cast off Hortense, after learning the truth about her. The couple needs worry no longer about Barton since Mansauel killed him, earning their gratitude and a place in their household. Hortense heads to Baden-Baden and a continuation of her career as a gambling hall hostess. The New Orleans setting is a stereotyped one: a city riddled with gambling parlors and the hideouts of criminal gangs.

109. Collier, Julia. *Pirates of Barataria*. Illustrated by Judith Ann Lawrence. New York: Putnam, 1966. 158pp.

This work of historical fiction for young people is set during the War of 1812 and deals with the brothers Lafitte and the Battle of New Orleans. Ned Bishop, a seventeen-year-old orphan, hears of the British threat and travels from his home a few miles outside New Orleans to join the militia. However, he is concerned about his lack of experience and welcomes the invitation of eighteen-year-old David Matthews and his younger brother Joe to their cabin in Barataria to learn how to navigate swampland and stand up to pirates. Even before he leaves New Orleans he meets one pirate, Pierre Lafitte, who lets the boys sleep overnight in his blacksmith shop. The Matthews work for the Lafittes and Ned later witnesses the British meeting with Lafitte. Most of the book deals with Ned's efforts to free David from outlaws who have agreed to guide the British and aid them in capturing New Orleans. With the help of Jean Lafitte (c.1776–c.1823), Ned rescues David and helps capture a map showing the British plan of attack that will aid in the defense of the city. Although the novel is mostly set outside New Orleans, it provides another fictional account of the British attack on the city during the War of 1812.

110. Comfort, Mildred Houghton. *Search through Pirate's Alley*. Illustrated by Sari. New York: William Morrow, 1945. 200pp.

In 1900 twelve-year-old Pierre D'Orsay's family lives in their ancestral Royal Street house in the no-longer fashionable French Quarter. Ten years ago Pierre's grandfather died and the only will that could be found was an early one. His lawyer knows that the later one would have benefited Pierre's father. The will has come up again because the bank issuing the stock Pierre's father inherited has failed, impoverishing the D'Orsays. The family's only hope is to turn a building they own on Orleans Street, off Pirate's Alley, into an income producer. Constructed by Pierre's grandfather in anticipation of the arrival of Napoleon Bonaparte (1769–1821), the current inhabitant is a baker's assistant unable to work since the death of his employer the baker. The D'Orsays establish "The Pirate's Bakery." Pierre also dedicates himself to finding the missing will and makes friends with an elderly praline seller, Josef Garavalia, who had been his grandfather's friend. From Garavalia he learns more about his grandfather's role in a plot to rescue Napoleon from exile and give him the Pirate Alley house, as well as the man's activities as one of Jean Lafitte's men. Pierre's grandfather had an elaborate desk built for Napoleon and Garavalia thinks the will must be in the missing desk. Pierre eventually discovers the desk and its secret, but the adventure novel has many plot twists and includes a great deal of description of cultural practices, such as interactions with slaves, and the celebration of holidays such as All Saints Day, Christmas, Mardi Gras, and Spring Fiesta.

111. Conaway, James. *The Big Easy*. Boston: Houghton Mifflin, 1970. 216pp.

The New Orleans of this novel is so dangerously corrupt and racially divided that the city is unlivable. A failed academic, thirty-seven-year-old Comiski works as a police reporter and most of the plot is connected to his investigation into why the body of African-American businessman and racehorse owner, Parks, was dug up and his head taken. In addition to their open racism, the policemen with whom Comiski interacts believe they must use force to maintain a civil society and that the law merely protects criminals. A large subset of the officers are members of a private organization training to fight off a perceived attempt takeover the city through gaining control of city government. At first they had thought the plot was organized by homosexuals but have begun to believe that African-Americans are the conspirators. Comiski also comes into contact with white thugs who are part of a motorcycle gang and work on behalf of drug-dealing organized crime figures; and finally with Tea, a young African-American man who believes he has a violently messianic mission to revenge his race against whites. As a somewhat bumbling "man of sorrows," Comiski only finds comfort in the arms of the beautiful, mixed-race Carrie, Park's former mistress and Tea's lover. By the end of the novel, all of the characters with whom the reader has sympathized are either dead or have left the city, which is portrayed as irredeemable.

112. Conaway, James. *World's End*. New York: William Morrow, 1978. 323pp.

In this 1970s novel political offices and business operations are located in New Orleans, but suburbanites are in control. The O'Neill family of World's End Parish exemplify the system. Patriarch Rory O'Neill is the parish commissioner. To promote the interests of his family, O'Neill orchestrates a political campaign to get his puppet, Strather Ward, elected governor, and uses hired thugs to subdue the local Mafia, led by Salvatore Cinque, who had threatened the family business, Calliope Trucking. The bulk of the family wealth comes from Boreal Energy and Development, built on oil wells drilled all over World's End on land that O'Neill had obtained for a pittance. Former assistant district attorney, Michael Duran, a thirty-five-year-old with a struggling legal practice and an apartment in the Pontalba Buildings, is retained by O'Neill to raise money for Ward's political campaign. Through Duran's eyes the reader learns about labor unions controlled by organized crime, corrupt law enforcement and judicial officials, and self-serving politicians. A range of social issues fill the narrative, including ethnic and racial prejudices, class distinctions, and violence against women. While most of the women are subjugated by men, Erin, wife of

Strather Ward, has a more fully-realized existence. She works outside the home as a foundation fundraiser and is not afraid to express her opinions, even to Rory O'Neill. Duran also stands out in stark relief from his surroundings for his intelligence and bemused alienation from his social environment. Even though he grew up on the edge of Irish Channel, his family had a long tradition of being cultivated landowners before his grandfather died and O'Neill who, unlike the Durans, knew of the oil wealth beneath the swampland purchased his plantation for a modest price. In addition to the prevalence of organized crime in New Orleans, Conaway airs controversies over the construction of the Superdome and a deep-water port for New Orleans.

113. Converse, Florence. *Diana Victrix*. Boston: Houghton Mifflin, 1897. 362pp.

This vivid portrayal of upper-class family life in turn of the twentieth-century New Orleans is preoccupied with gender roles and the relationship between artist and society. Twenty-year-old Jacques has been head of the Dumarais family for many years even though his father, a skilled accountant, is still alive, since the older man is blind and preoccupied with his amateur scholarship. Jacques is practical-minded and ambitious and decided not to finish college but go directly into the Cotton Exchange where he has been successful. His stepbrother Jocelin was born with a beautiful voice, studied, and was taken up by an opera diva, but failed on the stage due to an inability to project. He was diagnosed with a vague physical condition, connected to a lack of manly vigor that prevents him from feeling amorous toward women, although, attracted by his gentility, they are his constant companions. Their sister Jeanne, a nineteen-year-old on the verge of her debutante year, has been kept close to home, and playing the piano and composing her own songs. The entire family is altered when Jacques persuades his parents to accept as long-term houseguests, Enid Spenser and Sylvia Bennett. Jacques claims it would be good for Jeanne to have these Bostonian, college-educated women in the household. Spenser and Bennett, friends since college, are each twenty-eight and devoted to each other. Spenser hopes that spending December through March in New Orleans will divert Bennett from her nervous illnesses. A social science teacher, Spenser has found an audience for her views on workers' rights and economic justice. Jacques finds her conversation stimulating, but is most interested in getting her friend Curtis Baird, a wealthy, thirty-year-old capitalist, to join him in a business partnership. Initially, the Dumarais family seems less influenced by their visitors than the Northerners are by the beauty of New Orleans and the charm of Southern culture. Through Baird, Spenser and Bennett meet Roma Campion, a woman their age who wants to escape tradition-bound New Orleans and devotes her energies to winning Baird as her ticket into New York society. Typically Spenser would have dismissed Campion as a frivolous society lady, but the appeal of Campion's dinners and Mardi Gras balls, coupled with Campion's perceptive conversation, get Spenser fantasizing about giving up her work-filled, intellectual life for life with Jacques as a society matron. Bennett takes an interest in becoming Jocelin's impresario and he fantasizes about marrying her and becoming the well-cared-for pet of the wealthy woman. Both women encourage Jeanne to place her art above typical debutante concerns. In the end these Northern women destroy both Jeanne and Jocelin and Jacques makes a narrow escape. The book presents aspects of the New Orleans social world through descriptions of dinners, balls, opera outings, and Mardi Gras entertainments.

114. Conway, Theresa. *Gabrielle*. Greenwich, Conn.: Fawcett Books, 1977. 510pp.

Set in the years immediately prior to the War of 1812, this historical romance depicts a New Orleans in which prominent people that can now be found in history books mingle freely, whether they are government officials, society figures, mistresses, or prostitutes. The focus of the book, French aristocrat Gabrielle de Beauvoir, is orphaned shortly after the Revolution and her guardian cheats her inheritance away from her. Raped, sold into slavery and captured by pirates on a ship to the Caribbean, her life is spared by Jean Lafitte (c.1776–c.1823). He takes her to Barataria, subdues her, and makes her his mistress. Eventually Gabrielle persuades Lafitte to take her to New Orleans, where she gets to accompany him to the theatre and a ball. However, most of her time is spent in a locked room in an expensive brothel, under the watchful eye of Renee, an accomplished madam. When she becomes pregnant with Lafitte's child, Gabrielle's relationship with the pirate deepens, but when she miscarries, she flees without Lafitte pursuing her. Throwing herself upon the mercy of Renee, she is soon the mistress of Bernard de Marigny (1785–1868). However, at the crucial moment when he is about to install her in her own house with a servant, she offends him by her behavior in the company of Rafe St. Claire, the wealthy heir to a Virginia fortune. The twenty-five-year-old man, relocated to New Orleans to escape the more conservative society of his family, has quickly become a fixture in New Orleans society where his womanizing, often with prostitutes, does not prejudice society people against him. Despite their supposed animosity for each other, Gabrielle is soon living openly as Rafe's mistress in a grand house he rents for her only a few doors away from Governor Claiborne's residence. When Mrs. Claiborne meets Gabrielle for the first time she realizes that Gabrielle was raised as a lady and insists that Rafe marry her. He is unwilling, even though she is carrying his baby. However, soon afterwards he fights a duel with Bernard de Marigny, who spares his life after extracting his promise that he marries Gabrielle. By the War of 1812, Gabrielle has become a figure in New Orleans society as the friend of the governor's wife and mother to Rafe's heir. When she learns in confidence from the governor that there is a shortage of arms, she gets his promise that he will stop prosecution against the Lafitte brothers if they join the fight against the British. Convincing Jean Lafitte of the genuineness of Claiborne's offer, she plays a crucial role in saving the city.

115. Cook, Ella Booker. *A Magnolia for Joan.* New Orleans: Pelican, 1951. 246pp.

In Depression-era New Orleans, nineteen-year-old Joan Shannon holds her family together after her father's premature death. The Shannons live in a house whose lot takes up a whole block on Coliseum Street, but the sense of security the massive structure lends is illusory as William Robert Shannon had borrowed against his life insurance policy and mortgaged the house in order to send his four children to private schools and maintain the style of life that Bettie Joe, his impractical wife of twenty-two years, expects. Oldest son, twenty-one-year-old Bill, drops out of the University of Virginia to help the family by taking an engineering job with a South American mining firm, but actually adds to their burden by marrying Clarice Lowe, a young woman even more improvident than Bettie Joe, who socializes in a fast, less than respectable set and drinks heavily. Through the family lawyer, Joan gets a secretarial job in a legal firm, hoping to keep her younger siblings, seventeen-year-old Robert and fifteen-year-old Honey in school. Her smallest attempts to economize, however, face resistance, as her mother charges expensive new clothes and travels to resorts. The sole family servant, Aunt Het, a loyal African-American cook, economizes and goes unpaid to help out. Fortunately, both Joan's affluent Uncle John and the heir to his neighbor's plantation, Donald St. John, attractive and Harvard-educated, both take note of Joan's common sense and uncomplaining sacrifices. After Joan loses her job and the Shannons have spent all their savings, the bank takes their house. Bill is missing in South America and in this dark hour word arrives that Uncle John is dead and Joan is his sole heir. As the Shannons take up country life new problems and several tragedies ensue. Although much of the novel is set in New Orleans, the city has little presence beyond references to restaurants and addresses. The city is contrasted unfavorably with life in the country. The book's racism hearkens back to novels of the nineteenth century in presenting images of African-Americans who delight in subjugating themselves and serving their good masters. Although Joan would seem to present a strong female character whose independence puts her on an equal footing with men, she indulges the weaknesses of others, even to their own detriment, and enters into a self-abnegating romantic relationship.

116. Cook, Petronelle Marguerite Mary [Margot Arnold, pseud.]. *Marie.* New York: Pocket Books, 1979. 486pp.

In this historical romance novel, 1970s women's issues shape the account of Marie Laveau (c. 1801–1881) and her daughter, namesake, and heir to Voodoo queenship. The story begins in 1844 when the younger Laveau has just reached puberty and ends in 1918. Under her mother's tutelage, Laveau develops Voodoo powers, and also develops her ability to control powerful men and accumulate wealth and influence. One tenet of Laveau and her mother is that powerful Creole men marry to enhance their social status and treat their wives as expensively maintained acquisitions. Although their wives may bear them heirs, their sexual relations with them are perfunctory. They find passion in their illicit affairs with women of color, which is socially acceptable if the women are quadroons. Whereas the older Laveau has had many lovers by whom she had a number of children, her daughter longs for and finds true, if thwarted, love. The novel incorporates a good deal of physical description and summarizes major historical events affecting New Orleans, including flooding, fever outbreaks, the Civil War, Reconstruction, and the Cotton Exposition. Throughout the book, treatment of slaves and people of color is a major theme, as well as the social status of women. Treatment of the Laveaus' acumen as businesswomen parallels some fictional accounts of powerful New Orleans madams, with the distinction that the Laveaus are also powerful spiritual leaders.

117. Cooke, Grace MacGowan and Annie Booth McKinney. *Mistress Joy: A Tale of Natchez in 1798*. New York: Century, 1901. 370pp.

Approximately eighty pages of this historical romance novel dealing with frontier Methodism is set in New Orleans, where the female protagonist learns the pleasures and evils of the fashionable world. After the death of her mother, twenty-year-old Joyce "Joy" Valentine grew up maintaining her father Tobias's rural household outside Natchez. Tobias lives the tenets he preaches as a circuit rider and his household often includes guests in need of charity. One of these, Jessop, comes to Tobias in the tattered clothing of a gentleman, having not eaten for days. He soon falls ill of fever and as Joy nurses him the two fall in love. When Jessop pleads his suit with Tobias, he reveals that he is the youngest son of the Earl of Shropshire and that although he has run through a fortune, another will be provided when his father hears the news that he will settle down and establish a plantation. Joy had been courted by Methodist David Batchelor, a successful planter, and Tobias is surprised when Batchelor suggests Joy be sent to New Orleans to live with the family of Tobias's affluent brother, Henry Valentine, to test whether her true nature lies with the Primitive Christianity of the Methodist frontier settlement, or fashionable society. The spiritually vigilant Joy is surprised when she enjoys the frivolity and indulgences of her uncle's household, presided over by his wife Ausite, the daughter of a French nobleman displaced by the Revolution. For the first time, Joy is treated as a beauty, and becomes a favorite of the young gentlemen who escort her to dinners and balls. The epitome of her social success comes at a ball her aunt holds in honor of Louis Philippe, Duc d'Orleans, during his 1798 visit to New Orleans. Just as she is enjoying the company of the Duke, upon whom she makes a great impression, Joy espies Jessop, who had pledged to stay laboring on the frontier, proving his love and avoiding contact with Joy for one year. When the two hold a private conversation the gossip travels back to the immediately alarmed Ausite, for Jessop is now a married man. After losing everything in a gambling parlor operated by a woman known only as Madame, he had been forced into marrying his creditor. Shaken by the failure of her spiritual insight in falling in love with such a man, Joy only remains in New Orleans at the pleading of her aunt to entertain the Duke until his departure from the city. The novel establishes the pleasures of eighteenth-century New Orleans for the upper classes, even while condemning the empty frivolity. Several characters in the novel introduce the plight of Native Americans and African-American slaves. Several historical figures appear in the novel and Aaron Burr and his schemes are given full treatment.

118. Cooley, Stoughton. *The Captain of the Amaryllis.* Illustrated by Leslie L. Benson. Boston: C.M. Clark, 1910. 416pp.

Although most of the action of this book transpires aboard a steamboat, the romance novel presents the importance of the steamboat industry to the life of the city and indicates the ways in which the boats were an extension of the city's social life. Captain Ingraham, though still a young man, is an admired riverboat owner, following in the footsteps of his retired father. At the beginning of the novel he has just repaid the mortgage on his boat and has in prospect a meeting with Sally Heath, the young woman he wants to court. However, he has two rivals for her hand. Heath's family had long ago arranged a marriage between Heath and Sidney Drake, who owns the plantation next to that of the Heath family. Ingraham's other rival is Henri Mollison, the son of a wealthy New Orleans businessman. Ingraham knows that Drake gambles and drinks heavily and hopes Sally will realize the greater value of his own love for her. Unfortunately, Mollison pére decides to bolster his son's chances through economic warfare on Ingraham. During the course of the book Ingraham's moral superiority is demonstrated repeatedly and finally, even the elder Mollison acknowledges it when Ingraham refuses to file a claim, as he is legally entitled to do, on a percentage of a highly valuable cargo on a Mollison boat that he heroically saves from wrecking.

119. Cooper, Parley J. *Dark Desires.* New York: Pocket Books, 1976. 312pp.

In this sensational romance novel the spoiled daughter of a wealthy senator is forced to leave the refinement of Savannah and travel to frontier Louisiana, when her husband, a promising politician, decides to establish a sugar plantation to take advantage of opportunities presented by the Louisiana Purchase. Zelma had married Dester (sic) Granville because he was handsome and wealthy, but also because she could imagine him becoming a revered politician like her own father. She so resents being taken to Louisiana, that she refuses to even visit his land, known as Riverbend Plantation, until the elaborate mansion he is constructing for her is finished. Along with her infant children and several trusted house slaves, she settles into the New Orleans house of Madame Celine, not understanding that the woman owns and operates a successful brothel in a different section of the city. From Celine she learns to develop some independence from Dester, both financial (by investing in Celine's brothel) and emotional. With Celine's encouragement she begins an affair with Emile Faviere, not realizing that his father owns the plantation next to Riverbend. While she eventually rejects Faviere for his immaturity and realizes the value of the love she has for Dester, she never asks for her investment in Celine's brothel returned and continues her friendship with the woman even after taking up her life at Riverbend. Although New Orleans is repeatedly used as setting in the novel, the focus is primarily on the emotional and sexual liberties the city affords, which eventually ruin Zelma's son when she is a widow running Riverbend plantation with little help. The novel attempts to portray what a liberated nineteenth-century woman would have been like and presents a vision of enlightened slave ownership based on a respectful relationship between master and slave.

120. Corrington, John William. *The Upper Hand*. New York: Putnam, 1967. 383pp.

In the years immediately after World War II a lapsed Roman Catholic priest relocates to New Orleans. Twenty-nine-year-old Christopher Nieman's crisis of faith comes five years into his ministry when he reaches a sudden conviction that God is dead and that his call to the ministry was a youthful confusion. Returning to his hometown of Shreveport, almost immediately he picks up waitress Mary Ann Downey. As he is engaging in foreplay in a family-owned apartment, Billy Bob Stoker, a man to whom Nieman's mother rented the apartment without informing Nieman, fumbles through the door. Although Nieman does later bed Downey, shortly afterwards she disappears and Nieman and Stoker end up moving together to New Orleans. Soon after arriving in the city, Nieman gets a job as an early morning deliveryman for the Staff-of-Life Bakery, purveyors of inedible, processed white bread. Stoker's job offer comes after a night of drinking with Benny Boundoch, who operates a brothel using the girls he features in his sado-pornographic films. There, Stoker finds Downey and soon becomes one of Boundoch's actors. Nieman also becomes tangentially linked to Boundoch through his upstairs neighbor Dr. Aorta, an abortionist, some of whose patients are Boundoch's prostitutes. Aorta uses Christian Blackman, an African-American truck mechanic at Staff-of-Life bakery, to dispose of the corpses of his patients who do not survive, by cremating them in an old bakery oven. On one occasion Nieman inadvertently becomes involved in a cremation, which is how he finds out about Aorta's profession. When Downey reveals her pregnancy and anticipated visit to Aorta, Christopher Nieman believes he has found his purpose in life and offers to marry her. In the end, however, it is Stoker who leaves New Orleans with Downey, having taken more direct action to save her from Aorta. Nieman's experiences in New Orleans bring him into direct confrontations with evil, but he is unable to rediscover his faith in God and his only consolation comes from New Orleans' bars. In this novel, the vice with which the city had been identified in the late nineteenth and early twentieth century has expanded and been strengthened by World War II.

121. Costain, Thomas B(ertram). *High Towers.* Garden City, N.Y.: Doubleday, 1949. 403pp.

Through this work of historical fiction Costain details the importance of the eleven Le Moyne brothers during French colonization of Quebec, Montreal, New Orleans, and the frontier areas along the waterways in-between. To create a romantic plot he interweaves the story of Félicité, a French Canadian orphan, adopted by the Le Moynes, who is forced to marry an evil royal advisor so that Jean-Baptiste Le Moyne can retain his position as Royal Governor in New Orleans. Although the book's contents are dominated by Canadian history, the novel does present the early history of New Orleans, including the issues faced by colonists and administrators.

122. Cowdrey, A(lbert) E(dward). *Elixir of Life: An Historical Novel of New Orleans.* Garden City, N.Y.: Doubleday, 1965. 270pp.

In the summer of 1853 nineteen-year-old John Samson Donnelly experiences plague-ridden New Orleans. Born in rural Mississippi, Donnelly alternates between despising urban life and yearning for the city during rural interludes. A skilled gambler, Donnelly had begun to establish himself in the New Orleans underworld through his association with Harry Stapleton and H.A. Macvaine, proprietors of a modest gambling parlor. However, when he falls in love with Marie Cousin, a mixed-race, seventeen-year-old serving-girl in a coffeehouse, he abandons the faro table for her bed in Carrollton. When he is forced to return to the city after running through his money, yellow fever has forced Stapleton and Macvaine to close their business. They decide to capitalize on Donnelly's background in quack medicine and turn the boarding house in which they live into a "hospital" in order to steal their patients' hidden money. Disgusted by his involvement, Donnelly runs away to Carrollton to find Marie's father ill. When he tries one of his medicinal preparations the man's recovery inspires visions of wealth and fame until Marie falls ill, his concoction fails, and she dies. Returning to New Orleans, he lives on the streets for a time but, nearing starvation, returns to the boarding house to find that after surviving yellow fever, strongman Stapleton is chastened and Macvaine less truculent. Along with their landlady, Maydee, they form a plot to cheat a foolish young man out of his money. After suffering and illness, the success of their plot establishes a bond and by the end of the novel they are presenting themselves as members of an extended family residing together in a Shreveport house from which they operate a high-end gambling parlor. The novel captures some aspects of conditions in plague-ridden New Orleans. While focusing on socially marginal characters, it touches upon issues of race and gender, particularly through Donnelly's relationships with mixed-race women and the implied homosexual relationship between Stapleton and Macvaine.

123. Cox, George D. *Run Down: A Psychological Novel.* Philadelphia: Peterson, 1888. 242pp.

When a steamy love song is published as his work, Jesuit priest Father William Fano believes he has an evil doppelgänger. Fano has developed a following in 1880s New Orleans through his sermons at the fictional St. John's Cathedral and his gift for pastoral care that takes him to the humblest neighborhoods and most modest dwellings. Among his admirers and friends is Dr. Corliss who becomes his confidante when he finds the priest stricken with terror over the doppelgänger's apparent intent to destroy his reputation. In addition to the love song promoted all over

New Orleans, people claim to have seen Fano patronizing the city's most notorious gambling parlors. These matters concern his Jesuit superiors, but when a painting of "Three Goddesses on Mount Ida," featuring sensual nudes is signed by him and exhibited to wide-acclaim in New Orleans, he is formally censured. Kept under watch for a time, there are no further incidents until wealthy and distinguished Francis Grace accuses the priest of misrepresenting himself to Grace's daughter Mary, becoming romantically attached to her, and successfully proposing. The Jesuits remove Fano from his position, but he escapes before reaching the monastery to which they exile him and he makes his way to Dr. Corliss. The physician hires a private investigator who sees Fano gambling and finds incriminating documents that appear to be in Fano's hand. The doctor consistently maintains his friend's innocence, but has no way to explain the mystery. When Fano disappears, Mary Grace falls ill and her father recruits Dr. Corliss to aid in the search. Fano is discovered with a grave sickness in Denver, Colorado. While nursing him Dr. Corliss and Mary Grace solve the mystery when they realize he is subject to "exalted somnambulism." Reclaimed in the eyes of Francis Grace, who approves marriage and settles money on the couple, Fano begins a career in the Protestant church. While lacking in physical description of New Orleans, almost the entire novel is set there.

124. Coxe, George Harmon. *One Way Out*. New York: Knopf, 1960. 214pp.

In this tale of international espionage, journalist Rick Marston has the ill fortune to closely resemble Raul Delgado, a patriot of the imaginary Latin American country of Maraguay. While Maraguay has been friendly to the United States, a new dictator has begun welcoming Communist sympathizers and Delgado and his compatriots are preparing for a violent coup. Exiled in New Orleans, Delgado is under the surveillance of a brutal assassin. When one of his associates encounters Marston, Delgado offers the reporter a huge fee to impersonate him. Just after Marston refuses, he narrowly escapes the assassin with the aid of a female burlesque performer. When she is murdered, he hires detectives to protect him and bring the killers to justice, before the police follow the evidence trail to him as the mysterious man in the performer's apartment just before her death. Much of the action involves chases through New Orleans streets, but the narrative also mentions locales and describes some of the city's popular hotels, restaurants, and bars.

125. Craddock, Irving. *The Yazoo Mystery*. New York: Britton, 1919. 302pp.

A World War I adventure story, featuring the latest machines and engines, this novel trumpets the superiority of "white blood." Twenty-four-year-old Hiram Strong, Jr. epitomizes Anglo-Saxon virtue. He is intelligent, attractive, capable of hard physical and intellectual labor, and absolutely honest. During the course of the novel he faces a series of tests. Disinherited by his wealthy, financier father, he gets a job as a fireman on a steamer with the help of Ben Taylor, and outworks the experienced African-American, Mexican, Polish, Italian, and Greek firemen. When the ship begins sinking he continues firing the engine with a skeleton crew in order to get the boat close to the shore, exhausting himself to the point of hospitalization. While in New Orleans with Ben Taylor, looking for his next job, Strong completes a course in telegraphy and is soon hired by the Yazoo & Mississippi Railroad to run a small office just outside New Orleans. When a case of dynamite goes missing, Taylor clears Strong, and shortly afterwards the company puts him in charge of a four-track wharf in New Orleans that receives fresh meat and ships out fruit. Once again Strong is at the center of scandal when tons of meat disappear, but he and Taylor devise an elaborate, successful plot to catch the perpetrator. By the end of the novel, Strong owns a business with assets that include a steamer, a tract of lumber, a sawmill, and tens of thousands of dollars. He marries an all-American girl and shortly afterwards Taylor reveals that Strong's father had employed Taylor to observe him to see how he dealt with various tests of character engineered by Strong's father. Although a considerable portion of the novel is set in New Orleans, there is little description of the city beyond the docks. New Orleans is depicted as the center of a vast transportation network of great importance to national defense. Throughout the book race and ethnicity are used as criteria to assess the relative virtues of individuals.

126. Crane, Frances. *The Indigo Necklace.* New York: Random House, 1945. 238pp.

One of a series of murder mysteries featuring husband and wife Patrick and Jean Abbott, here the couple has relocated to New Orleans where Patrick, a U.S. Marine with ties to the Intelligence Service, is stationed as a medical officer. The novel gives a sense of the city during World War II shortages, particularly in housing, due to the dramatic population increase caused by the city's use as an embarkation point, naval installation, and center for wartime industries. With the aid of Patrick's colleague, Major Roger Clary, the Abbotts rent one of the apartments in the historic Clary mansion, a portion of which is still home to the Major, his ill wife, and her nurse, as well as Clary family members. Other apartment renters include Toby Wick, a womanizing nightclub proprietor; the Graham sisters, Ava and Carol, distant cousins of Roger; and George and Dolly (Clary) Sears, forced out of their Paris home by the war. The main house is the domain of Dolly's widowed sister Rita Clary. When Roger's wife is killed, he reveals she was mentally disabled by a brain fever she suffered a few years before. Her physician discourses at some length on her medical history revealing attitudes of the time toward the mentally disabled. When local police detective Captain Jonas, appears on the scene, he casts suspicion on the African-American nurse of the deceased, using a whole line of racist reasoning to make her seem the most logical suspect. However, there are many who would have benefitted from Mrs. Clary's death including her husband, for she was much wealthier than him and he and Carol Graham are in love. While the focus is on the Clary mansion, the epitome of a grand New Orleans house, the city backdrop mostly features well-known restaurants.

127. Crossen, Kendell Foster [M.E. Chaber, pseud.]. *A Hearse of Another Color.* New York: Rinehart, 1958. 250pp.

In this noir murder mystery set in the 1950s, New Orleans is a dark, bar-filled city of rampant crime. Private detective Milo March lives in New York and specializes in uncovering insurance fraud. On assignment in New Orleans with an insurance company, he investigates the mysterious death of two men. The deceased, along with a third man, had taken out new life insurance policies making each other beneficiaries. The three men thought they owned a treasure map and the two missing men disappeared from the swampy island where they expected to find riches. Although the island has quicksand, March and the New Orleans police are skeptical that the men died accidentally. March is warned off his investigation by notorious thug, Eddie Capo, introducing an apparent connection to organized crime. Among the characters with whom March interacts are members of the New Orleans police force, a Creole undertaker, a professional skin diver and fishing boat captain, and the elegant, wealthy, seventy-year-old, Raoul Rouen, who despite several generations of society ancestors and his residence in a historic family mansion, proves to be the king-pin of a drug-smuggling operation. Although written in the era of Jim Crow, the novel's African-American character Willie Morell proves more complex than one might expect. He uses the accent and servile behavior of an impoverished black while getting tourists to pay him for his supposed skill as a spiritual medium. However, he is actually a sophisticated graduate school student on a break from the University of Michigan. March hires Morell as his sidekick and at one point deplores the way in which Morell is treated at a "whites only" establishment.

128. Crossen, Kendall Foster [Clay Richards, pseud.]. *The Marble Jungle.* New York: I. Obolensky, 1961. 183pp.

Primarily set in 1890s New Orleans, this book presents a city filled with corruption. Protagonist Grant Kirby, a U.S. Postal Inspector, is there to investigate a syndicate that he believes responsible for stealing money from locked mail pouches on stagecoaches between New York and Philadelphia, and for murdering his partner, John Hargrave. Corruption is so widespread that

Kirby cannot trust officials to help him. So he goes undercover as a riverboat gambler. An aging "butting-fighter" becomes his primary informant. (Instead of boxing or wrestling, butting-fighters literally butt each other with their heads until one or the other falls unconscious.) Although the author researched the city (he references publications like *The Scarlet World*, a nineteenth-century newspaper that listed brothels and gambling parlors), his interest in New Orleans is narrowly focused on organized crime and gambling.

129. Curtis, Alice Turner. *A Little Maid of New Orleans.* Illustrated by Hattie Longstreet Price. Philadelphia: Penn, 1930. 224pp.

Events leading up to the Battle of New Orleans are presented through the eyes of twelve-year-old Dulce Evelyn Carroll Ferrand, the daughter of a wealthy family. The book begins with the arrival of General Jackson in the city on December 2, 1814. Not wanting to miss the excitement, Dulce disguises herself as a boy and rides her brother Francis's pony to watch. She is intercepted by a man who asks that she deliver a letter to the general and rewards her with a ring. Only later does she realize that the man was Jean Lafitte (c.1776–c.1823). Dulce tries to maintain the charade that her brother delivered the letter, but the truth comes out. Lafitte, the first to recognize her, rewards her with a pony and puppy. Accidental circumstances sweep Dulce into the center of events several more times before General Jackson honors her after the end of hostilities by attending a "fairy play" she performs with her friends. The book explains aspects of New Orleans history, details events during the War of 1812, and is unusual for the time in putting a female at the center of the action.

130. Cushman, Jerome. *Tom B. and the Joyful Noise.* Illustrated by Cal Massey. Philadelphia: Westminster, 1970. 110pp.

This work for children celebrates New Orleans jazz music by narrating one boy's discovery of the city's musical heritage. The eponymous Tom B. (Thomas Boynton Fraser) lives in the St. Bernard Housing Project at 3266 Gibson Street with his grandmother, who allows him to shine shoes on the streets but, as a deaconess in her church, is opposed to jazz as the devil's music. When Tom B. goes to the French Quarter for the first time to increase his shoeshine earnings, he immediately falls in love with the music. He meets the proprietors of Preservation Hall, Allan and Sandra Jaffee, as well as Willie Lewis, the leader of the Eureka Brass Band. When his grandmother finds out, she forbids contact with jazz men. When she takes away the mouthpiece Lewis gave him so that he could begin learning trumpet, he runs away. Although he is separated from his grandmother for only a little more than a day, his experiences strengthen his interest in jazz and he walks in a funeral procession, participates in a parade sponsored by the Tulane Aid and Pleasure Club, and visits the Jazz Museum. However, he also has an accident that reunites him with his grandmother and frightens him enough to pledge that he will not run away again. The book describes the riverfront with its warehouse operations and the diversions of Bourbon Street, as well as the liveliness of city streets, revealing their importance as spaces for public events and social exchanges.

131. Daniels, Dorothy Smith. *The Duncan Dynasty.* New York: Warner Paperback Library, 1973. 190pp.

In 1885, seventeen-year-old Jana Stewart is traveling with her parents to New Orleans on the steamboat Orleana. Her father has sold his business in St. Louis to start a new enterprise in New Orleans and carries all of the family's substantial cash assets in a money belt. When the Orleana's boilers explode, he and his wife are below decks and perish with a large percentage of the boat's passengers. Stewart is rescued by David Brennan, who gets her to New Orleans, where he is to guest-conduct the orchestra of the French Opera House. While Brennan rushes to a meeting of the opera board, Stewart is directed to Probate Court, where she is nearly imprisoned as indigent, until she mentions her distant relationship to Claude Duncan. To her surprise, Duncan is the owner of a

theater, opera house, hotel, businesses, and houses in New Orleans, as well as an extensive plantation outside the city. After testing Stewart's mettle, Duncan allows her to be treated as a family
member in his household that includes his wife Celina, twenty-four-year-old son Walter, and
sister-in-law Augusta. Stewart's bereavement earns her little consideration in the odd household,
whose members dislike each other and resent Claude's strict control. Claude rapidly decides Stewart is to be Walter's bride and mother of the heirs that Walter's first wife, Marie, did not produce.
Immature Walter tries to drive Stewart away with dangerous pranks, since he still loves Marie,
who disappeared almost a year before, without anyone ever discovering where she went. Stewart
also opposes Claude's plan since she is in love with David Brennan and has nothing but distaste
for Walter. Fortunately, the Duncans are great opera patrons and Stewart gets to see Brennan make
a brilliant conductorial debut. Over the weeks that follow, Stewart and Brennan use the brief time
they can see each other during social events to declare their mutual love and come up with a plot
for freeing themselves from Claude Duncan, who has demonstrated that he will ruin Brennan's
career if he continues to pursue Stewart. Meantime, Stewart barely survives a series of mysterious
attacks (including a sabotaged equestrian jump, a shove into the Mississippi, and a murder attempt
on an abandoned steamboat) and her very life seems to depend of finding out what really happened to Marie. The truth and an unexpected patrimony free Stewart of her predicament. New
Orleans in this novel is controlled by wealthy people and serves as a backdrop for dining and
opera attendance. Although set in the 1880s, the novel tells readers more about 1970s cultural attitudes toward women than anything about nineteenth-century New Orleans.

132. Davis, M(ollie) E(velyn) M(oore). *The Little Chevalier.* Illustrated by Henry Jarvis Peck.
New York: Houghton Mifflin, 1903. 317pp.
     In 1752, when twenty-eight-year-old Henri Louis Nadan, Vicomte de Valdeterre, arrives in
New Orleans with his servant Chapron he is single-minded in his purpose to revenge himself on
Chevalier de la Roche. De la Roche had mortally wounded Nadan's father in a duel eighteen years
before, and had already been punished with royal censure, confiscation of his lands, and banish-
ment to Louisiana with his two children. Immediately upon arriving in New Orleans, Nadan challenges the Chevalier by letter and is shocked when the Little Chevalier meets him at the dueling
ground instead, explaining that the older man died some months before in a military campaign
against Native Americans. As the Chevalier's son, the Little Chevalier insists on responding to
Nadan's challenge, but Nadan faints from hunger before the duel concludes and the Little Chevalier is immediately sent to family plantations outside New Orleans. Although he is eager to return
to France, Nadan is the nephew of royal governor Marquis de Vaudreuil and has the social obliga-
tion of making an extended visit. At his first ball, he falls in love on sight with nineteen-year-old
Diane de la Roche before realizing her identity. The two publicly scorn each other but, after further contact at social events, they fall in love. Nadan enlists as a captain in the Company of Bachelors, a military deployment of gentlemen intent on responding to Native American frontier incur-
sions. After a battlefield wound nearly kills him, Nadan is miraculously nursed to health and reunited with Diane. A series of extraordinary revelations enable public acknowledgement of their
love and their eventual marriage. This historical romance novel includes descriptions of New Orleans in the 1750s, as well as a number of historical personages and incidents of the time period,
many connected to frontier battles against Native Americans.

133. Davis, M(ollie) E(velyn) M(oore). *The Moons of Balbanca.* New York: Houghton Mifflin,
1908. 180pp.
     A year in the life of an extended family of cousins provides a glimpse into late nineteenth-
century childhood. The household of Madame Jean Le Breton includes the Le Breton children,
offspring of a son and daughter-in-law now dead, and the Allison children, the offspring of Madame Jean's daughter and an American who are away on a business trip to Cuba exploring sugar
plantations. The Le Breton children include fourteen-year-old Raoul, twelve-year-old Odile, and

nineteen-year-old, Floris. The Allisons include eleven-year-old Rick and his thirteen-year-old twin siblings, Basile and Louisette "Zette," The cousins' lives center on Madame Le Breton's historic Royal Street house where various African-American servants, most prominently "Maum" Angelique, care for them The Balbanca of the title is defined as an early name for New Orleans, meaning, "the talking place," and the moons refer to the main events of a year as identified by the children with games, holidays, and celebrations. The book begins with the Feast of Epiphany and a King-Cake Party and continues through Mardi Gras, before Mr. and Mrs. Allison return in May and the scene shifts to Mandarin, their sugar plantation, where summer through Christmas is spent before a return to New Orleans for Christmas Day and the beginning of a new year. Although Americans are still treated as different from Creoles, the Allison/Le Breton alliance is clearly successful. African-Americans are portrayed as faithful servants who love their employers, and whose folkways and aspects of their traditional religion, Voodoo, are treated with respect (a Voodoo woman is even called to help heal one of the younger white children). However, Italian and Irish immigrants are portrayed unfavorably.

134. Davis, M(ollie) E(velyn) M(oore). *The Price of Silence.* New York: Houghton Mifflin, 1907. 280pp.

During Noémie Carrington's debut year, events of the Civil War are still alive for most of those closest to her. Her parents, Richard and Mathilde Carrington, are both dead. Carrington, a Northerner, had come South after the War and brought the money needed to revive Lady's Rule, the Laussan sugar plantation that had been in his wife's family since the mid-eighteenth century. Carrington's grandmother, Madame de Laussan, lost both her husband and only son to war. The young men vying for Carrington's hand are both objectionable to her grandmother. Sidney Courtland's family is Southern, but they were poor before the War and his father was a Union officer. Maxime Allard is a Creole with a notable family, but his father and grandfather had long-standing feuds with Carrington's guardian, Confederate General Leon Grandchamps. Allard is also objectionable for attending West Point, accepting a commission in the U.S. Army and serving in the Spanish-American War. The immature Carrington is swayed by Courtland's physical attractiveness, and does not realize that he presses his suit with her grandmother by revealing that Carrington is of mixed race. At first he asks for and gets money for keeping quiet, and then demands marriage. With no alternative, Grandchamps commissions Allard to go to France and discover the truth. He returns in time to dance in the 1903 Louisiana Purchase Centennial Ball with Carrington, assured of the purity of her blood. However, Courtland forces a crisis by telling Carrington the now disproven tale of her mixed race, after which she flees before anyone can tell her the truth. All ends well however, and Courtland banishes himself to San Francisco. The novel includes extended descriptions of social events and family life, including a visit to the family sugar plantation and is filled with dialect-speaking African-American characters who are beloved family servants. One of the oldest, Uncle Mink, has the gift of second sight.

135. Davis, M(ollie) E(velyn) M(oore). *The Queen's Garden.* New York: Houghton Mifflin, 1900. 142pp.

After the death of her mother and later her father, Noel Lepeyre moved from the Texas households of one unmarried woman after another as maternal aunts and distant relations took responsibility for her. When she was nineteen-years-old and had just begun teaching school, the last of these women died and among her possessions Lepeyre found the address of a paternal aunt in New Orleans. When she arrives in the city to meet her aunt Marguerite Chretien, the woman is gravely ill with yellow fever and all of her servants, except for elderly Marcelle, have fled. Lepeyre is happy to explore the beautifully appointed house in which her father grew up and the well-tended courtyard garden, even though she is anxious about her aunt. During one of her walks in the garden, Lepeyre realizes a young man from the adjoining house is observing her across the courtyard wall and he introduces himself as Richard Strong. Although their contact is brief, the two are rapidly smitten. Each contract yellow fever and are discovered by Dr. Andrew Grafton as he is coming back from Marguerite Chretien's funeral. Dr. Grafton nurses the young people to health and returns them to each other's arms. The novel conveys some of the isolation of traditional French Quarter residences and the horrors of living in the fever-stricken city. Much of the plot is devoted to a long-ago love affair thwarted by familial opposition.

136. Decoin, Didier. *Laurence: A Love Story*. Translated from the French by Helen Eustis. New York: Coward, McCann, and Geoghegan, 1971. 156pp.

In this romance novel the first-person narrator is a French doctoral student in economics working on his dissertation about hospital management. He arrives in New Orleans to conduct research, but has difficulty getting time with any physicians, except for pediatrician Dr. Morrison. Although he finds Morrison's work admirable, he is really drawn to him through one of his patients, a thirteen-year-old girl named Laurence. She and her mother are French and came to the United States to live with Laurence's aunt, who had invested in a textile dying firm and ended up one of the principal shareholders. The aunt died in a bizarre accident and Laurence's mother is in the midst of settling her estate before returning to France. Laurence's mother initially welcomes the narrator as a Frenchman and later as Laurence's "lover" . . . for it is soon obvious that the twenty-four-year-old is obsessed with the girl. Even Morrison realizes the young man's infatuation. Laurence is dying of leukemia and Morrison and Laurence's mother think that the dying girl deserves to experience a love affair. Laurence's mother also knows that she will not be able to withstand the emotional devastation of remaining with Laurence to the end and welcomes the opportunity to leave her daughter in the emotional embrace of the narrator. The narrator, who makes clear his bisexual experiences with adults, devotes a good deal of text to explaining the nature of the love and why it is acceptable. The reader's sensitivity to pedophilia may make aspects of the narrator's interaction with Laurence, which does not go beyond kissing and shared nudity, disturbing. Furthermore, although the novel is explicitly set in New Orleans, the city gets little description, except for those that make it sound like a seaside community, which raises doubts as to the author's knowledge of the place. The narrative is also odd for only giving first names for Laurence and Morrison, as well as African-American servants (i.e., Delia a hotel housemaid; and Murdoch, a handyman).

137. De Forest, John William. *Miss Ravenel's Conversion from Secession to Loyalty*. New York: Harper and Brothers, 1867. 521pp.

Although on the surface this work is a romance in which a woman chooses the wrong man and is betrayed by him, on a deeper level the book is a complex social document of the Civil War and Reconstruction. Doctor Ravenel, a long-time professor at the Medical College of New Orleans, is forced out of the city as war breaks out, due to his well-known abolitionism. With his eighteen-year-old daughter, Lillie, he finds refuge in New Boston, a fictionalized New Haven, Connecticut. They socialize with Boston lawyer Edward Colborne, who is immediately smitten with Lillie. However, they are soon separated when Colborne enlists in the Union army, to the relief of Lillie, who finds him too serious and emotionally underdeveloped. In addition, as a product of the South, she is emotionally attached to and sympathetic with the region; a Secessionist in the rhetoric of many Southerners who thought they were acting defensively and combating an attack on their region and way of life. Not surprisingly, she is immediately attracted to Colonel Carter, a thirty-five-year-old widower from Virginia who has great physical appeal and is courageous in battle, but Dr. Ravenel objects to the man's weak moral fiber; he fights for the Union for practical and political considerations, not out of moral conviction. Both Colborne and Carter are in the regiments that capture New Orleans and Carter is appointed mayor. His opportunism becomes glaringly visible as he begins enriching himself and partaking in the sensual indulgences of the table and boudoir. Colborne resists temptation. When Ravenel and Lillie return to New Orleans, Colborne proposes, but Lillie rejects him, entranced by the dashing Carter. Only after she marries

Carter over the strenuous opposition of her father, who sees in him all the corrupting influences of a slave-holding society, does Lillie's emotional conversion to Loyalty begin. She is horrified when she learns about his womanizing. Doctor Ravenel promptly arranges passage for himself and his daughter back to the North. Carter leaves New Orleans a wealthy Brigadier-General only to meet a battlefield death. Colborne, on the other hand, remains poor, but entirely honest in the face of many temptations. However, his idealistic embrace of abolitionism and the Union cause has been tempered by his experiences in the Union Army and the Deep South. When he and Lillie become reacquainted and Colborne renews his marriage proposal, he is a more emotionally complex character and Lillie accepts, completing her conversion to Loyalty and vowing always to live in the North. Throughout the novel Ravenel and Colborne are disturbed by the open racism of Union troops and both men are involved in efforts to give African-Americans opportunities that place them on an equal footing with whites. New Orleans residents are outraged when Union troops treat African-Americans fairly and are incensed by social acceptance of "white negroes," i.e., people of mixed race. Ravenel is particularly aware of the mechanisms of racism that will continue to affect lives after the city's occupation comes to an end. Although the novel includes little physical description of New Orleans, the book is of great value in depicting social and cultural issues in the occupied city.

138. DeLavigne, Jeanne. *Ghost Stories of Old New Orleans.* Illustrated by Charles Richards. New York: Rinehart, 1946. 374pp.

DeLavigne created these forty short stories from newspaper accounts and oral traditions. The tales reflect the city's multicultural make-up, drawing upon the exoticism of African, Creole, French, Italian, Spanish, and Roman Catholic cultures as a starting point that takes readers out of the prosaic mainstream American culture of the 1940s in which they were written. The author includes a date with each story to indicate the relative age of the tale and they range from the eighteenth to early twentieth century and touch on most of the notable historical events in the history of the city. In addition to many specific houses (including that of Madame LaLaurie), settings include Old Parish Prison, Metairie Cemetery, the French Opera, the Seaman's Bethel, and the Shell Road.

139. DeLavigne, Jeanne and Jacques Rutherford. *Fox Fire.* New York: Duffield, 1929. 411pp.

David Carlin, an Episcopal priest in his early thirties, seems the most settled of men as this novel begins. Certain in his faith, he eagerly devotes his life to his parishioners at St. Stephen's Church in Winstead, Illinois. His fiancée is Roberta Winstead, the beautiful, twenty-something daughter of Anson Winstead, the wealthy owner of the local quarry for whom the town is named. Roberta, ambitious for herself and Carlin, gets her father to fund a grand new church, guildhall, and rectory for St. Stephens. In future she believes she can use her father to get Carlin a bishopric. However, Carlin's life is transformed when his bags get mixed up during a brief vacation and he is stranded at a country hotel with books about comparative religion from a stranger's bag. Under their influence he becomes convinced of the cultural relativism of religion and, rather unconvincingly, abandons his faith in exchange for an arid and not terribly learned, or intellectual conviction that religion is "bunk." In very short order, he breaks off his engagement, resigns his position, recants his priestly vows, and moves to New Orleans, a city he has never previously visited. While a churchman, he had diverted himself by unsuccessfully authoring stories and essays under the name "Quondam Railley," and after finding an apartment on Royal Street, he gets a lowly job with a newspaper under his nom de plume, writing novels in his spare time. He quickly learns journalistic practice, adapts to newsroom social life, and dates fellow reporter Sharon Moore. His love for New Orleans deepens over the seven years he spends there. That emotional attachment and his deeper one to Moore leads the reader to assume he will marry her and remain in the city, especially after he begins publishing novels at increasing levels of remuneration. By the end of the novel he and Moore are married, however, in the aftermath of being named heir to his great uncle, the Duke of Antledge, they anticipate a move to the vast estates attached to the title. In relatively ineffectual ways the novel raises issues connected to the conflict between religious fundamentalism, comparative religion, and public awareness of evolution (there are brief references to the Scopes trial). The novel conveys a sense of the beauty, history, and quirkiness of New Orleans in the last two hundred pages of the book. Both Carlin and Moore live in apartments that have been carved out of historic mansions and this type of accommodation is described in some detail as a common aspect of unmarried life. Carlin moves to New Orleans in 1919 and witnesses the burning of the French Opera House. A number of actual businesses and addresses are described, including Antoine's.

140. Delmar, Viña. *Beloved.* New York: Harcourt, Brace, 1956. 382pp.
      This fictionalized biography of Judah Benjamin (1811–1884) is not exclusively set in New Orleans, but the city is important for Benjamin and given full treatment. Benjamin arrives as a seventeen-year-old forced to leave Yale University prematurely due to a vicious act of anti-Semitism. He studies law and moonlights as an English tutor to more quickly repay money borrowed from family members. The precociously intellectual Benjamin is soon demonstrating extraordinary legal promise. When he opens his own practice and has little work he compiles an analytical compendium of Louisiana legal cases that becomes an important reference work and wins attention from the state's most respected lawyers, and from the opportunistic John Slidell, Jr. (1793–1871), his eventual law partner. Any social tensions over his Judaism are overcome when he marries Natalie de Martin, the daughter of a respected and well-connected Creole family. Her parents construct a mansion for themselves with a separate apartment for the newlyweds. Shortly before the wedding Benjamin had been made aware of why his in-laws did not oppose the marriage and opted for the odd housing arrangement. Natalie had earned a reputation outside of New Orleans for premarital sexual relations with a series of men, including a cousin. Benjamin is so enchanted by Natalie's beauty that he overlooks her behavior, even when she continues to be unfaithful. However, she does eventually establish a separate household in Paris. The ninety pages of the novel that are set in New Orleans depict the social establishment while emphasizing the opportunities available to a brilliant young man, such as Benjamin, to build a career and a significant fortune. The novel includes no description of the Jewish community in the city, but the Creole, legal, and political communities are depicted. While many historical figures are introduced, only Slidell is convincingly presented. Benjamin leaves New Orleans when he is elected to the U.S. Senate. Although he later reflects on the importance the city had for him, he does not return there. The novel presents a fairly compelling version of antebellum New Orleans from 1828 through 1852 although the divisiveness of slavery and Benjamin's own thinking on political issues are shallowly presented.

141. Delmar, Viña. *The Big Family.* New York: Harcourt, Brace, 1961. 375pp.
      New Orleans plays an intermittent role in this romance concerning historical figures of the Slidell, Belmont, and Perry families. John Slidell, Jr. (1793–1871), the oldest son of a respectable owner of a Manhattan shipping firm, is portrayed as morally corrupt. Although he studied law, he did not enter the profession, instead spending his days in New York coffee houses and his nights at the theater, engaged in a love affair with an actress. After a duel over her he is dismissed as irredeemable by his family and moves to New Orleans. He does, however, make the most of a connection to a cherished friend of his mother and father, Congressman Edward Livingston (1764–1836), a highly regarded man in New Orleans and the legal partner of socially prominent John Randolph Grymes (c.1746–1854). He gets legal cases through Livingston and through Grymes makes social connections in the hope of an appropriate marriage. Bored by respectable society, he amuses himself with women of the demimonde. When he finally marries, it is to the daughter of André Deslonde, a friend from his early days in New Orleans, who is experiencing financial difficulties that Slidell eases to secure the marriage. After the wedding, Slidell

establishes himself with a plantation and a town house on Royal Street. Through less than honest land transactions and shady political intrigues, Slidell enriches himself and extends his power, becoming a U.S. Representative and Senator, avidly supporting Southern rights. At the outbreak of the Civil War he leaves his beloved New Orleans to plead for French support for the Confederacy and is subsequently forced to end his days as an expatriate living in Paris. Although the novel has various settings, the work is extensively set in New Orleans and is filled with characterizations of historical figures.

142. Delmar, Viña. *New Orleans Lady.* New York: Avon Books, 1949. 189pp.

By the outbreak of the Civil War, thirty-six-year-old Eulalie de Ronciere has lived in New Orleans for twenty years, although during all that time she has considered herself French with no particular attachment to the city. Married off by her impoverished, noble family, to a man whose family wealth came after the Revolution, her new husband was at first delighted by her beauty, but found her prudish when she would not fully engage in the sensuality of his Parisian set. Abandoning her, he moved with a lover to Spain, offering a fortune for a divorce and threatening to claim that their son André was not his child when her religious convictions prevented her from granting his request. To protect her infant she moved to New Orleans to live with a friend from school. She is horrified when André enlists to fight with the Confederate Army under General Braxton Bragg. She does not have the romantic illusions of Southern belles and fears for André's safety. Known as the most beautiful and engaging of hostesses, Eulalie rejects any serious advances by New Orleans men, even after the death of her husband, but uses her charms to protect André. His immediate superior, Anthony Markland, a West Point instructor who resigned his federal commission to fight with the Confederates, is entranced with her, and accedes to her requests to protect André until his own son is killed in battle. Her longtime admirer, Lorenz Renault, has more patience in colluding with her. However, he makes a mistake when he outrages Markland by offering a bribe for André to be posted to Texas. As the war worsens for the Confederacy, André suffers a serious arm wound and returns to New Orleans around the same time as the more seriously wounded Markland has been invalided to the city, shortly before its capture by the Union. Eulalie can preserve her comfortable life if she presents herself as a Frenchwoman with no allegiance to the Confederacy, but dramatically stands by André and Markland. The author captures social life in New Orleans as the Civil War puts into relief the multiple allegiances of many Southerners.

143. Demarest, Donald. *Fabulous Ancestor.* Philadelphia: Lippincott, 1954. 288pp.

In this fictionalized autobiography set in the 1920s, ten-year-old Sonny returns from the Philippines ill with the measles. Most of his life he has lived outside the United States on his military father's various postings. In New Orleans, Sonny lives in the Felicity Street house of his maternal grandmother who conscientiously teaches him about his family's long and distinguished history in New Orleans as leaders of the Creole community. She strengthens his religious instruction by convincing the learned young Jesuit, Father Dagobert, to instruct him in Latin and mathematics. She also reinforces his French and teaches him about the Civil War from a Southern perspective. Having been forced into his grandmother's cultural milieu, he explores other milieux on his own. He assists an Italian-immigrant tailor and clothes presser who specializes in the gowns of society women and uniforms of sailors (his grandmother is horrified). He joins the Gas House Lions boys' gang, whose hangout is a tree house on Annunciation Square. Finally, he befriends a French Catholic worker-priest, Father Sebastien, who after decades serving on shipboard, heads a sailors' mission off Rampart Street. Sonny's experiences over ten months cover All Saints Day cemetery visiting, Mardi Gras, Lent, Easter, summer in Biloxi, and culminates with his eleventh birthday, while touching on customs, food, manners, and rituals. Most of Sonny's life focuses on his grandmother's residence, churches, and cemeteries. The novel provides contrasting views of the Roman Catholic Church and includes characters whose formative years predate the Civil War and were hardened by Reconstruction. As in many Southern novels, there is a beloved African-American servant—in this case a cook. However, her relationship with her employer is complex and her illiterate style of expression is treated respectfully. Finally, even though New Orleans' Creole life is lovingly presented, several characters have experienced life outside the limited social world described and offer trenchant critiques.

144. Denbo, Anna Margaret. *A Romance of Old New Orleans.* New Orleans: Pelican, 1949. 331pp.

Set in the period 1814 through approximately 1820, this romance novel uses the growth of steamboat travel on the Mississippi and the resulting economic growth of New Orleans as a backdrop. Henri Le Brun's parents migrated to New Orleans to escape post-Revolutionary France and they still live in a Francophone culture. Once Henri has become a law firm partner, they make an extended visit to France, leaving Henri responsible for entertaining Toinette Le Blanc, the orphaned daughter of friends who had grown up in Paris, while she visits her aunt and uncle in New Orleans. They hope that escorting her to social functions will inspire him to marry the convent-schooled girl. Serious, hard-working Henri fobs off the responsibility to his friend Pierre Benech. However, when he finally meets Toinette, he falls in love at first sight. Afterwards, Le Brun and Benech alternately escort Le Blanc until Benech informs Le Brun of his engagement to Le Blanc, leaving Le Brun heartbroken. One night when he and Benech are rowing, Benech irritates Le Brun with his dancing and singing and when he accidentally falls into the Mississippi, Le Brun clubs him with an oar. Suddenly aware that nearby sailors witnessed him, he flees rather than trying to rescue Benech. After Benech disappears, Le Blanc returns to Paris heartbroken. When she comes back to New Orleans years later, she and Le Brun reunite, marry, and have a child, Jeannette. By this time Le Brun is wealthy and, while traveling by steamboat with his family, is horrified to see Benech, proving rumors that Benech had survived, but suffered from amnesia. As soon as Benech espies Le Brun, he starts to strangle him just as the steamboat's boilers explode. The Native American boy Kawaska who, along with his grandmother Chicoula, had previously saved Benech's life after a disastrous night in Natchez-under-the-Hill rescues Benech and Jeannette. Le Blanc and Le Brun also survive and return to New Orleans. After months of depression over the loss of Jeannette and guilt over Benech, Le Brun dies. When Benech eventually makes his way to Le Blanc with Jeannette, their love is reignited and they plan marriage. While the novel portrays New Orleans as an emerging center of commerce, the book touches on unsavory aspects of the city, including lawlessness along the docks and in bars, attributed to the immorality of slave traders and slave culture. As a product of slave culture, Benech had not devoted himself to business, but focused on spending his cotton-rich uncle's money. Living on the land near Natchez with his Native American friends reforms Benech. The plans that he and Le Blanc have to live there rather than in New Orleans can be read as a judgment of the city.

145. Devereux, Mary. *Lafitte of Louisiana.* Boston: Little, Brown, 1902. 427pp.

This historical romance novel varies from other fictional accounts of Jean Lafitte (c.1776–c.1823) by focusing on his supposed childhood in France and acquaintance with Napoleon Bonaparte (1769–1821). (There is some confusion historically over whether Lafitte was from that country or Santo Domingo.) Throughout the novel Lafitte is portrayed as a cultivated French nobleman, rather than a mere brigand, and a good deal of the book focuses on life in France during the Revolution when Lafitte's father is killed and his exiled mother endangered in Toulon. Only after the fall of Toulon, almost one hundred pages into the novel, do Jean and Pierre Lafitte depart for New Orleans (after their mother retires to a convent). In Louisiana, Lafitte finds a multicultural community with many French expatriates still wealthy enough to live as aristocrats. Unsupported by inherited money, Lafitte distinguishes himself as a gentleman through considerate treatment of women and slaves and his fair dealings with New Orleans merchants. Echoing contemporary admiration for American businessmen, Lafitte is portrayed as the manager of a large, complex operation that includes an extensive transportation network held together by a system of communications and a significant shipbuilding industry. Lafitte is often in New Orleans at the house of Count Cazenau and at Pierre's blacksmith shop. Well before the War of 1812, even though Governor Claiborne declares him an enemy of the United States, he supports the country because of British opposition to Napoleon. More than one-hundred and fifty pages recount events leading up to the Battle of New Orleans. In this account Lafitte's patriotism earns him a presidential pardon and the woman he had long loved, a daughter of Count Cazeneau. The Battle of New Orleans reveals Lafitte's superior qualities to Cazeneau, she sets aside her objections to Claiborne's former accusations and accepts his marriage proposal, after which the two marry and return to France to live as nobility (the author claims that it was one of Lafitte's followers who took his name and established a port at Galveston). While this early twentieth-century book does not include extensive descriptions of New Orleans, readers may be interested to compare this account of Lafitte with those of authors from other eras. Here, Lafitte's services to Bonaparte are extensive and include rescuing him from Elba and hiding the imperial treasure in Louisiana for retrieval at the appropriate moment.

146. Dickson, Harris. *Children of the River: a Romance of Old New Orleans.* New York: J.H. Sears, 1928. 326pp.

The heroine of this novel, Mary Bullock, transcends her humble Kentucky origins to become an advisor to Governor Claiborne and marry a French nobleman. As a young man, her father Tige had been adventurous, serving in the Revolutionary War as a Green Mountain boy. Her brother Trigger has the same fearless personality. Tige decides the family should relocate to New Orleans in anticipation of the French ceding the Louisiana Territory and builds a riverboat on which they embark. Mary is in charge of three young children as well as general domestic duties, like caring for the family livestock, and is flattered when river men taking a barge to New Orleans become her protectors. One of them, Hob Puckett, even pledges his love and asks for her hand. Once they arrive in the city a jealous crewmate attacks Puckett and he falls into a coma, after which he only recovers part of his faculties. French nobleman Hugo d'Ardagnac witnessed the attack and becomes a patron of the Bullock household, getting his father the Chevalier to give land so that the river men can build a house out of barge wood for the family. He also arranges for Madame Athénée, an impoverished French noblewoman, to live with the Bullocks to improve their domestic life and teach everyone French. Lafitte also aids the Bullocks when he hires Trigger to trap fur. In 1814, when Mary is twenty-years-old, she starts a vegetable stand in the market that becomes a gathering place for Frenchmen and Americans, communities that the novel depicts as fiercely divided. Once she begins serving coffee, coffeehouse culture develops, and even Governor Claiborne (c.1772/75–1817) becomes familiar with Mary. In this account Mary persuades Lafitte to side with the Americans after she witnesses the British meeting with Lafitte. She also warns Claiborne that, should he reject Lafitte, the pirate might side with the British. When the fight begins Mary is on the battlefield loading guns and eventually becomes the American flag bearer. Her heroism wins over the Chevalier, who had opposed his son Hugo's marriage to the rude "Kaintuck."

147. Dickson, Harris. *Duke of Devil-May-Care.* Illustrated by H(arry) C. Edwards. New York: D. Appleton, 1905. 295pp.

Although most of the main characters in this book live on rural plantations near Vicksburg, more than half of the novel is set in New Orleans where they join other affluent people from across the country for Mardi Gras. Mrs. Ashton, a stern widow, operates her own plantation, Ivanhoe, with lawyer Joe Balfour as her advisor and her daughter Alice her only companion. Although Noel Duke, the overseer of the neighboring plantation, Devil-May-Care, has dramatically improved crop yields through his able management of resources and people, Mrs. Ashton has decided that he is beneath her notice because his father politically out-maneuvered her late husband and he lost his congressional race. Duke charms everyone he meets and only Mrs. Ashton's ability to continuously fuel her animosity with imagined slights keeps Duke her enemy. When Mrs. Ashton's orphaned niece Anita Cameron relocates to Ivanhoe, Duke takes an immediate interest in her, but is at a loss at how to win over Mrs. Ashton. He follows the family on their New Orleans trip for Mardi Gras, hoping to evade Mrs. Ashton and speak directly with Anita. However, his surveillance of their hotel seems suspicious and when Mrs. Ashton goes missing the police arrest him. Eventually, the hotel reveals that Mrs. Ashton had been secretly hospitalized with a mild case of small pox to avoid panic during Mardi Gras. Duke has enough time between his release from jail and Mrs. Ashton's recovery to propose to Anita and be accepted. Although the confusion and excitement of Mardi Gras New Orleans is used as a backdrop, the city garners little description. The novel does make a point of contrasting New Orleaneans with the honest, forthright Anglo-Americans who are presented as admirable. In the parlance of the book people of Spanish descent are excitable and those of French descent duplicitous.

148. Dickson, Harris. *Gabrielle Transgressor.* Philadelphia: Lippincott, 1906. 374pp.
    Although the action transpires in New Orleans in the 1750s, the immediate setting is a walled garden and the high-minded protagonists are so disconnected from the world that, except for scattered references to New Orleans' political figures and events, the book could have been set anywhere. Approximately twenty years before the novel's action a dramatic rift opened between two brothers, Paul-Marie and Jean, French noblemen who migrated to escape an antipathetic King. While waiting to follow Jean to Louisiana, Paul-Marie had Jean's wife thrown into a convent where she died soon afterwards. In despair over his wife's death, when his infant daughter Gabrielle arrives in New Orleans he places her in Ursuline Convent and joins the frontier Indian wars. The action of the story transpires in the weeks after Jean retrieves nineteen-year-old Gabrielle from the convent in preparation for her arranged marriage to Chevalier de Tonnay. Although Jean gives Gabrielle a rich trousseau, she prefers her school uniform and rejects social life for the overgrown, walled garden of Paul-Marie's house that is adjacent to Jean's and vacant since the brothers' enmity. When the exiled Prince Murad of Turkey is secretly brought to New Orleans and hidden in Paul-Marie's house, he and Gabrielle begin a courtly, platonic romance knowing that they will be separated by the complicated circumstances of their lives. Gabrielle must follow her father's wishes and marry the Chevalier while Murad has supporters on their way to New Orleans to aid him in deposing his illegitimate brother and taking the sultanate of Turkey that is rightfully his. Throughout the novel New Orleans is portrayed as slightly beyond the control of political regimes since European kingdoms are so physically remote. The book portrays Murad as an exotic representative of an Eastern tradition preoccupied by philosophical and spiritual matters, mostly expressed through astrology and gazing into a crystal ball.

149. Dorsey, Anna Hanson. *Warp and Woof.* Baltimore: John Murphy, 1887. 276pp.
    An historic house in New Orleans becomes an evocative reference point for an extended family and their social circle. Captain David Warner, his sister Gertrude and his uncle Max Ashton live in Washington, D.C. Both Warner and Ashton traveled to New Orleans years apart, but had related experiences in the del Alaya mansion. Before the Civil War, Ashton was visiting Raoul de Coucy, a wealthy Creole cotton merchant. Ashton's trip was shaped by Coucy's preoccupation with the high visibility of mixed race people and their plight. Neither family wealth nor social distinction can free them from denigration. They can only live isolated in Creole society; or, hide their identity and live in the North. Ashton becomes intrigued by a river mansion in the style of a Spanish castle, with a foundation stone dated 1647 and inscribed with the name of Dom Pedro del Alaya. Coucy is able to arrange a visit, knowing that the owner, Léonce de Moret, who owns large tracts of Louisiana, lives abroad. Moret's mother had instituted the expatriate existence to avoid the social disgrace of her husband's illegitimate son Eugenie, born of a quadroon mistress. While in the richly furnished house, a Raphael Madonna reawakens Max's Roman Catholic faith and he subsequently abandons his dilettante ways. Years pass before Warner enters the house as a Union

officer called in to investigate the scene of a death. He finds what appears to be a bludgeoned Léonce de Moret with Eugenie standing nearby, a near twin in appearance. Eugenie claims Léonce fell down a flight of stairs and the death is treated as an accident, although the scene haunts Warner. Years later in Washington he gets a new insight when both he and Ashton are reminded of the del Alaya mansion by a man going by the name of St. Aignan. He has the exact appearance of Léonce Moret and eventually reveals that he had reclaimed his family's good name by killing the illegitimate Eugenie and claiming that he, Léonce de Moret, had met his end. Long accounts of mixed-race people and foreign travels intervene before Ashton and Léonce return to New Orleans to salvage a vast treasure from the del Alaya house, part of which Léonce gives to a Roman Catholic convent and part of which he gives for the construction of a cathedral in Baltimore to redeem his father's sins of miscegenation and adultery. The narrative presupposes that readers will be shocked and sickened to realize that mixed-race people are going about in society (particularly in Washington, D.C. with its fluid population) under assumed identities. Although the portions of the novel set in New Orleans are mostly focused on the del Alaya mansion, the city is used to symbolize foreign cultures—Spanish, African-American, and those of mixed-race groups—that are on display in New Orleans and have a hidden existence in other American cities.

150. Douglas, Amanda Minnie. *A Little Girl in Old New Orleans.* New York: A.L. Burt, 1901. 325pp.

During the French Revolution, teenaged Hugh de Brienne, the son of Madame de Brienne, is married by proxy to six-year-old Sylvie Perrier. The noblewoman is on her deathbed and the rushed marriage is her way of both guaranteeing her son's happiness and keeping the Perrier fortune (distilled to a trunk filled with jewels) out of the hands of revolutionaries. The marriage is by proxy since Hugh is already safe in the New World. Gervaise Aubreton, a secretary to Madame de Brienne, is the proxy and, he along with other Brienne relations, including impoverished sixteen-year-old Angelique Saucier, make the trip to America to deliver the jewels. They survive a pirate attack and arrive in Spanish-controlled New Orleans. However, they live entirely within the city's French community. Believing Hugh to be in Detroit, Gervaise continues on with Englishman Roger Norton as a guide, leaving the rest of the company in New Orleans. Away from the terror dominating France and introduced to the warm climate and friendly African slaves, the party delights in New Orleans and a social life that centers on the house of Marquis Bernard de Marigny (1785–1868). The narrative is preoccupied with what it means for these forced immigrants to come to Louisiana. Like other French they want to maintain allegiance to France, but the country they know is disappearing. They despise the Spanish and are alienated from that cultural presence in New Orleans. In order to become fully American, they must leave the French community in New Orleans where they feel so comfortable. The little party of immigrants also faces some tensions in the French community over religion because they are Huguenots, not Roman Catholic. When it appears that Hugh is dead, the Roman Catholic Church takes over Sylvie's estates in France, since this was the provision made by her family, should she not marry. Hugh is not dead however, and when he arrives in New Orleans he volunteers to travel to France to recover Sylvie's estates. Years pass before his return and by then Sylvie is in love with Gervaise. Events in New Orleans provide distraction and the company is present for the return of New Orleans to France in 1803, but cannot fathom the significance. Within a short time the Louisiana Purchase is completed and a series of marriages occur. Gervaise marries Zenobie Lavalette, a Creole; Angelique weds Roger Martin; and Hugh and Sylvie finally progress to friendship and then marriage after Hugh helps defend New Orleans against the British in 1814. The subtext of the novel is the way in which immigrants with many allegiances come together to form the United States, even in New Orleans where European origins are so fiercely maintained.

151. Dresser, Davis [Brett Halliday, pseud.]. *Michael Shayne's Long Chance.* New York: Dodd, Mead, 1944. 218pp.

Florida private detective Michael Shayne is fed up with his life in Miami and accepts a job in New Orleans to get away from memories of a failed romance. His client, Joseph P. Little, a well-known, affluent editor, sends Shayne to the city to protect his daughter Barbara, who has ambitions to be a writer. As a twenty-three-year-old, she is beginning to despair of her lack of accomplishments, and recently attempted suicide. Little had brought Barbara to Miami to recover, but she ran away to New Orleans where she is living on Dumaine Street under the assumed name of Margo Macon. Her father fears for her life, because the drug dealer who got her addicted has found out she is in New Orleans and is searching for her there. Little hopes Shayne can gain Barbara's confidence and get her to see the danger of her situation. Unfortunately, she does not react quickly enough and is murdered. The police accept a deathbed confession of guilt that Shayne believes is contrived and he begins searching for the real murderer. Shayne knows members of the New Orleans police force and press corps and socializes with them as well as going out on his own to bars and clubs, giving the reader a very good sense of the French Quarter in the 1940s. By the end of the novel he has decided to stay in New Orleans and open an office. Lucille Hamilton, the woman with whom he has developed a romantic interest, agrees to be his secretary.

152. Dresser, Davis [Brett Halliday, pseud.]. *Michael Shayne's Triple Mystery.* Chicago: Ziff-Davis, 1946. 225pp.

In this Michael Shayne detective mystery, Shayne is settled in New Orleans with long-suffering secretary Lucy Hamilton managing his office. Shayne helps four sets of people vitally interested in a diary Jasper Groat kept while stranded in a lifeboat with two other sailors after their ship had been torpedoed. One of the sailors, Leslie Cunningham, survived to return to New Orleans with Groat. Albert Hawley, the other sailor, died at sea. In a strange coincidence, Hawley's multimillionaire uncle Ezra Hawley died around the same time and whether Hawley died before or after his uncle will determine who gets the fortune. Groat lives with his wife in the same apartment building on North Rampart in which Lucy Hamilton also lives. By the time Hamilton gets Shayne involved, the diary and Jasper Groat have disappeared. Before long, Shayne is also retained by Myra Wallace to find her missing husband, Leon, who had been Ezra Hawley's gardener at his Labarre Street estate. When Shayne visits the Hawley mansion Albert's mother brushes him off, but his drunkenly flirtatious sister quickly relates the family secrets. Ezra Hawley left his entire estate to Albert, surprising everyone. Even more surprisingly, the sole beneficiary of his will is Mrs. Theodore Meredith, his divorced and remarried wife. If Groat's diary documents that Albert Hawley died before his uncle, Ezra Hawley's estate will go to Ezra's other immediate heirs. The Groat diary is also important to powerful, scheming, Justin Cross, a famous journalist who wants to publish excerpts in his syndicated newspaper column. Shayne follows leads that mostly take him to lawyer's offices and apartment hotels in New Orleans' Central Business District. He does visit a number of bars that are described, along with drinks peculiar to New Orleans. The women in the novel are mostly vixens, plying men with alcohol to get their way. The plot turns upon a case of assumed identity.

153. Dresser, Davis [Brett Halliday, pseud.]. *Murder and the Married Virgin.* New York: Dodd, Mead, 1944. 179pp.

New Orleans private detective Michael Shayne solves four seemingly unrelated crimes that turn out to be connected. Shayne's office is in the newly refurbished International Building and his working relationship with his secretary Lucy Hamilton is verging on romance. Shayne agrees to investigate the death of Katrin Moe when her heartbroken fiancé, New Orleans Police Department Lieutenant Drinkley, tells him that Moe could not possibly have committed suicide on the day before their wedding. Around the same time the Mutual Indemnity Insurance Company hires him to recover an emerald necklace insured for one hundred twenty-five thousand dollars, that was stolen from the Nathan Lomax house where Moe lived and worked as a maid. The Lomax household is filled with tensions and Shayne soon has a number of suspects, including the Lomaxes' adult children Eddie, a twenty-one-year-old womanizer, drunk and gambler; and Clarice, who at nineteen is already spending late nights unchaperoned at private bars and clubs. Clarice is driven about town by the family chauffeur, a muscular young man with movie star looks who is also remarkably well spoken and intelligent for a low-paid household servant. Mrs. Lomax also arouses suspicion with her unconvincing account of the theft. Although set in New Orleans, the novel has a very narrow range of physical settings: besides the police headquarters, Shayne's office, the Lomax mansion, apartment-hotel rooms, and the Laurel Club, a private casino. Police interrogation techniques reveal a high tolerance for physical intimidation. As Shayne begins to investigate the Lomax household, descriptions of Norwegian immigrant Moe, by both the narrator and characters, border on ethnic slurring.

154. Dugan, James. *Dr. Dispachemquic: A Story of the Great Southern Plague of 1878.* New Orleans: Clark and Hofeline, 1879. 198pp.

Although satirizing members of the medical profession and social reform movements, this novel also provides information about daily life in fever stricken New Orleans. The protagonists, cousins Edgar Cecil Wilton and Mrs. Margery Summers, live in a tenement on Poydras Street in the center of an impoverished neighborhood where yellow fever is rampant. Both were accustomed to affluence and both have been wronged. Summers is the daughter of Judge Warfield whose wife was the sister of Edgar Cecil Wilton's father. Wilton's parents had died when he was just a boy, but they left a large estate that paid for his education abroad. His guardian was his aunt, Laura Latiel, a resident of New Orleans who was affluent in her own right. While finishing art school, Wilton received news of his aunt's illness. He rushed back to New Orleans to find her dead and her estate in the hands of lawyers who had seized it for unpaid fees. His precipitate return forced the managing agent to flee since that man had been embezzling for years from Wilton's now insolvent trust. Impoverished, he fortunately reconnects with a former family servant, Marie Foneau, before falling ill with fever. He is discovered by Summers in the course of her nursing visits to fever victims. She is living in the tenement because her father, Judge Warfield, disapproved of her marriage to a promising but impoverished young lawyer, James Summers. With no financial support from her father, when James disappeared on a business trip, presumed dead, Margery is forced to move into the tenement with her children. Although Foneau had secured the services of a physician through the local medical association, the doctor in question, Dr. Dispachemquic, is a hydrotherapist whose patients quickly die under his extreme care that involves ice and cold-water enemas. Fortunately, Summers adheres to common sense, resists Dispachemquic's proposed treatments, and Wilton begins to recover. Most of the other patients in the novel are not so fortunate, for although Dr. Kancurum treats some, most of the physicians are as misguided in their treatments as Dispachemquic. Summers discovers that Wilton had been cheated out of his aunt's estate and when her husband returns to New Orleans alive, she gets him on the case. With his health and fortunes recovered, Wilton is able to get James Summers started in a law practice and the Summers are established in middle-class comfort.

155. Duke, Mary Kerr. *The Mystery of Castlegreen: A Louisiana Romance.* New York: Broadway, 1913. 175pp.

When Dr. Pierre Postelle attends a young Acadian man, dying of a knife wound on Rue Royale near Lafitte's blacksmith shop, the victim only has enough energy to give the physician a quill with a map concealed in its cavity and utter two words, "Zurlee" and "Castlegreen," before dying. The remainder of the narrative is devoted to solving the meaning of these clues that eventually lead Postelle to rescue Irene Rondeau from gilded cage captivity in the household of Captain Blackmore, an honorable pirate at odds with his ruffian colleague Redbeard. Years before Redbeard captured the storm-raddled ship on which Rondeau had been journeying with her nurse and plantation-owning parents. Fortunately, Blackmore and not Redbeard discovered Rondeau and her nurse Queenie in the hiding place the faithful slave had devised. Blackmore put them under his protection and eventually kidnapped an elderly scholar to serve as her tutor. Queenie had assumed that Rondeau's parents had been killed in the pirate attack, but Mrs. Rondeau actually survived and joined the New Orleans household of her brother, Dr. Pascale La Montagne, a friend of Dr. Postelle. When Postelle solves the meaning of the Acadian's dying words he is able to present the map hidden in the quill to Louisiana's governor who forms an expedition to rescue Irene Rondeau. By the end of the novel, Irene has been reunited with her mother and married to one of her rescuers. In this novel New Orleans is a mysterious place on the edge of a swampland frontier filled with pirates. The book includes extended descriptions of African-American slaves, including Postelle's driver Zip and Rondeau's Queenie. Queenie's faithfulness is celebrated several times in conjunction with nostalgic observations about "mammies" in general and the novel ends with a plea that a monument be raised to the memory of such women.

156. Dunbar-Nelson, Alice Moore. *The Goodness of St. Rocque and Other Stories.* New York: Dodd, Mead, 1899. 224pp.

All but two of these short stories are set in New Orleans and tell of poor people who find dignity and self-worth in their devotion to a person or skill. Mr. Baptiste keeps himself alive by getting free baskets of over-ripe fruits on the wharf and exchanging them for meals in the kitchens of some of the finest houses. Monsieur Fortier has developed a more widely respected skill; he plays first violin in the French Opera House, but runs into trouble when a new concertmaster takes over. Camille employs religious practice to create a life for herself. She started her existence as an unwanted baby left on a convent doorstep. Knowing that she would never be able to marry without knowing her parentage and having a dowry, she becomes a nun as a practical matter. Another character, Miss Sophie, transcends her situation as an impoverished seamstress by working nonstop, sacrificing her life so that she can redeem a ring from a pawnshop. The man who gave her the ring now needs it to prove his identity and gain an inheritance. Most scenes in the novel transpire on public streets and there are several descriptions of Mardi Gras. The only historic event described is that of the 1892 Dock Strike.

157. Dupuy, Eliza A(nn). *Celeste: The Pirate's Daughter: a Tale of the Southwest.* New York: Ely and Robinson, 1845. 2 vols.: 195pp., 223pp.

Most of this romance novel, preoccupied with concealed, misrepresented, and unknown identities, is set in New Orleans. As Celeste Germain is about to leave Ursuline Convent a finished young lady of seventeen, Isola Moreau arranges to make her a part of her own household in the home of her guardian, Mr. Sinclair, at Magnolia Hall, on the outskirts of New Orleans in the absence of any plan from Germain's mysterious father, Victor Germain. Bachelor Sinclair has another young ward in addition to Moreau, his nephew Harry Sinclair, the offspring of a match between his brother and Mr. Sinclair's only love, who did not marry him. Upon the deaths of his sibling and sister-in-law, Mr. Sinclair became the guardian to his nephew. Some time later, his great friend Mr. Moreau died, making Mr. Sinclair the guardian of his daughter Isola as well as the administrator of Isola's rich trust from which she will benefit immediately on her eighteenth birthday. Before his death Mr. Moreau had openly expressed his wish that Isola marry Harry Sinclair, continuing the protection of the Sinclair family over her in adulthood. Mr. Sinclair would have had an additional ward, his niece, but she went missing at the time of her parents' death and her whereabouts remain unknown. Before the girls arrive to take up residence at Magnolia Plantation, Mr. Sinclair hires Mrs. Susan Ernest as a chaperone and companion for them. Upon her arrival, Celeste Germain's appearance surprises Mr. Sinclair, who thinks (in heavy fore-shadowing) that she strikingly resembles his dead sister-in-law. Germain's appearance has an impact on Harry Sinclair as well, as he is immediately smitten with her. Although Germain also impresses Mrs. Ernest, she is more concerned with Isola, the beautiful heiress she is determined her son Richard Ernest will marry. The rest of the two-volume novel is devoted to working out who will marry whom and the true identity of Germain (who, to her own horror, turns out to be a pirate's daughter). Harry Sinclair, who has steadfastly violated the wishes of his elder, in part by becoming a naval officer, marries Germain before her true identity is known and long before Isola is wed to Charles Langley. Langley and Richard Ernest are lawyers who, through a strange coincidence, become legal partners and then, over hundreds of pages, engage in a rivalry for the hand of Isola, even though Ernest already has a common-law wife, Annette Butin, a naïve young woman he maintains in a New Orleans residence. The city has little presence in the novel. While a pirate character places the book in the company of a large number of New Orleans novels, here the pirate remains a criminal, unlike books featuring a redeemed Lafitte.

158. Dupuy, Eliza A(nn). *The Planter's Daughter: A Tale of Louisiana*. New York: W.P. Fetridge, 1857. 416pp.

Significant portions of this tale of the Harrington family's redemption from frivolous dissipation are set in New Orleans. The Harringtons' Wavetree sugar plantation along the Mississippi River above New Orleans is casually managed by Charles Harrington whose wife died five years into their marriage, leaving him a son, Victor, and twin daughters, Adele and Pauline, whom he raises with the help of his unmarried sister Gertrude. If he focused on improving his plantation, the operation could be much more successful financially. However, he has gotten into the habit of using any money he earns on speculative ventures brought to him by his friend Reginald Malcolm, not realizing that Malcolm keeps the bulk of the profits for himself. By the time Victor is twenty-three and his sisters are twenty, Malcolm, who has plotted for years to get the Harrington family under his absolute control, lays a trap for Harrington, promising him an extraordinary profit if he will only borrow a substantial amount for which he must use the plantation as collateral. When the money is lost, Malcolm saves Harrington by acquiring the Wavetree Plantation mortgage. Secretly, he tries to extract a promise from Harrington that one of his daughters will marry him, although Harrington tells him that he needs to romance one of the girls to fairly win a bride. The narrow escape from financial disaster inspires Harrington to apply himself to running his plantation with the help of a family friend, Philip Evelyn, who is an engineer who has come to the South to recover his health. In the meantime, the reversal in family fortunes has forced a postponement of Victor's marriage to Louise Ruskin. Ruskin and her mother, near relatives of the Harringtons, reside in New Orleans and only consented to Victor's suit when he was an heir. Now, Mrs. Ruskin insists that the couple may wed only when Victor begins earning enough money to underwrite her daughter's expensive, urban tastes. Although Victor starts learning accountancy in a brokerage house, he quickly abandons office life to earn money in the theater under an assumed name, at which he achieves some success. However, he loses all of his money in repeated attempts to earn a fortune through gambling. Back at Wavetree, Malcolm has begun courting Pauline and won her devotion, but during an extended stay in New Orleans on business decides that Adele is the better choice and sends her a long love letter. She has fallen in love with Evelyn and is shocked at Malcolm's duplicity. When the sugar crop is harvested and proves more profitable than anticipated, the Harringtons pay off their mortgage and free themselves from Malcolm; not, however, before Pauline learns of his letter to Adele and suffers a health crisis. Further crises befall the Harringtons before they are driven off their plantation when a levee breaks, forcing them to seek refuge in the New Orleans residence of the Ruskins, where Charles Harrington finally succumbs to the illness brought on by the shock of losing the plantation. All of the Harringtons follow their father's deathbed entreaty to work toward financial security, except for Victor, who falls mad and into violent death. Gertrude establishes a school on a remaining family property, quickly achieving success with the help of Adele and Pauline. Adele finally abandons her former hauteur, and accepts a marriage proposal from Philip Evelyn. Pauline marries a penitent Malcolm. New Orleans in the novel is a frequent destination and occasional home for most of the characters in the book and is the center for commercial activity.

159. Duralde, H. Eduardo. *Louisiana: A Tale of the Old South.* New York: Exposition, 1965. 304pp.

   This indictment of racism is set in 1841 New Orleans and recounts the plight of Gustave Stuart, a wealthy, socially-respectable young man who has, far back in his mother's genealogy, an African-American ancestor. Twenty-four-year-old Stuart is wealthy through inheriting the estates of his uncle and father after a yellow fever epidemic (his mother had pre-deceased his father). With social connections and inherited wealth he is the foremost of New Orleans bachelors and courts Hortense Crozat, from one of the most respected families in the city. His rival is Edwin Dixon, the heir to a vast plantation fortune. In contrast, Stuart's wealth is mercantile and founded on the businesses of his father and uncle who had come South from Ohio. Stuart's family was educated and cultured and his uncle's friend, Professor Dietz, gradually became his friend and mentor. Dietz is outspoken in his social views and declares that slavery is merely the issue of the moment and that full social acceptance of African-Americans will in future become the norm, no matter the hostility of southerners. The author pointedly contrasts the plantation system as epitomized by the Dixons with the mercantile and corporate system of the wholesale grocer and cotton business of the Stuarts. In addition to this exposition, most of the narrative deals with the various plots and revelations that would seem certain to ruin Stuart. The worst of these emerges after he gravely wounds Dixon in a duel and must deal with the disgrace of being accused in a scurrilous newspaper of having African-American blood, after which his household is set upon by a mob demanding his ejection from New Orleans. The Crozats seclude their daughter and she dies of a broken heart. Stuart, who decides he cannot live in such a city, closes up his businesses and departs with much of his wealth to California. In addition to giving Stuart the qualities of a saint, the author shows that even the most evil of men, like Dixon, can be redeemed and can give up their racism. Although clearly written from the perspective of 1960s civil rights activism, the author makes great efforts to accurately present his story, which was based on an actual case. He portrays New Orleans as diverse, with many mixed-race people holding social positions without their racial identity becoming an issue.

160. Eads, William J. *Listen to the Termites.* New York: Vantage, 1977. 582pp.

   After serving in the Navy during the Korean War, Rod Murray decides to become an insurance salesman. Initially, he takes satisfaction in providing a needed service. As time passes, he is disillusioned and becomes a "Termite," recommending term life insurance for almost every situation. Eventually, he decides to become an instrument of change within the industry, and successfully runs for Louisiana Insurance Commissioner. While in office he runs into many obstacles, including a female industrial spy with whom he has an affair before realizing her identity. His exposure to politics and disillusionment with "creeping socialism" leads him to run for President in 1976 on a reform platform in which big business should more openly control the country. Most of the novel is set in Baton Rouge, but Murray frequently visits New Orleans for insurance conventions and political caucuses. The city is mostly described in touristic ways.

161. Easterling, Narena (Brooks). *Peter and Anne.* New York: Gramercy, 1942. 256pp.

   In this romance novel set on the verge of World War II, Anne de Joffrion's life is transformed in a few dramatic days after many years of quiet desperation. From the time of her father's death when she was a teenager, Anne has provided for her family by operating a café and gift shop on the lower floors of the family mansion in the French Quarter. Her younger stepsister Nolia helps by cooking and supervising a kitchen staffed with African-American family servants. The family's main support, however, comes from the money Anne gets for her paintings of local scenes that she sells in the gift shop. Her mother, Celeste Valadier de Joffrion, is permitted the illusion that she is still a wealthy society lady and spends much of her time resting when not entertaining friends and dining out. Raised in a male-dominated culture, she never acknowledges Anne as de facto head of the family, deferring to Anne's twin brother André, a womanizer who has continuously lost significant sums of money on sugar and cotton futures, further impoverishing the family. Although his behavior has exasperated Anne in the past, she is strident in her opposition when she finds out that he has power of attorney for their mother, and made a deal to sell the family mansion. Shortly after André's revelation she discovers that while carrying on an affair with a Russian immigrant named Venna Varensky, he also secretly tricked Nolia into having sex with him by getting her drunk and convincing her that a sham ceremony performed by his friend was an official civil ceremony. If that were not enough, she discovers that he is trying to get wealthy, eighteen-year-old Northerner Grace Axline to marry him by convincing her that she must be tubercular since her mother died of the disease and that she should marry fast before the condition manifests itself and scares off suitors. He has also convinced Grace's brother Harry Axline, a multimillionaire ten years Anne's senior, that Anne will marry him, even though she has a long-standing engagement to an inventor/chemist named Peter Adams. André's transgressions go beyond those listed above and when he is found dead of cyanide poisoning the list of those he wronged is lengthy. While much of the novel is devoted to cataloging André's bad behavior and detailing Anne's patience with him and her struggle to quell the doubt he has cast in her mind about Peter Adams' faithfulness to her, the book provides insight into the status of women in mid-twentieth-century New Orleans.

162. Easterling, Narena (Brooks). *Southern Moon.* New York: Gramercy, 1938. 253pp.

This romance novel is almost entirely set in New Orleans where Gail Marshall finds romance on Mardi Gras streets. As an eighteen-year-old orphan, Gail suddenly has bright prospects, when her grandmother D'Aubigny dies and she finds herself to be the principal beneficiary of an estate consisting of a mansion filled with valuable antiques and a plantation named Bayouville outside New Orleans. However, the will stipulates that Gail cannot take possession until she either turns twenty-one or marries. In the meantime, she has no income and is forced to live with her Aunt Felice, who has a roomy apartment in New Orleans. The other person Gail knows in New Orleans is lawyer Peter Guitry, whose parents are long-time caretakers of Bayouville. Immediately after the will is read Guitry proposes marriage to Gail, but she is too taken aback to accept. Gail begins learning family secrets as she becomes more mature, some of which are troubling. When she accepts a marriage proposal it is from Sydney Llewellyn whose family is wealthy. Over time she comes to understand that Llewellyn is a weak-willed drunk and breaks off the engagement to discover that her true mate was a man she has known all along. The novel conveys the excitement of a young woman living in New Orleans for the first time and beginning a social life that includes dates with many attractive, eligible young men.

163. Eberhart, Mignon Good. *The Bayou Road.* New York: Random House, 1979. 231pp.

This historical romance novel is set in the occupied New Orleans of 1863. Marcy Chastain can hardly bear up under the stress of her situation. Her brother Brule, a Confederate soldier, was killed in battle and her father, Henri Chastain, maintaining his allegiance to the cause for which his son died, refused to take the loyalty oath after the capture of the city and was marched off by Union soldiers. Chastain has been left to manage a household that includes the infant, illegitimate son of her brother and her beautiful but emotionally challenging sister-in-law Claudine. Fortunately, Liss, her African-American servant, formerly a slave, has remained with Chastain and undertaken the challenging task of operating the household, contending successfully with wartime shortages. Like many of her neighbors, Chastain knows she must endure having a Union soldier billeted in the house to avoid confiscation. Although the payments in gold will be welcome, the emotional tension could be unendurable. So, she is pleased when Major John Farrell appears as her new boarder. Chastain had known the handsome young man in Washington before the war. The fact that they had been romantically linked is no longer relevant since Chastain has a fiancé, Armand Ortega. Then, the old feelings Chastain and Farrell had for each other reawaken and Chastain regrets her hasty engagement to Ortega before the war. She had known and admired

Ortega's father and Armand was considered an extremely good match since he was handsome and wealthy. As a recently returned soldier, however, Ortega is not the same man. His family's wealth had been wiped out, his father is dead, and his battlefield engagements had left him with emotional lability and an inability to control his temper. At first violently opposed to the presence of Farrell in the Chastain household, when Armand discovers that Farrell is intimate with General Grant, he wants Chastain to help obtain secrets useful on the battlefield. Chastain resists and Armand is murdered soon afterwards; then, a woman claiming to be his wife appears. Chastain longs for her family's Nine Oaks Plantation on the Bayou Road, although it is unclear if she will ever regain possession. The author thoroughly researched the wartime occupation of New Orleans and makes clear the physical and emotional situation in the city for longtime residents. She also presents the challenges faced by affluent New Orleans residents, and Southerners in general, who had been close friends with Northerners before the war.

164. Ebeyer, Pierre Paul. *Gems of the Vieux Carré*. New Orleans: Windmill, 1945. 348pp.
    The author is open in his goal for this book. A lecturer on Creole history and culture, he wants to present his knowledge in a lively format. So he relates information via four love stories: "Inseparable," "Petite," "And Obey," and, "Mine." In the first story a Caucasian boy and mixed-race girl grow up together and want to marry, but must deal with social sanctions against such a union, even though the girl is more than 98 percent white. The second novella is set in 1814 and presents Jean Lafitte (c.1776–c.1823) as a patriot through an account of the experiences of French immigrant Antoine, the fiancé of a New Orleans Creole woman named Petite. In the third novel, "and Obey" the topic is respect for women and the way in which they dominate the Creole household, bending their husbands to their will. "Mine" includes a lengthy account of a historical Mardi Gras celebration as well as a description of an 1830s cholera epidemic.

165. Ebeyer, Pierre Paul. *Paramours of the Creoles*. New Orleans: Windmill, 1944. 178pp.
    This examination of Creole culture and the historical custom of Creole men having children with mixed-race women outside of marriage are presented in the guise of fiction. When twenty-two-year-old May visits New Orleans for a winter break she becomes fascinated by Creoles and befriends Jeanne, a recent college graduate, who is of mixed race (although she is described as 99.24 percent white), as well as forty-nine-year-old Pierre, a Creole whose grandparents were French, who has lived all of his life in the French Quarter. Although surprisingly open in its racism, this work provides an extensive rhetoric defending the custom of extramarital relationships, in part referencing the ways in which European royalty, who had officially arranged marriages, found love outside these legal bonds. The book also takes on the issue of slavery, claiming that slaves were treasured members of Creole families. The interest of the book lies in its thinly fictionalized nature. Ebeyer seems to have drawn on his own family stories and personal knowledge of New Orleans to construct this narrative that consists of Jeanne and Pierre relating their knowledge to May. Jeanne, her thinking clarified by interacting with May, decides that she has a right to marry Paul, the white man she had refused in the past because her mixed race makes the union illegal.

166. Edmunds, (Thomas) Murrell. *Passionate Journey to Winter*. New York: T. Yoseloff, 1962. 156pp.
    This romance novel is unusual for being told from the perspective of an African-American servant, Lucy, who entered a Royal Street household when her mistress Cora married Pierre LeBrun. As a servant, she can only watch as the people around her make choices that endanger themselves and the entire LeBrun household. Pierre married when he was already middle aged and by the time his only child Paul was a schoolboy he had already aged to the point that he was no longer sexually interested in Cora, who was still a relatively young woman. Lucy watched as the frustrated Cora descended into alcoholism, Pierre sickened with cancer, and Paul began to live

independently as a young man. Although most of Pierre's income was from landholdings and investments, he had always operated an antiques shop out of the ground floor of his house and rented out an apartment that had been created out of the servants' quarters that surrounded the house's courtyard. When Paul returns home to move back into the house with his beautiful wife Maude-Ellen, he finds that Stuart, a very attractive young man (only referred to by his last name throughout the novel), has insinuated himself into the household. Stuart had tried unsuccessfully to work as an actor in Hollywood, and initially rented LeBrun's apartment, but as Pierre became sicker, he started working in Pierre's antiques shop, eventually taking over the management, as well as becoming Cora's lover. In a strange coincidence, he and Maude-Ellen were lovers when they were both striving actors in Hollywood and he is prepared to blackmail her. For a time it seems that the two will team up to defraud the LeBruns of their wealth, with Cora as an unwitting accomplice. Paul's work as a cotton factor keeps him preoccupied and away from the house, enabling Stuart's scheme. After Maude-Ellen becomes pregnant, she genuinely falls in love with Paul and tells him the truth about her past while revealing Stuart's embezzling. After Paul's attempts to address the situation through legal means are delayed, he surprises Stuart beating Maude-Ellen and tragedy ensues. The novel is of interest for being narrated from the perspective of an African-American servant and for exploring the impact of traditional architecture on daily life in the French Quarter (the first floor commercial space, converted slave quarters, and the shared courtyard walls with the convent next door).

167. Elliott, Maud Howe. *Atalanta in the South: A Romance.* Boston: Roberts Brothers, 1886. 345pp.

Personality is attributed to sectional origin in this account of romance between a Northerner and Southerner. When Margaret Ruysdale brings her father Stuart Ruysdale to the South for his health, she does not expect to reconnect with Philip Rondelet. The two had met and become interested in each other in Paris where Ruysdale was studying sculpture and Rondelet medicine. Stuart Ruysdale had been a well-known sculptor before the Civil War, but lost his arm to battle wounds and has been left with chronic health problems. Not surprisingly he has deeply held convictions about the South and the causes of the war. While Southerners may perceive Margaret as a typical, Northern Puritan, both cold and heartless, General Ruysdale disdains Margaret's interest in Rondelet, since he believes him to manifest the corrupt qualities of slaveholding Southerners—soft from lack of labor and womanlike in temperament. Ruysdale's assessment seems to have some validity since Rondelet is so tenderhearted that he is ineffective as a surgeon. Even though the novel presents an ameliorative position on North-South relations through the voice of a Rondelet friend who opines that intermarriage between cold intellectual Northerners and passionate Southerners is important to strengthen the nation, personal tragedy prevents the marriage and the Ruysdales eventually return to the North.

168. Ellis, Julie. *Eden.* New York: Simon and Schuster, 1975. 350pp.

Most of this novel about the lurid sexual relations between slaves and their owners is set on Eden Plantation in the 1850s, but New Orleans settings have enough interest to justify inclusion here. Victoria Wickensham, an Englishwoman whose soldier father was disinherited by his titled family when he married a music hall singer, was orphaned before she was a teenager and moved to live with her only relative, a New York City aunt. Barely surviving in a Five Points slum household, Vicky meets Southerner Michael Eden by accident and Eden, a twenty-four-year-old lawyer being forced by his mother into a loveless marriage, makes a business arrangement with Vicky. If she marries him, he will provide her with the life of an affluent Southern lady, and only the two of them will know that the marriage of convenience will entail no emotional or sexual connection. Vicky soon finds much to admire about Michael, who believes slavery should gradually end, who takes legal cases to fight for right principles regardless of how they may harm his business, and who has a Jewish man as his closest friend. Vicky falls in love with him, but he keeps her at arm's length due to a secret in his past. While her discoveries about Michael draw her to him, the more she finds out about his family, the more she is repelled by them, mostly due to their scandalous sexual relations with slaves. A New Orleans office, a carriage ride away from Eden, is Michael's daily escape from his family and, over time, Vicky gets to escape to the city as well to attend the opera, go to Mardi Gras, and socialize with Michael's friends, mostly the Jewish Wasserman family. On one occasion Vicky and Michael witness an African-American child being pushed to her death from a window of the Coligny mansion and much later Michael, Vicky, and the Wassermans are driving by as a house fire is burning on the upper floors of the mansion. Michael and Wasserman break into the attic slave quarters and find grotesquely tortured slaves there. From then on, events at the Coligny house become a subplot that is clearly a re-telling of the Madame LaLaurie (1775–1842) scandal. Michael, the Wassermans, and other opponents of slavery, use the evidence of torture in their attempts to organize what they refer to as a pro-Union stance in opposition to the dominant Southern voices calling for states' rights and the protection of slavery.

169. Ellis, Julie. *Kara.* New York: Dell Books, 1974. 271pp.

Covering the years 1852 to 1860 this romance novel uses a fictional plantation family to relate the evils of slavery and local and sectional political issues New Orleans residents confronted in the period. After she has watched her brothers, sisters, and mother die over a period of potato famine years, Kara Thomas is given steerage fare to New York by her father. An eighteen-year-old, she finds a job at the lowest rung of household service with an affluent Manhattan banking family. Her life is soon transformed when Timothy Rankin, the Southerner who had been diffidently courting the daughter of her employers, chooses Kara instead to take back to his family's plantation near New Orleans. The extended Rankin family, patriarch Amory and his wife Emilie, their oldest son Charles and his wife Annabel, all live at Manoir Plantation and Timothy's choice for a bride is roundly opposed by Emilie and Annabel. Fortunately, Amory is immediately delighted with his new intelligent and beautiful daughter-in-law and becomes her ally. Kara finds ways to ease tensions while maintaining her strongly held commitment to treating others compassionately. Many aspects of her situation are outside of her control: Timothy ends conjugal relations with her as soon as she is pregnant with their daughter since he prefers the company of men; she opposes slavery but can only express her opposition by finding minor ways to improve their treatment at Manoir; she realizes that she and Charles have fallen in love, but respects his marriage bond to his frigid wife Annabel. She pursues social causes through Timothy's political career, which is fueled by Amory's own political interests, and over time the two of them find ways of advancing him from office to office until he is on the verge of election to governor. Throughout the novel trips to New Orleans are important to the plot. Charles maintains a placée and, later, an illegitimate child in a Rampart Street house and as Timothy gets elected to public office in the city he keeps a residence there from which he and Kara entertain. The work details New Orleans civic improvements, public health issues, corruption, and major political issues, such as anti-immigration prejudice and violence against Italian and Irish immigrants. Although it deals fairly with issues like racism and ethnocentrism, the work is homophobic in treating Timothy's sexuality.

170. Ellis, Julie. *Savage Oaks.* New York: Simon and Schuster, 1977. 345pp.

This work of historical fiction is preoccupied by social issues of the 1970s, including the role of women in society and prejudice against mixed-race people. Protagonist Suzanne Duprée was raised in a French convent school, but remains self-consciously American through reading American newspapers sent by her guardian Gilbert Mauriac. Although she is well provided for, she longs for connection to family, having been orphaned at age three when her parents died in a steamboat explosion. When Mauriac abruptly decides she should return to New Orleans in 1855, she is seventeen and hopes to find out more about her parents and members of her family. Mauriac purchases Tintagel Plantation for her, located an hour's carriage ride outside New Orleans and immediately adjacent to Savage Plantation, one of the South's largest and best known sugar plantations.

Even before she arrives, Mauriac has made arrangements for Keith Savage, the young master of Savage, to marry Duprée and solve his financial crisis that will otherwise end with bank foreclosure. Although Duprée is attracted to Savage and agrees to matrimony, she thinks the betrothal rushed. Soon after the wedding, she realizes Savage's proposal was forced and with the connivance of Savage's randy, younger brother, Phillip, discovers that Savage is keeping a mulatto mistress on the plantation grounds. To these challenges and others, Duprée responds with courageous strength while continuing to investigate her family origins, concerning herself with the welfare of plantation slaves, and starting a school for impoverished whites. Told various stories about her parents that she disproves, she still believes there is some scandal in her origins but is entirely unprepared for the revelation that comes immediately before a hurricane and, oddly, finally bridges the rift between her and Savage. Characters in the novel make frequent trips to New Orleans to attend social events, the opera, shop, and visit exclusive brothels. Actual restaurants and shops are mentioned and the author includes conversational exchanges that reveal political and social issues being debated in 1850s New Orleans, as well as describing William Makepeace Thackeray's lecture visit to the city.

171. Emery, Anne. *A Spy in Old New Orleans.* Illustrated by Emil Weiss. New York: Rand McNally, 1960. 237pp.

During the War of 1812, Hugh Greentree decides to give up the Kentucky farm where, with the exception of fourteen-year-old Ned, his wife and all of his children died. He intends to pilot a flatboat laden with all of his saleable goods to New Orleans to find his brother Charlie. Almost as soon as he arrives Hugh offends a Native American who promptly knifes him to death and throws his body in the Mississippi. Although Ned grieves, he believes it was only a matter of time before Hugh's quick temper and lack of respect for people with backgrounds different from his got him killed. Although Ned is also easy to anger, he is more curious than disrespectful about others. Through French-Americans who help him sell his Kentucky goods and find a place to live, he meets Jean Lafitte (c.1776–c.1823) . Lafitte takes pity on the orphan and employs him for his skills at written and spoken English, marksmanship, and tracking, His first assignment is to befriend a Spanish boy of his age, Jaime d'Alkhala, another orphan in Lafitte's camp, whose parents were killed when Lafitte captured the ship on which they were sailing. The two boys do not become friends but Lafitte teaches Ned to control his temper when interacting with the offensive Jaime. As Lafitte's assistant, Ned takes minutes at meetings with the British and carries messages to New Orleans. He also thwarts Jaime's plot to get a hidden cache of Lafitte's weapons into British hands and fights in the defense of New Orleans. By the end of the novel Ned is eager to join his newly rediscovered Uncle Charles in New Orleans with the prospect of starting a steamboat business. Although this account is similar to other juvenile literature that deals with the Battle of New Orleans, the slave trade, of which Lafitte was so much a part, is not discussed, nor are the varied cultural and political allegiances in New Orleans that complicated the populace's immediate embrace of the American cause against the British.

172. Erskine, John. *The Start of the Road.* New York: Frederick A. Stokes, 1938. 344pp.

The road in this novel is the path that Walt Whitman took to become a poet. As biographers have come to realize, Whitman's three-month stay in New Orleans in 1848 was crucial to his development as a writer. Without knowing specific incidents or people that influenced him, Erskine posits a fictional woman named Annette Clovis as transformative for her beauty that inspired romantic devotion and for her role as a first reader of his news stories for *The* (New Orleans) *Crescent* and critic of his poetry. Erskine conveys a great deal of cultural and social history of the nineteenth century in general and New Orleans in particular in the context of this fictionalized biography. However, his characterization of Whitman is so at odds with the current emphasis on the poet's homosexuality that the book may seem less than insightful. Only the first half of the novel is set in New Orleans; the rest of the book deals with Whitman's life in Manhattan and in

Washington, D.C. In this latter half of the book Annette remains an influence through her correspondence with Whitman.

173. Escoffier, Lillian Ann DuRocher. *Heartbreak*. Ann Arbor, Mich.: Edwards Brothers, 1954. 282pp.

This indictment of New Orleans poverty and the special plight of women in such an environment is set in the years 1901 to 1918 and tells the story of Shalimar Dauvillier. Dauvillier's mother Aline O'Dair loved Nick Dauvillier but when he died in the Spanish-American War, the two had not yet married and Aline was pregnant with Shalimar. To give the girl a name, she married Nick's brother Anthony, a weak alcoholic who had been raised by his sister Cora. In their poverty, the Dauvilliers rented a ramshackle house at 821 Royal Street and sublet rooms. As a five-year-old, Shalimar witnesses Anthony killing her mother and then taking his own life. Cora only lets her live with her to take advantage of her labor. School as a charity student at the Ursuline Convent is her only consolation, but when her aunt becomes bed-ridden with tuberculosis and dies, her school days end. Only sixteen-years-old at this point, she is threatened by her neighbors Joe and Rose Angelicos with being sent to an orphanage unless she works full time for them. When Joe forces himself on her, Rose throws Shalimar into the street and when Shalimar goes to the convent for help she learns that the Angelicos have already been there to falsely accuse her. Soon after getting a job at Charity Hospital she is wrongfully accused of wantonness with one of the doctors. Emotionally confused and naïve she is sold into white slavery and eventually bought by Ulysses Grant Bisco, who keeps her in a Pontalba Buildings apartment. Rarely left alone, except to visit the cemetery, she there meets and falls in love with young Louis Fontanille, who is in mourning for his wife. The romance proceeds with lies on both sides to conceal poverty and the fact that Fontanille has a baby. When the two are about to marry, Fontanille learns Shalimar has been the mistress of Bisco and Bisco learns of Fontanille. Forced onto the streets once again, Shalimar runs into a kind doctor from Charity Hospital who lets her know that the accusations against her have been disproved. She returns to work and begins to progress until Fontanille is brought in near death and his family manipulates her emotions in order to get her to leave her job and care for his baby in the squalor of their home. By the time she returns to Charity Hospital she is dying from pneumonia. The novel elucidates the plight of young women in the harsh environment of the French Quarter in the early twentieth century and shows that their lot actually worsens once the area gets discovered by the wealthy who are able to take advantage of their poverty. The book is filled with descriptions of streets, shops, and residents that have the authenticity of direct observation.

174. Evans, Lawton Bryan. *The Pirate of Barataria*. Illustrated by Oliver Kemp. Springfield, Mass.: Milton-Bradley, 1926. 298pp.

This retelling of Lafitte's story focuses on his origins and the events that turned him into a pirate. The tale commences in Bayonne, France with Jean Lafitte (c.1776–c.1823) a thirty-year-old soldier of fortune, and relates a series of adventures in Barcelona, Cartagena, and on the ocean before Lafitte, reunited with his brother Pierre, gains control of a ship that gets them to Louisiana before sinking. Making their way to Grand Terre, an island already known as a center for pirates, they join a group of men over whom Lafitte eventually wins control and through savvy management establishes a much more lucrative operation of smuggling and piracy that wins their loyalty. The final ninety pages of the book describe Barataria and Governor Claiborne's attacks on Lafitte. The book includes an extended description of a masked ball in New Orleans at the end of which the Lafittes dramatically escape after revealing their identity. In the book's final pages, Lafitte rejects the British offer to fight with them for a substantial amount of money and plays a heroic role in the Battle of New Orleans. The novel is interesting for the way it rationalizes Lafitte's piracy and ascribes a morality to his behavior, as well as dealing with the polyglot, racially diverse Baratarians as representative of the new country that was becoming the United States.

175. Eyster, Nellie Blessing. *Tom Harding and his Friends*. Philadelphia: Methodist Episcopal Book Rooms, 1869. 368pp.

Fourteen-year-old Tom Harding of Harrisburg, Pennsylvania travels by ocean steamer to visit relatives in New Orleans from December through the early days of Lent. Approximately half the book details Tom's shipboard experience. In New Orleans, Tom lives on the upper floors of a Canal Street house with his cousins; sister, Mary; and his childhood nurse, Maum Sara, the household's cook and maid of all work. Through Sara and his cousins, who have already been in the city five weeks, Tom learns about local customs and food ways (and the tradition of the lagniappe). One Sunday he gets lost and ends up spending much of the day in a cemetery, where he is entranced by the music, pageantry, and above-ground tombs, but dismayed by the brevity of the interment ceremonies. He also finds the flurry of commercial activity on Canal Street objectionable on the Sabbath, although he describes at length the merchandise of toy and pet stores, as well as the elaborate displays and street buskers with their performing birds and monkeys. Later, he experiences a minor flood, helps nurse his sister through a fever, and participates in Mardi Gras, for which even Maum Sara gets to take the day off and participate in street parades in a costume. The Hardings take several excursions to Lake Pontchartrain; travel on the Shell Road; and on the anniversary of the Battle of New Orleans visit Jackson Square and a monument in Algiers, where they hear about the battle from an eyewitness. In addition to descriptions of shops, street life, and cemetery culture, the book is of interest for digressions on the nature of African-Americans and mixed-race people who, while being God's children, must both experience the redemptive power of Christian salvation and give up their animal nature to become human.

176. Faulkner, William. *Mirrors of Chartres Street*. Minneapolis, Minn.: Faulkner Studies, 1953. 93pp.

These eleven pieces were originally published in the *Times-Picayune* in 1925 and capture life in the public spaces of New Orleans, mostly streets and public squares. The characters tend to come from the city's underclass and include inebriates and criminals, as well as street vendors and the marginally employed, who frequent balconies, corners, parks, and general stores. In addition to several bohemian artists, characters include Italian immigrants, an African-American, several people from rural areas, and a bootlegger, conveying a sense of 1920s New Orleans.

177. Faulkner, William. *Mosquitoes*. New York: Boni and Liveright, 1927. 349pp.

Even though most of Faulkner's 1920s novel is set on board a yacht sailing on a weeklong voyage, his New Orleans characters are fully formed and their physical and social milieus in the city are convincingly detailed. Mrs. Maurier is determined to be the patroness of a circle of artists who will behave in delightfully bohemian ways—perhaps one of them may even develop a passion for her, or at least create a work of art in her honor. The artists of her acquaintance, however, are tiresomely unforthcoming, even when she gets them all together for a yachting party. They spend most of their time drunk and sullenly resist the shipboard diversions she has planned. Even Ernest Taliaferro, whom she considers an aesthete and guide to the world of art and artists, is of no useful assistance. This is not so surprising since Taliaferro, whose actual surname is Tarver, is from a northern Alabama family of strivers and picked up his veneer of culture on a single holiday tour of Europe. His only connoisseurship is as a buyer for the women's department of a major New Orleans' emporium. Although he has been married, and is supposedly looking for a new wife, his deceased spouse had been an invalid and the male artists upon whom he dances attendance seem to be of more sexual interest to him than women. Among the artists dragooned onto Mrs. Maurier's yacht are writer Dawson Fairchild, poet Mark Frost, sculptor Gordon (always "Mr. Gordon"), and Julius (always "the Semitic"). The only true artist among them is Gordon, who upon returning to his studio produces a bust of Maurier in a single night that captures her completely, just as Faulkner captures an entire social class in her character, as well as those of Jenny and Pete, two young people Maurier's cheeky niece Pat recruits for the cruise on the spur of the moment after a chance meeting. Jenny is the daughter of a German-American policeman and Pete is an Italian-American whose family has turned their modest Italian restaurant into a high-income producer by taking advantage of Prohibition. Both represent immigrant groups that began to dominate and alarm old New Orleans families. Although Maurier comes from an old family, it is based in New England and she also represents a type, a Northerner who moved to the defeated South after the Civil War. Maurier's husband leveraged his Civil War service to take advantage of the patronage opportunities of Reconstruction to build a huge fortune, acquiring plantations and houses to which his Northern society bride provided a veneer of gentility he did not have. While most of what Faulkner has to say is about art and American culture, he memorably captures aspects of 1920s New Orleans by characterizing bohemian artists, second generation European immigrants, and Northerners made rich by the lost properties of Southerners.

178. Faulkner, William. *New Orleans Sketches*. Edited by Carvel Collins. New Brunswick, N.J.: Rutgers University, 1958. 223pp.

This collection includes many of the same stories published in the earlier *Mirrors of Chartres Street* (above), but is augmented by five additional works (of a similar type) and a piece of literary criticism.

179. Feibleman, James K(ern). *Great April*. New York: Horizon, 1971. 267pp.

This novel about boarding house life focuses on personalities, rather than place, but it does evoke some aspects of life in 1970s New Orleans. Otis Maldorf, a neurotic man of significant wealth, has increased a family fortune founded in the nineteenth century on South American sugar plantations, by establishing a department store and wisely investing the profits. He spends his life entertaining himself with a series of mistresses and with the boarders he keeps in his house at 2330 Britannia Street. Although he is married, his wife Hester does not manage his household, but his butler Lucius and, in another novelty, his boarders do not pay rent. Instead, Maldorf pays them an allowance, enabling several of his boarders do nothing at all. Lawyer Milo Hileman spends his time on one of the galleries hoping for glimpses of an attractive female neighbor. Xanthine Carney, a woman from a wealthy and socially prominent family, is the last of her line and depends on her Maldorf beneficence to remain inebriated most of the day. Dr. Leslie Cottus operates a practice on the first floor of the boarding house, mostly for the enjoyment of browbeating his intern, Dr. Brown. Unlike his fellow residents, John Woolford has a significant income stemming from the innovative toilet seats he manufactures. He devotes his time in New Orleans to visiting physicians to find cures for his mostly imaginary maladies. The only other boarder with an occupation is Charles Radovitch, barely twenty-one, who is searching for his father Hugo and is only in town temporarily from Breaux Tree Bayou. At the age of seventy-one Hugo turned his cannery over to Charles and left for New Orleans, giving no explanation to his wife. By the end of the novel, Charles discovers that his father died and was buried in Potter's Field. Although other boarding house residents also receive life-changing news, Dr. Cottus and his wife adopt a baby, and 2330 Britannia catches fire, it seems as though the little world of the boarding house will continue on unchanged. The novel captures neighborhood life and aspects of boarding house life in twentieth-century New Orleans.

180. Feibleman, Peter S. *Charlie Boy*. Boston: Little, Brown, 1980. 362pp.

On the surface, this book is another modern crime novel that gets inside the head of a psychotic killer. However, the novel also presents a subtle description of New Orleans' French Quarter in the 1970s, through the eyes of bartenders, hotel workers, panhandlers, and prostitutes. The killer, Charles Breaux, the eponymous "Charlie Boy," is an opportunist. While in prison, the Midwesterner, raised in poverty, becomes interested in a series of unsolved killings in New Orleans and claims responsibility through letters to newspapers. Released from prison, he moves to New Orleans and begins a life of crime that includes killing tourists. He falls ill and Maggie, the woman who runs the flophouse where he stays, recruits an odd, thirty-something physician from Boston, Josiah Moment, to save Breaux's life. Maggie, who acts like a crazy derelict in order to panhandle, has observed Moment, who stayed on after his American Medical Association conference, to be guided around the city by African-American teenager E. L., whose life he surreptitiously seeks to improve. An atypical conference-goer, the abstemious Moment's visit to New Orleans triggers self-revelations that permanently transform him. Moment is a compassionate, almost Christ-like figure, whose reticence people typically interpret as hauteur. Once he starts seeing himself through the eyes of others he matures into a fully realized adult. He accurately understands that Breaux is innocent of most of the crimes he claims. However, Moment does not fully acknowledge Breaux's identity as a psychotic killer and only after smuggling him out of New Orleans with the help of E. L., does he realize the danger and need for the police, leading to a dramatic conclusion. The novel touches on current social issues including urban hunger, poverty, and racism.

181. Feibleman, Peter S. *A Place Without Twilight.* Cleveland, Ohio: World, 1958. 382pp.

Through the story of the Morris family, the novel presents the emotional, physical, and psychological costs of living as a mixed-race person in the racist world of New Orleans in the 1930s and 1940s. Serge and his wife "Mama" Morris moved to New Orleans from Atlanta as a place more accepting of mixed-race people after their first child, Clarence, was born with light skin even though they are dark-skinned. Their other children, Lucille and Dan, are also light-skinned (Serge believes his enslaved ancestors had their white master's children). The Morrises live in Back-of-Town at the corner of Millicent and St. Thomas Street and for some years Serge is a well-paid cook. Then Serge falls into a period of depression, drinking, and job loss followed by a mortal illness. Seventeen-year-old Clarence and twelve-year-old Lucille, who are both good students, are forced to leave school and get work to supplement the money their mother earns from taking in laundry. Ten-year-old Dan is still too young to work. Clarence soon begins spending more time away from home in a mysterious new job that provides income that far exceeds his mother's earnings. When he gets drafted to fight in World War II, he at first declares he will not fight for white men and implies that he will reveal his homosexuality. His mother declares him dead to her and within a few years the telegram comes announcing Clarence's death on the battlefield. By this time both Dan and Lucille work as live-in household servants for wealthy white families. Dan eventually has a psychotic breakdown and cripples a white boy while strangling him almost to death. The boy's liberal Northern parents see that Dan is institutionalized, rather than incarcerated (or worse) and continue Lucille's employment. Within a year of the scandal Mama Morris dies and Lucille is free to accept her employers' offer of work in their New York City household (where she would presumably be able to pass as white). She arranges to move but the action takes an unexpected turn on the day of her departure. In addition to issues of race (including prejudice in the African-American community) and social class, the book deals with the repression of female sexuality and touches on homosexuality.

182. Feibleman, Peter S. *Strangers and Graves.* New York: Atheneum, 1966. 351pp.

Two of the four novellas in this book, totaling approximately half the page count, are set in New Orleans. The first, "Death of Danaüs," tells of the relationship between Edmund Choate and his daughter Mayann. Choate began adulthood as the dissipated scion of one of New Orleans' richest families. He left the city for the continent and came back married to an Italian woman he claimed was the daughter of a count, but was rumored to be a prostitute with whom he had fallen in love. She died within a few years and he married Anne LeGrange, the New Orleans society woman who had designs on him before his adventure. LeGrange transformed him by instilling moderation and getting him sober. When LeGrange died in childbirth, Choate devoted himself to his daughter. In the story's present, Choate lies dying in a Biloxi hospital while Mayann and his aunts reflect on his life. The novella makes little use of the New Orleans setting. A second novella,

"Fever," captures street life in New Orleans and the sequestered environment of a Bourbon Street brothel. Robert Whiteacre, a twelve-year-old whose mother died when he was a toddler, has been feeling abandoned since his brother joined the army and a neighbor friend went to boarding school. His father, an undertaker preoccupied with his job, is usually away from home, leaving African-American servant Thelma in charge. Except for school, where he has difficulties because of a speech impediment, the only time he spends outside his house is in the company of two relatives, elderly French Quarter sisters. Wanting to call attention to his loneliness, Robert leaves home to "commit suicide" by walking in the French Quarter where he has been warned never to go. While escaping from a predatory homosexual sailor, he randomly rings a doorbell and eventually gets welcomed into Madame Ladybird's house. A friendship develops that changes Robert's life and reveals Ladybird's past.

183. Ferber, Edna. *Saratoga Trunk.* Garden City, N.Y.: Doubleday, Doran, 1941. 352pp.

Approximately half of this novel dealing with revenge and romance is set in New Orleans. Clio Dulaine and Clint Maroon meet and become interested in each other on their way to the city. Each has long-held and complicated plans for revenge. Clio is the daughter of Nicolas Dulaine by his octoroon mistress Rita. When Nicolas committed suicide his family exiled Rita and Clio to Paris. After Rita's death in 1875 Clio returns to New Orleans with her maid Angelique and dwarf manservant Cupidon to revenge herself on the Dulaines. Maroon holds the railroad establishment responsible for his father's death and has a complicated plan to make the principal figures suffer by gaining control of the Saratoga trunk line. Clio's story dominates the novel's New Orleans section. She arrives to find that the only Dulaines still alive are Nicolas' widow Madame Dulaine, and Charlotte Thérèse, Clio's half sister. Intent on scandal, Clio very publicly reoccupies the Rampart Street house Nicolas gave her mother and appears at public functions announcing herself as a countess and relative of the Dulaines. To avoid a scandal at Charlotte Thérèse's debut, the Dulaines accede to Clio's wish that her mother be buried in an ornate New Orleans tomb and give her ten thousand dollars to leave town and never contact them. Clio departs for Saratoga Springs to pursue a romance with Clint and is drawn into his plan. The New Orleans section of the novel describes famous restaurants, locales, and social events (where Clio tries to embarrass the Dulaines), and it depicts the injustices experienced by mixed-race women.

184. Ferrall, Robert J. [Pierre Beaumont, pseud.]. *The Lanfer Case: A Tale of Hypnotic Passion.* Illustrated by Edward Mason. Chicago: Bow-Knot, 1892. 248pp.

Based on an actual murder committed in 1883 and detailed in the book's appendix, this fictionalized account includes information about the practice of hypnotism, a central feature of the crime. When a popular and admired young lawyer, Frank Legarde, goes missing, a note signed Carl Vonne directs the police to the murder victim's body. This mysterious circumstance makes police wary when Louis Lanfer offers assistance with the case. Upon investigation they learn that Legarde had been the rival of Lanfer's younger brother Bertrand for the hand of Ida, whose affections Legarde won, and later married. Publicly, Louis Lanfer declared that the better man had won and he became a great companion of Legarde. However, the friendship was only a means to spend time with Ida, whom he had come to love. The novel lays out the steps by which Louis executed a scheme for his brother to murder Legarde. The crime was meant to look like a suicide; however Bertrand bungled it. Louis tries to alter the crime scene, but cannot, and is pleased when the police suspect an Italian Mafia member. In the interim, he arranges for Bertrand to flee the city, while he successfully courts Ida Legarde. At the same time, however, he becomes intimate with Laura Larue, a woman with a black widow reputation earned in foreign capitals. Jealous of Ida, Larue (overheard by her African-American servant) threatens that she will reveal Lanfer had Legarde murdered. When Larue's butler tries to sell the information to the police (only to be met with physical abuse) they have grounds to arrest Lanfer. A newspaper sensation over his arrest reaches Bertrand, who returns to the city and confesses. However, the prosecutor contends that

Louis controlled Bertrand's actions through mesmerism and the execution is stayed at the last minute. In addition to references to locations, mostly in the French Quarter, the book includes a description of Mardi Gras.

185. Finley (Witte), Glenna. *Love's Magic Spell.* New York: New American Library, 1974. 197pp.

Sara Halliday Nichols travels to New Orleans from Chicago as a favor to her Aunt Prue, who has inherited Bellecourt plantation outside the city and wants to sell the property due to the expensive upkeep. Fortunately, Nichols soon gains a local guide in Piers Lamont, a wealthy young man who is friends with the owners of the Lafayette Hotel where she is staying. Piers, whose family has lived in New Orleans for many generations, so inspires Nichols with his enthusiasm for local history that she begins to think of staying in New Orleans. Piers, educated in the North and only in the city to reconnect with family after Peace Corps service, had intended to move to a more forward-thinking part of the country. As the two fall in love with each other and Bellecourt, their plans begin to change. This romance novel portrays the beauty of New Orleans and captures the preservationist fervor of the 1970s.

186. Fisher, Steve. *Saxon's Ghost.* Los Angeles: Sherbourne, 1969. 211pp.

Joe Saxon, "The Great Saxon," a forty-four-year-old magician, has honed his faculties in extrasensory perception (ESP) and employs them in an act that has made him a celebrity within the magic community. In his show's finale he seems to make a ghost materialize and then dematerialize in his arms just as the audience is convinced that the illusion is a scam. Ellen Hayes, the real girl who appears as the ghost, has no idea how he creates the illusion. A twenty-three-year-old beauty from Baton Rouge, Hays is a hippie and was working as a go-go dancer when Saxon discovered her. At first he paid no attention to her flirtation with him and ignored her interest in learning magic. Traveling on the road by the cheapest means, Saxon eventually lets Hayes share his bed and begins to train her in ESP. Once they get to Las Vegas, however, he leaves her behind, assuming she will find a wealthy man or skilled impresario. Instead, she disappears and begins appearing to him through ESP, asking for help. He becomes obsessed with finding her and while visiting her hometown, gets a call from a New Orleans police detective begging for help solving the mystery of nightly screams emanating from Room 104 of the Royal Orleans Hotel, a sleazy drug den, where the hotel owner was found dead of a heart attack. When Saxon witnesses the haunting, he realizes that Ellen is the ghost and employs his skills to help police uncover what happened to Ellen. Although Saxon lives in San Francisco and much of the novel is set there and on the road, the sections set in New Orleans are the most evocative and central to the plot. The use of the city as the setting for a violent death and dramatic haunting is consistent with popular images of the city.

187. Fleming, Rudd. *Cradled in Murder.* New York: Simon and Schuster / An Inner Sanctum Mystery, 1938. 293pp.

This murder mystery describes seedy, 1930s New Orleans and conveys social attitudes toward sexuality and race. While college professor Huymer Van Ravensway is grading an autobiographical writing assignment, he is shocked by Eugenie Fourain's work. She indicates that her mother and father were murdered and that she will be killed as well, prior to her approaching twenty-first birthday. As Ravensway investigates, he discovers that Fourain is to inherit the Talliefer fortune and plantation due to a will that many family members consider unfair. Eugenie's great-grandfather left his estate to his eldest son, Philip, leaving his other children, Eustache and Helen, Philip's dependents. Philip made his daughter Lilian (sic), Eugenie's mother, his sole heir. Lilian married Nicolas Fourain while she was a student in France. After Lilian's early death, Nicolas made a will that solely benefited Eugenie, excluding his son Maurice from a previous marriage. After his death the entire estate was put into a trust for Eugenie. Not only is everyone dependent upon the trust, they all live in the same house on Prytania Street. The residents include: the elderly Helen and Eustache; Lilian's sister Constance and her husband, Henry Perdeleau; and the youngest generation, Maurice and Eugenie. Ravensway tries to protect Eugenie, but cannot immediately assess her sanity or the motivations of anyone in the Prytania household. He intervenes when a drunken Maurice becomes physically abusive toward Eugenie, but is then ejected from the house by a servant. When Eugenie smuggles him into the house after dark, it is for passionate sex, after which Ravensway unwittingly poisons Eugenie by giving her water from a bedside carafe. Fearing conviction for the murder, Ravensway travels to the Talliefer plantation to gather evidence from African-American servants, witnesses Maurice accidentally shoot himself, and then hides from police in the French Quarter, where, unshaven and unbathed, he blends in. His break-through comes when he recovers a diary from an Ursuline Convent nun. Throughout the book sexual expression is feverishly pursued and the African-Americans who labor on the Talliefer plantation are made to seem bestial and sexually available. The time Ravensway spends on the plantation and in seedy French Quarter bars and diners, where needs are openly expressed and satisfied, make a vivid contrast with the psychologically twisted atmosphere in the upper-class Prytania household.

188. Fortmayer, Aenida V. Gonzalez. *Came a Gentleman*. New York: Vantage, 1956. 287pp.

When Val Perez, the gentleman of the title, is befriended by twenty-two-year-old Eugene Lafont, a fellow student at Tulane University, he gets drawn into a series of domestic situations and relationships, many of which end in tragedy. Perez, an engineering student, is from Buras, Louisiana, where his father owns an orange grove and winery, and he lives in a boarding house on Dumaine Street. Lafont, a law student, introduces Perez to the Coulon sisters, Honorine and Collette, since his sister Mercedes is best friends with Honorine. The Coulons are daughters of René Coulon, who had owned a restaurant, but lost it due to his chronic alcoholism. Now, he supports himself and daughters by working in the French Market and owning a boarding house located near the corner of Dauphine and St. Anne Streets that is mostly patronized by theater people. Mostly, however, he womanizes and drinks, forcing Honorine to manage the boarding house. The group of young people socializes, having dinners at Antoine's, Tujague's, Arnaud's, and the St. Charles Hotel, as well as attending the circus at Audubon Park. Although Collette and Val take an immediate interest in each other, any development of their relationship gets thwarted, at first because Collette makes it seem that she is interested in Eugene. She gets Val to pledge to try to influence him to stop drinking and gambling. However, when Val takes Eugene to Buras, away from the temptations of New Orleans, he still manages to cheat at cards, get publicly drunk, and bed a local girl, necessitating Val's aid in smuggling him back to the city. Shortly afterwards, Mercedes gets involved with a boarding house actor, Marcel Comos, gets pregnant by him, and, after they are married, gets abandoned by him. Around the same time, Eugene gets his fiancée Louisa Castain pregnant and marries her. Val helps Mercedes financially after taking a two-year contract with a South American mining firm. While he is away, Eugene is transformed into a responsible character through his marriage, but falls into alcoholism and depression after tragedy strikes. When Val falls ill and returns to Buras to recover, Collette goes to nurse him and the two finally can devote themselves to each other.

189. Foster, John T(homas). *Marco and the Sleuth Hound*. Illustrated by Lorence F. Bjorklund. New York: Dodd, Mead, 1969. 153pp.

In this book for children featuring boy detective Marco Fennerty, Jr., the August heat has driven most of Marco's friends from the city. He is relieved of boredom soon after he meets Larry Larue, a deep-sea diver, and overhears a conversation between Larue and men employing him for a one-time job. Marco's sleuthing instincts are awakened when he hears Larue's instructions that he will be forced to dive at night and will need to wear a blindfold while driven to the job site. Based on the conversation, Marco decides Larue will be diving for cannonballs at Fort Beauregard, one of New Orleans' abandoned Civil War forts. Enlisting Sally Westgate and her basset hound, he investigates the fort and is surprised to find Larue's valuable diving equipment, and a Civil War era diary kept by the fort's commander. Soon afterwards, Larue's employer, Jacob Q. Finger, and his henchman, Phil Bragg, discover the children and give chase to recover the diary. Marco outsmarts them and uses the diary to figure out the location of the gold that Finger hoped to find at the fort, before turning the manuscript over to the head of the Civil War Round Table, Leonidas Plum, a retired Tulane University professor who lives on Algiers. By the time Marco returns to Fort Beauregard, his police detective father has detailed an undercover police presence, but a dramatic chase for a time clouds the final outcome of the treasure hunt. In addition to relating some aspects of Civil War history, the book conveys a good sense of New Orleans in the summer, the bayou country surrounding the city, and the accessibility of Civil War forts and artifacts that had not yet been preserved.

190. Foster, John T(homas). *Marco and the Tiger.* Illustrated by Lorence F. Bjorklund. New York: Dodd, Mead, 1967. 127pp.

Another in a series of books for children featuring boy detective Marco Fennerty, Jr., whose namesake father is a New Orleans police sergeant, in this novel the fearless eleven-year-old has persistently tried to collect newspaper route money at 420 Royal Street. One day he finally enters the house's courtyard and discovers a tiger. He immediately befriends the animal that knows the tricks of a circus performer. By the time Fennerty finally meets the owner, Oscar Kermet (sic) Perry, the boy has become emotionally attached to the tiger and is alarmed to learn that the cat, that Perry had received years ago as a debt payment, is twenty-years-old, too old to sell, or give to a zoo. Unemployed, Perry is going out West in search of a job and gives the tiger to Fennerty. As the boy pursues schemes to give the tiger a future, the French Quarter and waterfront of New Orleans are brought to life for young readers. Only after investigating the costs of shipping the tiger back to her native India (prohibitive), and being failed by a sailor who promised to get the tiger on a Calcutta-bound boat, is he forced to return with the tiger to his father's apartment. The housekeeper discovers the cat and her screams get the feline roaring in agitation. Marco flees through Mardi Gras streets and eventually sets on the plan of releasing the tiger in Audubon Park. Getting the tiger there on a night-dimmed streetcar, he is soon followed by police and finally convinces a zoo attendant to let his tiger in for protection. When the newspapers feature headline stories the next day, the zoo is shamed into permanently taking the tiger that they had earlier rejected. The book conveys a sense of neighborhood life in 1960s New Orleans.

191. Gardner, Erle Stanley [A.A. Fair, pseud.]. *Owls Don't Blink.* New York: Grosset and Dunlap, 1942. 277pp.

One in a series of detective novels featuring Donald Lam and Bertha Cool, here their assignment is to find Roberta Fenn in New Orleans. Lam, who is slight, short and unintimidating solves crimes through intellect and street smarts and his partner, Cool, is a tough-talking woman with a passion for food and ability to get high client fees. Their client, Emory Garland Hale, a New York City lawyer, makes Lam uneasy. First, Hale cannot explain why he contracted with the Los Angeles-based Lam and Cool, rather than a New Orleans detective agency. Second, even though Fenn has been missing for three years, Hale has no explanation of why she is being sought only now. Finally, Lam is able to locate Fenn within only a few hours of arriving in New Orleans. Lam discovers that Fenn has been unwittingly involved in a scheme due to her resemblance to a woman named Edna Cutler who is involved in a messy divorce case. Most of the novel is set in New Orleans in the early days of the United States' involvement in World War II and through the book Lam increasingly resents Cool's domineering attitude and secret plot to keep him from being drafted. The New Orleans setting is mostly that of hotels, restaurants and bars, and is of interest for detailing bar culture and the many scams perpetrated on the unsuspecting. In addition, Lam details the lax security of the time that enabled him to get into people's offices and hotel rooms and the ploys used by bars to get female employees to prey upon visiting businessmen. In general women in the book are presented as strong to the point of being predatory.

192. Garfield, Dick. *Mardi Gras Madness.* Chatsworth, Calif.: GX, 1973. 185pp.

Mardi Gras revelry leads to life changing sexual exploration in this explicit gay pulp novel. After breaking up with his lover, Sid needs a vacation and invites his sister Fran and her fiancé, Doug, to New Orleans. Amidst the parades and drinking on Bourbon Street, a flirtation develops between Sid and Doug that leads to a sexual encounter. For Sid the experience, if not trivial, is nonetheless in the nature of a one-night stand. For Doug, the experience brings his whole life into question. Sid is forced to help Doug navigate the shoals of his emotions while trying to protect his sister Fran. The descriptions of 1970s bar culture and references to gay life make this book distinctive, although the New Orleans of the novel is mostly composed of tourist landmarks.

193. Gayarré, Charles. *Fernando de Lemos.* New York: R.F. Fenno, 1871. 486pp.

This first-person narrative presents the adventures of the eponymous Lemos, beginning with his school days at the College of Orleans, shortly after being forced out of Santo Domingo by the revolution there. One of his classmates, Trevigne, after coming into his estate in Spain, sends Lemos a check for ten thousand dollars, enabling him to travel to Spain and throughout Europe. When Lemos returns to New Orleans he reconnects with acquaintances, including Augustin Calandro, the sexton of St. Louis Cemetery. Lemos records the stories he hears from Calandro about the people interred in his cemetery, including the dissipated atheist, Henry O'Neill (originally of New York City), the German merchant Valdeck and his Portuguese widow, members of New Orleans' Jewish community, and jurist Francis Xavier Martin. Calandro makes asides about historical figures Dominique You and Theodosia Burr and slavery. Lemos' friendship with Calandro is interrupted by service in the Confederate Army. He returns to New Orleans as a sixty-year-old man and for the first time in his life has no inherited income on which to live. He describes the enormous social changes in the city after the war and shares stories of some of the people who, like him, lost everything with the collapse of the Confederacy. Although Lemos is able to secure a job in a printing factory, since he had saved the life of its Northern owner, he chafes under the indignity of being a wage slave. Fortunately, Calandro appears to him in a dream and tells him to open the back of the portrait Calandro bequeathed him. There, Lemos finds enough money to regain financial independence and begin a modest life near St. Louis Cemetery.

194. Genois, Renald H(enry). *Forge of Destiny.* New York: Vantage, 1972. 337pp.

In 1794, French revolutionaries beat and imprison Paul Perret, even though his connection to the monarchy was remote. Aided by his family, Perret escapes and sails to New Orleans where his father, the owner of a shipping firm, has established a bank account for him with significant funds. The author researched the time period and conveys the frontier nature of the city and the ways in which young men like Perret could create their own destinies. The bankers holding Perret's money realize that the secret transaction and subsequent death of the senior Perret mean that if Paul dies they can keep his money with no repercussions. They plot for Paul's death in a duel. The challenge is issued during a Cordon Bleu ball that is described in great detail. Paul survives and negotiates to purchase land outside New Orleans. However, he forms friendships that yield a land grant of two thousand acres in the Atchafalaya River Valley. As he departs for the frontier to begin improving his land, his crooked bankers continue to hope he will be felled by a fatal accident. This never happens and Perret establishes himself as his friends create plantations on adjacent tracts. Throughout the novel, historical details are introduced and the mingling of Spanish and French cultures plays a significant role in the book that includes descriptions of buildings, streets, and households in eighteenth-century New Orleans.

195. Gerson, Noel Betram [Carter A. Vaughan, pseud.]. *The River Devils.* Garden City, N.Y.: Doubleday, 1968. 239pp.

Gerson uses a fictional, atypical "river devil," Andrew MacCullough, to relate events between 1799 and 1803 that protected the Mississippi River as a transportation route for frontier Americans. The multi-lingual MacCullough attended Harvard College, studied in Paris, and travelled widely, but has a restlessness that makes him ill-suited to most occupations. At the beginning of the novel he is a river devil, transporting goods from Mississippi River ports to New Orleans. When Spanish customs officials prevent him and his fellow devils from reclaiming their barges, MacCullough organizes the men to resist and, when they are jailed, he engineers their escape with the aid of his beautiful female friend, Beatriz de Santos. After the escape he stays with Santos until he learns that she is betrothed to Don Felipe de Guzman, the new Deputy Governor of Louisiana, who is soon to arrive from Spain. He escapes from New Orleans under the protection of Abel Hillery, a U.S. diplomat who is impressed by MacCullough's combination of intelligence, patriotism, and fighting skills. After MacCullough has returned to the North and begun homesteading in Tennessee, Hillery hires him for a reconnaissance mission to New Orleans to assess the truth of rumors that Spain is to cede the Louisiana Territory to Bonaparte. When the transfer is imminent and the U.S. government is concerned that the French may close New Orleans to Americans, MacCullough is made the commander of an unofficial regiment of frontiersman to keep the port open. By the time MacCullough makes his final entry into New Orleans the transfer of Louisiana to the United States is about to happen and MacCullough has been offered a position as a warehouse superintendent by the Spanish businessman who is about to become his father-in-law. The novel emphasizes the importance of New Orleans as a port crucial to the development of early nineteenth-century frontier areas and claims for frontiersmen a role in protecting the port for the United States that they may not have played.

196. Gibbs, George. *Isle of Illusion.* New York: J.H. Sears, 1929. 301pp.

When a levee breaks in northern Louisiana, the water rises so quickly that two young strangers, lawyer Phil Hepburn and heiress Rita Perot, are stranded on the second floor of a farmhouse and must help each other survive over the course of three days. Not until they resume their normal lives do they realize that they are on opposite sides of a legal dispute. Hepburn believes that the Perot family wrongfully claimed a tract of Louisiana land that should have been part of his deceased mother's estate. If he is correct, the reputation of Rita Perot's father, a well-respected judge at the time of his death, will be besmirched. Most of the plot centers on the search by the opposing sides for old documents and buried pearls. Other characters, in addition to Perot and Hepburn, include a wealthy playboy interested in Perot, a less than scrupulous lawyer, and a society girl. While much of the novel is set in New Orleans, the work incorporates little physical description of the city beyond the generic: affluent residences, private clubs, legal offices, pawn shops, jazz clubs, and ancient French Quarter tenements occupied by people of color.

197. Gibbs, George. *The Shores of Romance.* New York: D. Appleton, 1928. 292pp.

In this take on Jean Lafitte (c.1776–c.1823) and New Orleans during the War of 1812, the two key figures are Francophone Marguerite de Jarnac and Irish-American naval officer Barry O'Shaughnessy. When O'Shaughnessy witnesses Jarnac's arrival in New Orleans, he assumes that she shares the perspective of her father Etienne, a legislator who votes to protect slavery and who supports Jean Lafitte, presumably sharing in the profits from his smuggling empire. Nonetheless, when Pedro Martinez, one of Lafitte's men, forces his attentions on Jarnac, O'Shaughnessy intervenes. The Baratarian challenges him to a duel that is broken up by Jean Lafitte and soon afterwards Jarnac appears at the dueling ground to apologize for causing the argument. O'Shaughnessy's opinion of her softens and soon afterwards he discovers that, like him, she opposes slavery and the lawless Baratarians. Through social events that bring French, Spanish, and American New Orleans residents together, O'Shaughnessy socializes and begins to fall in love with the outspoken Jarnac. Recently graduated from school, Jarnac is newly aware of her father's support of Lafitte and opposition to the politics of her American friends, Governor Claiborne (c.1772/75–1817), and Gordon Hartley. Although she is outraged, she finds no way of reasoning with her parent. When O'Shaughnessy asks for her hand, her father considers the proposal outrageous and schemes to kill O'Shaughnessy. Employing a quadroon prostitute, he lures O'Shaughnessy to a masked ball in order to compromise him in the eyes of Marguerite and then have him murdered. The plot succeeds in alienating Marguerite from O'Shaughnessy, although a miscue prevents the murder. However, when O'Shaughnessy is spying in Barataria Lafitte captures him and Jarnac comes to his aid since he is an agent of her beloved United States. When she witnesses the British approach Lafitte, she uses his attraction for her to influence him to refuse. She then helps O'Shaughnessy escape and shortly afterwards he repays her by courageously rescuing her from Lafitte. In doing so, he captures Lafitte and forces him to pledge his arms and men to Andrew Jackson. The New Orleans setting is mostly focused on historical events, rather than physical description and is occupied by several iterations of the issues dividing slaveholders, pirates/smugglers, and the American people. Throughout the book aspects of character are ascribed to ethnicity. For instance, Creoles are depicted as pleasant, but simple, indolent, and unconcerned about the immorality of smuggling and Lafitte's slave market, which is active even though the importation of slaves to the United States has been banned.

198. Grau, Shirley Ann. *The Condor Passes.* New York: Knopf, 1971. 421pp.

In the present of this family saga, New Orleans is still visited by Oliver family members, where they maintain one of several residences, but the city is most vividly connected to the family's past when patriarch Thomas Henry Oliver, now ninety-five, was building his fortune. Born in 1870 in Edwardsville, Ohio, at thirteen Oliver leaves the impoverished home of his widowed mother to make his fortune. He accumulates enough money by the age of seventeen to move to the West Coast and, after working as a sailor, begins smuggling guns, opium, quinine, and women into San Francisco. At twenty-seven, he sails for exotic ports, continuing to add to his savings, until he finds himself on a ship quarantined near the mouth of the Mississippi due to a smallpox outbreak. He escapes and makes his way to New Orleans. After a short time as a brothel bartender, Oliver goes into partnership on a bordello with Alonzo Manzini, a fruit importer and Italian immigrant with family connections throughout the city. With skilled management and savvy bribery the place flourishes and Oliver reinvests his profits in land, rental properties, and a dock. He eventually sells his share in the brothel to open a gambling parlor. By the time Prohibition begins, he is positioned to make huge amounts of money by smuggling alcohol. With his fortune secured, he marries the daughter of a city judge. The couple has five children, only two of whom survive, daughters Anna and Margaret. Widowed early, Oliver goes back to business, eventually adopting Robert Caillet, a young Cajun who worked as a bootlegger and prevented Oliver from suicidal despair after the death of his wife. During World War II when Robert is in the army, huge profits cause Oliver to structure a complex international corporation that Robert is never really able to grasp when he returns, even though he is the CEO. Throughout the novel the New Orleans setting is mostly of interest for the varying business opportunities its development presents. Even though Oliver is involved in illegal activities, his main emphasis is on accumulating legitimate assets and he is quick to perceive the incursion of organized crime into the city, willingly giving up bootlegging and even some legitimate businesses to avoid contact with criminals. In the post-World War II era Oliver mostly has offices in the city with his actual companies located elsewhere.

199. Grau, Shirley Ann. *The House on Coliseum Street.* New York: Knopf, 1961. 242pp.

Grau describes a household of women in New Orleans whose affluence has liberated them from traditional gender roles. Matriarch Aurelie Caillot's great-great grandfather built the house on Coliseum Street. Her wealth has allowed her to choose husbands and she has had five with whom she has had five daughters: Joan, Doris, Phyllis, Celine, and Ann. Her current husband,

Herbert Norton, retired from the U.S. Navy, lives on the top floor, devoting himself to whiskey. Aurelie had her oldest child, Joan, now twenty, with Anthony Mitchell, a lawyer and gambler, from whom she was divorced soon after Joan's birth. Mitchell accumulated a fortune that continues to benefit Aurelie and Joan ten years after his death, through trust fund payments. Joan's income is a source of resentment to her younger sister, eighteen-year-old Doris, whose father, though handsome, made no financial provisions. The disparity exacerbates sibling rivalry and when Doris and her boyfriend Michael Kern, a Tulane University instructor, have a fight, Joan accepts a date with him, even though she has been going steady with Fred Aleman, a young lawyer. Joan and Kern spend a long evening that includes Lake Pontchartrain, a French Quarter jazz club, and a "fairy" bar off the highway. Joan is left muzzily smitten, as well as pregnant, as she realizes three months later. Aurelie decisively arranges for an abortion and a summer for Joan with her Aunt Ethel in Pass Rigaud where the girl experiences no recriminations and luxuriates in genteel comfort, chauffeured about in a Rolls Royce, and provided with expensive bed-jackets and cosmetics. From Aurelie's perspective, by the time she fetches Joan back to New Orleans with the help of Fred Aleman, the matter is over. However, Joan feels a deep loss over the unborn child and still longs for Kern. While taking classes at Tulane to pass the time, Joan discovers Kern is having an affair with a freshman girl; a poison pen letter ends the romance. Then, after Joan finally reconciles herself to marrying Aleman, Doris and Kern renew their affair, leading Joan to make accusations against Kern to Tulane authorities that will probably lead to his dismissal. Throughout the novel New Orleans' Garden District has an evocative physical presence with descriptions of beautiful old houses and gardens. The workers supporting this life—maids, drivers, houseboys, and gardeners—remain faceless presences that are there, but are beneath comment. New Orleans' gay subculture is mentioned several times and Aurelie's refusal to have anything to do with gay men becomes another in a long list of social codes she observes and forces upon her daughters. Other social codes include partaking of a formal breakfast, having a male escort when going out in the evening, and being appropriately dressed on even informal occasions.

200. Grayson, Charles (Wright). *Original Sin.* New York: Alfred H. King, 1933. 254pp.

    Three young people fall in love in this romance novel and Mardi Gras madness brings clarity that unites two of the lovers without malice on the part of the third. Advertising man Hart Mallory falls in love with Helen Cassell on sight, but their meeting is random and he never expects to see her again. Then, his best friend, Jerry Coyle, finally introduces him to the woman he has been rhapsodizing about marrying and Mallory realizes that she is Helen Cassell. Mallory is pledged to the highest personal standards and suffers agonies at being disloyal to Coyle, even in thought. After a period of socializing that is torture to Mallory, all three young people leave their native New York for a variety of reasons. Cassell goes on an annual family vacation in Florida, Mallory to a remote island off Key West to meet with the vacationing manager of the coffee plantation he owns in Colombia, and Coyle sets off on a bizarre quest. Cassell, a practical-minded settlement house volunteer, wants Coyle, a wealthy, dilettante poet, to demonstrate initiative. Her father collects historical jewelry and the orphaned Coyle's guardian is Harrison Brower, a famous New Orleans antiquarian who just acquired a rare Egyptian scarab. Cassell sets Coyle the test of getting his uncle to give him the scarab so that he can impress her father by giving the jewel to him. While Coyle is in New Orleans, fate brings Cassell and Mallory together in Florida and although Cassell seems receptive to a new level of friendship, Mallory awkwardly resists. They separate, but are soon reunited in New Orleans to which they have been summoned by urgent telegrams. They arrive to find that Coyle is in jail accused of murdering his uncle and stealing the man's scarab collection. Mallory finds the real culprit (even though he realizes that if he makes no efforts Coyle will hang and he will get Cassell). The released Coyle, wanting to surprise Cassell with his prison release, assumes the Mardi Gras costume she knew Mallory would be wearing and is startled to hear her confess her love for Mallory. Fortunately, Coyle has come to realize he will never be able to live a stable, married life and can wish Mallory and Cassell wedded bliss with no hard feelings.

The New Orleans description is almost exclusively preoccupied with Mardi Gras balls and parades.

201. Greene, Frances Nimmo. *Into the Night: A Story of New Orleans.* New York: Grosset and Dunlap, 1909. 370pp.

In the aftermath of the 1890 assassination of New Orleans Police Chief David Hennessy (1858–1890) and the subsequent lynchings of supposed Italian-American Mafia members, the Laurence family undergoes a period of dramatic soul-searching that focuses on the romances of two family members. These are Helen Laurence and a young lawyer, Herbert Girard, she had intended to marry. However, Girard played a significant role in the jailhouse lynchings and Helen immediately decided that anyone who could participate in vigilante justice was an unsuitable husband. Helen's father, sixty-year-old John Laurence, had concerns about the match prior to the lynchings and became much more vocal afterwards. Zoe Laurence, Helen's eighteen-year-old adopted sister is the only family member that feels that Girard is being wrongly treated. Zoe appeared in the Laurence household as a foundling retrieved from the doorstep by John Laurence. He insisted that the baby be adopted over the objections of Susan Hopkins, John's sister-in-law, who had become a surrogate mother to the Laurence children after the death of John's wife Adele. Susan was concerned about Zoe's unknown parentage. A strong adherent to the view that genealogy shapes character, Susan considers the romantic relationship that Helen discovers between Zoe and Frank Laurence, John's only son, proof that her original qualms about Zoe were justified. When John hears of the romance he privately tells Frank that he has papers that prove that Zoe is "not white," but part Italian. She actually turns out to be the daughter of an Italian plotting vengeance for his lynched comrades. Both Girard and Zoe redeem themselves by playing heroic roles when John Laurence is kidnapped as part of the Mafia's revenge. The novel is interesting for revealing the depth of ethnic hatred in late nineteenth-century New Orleans and the very clear geographic boundaries of such areas as the Italian Quarter during the time period.

202. Grethe, James. *Misses, Martyrs, Mayhem.* New York: Vantage, 1966. 172pp.

Seymour Lee Fairchilde, III is the first-person narrator of this risqué satire of upper-class life in New Orleans. The scion of an affluent family with diverse international holdings, Fairchilde has scandalized his family since youth by drinking and philandering. After serving as a pilot in Korea and later operating a brothel-like servicemen's private club in Tokyo, Fairchilde returns to the family mansion to find only the servants in residence, along with some visiting twin "cousins" from Charleston—Gwendolin and Cynthia Breckinridge, who are distant relations. The girls are in town to study art at Newcomb College and they persuade him to share an apartment in the French Quarter and be their guide to cutting edge avant-garde art. Beatniks, who make him their poster boy for capitalist oppression, mistake the heavy-drinking Fairchilde for a downtrodden worker. Organized crime figures resent Fairchilde's ability to draw crowds that attract police to beatnik hangouts that are actually fronts to more lucrative Mafia businesses. Mafia threats, along with troubles at the shared apartment (Cynthia marries one of the beatniks and Gwendolin has declared her love for him), are compounded by an impending visit by the Breckinridges. The whole ménage returns to the Fairchilde mansion and adopts a veneer of respectability long enough for the Breckinridges to accept Fairchilde as a son-in-law. The novel captures some of the bohemian culture of the French Quarter in the 1960s.

203. Grice, Julia. *Lovefire.* New York: Avon Books, 1977. 373pp.

In this bodice-ripper set in the early nineteenth century, men are immediately drawn to the beautiful Brenna Laughlin. As soon as she is of age, Neall Urquhart agrees to pay her father's debts and keep him out of prison if he will give Brenna to be his bride. On their wedding night, Urquhart discovers that Brenna is not a virgin, but after a struggle falls out a window before he can create public scandal. Unable to return to her dying father's house, Brenna gets his help to leave Ireland and escape to the United States and a new life. She arrives in New Orleans in 1819 to live with her Aunt Rowena Butler on Prytania Street in the American section, where her uncle Amos is a prominent businessman. Her two cousins Arbutus and Jessica introduce her to New Orleans society, but her transition is complicated by the arrival of her brother Quentin, a drunkard and womanizer who develops a preference for quadroon women. Not long afterwards Toby Rynne forces himself on Brenna after a social event and when she is seen with few clothes intact, her relatives tell her that no matter the truth she will be faulted. The only solution is to marry Rynne, whom she finds repugnant. Fortunately, she has met Kane Fairfield, one of the wealthiest men in New Orleans, who is a social iconoclast. He rescues her on her wedding day and although he will not marry her, he can offer safety and love. They begin a peripatetic life that takes them to Cuba and the Caribbean. The novel conveys a version of New Orleans society in the early days of the Republic, while addressing fantasies of 1970s American women.

204. Gross, Josiah. *Ondell and Dolee: A Story of Mysticism.* New York: Abbey, 1902. 260pp.

This novel uses a slight plot as an excuse to expound tenets of mysticism and the occult; so, although the work is set in New Orleans, there is little physical description that is identifiable with the city. Dolee Antieth gives in to a hypnotic suggestion and abandons her lover Ondell Urmoden for Daltil Sondalere. After a time she realizes her mistake and marries Ondell, who lives in a house called Thousand Stair Mansion, filled with occult objects and books. The book is included for the association between New Orleans and the occult, and may be of interest to cultural historians for the ways it attempts to connect science and mysticism.

205. Gunter, Archibald Clavering. *Bob Covington: A Novel.* New York: Home Publishing, 1897. 313pp.

When Robert Boone "Bob" Covington visits New Orleans in 1854 for the racing season, he reconnects with his cousin, Louise Tournay, and falls in love. The races entail a range of social events and attract people like Covington (affluent and able to travel from one social event to another for diversion) from across the South. His maternal cousins, Louise and Nita Tournay, are just coming out of mourning for their father and have begun living a chaperoned life in New Orleans, living on trust payments made by Arvid Martineau, the lawyer managing their father's estate. Seeking an explanation for Martineau's niggardliness, Covington discovers that there is an anticipated claim on the estate that could impoverish the girls. Unfortunately for them, a sharp lawyer, Kitson Jarvis, has been secretly preparing the claim. Jarvis gets Covington to sign a retainer agreement leaving secret the property to which he is entitled. While traveling in New York, Covington learns that Jarvis has laid claim to the Tournay estate and seized Louise and Nita as chattels since unexecuted manumission papers seem to indicate they are mixed-race slaves. Dismayed by the situation, Covington hires the despised, but cunning, Kitson to find a means to legitimize the Tournay girls. His only hope stems from the fact that their mother, Eulalie Camile, seems to have been owned by one of Lafitte's pirates, Faval Bigore Poussin, before appearing in Prosper Tournay's household as his wife. The Baratarians sometimes enslaved white women, some of them Castilian noblewomen. The legal complications of a mixed-race identity and slave status are parsed over a number of pages as Covington rapidly depletes his liquid capital on legal fees and investigations. Finally, through a complicated arrangement with Poussin, he gets the evidence that Eulalie Camile was a white Castilian, knowing that Louise and Nita will be able to use the document to prove their racial identity and come into the unencumbered Tournay estate, even though this could guarantee his financial ruin since they may not repay him for legal fees and bribe money. This is a likely outcome since Louise has been alienated from Covington by Kitson's behavior. While the novel is focused on the plight of mixed-race people in slave culture, the book gives a sense of antebellum social life in New Orleans. In addition to dealing with issues of race, the work pays a good deal of attention to the social status of women.

206. Guyol, Louise Hubert. *The Gallant Lallanes.* New York: Harper and Brothers, 1929. 251pp.

In the absence of reliable men, the Lallane women address a financial crisis that threatens their inherited life of privilege in this novel that tacitly deals with the social status of women. The recently widowed Mrs. Lallane owns a house on Prytania Street that has been in her family, the Warrens, for generations. In addition, along with her brother Harry Warren, she owns a plantation in Plaquemines Parish, but even though formerly enslaved servants tend the place, it has not been farmed since the Civil War. Historically, the Warrens had spent the social season in New Orleans, and through much of the novel Harry, his wife, and their four sons are living in a wing of the thirty-room house (the architecture and contents of which are described in some detail). Mrs. Lallane has three daughters, the oldest, eighteen-year-old Marguerite, being the only one of importance to the plot. The Lallanes enter a period of crisis when they find that Timothy Nestor, the manager of Mr. Lallane's estate, invested their only liquid capital in stocks just before the crash. The girls are forced to drop out of private school and Mrs. Lallane takes in boarders, much to the resentment of her African-American servants, who do not consider the interlopers people of quality, (even though one of them is St. George White, an English widower with a country estate who comes to town for the social season and treats the Lallanes to drives in his limousine). Admittedly the others, unmarried women who work as schoolteachers and book reviewers, seem to fit the assessment of the servants. One of the Lallanes' boarders is a Boston relative who is a schoolgirl, and traditions and aspects of local culture are detailed for her benefit. As time passes, the Lallanes and Warrens reluctantly make plans to lease the plantation property and give up their cherished sojourns in the countryside, while practical-minded Marguerite gets a job as a stenographer at the Gates Mahogany Company. When one boarder returns from her summer in New England with a wealthy relative, Marguerite is able to use the information she has gathered on the value of the plantation timber to sell the expensive mahogany and cypress to him and restore the Lallane family fortune, enabling the family to cancel the plantation lease and enroll the girls in private school again. Soon afterwards, Marguerite discovers a fiancé supportive of her business and intellectual interests. Although the book includes African-American characters, they are all child-like servants who must be indulged and looked out for in paternalistic fashion. Furthermore, although the women solve their own financial crisis, they harshly judge their spinster boarders and have married life as their goal even though Mr. Lallane made poor financial choices, as did his estate manager, the same man who eventually becomes Marguerite's fiancé.

207. Hagen, Annunciata. *The Unflinching M.D.* New York: Fortuny's, 1939. 262pp.

A great deal of verbiage is expended on a very modest plot as twenty-three-year-old Agnes Hammond navigates her first foray into adulthood. Soon after the death of her father, she decides to leave Hill Crest, her family's Shreveport mansion, before the property's sale is finalized, and starts work as a paid companion to a New Orleans society lady named Julia Wilbur. In a strange coincidence, Wilbur's nephew, Sidney, a physician who has been in Vienna engaged in research, is on the same train as Hammond and they are immediately attracted to each other. However, Florence Archer, a childhood friend of Sidney's, is determined that she will marry him and free herself from the embarrassment of no longer having an adequate allowance from her father (who lost his fortune in the stock market crash of 1929), or any expectation of an inheritance. Once she realizes Sidney's interest in Hammond, Archer makes efforts to remind the Wilburs and everyone in their social circle that Hammond is a servant. When this fails she accuses Hammond of stealing a watch from her purse, but Sidney soon gathers evidence to discredit Archer and by the end of the novel, alienates all of her acquaintances by this evidence of her meanness. Current readers may be interested in the formality between the sexes among the upper classes (Hammond and Wilbur know each other for months before they progress to a first name basis), the supposed novelty of anyone as wealthy as Sidney having a career, a character who suffers from drug addiction, and the fact that medical offices could be housed in the wing of a private residence. Given the female authorship, the novel is surprisingly misogynistic, with a subplot involving the behavior of a scorned woman as an added example of feminine vindictiveness. New Orleans is mostly represented by society events, the romance of the French Quarter, Audubon Park, and Mardi Gras.

208. Hailey, Arthur. *Hotel.* Garden City, N.Y.: Doubleday, 1965. 346pp.

While focused on the inner workings of the fictional St. Gregory Hotel, a hostelry known for elegance and tradition on the edge of New Orleans's French Quarter, aspects of hotel life and the diversions of guests and employees describe 1960s social life in the city. William Trent has principally owned the St. Gregory for thirty years. Trent is proud of the hotel's long history and the number of employees who have worked there for decades. However, he has closed his eyes to abuse of trust by long-timers and not been receptive to improvements suggested by Peter MacDermott, his newish assistant general manager, and graduate of the School of Hotel Management at Cornell University. Over the four-day span of the novel the hotel faces a crisis in which a two million dollar mortgage, which the bank has refused to renew, is coming due. Self-made Texas hotel magnate Curtis O'Keefe is prepared to pay the mortgage and buy out Trent, but O'Keefe's plan to make the St. Gregory a part of his well-managed chain will replace the charm of the St. Gregory with corporate uniformity. Several subplots demonstrate the hotel's character, including the way the attempted gang rape of a society heiress, after a fraternity social, is handled. In another instance, Christine Francis, personal secretary to Trent, is instrumental in committing hotel resources for an elderly male guest experiencing a health crisis, even though the guest will probably not be able to pay for the private nurse and suite. The old-fashioned nature of the place nearly ruins Trent's plan to sell the St. Gregory to a labor union intent on organizing the hotel industry, since he has followed tradition and kept the hotel white-only, refusing African-American guests. Unfortunately, a *New York Post* reporter is on hand when a distinguished African-American dentist is turned away from the St. Gregory, unable to attend a professional convention at which he was to speak. The union backs out of the purchase, but a mysterious buyer completes a deal with the proviso that MacDermott takes over as chief executive. Details of hotel operations and the general philosophy of management were taken from New Orleans' Roosevelt and St. Charles Hotels. Settings outside the hotel include Jackson Square, Brennan's, Galatoire's and others of New Orleans's best-known venues. The novel was adapted into a movie of the same name (Warner Brothers, 1967) and in 1983 Aaron Spelling created a television series based on the book that aired for five years on the ABC network, although he changed the location to San Francisco.

209. Hale, Edward Everett, Sr. *Philip Nolan's Friends: A Story of the Change of Western Empire.* New York: Scribner, Armstrong, 1877. 395pp.

Aspects of Louisiana's transfer from Spanish to French to American control are related through the experiences of Silas Perry, his family, and friends. Perry, a New Englander, relocated to New Orleans in 1763, when Louisiana was transferred to the King of Spain, and built a successful business as a shipping merchant. Through his travels to Cuba he met and married a beautiful Spanish woman with whom he had one daughter, Iñez. Widowed when Iñez was still an infant, he called upon his sister, seventeen-year-old Eunice, to join his household. Sixteen years later, in 1800, Perry leaves on an extended trip to Paris and sends Iñez and Eunice to San Antonio to visit his sister-in-law, Maria Dolores Barelo, whose husband is a high-ranking military official. The women travel under the protection of horse trader Philip Nolan, who gets captured and executed by the Spanish Governor of Texas. The women, in turn, become protectors of White Hawk, a Caucasian girl who had been an Apache captive, before returning to New Orleans. Further adventures come two years later when Iñez must get Silas Perry released from prison during Spain's embargo on U.S. ships entering New Orleans, which Perry had plotted to violently oppose. Fortunately, she has American Daniel Clark (1766–1813) and Eunice's fiancé, an Englishman, to aid her. Nothing is effective, however, until word comes that Napoleon Bonaparte (1769–1821) is ceding the Louisiana Territory to the United States (the secret treaty through which he had acquired Louisiana was already known to Spanish Governor Salcedo). The novel reveals the efforts taken by Americans to end the Spanish embargo and the conflicted loyalties of people living in New Orleans in the early nineteenth century.

210. Hales, Carol. *Wind Woman.* New York: Woodford. 1953. 288pp.

Although this novel is in some ways a psychological case history of a lesbian, the New Orleans setting plays an important role. When Laurel Dean is twenty-four she meets Zalda Farrar at a musical salon in the French Quarter and the two immediately form an emotional attachment. Dean is a concert pianist and composer and Farrar is a concert violinist who has recently moved to New Orleans and purchased a house on Esplanade. From her early childhood, Dean has sought her "Wind Woman," a female companion who will be emotionally available to her, but not physically demanding. Farrar fits this typology. She was married, but found the sex act distasteful and has no plans to remarry, because she enjoys the independence of unmarried life. As a heterosexual, she appreciates the emotional friendship she forms with the younger Dean, but is not open to any physical contact, even an embrace. Eventually, Dean realizes she needs some physical contact with Farrar. To complicate matters, Bert Dexter, one of New Orleans' wealthiest and most eligible bachelors, is in pursuit of her. Since she lives at home with her mother, Dean must endure both Dexter's hectoring pursuit and her mother's use of emotional warfare to get her to marry Dexter. Fearing she is on the verge of a crisis—she had previously had a nervous breakdown—she begins daily sessions with Dr. Garner, a female psychoanalyst. Although the novel advocates acceptance of homosexuality, as Dean relates incidents from her past, an etiology emerges that follows traditional notions (an emotionally distant mother and abusive relationships with men). Dean's account of her personal history is event-filled, including an attempted rape by a tramp; a bizarre ménage with a married doctor and his wife in which the frigid woman encouraged a sexual relationship between Dean and her husband; and an extended sexual relationship with a divorcée, although the woman's son (who was Dean's age) repeatedly broke in on their love-making. Even her relationship with Dr. Garner is somewhat sensational because by the end of their sessions, the doctor has fallen in love with her and they seem about to embark on a relationship. In the course of the novel, scenes transpire in French Quarter venues, at the New Orleans Yacht Club, and in a gay nightclub. New Orleans weather plays a significant role in the narrative as heat and storms exacerbate Dean's emotional state. Finally, New Orleans in this book is a center for classical music in the South, with talent agencies booking performers for events throughout the region, illustrating the extent to which live musical performances were mounted in schools and church halls, had a role in meetings of associations and clubs, and were used as fund-raisers for even small organizations. The book is unusually open in describing sexual encounters, given the era in which it was published.

211. Hall, Georgette Brockman. *House on Rampart Street.* New York, Vantage, 1954. 291pp.

Although this novel spans a time period of only two years, the settings include the Texas frontier, a plantation near Baton Rouge, and grand and modest residences in New Orleans. Through murder, yellow fever epidemics, false accusations, and flight from Santa Ana's troops, Kay Callahan maintains her faith in God, cares for her orphaned sisters and brother, and remains pure for her man, Hunt Randolph, even after they are separated for several years and she finds that he has married. The story begins in 1833 with the death of Melo Callahan on her family plantation, now in the hands of her alcoholic husband, Dudley. He has nearly bankrupted the place and, soon after she dies giving birth to his namesake, he remarries Vivienne Gaspard, a temporarily displaced New Orleans courtesan. She insists that Dudley sell the plantation and all of Melo's family heirlooms, so that they can move to New Orleans. On the steamboat trip to the city, Vivienne murders Dudley after grabbing the sale proceeds and when she arrives in New Orleans quickly latches onto steamboat entrepreneur Gilbert de Latour. She abandons her Callahan stepchildren and nineteen-year-old Kay struggles to keep her three siblings clothed and fed. Throughout her travails Kay maintains an unwavering morality that earns Latour's admiration; so, when Etienne dies of yellow fever, Latour makes provisions for the Callahans, eventually proposing marriage to Kay. Still in love with Hunt Randolph, who had grown up on the plantation neighboring the Callahans, she is urged by her evil sister Diana to take the family to the Texas frontier where Randolph is making a name for himself. Diane wants to escape to the frontier where her bad reputation will have little impact. Already aware that Randolph is married, she gloats when Kay finds out the truth after they reach Texas. After Randolph's wife dies, Diane tries to poison him against Kay, but Kay's virtue is so obvious that Randolph is not long in realizing the truth. The New Orleans of the novel is one in which fortune and disaster quickly follow each other and with the right lover a woman can go from desperation in a hovel to a mansion on Esplanade Avenue overnight. Much of the action takes place in gambling parlors, whorehouses, and the boarding houses of the desperately poor.

212. Hall, Georgette Brockman. *The Sicilian*. Gretna, La.: Pelican, 1975. 264pp.

Focusing on ethnic violence in New Orleans, inspired by hatred of the Mafia, this novel illustrates the danger of maintaining long-held hatreds. The book starts with an account of police chief David Hennessy's 1890 murder and the resulting violence against Italian-Americans. In a dragnet the police had arrested a large number of immigrant Italians not connected to the murder. After the few men directly involved were convicted, the rest of the men were acquitted and scheduled for release. However, enraged by the verdict, a citizen mob of six thousand people, organized by Edmond Gironde, captured the prison holding the plaintiffs and gunned down everyone who was Italian-American. The novel flashes forward to Italy in the 1950s where Nicosia Savelli has been raised by his uncle to believe that he is the son of one of the innocent men. Savelli is a trained opera singer and his uncle funds a touring opera company that will travel to New Orleans where Savelli will dramatically avenge his father. Instead, Savelli becomes enchanted with a woman he meets on the street, who turns out to be Contessa Gironde. From her he learns that his target, her father, had died in an accident six months before. He falls in love with her even though his uncle insists he must kill her. Eventually he learns from her that the Girondes were not responsible for the massacre and that he could not even be the son of any of the victims. Savelli falls in love with New Orleans, as well as with Gironde, and seems poised to take up residence. The book can be seen as part of the larger cultural movement of the 1970s to reclaim ethnic heritage and end stereotypes.

213. Hallbing, Kjell [Louis Masterson, pseud.]. *New Orleans Gamble*. Translated from the Norwegian by Jeffrey M. Wallman. London: Corgi, 1975. 110pp.

One of a series of books featuring nineteenth-century Texas Ranger Morgan Kane, in this adventure novel, Kane goes undercover as a riverboat gambler to capture Louis Bellamy and his henchman. They killed undercover policeman Alex Gorman while he investigated the River Rats, a ring of thieves who prey upon riverboat card games. Bellamy had also earned Gorman's enmity by falsely courting his daughter and abandoning her when he learned of her pregnancy. On his first foray on board ship, Kane espies a group of ultra-refined Creole gamblers and he suspects them of being River Rat conspirators (while expressing distaste for their effeminate behavior). Returning to New Orleans, he waits for Bellamy to emerge from his bayou hideout. When Bellamy shows himself, Kane strikes. Much of this thinly written and plotted novel is set in New Orleans, as well as on Mississippi riverboats and in Louisiana bayous.

214. Hallman, Ruth. *Gimme Something, Mister!* Philadelphia: Westminster, 1978. 103pp.

When Jackie's parents travel to England for her father's job, she stays in New Orleans with her great-aunts, Colette, Odelia, and Violetta de la Fouches, in the French Quarter house on Royal Street that her family has had for generations. Chafing under their watch, when Mardi Gras comes she breaks free long enough to attend the festivities with the help of her friend Bertha, an African-American stall owner in the French market, who thinks it is a shame for the girl to miss the King Rex parade. Bertha helps her create a costume so that she can mask and at the parade receives a marvelous antique jade necklace as a throw, after which a man dressed in a Voodoo costume mysteriously gives chase until passersby rescue her. She gets back to Royal Street just in time to prepare dinner for her aunts and learn about the Comus Ball, that they are all about to attend. When she receives a necklace as a call-out gift that is identical to the one she got as a throw, Jackie becomes so frightened that she pleads illness in order to be taken home. The mystery of the necklaces is eventually solved, but not before a visit to the tomb of a Voodoo priestess is organized by Bertha and the only one of her aunts who believes in the practice. This work for children conveys little information about New Orleans or Mardi Gras, but does use the festival as an exotic backdrop for a tale meant to inspire girls to choose appropriate risks on the road to maturity.

215. Hamilton, Harry. *Banjo on My Knee.* Indianapolis, Ind.: Bobbs-Merrill, 1936. 320pp.

A significant portion of this novel about river folk who fish between Tennessee and Arkansas is set in New Orleans. Pearl Peters, a "land girl," marries Ernie Holley and moves onto the boat on which he had grown up and still lives with his widowed father, Newt. Soon after the marriage, in the midst of the Depression, Ernie gets work as a sailor on a cargo ship and Pearl is left with Newt. Deeply in love with Ernie, but powerless over his decisions, Pearl decides to escape her isolated life by letting itinerant photographer Warfield Scott take her to New Orleans. Scott promises to teach her retouching in his photographic studio, but secretly just wants a sexual relationship with her. When Ernie tries to find Pearl, he gets shanghaied without Pearl or Newt's knowledge. When Newt, who has never traveled more than a few miles along the river, sets off to retrieve Pearl, he supports himself by playing an assemblage of musical instruments in one-man band fashion and soon gets a job at the Creole Café, replacing Chick Bean, a male crooner. Months pass before Newt realizes that Pearl is a dishwasher in the café (she was forced upon her own resources after rejecting Scott's advances). With Newt's help she starts working as a waitress. However, Bean tries flirting with her heavily enough that she will leave New Orleans and take Newt with her so that he can resume his job. When Ernie's ship returns to port, misinterpreting the interaction between Pearl and Bean, he becomes violent and is arrested. A tense period follows in which Pearl must decide whether she will stay in New Orleans or return to live on the river. New Orleans in the novel represents the broader world to the river folk, but the anonymity of city life violates their sense of appropriate social interaction and the consumer goods on offer are of slight interest to them. A screenplay based on the novel was written by Nunnally Johnson and produced under same title by Darryl Zanuck, starring Barbara Stanwyck, Joel McCrea and Walter Brennan (Twentieth Century-Fox, 1936).

216. Hammond, Hilda Phelps. *Pierre and Ninette in Old New Orleans.* Illustrated by Elizabeth Urquhart. New Orleans: Hauser, 1946. 80pp.

In this book for children, Pierre and Ninette, who live on a Louisiana sugar plantation, travel to New Orleans to visit their cousin Louis during Mardi Gras season. However, their visit is occupied with touring historical sites, shopping, and fine dining. Although many of the places they visit will be familiar to present-day tourists, the 1940s social and cultural context, often presented via the mouths of locals, may be of some interest to scholars, particularly as the focus is on Francophone people who still practice artisanal trades, including wood carving, toy making, and mask and costume making.

217. Hancock, H(arrie) Irving. *Detective Johnson of New Orleans: A Tale of Love and Crime.* New York: J.S. Ogilvie, 1891. 247pp.

A young man gets a second chance at pursuing love when a defenseless schoolgirl becomes the victim of a plot on her inheritance. Thirty-year-old Reginald Prentiss, returning from a trip to St. Paul, Minnesota to purchase lumber for the restoration of his family's plantation house, is detailed to escort his cousin, eighteen-year-old Elsie Prentiss, from school to home for Christmas via steamboat, and is smitten with her school friend and companion Dianne Lorraine. After witnessing Frank Streator, an acquaintance from a neighboring plantation, being cheated at poker, accusations lead to a duel between Prentiss and a player who turns out to be Dianne's brother, Gaspard Lorraine. Prentiss seriously wounds Lorraine and, out of respect for Dianne, stays behind in New Orleans hoping for Gaspard's recovery. He is treated to further contact with Dianne when she comes for visits. On one of these, she is shocked to learn that Gaspard has arranged for her to marry forty-year-old Captain Lipscomb (their parents are dead). After escaping to family friends Major and Mrs. Delaporte, they hospitably invite her to stay for the winter, and Elsie soon joins the house party. When Dianne is kidnapped, Prentiss and Streator search for her and recover her from the street after a servant helps her escape. In the meantime, Major Delaporte has hired detectives who discover Lipscomb and Gaspard are plotting to get Dianne's inheritance. When Dianne is kidnapped once again by the duo they get her aboard a steamboat by pretending she is an insane patient bound for a St. Paul sanitarium. In their pursuit, Prentiss and Streator board the wrong the boat. A steamboat race ensues and just after the heroes rescue Dianne the steamboat boiler bursts. A happy ending follows, however, with Lipscomb and Gaspard captured alive and a marriage between true loves in prospect. New Orleans has little presence in the novel, although some neighborhoods and private clubs are mentioned. African-American servants repeatedly help Dianne in her escapes.

218. Handl, Irene. *The Sioux*. New York: New American Library, 1965. 308pp.

As a domestic novel concerned with a clannish, French-American family, this book is little concerned with settings outside the walls of mansions occupied by members of the international set. The Benoirs of France, Martinique, and Louisiana, call themselves the Sioux to indicate their tight social bond. When English banker Vincent Castleton weds Marguerite Benoir, he willingly tries to acclimate to the social milieu of his wife's family and believes he will have most difficulty forging a relationship with "the Dauphin," Marguerite's son George from her first marriage to her cousin at the age of sixteen, which ended with his youthful death in an automobile accident. Nine-year-old George, heir in his own right to a large fortune, suffers from a rare illness and, in addition to upgrading a New Orleans house with bidets for Marguerite, Castleton must install elevators for George. To his surprise, George is immediately friendly but Marguerite and other Benoir family members treat George in overly protective ways that Castleton considers problematic. When he tries to address the situation, he makes enemies and begins to experience angered outbursts from Marguerite that are so shocking as to seem unbelievable. For the survival of his marriage (and possibly himself), Castleton must bring to light the hidden family conflicts that lie beneath the close-knit façade of the Sioux. Although mostly set in New Orleans, the novel has little concern with the city, except as an appropriate fictional setting for a family such as the Benoirs, who live in great luxury, maintain a French cultural heritage, and spend their lives traveling among houses, some of which are located outside the United States.

219. Harrington, Dare. *Fun Was Where You Found It.* Jericho, N.Y.: Exposition, 1974. 130pp.

Many of these short stories are set in the French Quarter, but the focus is on conveying strong, mostly eccentric personalities, so the stories provide little physical description. Events include New Year's Eve, Christmas, a meeting of a Women's Writers Club, and a hot summer day. People include a man who devotes his whole life and estate to his house, several football heroes, and a neighborhood handyman who has spent his life keeping the houses on his street habitable.

220. Harris, Thomas. *Black Sunday*. New York: Putnam, 1975. 318pp.

This story of international espionage, inspired by world events (the Munich Olympics and the controversy over the Vietnam War), is partially set in New Orleans. Michael Landers, a former prisoner of war in Vietnam, has been recruited by the Palestinian terrorist group, Black September, through their agent, Dahlia Ilyad, a beautiful young woman who takes an important role in Landers' life. After his service, Landers returned to the United States to find that his wife was having an extramarital affair, and promptly divorced her. Although he still suffers from posttraumatic stress syndrome, Ilyad has been able to restore his sexual confidence and cure his impotence, earning his devotion and easing his agreement to detonate a bomb during the Super Bowl to be held in New Orleans at Tulane University stadium. Landers is the pilot of the Aldrich Blimp, a fictional version of the Goodyear Blimp, and fabricates a special nacelle compartment, containing plastic explosive smuggled into the country by the Palestinians, and a quarter million steel darts, that, after much suspense, is fit onto the blimp at the last moment. American and Israeli intelligence were alerted about a plot and Mossad agent David Kabakov and FBI agent Sam Corley are eventually able to follow the trail of the explosives into the country and Ilyad's movements in order to race to New Orleans to prevent a large-scale catastrophe. Approximately seventy pages of the novel are set in New Orleans as various principal characters arrive there and perform reconnaissance, settle into expensive hotels, dine out at famous restaurants, and rendezvous in the French Quarter.

221. Harrison, Edith Ogden. *Gray Moss.* Chicago: Ralph Fletcher Seymour, 1929. 205pp.

Many of the romantic stories in this volume are set in New Orleans and, for the most part, draw upon traditional images of the city as a place of mystery where destiny brings lovers together. In "Two Portraits," paintings of seventeen-year-old Ninette's great grandparents determine her own marriage to Robert, for she is the twin of her great grandmother and for a costume ball he appears dressed like her great grandfather. One of the more interesting tales, "Brilliant Plumage," concerns the impending marriage of a thirty-three-year-old "spinster" who has received a proposal via correspondence with a childhood friend whose wife has died. The ladies of New Orleans, who are fellow volunteers at the bride's charities, are concerned that her plainness will derail the marriage and use their skills to transform her into a beauty. "Queen of the Carnival" depicts people descending upon New Orleans from all over the South to participate in Mardi Gras. On a steamboat en route, a soon to be King Rex espies a woman in the distance who he wishes to choose as his Queen. She had dreamed her destiny would be determined at a Mardi Gras ball and King Rex finds her there. In another story of inevitable destiny, "Pink Oleanders," John Barrington, about to depart northwards on business, takes an early morning walk in New Orleans and happens upon a beautiful young woman. When he meets her again on the train, he realizes that she is his cousin, Constance, whom his mother has thought he should marry. He has not seen her for years, resenting his mother's intrusiveness. Now he realizes this is the woman he can love for the rest of his life.

222. Harrison, James Albert. *Autrefois Tales of Old New Orleans and Elsewhere.* New York: Cassell, 1888. 294pp.

This collection of gothic romances and supernatural stories includes many tales set in New Orleans. The stories are distinctive for capturing settings peculiar to the city, including: a period of plague when a nun sings as her way of nursing fever victims and fires are set to stop the fever's spread; elaborate entertainments on Congo Square; and the celebrations and optimism at the outset of the Civil War. In several cases, mysterious women woo confirmed bachelors—including a man who has lived most of his life in the world of books—into marriage. The descriptions of the city are evocative and much is made of the exoticism of Creoles and African-Americans.

223. Harrison, William. *Pretty Baby.* New York: Bantam Books, 1978 184pp.

A novelization of the movie of the same name, directed by Louis Malle and released by Paramount Pictures in 1978, this work of historical fiction includes characterizations of actual people, including photographer E.J. Bellocq and various jazz musicians. The simple plot focuses on Storyville in 1917 in the months before the officially sanctioned houses of prostitution are closed by government order. The romanticized version of life in one house, Nell Livingston's, is as much a cultural artifact of the so-called sexual revolution of the 1970s as it is an evocation of the earlier historical period that it describes. When Violet, the daughter of prostitute Hattie Marr, turns thirteen, the house's madam, Nell, holds an auction for the opportunity to deflower her. When Hattie, who had long dreamed of marrying and leading a respectable middle-class life, weds a St. Louis paving contractor, she is convinced that Violet will not fit into her new household and leaves her behind. Bellocq, who had become an intimate of Nell's through photographing the women in a respectful manner, marries Violet when word begins to circulate that Storyville will be closed. His love for her is genuine and he grieves for the rest of his life when Hattie returns to separate them. Although the book relates some details concerning the history of prostitution in New Orleans, since the characters rarely leave Nell's house there is little general description of the city.

224. Hay, Corinne. *Light and Shade 'Round Gulf and Bayou.* Illustrated by Julia Ann Mountfort. Boston: Roxburgh, 1921. 222pp.

More than half of this collection of short stories is devoted to the Gothic murder mystery entitled "The Flaming Sword," in which an artist enamored of New Orleans solves the mysterious death of Henrique Jacquard, the last of his line, by looking into history and discovering a curse made by a wronged woman. However, he also discovers that although practitioners of Voodoo and a mysterious "Hindoo" are involved, the murder and previous tragic deaths all have their basis in human evil. The narrative takes full advantage of romantic images of New Orleans and includes several visits to cemeteries, abandoned houses, and Voodoo gathering places.

225. Hedden, Worth Tuttle. *The Other Room.* New York: Crown, 1947. 274pp.

Although this novel is almost entirely set in New Orleans, most of the action transpires on the grounds of a school and readers are provided with more insights about racism in the South than about New Orleans. Nina Latham interrupts her master's studies at Columbia University to take a teaching job at Willard College in New Orleans, not realizing the college is a high school for African-Americans. A native of Virginia who proudly traces her family in the state back to the eighteenth century, Latham is possessed of all the prejudices against African-Americans typical of someone with her upper-middle-class social status. After thinking over the challenges she would face if she fled (financial issues and the explanations she would have to make to family and friends) she stays and gets swept up in the work of teaching English to one hundred fifty students in a series of classes. The capabilities of several students transform her assumptions about the capabilities of African-Americans. Her social life also forces her to examine her assumptions. Because Willard is resented by New Orleans residents who think the teachers there, mostly Northern, are violating segregation and coaching African-Americans to have a false sense of their social class, Latham must build a social circle drawn from her fellow teachers. Even though the book is about overcoming prejudice and seeing worth in individuals, Latham harshly judges all of her Caucasian colleagues (for their manner, implied lesbianism, appearance, lack of culture, etc.). However, she befriends Leon Warwick, a man of mixed race, who received his master's degree from Harvard University, and his friend, Erma Clinton, an artist who has studied in Paris and is also mixed-race. When she is out in public with Clinton or Warwick she must deal with Jim Crow laws and when she realizes she is in love with Warwick, is forced to reflect upon anti-miscegenation laws and the costs of "passing" for individuals like Clinton and Warwick, who have decided to embrace their African-American identity when they could so easily live outside the United States and not have to deal with racism. The book touches on the psychological issues with which Latham must deal (she has a persistent cough that is diagnosed as a revulsion at talking to African-Americans as equals, and she is unable to engage in physical intimacy with Warwick). The book is specific about racism in New Orleans in several ways, but mostly in explaining the backlash against mixed-race people that occurred during Reconstruction and worsened in the twentieth century. In another example of prejudice, a Jewish doctor in the novel who has experienced anti-Semitism in the North finds he is treated fairly in New Orleans, so long as he is outspoken in supporting local prejudice against African-Americans. The book touches on the Garvey Movement and racism among African-Americans, who evaluate their fellows by degree of blackness. A Mardi Gras celebration is evoked in some detail to describe the distaste and titillation some participants experienced in knowing that African-Americans could be brushing up against them in disguise, something that could never happen in segregated daily life.

226. Hicks, John (Kenneth). *The Long Whip*. New York: David McKay, 1969. 344pp.

In this salacious novel about an African-American's experiences of slavery and freedom, a Caucasian author takes on the issue of black identity. Ben is born on Seven Oaks Plantation in Franklin Parish, Louisiana, in 1840. Even in his youth, his experiences are different from many slaves, for he is selected by the mother of plantation owner Otto von Gruber to receive her instruction in reading and writing, becoming her most promising pupil. He would have been destined for life as a house slave had his body not begun to mature so early. By the time he is fourteen he has a man's body and genitals and is successfully mated by von Gruber to a series of female slaves. Unfortunately, he is also employed by von Gruber to punish runaways and other slaves with lashings from a leather whip. On Ben's first visit to New Orleans, von Gruber sells him to Etienne LeGrand, a wealthy and politically influential Creole. Unlike von Gruber, LeGrand regrets the institution of slavery and is pleased that Ben has been educated. However, he is most interested in Ben's physical prowess. A gambler, LeGrand is always accompanied by a bodyguard on his visits to New Orleans and his current one is aging. Ben is trained in the arts of defense and begins living in comparative freedom. LeGrand has clothes made for him by his own tailor and Ben has a great deal of freedom in his movements while in New Orleans, living on the grounds of the LeGrand mansion on Iberville Street. In his discussions with Ben, LeGrand tries to get him to think about his identity. As war approaches, LeGrand preemptively frees his slaves and Ben joins the Native Guard that becomes part of the Yankee occupation force when New Orleans falls. The novel includes a good deal of New Orleans history for the period 1858 through 1865 and articulates the troubled identity of some African-Americans, as well as the great betrayal they experienced as the Civil War ends and Reconstruction begins.

227. Higginbotham, (Prieur) Jay. *Brother Holyfield.* New York: Thomas-Hull, 1972. 377pp.

Higginbotham teases out what might happen if a respected white Baptist minister became convinced that he should spread his ministry to African-Americans and poor whites of the sort who frequent the area around Bienville Square. Set in 1968, the book thoroughly evokes the social and racial dividing lines in New Orleans during the time period. At home Holyfield must deal with his wife Pauline's opposition to any violation of social rules, while the most powerful members of his church (First National Baptist—people joke about the bank-like name) are more concerned with building a new church with spectacular architecture, than about social justice issues. Pauline becomes more vocal when Holyfield begins telling her about a young woman, Reena, who mysteriously appears in various settings, always with the same appearance but with varying identities, and who is prodding him to question his assumptions about his ministry. As he begins to spend more time outside his church, he comes into contact with a diversity of residents, including Cajuns, Native Americans, Catholics, "mulattos," and a "Mongoloid." When a wealthy member of his congregation begins to negotiate to buy a property neighboring the church, Holyfield gains a new appreciation for the confidence with which such men believe they can use their money to get their wishes, no matter the implications for other people. Holyfield's new perspective on his congregation descends with sickening clarity during the fervor of Mardi Gras when he witnesses a dramatic desecration of his church when Reena is "stoned" with hymnals. Although this social satire is focused on the conflict between lived Christianity and the hypocrisy of contemporary organized religion, the author chose to set the work in New Orleans and uses his perspective on the social and economic divisions in the city to illustrate his parable.

228. Hills, Alfred C. *MacPherson, the Great Confederate Philosopher and Southern Blower: A Record of his Philosophy, his Career as a Warrior, Traveler, Clergyman, Poet, and Newspaper Publisher, his Death, Resuscitation, and Subsequent Election to the Office of Governor of Louisiana.* New York: J. Miller, 1864. 209pp

This Civil War era satire of the Southern Cause features protagonist James B. MacPherson whose letters to a New Orleans newspaper articulate his political stance and his analysis of public events. Although MacPherson resides in Madisonville, Louisiana, he describes trips to New Orleans and comments on the Union occupation. He takes the loyalty oath in the city and attends a charity fair, as well as encountering a variety of citizens. The nature of the work makes the New Orleans content difficult to assess, but the author seems to have considered that city more than any other to be the capitol of the Confederacy.

229. Hilton, Alice Howard. *A Blonde Creole: A Story of New Orleans.* New York: J.S. Ogilvie, 1891. 270pp.

This romance novel, a sequel to the author's *Paola Corletti*, touches on issues of racial prejudice, including that experienced by Creoles who were sometimes classed as non-white and subjected to the same racism as African-Americans. Lucia Corletti is the granddaughter of an American blonde who married the Italian Count Martini. Her mother Paola had been orphaned young and married Marco Corletti, a tenor in a cathedral choir. They couple migrated to New Orleans, where Lucia was born. After the death of her parents in the yellow fever epidemic of 1878, Doctor Orlando, a Creole, adopted Corletti. Convent-educated, Lucia makes her social debut at seventeen as the granddaughter of an Italian count. Still, her suitors are less than appealing. She likes her stepbrother, Frank Orlando, and is ready to accept him, until she discovers he had been engaged to Aline Blanc, the mother of his child, but broke off the relationship when he learned that she has African-American "blood." Robert Bruce, a Northern businessman, becomes Frank's substitute after he wins over the Orlandos with his charming stories. Unfortunately, Florry Monroe appears during the Bruces' wedding tour with proof that Bruce is her husband. Bruce has a plausible, if lengthy, explanation. He married Monroe out of gratitude that she nursed him through an illness and only later learned that she suffers from mental instability. She refuses to recognize the divorce Bruce obtained on the advice of physicians. A devout Catholic, Lucia does not recognize the divorce either. To conceal her disgrace she goes to New York City to teach music and makes friends with Mrs. Francis, a Southerner, who helps her get work as an actress. Eventually she falls in love with impresario Will Carrol, though she remains chaste through the chaperonage of Mrs. Francis. Then, the newspapers are filled with the murder-suicide of Robert Bruce and Florry Monroe. The happy ending includes Lucia's marriage to Carrol, the news that she is a countess and has inherited her grandfather's palace, and the revelation that Mrs. Francis is actually Aline Blanc, with whom Frank Orlando reunites, this time in marriage, now that his parents, who had opposed the union, are dead.

230. Hilton, Alice Howard. *Paola Corletti: The Fair Italian.* London: James Henderson, 1897, 153pp.

The eponymous Corletti is the daughter of Count Martini, a Neapolitan count who had married a wealthy American girl to recover his family fortune. She died giving birth to Paola, whose lonely life was transformed by meeting Marco Corletti, an attractive tenor in the cathedral choir. When her family opposes the match, the couple elopes to New Orleans. Although their love remains strong, they face severe financial hardships, but do find a place in the Creole community, which is described in some detail. The couple has a daughter, whose story is told in a sequel, *The Blonde Creole*, included here. The author treats New Orleans as an international setting, closer to Europe in culture than the rest of the United States.

231. Hoerner, Aline. *Song of the Bayou.* New York: Vantage, 1960. 135pp.

Ann Dupre and her husband Steve move to New Orleans in 1942 with very different expectations. Steve had grown up in New Orleans as the artistic son of a wealthy family, but he returns a penniless prodigal who has yet to establish himself as an artist. Ann has never been to New Orleans, but her image of it is based on novels describing the antebellum South. Both of them are disillusioned by modern New Orleans. Steve must work as a ship fitter's helper and is surrounded by friends from his affluent youth whose socializing focuses on gambling and bars. He resents his lost youth and fortune, as well as changes in the French Quarter and city as a whole. The Dupres have also experienced change. The family mansion lies in ruins, and only Steve's sister still has her share of the family money (a source of resentment for Steve). So, although Ann may have married into a family that would have fit her stereotype of Southern affluence, she suffers the squalor of an overcrowded wartime boarding house on St. Charles Avenue. Out of desperation, she flirts with a contractor who is able to get them a rental house in a newly constructed development near Pontchartrain Boulevard. She soon regrets her behavior, but the regret, along with her disillusionment over her husband, reflect her maturing judgment. Both Steve and Ann realize that they must leave the South if they are to build a life together and when Steve is offered a job in California, they sell off his remaining family heirlooms to fund a new car for the trip. New Orleans in the novel is a place of bad influences and harsh living conditions exacerbated by World War II.

232. Holcombe, William H(enry). *A Mystery of New Orleans: Solved by New Methods.* Philadelphia: J.B. Lippincott, 1890. 332pp.

A thirty-year-old Chicago architect employs the occult to solve an old mystery and win a sizable reward. Hugh Stanford seems to regard spiritualism as a little-explored adjunct of the modern scientific age that may yield a new metaphysics with more explanatory power than current science. While engaged in his explorations, he convinces himself that he has discovered the solution to the mysterious 1865 disappearance of Gordon Clarke and his daughter in New Orleans. He has had a revelation that Gordon Clarke was killed and his daughter put up for adoption. Stanford approaches Clarke's brother, Chicago millionaire Ephraim Clarke, requesting travel expenses to New Orleans in order to prove Gordon Clarke is dead and recover Mary Gilford Clarke. Ephraim not only agrees to fund the undertaking, but also pledges Mary's hand in matrimony to Stanford and a dowry of five hundred thousand dollars. Upon arriving in New Orleans, Stanford is soon convinced that a hypnotist was guilty of the murder and that Ninette du Valcourt is the missing heiress. The rest of the novel describes the ways that Stanford proves his hypotheses through the skills of mesmerists, magnetizers, and psychometrizers. The novel includes physical descriptions of New Orleans, but is most interesting for addressing social issues, such as racism and continuing regional divisions and hostilities decades after the Civil War.

233. Holland, Rupert Sargent. *Pirate of the Gulf.* Philadelphia: J.B. Lippincott, 1929. 270pp.

This account of Lafitte and his pirates differs from others by portraying them as successful merchants in 1814. Nineteen-year-old Joseph Lyman travels from Boston at the behest of his father to find his cousin, Philippe Lyman, the son of Joseph's oldest uncle, Frederick, who had moved to New Orleans and married a wealthy Spanish beauty. Frederick had started a cotton exchange and had been selling the cotton through Joseph's merchant father. After Frederick's death Philippe had taken over the business, but shipments have stopped and Joseph's father wants to find out why. In New Orleans, Lyman has difficulty finding Philippe, although he haunts his business in the city. He is told that Philippe is a Baratarian, but does not quite know what this means. When Lyman is introduced to Jean Lafitte (c.1776–c.1823) the Bostonian finds him charming and cultivated. Then, shortly after a masked ball at Lafitte's mansion, a beautiful young lady, Juliette Bienville, entrusts him with a package for Lafitte, compelling Lyman to travel to Grand Terre, where he meets his cousin and learns about the operations there, which are legitimized by referencing the tradition of letters of marque. On a second trip, Lyman witnesses the British offer to Lafitte and, after their departure, Lafitte's avowal of American patriotism. Just as Lafitte is setting off to Governor Claiborne to offer information and support, he is shown a flyer issued by Claiborne offering a reward for Lafitte's capture. Lafitte promptly heads for New Orleans with Lyman in tow to be presented to the Governor as a witness that Lafitte and his men are not criminals. In this account, Claiborne is persuaded, but his council is not, and Lafitte realizes that General Jackson (1767–1845) should be approached directly, which Lyman undertakes. Although he fails, he is present when Lafitte successfully pleads his own case after Jackson arrives in New Orleans. Lyman participates in the Battle of New Orleans and subsequently helps recover the Bienvilles' treasure and presents it to Juliette. The New Orleans of the novel is the setting for a "swashbuckling" adventure, at the end of which Lyman is preparing to return to the counting-house world of Boston.

234. Homes, Mary Sophia Shaw [Millie Mayfield, pseud.]. *Carrie Harrington, or, Scenes in New-Orleans: A Novel.* New York: A. Atchison, 1857. 354pp.

In this morality tale concerning the nature of social status and gentility, an impoverished girl descended from a wealthy family, suffers the death of her parents and the embarrassment of poverty. Carrie Harrington's mother grew up in Bostonian affluence, but was disowned when she married her true love, Ezra Harrington, whose origins were humble. Although Ezra worked hard, he remained a clerk, barely able to provide for his small family that included Carrie and her older brother Robert, who went to sea as a boy to help the family finances. When Ezra gets an opportunity to invest his savings in a new, New Orleans branch of his employer's company, he welcomes the chance and relocates. However, within two years the firm is bankrupt and Ezra's mind permanently unstable from his worries. In a short time Ezra is a suicide and Mrs. Harrington dead from yellow fever. Fortunately, Carrie finds a patron in Mrs. Ella Percival, a woman who has tentatively advanced in society, based on her husband's business success, but has never fully arrived, due to her malapropisms and lack of refinement. Her good-heartedness is unquestionable and she takes Carrie into her home. Her daughter Nelly is of a similar age, although she is distracted by her love for Horace Nelson, a Bostonian, visiting New Orleans with his wealthy uncle. Nelson considers Nelly Percival, a merchant's daughter, beneath him, even though she is entirely refined and genteel. He focuses on a judge's daughter, although she has little interest in him. When Carrie is discovered to be Nelson's maternal cousin, she and Robert (who has returned from the sea) are welcomed into their mother's affluent family, make attractive marriages and enter New Orleans society. The New Orleans of the novel is one of drawing rooms, ballrooms, and ladies' boudoirs where tête-á-têtes occur with dressmakers and the subject of concern is the fluidity of social class. Despite the reserve expressed by some characters, clearly the ability to move from one social class to another is considered good. Furthermore, while proper deportment may be necessary to advance, money is equally necessary, since the Harringtons' situation is desperate until they have money, even though their deportment is superb. While mostly about high society in New Orleans, the novel touches on public education; Carrie Harrington teaches in a school for which Mr. Percival serves as a board member and there is a significant digression on the nature of teaching in New Orleans.

235. Houston, Margaret Bell. *Moon of Delight.* New York: Dodd, Mead, 1931. 282pp.

Set in 1920s New Orleans, this crime novel of suspense, intrigue, and romance limns two very different and very private worlds: that of a household of French Quarter criminals and that of a very affluent family on upper St. Charles Avenue. Jason Divitt masterminds the criminals. He owns the French Quarter Hotel Tijon and an adjacent gambling parlor that occupies part of a mansion. Around the courtyard of the mansion, in the rooms formerly occupied by family members and slaves, live Divitt and his wife Molly (a troubled woman who served time in prison for forgery); the Italian strongman, Umberto; and Conchita and her dwarf son Gabreau (who claims descent from Napoleon Bonaparte). Between the hotel and casino Divitt finds many opportunities for theft that he gets Umberto and Gabreau to carry out. Occasionally, larger operations fall in his way, including stealing from ships docked in New Orleans harbor. On one of these operations, Umberto and Gabreau carry back chests from a South American steamer to discover that one is filled with opals and the other conceals a beautiful young woman who claims she is Juanita Basare from Argentina, and was bound for Vera Cruz as a ticketed passenger, but she lost her ticket and had to stow away. Clearly on the run for some reason, Juanita is persuaded by Divitt to hide, and Molly, whose illness prevents her from being the casino cigarette girl, gets Juanita to substitute for her, disguised in a veiled, Turkish, harem costume. This is one of a series of disguises and costumes that Divitt has Juanita adopt to get her introduced into the household of his wealthiest casino patrons, Kirk Stanard and his grandmother Nelly Sartoris Belaise, who owns a fabulous jewel collection. At first Juanita is unaware of Divitt's purpose; when she discovers she is to be a pawn in the theft of Belaise's jewels, she devises her own plot to thwart Divitt, while protecting herself, the secret of her true identity, and her engagement to Stanard. The novel gives unusually detailed accounts of Divitt's French Quarter house and businesses, aspects of street life in the Quarter, and the clothing, food, and entertainments of the upper-class Stanard, his grandmother, and their circle of friends.

236. Huff, Lawrence. *Dome.* New York: Pocket Books, 1979. 296pp.

As a recently constructed nuclear power plant on Lake Pontchartrain powers up for full implementation, a flaw emerges that threatens the plant with an explosion that could annihilate the communities around the lake and New Orleans. Most of the novel is set in and around the power plant. However, the key figures, nuclear scientists Dan Mason, George Slayer, Mayor Dorothy Mathieu, and her husband Lawrence, all spend some time in the city and have flashbacks to events in their personal lives that occurred in New Orleans. Among the New Orleans settings are Tulane University (the only place where Lawrence can find a computer for his probability analyses), City Hall, and New Orleans streets. Once the electricity goes out, people suffering from July 4 heat without air-conditioning take to the streets that are later filled with evacuees. In addition to fears of nuclear power, several aspects of the novel connect with 1970s American culture, including women's rights and opposition to the federal government (which acts clandestinely throughout the novel to control events).

237. Huff, T(om) E(lmer) [Jennifer Wilde, pseud.]. *Love's Tender Fury.* New York: Warner Brothers, 1976. 466pp.

This historical romance deals with the inequities of indentured servitude, and the challenges for women living in a male-dominated society. After the English lord for whose children she is a governess rapes Marietta Danver, she is wrongfully accused of stealing jewelry; however, her death sentence is commuted to transportation to the colonies to be sold into indentured servitude. She falls in love with her first master, Derek Hawke, but when she engineers the escape of one of his valuable slaves, he sells her to Jeff Rawlins, a dealer in indentured servants. Rawlins subjects her to an overland journey to Natchez that nearly kills her, all the while claiming that his object is to sell her to a New Orleans brothel. After she heroically escapes and he recaptures her, Rawlins reveals his love for her and tears up her indenture. She goes with him freely to New Orleans to open a gambling house where she serves as hostess, but refuses to marry him. When he dies, she is left with nothing but some jewelry to sell, although she garners enough to open a dress shop in Natchez. Almost as soon as she has married a respectable, affluent man, however, she learns that Derek Hawke has come into his inheritance and is seeking her. Approximately ninety pages of the novel is set in New Orleans in 1774 and the author makes efforts to describe the social setting, including the prevalence of smuggling, practice of taking "mulatto" mistresses, and existence of upper-class gambling houses as gentlemen's clubs.

238. Imbert, Dennis I(gnatius). *The Colored Gentleman: A Product of Modern Civilization.* New Orleans: Williams Printing Service, 1931. 86pp.

In the guise of fiction, the author advocates political views, mostly concerning racial equality. Protagonist Francis Lafarge is the son of a wealthy West Indian who is the agent for a steamship company and owns retail stores, a sugar plantation, and a rum distillery. Although Lafarge is mixed race, he has lived an affluent life in his home country and experienced no racial prejudice in England while attending Oxford University and reading for the bar in London. Returning to his country as a twenty-four-year-old, he is quickly bored and finds no educated women to date. Entranced with the United States' lead in modern inventions, Lafarge emigrates to New Orleans with a letter of introduction to attorney Charles T. LeBlanc, who becomes his mentor when he hears that Lafarge wants to become a U.S. citizen and practice law. Lafarge's political views later attract another mentor in Senator Shrewsbury who helps him successfully campaign for the Louisiana Legislature. Lafarge bases his campaign on opposition to Prohibition and the Exclusion Act. He warns that the racism behind the Exclusion Act will eventually lead to war with Japan. The racism he experiences in his personal life is confined to his rivalry with Major Reilly for the love of Charles LeBlanc's daughter Juanita. Unlike immigrant Lafarge, Reilly is from an old Virginia family and, as a six-foot-four blonde, has an All-American appearance. Reilly is an important man in the Ku Klux Klan and plots clandestinely against Lafarge, using direct violence in the form of a bomb and a smear campaign based on a libelous charge of sexual misconduct. Lafarge is victorious against Reilly's criminality, and even Reilly's charge that Lafarge is of mixed race does not prove consequential, since Juanita's father reveals that she too is mixed race. Although set in New Orleans, the novel is much more concerned with exposing political viewpoints than with physical setting; however, in an appendix, the author lists the "Prominent Leaders of the Colored Race in New Orleans Who Have Achieved Success."

239. Ingraham, Joseph Holt. *Lafitte: The Pirate of the Gulf.* New York: Harper, 1836. 2 vols.: 211pp., 216pp.

This work of historical fiction tells the stories of Achille and Henri Lafitte, American substitutes for Jean and Pierre Lafitte. These Lafittes grow up on the Kennebec River in Maine, not Haiti or France, although they, too, end up as buccaneers in Barataria. The book mostly consists of melodramatic acts of piracy, pursuit by government authorities, and chivalrous treatment of young women, while the action ranges over a wide territory, including Britain, France, Haiti, Ireland, and Jamaica. Only the last one hundred and twenty pages deal with New Orleans and tell of the Lafittes' deception of the British commander in charge of invading New Orleans. They gain his confidence, get his plans of attack, and turn them over to Governor Claiborne, winning pardons for themselves and all of their men, and aiding in the defense of the city.

240. Ingraham, Joseph Holt. *The Quadroone, or, St. Michael's Day.* London: Richard Bentley, 1840. 2 vols.: 244pp., 253pp.

Although this novel presents historical events connected to Spain retaking control of Louisiana in 1769, the book is much more focused on the personal struggles and romances of the divided de la Caronde family. The Marquis de la Caronde married and had a son, Jules, his legitimate heir. However, he also took a mixed-race lover, Ninine, with whom he had two children, Renault (the "Quadroone" of the title) and Azelie. The Marquis treated Ninine well, emancipating her and educating the children abroad. However, upon his sudden death, no manumission papers could be found, and Jules declares them his slaves, unless Azelie will become his lover. When the Spanish governor of Louisiana, Garcia Ramarez (sic), Count of Osma, tries to take control of New Orleans' public buildings, the resulting confusion and social disruption gives the family a reprieve from Jules threats. Both Jules and Renault raise militias of armed citizens to oppose Ramarez, in the name of loyalty to France. Jules only leads forty men, but possesses the primary municipal building and declares himself governor. Renault leads three hundred men and opposes Jules, as well as Ramarez. After an initial skirmish, Renault begins to consider the benefits of Spanish rule, since Jules' power would be destroyed. However, he quickly realizes that Ramarez is an evil man when the insurgents' plot to burn New Orleans and murder the city's judges is uncovered. Ramarez's own daughter, Estelle, is horrified by the plan and aids Renault in rescuing the judges. When her complicity is revealed, her father banishes her and she finds sanctuary with Renault and his family. A series of revelations by the sorceress Zillah reorder the social universe. Jules is actually Ninine's son and Renault the Marquis' legitimate heir. He takes the title of the Marquis del la Caronde. Furthermore, Ramarez's older brother is actually alive, not dead as everyone had assumed. As the legitimate ruler of Louisiana, this more enlightened man will make an acceptable governor and is welcomed by Renault and the citizens of New Orleans. Ingraham's fascination with Orientalism, courtly love, and codes of honor, make the Louisiana of his novel seem like a European country.

241. Ingraham, Colonel Prentiss. *LaFitte's Lieutenant.* Cleveland, Ohio: Arthur Westbrook, 1931. 196pp.

The eponymous lieutenant of the title is Ted, a seventeen-year-old, rescued from a wreck off the coast of Africa by Achille LaFitte (sic), with the bulk of the book telling of his experiences after LaFitte's death. Written for young men, the adventure story commences with British attempts to suborn LaFitte and get his aid in capturing New Orleans. Considering himself an American, LaFitte reports the British overture to Governor Claiborne, even though the governor has previously charged him with a series of crimes. Although Claiborne makes no official response, LaFitte goes on to fight against the British in the Battle of New Orleans, and soon afterward dies of a sword thrust. Ted assists in carrying LaFitte to the Ursuline Convent and witnesses the dying pirate's exchange with the nun caring for him, who turns out to be a former lover, over whom he had gotten into a murderous rivalry with his brother. In his dying moments, LaFitte learns that he did not, as he assumed, kill his brother. A final revelation occurs years later when the brother of Lord Clarence meets Ted on the Mississippi estate of Count d'Oyly and realizes that Ted is the late Lord's son. Although much of the book is set on the ocean, in Cuba, and in Mississippi, the book does recount aspects of the Battle of New Orleans and a version of the legend of LaFitte, who is so closely identified with the city.

242. Isham, Frederic Stewart. *The Strollers.* Illustrated by Harrison Fisher. Indianapolis: Bowen-Merrill, 1902. 499pp.

Much of this historical romance novel is set in 1840s New Orleans and deals with forgotten, mistaken, and redeemed identities. English actress Constance Carew is in New Orleans to establish a reputation in the United States with a successful play at the St. Charles Hotel. She travels with a theater company headed by Barnes, who has also been her guardian since the death of her mother when she was still a child. Her father never married her mother and Carew has no idea as to his identity. Ernest Saint-Prosper, recently a French military officer stationed in Algiers, meets Carew soon after the company arrives in New York City and immediately falls in love. Even though Carew also falls for him, a number of interlopers and misapprehensions must be overcome before the lovers can unite. Saint-Prosper is generally able to deal with open rivals, even wealthy ones, but he has little recourse against a whisper campaign that claims he was a battlefield coward in Algiers. Saint-Prosper is also wary of openly declaring his love, since he only has his income as soldier. Like Carew, Saint-Prosper grew up in the care of a guardian after his parents' deaths. He is in New Orleans to meet with the Marquis de Ligne, who has come to despise his ward, for the Marquis is a monarchist and Saint-Prosper is a republican. As New Orleans fills with troops gathering under the command of Zachary Taylor (1784–1850) for the Mexican War, Saint-Prosper enlists, not realizing that Carew's odd coolness stems from her having heard he is a coward. Carew's debut is a success and when Marquis de Ligne attends he realizes Carew is the daughter of the actress he had married in England, but abandoned when he returned to France, in order to marry a French noblewoman who was connected to the royal household. To correct this wrong, he makes Carew his sole heir, disinheriting Saint-Prosper, and promptly dies. By the end of the novel Saint-Prosper has returned to New Orleans a hero and clears up the misunderstanding about Algiers (his older brother was the coward) The novel includes many topical references to events and people of the 1840s, as well as general descriptions of New Orleans, Mardi Gras, and All Saints Day.

243. Jackson, Charles Tenney. *Captain Sazarac.* New York: Grosset and Dunlap, 1922. 332pp.

This novel imagines Jean Lafitte (c.1776–c.1823) and some of his men reuniting in New Orleans in 1821 to join a plot to rescue Napoleon Bonaparte (1769–1821) and bring him to New Orleans. A house for the deposed emperor has been elaborately constructed on Rue de Chartres and an expensive, fast, sea-going ship, the Seraphine, is waiting for the expedition. René Beluche (1780–1860), now an admiral in a South American navy and Dominique You (1774–1830), now a New Orleans alderman, are both leaders in the plot and when Jean Lafitte now a forty-two-year-old, appears in the city under the assumed identity of Captain Gaspard Sazarac, they try to recruit him. Lafitte is reluctant, but when a beautiful young lady, Louise Lestron, is kidnapped and he is accused of the crime, he sees the Bonaparte plot as the perfect cover for rescuing Lestron. Sixty four New Orleaneans join the expedition, among them, Count Raoul de Almonester, a nephew of Marie Pontalba; and the bohemian painter John Jarvis (1781–1839). After rescuing Lestron, Lafitte is determined to return her to New Orleans, but the crew wants to continue on their mission to Bonaparte. After a mutiny they set Lafitte and his followers ashore. Fortunately, the mutineers' ship is becalmed long enough that Lafitte is able to recapture the vessel. When word arrives that Napoleon is dead, Lafitte decides to buy the Seraphine and set off on new adventures. Approximately the first half of this novel is set in New Orleans and retells Lafitte's history in the city, as well as recounting current conditions there, making much of the changes brought by the incursion of Americans.

244. Jackson, Charles Tenney. *New Orleans Adventure: A Story of the Last Romantic Flicker of Piracy-Privateering in the Gulf and New Orleans of the 1830s.* Philadelphia: Dorrance, 1955. 261pp.

In this Jacksonian-era adventure novel, nineteen-year-old Dade Watt gets a chance to leave his native Skinquarter, Kentucky and see New Orleans, where his father died while serving with General Jackson (1767–1845). Hired to guard a load of buffalo pelts, he travels with the cargo on a steamboat and meets, Aurelie D'ulac, a granddaughter of Armand D'ulac, an associate of Jean Lafitte. Through her, he meets André Noyon who can talk of nothing but an anticipated trip to the Yucatan to recover a fortune in silver before the Spanish can reclaim the bullion. When they arrive in New Orleans, Noyon expensively clothes Watt and presents him as a wealthy descendant of James Watt, referring to him as the "Admiral of Kentucky." When Noyon takes him to gambling houses Watt has remarkable luck in winning money to fund the Yucatan expedition. When the two finally leave the city they first go to Grand Terre to assemble a company of retired pirates and meet D'ulac. She continues to flirt with Watt, but when the expedition is a success, she reveals that she has always intended to marry Noyon, although she helps Watt get back to New Orleans and insures that he shares in the treasure. He returns to Skinquarter and his girlfriend there with a fortune of six thousand dollars to buy a farm. In the novel New Orleans is filled with excitements that the innocent Kentuckian must resist, overcoming temptation and behaving honorably in order to win his fortune and to return home to his girl.

245. Jacobs, Howard. *Charlie the Mole and other Droll Souls.* Illustrated by Eldon Pletcher. Gretna, La.: Pelican, 1973. 152pp.

The introduction to this book of short character sketches announces the author's purpose to illustrate the way in which social tolerance in New Orleans has created a society filled with distinctive individuals. More than forty chapters present a wide series of non-conformists, including journalists, politicians, criminals, tattoo artists, gamblers, and various scammers, many in the guise of entertainers.

246. Jahncke, Carol Saunders. *Louisiana Visit.* Illustrated by Yvonne Voorthuysen. New York: Carlton, 1976. 94pp.

In this work of juvenile fiction, when twelve-year-old Laura Lowery is sent to stay with her Aunt Wisby and Cousins Catherine and Walt in Vachere, Louisiana, she knows nothing of the South. Her mother is from there, but had fled Louisiana to live in New York City and, later, married an affluent man. When he died she went on a two-year trip to Europe with seven-year-old Laura. Only afterwards did she learn that her inheritance was poorly managed. Now that she needs an operation she has realized she is almost out of money. Even though necessity forced her move, Laura enjoys visiting her aunt and she and Catherine immediately become friends. Their horses are boarded at their next-door neighbor, Mr. Putts, whose wife has been dead for five years. A correspondence begins between Putts and Laura's mother that leads to romance when they meet. Fortunately, Mr. Putts is a wealthy man with a historic plantation that will make a beautiful new home for Laura and her mother. The Wisbys visit New Orleans frequently. One daylong outing in the city ends with dinner at Antoine's. Clearly the attractions of New Orleans are meant to seem an adequate substitute for the cosmopolitan life Laura and her mother are giving up by moving to Louisiana.

247. James, Samuel Humphreys [A Man o' the Town, pseud.]. *A Woman of New Orleans.* The Author, 1889. 238pp.

The story of the post-Civil War life of Mildred Girault, the daughter of Benjamin Rankin, a Mississippi State senator, is that of a struggling widow managing to retain her self-esteem and public image. A great beauty before the war, Girault had many wealthy suitors but out of love married a young physician. He was killed, a Confederate hero, and in the hard years after the war, she moved to New Orleans to provide for her six daughters, operating a boarding house on the 200 block of St. Charles Avenue. Although driven by financial necessity, she is far from mercenary and uses her modest savings to help a wide variety of boarders, drawing her eldest daughter's criticism. While establishing a stance between benefactress and landlady, she also balances enjoying the attentions of men who relish her beauty, while protecting her good name and that of her daughters. The book provides many details about boarding house life in New Orleans, including the operation of such houses and their clientele. The unquestioned respectability of Girault's boarding house means she attracts some society people who come to New Orleans for the season, although financially embarrassed young men (e.g., an unsuccessful lawyer and a German traveling salesman) are her usual clientele. When the boarders gather at dinner, conversation touches on the debate over evolution, the superiority of German culture, and the powerful and wealthy men pursuing Girault. Only a few of the novel's scenes transpire outside the confines of Girault's house and these are in court and in church. Girault remains single, but inherits a fortune from a relative, and she sees her daughters married to young men whom she had started on their careers while they were living in her boarding house. With all of her daughters married, Girault devotes herself to women's clubs and women's reform issues. The novel is clearly the author's homage to his mother-in-law and meaningfully deals with the means by which a woman can live independently in a sexist society.

248. Jamison, C(ecilia) V(iets) Dakin Hamilton. *Lady Jane.* New York: Century, 1891. 233pp.

Traveling from San Antonio to New York City, the refined Mrs. Chetwynd and her daughter, Lady Jane Chetwynd, must transfer to a boat in New Orleans; the experience has disastrous consequences. At this point in their journey Mrs. Chetwynd is becoming ill and after being misdirected to Gretna, swoons in a faint on the street, attracting the attention of the "evil Creole"

Madame Jozain. Suspecting from their garments that the Chetwynds are affluent, she offers them hospitality, while scheming ways to take advantage of them and free herself of the burden of earning a living by making lace. She must proceed cautiously, however, for her son Adraste "Raste" Jozain is even wickeder than she is and could do something precipitous. To appease him, she steals the Chetwynds' railway tickets and a small sum of money. Before Madame Jozain's plotting gets very far, Mrs. Chetwynd dies while Lady Jane is desperately ill with a fever. Lady Jane slowly recovers but has lost her memory and is easily convinced that she is Madame Jozain's Texas niece. To avoid questions from neighbors, Madame Jozain moves to Good Children Street (renamed St. Claude Avenue after 1850), but does not take into account the ease with which Lady Jane will make friends. Before long she has attracted the attention of Modeste, the wife of an affluent dairyman, who is not convinced that Lady Jane is a relative of the Jozains and begins making private inquiries. Lady Jane befriends the D'Houtreves, impoverished French nobility who live in great privacy in a large house on her street. When Diane D'Houtreves notes Jane's interest in music, she teaches her the piano. After a year passes, Jozain and her son begin disposing of valuable linens, jewelry, and money from the Chetwynds' luggage. However, Madame Jozain holds back a substantial sum that she hopes to use to change her circumstances in an undefined way. When Raste absconds with the money, Madame Jozain's health fails and she eventually dies. Lady Jane ends up in an orphanage, but her friends rescue her and reunite her with the woman she and her mother were on their way to visit, Mrs. Lanier. She is restored to her to rightful place in society as the heiress to a French fortune (her mother had gone against family wishes and married an Englishman who took up a land claim in Texas, only to die). The novel reveals a good deal about lower and middle-class life in New Orleans, as well as the way daily contact brings social intimacy among people of various classes. In recounting neighborhood life, the novel introduces modest shops, such as that of a milliner, a greengrocer, and a dairywoman who sells milk and cream cheese.

249. Jamison, C(ecilia) V(iets) Dakin Hamilton. *Seraph: the Little Violiniste.* Illustrated by Frank T. Merrill. Boston: W.A. Wilde, 1896. 298pp.

In this novel for children, a daughter must struggle to honor the legacy of her deceased father. Although Seraph Blumenthal inherited a fine del Gesu violin from her musician father and had the talent and dedication to play the instrument beautifully, her invalid, impoverished mother is beholden to her closest relative, Franz Arnet, a Lutheran pastor, and she accedes to his insistence that the violin be sold and that Seraph should learn to play and teach the piano. Fortunately, heartbroken Seraph has befriended Leonidas Nardi, a knowledgeable bibliophile and bookstore owner, who is convinced of her talent. She wins another supporter when Arnet recruits Professor Vortman to teach piano to his own daughter, Madge, and he pays for Seraph's lessons as well. Vortman quickly discovers Seraph's talent on the violin and allows her to play his own instrument. Nardi and Vortman conspire to get wealthy Royal Street art patroness Madam St. Maxent to become Seraph's benefactress and Seraph gets a Cremona violin as a birthday gift. St. Maxent's son Maurice takes on the quest of recovering Seraph's father's violin, which he does just before Madame Maxent sponsors a musical evening to debut Seraph's talent. This is after Nardi announces that he has provided for Seraph in his estate planning and will pay for her conservatory education in Paris. The major theme of this may have been unusual at the time; instead of advocating obedience to parental authority, young people are encouraged to work hard at perfecting their talents and letting their skill overcome parental opposition. The novel is mostly set in the French Quarter's German immigrant community where music and culture are highly valued. The book reveals the range of artisanry practiced there. Seraph's mother creates elaborate, paper floral displays for weddings and other celebrations, and other French Quarter artisans include seamstresses and milliners (Madge disdains the plan that she become a German professor and longs to become a milliner). Furthermore, Nardi's success as a dealer in early printed books evidences a community of knowledgeable collectors in New Orleans, revealing another aspect of culture in the city.

250. Jamison, C(ecilia) V(iets) Dakin Hamilton. *Thistledown.* New York: Century, 1903. 269pp.

In this tale of lost identity a twelve-year-old boy with acrobatic skills is believed to be the lost member of a well-connected French Quarter family and most of the book is devoted to uncovering the necessary evidence, beginning with an extensive tracing of family history that goes back to 1859. Brothers Anatole and René Chapelle loved wealthy plantation heiress Estelle. She chose René and their marriage produced four children: Honoré, Maurice, and an infant boy and infant girl. While vacationing on an island in 1859, a tidal wave devastated the household, killing all the family, except Honoré and Maurice. Anatole Chapelle raised the boys as his own with the help of his two friends, music engraver Josephe Aubert and his wife, Madame Aubert. Honoré and Maurice lived with the Auberts while Chapelle fought in the Civil War, and even though the boys returned to the Chapelle household, remained close to the Auberts and their daughter Celeste. Maurice later married Celeste (Honoré wed Gabrielle Kenyon, the daughter of a wealthy New Orleans cotton broker). A few months after a girl, Mignon, was born to Maurice and Celeste, they died of fever and, since Josephe Aubert was also dead by this point, Madame Aubert and Chapelle raised Mignon. All would have been well, had not Honoré behaved disgracefully. Chapelle, a Harvard educated lawyer and gentleman banker, had gotten Honoré a job in his bank. Honoré embezzled a large sum of money and absconded to Paris. Out of a sense of honor and fear of scandal, Chapelle secretly covered the debt (using all of his assets). He then resigned from the bank and opened a legal practice. His sacrifices were unknown to Gabrielle Kenyon Chapelle, who falsely believed that Chapelle had driven Honoré away over some family disagreement, and she alienated her oldest son Silvain against Chapelle. When Mignon and Madame Aubert come across the twelve-year-old boy acrobat nicknamed Thistledown performing in a New Orleans park, Madame Aubert is reminded of the young Anatole Chapelle and Mignon is disturbed by the cruelty of Thistledown's caregiver, an Italian fisherman named Costanza. When Chapelle meets Thistledown he is convinced that the boy is René Chapelle's missing baby boy. Thistledown grew up and lives on the island of Pont aux Chenes and Chapelle's investigations take him to the parish priest there. Silvain is drawn into the project and by the time Thistledown is proved to be the missing boy, Silvain has learned the truth about his father and Chapelle's sacrifice. Although Thistledown becomes a part of Chapelle/Aubert domestic life, his childhood friend Tessa, who is later proven to be his sister, prefers island life with her friend, the parish priest. Under the name, Beppo, that he was given in childhood, Thistledown goes to school, but remains undomesticated and, to his uncle's horror, occasionally performs acrobatic tricks in public. After promising to no longer do so, Beppo secretly finds an outlet for his athletic energy by becoming a jockey. In an odd coincidence, the owner of the horse is Senator Kenyon, the brother of Gabrielle Kenyon Chapelle and Silvain's uncle. Silvain witnesses Beppo ride Kenyon's horse to victory, but also sees the horse throw him. He comes close to being permanently crippled and dedicates himself to training for a profession, in which he is aided by Senator Kenyon's influence and a substantial financial settlement. Around this time, Anatole Chapelle recovers his title to a tract of land and his family's financial troubles are solved for generations when a petroleum company discovers oil. Although there are New Orleans-specific references throughout the novel (the Chapelles and Madame Aubert live on St. Phillip Street), the main focus is on family life as exemplified by the close-knit, honorable French Quarter Chapelles.

251. Jamison, C(ecilia) V(iets) Dakin Hamilton. *Toinette's Philip.* New York: Century, 1894. 236pp.

In post-Civil War New Orleans the lives of a group of people struggling to support themselves are transformed when a New York City artist employs several of the children in the group as models and the mystery of their family background is solved. The Toinette of the title is the "mulatto mammy" of the boy, Philip, who lives with his dog Homo in a mansion abandoned after the death of the owner, General Detrava. His closest friend is the girl he regards as his sister, Dea. Dea lives with her ill father in a cottage on Villere Street and a "mulatto" servant named Grande Seline (she is quite stout) who has an oddly named son younger than Philip and Dea called Lilybel. Everyone in this circle practices a craft in order to contribute to living expenses. Toinette makes flowers on wire forms that Philip sells on the street. Dea sells wax models her father molds with subjects from Victor Hugo's books. Seline sells refreshments near a theater. When New York artist Edward Ainsworth is in town painting New Orleans' picturesque streets, he is entranced by the children and their dog and hires them to model for him. When Toinette dies, the childless Ainsworth and his wife unofficially adopt Philip. By a bizarre coincidence, Philip turns out to be the son of Ainsworth's brother who had died in the Civil War. Philip's father had secretly married the daughter of Confederate General Detrava while stationed in New Orleans. So Philip is the rightful owner of the Detrava mansion and stands to inherit several Ainsworth family fortunes. Dea turns out to be an heiress as well. Her father was a member of the extended Detrava family who never talked about his origins since he had been disowned for marrying a French governess. Through a rich Detrava uncle Dea is returned to the family. Although the book includes little general description of New Orleans, the camaraderie of street life is depicted, as well as the lingering effects of wartime economic devastation and social dislocation. Although there are several African-American characters to which white characters are emotionally attached, the book makes clear that they are "mulattoes" (i.e., have been improved by white blood) and not "negroes" (i.e., pure black).

252. Janas, Frankie-Lee (Salliee O'Brien, pseud.]. *Black Ivory*. New York: Bantam Books, 1980. 354pp.

In this historical romance novel, Hester Bell is the focus of lust more often than love. Born in 1843 to African-American slaves on Wabash Thorne's Thornton Plantation, Hester appears to be white and when she is fourteen-years-old trouble begins when a young Thorne family friend named Philip Bennett falls in love with Hester and tries to arrange a marriage. The Thornes and Bennetts are horrified and Hester is immediately consigned to the auction block in New Orleans. The plantation overseer rapes her while she is in confinement and she is sold to Edward Dalton, the thirty-six-year-old owner of a New Orleans clothing factory. Although Dalton is married, he chose his wife Mildred for the dowry that came with her, and even though she has not produced an heir for him (giving him two girls, instead), she rarely permits sexual intercourse. He has an octoroon mistress, Clio, in a house on Rampart Street, with whom he has had two boys that he is raising as white gentlemen in England. However, Mildred has recently heightened her jealous watch over him and he rarely gets to enjoy Clio. So, he immediately takes advantage of the physical availability of Hester. Unfortunately, even through the haze of laudanum addiction, Mildred discovers the couple in flagrante and promptly stabs Dalton to death. Hester flees New Orleans on a showboat and the rest of her dramatic story proceeds after she and Bennett reunite and a startling revelation about her identity means she can lay claim to Thornton. Although more than half the novel is set in New Orleans, the narrative's close focus on issues of race and sexual concourse means that the setting is not fully realized.

253. Janssen, Milton W. *Divided*. New York: Pageant, 1963. 141pp.

Although set in the 1940s, this coming-of-age novel is written from the perspective of the later, post-World War II youth rebellion. The outbreak of World War II forms the backdrop for action that transpires in New Orleans, San Francisco, and Pineville, Virginia. Protagonist Billy Anderson is an angry eleven-year-old at the beginning of the novel. His mother died several years before and he has seen his older brother Johnny and his father, an engineer, become even closer and more distant from Billy as Johnny enters adulthood. In his affluent middle-class house, Billy spends more time with the African-American cook and housekeeper Henrietta than with his father, who works long hours; or with his brother, who is frequently in his car and out on dates. He does have one neighborhood friend, Sammy White, with whom he smokes, reads books on sex, and eventually teams up to force a sexual encounter on a girl their age. Once Billy enters adolescence, reaching six feet by the time he is fourteen, he becomes totally preoccupied with sex. While at summer camp, around the time Germany invades Poland, Billy tries to rape a girl. He is sent home, as he had wished, but quickly gets beaten up by Johnny for peeping while Johnny has sex with his girlfriend Margaret. Once school starts he joins a fraternity and socializes with boys who drink heavily. Billy wrecks both his father's car, and his brother's (once Johnny enlists). Besides drinking and sex, Billy is obsessed with joining the army and eventually enlists with falsified papers. He completes basic training at Fort Sill before anyone finds out his real age. His enraged father allows him to return home, but ends his substantial allowance, forcing Billy to get an after-school, gas station attendant job. He soon breaks his routine for a cross-country trip to Johnny's army base near San Francisco. His father forces him home and mandates his enrollment at Virginia Tech Military Academy in Pineville. During his brief layover in New Orleans he flirts with and eventually rapes Margaret. Although he does well in the harsh environment of military school, he craves freedom and forces the administration to give him his diploma early after he falsely, but credibly, accuses a gym instructor of sexual advances. Returning to New Orleans, he drops Margaret when he finds out she is pregnant with his baby and he becomes a habitué of the French Quarter, dating drug-abusing stripper Cookie Weaver, while earning spending money working in a brokerage firm. After he enrolls at Tulane University, he works as a desk clerk in a Bourbon Street hotel and earns money setting up dates between strippers and college boys. Several crises ensue, including a fight with Johnny during which his brother severely beats him, even though he has returned from war service with one leg. After Margaret and Johnny are engaged to marry (her baby aborted), Billy accedes to Weaver's marriage proposal and a civil wedding. However when Billy confronts his new bride with her rumored lesbianism, she confesses, and when Billy tries to shoot her she is nearly successful in knifing him to death. In recovery, Billy learns from Margaret that she did not marry and a pat conclusion follows that ends the sibling rivalry that has been a controlling factor, although any character reform on Billy's part seems unlikely. New Orleans in this novel is a venue for womanizing and drinking. Some of the establishments that get frequent mentions are the Old Absinthe House, the Roosevelt Hotel, and the Napoleon House.

254. Johnson, Barbara Ferry. *Delta Blood*. New York: Avon Books, 1977. 407pp.

This novel tells the experiences of seventeen-year-old Leah, an octoroon born to quadroon Clotilde, a free woman of color, and Jean-Paul Bonvivier, the son of a white sea captain and Polynesian woman. From early childhood Leah has been made to understand her position. As a woman of color she is not able to legally marry a white man but must find one who will love and protect her, even though she will never be publicly acknowledged as his wife. When Charles Anderson, a Northerner, forces himself on her at a quadroon ball in 1858, Baptiste Fontaine, Creole gentleman, rescues her. Fearing reprisal, she flees her mother's house that very night. On the Natchez Trace white men who claim she is an escaped slave kidnap her. Before they can get her to the Baton Rouge slave market, she is rescued once again by Baptiste Fontaine. When Fontaine rescues her a third time, after she has been falsely accused of theft, she can no longer resist him and becomes his placée. Even though he has a wife, he was forced to wed her through an arranged marriage, and his romantic attachment is to Leah, even though her emotions toward him are too immature and confused to be love. Before long the two have a son, René. After a yellow fever epidemic tragically kills both Clotilde and René, Leah experiences the depth of Fontaine's support and realizes her love for him. The rest of the novel details how she expresses that love in caring for Fontaine after he is badly wounded in battle and must have his legs amputated. The amputation alienated his wife and Fontaine would have been imprisoned by Butler's army of occupation had Leah not hidden him. Just as she believes she has Fontaine safe, Charles Anderson appears as a Union officer and has her imprisoned for being a Confederate spy. The novel describes Voodoo religious ceremonies as a way in which African-Americans maintain their culture, goes into great detail about social conditions for mixed race people, and relates a good deal of history about Civil War New Orleans.

255. Johnson, Barbara Ferry. *Homeward Winds the River* New York: Avon Books, 1979. 471pp.

In this continuation of the author's book *Delta Blood*, the Civil War is over and Leah helps Baptiste Fontaine adjust to the physical challenges presented by his war wounds and his new economic situation. Leah even works to pay back taxes on his plantation, Belle Fontaine. Then a Union officer forces himself on Leah and when he is found dead, she is charged with murder. Fortunately, James Andrews, an Indiana lawyer, concerned that she will not get a fair trial, becomes her defense attorney. During the course of the trial he falls in love with her and proposes marriage. Although she loves Fontaine, Leah knows that they will never be able to marry and that Fontaine should choose a woman from his own social class with whom he can produce heirs. Tantalized by the prospect of freedom and living as a white woman, Leah accepts Andrews' proposal and moves with him to Indiana. As her fear that her race will be discovered wanes, Leah becomes relaxed enough around her neighbors to be appalled by their behavior. She witnesses the physical abuse of an African-American man and the arson of the local Catholic church during a Protestant revival meeting. While Leah is with Andrews, Fontaine reopens his import business in partnership with members of Leah's father's family. He also marries a woman of his own social class. Although Fontaine's business flourishes, his marriage is disastrous and after his wife attempts suicide, the couple becomes estranged. Soon after Andrews dies, and Leah returns to New Orleans; a short time later word comes that Fontaine's wife has drowned. Once again Leah insists that she does not want to follow the traditional role of octoroon mistress and as the novel ends, the couple plans a move to France where they will be able to marry. While the novel is not exclusively set in New Orleans a good deal of the action transpires there and the city is the focus of Leah and Fontaine's emotional life. The novel includes some evocative physical description of the city, but it is mostly focused on social customs, particularly those involving marginalized women (octoroons and prostitutes) and privileged men.

256. Jones, Alice Ilgenfritz. *Beatrice of Bayou Têche.* Chicago: A.C. McClurg, 1895. 386pp.

This novel uses the plight of a mixed-race person to explore racism in the United States. Only the first fifty pages are set in New Orleans. Much of Beatrice's childhood is spent with her grandmother Mauma Salome in the service areas of a French Quarter mansion owned by her white aunt Rosamond La Scalla. Beatrice is the child of René, Salome's daughter, and Ralph La Scalla, Rosamond's brother. After René's premature death, Salome had successfully pleaded with Ralph to emancipate her and Beatrice, but he had not completed the paperwork at the time he died. Salome continued to plead her case with Rosamond, but as she is on her deathbed her distant relation, Madame Maurice La Scalla, easily persuades her of the foolishness of granting Salome and Beatrice their freedom since Salome is an excellent cook and Beatrice will make a perfect maid for Madame La Scalla's daughter Evalina. Soon after Rosamond's funeral Beatrice is taken with her grandmother to live at the La Scalla sugar plantation in Bayou Têche. The New Orleans portion of the novel captures domestic life in the French Quarter from the perspective of servants. Beatrice rarely leaves the confines of the mansion's service yard from which she has views of nearby businesses, including laundresses, a wig-maker, and a glove-cleaner. Protected from social contact, Beatrice develops no self-awareness and does not need to confront the social status incumbent upon her racial makeup until after Rosamond's death, when she is for the first time treated as a slave.

257. Joseph, Robert F(arras). *Odile.* New York: Ballantine Books, 1977. 437pp.

In 1835 in Ohio young Jim MacKay leaves the farm he had helped his family carve out of the wilderness after they all died in an epidemic. Having sold everything to buy goods to resell in New Orleans and establish himself there, Mackay pilots his own flatboat. Near Natchez, he meets

Isaac DaCosta, a Jewish peddler, who guides him through the most dangerous stretch of the Mississippi. Since DaCosta is based in New Orleans, he uses his connections to aid MacKay in profitably selling his goods and shares his boarding house room with him. Determined to open a store, Isaac fails to get MacKay to go into a partnership since MacKay disdains the city life of New Orleans and wants a plantation. He buys land from Placide Martinon, the owner of a huge sugar plantation named Mandragore. MacKay later realizes that Martinon cheated him and sold him swampland that will be difficult to reclaim and the two become rivals. Disdainful of slavery, MacKay labors alongside his workers in draining the swamp and building a house. His social life is still centered on New Orleans where he falls in love upon first sight with Delphine, a quadroon and mistress of the powerful Etienne Bourrier. In the absence of Bourrier in Martinique, the two carry on a romance and MacKay learns of the plight of mixed-race people. Around the same time, Isaac introduces him to Roger Guillon, a Frenchman with a newly patented type of sugar mill. To thwart MacKay's rapid progress, Martinon tells Bourrier of MacKay's affair. However, when the two duel, MacKay wins a hollow victory since he only cripples Bourrier, who then takes Delphine with him to live in Martinique. Later, MacKay focuses his romantic interest on Martinon's sister, Odile. When Martinon discovers them together, to everyone's surprise, he calls no duel, but insists on a wedding, after which MacKay's visits to New Orleans become more intermittent, but throughout the novel the main characters are in the city for entertainments, legitimate and illicit affairs, and for consultations with voudons and Catholic priests. Covering both the Civil War and Reconstruction, this bodice-ripper interjects observations on the evils of slavery, the plight of nineteenth-century women, and the ingenuity of Northerners like MacKay, undiminished by the deleterious effects of slave culture and able to help redeem the South through innovative thinking that made prosperity possible after slavery ended.

258. Judson, Clara Ingram. *Pierre's Lucky Pouch: They Came from France.* Illustrated by Lois Lenski. New York: Follett, 1943. 245pp. (alternate release of the work below)

259. Judson, Clara Ingram. *They Came from France.* Illustrated by Lois Lenski. Boston: Houghton Mifflin, 1943. 245pp.

This work of juvenile fiction presents New Orleans in the early settlement period from the vantage of Jules Remy's family, French immigrants arriving in 1741. Jules Remy had already been to the Louisiana colony to fight in the French-Chickasaw War of 1736. For his service Governor Bienville awarded him a tract of land in New Orleans. However, he returned home to the Remy family in Paris, treating the land as a joke until the Paris house in which the Remys were living burned down, and he needed to recover his fortunes by pursuing information he had gathered about frontier silver deposits while in Louisiana. He leaves his family in New Orleans with his wife's sister, Therese, who had arrived in 1735 as a casket girl and married John Barth, the owner of a lumber mill. Soon after their arrival, the Remys can build a house since wood is cheap and their small amount of Parisian gold is worth much more in New Orleans where hard currency is rare. Remy's son Pierre, a fourteen-year-old who had worked in a cannon makers' shop easily gets a metalworking job since skilled trades are in high demand, and his mother gets work as a skilled seamstress. Much of the narrative is devoted to the ingenious ways in which the Remys gather raw materials to make items they need, establish a garden, and participate in the local economy. Many of their techniques would have been common to other New World colonists, but the book also points out conditions peculiar to New Orleans, such as free wood from abandoned flatboats and wax myrtle plantations. Even in this early period, affluent New Orleaneans travel back and forth to France and French luxury goods are available. Pierre's father Jules returns to New Orleans empty-handed, but the new governor, Marquis Vaudreuil commissions him as captain of a local regiment and the family makes plans to stay in a city that has more opportunities than their native Paris.

260. Judson, Edward Zane Carroll [Ned Buntline, pseud.]. *The Mysteries and Miseries of New Orleans.* New York: Akarman and Ormsby, 1851. 104pp.

One of a series of scandal novels with urban settings printed in cheap editions, this work is mostly set in New Orleans, although the culminating scenes transpire in Cuba. Two roués, Orrin Bird and Mr. Malpin (a Chartres Street merchant who is never given a first name), compete to win the affections of two different women. Each of them faces unique challenges. Adalie d' Bouligny has grown savvy from working in the theater and Fanny Gardner is a married woman. Malpin is aided by Adalie's mother, Minervie (sic) d'Bouligny, a woman for whom money is the ultimate good. Minervie has opposed Adalie's romance with a poorly paid writer named Eugene Beverly and welcomes the rich Malpin's suit. After several expensive dinners and Malpin's promise of a house in her name, Madame d'Bouligny is ready for a wedding and when Adalie continues to resist, Minervie comes up with a scheme involving an Italian seer, Salvi "The Sybill" Medici, and a poison that gives the appearance of death until the antidote is administered. Fanny Gardner's own husband, Charles, an alcoholic gambler who has tested Fanny's love in many ways, furthers Bird's suit. Now, Charles' gambling losses, the effect of falling cotton prices on his income, and his constant drunkenness has brought a crisis. Bird befriends Charles and cautions him against gambling and drinking while taking him to bars and gambling parlors. After Bird pays off Charles' gambling debts, gives Fanny an expensive piece of jewelry, and saves the lives of both Gardners during a yachting accident, Fanny welcomes Bird's overtures and becomes his mistress. With arrangements in place for Madame d'Bouligny to deliver Adalie to Malpin and the consummation of Bird's pursuit of Fanny, the two meet to celebrate their conquests at The Verandah restaurant. A "Yankee reporter" working for *The Picayune* informs Charles Gardner and goes with him to The Verandah where he preemptively informs Malpin that Eugene Beverly was killed in a duel over the honor of Adalie, who died of shock over the news, and has been entombed with him. Then, Gardner kills Bird and escapes New Orleans to Cuba, where he falls in with insurgents. Fanny, seeking revenge, follows Gardner to Cuba and associates with the ruling political party. Before the inevitable capture of the insurgents, Fanny has secured a promise that her husband will be executed with her as a private audience. When the hour of execution comes, Fanny subjects Charles to a lengthy tirade in which she justifies her adultery on the grounds of his years of bad behavior. While this novel references streets, gambling parlors, restaurants and theaters in the French Quarter, it makes slight use of the setting. The book touches on issues of ethnicity in dealing with Italians and Irish people, as well as gender issues.

261. Judson, Jeanne [Frances Dean Hancock, pseud.]. *The Flowering Vine.* New York: Avalon Books, 1964. 192pp.

In this romance novel Cecily Pinchon must begin her adult life by choosing a husband. With her parents both dead, she was raised by her Grandmother Pinchon. Madame Pinchon is affluent and her house is a mansion, set in a park and maintained by African-American servants watched over by a butler/major-domo. Although Cecily socializes with debutantes, she did not come out and instead of continuing her education after high school, decided to work as a hostess at Madame Blanchard's French Quarter restaurant, The Flowering Vine. Both Madame Pinchon and Cecily's boyfriend, third cousin Simon Beaufort, are puzzled by her decision, but consider her job a whimsical notion that will eventually pass. Everyone in Cecily's acquaintance assumes she will marry Beaufort, a newly minted lawyer. However, Cecily has difficulty thinking of him as a lover since they were childhood friends and he is more like a brother. She has concerns over his maturity. He lacks the poise or experience to handle difficult situations in the way she would expect of her husband. When Dr. Theodore Cheney arrives in New Orleans with a letter of introduction to Beaufort, Beaufort and Cecily feel obligated to assist him in his research on extrasensory perception (ESP) that involves nighttime visits to the Bondurant mansion, even though everyone Cheney meets in New Orleans considers him a fraud, despite his academic degrees, and believes he is mostly concerned with money and social advancement. The way in which Beaufort handles the situation provides further evidence of his immaturity. Eventually, Cecily realizes that art gallery owner Vincent Leary, who is a few years older than Beaufort, handles social challenges, like those presented by Cheney, with ease, and begins to accept his interest in her. When Cecily accompanies Cheney and his medium, the simple-minded young Tessie, to the Bondurant mansion, Leary secretly follows them. When Leary resolutely steps in to prevent a near tragedy he confirms Cecily's estimation of him and wins her love and Madame Pinchon's approval. New Orleans in this romance novel is a place where lineage still matters and social interactions reveal the quality of one's family origins. Physical settings are mostly drawn from the French Quarter and history is treated as romantically and tastefully present through architecture, furnishings, and genealogy. Finally, strong characters such as Madame Pinchon and Leary treat less capable persons, like household servants and Tessie, with paternalism.

262. Kane, Frank. *Poisons Unknown.* New York: Dell, 1953. 192pp.

In this noir detective mystery, New York private eye Johnny Liddell is hired by a Southern, organized crime boss, Mary Kirk, to find self-denominated Brother Alfred, a New Orleans religious figure. Since Alfred, had mounted a public campaign against Kirk's bars and gambling parlors before disappearing, Kirk fears that she will become the prime suspect if Alfred does not turn up soon. Liddell's sidekick in New Orleans is beautiful, blonde, twenty-five-year-old Gabby Benton, the owner of a legally registered detective agency that can provide Liddell with a cloak of legitimacy. Benton lives in the Central Business District on Carondelet Street in a multi-story building described as a cliff dwelling. When Brother Alfred contacts Liddell through an underling, Wanda, Alfred indicates that he fears for his own life. When he later dies in a car crash, Liddell believes Alfred has been murdered, despite the police determination of accidental death. Police Chief Sherriff Lalonde is entirely corrupt, in league with criminal organizations, and intimidates private detectives and journalists with beatings and, if violence and threats fail, murders to them. Liddell exonerates Mary Kirk by uncovering a connection between Brother Alfred's apparent murder, international drug dealing, and connections to a syndicate assembling financing to overthrow the government of the Dominican Republic. Finally the "temple" Brother Alfred and Wanda operate is the setting for drugged sexual encounters that are filmed and later used to blackmail participants. The book is of interest for including a *New Orleans Dispatch* reporter, who aids Lidell and introduces the world of investigative journalism, as well as for describing investigative tools of the time like: infrared binoculars and cameras, and a chemical for detecting arson. In addition, the New Orleans police department is shown to be entirely corrupt through the character of Police Chief Sheriff Lalonde. Among the locales mentioned are the Blue Room at the Roosevelt, the Delgado Museum, the Carter Arms Hotel on Lafayette Square, City Park, and the French Market.

263. Kane, Harnett T(homas). *New Orleans Woman: A Biographical Novel of Myra Clark Gaines.* Garden City, N.Y.: Doubleday, 1946. 344pp.

In this fictionalized account of the life of Myra Clark Gaines (1804–1885) the plaintiff in the lengthiest lawsuit in American legal history, Myra is the adopted daughter of military hero Colonel Samuel Davis. Soon after her 1832 marriage to Will Whitney, Myra discovers that property she should have received as a bequest from estate of her biological father, Daniel Clark (1766–1813), a wealthy Southern landowner, was misappropriated. The novel, set in New Orleans as well as Washington, recounts in lengthy detail Myra's struggle to gain her inheritance. After Will Whitney dies, Myra eventually marries the powerful General Edmund Gaines. Through his efforts, parts of her case are argued before the Supreme Court in the 1840s. After winning her court case to prove that Clark was her father and she is his legal heir, further court cases loom, but the death of Gaines, her most powerful advocate adds decades to her struggles. The novel includes physical descriptions of New Orleans, analyses of its qualities, and accounts of social customs as Myra tries to befriend influential people who may help with her search for justice. Through her eyes the reader sees all the changes that have occurred. After the war, land records in the South are in disarray. She continues her legal struggle and returns to Washington to live in a boarding house in 1873. However, by the time of her death in New Orleans in 1885 her legal case is still not settled. Only in 1896 is the suit resolved and Myra's heirs receive $923,788.

264. Kane, Harnett T(homas). *Pathway to the Stars: A Novel Based on the Life of John McDonogh of New Orleans and Baltimore.* Garden City, N.Y.: Doubleday, 1950. 312pp.

This fictional biography of John McDonogh (1779–1850) details the merchant's early nineteenth century rise, to become the largest land owner in the United States, emphasizing McDonogh's ability to make shrewd investment decisions by rapidly assessing changing political conditions and their economic implications. The son of a Baltimore brick maker, McDonogh first appears in New Orleans as an agent for the Taylor family, but starts his own firm as he quickly realizes the importance the city will have as the frontier develops. Harshly judgmental against Roman Catholics, Spaniards, and Creoles, McDonogh would appear to be ill suited to function successfully in a multicultural environment but—surprisingly, he makes some friends. One is his partner Edward Jones, initially sent by Taylor to oversee McDonogh. The other (in this account) is Madame Desiree Boisblanc, a woman he meets on his way to New Orleans. She is a wealthy widow, but is cursed by having sons more concerned with fighting duels than managing property. McDonogh understands the importance of social life to business relationships and establishes an appropriate townhouse in the French Quarter, but he makes little headway in the social realm and even becomes a figure of ridicule when he pursues Micaela (1795–1874), the daughter of Madame Almonester. He finally becomes acquainted with the Johnstons, a family newly arrived from his native Baltimore. Susan, the daughter of the family, is responsive to his attentions, but he is inept in timing and she enters Ursuline Convent. McDonogh stays in New Orleans through the famous battle of 1815, but then closes up his house there to reside on one of his plantations. The novel provides a great deal of historical information and tries to give a sense of the cultural milieus in New Orleans that so challenged McDonogh. Because of his bequests, McDonogh is still known for his philanthropy and the novel makes much of incidents that demonstrate his pragmatism in helping others. The book also presents detailed information about his position on slavery. He did not want to own slaves, but when he purchased land, in the form of plantations, he was also buying slaves. He developed a system by which they could earn their freedom over a period of years. After his difficult courtships, McDonogh remained single, unlike his partner, Jones, who took a quadroon mistress soon after arriving in New Orleans and had a son by the relationship, whom he acknowledged. Concerning this other aspect of race relations, the author claims McDonogh looked askance at miscegenation because of the social status of the children of such relationships.

265. Keating, Lawrence A. [H.C. Thomas, pseud.]. *A Boy Fighter with Andrew Jackson.* Illustrated by Henry E. Vallely. Racine, Wis.: Whitman, 1946. 249pp.

In this retelling of events leading up to the Battle of New Orleans, orphaned teenager Lee Baird plays a crucial role in facilitating Jean Lafitte's (c. 1776–c.1823) alliance with Andrew Jackson (1767–1845). Baird first meets Jackson in 1813 through his father, a former sergeant in a militia commanded by Jackson. When bushwhackers invade the Bairds' frontier home, only the young Baird escapes death. When he seeks Jackson's assistance, the general aids him in securing his father's warehoused goods (cotton, tobacco, and hides) and lets him transport them on a keelboat for sale in New Orleans in return for overseeing the transport and sale of goods for Jackson. After a dangerous river adventure, Baird overcomes the difficulties of selling the keelboat's contents and must then safeguard seven thousand dollars in gold (most of which is Jackson's, eventually with the aid of lawyer and politician Edward Livingston (1764–1836). Shortly afterwards, he is dragooned into sailing with Jean Lafitte's pirates but when it is discovered that he can maintain a ledger, Baird is soon balancing accounts at Lafitte's headquarters on Grand Terre Island. As the British approach New Orleans, the pirate sends Baird to Governor Claiborne to convince him to accept the aid of Lafitte and his men in defeating the British. When Baird meets with Jackson, the general accepts Lafitte's offer, with Baird becoming a liaison between the general and the pirate during the course of the British siege and later seeing action in the battle. By the end of the novel, Lee has returned to Tennessee with his money and begins to prepare for his future as a lawyer. An extensive section of the novel is set in New Orleans and presents a good deal of historical information about the city during the War of 1812 and coverage of Jackson's defense of the city.

266. Keeler, Harry Stephen. *The Voice of the Seven Sparrows.* London: Hutchinson, 1924. 284pp.
　　A substantial portion of this convoluted novel is set in New Orleans; other settings include New York City, Chicago, and on board a ship at sea. When Beatrice Mannerby, half-owner of the *Chicago Morning Leader*, disappears, twenty-nine-year-old reporter Absalom Smith goes on assignment to discover what happened to her. Mannerby's friendship with Sara Fu, a Chinese-French woman she met while studying in Paris, is considered an ominous clue to her disappearance. Since Mannerby's father had considered any contact with a mixed-race person inappropriate, she maintained the friendship through a clandestine correspondence. As Fu, an expert in creating artistic silk-weavings, relocated to New Orleans after Paris, Smith focuses his efforts to locate her in that city's Chinatown, which is described here as one-block long, the 1100 block of Tulane off South Rampart. As with other Keeler novels, there are numerous disguises and mistaken identities. Sara Fu (herself an imposter) is being simultaneously pursued by U.S. government agents for illegal immigration, the Seven Sparrow T'ong (more commonly tong), and another reporter. Smith lives in the French Quarter in the boarding house of a Frenchwoman at 624 St. Anthony's Alley and the novel includes descriptions of the neighborhood, as well as of St. Louis Cemetery and Prytania Street. As with many Keeler novels racism is explicit and focused on Asians and African-Americans.

267. Keene, Carolyn [house pseudonym]. *The Ghost of Blackwood Hall.* New York: Grosset and Dunlap, 1948. 216pp.
　　Although the book jacket synopsis prominently mentions New Orleans, in fact most of this detective mystery for children takes place in Nancy Drew's hometown, River Heights. After a widow retrieved the jewelry she had buried at the request of her husband's ghost, she discovers that the gems are fakes and retains Nancy Drew to recover the real stones. When Drew shows the imitation jewelry to experts, they quickly attribute the work to traveling jewelry salesman, Howard Brex of New Orleans, who has recently been released from a Louisiana prison for fraud. Drew and her girlfriends, chubby Bess Marvin and the oddly named George Frayne, leave immediately for the Southern city, eager for adventure, (and, in Marvin's case, Creole cuisine). On their relatively brief visit, Drew talks with Brex' former employer, but her true leads come from attending a séance and sitting for a spirit photograph. Shortly after she realizes that a woman who attracted her attention on the plane for New Orleans is working in the darkroom, the lights go out and she is abducted. Fortunately, she is able to free herself and escape from an abandoned house. The girls return almost immediately to River Heights where they have many more ghostly adventures. The New Orleans setting is used both as an exotic locale (with women in colorful costumes and talking parrots in abundance), as well as one where various frauds are perpetrated upon tourists.

268. Keene, Carolyn [house pseudonym]. *The Haunted Showboat.* New York: Grosset and Dunlap, 1957. 184pp.
　　In this detective novel for children, Nancy Drew is invited to Mardi Gras by Colonel Havers and his wife Stella in order to engage her assistance in solving a mystery. The Havers will be announcing the engagement of their daughter, Donna Mae, to Alex Upgrove, an Oxford University graduate, during a grand Mardi Gras ball on a retired showboat moored at their plantation, Sunnymead. Workmen have complained of strange accidents on the boat and Drew must solve the mystery in order to get the men to resume work in time. Drew is distracted by the suspicious

behavior of Upgrove, and the suddenness with which he usurped Charles Bartolome (sic) in Donna Mae's affections. Although much of the book is set at Sunnymead and in the bayous, Drew and her friends make several trips into New Orleans where they learn about the city's history, observe a Mardi Gras parade, and have dinner at Antoine's where they are delighted with their oysters Rockefeller and chicken in a bag. Elderly Henry de la Verne and his widowed sister Mrs. Claiborne Farwell, who live adjacent to Sunnymead and whose father used to own the showboat, clear up much of the mystery of the showboat. De la Verne, a cultured bachelor, graduated from Oxford, is able to show that Upgrove is an imposter and Drew uncovers his role in causing the mysterious accidents. African-Americans in the book are presented in the broadest caricatures through the servants Mammy Matilda and Pappy Cole, and Uncle Rufus, a Voodoo priest who lives in the bayou near the showboat.

269. Kelly, Regina Zimmerman. *New Orleans: Queen of the River.* Chicago: Reilly and Lee, 1963. 176pp.

Using four generations of the fictional LaPlace family to bring immediacy to her account, the author presents the history of New Orleans from 1718 to 1877 in this work of juvenile fiction. The account emphasizes the importance of French culture and the Roman Catholic Church. Spanish control is mostly discussed in terms of the resentment of New Orleans residents. The LaPlace family eventually incorporates people from several cultural traditions. In the context of the Louisiana Purchase, the LaPlaces are used to exemplify the positive outcomes of cultural blending that will strengthen America. In recapping New Orleans' history, the book pays most attention to the Battle of New Orleans; the era of steamboat travel when, by many accounts, the city was at its apogee; and the city's occupation by Union troops. The book ends with the withdrawal of federal troops in 1877. Once Kelly abandons the fictional LaPlace family, and catches readers up on what happened after Reconstruction, she mostly emphasizes the preservation efforts that protected and restored the French Quarter.

270. Kelly, Regina Zimmerman. *One Flag, One Land.* Illustrated by Wendy Kemp. Chicago: Reilly and Lee, 1967. 115pp.

In 1802, recently orphaned David Coleman is sent to live with his maternal Francophile uncle Louis Bougeron, a New Orleans printer and newspaper publisher, who resides on Toulouse Street near Royal. In this book for young adults, Coleman arrives to find the port closed to Americans by the Spanish. Coleman's flatboat docks outside the city and he is able to locate his uncle. Instructed in French by his mother, Coleman adapts to the French household that includes, in addition to his uncle, his Aunt Marie and the household "servants," Big Jule and Celeste and their son Miche, who becomes Coleman's personal servant and playmate. Bougeron has long opposed Spanish rule in New Orleans and is eager for the transfer to the French, even though many of his fellows despise Napoleon Bonaparte. Bougeron urges the French to help the American flatboat men and defy the Spanish. In this account, Jean Lafitte (c.1776–c.1823), who plays a prominent role, is a French hero because he defies the Spanish, plunders goods only from their ships, and sells exclusively to the French population in New Orleans, who would otherwise have to pay high prices because of Spanish duties. From the perspective of the novel, French culture dominates New Orleans, as food, language, clothing and architecture demonstrates. Bougeron is soon imprisoned and held for months until the new French government is about to be installed in 1803. He witnesses the transfer to France, but knows this is temporary because of the Louisiana Purchase. Even though Bougeron is supportive of Americans on a personal level (he is a friend of American businessman Daniel Clark, 1766–1813), he is opposed to American control of the city. Just as New Orleans is gathering to hear Governor Claiborne speak during the American takeover, Coleman gets exciting information from Lafitte. A mysterious map that Coleman had inherited from his father documents Lafitte's transfer of valuable land to Coleman's father as payment for legal fees. When Clark learns of Coleman's inheritance he immediately begins to strategize to get the land for a low price.

Lafitte offers to act as Coleman's agent in the sale so that, in obtaining the best possible price, he can get his uncle's business out of debt. The novel's descriptions of New Orleans are shallow, but the 1960s presentation of cultural and political history and acceptance of slavery as a fact of nineteenth-century culture is of interest for their distortions.

271. Kent, Madeleine Fabiola. *The Corsair: A Biographical Novel of Jean Lafitte, Hero of the Battle of New Orleans.* Garden City, N.Y.: Doubleday, 1955. 299pp.

This version of Lafitte's (c.1776–c.1823) life deals extensively with his youth in Haiti and the ways in which the cruelties of revolutionaries there influenced him to treat both his own men and the crews of boats he captured with fairness and respect. The book also elevates Lafitte's role in the Battle of New Orleans to the level of hero. Even prior to the battle, the book claims, Lafitte captured British ships and repeatedly sent messengers to warn the federal government that British agents provocateurs were riling the Indian tribes and that the British planned a full-scale invasion of Louisiana. Lafitte also tried to warn New Orleaneans but anything he said was discredited by focusing on his piracy. In this context Governor Claiborne (c.1772/75–1817) is represented as having a one-sided animosity toward Lafitte. Even though he was continually wronged by Claiborne and could have been affronted by silence from Washington, Lafitte persuades his council to side with the Americans and when American troops attack Grand Terre, he mounts no resistance beyond burning warehouses. Even after this provocation, Lafitte goes directly to General Andrew Jackson to offer him six thousand men to effect a successful defense of the city. Although the book has various settings, it is primarily another retelling of events that led up to the Battle of New Orleans.

272. Keyes, Frances Parkinson. *The Chess Players: A Novel of New Orleans and Paris.* New York: Farrar, Straus and Cudahy, 1960. 533pp.

Nineteenth-century chess champion Paul Morphy (1837–1884) has long been proudly claimed as one of New Orleans most famous native sons. Keyes' fictionalized account of his life is unusual both for devoting considerable attention to his grandparents and for imagining his life during the more than twenty-five years between the time he became an adult and his death at age forty-seven, a time period about which little is known. About Morphy's grandfathers, much is known. Diego Morphy, his paternal grandfather, was Spanish Consul in New Orleans and had a far higher social rank than Joseph Le Carpentier, Morphy's maternal French grandfather, whose wealth stemmed from a successful French auction house. However, both men loved chess and had frequently competed against each another. So, Diego stipulated that his son Alonzo could marry Telcide Le Carpentier, if the father of the bride would provide a rich dowry and a luxurious bridal residence. Alonzo, a young lawyer of promise, went on to become a justice in the Supreme Court of Louisiana. Given the social prominence of the Morphys it is not surprising that much of the New Orleans section of the novel deals with social events and prominent antebellum historical characters. The Morphys consider chess playing a pastime and Paul does not play competitively even after beating a chess master when he is twelve. He continues to study, finishing college earlier than usual, and receiving his law degree from Tulane University in 1857 when he is nineteen. Still too young to practice law, he spends time playing chess and is invited to play in the first American Chess Congress in New York City in 1857. Victorious in his matches, he is acclaimed America's champion and he goes on to play in European competitions. In this account Morphy has a thwarted love affair with Charmian Sheppard, a woman Paul's family considers inappropriate since the Sheppards are Yankees and a mercantile family. When Charmian marries someone else Paul suffers a nervous breakdown and stops playing chess. He then returns to New Orleans after accidentally coming upon Charmian's body soon after she has murdered her husband and committed suicide. The novel provides description of upper-class family life and tells the story of one of New Orleans' most famous native sons.

273. Keyes, Frances Parkinson. *Crescent Carnival.* New York: Julian Messner, 1942. 807pp.

Covering three generations of love affairs, economic and personal triumphs, and dozens of social events, this society novel focuses on the cultural conflicts that still remained in New Orleans into the mid-twentieth century and that divided traditional Creole families from other wealthy Americans. In 1890, the Breckinridges, originally from Kentucky, have a magnificent plantation, Splendida, and fine townhouses. However, they have not been accepted by Creole families because they are Protestants and do not follow any of the Creole traditions that focus social life on family gatherings where behavior is closely prescribed, especially for women. When Andrew Breckinridge takes an interest in debutante Estelle Lenoir, there is no official way in which he can make her acquaintance and he begins meeting her surreptitiously, waiting for her before and after Mass, for instance, when she is unchaperoned. Any direct approach to her family is rebuffed. Lenoir rapidly falls in love with Breckinridge, but when he proposes elopement, she refuses and marries the man chosen for her by her family, Marcel Fontaine, the brother of her close friend Clarisse, and a man from her social class and cultural milieu. Years later, Estelle's granddaughter, Stella, defies her parents and marries a politician, Raoul Bienvenu, ignoring Estelle's suggestion that she return the interest of Breckinridge's grandson, who ends up making his own unlikely but fortuitous choice of a wife. As in others of her novels, Keyes provides an incredible amount of social history, describing actual society events and figures, traditions, aspects of household management, clothing, and menus. Several Louisiana and New Orleans political issues are presented in some detail, including the Louisiana Lottery.

274. Keyes, Frances Parkinson. *Dinner at Antoine's.* New York: Julian Messner, 1948. 422pp.

Both murder mystery and romance, this work is above all a society novel presenting upperclass life in post-World War II New Orleans. The dinner of the title begins the novel. Wealthy shipping magnate Orson Foxworth hosts the event to celebrate his return from an extended business trip to Central America and to introduce his niece Ruth Avery to his New Orleans circle as she begins a six-week Mardi Gras visit. Although Avery is the youngster in this group of thirty and forty-year-olds, she is in some ways the most perceptive and mature. Her uncle, for instance, a most eligible bachelor because of his wealth and appearance, has for years been enamored of Amélie Lalande, a young widow with two adult daughters, Caresse and Odile Lalande St. Amant. Although Lalande returns Foxworth's affections, her stipulations that she must continue to live in the family mansion on Richmond Place and that any romance must lead to a cathedral wedding continues, to make Foxworth hesitate instead of taking action or looking elsewhere for love. Lalande's daughters continue to live in wings of the Lalande mansion, a slightly scandalous situation since Odile's husband Léonce is carrying on an affair with Caresse, while his wife's health deteriorates from paralysis agitans. Léonce is a "sensualist" and "gourmand" (rather than gourmet), who has made so poor a match with Odile, that even during courtship days everyone assumed his aim was to marry Amélie. Odile had for several years before her marriage been romanced by an idealist, the cultured artist and connoisseur, Sabin Duplessis, with whom she continues platonic meetings, unaccompanied by her husband. Should Avery (or the reader) be in doubt about Duplessis' over-refinement having prevented a marriage, Foxworth asserts that Duplessis is not a "pantywaist," having been a decorated captain during the war. With Odile unavailable, Foxworth makes certain that Avery meets both Duplessis and the wealthy young archeologist Russell Aldridge, whose travels to remote digs is cited as a guarantee of his manliness, while his love for camellias and gardens is said to merely indicate his idealism. In this atmosphere of Mardi Gras excitement and romance, a murder is committed. In contradistinction to the terse noir detective mysteries of the time period, this book overflows with descriptions of meals, furnishings, clothing, and social events that could prove of great interest to cultural historians. Keyes furthers the authenticity of her work by including actual friends and acquaintances, including restaurateurs, reporters, and police detectives.

275. Keyes, Frances Parkinson. *Madame Castel's Lodger.* New York: Farrar, Straus and Cudahy, 1962. 471pp.

Keyes took a great deal of interest in Confederate General Pierre Gustave Toutant Beauregard (1818–1893), in part because she owned the New Orleans house in which he lived immediately after the Civil War. Here, Keyes envisions Beauregard's emotional situation after the war. Impoverished and twice widowed, he refuses to take the loyalty oath and, as an unreconstructed Confederate, is a worry to his children and many relatives in the area, since he could be subject to harsh treatment by the U.S. government. He lives at 1113 Chartres Street, the same house where he had honeymooned years before with his first wife, Caroline Deslonde. His days are spent sifting through salvaged personal papers, piecing together the story of his life, and documenting his Civil War actions. His social life focuses on Simone Castel and her mother, boarders in another wing of the house, who are also caretakers for the house as the owner makes final arrangements for its sale. Beauregard helps Castel by using his connections to get information about Castel's missing son, a very young Confederate drummer boy but he never returned. As Keyes tells her story, she emphasizes the ways in which Beauregard's sophisticated cultural perspective (he was educated in New York City and graduated from West Point) put him at odds with other Confederate generals. According to her, he was also often in conflict with Jefferson Davis, due to aspects of his Creole identity (which Keyes goes at great lengths to elucidate). Although the narrative is mostly concerned with past events, Beauregard's occasional forays beyond his lodgings give some indication of conditions in New Orleans in the years immediately after the Civil War. This was a time in which so many people who had once been wealthy social leaders were reduced to poverty and newly moneyed people, often Northerners, took prominent roles in society and politics. By the end of the book Beauregard has become chief engineer and general superintendent of the New Orleans, Jackson, and Great Northern Railroad and his anxiety about the financial circumstances of his three adult children eases. (Beauregard went on to wealth after he was appointed supervisor of the Louisiana Lottery in 1871 following a series of engineering positions, including one in which he created a system of cable-powered street railways for New Orleans.)

276. Keyes, Frances Parkinson. *Once on Esplanade: A Cycle Between Two Creole Weddings.* New York: Dodd, Mead, 1947. 202pp.

In this fictionalized account of Marie Louise Villere Claiborne's (1867–1963) girlhood in the 1880s, young readers learn about affluent Creole family life in the time period. As Keyes indicates in her preface, she based her account on a series of conversations with Mrs. Claiborne. After an account of the wedding of Marie Louise's sister Helmine to James Dupas, a French vice-consul to New Orleans, the book describes the protected life of girlhood, school days at the Cenas Institute at the corner of Claiborne and Esplanade avenues, daily and specially-prepared family meals, annual holidays, such as graveyard visits on All Saints Day, Race Day, visits to the family plantation and to the Gulf of Mexico, opera attendance, and Mardi Gras. The Villere family goes into mourning upon the death of their mother and Marie Louise, as the oldest girl still at home, becomes the hostess at events in the family home, even though her activities in general are very restricted, since she is an unmarried woman. She later makes her social debut in typical fashion, seated in a box at the opera, receiving callers, and bouquets. Later that year she is in the court of a Mardi Gras queen and attends a series of balls and entertainments. While the book touches on controversial matters, such as dueling and the Civil War, the work is mostly a sentimentalized view of a life in a very privileged household and matters such as Reconstruction politics, social class, and racism are not even obliquely raised. The novel ends with Marie Louise's marriage to Fernand Claiborne, through which the family of the first Creole governor of Louisiana is linked to that of the first Anglo-Saxon governor of the state.

277. King, Charles. *Kitty's Conquest.* Philadelphia: J.B. Lippincott, 1884. 302pp.

This romance novel set in the Reconstruction-era South promotes an end to regional antipathies through increased contact among civilians to defuse lingering animosities. As a case in point, the narrator, "Mr. Brandon of New Orleans," observes the whole course of a romance between Kentuckian Kitty Carrington and Union soldier Frank Amory. Brandon, originally from New York, graduated from Columbia University, and fought in the Union army. However, he lives in New Orleans, and has no lingering animosity toward Southerners, although he is a fierce critic of the Ku Klux Klan. By contrast, Kitty hates anyone from the North. However, when recent West Point graduate Frank Amory behaves chivalrously toward her, she begins to change her mind. The beginning of the novel is set during a house party at a country plantation owned by Kitty's uncle. However, the last one hundred and seventy pages are set in New Orleans, to which Brandon has returned and Amory is drawn when a friend of his falls ill with fever. Kitty soon follows to aid the fever-stricken, while secretly hoping to spend more time with Amory. When he falls ill, Kitty assists his mother in nursing him, socializes with her, and is drawn more closely to Amory. Not long after Amory recovers, his regiment is called to the Dakota Territory and, amidst departure preparations, he and Kitty become engaged. The New Orleans content of the novel mostly consists of descriptions of street scenes and socializing at public venues (Moreau's, The Varieties Theatre, the opera, and a military review).

278. King, Grace Elizabeth. *Balcony Stories.* New York: Century, 1893. 245pp.

King describes her stories as those of a type that would be told on a balcony after dark in a family setting. All of the stories capture the suffering of women, most of them are clearly set in New Orleans, and many deal with the financial and social losses brought by the Civil War. For example Idalie Sainte Foy Mortemart des Islets, a plantation belle before the conflict, is reduced to poverty and works as a schoolteacher after the conflict. A cantankerous perpetual bachelor who marries her out of respect for the old days rescues her. The Mimi of "Mimi's Marriage" has a more pleasant escape from post-bellum poverty when a Northerner, who is not wealthy, but kind and hard working, proposes and agrees to care for her sister and mother. She must give up her romantic notions of a suitor, but comes to believe her real-life husband far preferable to her imaginary prince. The settings of other stories include a riverboat, a slave pen, a girl's school, and a bayou.

279. King, Grace Elizabeth. *La Dame de Sainte Hermine.* New York: Macmillan, 1924. 296pp.

As this novel opens in 1720, the ship on which Marie Alonge sailed from France arrives in the port of Mobile, Alabama. Alonge's mother died when she was a child and her father maintained her in a convent school until his death around the time she was sixteen. At that point, her uncle, the unscrupulous Raymond de St. Hermine, became her guardian, and in order to gain control of the two rich estates to which she was heiress, deceived her into marrying his son. When she refused to consummate the union, or even acknowledge it, he had her sent to the Louisiana Territory under a *lettre de cachet.* Fortunately, upon her arrival in Mobile she falls under the protection of Governor Bienville (1680–1767), the widow Madame Catherine, and the Chevalier Henri de Loubois. Madame Catherine takes her into her household and when Bienville moves to New Orleans in 1723, he gives the women a house and property in the city. Alonge's plight inspires semi-official investigations on her behalf that transpire over a number of years. She is finally offered the opportunity to return to France and live under the protection of a noble family, but rejects this offer for she has become fond of her life on the frontier and fallen in love with the Chevalier de Loubois. When she finally learns that her uncle is dead after his son, her husband, assaulted him and absconded, she is told that she will never be able to recover her estate, but can legally marry, now that her husband is a fugitive. Although significantly set in New Orleans, the book is most concerned about the Louisiana Territory and recounts historical incidents, focusing mostly on extended periods of Indian warfare and changes in political control of the territory.

280. King, Grace Elizabeth. *Monsieur Motte*. New York: A.C. Armstrong and Son, 1888. 327pp.

Marie Modeste is a seventeen-year-old girl who graduates from the Institut de St. Denis in the French Quarter where she has been a boarder for thirteen years. When her guardian, Monsieur Motte, does not claim her, the school directress, Madame Lareveillere, realizes that she has never had any direct contact with Motte. A mixed-race hairdresser named Marcelite Gaulois, who sometimes does the girls' hair, confesses that she has secretly been paying for Modeste's education. She cared for Modeste's mother in her final illness and took pity on the orphaned child. Gaulois is reviled for her presumption and Lareveillere actively employs the old girl network to find a wealthy man to marry Modeste before any scandal can attach to her. Modeste is presented at a series of debutante balls and the novel provides a great deal of information about the tradition of such events, as well as using them to reveal social tensions of 1870s New Orleans, mostly focused on shifting social status. There is much open evaluation of marriage prospects based on a combination of ancestry and wealth. The dowerless Modeste is not highly rated, but nonetheless the most eligible man, Charles Montyon, recently arrived from Paris with his wealthy stepmother, notices Modeste. The romance progresses, but is almost derailed when Modeste refuses to sign a marriage contract that excludes her from any right to Montyon's wealth or property. By the time of the wedding, however, she is the wealthiest partner in the marriage, for long-suffering Gaulois has been able to reclaim Modeste's rightful inheritance, a sugar plantation. While on the surface a somewhat frivolous society novel concerned with the friendships and personal rivalries of a set of women, most of whom graduated from the Institut de St. Denis, the book raises issues of gender, race, and status anxiety in 1870s New Orleans.

281. King, Grace Elizabeth. *The Pleasant Ways of St. Médard*. New York: Henry Holt, 1916. 338pp.

In 1865 the Charles Talbot family, dispossessed former plantation owners, and their freed African-American slaves, arrive in New Orleans to settle in the fictitious St. Médard Parish (probably based on St. Bernard Parish since it is described as one of the farthest outlying neighborhoods of the city still reachable by city horse-car and has a large military barracks on its boundary which was established by General Jackson in 1832). Although the Talbots had not had great monetary wealth, they had owned a considerable property, including some slaves, and benefited from their social prestige to get political and social positions. While most of his income was derived from agriculture, Charles Talbot maintained a law office in New Orleans, mostly for social and business contacts. After serving as a Confederate officer, he finds his land confiscated and is relieved to discover that his office boy, Tommy Cook, has kept his legal practice intact. Talbot, a cultivated man resigned to his post-war poverty, is glad to have some profession, even if he takes no pleasure in practicing law. He faces intense competition from other formerly non-practicing gentleman lawyers and newly arrived Northerners who get preferential treatment. While Talbot is resigned, his wife, from whose perspective much of the story is told, is not. She is particularly offended by the only rich family in St. Médard, the San Antonios, Italian immigrants and antebellum saloon owners, who quickly built a fortune originating in the purchase at low cost of valuable possessions and commodities from desperate Confederates. While the San Antonios thrive in a new world in which the prerogatives of birth are gone and replaced by business competition, the Talbots decline. Mr. Talbot is passed over for jobs and reduced to working for a pittance for lawyers who are retained at high pay as legal counselors, but have not even the basic skills to write their own briefs. Mrs. Talbot secretly goes to newly powerful men and women to try to barter pre-war status for employment for her husband only to be scorned and slighted. The final blow strikes when Talbot dies of fever. Fortunately, self-taught Tommy Cook has passed the bar and becomes the sole support of the ever-haughty Mrs. Talbot, maintaining her and her children in their St. Médard hovel. In a delicious irony, when the patriarch of the San Antonios dies at the same time as Talbot, Tommy Cook becomes the wealthy widow's financial and legal advisor, making a handsome living. King uses the Talbots' former slaves to show the plight of "good Negroes" who thrived under the control of a benevolent master and fall into laziness and outright villainy in their new, undisciplined state, under the influence of "city Negroes." Through the stories of the families of St. Médard and Mrs. Talbot's trips to business and residential districts in better parts of New Orleans, King provides a wealth of social detail about the city immediately after the Civil War.

282. King, Grace Elizabeth. *Tales of a Time and Place*. New York: Harper and Brothers, 1892. 303pp.

Three of the five stories in this volume are set in New Orleans. The Reconstruction story "Bonne Maman" tells the story of the impoverished final years of Mademoiselle Nenaine, a once wealthy woman reduced to taking in sewing and living in the Back-of-Town neighborhood with her orphaned granddaughter Claire, whose father Edgar was killed in the war and whose mother died shortly thereafter. In "Madrilène, or Festival of the Dead" the title character, who has been told she is of mixed race, lives in poverty as a lowly domestic in the boarding house of Madame Laïs, where she is mistreated by Laïs and her daughters, all of mixed race. Madrilène looks forward to the Day of the Dead when she sells funeral wreaths, fantasizes about going to sleep in one of the beautifully maintained tombs, and visits the grave of her putative mother Rosémond Delauney. After a public fight with a Laïs daughter, who she stabs, Madrilène discovers she is white and not the daughter of Delauney. The story details the celebration of All Souls Day and explores the implications of mixed race heritage. The story "In the French Quarter, 1870" presents tensions brought by the Franco-Prussian War to New Orleans residents who trace their heritages respectively to France or Germany. In a subplot concerning the plight of learned Monsieur Villeminot, the conflicted social status of impoverished scholars is raised. The characterizations, obviously based on first-hand observation, provide a valuable social document of New Orleans during the 1870s.

283. Knapp, George L. *A Young Volunteer at New Orleans*. New York: Dodd, Mead, 1930. 271pp.

In this boys' adventure novel, John Preston, although a teenager, has already served with General Jackson (1767–1845) and behaved heroically during the Creek Indian War. In 1814, he is determined to fight with Jackson in the defense of New Orleans. Since the book is intended for children, the narrative is interrupted by digressions that inform readers about many aspects of New Orleans history, the ethnic makeup of the city, the nature of piracy (and the relative morality of the undertaking in this time period), as well as the events leading up to the Battle of New Orleans. Preston is waylaid by Lafitte's pirates on his way to Mobile to join Jackson, and while their prisoner witnesses the British appeal to Lafitte. Lafitte associate, Edward Livingston, then sends him as an official emissary to Jackson in Mobile, bearing information about the British plans for attack and Lafitte's offer of support. After Preston returns to New Orleans via Grand Terre, Lafitte includes him in a meeting with Governor Claiborne as a witness to the British offer. More than half the book recounts preparations for hostilities and the tactical actions against the British. In this novel, Preston plays the instrumental role in getting Jackson to accept Lafitte's assistance.

284. Knight, Gladys. *Binny's Women*. New York: Century, 1931. 310pp.

This novel about social class in New Orleans focuses on the McElroy family. Binny McElroy arrived in the city as a poor carpenter and through hard labor had established a successful contracting business. His wife Netta died when his daughter, the oddly named Joel, was eight, nine years prior to the action of the novel. When Joel returns from boarding school to the McLeroy's servant-manned house on Prytania Street, Binny is contemplating a second marriage to twenty-seven-year-old Georgia Tabor, an impoverished society woman from St. Louis. Even though Joel is scandalized that her father is twice the age of Tabor, the wedding proceeds and Georgia takes control of Binny and his house, banishing Joel's dog, remodeling, and having frequent guests. She even suggests that Binny sell his house and move to Audubon Park. The tensions in the household are described in great detail, although Joel cannot articulate her most substantive complaint about

Georgia, for she believes her stepmother and Nick Spalding are having an affair. When Joel finds her father dead from a heart attack, with a poison pen letter revealing the affair clutched in his hand, Joel considers Georgia a murderess. Binny's will stipulates that Joel's half of the estate be held in trust by her stepmother until she reaches the age of twenty-one. Intent on freeing herself from Georgia, Joel moves out and gets a job in a large music store. Although she had despised society people for their shallowness and meanness, she comes to realize that her co-workers also have their shortcomings and she eventually reaches a rapprochement with Georgia. The focus of this novel is domestic and the descriptions of New Orleans remain fairly general. Some details are provided concerning the operations of an upper-class household, working life in a department store, and social gatherings.

285. Knipe, Emilie Benson and Alden Arthur Knipe. *The Treasure House.* Illustrated by Margaret Ayer. New York: Century, 1930. 300pp.

In this adventure tale for children, a brother and sister go to New Orleans to find their unjustly banished father. Out of favor with Louis XV, the Marquis de Montrouge-Laborde is an easy prey for his nephew, the Chevalier de Laborde, who, in 1763, has exiled him to New Orleans. His pregnant wife is left behind in France with their six-year-old son Joseph. In 1770, weakened by illness, she sends thirteen-year-old Joseph and his now six-year-old sister Corinne to New Orleans under the protection of nuns from the Ursuline Convent to protect the children from the evil Chevalier de Laborde. After several adventures, Corinne charms a man named Rougemont in Cuba, who makes arrangements for her and Joseph to live in his house in New Orleans. The house, under the care of a family of free people of color and the oversight of Father Dagobert, turns out to be the treasure house of the title, where Rougemont was protecting the valuables of members of the Rebellion of 1768, which for a time had prevented the Spanish governor from taking control of New Orleans. The reason he had been in Havana was to plead for their release from prison. Most of the narrative is devoted to the children's efforts to find their father, protect themselves from being kidnapped by agents of their evil relative, and protect the Rougemont house from thieves (in this they are eventually aided by the governor's troops). New Orleans history between 1770 and 1778 is mostly conveyed through changes in Spanish governors. When Corinne befriends Philadelphian Lewis Bruce, an assistant to Oliver Pollock (1737–1823), who is in New Orleans in 1777 to persuade the Spanish governor to aid the Americans in their fight against the British, the novel begins to introduce details about the American Revolution and the debate over Spanish involvement. Unlike other novels of the time period, African-Americans are described with great respect.

286. Knoblock, K(enneth) T(homas). *There's Been Murder Done.* New York: Harper and Brothers, 1931. 337pp.

The omniscient, anonymous narrator of this account of a sensational murder at first seems to admire Police Captain Timothy Hogan of the tough Fourth Precinct, who had won attention early in his police career for his six-foot-four-inch stature and muscles. Now in his fifties, Hogan enjoys broad popular support for crime fighting. His techniques, involving intimidation, psychological humiliation, and the use of force, bother no one since he keeps order in the city's worst neighborhoods. The book's extended account of the murder investigation of the decapitation of two sisters and a man, serves as an example of Hogan's techniques, although the reader may begin to doubt the public estimation of Hogan. He is unconcerned about seeing an innocent man hang for the crime, thinking it more important to public order to "solve" the crimes rather than investigate them. The victim of Hogan's criminal investigation is Frank O. Landry, the thirty-two-year-old husband of murdered Marie Thibault Landry. Frank grew up in rural Louisiana and rose to management positions in grocery stores. Unfortunately, his business acumen did not translate into savviness in his personal life and he married a woman who was never content with the money he earned. When the couple moved to New Orleans after a promotion, Marie's sister Theresa came along and led Marie into casual prostitution to finance the jewelry and clothing Landry's salary could not support. Days after the police discover the decapitated bodies of Marie, Theresa, and a "john," they pick up Landry. He claims that after too much to drink he bemoaned his situation to a red-haired sailor and before he knew it, the two of them were hiding in Landry's apartment. When his wife, sister, and their client appeared, the sailor hacked them to death with a machete. The horrified Landry fled. After a half-hearted attempt to find the red-haired sailor, Hogan charges Landry and falsifies evidence to get him convicted, even though, had he investigated, he would have found the red-haired, sailor. In addition to depicting the physical environments of the New Orleans criminal justice system (police station, jails, courtrooms), the novel describes the French Quarter, Kenner, and Fort St. Philip and surfaces a range of social attitudes on race and gender. African-Americans in the novel are treated in demeaning terms and the lynching in which Hogan participated is sickeningly recounted. The Prohibition-era New Orleans of the novel is an entirely corrupt place where alcohol is widely available and prostitution rampant.

287. La Farge, Oliver. *The Copper Pot*. Boston: Houghton Mifflin, 1942. 295pp.

In this novel of a young man's journey of self-discovery, immediately prior to World War II, New Englander Tom Hartshorn lives in New Orleans' artistic French Quarter, associating with a whole circle of aspiring artists. The Depression and war in Europe mean that they flock there, as earlier they would moved to Paris and Montmartre. Unlike many of his friends, Hartshorn has the security of steady trust fund payments. Orphaned as a youngster, he was raised by an aunt and uncle, but his Rhode Island family goes back many generations and he benefits from their industry and thrift. His guardian uncle has been surprisingly indulgent, allowing Hartshorn to drop out of Harvard College as a sophomore and move to New Orleans on his own. By the time the novel commences, Tom has lived in New Orleans for several years and won respect as a promising artist. He rents the entire floor of a house on St. Peter's Street and employs a daily maid who cooks and cleans for him. The members of his circle frequent the Pen and Palette Club, a kind of artists' cooperative where art supplies are sold, a rental library operates, and the artists sell their work to tourists. The artists patronize cheap French Quarter restaurants, drink gin and absinthe at local bars, and gather in each other's studios, where they often live and sometimes cohabit with members of the opposite sex without formally marrying. Despite their bohemianism, the painters in this circle do look for external validation in the form of the New Orleans Art Institute Goldwater Prize, which entails a five hundred dollar prize and exhibition in New York City. While his friends consider Tom a major contender, they also believe he has not entirely thrown over his Puritan upbringing, making his artwork cautious and bringing frigidity to his relations with women. Throughout the novel Tom yearns after women who end up with other men. The book details French Quarter life in the 1930s and the great impact that seasonal heat waves had on garret dwellers. In this social milieu one finds prostitutes, homosexuals, women who are openly seeking husbands out of economic necessity, and women living independently and working as artists or writers. However, African-Americans are still not encountered as social equals, and French Quarter artists, whether they are painters or writers, tend to be from outside the Deep South. Even though the Depression continues for many Americans, affluent tourists escaping Northern winters contribute importantly to the New Orleans economy. Boarding house life and the frequency with which people entertain guests in even modest apartments are major factors for the novel's characters.

288. Laing, Sallie Wear. *Her Black Body*. Newark, N.J.: Essex, 1921. 324pp.

The narrator of this disjointed tale of the occult notes in a preface that she based it on the life of Mona Middleton, a member of her social set in the Reconstruction South, but enriched the story with details from her own experiences. The affluent protagonists all stay in family houses in New Orleans from time to time and many of their most important social events are held in the city. However, they travel to East Coast resorts, South America, and their plantation homes as well.

The book deals with race and gender and the title refers to the conviction of an African-American seer, Bet, that all of her powers and her entire spiritual nature can be attributed to a higher "white" self that she also comes to identify with Mona Middleton, her patroness. Bet comes to hate her black body so much that she commits suicide. The novel describes social events, details the foods served, and relates conversations between whites and African-Americans that reveal social attitudes.

289. Laird, Marion Murdoch (Lind). *Impounded Waters: A Novel of John McDonogh*. New Orleans: The Author, 1951. 114pp.

An admiring, distant descendant wrote this fictionalized biography of McDonogh's life. McDonogh, who was born in Baltimore in 1789, had his whole life course altered by his first job with an important shipping firm. Around his twenty-first year he was sent with a cargo to New Orleans and, realizing the importance of the developing city within international shipping networks, began a shipping and exchange business. Although the firm got off to a slow start, business flourished after the Louisiana Purchase. He became a wealthy man and was thus entitled to an important position in New Orleans society, but his Presbyterian religion, commitment to temperance, and opposition to slavery all worked against him. Since the real-life McDonogh was considered a miser and recluse during his lifetime, Laird takes pains to describe the ways in which he aided his family, treated his slaves respectfully, and practiced his religion. Laird also tries to unravel the rumors concerning his romantic life. Supposedly two disappointments in love kept him from marrying and propelled him to increasingly withdraw himself from society. The first misalliance was with the daughter of Don Almonester. Although the Creole family at first permitted the suit, the dowry arrangements were not concluded before the visiting Count Pontalba made a proposal and Don Almonester dismissed McDonogh as a commoner and a Protestant. Having been rejected once on religious grounds, it may seem surprising that the object of McDonogh's second romance was Suzanne Johnston, the daughter of a Roman Catholic Baltimore family, friendly with Governor Claiborne. Laird presents Suzanne as in love with McDonogh, but prevented by her priest from entering into marriage with a Protestant. Instead, she became a nun at Ursuline Convent. According to Laird, Johnston's vows inspired McDonogh's decision to sell his New Orleans mansion at Chartres and Toulouse Streets to live a secluded life on his plantation in what is now Algiers. Much of the rest of the book describes McDonogh's acquisition of land and slaves as part of a plan to end slavery, since his slaves were able to earn their freedom through their work and received an education on McDonogh's plantations (in violation of the slave code). By his death in 1850, McDonogh was supposedly the largest individual landholder in the United States and one of the largest slave owners. His will stipulated a plan for the manumission of his slaves and created a trust to fund free public education for whites and freed blacks in Baltimore and New Orleans. As part of her narrative, Laird summarizes the history of New Orleans between 1800 and 1850, spending most time on the War of 1812, and the Baratarian pirates.

290. L'Amour, Louis. *Treasure Mountain*. New York: Bantam Books, 1972. 187pp.

Roughly fifty pages of this Western adventure novel take place in 1870s New Orleans. Twenty years prior to the events recounted here, Pierre Bontemps hired Orrin Sackett, a frontiersman who spent most of his time in Tennessee and Kentucky, as a Western guide. The Sackett family never heard from Orrin again and to ease their mother's mind in her advancing age, two of Sackett's sons, his namesake Orrin, and William "Tell" Sackett, travel to New Orleans from their current property holdings in New Mexico. Orrin, a lawyer accustomed to cities, arrives first to gather leads. When Tell arrives at their designated rendezvous point at the St. Charles Hotel, Orrin does not appear and Tell realizes something untoward must have happened. He quickly learns that Orrin was witnessed having a mildly heated exchange with André Baston, a member of the well-known affluent Creole family, of which Pierre Bontemps was a member. With the aid of a local Gypsy named Tinker, Tell rescues Orrin from a bayou houseboat, where he is being held captive and interrogated by agents of the Bastons. The Sacketts then leave New Orleans to regroup in New Mexico before following their father's route to the West, now that they know that Bontemps had a map to thirty million dollars worth of gold. In addition to the St. Charles Hotel, the book mentions the Absinthe House and a whole series of dive bars on Gallatin Street.

291. Lane, Frederick A. *A Flag for Lafitte: Story for the Battle of New Orleans.* Illustrated by Leonard Vosburgh. New York: Aladdin Books, 1954. 191pp.

This work of juvenile fiction describes events surrounding the Battle of New Orleans from the perspective of Philip Duvall, a teenaged office boy for the law firm of Edward Livingston (1764–1836) and John Randolph Grymes (c.1746–1854). Duvall is an Acadian and has strong feelings against the British that are aroused when he hears about the burning of Washington, DC in 1814. Initially, however, he has difficulties siding with Americans who are still much resented in New Orleans. He is not surprised that his grandfather, an ardent patriot, is eager to defend New Orleans. However, he is taken aback when his father, who for years has declared he would take his family to France were it not for the political unrest there, actually begins making plans for the move in light of the city's imminent invasion. Duvall is devoted to his job and resists his father's plans. Then Livingston dispatches him with a letter to Jean Lafitte, requesting the pirate's support of the American cause, since Livingston believes that Lafitte and his men may prove crucial in the defense of the city. Duvall makes the journey with his friend Gumbo Ferrier, a Creole who lives in the bayous and knows the intricate waterways, and the boys witness Lafitte's meeting with the British. The boys return to an uneasy city where divided allegiances on all sides cause distrust. Duvall later carries a secret message from Lafitte to Governor Claiborne, witnesses the arrival of General Jackson, is sent on a mission by Lafitte and Jackson to retrieve a cache of flints from Barataria (necessary for flintlock guns), and serves on a boat defending the harbor. By the end of the book the city is no longer divided and even Duvall's father has become a fervent supporter of the United States.

292. LaScola, Ray(mond). *The Creole.* New York: William Morrow, 1961. 311pp.

Unlike other stories of Creole men and women, in this book, heroine Camille Broussard, has no close-knit family to care for her and does not enjoy a genteel childhood in the French Quarter. Her mother, a gentle Spanish lady, made a misalliance with Frenchman Jacques Broussard whose ne'er-do-well ways put her in an early grave. Although Camille's aunts want her to live with them in New Orleans, in 1868, when she is eighteen, her father insists that she accompany him when he commences a job as plantation manager in Amantville, outside Baton Rouge. There, for the first time in her life, she enjoys keeping house and meets Raoul Amant, the plantation owner's son. The pair fall in love and Raoul promises marriage, although he knows his parents, and even Jacques, will never permit the match. While his parents are away, he repeatedly makes the alcoholic Jacques drunk and consummates his relationship with the naïve Camille. By the time his parents return, Camille realizes she is pregnant. The Amants deceive Camille and Jacques into thinking they will agree to the marriage. They surreptitiously get Raoul out of the country to France, and then fire Jacques on false accusations and declare Camille an unsuitable bride. When Jacques pursues one of his hopeless moneymaking schemes she is forced to return to New Orleans on her own and the novel describes the difficulties she faces as a single pregnant woman in the Reconstruction-era city. Taken in by nuns, she daily awaits Raoul's return in response to a letter that she is able to send to France with a sea captain. Needing to feel active and hoping to pay her way, she takes a nursing job outside of New Orleans, caring for an invalid wife addicted to drugs, but is forced to leave when her husband, businessman Gerald Romalda, forces himself on her. When Raoul comes back from France, he is determined to get his mother's approval of the marriage. Camille, newly matured, knows this will never happen. She does not realize the lengths to which Madam Amant will go. She is soon subjected to investigation by a private detective that falsely, but publicly, discredits her. When she observes Raoul in this stressful situation, his increasing drunkenness and distrustfulness force her to realize she has made a mistake in loving him. By the end of the novel her circumstances have changed dramatically and her future looks hopeful. The New Orleans content mostly focuses on family relationships and makes little use of the setting.

293. Lattimore, Eleanor Frances. *Christopher and His Turtle.* New York: William Morrow, 1950. 126pp.

In this work of juvenile fiction, five-year-old Christopher lives on St. Denis Street in the French Quarter with his parents and older brother Larry, who is already in school. His days are spent at home with live-out housekeeper Queen, since his father works in an office and his mother in a gift shop. When the gift shop gets a shipment of miniature turtles, Christopher and Larry each receive one from their mother. Hoping to show his new pet to Antonia, a girl his age who lives across the street, Christopher leaves his family's apartment while Queen is vacuuming. Unfortunately, he gets swept up with a group of school children on their way to the nearby museum and is soon lost. During the few hours he is gone, he meets a nun, a grocer, a street sweeper, an African-American boy his age, a boy older than him whose bad influence he resists, and a girl whose nanny brought her to Jackson Square so that she could ride her new tricycle. The book captures neighborhood life and gives a sense of what it was like to be a French Quarter child in the 1940s and 1950s in a house dominated by one's gallery and garden.

294. Lawrance, William V(icars). *Defeated but Victor Still, or, Heirs of the Fonca Estate: A Story of the Mysteries of New Orleans, following the Civil War and Reconstruction.* New York: F. Tennyson Neely, 1898. 424pp.

The mystery in this novel is about what happened to Spanish record books that could establish a New Orleans family's rights to a large tract of land in the city, the Fonca estate. The record books went missing during Reconstruction and the novel has a certain amount to say about corrupt Northerners. One of the interested parties in the matter is Dr. James Hemstead. Hemstead learns from a man, named George Quitman, of the Fonca estate, his relationship to it, and the branch of his family, the Sandovals, living near New Orleans, on whose behalf Quitman is working. The claim of this family is contested by the Constantos. The book is filled with genealogy, mistaken and false identities, and missing rings and lockets, originally attached to babies, which would prove true descent. Several houses in the French Quarter that are considered romantically ancient in the present time of the novel, serve as settings and family servants are mostly freed slaves who remain loyal to their impoverished families. Both the inadmissibility of evidence by African-Americans in the courtroom and the barring of women from such settings get a great deal of attention, as do the immigration patterns that are changing New Orleans and the contrast between the American section of the city and the French Quarter.

295. Lea, Fanny Heaslip. *Chloe Malone.* Illustrated by F. Graham Cootes. Boston: Little, Brown, 1916. 292pp.

The debutante year of Chloe Malone, a New Orleans girl, takes an unexpected turn when a taxicab collides with the hired limousine in which she and her widowed mother are riding to the first opera performance of the season. The brief contact with cab passenger Courtenay Wheeler, an entomologist from Boston studying ways to rid the South of boll weevils, eventually transforms her life. Malone's debutante year centers on Dan Kinloch, the owner of three cotton plantations around Natchez, who principally resides in New Orleans. As Malone attends one ball after another, Kinloch is constant in his attention and, at the Comus Ball where she reigns as queen, he proposes. In doing so he fulfills the hopes of the Malones for he is wealthy, attractive, considerate, and well connected. The Malones, descended from the Jumonvilles and once wealthy, were impoverished by Chloe's father who squandered his own and his wife's fortune before dying. Mrs. Malone sold family antiques and jewelry piece by piece to continue to living respectably in a house on Dufossat Street, dressing Chloe appropriately, and sending her to the right schools and social events. When Wheeler unexpectedly writes to Malone after seeing her Comus Ball picture in a Boston newspaper, she is unsettled because of her interest in the young man. However, she accepts Kinloch's proposal while forthrightly telling him that she does not believe in marrying for love (as her mother did). When her godmother takes Chloe on a cruise, a series of strange coincidences lead her to meet and spend time with Wheeler, during his search for a tropical parasite that will feed on and kill boll weevil larvae. Although she returns to New Orleans still determined to marry Kinloch, she tries to inspire him to do more than simply live off his rents and investment income and she starts to long for more purpose in life than ornamenting a man's arm. Through the rest of the novel she struggles with defining herself. The book raises issues of gender roles and touches on aspects of feminism in a cursory way, for Malone is not looking for independence and self-determination, but a companionate marriage in which she can share in and support the goals of a husband committed to social good.

296. LeBlanc, Doris Kent. *One Was Valiant*. New York: Arcadia House, 1939. 318pp.

The Ashton family lives in Côte Verte, Bayou Têche. Myrthé grew up in New Orleans where one branch of her family was affluent enough to have daughters reign as Mardi Gras queens. The orphaned Myrthé lived with her seamstress aunt and spent her days sewing gowns that she would never wear. When she married Stephen Ashton, the couple moved into the sizable house he had inherited from his parents and Myrthé settled into the life of a society lady, using references to her fashionable days as a New Orleans belle to bolster her position. As the couple's three daughters, Gratia, Ninette, and Zoe mature into young women, Ashton, who works as a salesman, is overwhelmed by the costs of maintaining the illusion of affluence demanded by Myrthé, and he eventually dies from a heart attack brought on by stress and lack of sleep. His only realistic daughter, Ninette, initially tries to take over his role, but when her fiancé makes her choose between him and her family she goes away with him, leaving her mother and sisters to gradually adjust to their real situation in life. Although little of the novel is physically set in New Orleans, the book illustrates how the city dominates the thinking of Louisianans like Myrthé, who credit the place with all that is fashionable and of good quality. Gratia wins a scholarship at Newcomb College and after she graduates as valedictorian she completes a master's degree at Tulane. When her sister Zoe travels to New Orleans it is to obtain an illegal abortion.

297. Le May, Alan. *Old Father of Waters*. Garden City, N.Y.: Doubleday, Doran, 1928. 329pp.

This book about the steamboat industry on the lower Mississippi in 1858 focuses on twenty-seven-year-old Arnold Huston. At the beginning of the book Huston captains his own boat and has retained control of his father's plantation mansion in Natchez. His fortunes change dramatically when his boat burns and his grasping cousin, Will Huston, forecloses on the Natchez mansion. In the course of receiving the news about the foreclosure, Huston punches his cousin, who promptly challenges him to a duel. Huston travels to New Orleans to arrange for Mark Wallace to be his second. Wallace, correctly, considers the duel a minor setback and takes advantage of Huston's unsettled circumstances to get him to agree to a business proposal in which Wallace will raise money from silent partners and use his connections and business savvy to build a steamboat empire based on Huston's knowledge of the Mississippi. One of the partners is the beautiful, twenty-four-year-old widow, Jacqueline DuMoyne. Huston is immediately smitten but proceeds very cautiously since DuMoyne's husband disappeared, but was never declared dead. Huston's visits to Wallace and DuMoyne mean that significant parts of the novel are set in New Orleans, although the book is mostly concerned with river adventure and a great steamboat race. The city is represented as an exotic place of cultures foreign to Huston in which he can nonetheless achieve distinction for his mastery of the river.

298. Le May, Alan. *Pelican Coast.* Illustrated by George Illian. Garden City, N.Y.: Doubleday, Doran, 1929. 329pp.

Although this is typically identified as a New Orleans novel, the book is mostly set in Barataria and deals with a period of crisis in the life of Lafitte (c.1776–c.1823) and his privateer associates when letters of marque, enabling the capture of French ships, expire. The U.S. government begins attacking piracy and the sale of goods becomes more difficult as New Orleans merchants are concerned with prosecution. At the same time, Northerner, Job Northrup, appears and wins Jean Lafitte's confidence and that of Roman Catholic priest, Père Miguel. At the priest's urging Northrup pursues a romance with Madelon de Verniat, even though her mother has been conspiring to marry her to Jean Lafitte. Lafitte needs Northrup in his efforts to get letters of marque from Cartagena and he indulges Northrup. The Northerner turns the tables on Lafitte, enriching himself by capturing a ship and its gold. Northrup leaves New Orleans forever with Madelon on board. The book includes descriptions of the Lafitte blacksmith shop and interactions with New Orleans businessmen, as well as recaps of the changing legal situation of the Lafitte brothers and the merchants who dealt with them.

299. Le Moine, Weston J. *The Sacrifice: A True Story.* Illustrated by W.E. Greer, Jr. New Orleans: Cox, 1919. 212pp.

Lewis Ferry's father was so poor that he took over a farm that had been abandoned because everyone considered the place haunted. After the death of his father, his mother could not adequately feed and clothe Ferry and got him admitted as a charity student at a boarding school, while she began supporting herself by renting out rooms to an African-American woman and her son. At about the time he comes of age and begins looking for a job, Ferry's mother dies and leaves behind a fortune that her son discovers while cleaning out her house. Joining his friend John Russell in New Orleans, Lewis is introduced to upper-class society. Russell, a physician with an inherited income, married Edna Miller, an heiress, and, as the couple's long-term guest, Ferry participates in their social life and joins Russell's club, where he meets Mr. Blake, who is having an affair with Russell's wife. When Russell realizes he is being cuckolded, he suspects Ferry. Breaking in on his wife in flagrante, Russell shoots her and pursues her paramour, who escapes without Russell determining his identity and so shoots Ferry when he appears on the scene. Recovering from his wound, Ferry marries the deceased Edna's sister, Helen, and departs for California to escape his association with the scandal. Russell leaves New Orleans as well, and successfully evades prosecution by taking on an assumed identity in Mexico. When Ferry returns to New Orleans he begins a life of philanthropy and adopts Russell's orphaned daughter, Edna. Having accumulated a fortune, Russell also returns to New Orleans, but in the guise of Carlos Rodriguize (sic), secretly intent on revenging himself on Ferry. Fortunately, when Ferry is violently confronted he can produce Blake's deathbed confession. Russell dies soon after the reconciliation and his daughter Edna becomes a nun, playing an important role in nursing yellow fever victims. Similar to other scandal novels, this book portrays a New Orleans in which even society figures are corrupt. However, Ferry demonstrates that a moral life dedicated to one's wife and family and spent working for the public good can be lived in the morally bankrupt city. The book places great emphasis on the social value of Roman Catholicism.

300. Linfield, Mary Barrow. *Day of Victory.* Garden City, N.Y.: Doubleday, Doran, 1936. 239pp.

On his forty-eighth birthday, John Chapman, an officer of the St. Bernard Yellow Pine Company, is forced by a series of circumstances to reflect upon his life and loves. His day begins with the death of a visiting salesman who is almost exactly his age and it ends with the death of his unmarried secretary, who had remained home, sick from an accidental overdose of prescription medication. Much of Chapman's day in this Depression-era novel is occupied by business and observations about his colleagues, including several Creoles who he admires for their politeness. Chapman grew up in humble circumstances and whenever he begins to take satisfaction in what he has achieved, he hears his mother declaring that none of her children will ever be successful. The New Orleans setting of the novel is most vivid when Chapman leaves the office to have lunch with some colleagues and when he thinks back to his marriage to his first wife Imelda, after an earlier romance with an impoverished daughter of Southern aristocracy was terminated by her family. When he met Imelda she was teaching dance in a public school and had a studio in the French Quarter. Their marriage ended early when she asked him to release her from her marriage vows so that she could become a nun. The novel touches on issues of gender, race, and religion, as Chapman's observations often reveal underlying prejudices. Descriptions of social class are also present as Chapman digresses on the pleasure he takes in squiring his current wife (also of modest background) to orchestra concerts and the right church.

301. Linfield, Mary Barrow. *Young Woman in Love.* New York: Macaulay, 1929. 322pp.

In this semi-autobiographical coming-of-age novel, mostly set in the 1920s, Héloise, orphaned by a yellow fever epidemic at an early age, is raised by her uncle near Bayou Melpomène, an area dominated by the plantations of her extended family, the Claverhouses. Only about forty pages of the novel are set in New Orleans, however throughout the novel, family members travel to the city for business and socializing. While attending college, Héloise lives in New Orleans in the house of an aunt, Madame de Rubia. The narrative includes vivid descriptions of the residence on Esplanade Avenue, since Rubia rents rooms to some very respectable elderly women (who spend their time knitting and churchgoing), and allows several equally respectable men, who rent rooms in the neighborhood, to board at her table. One of these men, Mr. Karama, is a bank clerk and musician who coaches Héloise in piano performance (she is a voice student). Although Héloise socializes with her sorority sisters and some of her many cousins in the city, she forms a close friendship with Karama and the two engage in the sedate activities of middle age, including dinner at old-fashioned restaurants like Galatoire's, attending church services at Our Lady of the Sacred Heart, coffee at Bijou Pharmacie, visits to the Delgado Museum, and strolls in City Park. When Héloise eventually marries a cousin who is several decades her senior, the two live in the Carrollton district of the city. Her husband is a reporter and the two socialize with his artist friends in the French Quarter.

302. Lipscomb, Marie Lauve. *The Lost Treasure.* Grand Rapids, Mich.: Zondervan, 1959. 118pp.

Sixteen-year-old André Farel is delighted to have his father home, after he has given up the sailing life to establish a boatyard. André tries very hard to help save money and make his father's modest business a success. However, he has many challenges. An arson attack on the boatyard injures his father, and later André must fight off intruders who come searching for a treasure that his father's cruel, pirate brother, Tigre Farel, supposedly buried in the vicinity. To help support his family, he also makes a dangerous trip to Kentucky with an Indian trader named Ortho Bond. In this religious novel, André draws strength from his Christian faith and when he finds the pirate treasure, he plans to redeem the blood money by using it to build a church.

303. Little, Paul H(ugo) [Marie De Jourlet, pseud.]. *Return to Windhaven.* Los Angeles: Pinnacle Books, 1978. 552pp.

One of a series of historical romance novels featuring the travails of the Bouchard family, this book gives a sense of life in New Orleans during Reconstruction. Fifty-year-old Luke Bouchard establishes a ranch in southeast Texas after Union troops drive him and his extended family from Windhaven Plantation near Lowndesboro, Alabama. He is fortunate in having inherited gold held in British banks accounts. After the death of his wife, Bouchard returns to New Orleans intending to marry Laure (sic) Brunton, the widow of Bouchard's banker John Brunton, and, the secret mother of his son, the result of one passionate, adulterous encounter. Arriving in New Orleans in 1866, he finds Laure plans to establish the bank her husband had operated privately as a financial institution officially recognized by the U.S. government. Her husband had previously operated this as a sideline, holding secret accounts for patrons of the bordello he owned and operated. Instead of marrying her, Bouchard becomes Laure's partner, investing forty thousand dollars in gold. He also helps Laure find jobs for the young women who had worked in her brothel and whose life stories often entail war-related impoverishment that drove them into prostitution. Bouchard also secures bank investors and a building in the city's American quarter, near city hall. Many aspects of living in a New Orleans overrun with carpetbaggers and Northerners filling government jobs are detailed, as are current events like the race riots brought on by the prospect of the Fourteenth Amendment to the Bill of Rights. In a specie-poor city, Brunton and Brouchard can take advantage of significant investment opportunities, including buying land and warehouses, and loaning money to promising sugar plantations. Although Bouchard wants to make enough money to get back Windhaven plantation (located in Alabama), he is also unselfishly concerned with re-building the South. Bouchard restores a fine New Orleans mansion, employs Marius Thornton, a former African-American slave, as his factotum at an attractive salary after rescuing him from a mob, and eventually marries Laure. With the success of the bank, Bouchard anticipates regaining Windhaven when he learns that allies of his former nemesis Pierre Lourat, have become signifi-cant figures in the Ku Klux Klan and are attempting to seize the plantation by driving out the African-American caretakers of the remnant of Windhaven Plantation. In a duel at Allard Plan-tation Bouchard kills the men scheming against him and sets out for Alabama to fight the Klan. Introducing data about economic conditions and information about legal decisions, this book pre-sents a view of Reconstruction New Orleans.

304. Little, Paul H(ugo) [Marie De Jourlet, pseud.]. *Storm Over Windhaven.* Los Angeles: Pinna-cle Books, 1977. 528pp.

At the center of this historical romance novel is the Bouchard family of Windhaven plantation in Alabama. New Orleans figures prominently in the novel as a center for banking, the slave trade, and luxury goods, as well as less legitimate forms of financial transactions, such as gambling, and prostitution. The patriarch of Windhaven, Lucien Bouchard, is now too elderly to travel the four hundred miles to New Orleans even by riverboat, but his son Henry, the current proprietor of the plantation and his grandson, sixteen-year-old Mark, make the trip after the cotton harvest in 1834 when the city is filled with planters flush with money. Henry, with his eye on small plantations adjoining his land, takes their owners with him to the Chartres Street establishments of Pierre Lourat. The Creole businessman operates a slave auction block, a gambling parlor, and brothels. Here Henry entertains his prey and plies their weaknesses for gambling and illicit sex in ways that will eventually bring their downfall. Although Henry gives Mark a small amount of money to gamble and condones Mark using his funds to hire prostitutes, he does not realize Lourat's own designs. By the end of the trip, Mark owes Lourat a huge gambling debt and has fallen to the wiles of one of his gambling parlor hostesses. Mark is shocked to later learn that the beauty is forty-years-old, a quadroon, and the daughter of Lucien Bouchard through an affair with one of his slaves. Even Henry's purchase of the African chief, Djamba, who is intelligent and exceptionally strong, turns out to be a miscalculation that will further his undoing. Subsequent trips to New Or-leans are less consequential, but usually involve visits to banks, gambling houses, and brothels. By the end of the novel in 1865, several more generations of Bouchards appear and begin to redeem the line, by acting on the behalf of the Creek Indians, secretly aiding the abolitionists and the Un-derground Railroad, and shifting the family business from growing cotton to growing food. While on the whole a bodice-ripper, the author does provide brief references to historical events over the time period.

305. Llewellyn, Michael [Maggie Lyons, pseud.]. *Bayou Passions.* New York: Jove / Harcourt, Brace, Jovanovich, 1979. 383pp.

Orphaned at an early age, Marie Boudreaux was raised by her spinster Aunt Alice in their important New Orleans family mansion. By 1840, at the age of eighteen, Marie has been a debutante for two years and has young men from the most important French Quarter families as suitors. None of them intrigue her, however, except the fabulously wealthy sugar plantation owner and investor Morgan Davies. Initially her interest seems inspired by a desire to violate social convention. Her aunt's friends discuss his vulgar wealth, and interacting with Americans is generally taboo. At Marie's instigation, one of her friends brings Davies to a ball, and Marie boldly asks him to dance and goes alone with him onto a darkened balcony. Her behavior is considered scandalous, but she is even more shocking in secret when she takes a public hack to his Garden District mansion at one o'clock in the morning. The two proceed to construct a plan for how they can marry at a time when Americans are even blocked from purchasing real estate in the French Quarter. Marie devises steps to effect Davies' social acceptance, knowing that his wealth will be irresistible to cash poor Creoles in need of currency to feed their speculative ventures and banking firms. A grand dinner at his plantation, the largest and most beautiful on the River Road, is a great success and leads to invitations from social arbiters. However, soon afterwards, Boudreaux is seen leaving Davies' house early in the morning and he is challenged to a duel in defense of the honor of all French Quarter debutantes. Marie's presence at the duel outrages society and Davies is nearly killed, but he preserves his honor by the skill he demonstrates in shooting his opponent. Having already violated social conventions, the two announce their engagement. It would seem that Davies' lack of a past and the French Quarter's great insistence on genealogy have been overcome until a meddlesome, scorned woman hires a private detective to investigate Davies. If the discoveries were made public, he would be ruined. Before the dramatic and happy conclusion of the novel, another duel is fought, a long-lost son returned to his father's household, and a hurricane survived. The novel provides many details of New Orleans social history. Throughout the book, African-Americans are cast as beloved, trusted servants and women have the true power.

306. Lockwood, Myna. *Beckoning Star: A Story of Old Texas.* Illustrated by Myna Lockwood. New York: E.P. Dutton, 1943. 242pp.

   In this work of juvenile fiction, a sequel to the author's *Free River*, Guita is married to Frank Paine, a former New Englander and affluent merchant. The couple have three children, a baby named Nancy, thirteen-year-old Margot and her older brother Lee. During the first half of the book the Paines live in New Orleans, which is described from the perspective of Margot. Even though she is constantly attended by an African-American servant and lives a sheltered life, she clearly has the pioneer spirit that her brother Lee seems to lack. Frank Paine wants his son to go to the Texas frontier with a new acquaintance, Stephen Austin, since he is trying to find settlers to take up land grants being offered by Mexican ruler Agustin de Iturbide (1783–1824) in 1822. Lee is proving himself something of a ne'er-do-well, acting on the belief that as the son of a wealthy man he should not be expected to have any occupation. Margot is embarrassed that her brother is not more adventurous and thinks young Creole men of his acquaintance are corrupting him, particularly with gambling. Eventually, Margot is instrumental in shaming Lee to go to Texas and heartbroken when the ship on which he was traveling sinks. Later, Margot and her family relocate to Texas and are surprised to find that Lee survived the shipwreck and became one of Austin's Old Three Hundred along the Brazos River. In 1830 when Mexican Texas prohibits continued immigration from the United States, Frank Paine decides it is too dangerous to keep his family there and they return to New Orleans, with the exception of Lee, who stays behind with Stephen Austin, having discovered courage and strength through his adventures. Although the novel describes daily life in a New Orleans household of the 1820s and relates some of the excitement Texas aroused in the city, the book is of most interest for trying to introduce a female presence on the historical stage for young adult readers.

307. Lockwood, Myna. *Free River: A Story of Old New Orleans.* Illustrated by Myna Lockwood. New York: E.P. Dutton, 1942. 255pp.

The history of New Orleans during the period when city control shifted from Spain to France to the United States is related through the experiences of an orphaned girl in this juvenile novel. During the period of Spanish rule, French-speaking New Orleans residents try to smuggle French noblemen escaping the Revolution into the city, even though the Spanish strictly prohibit this. When orphaned infant Guita is found on the steps of the Ursuline Convent, her discoverer, Spanish nobleman Don Carlos Hoyos, suspects she may be of noble birth, because of her beauty and elaborate wrappings (American homespun, French velvet, and a Spanish shawl) and makes her his ward. As a ten-year-old, Guita begins to question her origins around the time that New Orleans is to be ceded to French control and the status of Don Carlos Hoyos may dramatically change. Soon after Hoyos learns that France has sold the Louisiana Territory to the United States he dies of a heart attack. Uncertainty surrounds the settlement of Hoyos' estate, and a Spanish relative takes great interest in the matter, since if Guita does not inherit Hoyos' fortune, it will come to him. However, Hoyos had made a mysterious alliance with John Adams, the ex-vice president, who becomes Guita's ward. In addition to Adams, Aram, a mulatto Voodoo practitioner, who has been Guita's servant since she was an infant, also remains as her protector. Other historical figures in the novel include General James Wilkinson (1757–1825), Abigail Adams (1744–1818), Aaron Burr (1756–1836), and Jean Lafitte (c. 1776–1823), who Guita believes knows her origins. On Aram's deathbed, as a slave uprising is threatened, she reveals that Guita is the infant daughter of a Mississippi family named Leonard who had been killed in an Indian attack. Throughout the novel, Guita's identity is paralleled with that of New Orleans as she has connections to France, Spain, and America.

308. Long, Amelia Reynolds. *Murder by Scripture.* New York: Phoenix, 1942. 254pp.

In search of inspiration for a new novel, Philadelphia author Katherine "Peter" Piper travels to New Orleans at the suggestion of her fiancé Amédée Dumont. She soon hears of a dramatic murder in which the apparent murderer, Kane Moyer, is accused of bludgeoning his brother Arnold in the billiard room of the affluent townhouse they shared. The motive for the crime is unclear, but the brothers were members of the Cult of Gabriel, a group of occultists headed by Dr. Gabriel Devereux, who claims direct descent from Count Cagliostro, both genealogically, and in terms of necromantic powers. Each brother had willed his entire estate to the cult and over the past several years, other members died suspiciously. Piper checks into a French Quarter hotel and becomes obsessed by the murder investigation, but Dumont wants to fill her time with touristic outings and lavish restaurant dinners. She is soon staying with friends of Dumont outside the city proper. Their house, and a neighboring abandoned plantation mansion (complete with garçonnières), become the venue for dramatic revelations, nighttime disturbances, and the announcement of further murders (each with an accompanying biblical verse). Additional settings include a New Orleans cemetery, the New Orleans Police Department headquarters, and its holding cells. Issues of gender and race are prominently featured in the novel, particularly as Piper's bravery is contrasted with the cowardice of inferior races.

309. Louisiana [pseud.]. *Blue and Gray, or, Two Oaths and Three Warnings.* New Orleans: L. Graham, 1885. 169pp.

Although much of this novel is set in Texas and rural Louisiana, the book is included here since extended sections transpire in New Orleans and the work describes conditions there during the Civil War and in the Reconstruction era. The novel rehearses the injustices experienced by Confederates at the hands of African-Americans and their supporters. At the center of the story is Jenny June Bancroft who, as a sixteen-year-old, was duped into marrying Richard Bancroft, an alcoholic twenty-two years her senior. Even though the couple had several children, Bancroft did not reform and absented himself for long periods of time, even during the Civil War as Union troops approached. Not only did Jenny volunteer to nurse wounded soldiers, she also opened her rural home to them. In this way she meets Confederate soldier Harold Clinton who, thinking her a single woman, falls in love with her. Later, she also meets the Union officer Fred Manly. These men become her protectors, although over time Manly becomes more important as the Union takes control of the area. Clinton is wounded, captured, and, owing to Manly's influence, paroled to New Orleans. As Richard Bancroft falls into violent insanity, Manly also arranges for Jenny to move with her children and niece Maggie to New Orleans under Manly's protection. Most descriptions of the city focus on slights Confederate women experienced on the streets, particularly from African-Americans. These worsen after the war ends and Maggie devotes herself to unnamed organizations dedicated to maintaining Southern honor and suppressing aggressive African-Americans. Despite her political convictions she and Manly eventually marry, a union made only slightly plausible by the fact that Manly seems to have no political convictions, despite his service. Jenny is traumatized over her Bancroft's escape from an insane asylum and then falls ill with yellow fever, the disease that finally kills her Bancroft. Over time she and Harold Clinton finally marry—a fortunate union for Jenny since Clinton is an English aristocrat with property in California to which he can take her for her health before relocating with her to England where he succeeds to the baronetcy of his deceased father. In addition to describing New Orleans during a yellow fever epidemic and Reconstruction, the novel touches on the difficulties that Jenny and her family experience in such an urban environment, in great contrast to their earlier rural existence.

310. MacDonald, Edwina Levin. *Blind Windows.* New York: Macaulay, 1927. 383pp.

A significant portion of this romance novel focusing on a young woman's choice of a husband is set in New Orleans. Wilda Garnett was raised in her family's ancestral home, Fairmount Plantation, near Natchitoches, although her father had been a reluctant tenant who only returned to manage the property out of family loyalty after the death of his older brother, giving up his career as a physician in order to do so. As the story begins, everyone assumes that Garnett, about to celebrate her sixteenth birthday, will soon marry, although her choices are somewhat limited. Her childhood sweetheart Ned Turner lives on the neighboring Sycamore Plantation, but even to Garnett he seems immature, with no immediate plans except the desire to be a poet. The most eligible bachelor in the area, Jimmie Biggs, the attractive son of a major landowner, has shown an interest in her and could help her struggling family, but she has no interest in him. When one of Turner's friends, thirty-five-year-old widower Vallon Dupre, comes from New Orleans for a weekend visit, his maturity and sophistication are exciting distinctions in contrast to her other beaux. Even when Turner is finally provided with a future by his family's decision to sell their plantation and put him through law school, the prospect of waiting to marry for six or seven years until he can support her seems unbearable to Garnett. When the Garnett family cotton gin burns, forcing the immediate liquidation of their plantation and possessions, Garnett leaps into marriage with Dupre. She tries to settle into the marvelous Uptown house in New Orleans that he had built for his first wife, but the first wife's clothes are still there, and even her seven-year-old daughter is eventually in residence. The deceased woman's role in New Orleans' society is ever-present as well. Garnett soon realizes that she has made a mistake and over time separates from Dupre and returns to Natchitoches as the wife of Jimmie Biggs. When she is reunited years later with Turner, he has become a famous author and she again relives the choice she made as a sixteen-year-old. As a girl in Natchitoches, Garnett longs for a life in New Orleans, but when she walks into a ready-made existence, complete with an attractive husband, beautiful house, elegant wardrobe, and lively social set, the circumstances are more than she can manage and she longs for the simpler, rural life of Natchitoches.

311. MacDonald, Edwina Levin. *A Lady of New Orleans.* New York: Macaulay, 1925. 314pp.

Twenty-two-year-old Joan Beauseant is the last of a family that has lived on Esplanade Avenue since Louisiana was French. Descended from early settler Duc Louis Philippe de Beauseant, Joan grew up in a house filled with ancient heirlooms. The novel begins during Mardi Gras, on the day she is scheduled to wed Albert E. Durant, a young lawyer, with whom she will move to Jennings, Louisiana, a small oil town not far from New Orleans. When word comes that Durant has instead married wealthy oil widow Rita Newton, whose family owns Jennings, the explanation he gives Beauseant is feeble. However, while following through on Mardi Gras social commitments at the insistence of her family, she attends the Comus ball and is openly fascinated by King of the Carnival Dallas Randolph, contrasting the thirty-three-year-old physician's masculine assuredness and naturalness with Durant's immaturity. After a short romance, Randolph proposes marriage. Even though Beauseant does not believe he loves her, she cannot dissuade him and eventually consents. However, when she goes to Durant the day before the wedding, her ex-fiancé impulsively persuades her that they should run away to California. Joan goes even though Durant lets her know that his Catholic wife will never divorce him. Moving from place to place to avoid gossip, they live in San Francisco, Los Angeles, and Denver. Joan eventually sends Durant back to his wife after the revelation that he has not only had a series of affairs but also fathered a child. Fortunately, Joan makes friends with a free-spirited woman who pays for her to travel to the Riviera and arranges for Dallas Randolph to be there. They marry in Paris, but return to the United States to build a house together on the Hudson. Although only a small section is set in New Orleans, the book is included for its title and the romantic notion of New Orleans gentility that carries throughout. The notion contrasts with portrayals of the city as a place to which people go to avoid social convention. Once Joan's life no longer fits social norms, she never considers returning to New Orleans.

312. MacDonald, John D(ann). *Murder for the Bride*. New York: Fawcett / Gold Medal Books, 1951. 164pp.

Thirty-two-year-old Dillon Bryant is a World War II veteran whose prospecting work for TransAmerica Oil takes him to exotic South American locales. When he is introduced to Laura, a lovely young blonde who seems immediately as interested in him as he is in her, he follows his impulses and marries her within three days. After a weeklong honeymoon he is back in the field and assigns a tough female reporter friend, Jill Townsend, to keep an eye on his bride, Laura, in New Orleans. When he returns in response to an urgent message from Townsend, he arrives just in time to identify the body of his murdered wife. Determined to find the culprits, Bryant is surprised to discover that almost nothing he thought he knew about his wife (age, hair color, origins) was true. In fact, she was the former mistress of a Gestapo leader sought by the U.S. government as a war criminal. In a subplot, the Russian spy, with whom Bryant deals, is the beautiful Talya Dvalianova whose cover is employment as an exotic dancer in a Bourbon Street jazz club Bryant frequents. When she is found murdered, a police dragnet begins closing in on Bryant as the prime suspect. The streets and bars of the French Quarter provide much of the New Orleans backdrop, although the Garden District, the Algiers ferry, and Gentilly are also included.

313. Madere, Hubert. *Bachelor's Daughter*. Philadelphia: Dorrance, 1935. 259pp.

While mostly set on a sugar plantation, New Orleans is important to the social life of the protagonists in this romance novel that reveals contemporary attitudes toward race and gender. Twenty-one-year-old Bonny Wogan returns from four years abroad with her paid chaperone to Fashion, the Louisiana sugar plantation of which she is the sole owner after the deaths of a series of family members. While she finds there the same African-American servants she remembered from her childhood, the management of the plantation has been placed in the hands of a newcomer, thirty-year-old Rodney Schex. Unlike recent manager, Hugh Murphy, Schex is a graduate of Louisiana State University and the Audubon Sugar School. Wogan's father had let Murphy oversee the plantation, as he was the son of a friend who was also his sugar broker. Murphy is still on the scene to energetically romance Wogan, but Shex quickly finds a place in Wogan's affections and is soon claiming that with his modern production techniques there is no longer a need for the Murphys to broker the sugar. Much of the socializing transpires in New Orleans and as Murphy sees Schex and Wogan's relationship progress he uses a Mardi Gras ball as the setting to imply that he would still marry Wogan even though he knows that she is part African-American. When she refuses, he has her kidnapped and artificially inseminated with an African-American's "germs" before fleeing to Europe. Wogan thinks she has been raped and refuses to marry Schex, after which she discovers that her parents were never married and that her father had had sex with African-American women on his plantation. After the drama over her pregnancy and stillborn birth, a confessional letter arrives from Murphy that reveals he was lying about Wogan's identity and was responsible for the violence against Wogan, that did not actually entail intercourse.

314. Mally, Emma Louise. *The Mocking Bird is Singing.* New York: Henry Holt, 1944. 394pp.

Mally's family saga is unusual for detailing political and economic issues confronting Southerners from 1861 through 1873 and for plumbing very personal emotions connected to immigration, war, economic dislocation, and romance. The novel primarily focuses on two extended families: the Dancourts and the McClouds. The Dancourt banking family emigrated from France in the 1840s. Gustave Dancourt, fueled by a romantic notion of Louisiana he gained from reading Chateaubriand's novels, arrived in New Orleans and squandered his business capital on high living. Despite Gustave's personal failings, his father was confident in New Orleans' dramatic opportunities for economic growth and aided two more of his sons to settle in the United States, Michel in New Orleans and Auguste in Boston. Their sister Emilie married family friend Henri Beaumarc who invested in several businesses, but concentrated on a New Orleans pharmaceutical company. Emilie's family circle was enlarged after Michel's death in the 1853 yellow fever epidemic, when Beaumarc adopted her orphaned nephews Simon, Charles, and Michel. Much of the novel focuses on the impossible love affair between Charles and Emilie's daughter Therese, his first cousin. Just seventeen in 1861 when the novel opens, Therese is unusual among her New Orleans circle for having been educated in Boston and for being opposed to slavery (like the rest of her family). Two older men have courted her, both of whom were found inappropriate by her family. Charles, on the other hand, marries quickly, having met Miriam McCloud, a Calvinist Scot, while on an extended business trip to England. Miriam's attractive twin brother, Keith McCloud, arrives with the newlyweds as Charles' business partner in operating a fleet of blockade-runners. Therese, impelled by her thwarted desire for Charles and her burgeoning sexuality (frankly acknowledged by her mother), accepts Keith's attentions and eventual offer of marriage (his effort to strengthen ties to the well-connected Dancourts). Throughout the Civil War the Dancourts and McClouds are mostly located in New Orleans, while the novel includes extensive descriptions of wartime conditions and the implications of living in a Yankee occupied city. After the war the families move to Jackson, Texas, and take important roles in the development of the state. The novel presents in detail aspects of the history of New Orleans from 1861 through the Civil War, and touches on issues of race, miscegenation, immigration, and women in society.

315. Margulies, Leo and Sam Merwin. *The Flags were Three: A Novel of Old New Orleans.* New York: S. Curl, 1945. 283pp.

This work of historical fiction relates the story of New Orleans from the period of French rule, through Spanish control, to the beginnings of U.S. sovereignty. The story is told through the lives of three generations of women. Juliette Michaux, orphaned soon after she was born in 1732, grew up New Orleans' Ursuline Convent. Though intent on being a nun, she accepts ball invitations from wealthy school friends, is introduced to society during the days of Governor Pierre de Rigaud, Marquis de Vaudreuil-Cavagnial. Romance and marriage ensue when she meets wealthy Henri de Carrere, a close aide of the governor, but the relationship is soured for Juliette by Carrere's love of wealth, the frivolous social life the Governor expects him to pursue, and the patronage he must pay to retain his social position. After Spain takes control of New Orleans, Carrere is implicated in a plot to reestablish French control and executed. As a result, Juliette hates the Spanish and when her daughter Adrienne falls in love and marries Carlos de Sedella, a Spanish nobleman, permanent estrangement follows. Adrienne's own children also disappoint her. After the Battle of New Orleans, Adrienne reluctantly permits wounded Asa Harvey to be nursed back to health in her household. She is outraged when her daughter Francisca falls in love with the American, who eventually establishes a steamboat transportation company. The novel relates many aspects of New Orleans history, but spends little time describing the city.

316. Marko, Samuel. *To Struggle, to Laugh.* Boston: Chapman and Grimes, 1946. 236pp.

This romance novel, set almost entirely in New Orleans, portrays the city as an unhealthy environment to be escaped, in contrast to salubrious rural life. Protagonist Nancy Witherell is the daughter of a Parisian stage vocalist and Colonel Jefferson D. Witherell, a conservative, New Orleans society figure and businessman devoted to his international construction company. Left without a mother after a shipwreck during which her own life was rescued by affluent Louisiana farmer Pierre Ledoux, Nancy was educated in Buenos Aires and retrieved by her father only after she had graduated from college and could be an ornament to his St. Charles Avenue mansion. Fortunately, Sylvia Ashley, a young woman her age whose family lives next door, acts as her guide to the society life of New Orleans' private clubs that would be considered frivolous by the Colonel. Almost immediately Nancy falls in love with David Ralston, the chemist son of lumber baron Harold Ralston, an enemy of the Colonel, with whom he is engaged in litigation. Although David returns her interest, he remains distracted by his research to make gasoline burn more efficiently, until he sees Nancy win a club swimming competition. Shortly afterwards, however, the Colonel loses his lawsuit with David's father and throws a tantrum that leads to a stroke, recovery from which takes months. With much sentimentalizing over finding true satisfaction in life and rhapsodizing over love, Nancy talks herself into making a break with her father in order to elope with David. All of the characters (with the exception of servants and business managers) are wealthy and the settings are affluent. However, the shallow, backbiting social life of New Orleans is contrasted throughout the novel with the bayou family life of Pierre Ledoux. He remained close to Nancy and is one of the Colonel's few friends. Ledoux is comfortably upper-middle class but he focuses on managing his estate and enjoying rural pleasures. By the end of the novel, David and Nancy have settled on their own piece of land deeded to them by Ledoux.

317. Marshe, Richard [pseud.]. *Wicked Woman: A Novel.* New York: Woodford, 1950. 246pp.

The people she meets in New Orleans transform Desiré le Conte's financial and emotional life. A native of rural Southeastern Louisiana, she is the daughter of very young parents who were improvident and who died in an automobile crash in 1942, when she was sixteen. With no resources, she is forced to live with her maternal aunt, Celeste de Lesseps, in a household that includes her husband Charles; his son by a first marriage, Charles, Jr.; and Lesseps' daughter Joan from her first marriage. Living in near poverty, the slovenly Lessepses make no efforts to improve their lot and treat Desiré as their slave. Her only consolation is a physical relationship initiated by the amoral and pansexual Joan. Desiré's situation reaches a crisis when Charles, Jr. drunkenly rapes her and uses such force to restrain her that she is left unconscious. Fortunately, a Roman Catholic priest writes to Desiré's fifty-one-year-old paternal uncle in New Orleans, André le Conte. A man of wealth, le Conte rescues Desiré, adopts her, and takes her into his New Orleans mansion to be attended by servants and supplied with beautiful clothing. He accedes to Desiré's pleas on behalf of her friend Joan and makes possible the young woman's escape to New Orleans, providing her with a small income. In the city Joan continues to see Desiré and manipulates her into believing that she is physically unable to take pleasure in sex with men. Without her knowledge, André le Conte has begun to realize that he is on the verge of bankruptcy but decides to proceed with a lavish debut for Desiré in the hope that she will find a wealthy husband. However, when Philip Grand, whose income is over one million dollars a year, proposes, she rejects him, not because she does not love him, but out of a morbid fear of sexual intercourse. Soon after André dies in 1947, Desiré receives word that Grand has been gravely injured during training exercises in a military camp. Desiré's impulse to rush to Grand's bedside is supported by André's octoroon mistress, Angelique de Brissac. Believing Grand to be near death, Desiré consents to his renewed marriage proposal and when he recovers is forced to confront her fears of intimacy by Brissac's worldly daughter Lillie. New Orleans receives little physical description but is filled with the socially sophisticated people who facilitate Desiré's growth into womanhood. The book references the tradition of octoroon mistresses, since Angelique had been obtained for André by his uncle through a legal arrangement in which she agreed to be his mistress for a ten-year term so long as he supported her in luxury. Clearly the book reveals a good deal about 1940s attitudes toward female sexuality and a woman's place in society.

318. Martin, Aylwin Lee. *The Gambler.* New York: Thomas Y. Crowell, 1929. 350pp.

Shortly after riverboat gambler Sam Caxton wins Stewart Mowbry's ancestral plantation home, the elderly Mowbry commits suicide, and Caxton travels to the plantation to claim his prize. He expects to find Mowbry's wife, but instead finds two slave women, one of whom is Mowbry's common law wife, Hannah, and the other his daughter, Carol. Caxton immediately falls in love with Carol and takes the women to New Orleans. In the antebellum world of the novel, racism and sexism shape Caxton's thinking and actions. He decides he is in love with Carol and assumes she will be thrilled by his announcement. Legally, he cannot marry her and does not anticipate taking her somewhere that he can do so. Instead, he tells her that she will in future be known as his wife (although he will wait for her to fall in love with him before consummating the relationship). Because Hannah is dark-skinned, he tells Carol that her mother will live as her maid. Arriving in New Orleans in 1849, the trio settles into the St. Charles Hotel. Carol, an intelligent girl, with culture acquired through wide reading, is delighted with city life. No matter what Caxton's shortcomings may be, he is truly in love with Carol and spends time indulging her in music and the piano. Soon after moving to the city, Caxton wins a famous gambling parlor from its owner and buys a mansion on Orleans Street. While living there, Carol falls in love with Charles Dalcour and tells Caxton, that despite his patient courtship she will never love him. She does not realize that Dalcour secretly considers her a "negress" and pursuit of her a game. After Carol's announcement, Caxton offers to sacrifice himself by losing a duel with Dalcour so that Carol can be with him. However, the duel has no definitive outcome and enrages Dalcour whose arm is irrecoverably injured. A short time later Dalcour inadvertently reveals his true feelings toward Carol and a little later Hannah makes a revelation that opens the way for Carol to marry Caxton, with whom she is finally in love. The New Orleans setting is employed to offer the titillation of mixed race encounters and gambling parlor challenges.

319. Martin, Fleming. *Despair in a Creole Garden.* New York: Vantage, 1967. 204pp.

Set during Holy Week, this novel is concerned with the casual immorality presented as typical of New Orleans. Seventeen-year-old protagonist Ronny Toole is described as an all-American boy who everyone believes is headed for the priesthood. However, he does not feel he can consider a religious vocation, as his father's poor health has reduced his family to impoverishment. Even so, Toole remains obsessed with moral judgments, particularly as they relate to sexuality. For instance, he considers his own father inappropriately flirtatious with young women. He partially excuses the open sexuality of his best friend Sero Daco because Daco is "Latin" and part of a culture that Toole considers to be awash in immorality. The boys share a birthday and most of the action focuses on a double date at Brendle's Creole Garden. Toole's girlfriend is Leah Webre (sic), of whom he is very possessive, even though, like everyone else, she thinks he is more likely to become a priest than a husband. Daco's date, Flo Seems, means little to Daco, but Flo is obsessed with her date and is known for being temperamental and envious. In the course of the evening, Toole discovers that Daco is in love with Leah and confronts him. When Daco falls dead from a gunshot wound, Toole, who was brandishing a weapon, assumes his gun fired the bullet. However, Flo, the daughter of a murderer, is in the end revealed to have committed the crime.

New Orleans settings are mostly in and around the French Quarter, which is portrayed as impoverished and fairly unsavory. Most of the novel is an exposition on temperaments formed by family life and genetic inheritance.

320. Martin, Valerie. *Alexandra*. New York: Farrar, Straus and Giroux, 1979. 179pp.

Low-level government worker Claude Ledet has managed to get to the age of forty-nine without significant romantic or social involvement. His few acquaintances are fellow accountants. When one of them sets him up with Mona, a widow his age whose inheritance allows her to enjoy a comfortable suburban existence, his life begins to change. Mona is aggressive in satisfying her sexual needs, mitigating any inadequacies of the inexperienced Ledet. She is also insistently social and focused on exploring New Orleans' nightlife. Although Ledet is indifferent to some aspects of his evolving relationship with Mona, including loud nightclubs with youthful clientele, he is adamantly opposed to Mona's attempt to propel him into marriage. At the juncture at which Mona's willfulness seems irresistible and marriage imminent, Ledet espies thirty-year-old bartender Alexandra. Her youth and beauty attract Ledet and, surprisingly, his inept advances are successful. Alexandra is another strong woman, but Ledet does not resist her will. When wealthy, young, pregnant Diana wants Alexandra with her during childbirth, Ledet complies with Alexandra's request that he quit his job, sell or abandon his possessions, and go with her. They arrive at a remote Lake Pontchartrain mansion that is set on expansive, maze-like grounds that can only be reached by boat. Once Ledet is in residence in the strange household, he discovers that his appearance matches that of an earlier lover, shared by Alexandra and Diana who came to a violent end. Approximately one-third of this novel is set in New Orleans and focuses on nightlife as seen from the perspective of a disaffected middle-aged man.

321. Martin, Valerie. *Set in Motion*. New York: Farrar, Straus and Giroux, 1978. 209pp.

Social worker Helene Thatcher illustrates many aspects of the independent, self-aware, strong modern woman celebrated in 1970s culture. However, her liberated sexually could also be read as a new form of subjugation to men. Thatcher works in a Louisiana welfare office and insulates herself from her clients' pain and systemic injustices while remaining committed to helping. In her personal life, she is in a co-dependent relationship with a drug-addict, Reed, and is envious of his ability to completely detach himself from reality. Frightened for her safety when a madman begins killing women, she seeks refuge in Reed's Esplanade Street house. However, there are impediments to her relationship with Reed in addition to his drug abuse. She allowed herself to be seduced by her friend Clarissa's fiancé, Michael, and not long after that incident became involved with her co-worker Maggie's husband, Richard. When Richard commits arson and is remanded to a mental hospital, disturbing notebooks reveal a psychotic obsession with Thatcher. Thatcher begins to see parallels between her own mental states, Reed's increasing overdoses, and Richard's suicidal obsession. By the end of the novel, Thatcher has found new strength to cast off these men, even if her alternative future is unclear. In addition to the main theme of the novel—women's liberation—the book touches on racism, French Quarter bar culture and street life, as well as the dangers faced by single women in an urban environment. Descriptions of nighttime French Quarter streets are particularly evocative.

322. Martinez, Raymond J(oseph). *In the Parish of St. John*. Thibodaux, La.: George A. Martin, 1925. 147pp.

Protagonist thirty-year-old Philip Dandolo lives on the Terragona sugar plantation thirty-five miles upriver from New Orleans, with his aged grandfather Pedro Dandolo. Unlike his ancestors who had committed their lives to the plantation, Philip longs for a more social life in New Orleans, and is only holding onto the place until his grandfather dies and his sister Elsie marries. A crisis comes when the firm holding the mortgage on the property, the firm owned by the family to which Philip's fiancée belongs, takes steps to foreclose. Just as the romance fails during the financial crisis, Philip meets and falls in love with Maria Lopez, an actress with a traveling stage company, and begins spending extended periods in New Orleans, courting her while staying at the St. Charles Hotel and the Hotel Prytania. His grandfather and sister are at first dismayed by the budding relationship until they meet Maria, and Pedro Dandolo realizes that he studied in France with Maria's grandfather and knows her to be from an old and noble Spanish family. Indeed, Maria spends most of her time in New Orleans with the Spanish consul and his circle. Because she is older than Philip and was once married, she tries to deflect Philip's interest in her and finally leaves New Orleans suddenly. In the meantime, a neighboring plantation owner who fears Terragona will be divided up for sharecroppers, saves the plantation from foreclosure. Within six months Elise Dandolo has married and Pedro Dandolo is dead. Just as Philip begins to plan his departure from Terragona, a storm drives the Spanish consul's boat to the plantation's shores and Maria is onboard. Inspired by the coincidence, Maria reciprocates Philip's romantic overtures and the two soon begin anticipating wedded life together at Terragona. New Orleans in the novel is the center of the social, civic, and political universe. The novel makes a great deal of the fact that the Dandolos and families like them are noblemen and contrasts them with the "shiftless" Creoles. African-Americans are described as less than human.

323. Mason, F(rancis) van Wyck. *Proud New Flags.* Philadelphia: Lippincott, 1951. 493pp.

The main concern of this work of historical fiction is to trace the development of the Confederate Navy in New Orleans. In addition to actual historical figures, Mason introduces Lachlan Brunter, an engineer from the North who is not committed to the Confederate cause, but thinks he can establish his career in the shipyards of New Orleans more easily than in crowded Union shipyards and be well-placed to take advantage of the burgeoning of the city into a world port once the war is over. He is soon joined by his fiancée, seamstress Christine Riegler, after she gets into a dispute with her employer and braves the trip down the Mississippi with the country on the brink of war. Her experiences in New Orleans give readers a chance to understand domestic life in the time period, just as Brunton's experiences in the Algiers shipyards reveals the administrative and other challenges faced by the Confederate Navy. The other main character, Samuel Seymour, resigns his commission in the U.S. Navy to take part in forming a Confederate one, illustrating the degree to which it mirrored the U.S. Navy, of which so many of its officers had been members. The book ends just as New Orleans is in a panic about its imminent fall to the Union. The defeat without a fight epitomizes for the author, the South's failure to realize the importance of a navy early enough and to take effective steps to thwart the blockade, to enable the flow of armaments and supplies from Europe that would have proved crucial to strengthening the Confederacy and the South.

324. Massena, Agnese M. C. [Creole, pseud.]. *Marie's Mistake: A Woman's History.* Boston: Pratt Brothers, 1868. 357pp.

The story of Marie Lafourche illustrates how little self-determination nineteenth-century women possessed in the United States, while encouraging women to transcend their plight through humble resignation, religious devotion, and selfless love for their husbands. Fourteen-year-old Lafourche, orphaned at an early age, and becomes the ward of her cousin Camille Lafourche, but stands to share the ownership of a large plantation when she reaches her majority. A New Orleans convent school girl, Marie becomes acquainted with Captain Jean Luzerne during his visit to the plantation where Camille lives. Luzerne decides to pursue Marie Lafourche for the considerable property that will come to her and be controlled by her husband, even though he is already the lover of a New Orleans woman, Julie de Bourghe. Luzerne knows that formal pursuit of Marie's hand will eventually be thwarted by her family's investigations, so after winning over the nuns of her school, he woos Marie by taking her away on daytime excursions, making her the envy of her classmates. When he gets permission to escort Marie home for the holidays, he marries her. The Lafourches immediately cut off her financial support and future expectations in order to prevent

Luzerne from any financial benefit and Marie is exiled to the poorly maintained New Orleans mansion of Luzerne's father. Although the elderly man is kind toward her, Marie is treated badly by Luzerne, and soon discovers his continuing affair with Bourghe. Luzerne eventually repents his cruelty and Marie steadfastly pledges her obedience to him, as the appropriate role of a wife. However, their reconciliation is troubled and not until the outbreak of the Civil War does their marriage take on any vitality. Luzerne enlists and forms a regiment, taking Marie with him to Richmond, where he allows her to socialize. However, in a fit of pique, he strikes her and she loses the baby she had been unwittingly carrying. Shortly afterward, Luzerne deserts from the Confederate Army, and is reported killed crossing to Union lines. In the last fifty pages of the novel, a more mature Marie falls in love with and marries an acquaintance from New Orleans, Henri Adrian, a business associate of Luzerne and who sympathized with Marie's plight. After he dies on the battlefield a short time later, Marie gives birth to his son, but the boy dies as an infant. Ill and impoverished in Virginia, Marie is returned by a benefactor to New Orleans for her health and is just beginning to support herself as a writer when Luzerne, who had not been killed in the war and now lives as a gambler, reappears to threaten Marie with scandal. He threatens to publicize her (unintentional) bigamy unless he receives a financial settlement. In despair, Marie enters the convent where a school friend is now the Mother Superior. She dies the day after taking her vows (by coincidence, Luzerne dies the same day). Although most of the novel is set in New Orleans, the book provides little description of the city, besides referencing well-known sites and locales. The work does touch on the Roman Catholic Church, role of women in society, and describes a number of faithful African-American slaves.

325. Massicot, Norita (Newman) [Norita, pseud.]. *The Beasts, the Sheep, and the Chariots.* Baton Rouge, La.: The Author, 1962. 88pp.

In this version of the Battle of New Orleans, corrupt European morals, as exemplified by the loose marital relations within a circle of young friends in England, are contrasted with the American morality exemplified by Andrew Jackson. The confusing tale begins in England when some members of a house party get drunk and a woman ends up in the bedroom of a man who is not her husband. Most of the guests later move to Maryland and some of the men and a few of their sons fight at the Battle of New Orleans. Jackson's victory is portrayed as a moral victory over such immoral Englishmen. The New Orleans setting of the last half of the book is entirely preoccupied with the battle.

326. Massicot, Norita. *The Refugees.* Boston: Christopher, 1963. 223pp.

Many sections of this novel tracing the fictionalized experiences of the author's family over several generations are set in New Orleans, but the city is represented only by the names of streets and an occasional landmark. The book covers a period of more than two hundred and fifty years and reads almost like a genealogy since there are so many characters and so little characterization. The essential source of pride in the family is noble French descent that could be used to make a claim on significant wealth in France. The most significant events in the history of New Orleans, including the battle of 1815, the Civil War occupation, and the Reconstruction period, are touched upon. Characteristic New Orleans' scenes include a quadroon ball, the brief description of a Creole household, and an account of an impoverished laundress who marries into the family in the early twentieth century.

327. Masters, Kelly Ray [Zachary Ball, pseud.]. *Bar Pilot.* Illustrated by Arthur Shilstone. New York: Holiday House, 1955. 218pp.

Set in New Orleans and the Mississippi Delta in the years 1859 through 1861, this adventure story for young adults conveys a great deal of information about river piloting and the Union capture of New Orleans. The main character, sixteen-year-old Jim Yorby, is suffering from amnesia at the beginning of the novel, but eventually remembers that his dying father made him promise to leave Pittsburgh and travel to New Orleans to find his grandfather, Grat Yorby. Jim's mother had already succumbed to the fever that shortly afterwards killed his father. Traveling on a paddle-wheel steamboat, Jim nearly drowned when the craft hit a river whirlpool and he fell overboard, and was rescued by an itinerant blacksmith who travels up and down the river, plying his trade on board ship. Jim arrives nearly penniless in New Orleans and he is still suffering from amnesia. Living under the wharves, he is befriended by Louis Mendoza, a coffee house errand boy who feeds him. Once he has regained his memory, Jim is able to find his grandfather, a well-known river pilot with a business guiding boats up the river to New Orleans. Although the older Yorby is gruff and emotionless, he lets Jim live with him and when his grandson begins teaching himself about the river, supports his ambition to become a river pilot. The Yorbys have a Spartan existence in a settlement Grat Yorby owns in the Mississippi Delta on the Southwest Pass. In addition to the early section of the novel, that gives a sense of street life and coffee shop culture in the city, the Yorbys visit the city on a shopping excursion, and near the end of the novel, they arrive with the Union fleet as militia men on Commander Farragut's ship as it sails into the harbor, witnessing the destruction along the wharves upon the approach of the Union troops.

328. Matschat, Cecile Hulse. *Murder at the Black Crook.* New York: Farrar and Rinehart, 1943. 250pp.

During World War II, David Ramsay, an architect assigned to the Department of Housing, is called upon for double-duty by the Army Intelligence Agency when huge supplies of crude oil are found missing from New Orleans' Youba Oil Company and are suspected of having gone to the Japanese. Under the direction of Major Cassius Hart, Ramsay and his wife Andrea, are placed in the historic plantation house of Robert Brook, president of the oil company. With the pretense that they are houseguests staying in a wing of the mansion on Moss Street, near City Park, the Ramsays are surrounded by a complex social set of family members, former and future spouses, and their offspring. Among the group are high-power lawyers, a novelist, and a famous actress, Erica Lange. Brook is so avid a supporter of the dramatic arts that he has built a home theater and is about to marry Lange, who is staging the play, "Murder at the Black Crook," in a USO performance. The first murder is committed during a dress rehearsal. As is typical of such mysteries, the close observation of behavior and personality is enabled by keeping the characters and action confined to the mansion house, so that, while set in New Orleans, the city has little presence. However, the mystery treats the city as a strategic military target due to its proximity to shipping, ship-building, and petroleum industries.

329. Matthews, Clayton Hartley. *New Orleans: A Novel.* New York: Pocket Books, 1976. 223pp.

In this sensational novel set over three days of Mardi Gras during the 1970s, all aspects of scandalous New Orleans are on display from political corruption to sexual obsession, religious mania to the violence of social protest movements. At the center of the story presidential aspirant Senator Martin St. Cloud, whose wife Raquel has become troublesome for thinking he should retire and for her increasing resentment over his extramarital affairs. One of these liaisons is with Audrey Fain, a self-possessed young woman with money and social influence, who thinks she would make a good First Lady. Other characters include Ebon, the head of an organization concerned with redressing African-American slavery through acts of violence, and Ando, a religious fanatic with high moral standards who is sickened by his knowledge of the senator's affairs. Calculated to titillate through descriptions of sexual intercourse, this book still includes a good deal of description of New Orleans interlarded with journalistic information about the city's social problems and criminal activity.

330. Matthews, Harold. *River-Bottom Boy.* New York: Thomas Y. Crowell, 1942. 354pp.

Capturing daily life for impoverished African-Americans on a farm and in New Orleans during the Depression, this novel traces the destruction of an entire family within a two-year time span. Protagonist Burden was born in the shack in which his parents, grandparents and great-grandparents lived on the now greatly reduced Musgrove Plantation. As the novel begins, he is sixteen and his sharecropper parents, Luella and Pentacost (sic), are anticipating their annual payment from the widowed Captain Berry Musgrove, whose four children have all begun adult lives far away from the remote plantation. Luella and Pentacost have begun to dream of an easier life than the constant physical labor of the farm and long for participation in the consumer economy. The Burdens are newly inspired at a party at Villere Plantation attended by several sharecroppers who have gone away and comeback for a visit. One, China Mary, is accompanied by the expensively dressed, automobile-driving Slack, who encourages Luella and Pentacost, assuring them that when they arrive in New Orleans they will help them find jobs. The worldly revival preacher Shadrack Kribs also impresses them. Even though Musgrove only gives them one hundred dollars, half the amount they had expected from their year of labor, they still load their modest possessions, along with Burden and his teenaged sisters, into a mule-driven wagon. After several days on the road, they arrive in the completely foreign environment of New Orleans, with no information about how to find housing or jobs. Accustomed to community life in the country, they experience social isolation for the first time, their only, rather remote, guide is a New Orleans under-cover detective named Videau. They inadvertently begin their urban life in the worst possible neighborhood, "Hell's Half Acre," and although they are able to move to Dryades Street after a few months, Pentacost and Luella can only find low-paid work unloading ships and washing dishes in an Italian restaurant respectively. Burden, who finds no work, spends his days searching for Slack and, when finally located, rushes his father to him for his promised job. Instead, Slack hustles Pentacost in a dice game and brings about his violent death. This event, which would seem to be the low point in the family's life, is actually just the beginning of tragedy and suffering at the hands of Slack and the Rev. Kribs, as well as an assortment of dishonest policemen. The only good man in the novel, Videau, comes from such a different socio-economic background that he remains a figure of distrust and his misinterpreted efforts to protect Burden eventually lead to his own death.

331. Maxwell, Patricia. *The Court of the Thorn Tree.* New York: Popular Library, 1974. 253pp.

Set in the early nineteenth century this novel deals with issues of gender and race, as well as describing domestic life in a French Quarter mansion during the time period. When Margaret Stuart's uncle remarried, she found that she was no longer welcome in the household and so a position as governess was arranged for her in the house of a recently widowed Creole gentleman named Charles Villars. In addition to the attractive Villars, the household includes an unmarried brother, Victor, and Charles' quadroon mistress Celeste. As if these strong personalities and their irregular relationships to one another were not enough to challenge even a no-nonsense woman like Stuart, her charge Amelina sometimes behaves so badly it is almost like she is being possessed by evil. Eventually, the little girl confesses that she is under the command of a faceless, ghost woman who comes to her at night. Although the Creoles with whom she comes into contact, at first resent Stuart's Americanness, she eventually earns their admiration and a marriage offer, since the mysteries in house are not of supernatural origin, but are problems the practical-minded Stuart can discern and resolve.

332. Maxwell, Patricia. *The Notorious Angel.* Greenwich, Conn.: Fawcett, 1977. 384pp.

Most of this romance novel revolving around the exploits of William Walker (1824–1860) in Nicaragua takes place in that country. However, the first section of the book is set in New Orleans and it shows how the principals in the Nicaraguan adventure come together in a city filled with excitement over Walker and sympathy for oppressed Central American peoples. The angel of the title, Eleonora Villars, is twenty when the book begins and has had to deal with discovering that her once revered and wealthy Creole family is impoverished. She endures the disgrace of operating a boarding house and no longer having any suitors because of her advanced age and lack of dowry. She has also begun to despair that her brother, Jean-Paul, two years younger than her, may never grow up. The fact that he has enlisted to be a soldier in Nicaragua is, for her, yet another example of his impetuous disregard for responsibility. When she is unable to get him released from his commitment, she too travels to Granada thinking that the money she is able to gather is going to purchase land that will enable a new start. Through her superior personal qualities she eventually helps many people and gains a husband, but returns to make a permanent home in her beloved New Orleans. New Orleans in the novel is a port city filled with peoples of multiple allegiances deeply affected by events in South America and on the Texas frontier.

333. Maxwell, Patricia [Jennifer Blake, pseud.]. *Love's Wild Desire.* New York: Popular Library, 1977. 384pp.

This romance novel raises issues of gender and social class in presenting the story of Eleanora Villars. At the beginning of the novel, Villars has been forced to support herself and her eighteen-year-old brother Jean-Paul, by turning their family home into a boarding house. Their father had abandoned the upper-class social position to which he was entitled, to train as a physician. In treating impoverished immigrants, with his wife as nurse, they contracted cholera during an epidemic and died. Eleanora and Jean-Paul then lived with their grandmother, a very elderly woman with a house on Royal Street, who spoiled Jean-Paul and considered Eleanora worthless female offspring. Although she lived as though she still controlled a fortune, her grandchildren learned after her death that she had little money. While the struggle to earn enough money on which to support them could easily take all of Eleanora's attention, she was constantly forced to rescue Jean-Paul from scrapes he got into at gaming tables and whorehouses. Finally, embracing the popular excitement over the war in Nicaragua, Jean-Paul volunteers for the Walker Campaign, and Eleanora feels compelled to follow him as a nurse. While abroad she falls in love with a Spanish nobleman and marries. By the time she returns, she is renowned as a heroine of the battlefield, and has regained social respectability as the widow of a Spanish nobleman.

334. Maxwell, Patricia [Maxine Patrick, pseud.]. *Bayou Bride.* New York: New American Library, 1978. 171pp.

In this romance novel, twenty-one-year-old Sherry Mason is secretary to an exasperating mid-level manager in the St. Louis office of a New Orleans-based shipping firm. Her life is suddenly transformed through her romance with Paul Villieré, a scion of the family that owns the corporation of which Mason's employer is only a small part. Twenty-five-year-old Villieré is a self-confessed womanizer and he asks Mason to masquerade as his fiancée at an important family event in New Orleans to forestall plans to reunite him with his socially prominent high school sweetheart Aimee Dubois. Mason agrees, but is secretly in love with Paul and tries not to take her role too seriously. She is surprised, however, when Paul's older brother Lucien, the CEO of the family firm, meets her in New Orleans instead of Paul. He has arranged for the limousine ride from the airport, the luxurious French Quarter hotel and, after a romantic carriage ride, dines with her at Antoine's. At first Lucien claims Paul will soon appear, but then acknowledges that he wanted to find out more about Mason to determine whether she was a suitable person for Paul to date. At the end of the evening, Lucien claims Mason meets with his approval and offers to take her to Paul. Only after a long boat ride through the bayous and their arrival at a remote mansion does Mason realized she has been kidnapped. Lucien assures her that she will be released after the weekend during which he is confident that Paul and Aimee will become engaged. However, when Mason tries to escape she encounters a hurricane during which Lucien rescues her and they realize their feelings for each other. Although the novel's portrayal of New Orleans has a touristic shallowness, the novel is of interest for cultural representations of gender roles reflecting the time period in which it was written.

335. May, Margery Land. *Such as Sit in Judgment*. London: Leonard Parsons, 1923. 287pp.

Most of this extended parable on the importance of not rushing to judgment is set in 1920s New Orleans and focuses on sexual morality. Thirty-six-year-old John Dawson spent most of his formative years in England and was schooled at Eton and Oxford, although he feels most at home on his family's plantation outside New Orleans and he spends as much time there as possible, while maintaining a social life in New Orleans, based in his French Quarter townhouse. Accustomed to looking out for his younger brother Robert after the death of their parents, John is worried over Robert's dissipated life in New Orleans and his romance with the mysterious older English divorcée, Angelique Dawson. After John insists she reveal to Robert that she is not interested in a serious relationship, Robert is crushed and travels to England on business for the family firm. In his brother's absence, John is increasingly drawn to the divorcée, whom he finds well read, cultured, and a subtle thinker. However, her past remains mysterious, as does her connection to Chapman Griswold, a roué with a well-earned record for spoiling the reputations of young New Orleans women. To complicate matters, Kitty Drexel, who remains in love with John, despite her marriage to his wealthy friend, James Dunstan Drexel, sets out to damage Mrs. Dawson's reputation and sets off a violent rivalry between John and his brother Robert over her. The situation causes seemingly endless soul-searching on the part of John, although he eventually proposes marriage to Mrs. Dawson, who accepts on the curious stipulation that the betrothal remains a secret until her sister marries Tom Eustace, another friend of John. When Robert learns of the impending marriage, he maliciously claims that Griswold spent a night with Mrs. Dawson at a notorious hotel. When she realizes that John believes the accusation, Mrs. Dawson breaks off the engagement. By the end of the novel, however, John realizes that he has rushed to judgment after he discovers Mrs. Dawson's impeccable social background and the fact that she was protecting her sister from Griswold. Much of the novel's action transpires at public social events in New Orleans; restaurants, private clubs, and residences are also referenced and described. Dual standards for the sexual morality of men and women are analyzed and an example of the "new woman," who is self-confident and defies traditional standards, is presented. The novel includes descriptions of relations between African-American servants and employers that are uniformly demeaning to the former.

336. McCormick, William Bennett. *The Wanton: A Story of the Red Light*. Shreveport, La.: The Author, 1925. 495pp.

This work presents exhaustive information about prostitution in New Orleans in the early twentieth century. Through the 1880s story of Ellen Landry, the author conveys the full import of crimes against women. Orphaned and needing to support herself, Landry gets a job playing piano at the Palais Royal, a bar with a floorshow owned by Jack Bruce. The novel provides a good deal of information about the ruses used to cheat the Palais patrons out of money and the Palais Royal's connection to houses of prostitution also owned by Bruce. Landry falls completely under Bruce's power when she prostitutes herself to him in order to pay for her sister's operation. As a steady stream of misfortune overtakes Landry's family, she is drawn into becoming Bruce's mistress. He eventually makes her one of his madams, renaming her Madame LeGrande. Secretly, she uses her position to help the girls working for her and get them out of prostitution. Later she hears the Rev. James Boland preach, becomes acquainted with him, and falls in love. The two grow closer when she nurses him during a fever epidemic. However, Bruce eventually discovers what is going on and revenges himself on Landry by having himself beaten up and falsely accusing LeGrande and Boland, who are tried for the crime with dramatic news coverage. Although the wronged couple is freed when Bruce is unmasked, they enjoy no happiness. The dark side of New Orleans is presented in this novel with great factual detail.

337. McCurtin, Peter. *The Assassin; New Orleans Holocaust.* New York: Dell / Lorelei, 1973. 191pp.

In 1972, after gun shop owner Robert Briganti refused to illegally supply firearms to the Long Island crime family of Joe Coraldi, mobsters murdered his wife and son, leading him to begin a vigilante campaign against organized crime. To counter Briganti's attacks, crime family heads meet in New Orleans' Fontainebleau Hotel to plan Briganti's elimination. Instead of being intimidated, Briganti decides to further his vendetta by attacking the gathering and is particularly excited that Joe Coraldi's brother, Benito "The Dick" Bonasera Coraldi, will attend. (Yes, Coraldi's nickname does refer to his physical endowment and sexual prowess and the book includes much sexual innuendo, mostly homophobic, or involving violence against women.) Sam Rubi, a retired Bourbon Street shooting gallery operator; retired policeman Mike Donofrio; and stripper Annie Murphy, a.k.a. Starfire LaFever, aid Briganti in his New Orleans campaign. After landing by helicopter on the roof of the Fontainebleau, Briganti kills a number of Mafia gunmen and escapes to be bandaged at Murphy's French Quarter apartment before going into hiding in the decaying Metairie mansion of Rubi's sister. Briganti is soon revenging himself on Murphy's killer, however, after she dies from vicious kicks received from a sadistic Mafia foot soldier and a gay Dominican immigrant, Eladio Connelly, who is the son of an Irish-American Voodoo priest. (To eliminate the latter, Briganti must visit a gay club.) Although Briganti later uses grenades to kill more than twenty Mafia kingpins at the Judah P. Benjamin Hotel, Coraldi is not among them and he must track him down using a bayou boat and finish him off in a swamp. In the midst of his killing spree, first-person narrator Briganti comments on changes in New Orleans, including urban renewal to attract tourists, and the increase in Latino immigrants and openly gay men.

338. McHale, Larry. *Dark Shadows.* Philadelphia: Dorrance, 1962. 269pp.

This historical romance novel presents the Battle of New Orleans through the characters of Richard Woods and Réné d'Estes. Woods grew up on the frontier and is an American in the mold of Andrew Jackson (1767–1845). When d'Estes, the son of a French fencing master who had grown up in New Orleans and St. Louis, is commissioned by Jackson to travel to his hometown to assess, and if need be, to influence New Orleans residents to support the United States against the British, he seeks out Woods to accompany him on his recognizance mission. Along the way, they meet seventeen-year-old Marie, traveling with Jean Bares, the old man she believes to be her grandfather. As the old man dies, he reveals to Woods and d'Estes that he had been a pirate with Lafitte and helped capture the ship on which Marie's mother, a noblewoman named Louise Lannoy, had been traveling. Lannoy bribed Bares with a cask of jewels to protect Marie and care for her. Bares had been on his way to New Orleans to place Marie Louise in a convent and deposit the remaining jewels in an account for her use. Woods and d'Estes set off to complete his mission and d'Estes is immediately smitten with the young woman, who soon reciprocates his feelings. When they arrive in New Orleans, d'Estes turns Marie over to the care of his aunt, Martha Doyle, a formidable society woman. He returns to the house on St. Anne that his father had sixteen years earlier left in the care of Ben, his quadroon wife Lucy, and his octoroon daughter Emma. As Doyle coaches Marie in the behavior appropriate to a Creole society woman, d'Estes begins a romantic relationship with Emma and has sex with her. However, he is disgusted to learn that she had been courted by an octoroon and breaks off contact with her. D'Estes then learns that his own father had a quadroon mistress and an octoroon daughter, Gloria. When Woods unwittingly falls in love with Gloria, d'Estes reveals her identity before leaving New Orleans. After d'Estes' departure, Emma dies in aborting his baby and Woods proposes to Gloria. Her mother does not regard him as suitable since he has no money and, at any rate, no priest will perform a wedding since Gloria is of mixed race. Although Woods pledges that if he survives the Battle of New Orleans, he will take Gloria to Missouri and marry her, just before the battle a Voodoo priest takes her captive and kills her when she tries to escape. With battle imminent, d'Estes returns to defend New Orleans and, in this version, is the one who gets Jackson to make a pact with Lafitte. Reacquainted with Marie, he falls in love, but she knows about his affair with Emma. After d'Estes is wounded, Woods effects a reconciliation by explaining to Marie that d'Estes' affair with Emma had just continued a childhood dalliance and never been love. In addition to presenting yet another retelling of the Battle of New Orleans, the book touches on issues of gender and mixed-race identity.

339. McKeag, Ernest Lionel [Roland Vane, pseud.]. *White Slaves of New Orleans.* Cleveland, Ohio: Kaywin, 1951. 128pp.

The orphaned Shirley Westford is trapped into white slavery when she is forced to sign a document stating she owes money to Jack Gutterman. After she is registered as a prostitute by the police and told she can never leave the "colored" district without attracting police attention, she becomes resigned to her fate, although she still initially believes Gutterman's assertion that he will release her after five years of work. However, one of her clients, Cal Wheeler, a wealthy, politically prominent lawyer, convinces her that she will never be free because the police have a file on her with false information supplied by Gutterman. Eventually, she thinks she has gained the upper hand when she finds a notebook in the drunken Wheeler's pocket that documents his ownership of brothels all over the city, including Gutterman's. Stealing the book in order to threaten his political ambitions, she gets him to procure her police file and make her one of his madams. Becoming wealthy through her new position, she is shocked when Wheeler reveals he merely gave her a copy of her police file. After introducing gambling parlors into her houses, she suckers a wealthy New York businessman, Roger van Tarlesan, and, to discharge his debt, he agrees to marry Shirley and help her change her identity. She easily manages the alcoholic Tarlesan, and lives the life of a New York society woman while building a new fortune by means of a yacht that sails between New Orleans and South America and functions as a luxurious private brothel for wealthy men. When Shirley decides to give up her life of vice, fate intervenes to punish her misdeeds. The book details twentieth-century white slavery and prostitution in New Orleans, but while at times sympathetic to the plight of white slaves, also takes satisfaction in describing their sufferings.

340. McNeill, Nevada [A.S.M., pseud.]. *The Yellow Rose of New Orleans: A Novel.* New York: G.W. Dillingham, 1895. 246pp.

In this attack on mixed-race people and miscegenation the life of an abandoned girl is used to present a racist lesson. Literally born on the street in Algiers, Rose is left at a Roman Catholic Church and raised in the priest's household until his death when she is thirteen. Although she is part African-American, Rose is filled with loathing toward "pure Negros," even though, according to the narrator, some aspects of her racial inheritance—superstition and the dominance of emotion and appetite over her intellect—keep her from progressing. At fifteen Rose is pretty and white in appearance and Mr. and Mrs. Douglas Chase, wealthy Northerners living near St. Louis Cathedral, informally adopt her, since they are childless. Around the time Mrs. Chase dies, twenty-three-year-old Rose marries thirty-year-old Geoffrey Marneff, a lawyer and cotton planter, never revealing her mixed-race identity. The two live quietly in Marneff's suburban house, Chateau Espagne, and rarely socialize due to Marneff's religiosity. However, two years after their wedding Marneff invites his Northern friend Dr. Juste to spend Mardi Gras with them. Subsequent to attending a ball, Rose falls ill and when Juste exams her, he realizes she is of mixed blood because of the color of her cuticles. Because Marneff has always been outspoken about his distaste for mixed marriages, Dr. Juste takes pleasure in revealing his discovery. Dr. Juste, enabled by his wealth to pursue private research, prides himself on his ability to detect the smallest amount of African-American blood. He tells Marneff horror stories about the ways in which mixed-race people (here referred to as Creoles), conceal their identity and marry whites. Marneff exiles Rose to her adopted father's house, where Rose falls ill and comes under the control of a savage Voodoo practitioner, filled with hatred over Rose trying to pass as white. Surprisingly, Marneff can hardly restrain himself from reclaiming Rose, so he leaves the city without her knowledge. When she musters all her waning strength to go to him and beg forgiveness, she discovers he has gone, and falls to her deathbed. When Marneff decides he can no longer be separated from her, he returns prepared to brave social censure and reclaim her. He finds her dead, dies himself three weeks later, and is buried at her side.

341. Michaels, Irene. *Frenchman's Mistress.* New York: Dell, 1980. 432pp.

This historical romance novel presents a heroic female character. Irish-born Tierney Chambers is forced to become a tavern servant girl after the death of her grandmother. To escape the unbearable life, at sixteen she disguises herself and gets work as a cabin boy on the boat of André de Montfort. After a period of tension, Chambers' sex is revealed and the two begin a sexual relationship. However, Montfort arrives in New Orleans in January of 1813 to get involved in the sugar trade through an alliance with Jean Lafitte, and having no time for teenage girls, places Chambers in Ursuline Convent. While Chambers quickly acclimates to convent life, when she is discovered to be pregnant she is sent to Pass Christian to work as a nanny. Unfortunately, Indians capture her and her baby, Rosalie Neal. Montfort rescues her and returns with her to New Orleans, however, the Indians had managed to conceal the whereabouts of her baby. Even though Montfort arranges a Roman Catholic wedding and settles with Chambers in a well-appointed townhouse, she is still agonized over the loss of her daughter. Distracted by the impending British attack on the city, Montfort is away from New Orleans when Jim Bowie (c.1796–1836) reveals the likely whereabouts of Rosalie in Mississippi. Too impatient to await Montfort's return, Tierney disguises herself as a man and travels with Bowie to recover her daughter. A snakebite forces her to return to New Orleans without reaching the Indian camp and the British approach forces Montfort to defer Rosalie's rescue. In this version, Montfort plays a crucial role in getting Governor Claiborne to make an alliance with Jean Lafitte and, while talks are underway, Tierney helps Pierre Lafitte escape from prison. As soon as the decisive battle ends, Montfort successfully recovers his daughter. The novel makes the argument that non-conformist women like Tierney are characteristic of the new American society that has emerged at New Orleans, although the character seems to tell us more about the period in which it was written than about historical New Orleans society.

342. Miller, Martha Carolyne Keller. *The Fair Enchantress, or, How She Won Men's Hearts.* Philadelphia: T.B. Peterson, 1883. 260pp.

Between the ages of seven and roughly eighteen, the long-suffering heroine of this novel lives through the murder of both her parents, an escape from her mother's murderer, life on the streets, a murder attempt on her life, a first romance, a yellow fever epidemic, the death of her first love, and marriage out of mature consideration, rather than love. When she was only seven-years-old Edna Mabrey's father was murdered and she was sent to a convent boarding school where she became the most studious of scholars. Called back to her mother at thirteen, Mabrey arrives at the bloody death scene of her mother to witness the murderer, Episcopal priest Rev. Dr. Cluny, before he escapes. After the funeral, when she is told Cluny is to be her guardian, she flees to New Orleans. With no acquaintances and unable to find a job, she lives on the streets and sleeps in a cemetery until thirty-year-old Dr. Erle Kingsley discovers her. Unfortunately, his home life is a less-than-promising refuge for the girl. As a youth, Kingsley had fallen in love with his stepsister, Netta Burbank. After he came into his inheritance, she agreed to marry him, although she wanted a settlement of eighty thousand dollars. He consented, but after the wedding Burbank claimed that because a Protestant minister performed the ceremony she did not consider them married (she is Roman Catholic). She kept his money and he traveled in Europe and the Far East before returning to New Orleans. In an attempt to force Burbank out of his house, Kingsley returns there with Edna Mabrey causing Burbank to be consumed by jealousy over Kingsley's affection for the girl. Kingsley offers to adopt Mabrey when she is fourteen, but she inexplicably changes her name to Mora Evans and says she would rather continue her schooling and eventually repay Kingsley. Shortly afterwards Burbank tries to poison her, but Evans/Mabrey forgives the distraught woman and even forces Kingsley to reconcile with her. By the time she is seventeen Evans/Mabrey has published newspaper articles and a book and attracts Sir Guy Lindsay. Kingsley prevents a marriage proposal in order to allow Evans/Mabrey time to consider if she loves the much older Lindsay. Working as a governess, she is traveling in the North when she hears of the 1878 yellow fever epidemic and returns to New Orleans to nurse the sick. The Rev. Dr. Cluny and Burbank are among the dying. In a bizarre coincidence Cluny married Burbank under an assumed identity to get control of her money, eventually murdering her parents to increase her fortune. In the midst of the epidemic Evans meets Orrick Graham, a gifted politician and man of wealth, who has dedicated himself to assisting the fever victims. When the two fall in love and pledge to marry after the epidemic ends, Kingsley breaks the news to her former suitor Lindsay. Autumn finally comes and the fever abates; however, on the evening of her wedding day Evans watches at the deathbed of Orrick Graham. When her erstwhile guardian Kingsley arrives from London in 1881, Evans/Mabrey is prepared to accept his marriage proposal. Though almost entirely set in New Orleans, the text includes little description of the city and contains extended philosophical discussions about suffering, death, and religion.

343. Minnigerode, Meade. *Cockades.* New York: G.P. Putnam's Sons, 1927. 374pp.

In this novel about French royalists in the United States, the author invents a fiction based on the idea that the Dauphin of France survived the French Revolution and was brought to the United States in 1793, by a group of French immigrants and Americans, including Aaron Burr (1756–1836), Edmond-Charles "Citizen" Genet (1763–1834), and Count Axel von Fersen (1755–1810). Most of the book is set in the political circles New York City and is preoccupied with a fictional presentation of the issues surrounding the relationship between the United States, France, and Britain, and the machinations amongst various factions. A crisis that lasts several years arises when the Spanish kidnap the Dauphin in 1798 and hide him in their New World colonies. By 1803 spies let the royalists know that the Dauphin is being brought to New Orleans and Raoul de Vendome is deputed for recognizance. Arriving shortly before Louisiana's transfer from Spain to France, Vendome hears diverse reactions in the city. The Roman Catholic population is especially concerned at the approach of French Republicanism. Then, suddenly, word comes that Louisiana has been transferred to the United States. Over the course of several months Vendome gets no clue as to the French royal's whereabouts. After killing one of the kidnappers he discovers many useful documents on the corpse, one of which indicates that the Dauphin is being held at the arsenal on St. Anthony's Alley. As a lone agent, Vendome can do little. Then, Louis de Valmy appears, a police detective for Napoleon Bonaparte (1769–1821). Believing him to be an ally, Vendome shares the Dauphin's location, leading Valmy to organize a plan with the brothers Lafitte to rescue the young man as he is being moved on the day of Louisiana's official transfer. The Dauphin himself short-circuits the plan. Suspecting the Spaniards are taking him to Havana, he escapes the carriage in which he is being driven to the ship. Tired of captivity, whether by royalists or Spaniards, he decides to give up his claim to the throne. After hiding briefly at the Ursuline Convent, he moves to a boarding house. Initially, only Vendome knows the truth, but eventually he is forced to tell double agent Valmy, who begins to plot the Dauphin's imprisonment. To avoid future interest, the Dauphin destroys the papers proving his identity, thwarting the royalists and causing Valmy to lose interest in him. The New Orleans of the novel is highly politicized and divided into factions based on European loyalties. However, the book reveals the strength of the United States in melding people from various nationalities; even a King of France decides to become part of such a country.

344. Mitchell, Carl. *Walk the Gay Night.* Van Nuys, Calif.: Triumph, 1967. 158pp.

In this erotic novel, Marine Lieutenant Drin Coty is on a ninety-day shore leave in New Orleans and the open sensuality of the town gives him the opportunity to explore his sexuality. His partner in this adventure is Troy Dean, a fellow sailor, who like him, is less than five foot five. Coty grew up in Mississippi hill country and Dean, who grew up in New Orleans, serves as a guide. Currently Dean lives in Algiers, but his mother has an apartment in the Pontalba Buildings, which she uses as her base for antiquing. The two get into a scuffle with Cubans, an ethnic group that is said to be filling up the streets of the post-World War II city. Plotting revenge, the two frequent Cuban hangouts, more often than not gay bars, where the Cubans are fetishized. The two young men share Dean's tastefully furnished apartment in Algiers during their adventure and become emotionally and physically intimate. The novel is filled with rhetoric concerning masculinity, as well as lists of bars and descriptions of them and the French Quarter in the 1960s. Mardi Gras is underway during part of the book and, later, the one hundred and fiftieth anniversary of the Louisiana Purchase is celebrated.

345. Moon, Ilanon. *Twilight on the River.* Austin, Tex.: Shoal Creek, 1977. 223pp.

Although most of this historical romance is set outside New Orleans, particularly in Natchitoches, the novel deals with French colonial identity in Louisiana between the years 1762 and 1768, when protagonist Gaston de la Mignet travels frequently to New Orleans to participate in political councils. One focus is the way in which frontier culture erodes notions of social precedence and nobility. Aristocrat de la Mignet is at first appalled and then angered that his rights as a nobleman are not respected. However, through the guidance of his friend, Athanase de Mezieres (1719–1779), whom he considers his social superior, de la Mignet comes to accept earned respect as the basis of frontier social structure. By the time France cedes Louisiana to the Spanish at the end of the novel, de la Mignet and his circle realize that Americans, not European governments, will soon control the continent. The New Orleans setting is mostly represented by historical figures and events, rather than descriptions of the place.

346. Moore, John Trotwood. *Hearts of Hickory: A Story of Andrew Jackson and the War of 1812.* Nashville, Tenn.: Cokesbury, 1926. 450pp.

Presenting vignettes of some of the officers and soldiers who fought with Jackson (1767–1845) on his War of 1812 campaign, this narrative begins shortly after the end of the Creek Indian War, provides an account of life on the Tennessee frontier, and presents events around Jackson and his men, from the declaration of war on Britain in 1812, through the Battle of New Orleans. Only the final eighty pages or so are set in New Orleans. Throughout the novel, fictional character Philippe Trevellian provides a foil to raise issues of immigration and social class. Trevellian was raised as a gentleman by his French tutor, even though his parents are dead and he has private doubts that they were legally married. Even as a teenager he is skilled in using a sword and a gun and follows a code of gentlemanly conduct that makes him conspicuous on the frontier. At times his aristocratic code inspires resentment since many frontiersman were forced out of their home countries by land seizures and dislocations caused by warring nobility. General Jackson respects Trevellian's courage in adhering to a strict code of conduct and accepts the teenager's enlistment, eventually promoting him to captain. During Jackson's 1812 campaign, Count de Chartres captures Trevellian. Concerned about rivals to the French throne, Chartres holds Trevellian because, with all the beheadings, he can probably claim the title "Duke of Orleans." Trevellian rejects any claim to nobility, preferring to be known as an American. He is soon rescued through the efforts of his frontier beloved, Pamela Crockett, and is able to fight in the Battle of New Orleans. Once the battle is won, he and Crockett return to the Tennessee frontier to marry.

347. Morrow, Susan. *The Insiders.* Garden City, N.Y.: Doubleday / Crime Club, 1967. 191pp.

An employment agency is at the center of this murder mystery. Anne Repplier is a strong-willed, successful, businesswoman, owning and operating her own personnel firm. Even the powerful Orenda Oil Company has retained her to recruit top executives. When one man she placed with the firm, Philip Lang, is killed by being flung from an oil rig in the Gulf of Mexico, Orenda vice president Hoyt Sullivan, shows up in New Orleans to investigate. Lang left behind a note, indicating he knew he would be killed, and mysteriously listing six men, all of whom Orenda had hired through Repplier. Sullivan, a self-made man, is less impressed by Repplier's connections (her father is a well-respected judge and friend of Eric Enders, a man with great power in political and financial circles). He is, however, immediately smitten with Repplier, but very cautious, since he knows his employer, John Ivory, is also in love with her. Soon, he learns that she has accepted a proposal from Enders, a considerably older man, on whom she earlier had a schoolgirl crush. What motivated Enders to propose so suddenly after Sullivan's arrival in town and what exactly is the relationship between Enders and Lang's widow Mira, the proprietress of a high-end Royal Street antiques shop? The evidence soon leads to insider stock trading with Enders at the center. Should he ever come to trial, however, there could be a crisis in the market that would bring economic collapse. Although Sullivan follows leads in Houston and New York City, most of the novel is set in New Orleans and settings include the Reppliers' Garden District mansion, the Boston Club, and exclusive restaurants. The novel deals with contemporary topics such as the challenges faced by families with developmentally disabled children, internalized racism, and efforts to overcome racism in the workplace.

348. Murphy, Edward F(rancis). *Angel of the Delta.* New York: Hanover House, 1958. 311pp.

The first one hundred and twenty pages of this fictionalized biography of Margaret Gaffney Haughery (1813–1882) covers her birth into poverty in Ireland, emigration with her family to Baltimore, her parents' deaths when she was nine-years-old, subsequent adoption, childhood, and marriage to Charles Haughery at twenty-one. Haughery's birth on Christmas Day was considered an augury and this hagiographical work makes much of sayings and actions that evidence her faith and charity. Courted by brothers Daniel and Charles Haughery, Margaret weds Charles, the weaker of the two, after headstrong Daniel leaves for the Ohio frontier. Charles' ill health prompts an 1835 move to the warmer climate of New Orleans. However, his health deteriorates further, after the death of their infant daughter, and, after returning to his family in Ireland, dies, leaving Margaret with modest savings and a small cottage in Irish Channel. A devoted parishioner of St. Patrick's Church from the time of her arrival in New Orleans, her parish priest, Father Mullon suggests ways in which she can focus her charitable nature to bolster church groups for women and aid the Sisters of Charity in operating their orphanage. Caring little for her own needs, Haughery spends her time soliciting cash and in-kind donations, while supporting herself as a laundress at the St. Charles Hotel. When Daniel Haughery reappears in her life, enriched by frontier land acquisitions, she rejects his marriage proposal to continue her charities. After a gift of land, she starts a dairy herd for the needs of the orphans and begins vending surplus milk and cream as another support for the orphanage. The success of this business leads her to invest in the D'Aquin Bakery so that the orphans will have a guaranteed bread supply, eventually becoming the principal stockholder after an economic crisis. Selling baked goods from a cart, the products become synonymous with her, and Margaret's Bread flourishes, eventually becoming the first steam bakery in the South. The book depicts ways in which Haughery, though devoted to her ethnic heritage and to the Roman Catholic Church, was also a unifying force in a divided city, as she befriended African-Americans, Voodoo practitioners (including Madame Laveau), Jews, Protestants, and immigrants from many countries. Although the novelist expresses rhetoric echoing what is known as the South's "Lost Cause" view of the Civil War, Haughery is shown to be a supporter of the federal government and devoted to the United States, despite her confrontations with Benjamin Butler. The book provides perspectives on the immigrant experience, Irish settlement in New Orleans, the social impact of the Roman Catholic Church, and the role of lay Catholics in funding Church projects and growth.

349. Murphy, Edward F(rancis). *Bride for New Orleans.* Garden City, N.Y.: Hanover House, 1955. 313pp.

In his telling of the story of the casket girls (women brought from France to be married), Murphy focuses on one beautiful woman, Yvonne Delisle. Delisle had gladly left her home in Paris'

Montmartre after her mother died and her father married a hostile new wife. Although innocent and pure, she is accused of bewitching men after she starts working in a dress shop. Ursuline nun, Sister Madeleine, believes in Delisle and thinks she might be called to the novitiate. She arranges for her to travel with other nuns taking casket girls to the New World in 1727. By the time they arrive in the Gulf of Mexico, several duels to the death have been fought over Delisle. When they arrive in Belize and the governor and two powerful noblemen compete for her, the nuns deflect their interest by leaving behind casket girls in her stead, disguising Delisle as a nun in anticipation of her future vocation. However, when Raymonde Massey, a wealthy young man under a vow to join the priesthood and evangelize the Natchez Indians, is smitten with Delisle, the nuns are finally exasperated. He resists contact with Delisle after his priest advises him that he cannot be released from his vow, but finally, overcome by passion, gets her to consent to go unchaperoned to his plantation. Immediately realizing his offense against God and the harm to Delisle's reputation, he leaves her, signing over to her his plantation, slaves, money, and deceased mother's jewels and he returns to New Orleans to take up his vow. After much tribulation, Delisle is able to repay Sister Madeleine's faith in her by reforming some prostitutes. Just as Delisle has begun to plead to become a nun, Massey returns from the wilderness, blinded and with his health shattered, causing Delisle to become first his nurse and then his wife. While roughly half the book recounts shipboard adventures, the one hundred and forty pages set in New Orleans cover a good deal of history, most of which focuses on competing Roman Catholic orders and political factions. Written in the 1950s, cultural attitudes toward female sexuality dramatically shape the narrative.

350. Murphy, Edward F(rancis). *Père Antoine.* Garden City, N.Y.: Doubleday, 1947. 304pp.

In this historical novel Murphy creates a psychological portrait of New Orleans' famous priest, Antonio de Sedella, O.F.M., Capuchin (1748–1829). The early part of the book is set in Granada where Antonio (born Francisco Ildelfonso Moreno) not yet in holy orders, falls in love with Anglice Hernandez. His boyhood friend, Emilio Fernandez, becomes his rival for Anglice and is able to make Antonio seem unavailable, due to his long devotion to the Church and clear priestly vocation. Anglice suppresses her love for Antonio and chooses worldly Emilio. Despite his boyhood friendship with Emilio, Antonio remains bitter over the way Emilio manipulated Anglice and, in Murphy's view, his animus fuels his passion to punish sinners. As a Capuchin, he embraces the Office of the Inquisition and upon arriving in New Orleans in 1774 and becoming pastor of the Church of St. Louis in 1781, he harshly pursues a series of heresy investigations as commissary of the Inquisition. His strict ideology causes trouble for political rulers, as does his pastoral role, vaunting the rights of the poor and African-Americans. In Murphy's account, Antonio's strict ideology plays a crucial role in the city's 1788 destruction by fire because he declared church bells could only be rung as a call to divine office, not as a warning. Murphy also presents ways Antonio fueled the rivalry between the Capuchins and other religious orders in Louisiana. In 1790 Antonio was forced to return to Spain and finds that Anglice has died. In Murphy's fictional world, Antonio's contact with Anglice's daughter converts him to a more loving form of Christianity. Then, on the long voyage back to New Orleans, he is subjected to prolonged contact with Terence McGovern, a merchant and Revolutionary War veteran, who instructs him as to the principles of the Declaration of Independence, as well as to the true meaning of shepherding a flock of sinners. Given Murphy's ethnicity and his assertion of the positive influence of Irishmen in New Orleans' development, this character and his influence is not surprising and the friendship between the two men continues in the novel. Under these influences, Père Antoine returns to New Orleans to become a long-serving, beloved figure as rector of St. Louis Cathedral until his death in 1829.

351. Murray, John. *Belle Esperance.* Notre Dame, Ind.: Ave Maria, 1942. 344pp.

This pro-Confederate book has many settings in addition to the Louisiana plantation of its title. New Orleans, however, is described in some detail before, during, and after the Civil War. The Cornevals, French nobility with a history in Louisiana dating back to d'Iberville, own the splendid Belle Esperance sugar plantation. Although slaves labor to operate the place, the visiting Michael O'Toole finds the Cornevals enlightened and cultured. O'Toole comes from Chicago, where his grandfather made a fortune in real estate, which his father enlarged considerably. Even in December 1860, as secession fervor is on the ascendant, he is treated cordially because his grandfather had saved a Corneval patriarch on a Mexican-American battlefield. Francois de Corneval, the current master, is nearly O'Toole's age, as is his sister Alice, with whom O'Toole falls in love. Anti-Northern sentiment begins to run so high that the Cornevals smuggle him off the plantation so that he can return to Chicago. O'Toole makes a chancy return to the South for the 1861 Mardi Gras in New Orleans. The author describes the parades and Comus Ball as enactments of tradition. Immediately afterwards the city returns to war preparations. The city is described once again when Alice returns to her aunt's house there during Buell's occupation to gather medical supplies for the Confederate hospital in which she works. Her aunt and the physician who aid her smuggling describe living under Buell and the impact of the Confiscation Act. (They take the oath of allegiance but remain loyal to the Confederacy.) In describing the city during Reconstruction, the novel continues a theme that runs throughout to show that African-Americans are incapable of self-determination and presents with horror the image of whites forced to submit to brutish African-American policemen and the power of un-enlightened blacks who control elections.

352. Murray, John. *Son of the Bayou.* Notre Dame, Ind.: Ave Maria, 1940. 317pp.

Like other novels concerned with antebellum laws that subjected people of mixed-race heritage to the same treatment as African-Americans, this book's protagonist is burdened by a mystery concerning his origin, that prevents him from pursuing courtship and marriage. For the reader there is no mystery. Joseph Lacorne, educated from the age of five in French boarding schools with a New Orleans guardian acting on behalf of an unnamed benefactor, is actually the son of Marie Lavasse and Louis de Corneval, the heir to one of Louisiana's most important fortunes. When Corneval met Lavasse he assumed she was Caucasian based on her appearance, but is later told that she is a quadroon. He persists in his love affair even after he is warned that such alliances can never be blessed by marriage. Corneval establishes Lavasse in a house on Rampart Street, the couple has Joseph Lacorne, and Louis de Corneval does not marry any of the New Orleans debutantes his parents parade before him. During the Asiatic cholera epidemic of 1832 Corneval flees the city to one of his family's plantations and Lavasse perishes (Corneval assumes Joseph has as well). Joseph is taken in by Antoinette Lavasse, the woman Lavasse knew as her mother. She has means, since as a free woman of color she owns a large boarding house on Canal Street and becomes Joseph's benefactress, sending him to France. There, his intelligence and physical strength well suit him to a military career and by age twenty-five he has served the French army in a number of military campaigns and published a military treatise. Wounded in the Crimean war, the nun who cares for him, remarks over his resemblance to her own brother, Louis de Corneval and, with a period of recuperation ahead of him before he can return to active duty, Joseph travels to New Orleans to solve the mystery of his parentage. His first steps lead him to the story the reader knows, but a deathbed confession by Antoinette, given to him by an aged priest, reveals that Marie Lavasse had been adopted by Antoinette after her poor German immigrant parents died of yellow fever. When Joseph meets Corneval shortly before that man's death he is able to tell him of Lavasse's racial purity and discovers that Corneval had actually married Lavasse. With proof of his origins, Lacorne returns to France, making no claim on the Cornevals. He takes the name of his mother's family, and successfully courts an upper-class woman. This novel makes an interesting contrast to abolitionist novels written in the antebellum period that also deal with mixed-race origins.

353. Neubauer, William Arthur [Norma Newcomb, pseud.] *The Heart Story.* New York: Gramercy, 1947. 254pp.

Although Phyllis Bradley moves to New Orleans for a job, the relocation is also an escape from a love affair gone wrong, allowing her to eventually find true love in the city. A native New Yorker, Bradley had qualms about Joe Endicott's possessiveness, but she was reluctant to end the relationship, since he had been her first love. However, when she and Endicott fight publicly over his paying attention to Lucille Tompkins, Bradley's wise employers, Miss Griselda and Miss Deborah, co-owners of the London Dock restaurant chain where she is their most successful waitress, quickly offer her an assistant manager job in New Orleans to separate her from a man they consider wrong for her. Once she is settled in, Miss Deborah insists Bradley go on dates with Andrew Penn, who had become smitten with Bradley when he visited New York. Although she issues warnings about his treatment of women, Miss Deborah wants Penn's family to invest in her restaurant chain and believes women should use their emotional control over men to advance their own interests. Miss Deborah has no illusions about Penn, a man she thinks should be jailed for the way he treats women. At first Bradley goes along, but then Penn's mother and his jilted lover, Isabel Queen, tell her that even Miss Deborah's promotion of her was part of a plot laid by Penn, to win Bradley. Outraged, and disgusted with the heat and over-emotional residents, Bradley leaves the city to return to wintertime New York. There she sees the happily married Endicott and pregnant Lucille and rues leaving him. Other emotional confusions follow before Andrew Penn reappears to defend his actions and take extraordinary measures to force Bradley to accept his marriage proposal and return to New Orleans.

354. Neugass, James. *Rain of Ashes.* New York: Harper and Brothers, 1949. 326pp.

As this family saga begins in 1913, patriarch Gunther Ewart, founder of the firm Ewart and Sons, has been dead for several years. He had built churches, hotels, stores, and street railroads, amassing a fortune as well as public acclaim, but his family being lesser creatures cannot carry his legacy forward. His wife took to his deathbed soon after he was gone, not truly ill but seeking sympathy. His oldest son Otto, who has never moved out of the family mansion on Bonaparte Avenue, is keen to take his father's place by pushing out his siblings. Otto's sister Sybil lives in a mansion next door with her handsome husband Charles Morand, who she chose less out of romantic love than a hope that he would take her father's place in the company and advance her children's interests in the firm. She has three offspring, Helen, Dennis, and Ralphie, all unpleasant personalities. The only Ewart heir with no designs on the company is youngest son Homer, who lives a dissipated life of women and alcohol. Charles Morand uses all of his energies to keep the Ewart family name from being tarnished by Homer's disgraceful behavior with a string of actresses, while grandly supporting his own wife and children in New York, at fashionable summer resorts, and on trips abroad. Feeling abandoned in New Orleans, Charles eventually commences a series of affairs. Through his social life, the wanderings of Homer, and Otto's self-important club activities, commissions and dinners, a good deal of information is conveyed about a male world in the city composed of private clubs and dining rooms. The book also provides rich detail about the furnishings and operation of upper class New Orleans households in the first half of the twentieth century.

355. Nixon, Joan Lowery. *Mystery of the Hidden Cockatoo.* Illustrated by Richard Lewis. New York: Criterion, 1966. 144pp.

A stereotypical French Quarter provides the atmospheric setting for this mystery novel written for young girls. Thirteen-year-old Pam Peters, the oldest of five children, is beginning to express frustration with the ways her siblings are holding her back from teen activities, when her mother arranges for Pam to visit her twenty-five-year-old aunt, Janet, who operates her own public relations agency in New Orleans. Janet collects antiques and lives in an apartment carved out of the historic Roche mansion. Soon after Pam arrives, Janet tells her the romantic story of a Roche girl who fell in love with a pirate from whom she received a valuable jeweled cockatoo pin, which she hid before dying of yellow fever. Pam involves her new friend Felicity in searching for the pin. Two other mansion tenants complicate their quest, Madame Lala—who operates a tearoom and reads palms—and her nephew Bert—a painter. A talking parrot, ghostly sailor, and a secret passage add to the atmosphere, but actual New Orleans locales play only a small role.

356. Nunez, Nemours Henry, Jr. *Chien Negre: A Tale of Vaudoux.* Aurora, Mo.: Burney Brothers, 1938. 278pp.

This tale of gothic suspense written by an African-American depicts the plight of blacks after the Civil War, when white racial hatred is exacerbated by the loss of land and wealth that is symbolized by freed African-Americans. Armand Garvais developed a great hatred for his father for leaving his dying mother and selling off his plantation and slaves to live with a quadroon mistress. As a riverboat captain, Garvais has numerous opportunities to vent his hatred of blacks, particularly when they are of mixed race. A man of towering height and daunting strength, Garvais cudgels his African-American workers and sometimes whips them to death. When the quadroon Chlora is discovered on his boat as a stowaway, Garvais' first mate assumes she will be dealt with violently and is surprised when Garvais treats her with consideration and allows her to remain on board. A sexual relationship develops between the two, and Chlora falls in love with Garvais. However, when Chlora becomes pregnant, Garvais is horrified that he has followed in the steps of his father and rages against Chlora, who flees. When she has difficulty giving birth to a boy she names Armand, Voodoo priest Tamor saves her life. The two fall in love and Chlora becomes a Voodoo queen. Tamor almost destroys the relationship by his virulent hatred of the young Armand, for Garvais had almost beaten Tamor to death years before. To save the relationship, Armand is sent away and Chlora is forbidden to ever have contact with him. As the years pass she becomes obsessed with seeing him and two of her friends help her escape Tamor's surveillance. She finds that her son, now a young man, has the violent temper of Garvais and, when Tamor learns of Chlora's disobedience, he lays a plot to have Armand kill Garvais. The novel describes an African-American world in New Orleans hidden from whites. The tributes Tamor receives allow him to live opulently in a French Quarter townhouse, although most of the African-American characters live in servants' quarters on plantations and in white residences in New Orleans. In addition to lurid descriptions of Voodoo ceremonies, the novel includes song lyrics.

357. O'Connor, Florence J. *The Heroine of the Confederacy, or, Truth and Justice.* London: Harrison, 1864. 432pp.

Commencing just after South Carolina's secession from the Union, this novel tells the history of the Civil War from the perspective of Natalie de Villerie. Villerie, an orphan and heiress to Rosale Plantation, was raised in the household of Creole relatives, Judge de Breuil and his sister, Madame de Breuil, on Esplanade Avenue. At the beginning of the novel Villerie is engaged to marry Clarence Belden. However, when Belden, whose family is Northern, enlists in the Union Army, Villerie immediately breaks off the engagement, even though Judge de Breuil reminds her of the wisdom of protecting her wealth by uniting with a Northerner so that, whether the South wins or loses, she will remain safe. She rejects such calculations and the attentions of Count Beauharnais, even though she is attracted to him, out of fear that people will think she broke up with Belden for a Count, instead of rejecting him on political grounds. Villerie remains in New Orleans, aiding in preparations for the war, including sewing uniforms and flags, planning celebrations for departing troops, and helping to raise money for the Confederate Army through benefits. At one of these events where women publicly donate jewelry, she contributes a necklace worth one hundred thousand dollars. After New Orleans has surrendered, Villerie defies the order that all Confederate flags be lowered and is shot by Union troops as she wraps her arms around a Confederate flagpole. After she recovers from her wounds, she persuades General Butler to issue her a safe passage document to Richmond. Once there she continues to raise and donate money for the war. When she returns to New Orleans after the conflict, a former Confederate general, Beaumont, seeks her out and reveals his true identity as Count Beauharnais. With the war behind them the couple is free to marry. In addition to presenting a history of the war and a rehearsal of the Southern perspective on the conflict and on slavery, the book describes historical events of the time period in New Orleans, including patriotic illuminations, the becalmed Camp Street district during the trade embargo, celebrations to greet Jefferson Davis, the first funerals for Confederate war dead, events surrounding the fall and occupation of the city, and the funeral of Mrs. Beauregard.

358. O'Donnell, Mary King. *Those Other People.* Illustrated by F. Strobel. Boston: Houghton Mifflin, 1946. 338pp.

Covering roughly twenty-four hours (4:00am to 1:00am) over two June days in 1930s New Orleans, this novel of daily life presents the residents of a few blocks along St. Philip Street and captures a social milieu that will be dramatically transformed by World War II housing shortages and the gentrification of the French Quarter immediately after the war. The most affluent family, the Websters, entail several households. Realtor Merlin Webster lives with his wife Marie and daughter Georgiana in a large, historic house, the slave quarters of which they have just converted into apartments. He has put his sisters Leah and Maudie in both halves of a double house a few doors away. One sister, Maudie, lives with her husband, Victor Peralta, a writer with the Works Projects Administration, and Italian-speaking mother-in-law. The other, older sister, forty-year-old, Leah, spends most of the novel trying to find a sailor she had met the night before and whose name she had never learned. To the distress of upwardly mobile Marie, within a one block radius live the Italian-American, Mr. and Mrs. Bruno Tarantino; the Filipino Mr. Gomez, his wife of indeterminate race and nationality, and their children; and African-Americans Dan and Iris Clark. Both Tarantino and Clark operate businesses from their properties. Tarantino, a former macaroni factory employee, builds skiffs for duck hunters and fisherman, and Dan Clark operates an automobile body and fender repair shop. Even if they have little direct contact, the neighbors take a great interest in what they can physically observe about each other and most of the novel consists of descriptions of daily activities. However, at least three subplots carry the narrative forward in desultory fashion. Leah searches for her sailor. Marie Webster prepares for and meets her first tenants and finds they do not measure up to her expectations (they are from the North and he will teach at Tulane, but he is a sociologist concerned with race issues). Finally, a hate-filled man, Mr. Graber, a former vendor of Eskimo pies from a hand-truck, has read *Mein Kampf* and convinced himself that he wrote the book and has a mission to prepare for an invasion and identify the people who will need to be eliminated. Dense with descriptions of everyday life, the novel presents a good sense of New Orleans in the years immediately before the entrance of the United States into World War II, including the social, economic, and racial tensions that shaped even the simplest interactions between people.

359. O'Hara, Edith C(ecilia) and Mary S. Ely. *Confidences.* New Orleans: Press of Louisiana, 1912. 142pp.

In this epistolary novel two school friends correspond during their first year out of the Ursuline Convent School. While Gretchen Vanderlind has returned to Huntsville, Texas (where her family has a house in town and one in the country), Carmen de Vasquez returns to her family in New Orleans. Although Carmen mostly describes events and sites in New Orleans, she occasionally talks about her family's mansion with its Corinthian columns, Bermuda grass lawn, and gardens maintained by a full-time gardener that include magnolias, rose trellises, and a grape arbor. The Vasquez family staff includes "Snowball," who is described as shiny black with "whitey white" teeth. Carmen later reflects on the great influence that her "Mammy," who had also been her mother's, still has on both women, despite being an uneducated former slave. Attitudes toward race and ethnicity also emerge when Carmen and her friends visit Chinatown along Tulane

Avenue and the Japanese stores below Canal Street. Mostly, however, the girls visit uplifting sites, such as the Custom House, St. Roch Chapel, Christ Church Cathedral, and the Charity Hospital on Rampart Street (one of Carmen's friends devotes herself to a children's' charity). Their social activities are usually organized and chaperoned and such as a debutante picnic in Old City Park, an afternoon tea at home, and a French Fete in City Park, that is an official debutante event and includes all of the girls, their formal escorts, and their parents. In relating her activities, Carmen sometimes takes the tone of a schoolgirl essayist and details the history of buildings and locales and recent social trends, such as the growth of non-Catholic religious institutions and families giving up their large gardens to build houses, as buildable land becomes scarce. Perhaps unsurprisingly, given her social status, Carmen only becomes slightly lurid once, when describing the LaLaurie mansion, even though New Orleans affords many such opportunities. She rarely opines, but does so on arranged marriages and votes for women (both of which she opposes). She becomes engaged to the socially acceptable Edward Crenshaw soon after they meet and the only slight detour on their way to the altar comes after Edward falls gravely ill after saving a boy from drowning, during a stroll with Carmen in Audubon Park.

360. Olivier, Robert L(ouis). *Pierre of the Teche.* New Orleans: Pelican, 1936. 236pp.

The eponymous Pierre Lanclos wins a scholarship to study at the University of New Orleans and about fifty-six pages of this book treat his experiences in the city, mostly dealing with the culture shock of living in a place so different from the traditional Acadian community, in which he grew up. He stays with the family of one of his high school teachers and their daughter, Lucille Saunhac, makes him welcome and helps him become acquainted with the city. At a fraternity subscription dance he meets Irma Cook and her former boyfriend, Joe Tremalusa, an Italian-American whose father runs a speakeasy. When he is invited to a party on St. Charles Avenue he is diffident but goes, due to Lucille's urgings. When he witnesses the hostess being robbed of her diamonds at gunpoint by Tremalusa, Pierre heroically subdues the assailant and warns off Irma, who had unwittingly awaited Tremalusa outside in his car. The Cooks reward him with an apartment and a position as family chauffeur. Although Pierre meets affluent people, he remains attached to his origins and decides that a degree in agriculture is best for him. When he seeks out a former resident of his hometown who has a job with the city as a street cleaner, he visits Irish Channel and is concerned about the urban poverty that his former townsman endures to live in the city. This is a type of poverty that he has not seen in the country and considers it an indictment of New Orleans.

361. Olmstead, Florence. *Madame Valcour's Lodger.* New York: Charles Scribner's Sons, 1922. 261pp.

The New Orleans setting is implicit in this novel concerning star-crossed lovers in the second decade of the twentieth century. Representatives of French culture in the household of Henri Valcour, the French consul in New Orleans for thirty years, provide the sophisticated insights young Americans in the novel require in order to begin independent and fulfilling lives. Henri's wife, Mathilde, conducts French language school and becomes involved in the life of one of her students, twenty-five-year old Georgina Burke who, orphaned at an early age and living with her aunt and uncle, is being forced to marry Herbert Peyton, her uncle's nephew. Although Peyton is wealthy and eager to provide a luxurious home for Georgina, she is adamantly opposed to the idea of not marrying for love. She has expressed her independence in another way, as well, by following her own counsel investing her inheritance. Having lost most of her money, and unable to bear her aunt's insistence that a wedding date be set, Georgina comes to Mathilde for a job. The other young American with a connection to the household is Luke Hampton, a bank clerk with ambitions to invent synthetic rubber who rents the Valcours' attic for use as a laboratory. The Valcours' long-term tenant Philippe Trudeau, a wine importer who has been put out of business by the Volstead Act, takes an interest in Hampton and becomes his advisor. Hampton's father died when he was two, and his mother, the proprietress of a shabby boarding house, has re-married several times. Trudeau, convinced that Hampton shows promise, introduces him to a member of his chamber music group, professional investor H.P. Dillingham, who begins raising the money needed to set up a factory and begin production of Hampton's invention. Trudeau also encourages Hampton's interest in Georgina. Because Georgina's father was a wealthy man, Hampton initially believes that the difference in their social status is too great. Just as Trudeau succeeds in disabusing Hampton of his notions, a lower-class young woman at Hampton's boarding house, Lizzie Wilson, makes a play for him and Hampton is convinced that he must marry her, even though he is in love with Georgina. When Georgina secretly invests all of her remaining inheritance in Hampton's company, he immediately realizes the identity of his secret patron and eventually confronts her, telling her he has been freed from his entanglement with Wilson and will only accept Georgina's money if she has invested out of love for him. The novel provides no physical description of New Orleans, but gives an indication of boarding house life and focuses on the ways in which French culture survives in the city and benefits those Americans who come into contact with it.

362. Ondaatje, Michael. *Coming through Slaughter.* New York: Norton, 1976. 156pp.

Eschewing the typical form of fictionalized biographies, Ondaatje instead presents the early twentieth-century cultural milieu of Charles Joseph "Buddy" Bolden (September 6, 1877–November 4, 1931). Bolden is now regarded as important to American music history for marrying ragtime and the blues in his compositions, resulting in a distinctively New Orleans sound considered formative in the development of jazz music. Although Ondaatje occasionally inserts succinct historical facts into the narrative (as well as poetry and song lyrics), he does not adhere too closely to what is known about Bolden and incorporates some legendary aspects. Another fictionalized historical figure, photographer John Ernest Joseph Bellocq (1873–1949), is also featured in this novel that gives a very good sense of life in early twentieth-century New Orleans for African-Americans and touches on the treatment of the mentally ill (Bolden lived with schizophrenia and was confined to a mental institution for the last twenty-four years of his life).

363. Onstott, Kyle. *Drum.* New York: Dial, 1962. 502pp.

The author of *Mandingo* here presents a sequel that provides the fate of Hammond Maxwell, although more than three hundred pages of the narrative flow before his first appearance in the novel. The first section of the book is set in Africa, where Tamboura, nicknamed Drum, grows up and is on the verge of manhood, when jealous relatives sell him into slavery the Royal Hausa who would rule the tribe. Eventually ending up in Cuba in 1800, the slave of Don Cesar. Drum's physical beauty and huge endowment win him the positions of groom and brood stud, respectively. For Cesar has realized that a fortune is to be made when the United States forbids the importation of African slaves, if he can substitute slaves bred in Cuba. Drum worships Cesar, but is led astray by his mistress Alix who has developed a taste for black men that is insatiable until she meets Drum. Their covert affair ends gruesomely when Cesar discovers their mutual betrayal and has Drum tortured to death. He exiles Alix to New Orleans. The narrative starts up again around 1820 when Drum's son by Alix (also named Drum) is ending his apprenticeship as a blacksmith to Jean Lafitte (c.1776–c.1823). At eighteen, he is even more impressive than his father. Alix is delighted with him, but does not acknowledge him as her son. Instead she makes him a barman and performer in live sex acts in her whorehouse, frequented by the most powerful men in New Orleans. She soon discovers that he has additional value to her as a fighter and her friend Dominique You (1775–1830) has him trained by an English boxer. He is felled in his prime, however, when a young mulatto boxer named Blaise whom he has trained, betrays him by bedding his wench Calinda. During the ensuing fight Blaise accidentally kills him. Approximately twenty years later, around 1840, his son, Drumson, is turning eighteen when Hammond Maxwell appears at Alix's seeking a white woman to run his household (having been cuckolded, he has no interest in a wife). He sees Mandingo in Drumson and latches onto purchasing the boy as a means of regaining his most valuable breeder (since his plantation Falconhurst grows no crops, it only produces slaves). The remaining one hundred and fifty pages of the novel are set outside New Orleans on Falconhurst Plantation and detail the disturbing relationship that develops between Hammond and Drumson. The intense racism underlying this narrative, filled with sadism and descriptions of sexual acts, is made more disturbing by its clear intent to titillate the reader to whom this sort of material is meant to appeal. Aside from references to historical characters and the supposed plot to rescue Napoleon Bonaparte (1769–1821) and bring him to New Orleans, the novel contains little material specific to the city, despite the extended portion of the book set there.

364. Osborn, Pete H. *The Morals of a Tomcat.* Gretna, La.: Her, 1980. 185pp.

After imbibing heavily at a cocktail party, a human tomcat dies in an automobile accident at the intersection of Apple and Third Street in 1959. Reincarnated in feline form, he quickly runs through his nine lives. Although he lives for a time in the open on Pirate Alley, quickly becoming the "Tom Cat" of the French Quarter. While spending most of his nine lives as a household pet, his experiences encompass a wide range of social milieus, including that of a retired, aging, alcoholic strip tease queen on Toulouse Street; that of a house of prostitution in which he saves a girl from suicide and himself from being a collateral victim; that of a medical student who kills his lover and best friend when he finds them in bed together; that of an affluent modern couple who are often engaged in drunken arguments prompted by their extramarital affairs; that of a prideful nun; and that of a Mafioso. He finally settles down in a family household and begins a committed relationship with a Persian cat, only to awaken from a dream and discover that he had not been killed in a car crash and is still a human. A reformed man, he pledges to become a citizen of substance and devote himself to one woman. In addition to individual households, the novel describes locales, sometimes providing historical background and defining boundaries of some neighborhoods.

365. Otis, G.H. *Bourbon Street.* New York: Lion Books 1953. 160pp.

The 1950s New Orleans of this work of pulp fiction is a dismal, impoverished place. The party may continue twenty-four hours a day on Bourbon Street, but it is populated by out of town drunks who are preyed upon by locals. The boom times of World War II are long gone, and a recent crackdown on organized crime has brought an end to prostitution and gambling. Digger had been far down on the vice food chain, but he had been enjoying a cash-filled few years, collecting payments for a bookie, prior to the crackdown. At thirty-six, and with no skills except working as hired muscle (he is six feet two and weighs two-hundred pounds), nothing has gone quite the way he has expected. Born Hector Patrick Mulcahy in Paterson, New Jersey, he ran away from his Irish/Polish home at fifteen, supporting himself picking fruit in California, cotton in Texas, and, later, working in construction. Hard manual labor left him with the body that he successfully employed as prizefighter until his license was revoked after a street brawl. Forced to enlist during World War II, to avoid prosecution for manslaughter, he learned to be a seaman in the Navy, so that after the war he got jobs on Gulf freighters, only to lose his union card for drunkenness. Digger's plan for fiscal security and legitimacy depends upon implementing a sophisticated smuggling operation to earn enough money to retire from crime. He establishes an oil exploration business as a legitimate cover and lets New Orleans organized crime boss, Vitolo Gianinni, become his partner to replace his lost gambling and prostitution revenue. Within a very brief time, everything has gone wrong and both vengeful crime figures and the police pursue Digger. The novel establishes a noir atmosphere through descriptions of French Quarter hotels and restaurants. Many businesses, most still in operation, are named. The material culture of the time period is captured in references to clothing, furnishings, food, and drink. Although the novel has one strong female character, Ma Vivaldi, who owns property and businesses, most of the women are scantily clad and sexually available. Inevitably, before "the pill," one of the women Digger beds, the daughter of a wealthy man, becomes pregnant and commits suicide. Although references are made to

Creoles, only one African-American appears in the novel, a low-level runner for a gangster, who Digger beats up to get information.

366. Oursler, (Charles) Fulton. *The World's Delight.* New York: Harper and Brothers, 1929. 425pp.

While on one level this is the tale of an independent woman able to support herself through her skills as a performer, on another level the novel reveals the distorting effects of a patriarchal society on the life of a young woman. This fictionalized biography of Adah Isaacs Menken (1835–1868) gives her a New Orleans background. Given the birth name of Dolores McCord, she is said to have been raised in an affluent antebellum New Orleans household. When her father died young, her mother soon married an Army surgeon. Her stepfather was tenderhearted and enjoyed life, but when he died suddenly it was suddenly revealed that he had spent the family inheritance on drink and frivolity. Soon afterwards a Cuban planter begins courting Dolores' mother. The part owner of an opera company, the planter arranges for the talented Dolores to become a member of the corps de ballet. She enjoys the work, but the job ends when he rapes Dolores (who gives birth to a daughter before she is sixteen). Forced to give up the child she finds a substitute in a neighborhood toddler, Patsy, whose mother Adelia abandoned her husband, Buddy Durand, a circus clown. Dolores gets a job as a trick horseback rider with Draconi's Imperial Hippodrome, for which Durand works, so that she can travel with Patsy and marry Durand once he gets divorced. Even though Dolores becomes a Draconi star, Buddy caves in to Adelia's pleas to reunite. Dolores runs away from the circus, is captured by Indians, escapes on her circus pony, and settles for a time in Galveston, Texas, where she studies voice with Isaac Menken, eventually marries him, changes her name to Adah Menken, converts to Judaism, and lives in subjugation to her mother-in-law. However, when Buddy appears with news that his wife and son have died of fever, she runs away from Menken back to New Orleans. By staying at the St. Charles Hotel to pose as a successful actress, she wins the post of leading lady of New Orleans' La Variété Association, a theatrical company supported by influential Southern gentlemen. With the guidance of the company's theatrical manager, Dolores' beauty and acting ability win her celebrity from her first performance, and she is soon able to reunite with her mother, who lives in a modest rental in one of the Thirteen Buildings in the 600 block of Julia Street. Dolores' daughter, now a young woman, has become part of the household after expulsion from her convent school for a love affair that produced an illegitimate daughter. Then news reports begin to identify Durand as Adelia's murderer. Dolores risks her career to get Durand to Germany and soon afterwards leaves New Orleans for New York. She creates her signature role of Mazeppa as the Civil War begins, and by the end of the novel has achieved artistic prominence in London and Paris, and earned the friendship of Dickens and, later, Swinburne. Although the book is not entirely set in New Orleans, the city is portrayed as a social center for culture and the arts that could produce a character like Dolores and support her with its highly developed theatrical community. The book includes some sentimental descriptions of French Quarter scenes and a lengthy account of one of La Variété's theater parties, at which an all-male assembly provides tributes to their star, Dolores, through expensive gifts of diamond necklaces and gold cups. Although minor references are made to historical events and figures to show the passage of time, the novel is so much set within the world of theater that such content never becomes particularly significant.

367. Parker, Walter. *New Orleans, The Hoe Doo Candle, and Other Stories* New Orleans: Rogers, 1939. 87pp.

The author moved into the French Quarter in 1894, a time of great change as the original Creole families were moving out and people from all over the world were moving in, to take advantage of cheap rents. The book contains brief, local-color stories that cover the period up to 1914 and feature bohemian writers, local characters, restaurateurs, and theater people traveling through the city on the theater circuit. Common themes are firsts (motorcycles, automobiles) and lasts (mule drawn streetcars and the African-American woman's maid who had been in service before the Civil War). Among the celebrities described are Sarah Bernhardt (1844–1923), Lafcadio Hearn (1850–1904), Eugenie Blair (1864–1922), General Fitzhugh Lee (1835–1905) and among the clubs and restaurants, the Tally Ho, Absinthe House, and Antoine's. The stories seem to have been written for readers with a shared acquaintance and past in New Orleans since they are brief, nostalgic, and provide few details.

368. Peacocke, James S. *The Creole Orphans, or, Lights and Shadows of Southern Life: A Tale of Louisiana*. New York: Derby and Jackson, 1856. 365pp.

New Orleans is a constant presence in this abolitionist work, even though the novel is not exclusively set there. On a trip to Martinique, Charles Ormond, a bachelor and owner of a successful sugar plantation, falls in love with Marie, a free woman of color. When she is unjustly sold in the United States, Ormond purchases her, but treats her as his wife on his sugar plantation outside New Orleans and at his city townhouse. Ormond gives their daughters, Zoe and Estelle, the best education, even sending them to Paris for further studies. Marie dies of a fever while the girls are abroad and shortly afterwards a man named Talbot arrives from the North, announcing that he is a distant relative and craving assistance in securing a job. When Talbot learns Marie was mixed-race and had been purchased as a slave, he begins strategizing with his evil friend Billy Stamps to become the sole heir to the Ormond estate. Ormond helps Talbot get a job as a New Orleans cotton broker and when he dies without a will, Talbot successfully applies to be administrator of the man's estate. With the help of an unscrupulous lawyer, he builds his case for sole proprietorship. To secure his position, he documents Marie's race and status and then makes arrangements to sell Zoe and Estelle into slavery. Fortunately, Northerner Louis Hartley is in love with Zoe and works to save her. After many reversals he discovers that Ormond had actually gone to Martinique, secured evidence that Marie was a free woman, and married her. So Zoe and Estelle are not only free, but the legitimate heirs to Ormond's estate. Although most of the narrative is devoted to presenting the plight of mixed-race people and the laws that suppress them, New Orleans is the setting for much of the book. The city receives little description, but is clearly regarded as the center of slave culture.

369. Peacocke, James S. *The Orphan Girls: A Tale of Southern Life*. New York: Derby and Jackson, 1857, 365pp.

This is a later edition of *The Creole Orphans*.

370. Peacocke, James S. *The Two White Slaves Later, or, The Creole Orphans: A Tale of the Power of Virtue over Dishonor*. Philadelphia: Columbian, 1890, 365pp.

This is a later edition of *The Creole Orphans*.

371. Peck, William H(enry). *The Conspirators of New Orleans, or, the Night of the Battle*. Greenville, Ga.: Peck and Wells, 1863. 132pp.

As Jackson's troops prepare for battle, a band of New Orleans residents too old for combat, thwart a plot to incite a slave revolt and larcenous riot, while the able-bodied men of the city are absent fighting British troops. Mario and Banditto suspect that Victor St. John, the conspirators' supposed leader, is actually Henri Le Grand, the villain who married and then abandoned Mario's daughter Clara, far from her home before she gave birth to his baby. Clara died and Mario never recovered his granddaughter, although he has begun to suspect that she is the young woman known as Rosetta and thought to be the daughter of St. Anne Street wine merchant Paul Amar. If true, this would be especially troubling, since she is the lover of the man she knows as Victor St. John, who actually may be Henri Le Grand and her father. Mario, Banditto, and Amar get Rosetta to disguise herself as a young man to infiltrate the conspirators where she gathers various code words that Banditto uses to thwart the plot. Although Rosetta is disgusted to learn that St. John is the leader of the dastardly plot and falls out of love with him, he plunges to his death before she learns that he is her father. In the final pages of the book most of the main characters reveal their true identities as European noblemen who took new names and identities when they came to the United States. This War of 1812 novel portrays New Orleans as though it were an Italian village filled with noblemen.

372. Peck, William H(enry). *The Fortune-teller of New Orleans, or, The Two Lost Daughters.* New York: Street and Smith, 1889. 215pp.

In this novel about misrepresented identities, two young people are shocked when they learn that their relationships to Laura Parnail are not what they believed. Residing in an elegant house at 926 Rampart Street, Parnail lives with the young Carola Fairmount, who has always believed she was the woman's niece. Twenty-six-year-old Dr. Robert Kampton, who is in love with Fairmount, has always been told he is Parnail's nephew. Early in the book Parnail is forced to confirm that Kampton is really her son and that his father is a former Portuguese bullfighter named Pedro Diaz, who goes by the assumed name Don Pedro del Amazor. Fairmount has another suitor, Alfred Raymond, the son of scheming lawyer, James Raymond. After the younger Raymond proposes to Fairmount, the elder Raymond is committed to deciphering the young woman's true identity, employing New York detective Roger Flaybank. When he realizes that a fortune-teller, called Señora Goliari, who is newly arrived in the city, is actually Duchess D'Ossiri, he is convinced that Fairmount is D'Ossiri's missing daughter. The girl had been kidnapped seventeen years before, driving Duke D'Ossiri into intermittent states of madness. Raymond makes a contract with Duchess D'Ossiri, obligating her to allow her daughter to marry Raymond's son, and let him take control of her estate if Raymond can supply the missing daughter. He is at first troubled when Prima donna Zaretta, a touring opera singer, approaches him about proving that she is the daughter of the Duchess, but when he sees the proofs supplied by her guardian Rosa Baretta (jewelry, clothing, papers), he latches onto them to support his claim that Fairmount is the missing heiress. The plot progresses with kidnappings, incarceration in mental institutions, attempted murder and no descriptions of New Orleans, although addresses in the city are conscientiously presented. By the end of the novel both Fairmount and Zaretta are proven to be missing heiresses and get to marry the men with whom they have fallen in love.

373. Peddie, Jon. *The Crawfish Woman, and Other Stories.* New Orleans: Wetzel, 1930. 79pp.

Filled with macabre stories set in and around cemeteries, this book evokes an aspect of New Orleans culture. The title story concerns an elderly woman who delights in an abandoned cemetery. In addition to looking at the graves, she gathers plants that grow there, finding them tastier than any in the market. She also brings her crawfish to the cemetery to fatten them on recently interred corpses. Another frequent visitor to the cemetery is a woman whose youngster choked on a marble. Over time she brings all of the child's toys to his tomb and when it is filled, demands the crypt be opened. So thorough is her delusion that in kissing the child's skull, she believes he has been revived. In another story, a skillful mortician is horrified when he realizes that in falling from the hands of drunken pallbearers, the body he had so carefully prepared to look lifelike, is transformed into a rotting corpse when it hits the ground. In a final story a skilled perfumer meets a St. Louis girl during Mardi Gras who dies before he can marry her. Recreating her scent becomes his obsession until he actually breaks into her tomb and pulverizes the bones of her arms to constitute an evocative aroma. The book contains vivid descriptions of unevenly cared for graveyards and the plants that thrive in them.

374. Pendleton, Don. *The Executioner: New Orleans Knockout.* New York: Pinnacle Books, 1974. 178pp.

This is one of a series of books in which Vietnam War veteran, Mack Bolan, pursues a vendetta against the Mafia in cities all over the United States. In this installment, the local don in New

Orleans, Marco Vannaducci, is being brought down by the Justice Department, leading to a fierce rivalry amongst the Mafia families, to gain control of the South. Bolan's efforts are extra-legal and despaired of by New Orleans Police Department Mafia specialist Jack Petro, even though Bolan wants to turn over records that show crime in the South is controlled by the Mafia. Bolan uses the huge sums of money he captures from the Mafia to fund sophisticated surveillance equipment (designed by a NASA engineer), as well as high-powered bombs and weapons. As with most Executioner books the setting is somewhat incidental. In this case, Pendleton's activities are set against the backdrop of Mardi Gras.

375. Percy, Walker. *Lancelot.* New York: Farrar, Straus and Giroux. 1977. 257pp.

The protagonist of this novel, Lancelot Lamar, is a New Orleans lawyer who is incarcerated in a New Orleans mental institution when, after discovering that he is not the father of his youngest child, he murders his wife. However, the New Orleans setting is inconsequential. Although Lamar talks about his household and the behavior of his wife and daughter while a Hollywood movie was being filmed there, in his conversations with a priest who had been a childhood friend, he is convinced that their character flaws are an expression of the emptiness of modern American culture on which he expatiates on at length. This universal concern that inspires philosophical discourse, along with the author's references to Arthurian legend through which he situates Lamar as a modern, if antithetical version of Lancelot, diminishes the importance of the New Orleans setting to a bare minimum.

376. Percy, Walker. *The Moviegoer.* New York: Knopf, 1961. 241pp.

Although concerned with presenting the interior life of the first person narrator, that character's existential crisis makes him the perfect guide to New Orleans in the late 1950s. John Bickerson "Binx" Bolling, born in approximately 1920, grew up in his Aunt Emily Bolling Cutrer's Garden District mansion on Prytania, after the death of his physician father during World War II. On track for a medical career before service in the Korean War, Bolling received a battlefield wound that left a huge chest scar and permanent pain and weakness. However, the deeper effect of the war is his malaise and a search for meaning and connectedness. His job as a stock and bond broker in his Uncle Jules Cutrer's office leaves him plenty of time for movie going, appreciating qualities of light in nature, and engaging strangers in casual conversations. However, his aunt finds such endeavors too petty for a Bolling and tries to awaken him. Eight years have passed since his return to New Orleans and he has not continued his education or married, preferring meaningless dalliances with his secretaries. When his cousin Kate, Emily's step-daughter, breaks off her engagement and seems on the verge of another nervous breakdown, Bolling's feelings for her take on a new dimension that lead to change in both their lives, although the reader is left wondering whether either of them have resolved their existential crises, or even found a means of successfully displacing them. The novel is notable for the narrative's intense observation of people and locales in New Orleans' French Quarter, Faubourg Marigny, and Garden District in the 1950s during Mardi Gras week. In conversation, the main characters reveal attitudes on race, gender, and social class.

377. Perkins, Kenneth. *Voodoo'd.* New York: Harper and Brothers, 1931. 289pp.

The distinctive New Orleans twists in this murder mystery include Voodoo and ancestry-based class distinctions. When young, wealthy Creole socialite Basil Boyean discloses that he has received a gland transplant to prevent repeated malarial infections, his fellow Bourbon Club members debate the negative impact a transplant would have on a man's personality, depending upon the source of the gland. With complete trust in the world famous surgeon conducting the operation, Boyean had never inquired about the source of the tissue he received. Afterwards, he discovers the donor was Bouche, a racing tout and murderer of Bertram Juvenal, who had escaped the gallows by leaping to his death out a courtroom window. Although Boyean had scoffed at the

Bourbon Club members, he finds himself drawn to a tailor's shop where he is fitted out in the showy garb of a racetrack habitué. He then proceeds to the track, gambles the day away, and forsakes his residence for the Auberge Juvenal, the scene of Juvenal's murder. Formerly, the Juvenal ancestral mansion, the structure is now part family home and part boarding house since the Juvenals' fortune has dwindled away through several generations of poor managers and gamblers. The novel provides a good sense of the physical and social awkwardness of the boarding house. After a nightmare-filled sleep, Boyean awakens to find that police are on the premises to investigate the murder of Lucien Juvenal in the room next to Boyean's. The police are flummoxed by the fact that Lucien's door and windows were locked from the inside, and believe they have solved the crime when they discover a secret passage connecting Boyean's room with Lucien's. However they consider Boyean above suspicion due to his social position. In fact, they soon involve him in investigating the crime. Several more Juvenals are murdered and through much of the rest of the book suspicion is cast on the "piebald" butler, who is also a Voodoo priest. When Boyean solves the crime, he realizes that Bouche's spirit had been influencing him to discover the real murderer and clear his name. Although much of the novel transpires within the Juvenal mansion, the novel captures many aspects of social life in the city during the time period, as well as detailing the architecture and operation of a large domestic establishment. A number of descriptions of Voodoo ceremonies are incorporated into the narrative and the book is openly racist, attributing all sorts of negative characteristics to racial origins. Perhaps, due to the Depression era in which the novel was published, or the associations of New Orleans with food, fish, lobster, oyster and shrimp dishes are mentioned frequently.

378. Perko, Margaret (Snyder). *The Other Side of Silence.* New York: Leisure Books, 1979. 285pp.

Although this novel is mostly set in Venezuela, it does have significant New Orleans content. Mary Beth Rolvaag grows up in the Garden District in the 1940s and 1950s, the daughter of a liberal Minnesota lawyer and opinionated New Orleanean, Ouida Trosclair, who grew up poor in St. James Parish and does not share her husband's political views, especially when they focus on racial equality. While Mary Beth is a student at Dominican College, a girlfriend introduces her to Eduardo Ortega, a wealthy, thirty-year-old Venezuelan. After a whirlwind romance the two marry and Mary Beth relocates to Venezuela. She maintains contact with New Orleans through her parents and family and friends who are members of the diplomatic corps or who are employed by American oil companies (part of her husband's wealth stems from oil leases). On visits home, Mary Beth witnesses New Orleans' struggle with desegregation. Near the end of the novel, Mary Beth's father engages the assistance of one of Mary Beth's college boyfriends to find her since she has disappeared. The novel includes significant content concerning the student community in New Orleans and the political divisions over desegregation.

379. Perry, Stella G(eorge) S(tern). *Melindy.* New York: Moffat, Yard, 1912. 250pp.

Written with the intent of humorously recounting the behavior of African-American servant girl Melindy in an affluent white household in New Orleans's Garden District, the novel unwittingly reveals a whole range of cultural attitudes toward African-Americans, children, women, and servants. Melindy was born in rural Louisiana and was brought to live in New Orleans by her sister Suky, the cook for the white household of Master George (the family is never given a surname), that includes George's wife Caroline, four children and an orphaned niece. Melindy's open, spirited nature and obliviousness to her social position brings her a wide range of acquaintances. Her white family is tolerant of the more disruptive aspects of her behavior because they embrace the notions that African-Americans are superstitious, have no sense of time, no recognition of moral imperatives, and are pagan, fetish-worshippers. Melindy has a number of adventures in the course of the novel. She rescues a stolen horse, gets a Baptist church congregation to forgive a female member accused of public drunkenness, and helps her grade school classmates overcome their graduation-day stage fright. She also transforms a number of white people's lives. When Melindy discovers that the Du Fossets are on the verge of financial ruin, she alerts their maiden aunt, Euphrosyne Myrtilla Du Fosset (who she helps with her gardening), and the crisis is averted. After she befriends a reserved, elderly bachelor and hears his regret over not having children, she brings him together with an Ursuline Convent School girl who has just learned that both of her parents died, leading him to eventually adopt her. As a servant Melindy carries out errands and comes into contact with a range of merchants and service providers, conveying a sense of daily life in early twentieth century New Orleans. Some of the pastimes of children and adults are also described, including sand dyeing and trading (children), trading plants (adults), and gathering to watch cereus cacti open their night blooms.

380. Pinkerton, Myron. *A Woman's Revenge; or, The Creole's Crime*. The Pinkerton Detective Series. Chicago: Laird and Lee, 1887. 152pp.

   This book, in which a man pieces together the truth of his stolen identity, manages to be racist, misogynist, and filled with ethnic slurs. At twenty-two Buckingham Broguand experiences an emotional crisis when Mrs. Bertha Broguand, whom he had always known as his mother, tells the story of his origins. She had never before told him anything of his father, leaving him to be filled with anxiety over his parentage. She says she grew up in Cuba, the daughter of a smuggler who owned his own ship that journeyed between New Orleans and Cuba, where he owned a plantation. Planning to marry his daughter off to a wealthy man and retire from smuggling, he was frustrated when seventeen-year-old Bertha chose her own boyfriend, Robert Barnard. When she and some of her friends were invited by their boyfriends to a mock wedding ceremony, her father heard of the event, and hoping to force a wedding, hired a priest to perform an actual ceremony for his daughter. Some drinking was involved and when she awoke the next morning her father told her that Benton had wronged her by asking his friend Benton Broguand to be her mock husband. As a result, Broguand, whose affluent family made him a much better match from her father's perspective, was her new husband. At this point, the new Mr. and Mrs. Benton Broguand were on her father's schooner bound for New Orleans, where Broguand could announce the match to his family. A series of disasters followed when Bertha's mother, sailing on a separate ship drowned, when the boat sank. A short time later, after Benton and Bertha had decided to make the best of the situation and began to fall in love with each other, Bertha's father discovered that he had been tricked and that the man he thought was a priest was not. In a rage, he murdered the wrongdoer, was convicted, and was publicly labeled a smuggler. Before Benton could have a wedding ceremony performed, he ran into Robert Barnard on the street, began a violent confrontation, and was killed. Bertha was left to pass herself off as a widow and bore Benton's child. On the basis of this story, Bertha gets Buckingham to pledge revenge on Barnard. The revenge she describes involves letting Buckingham pursue and marry Barnard's daughter, Bianca, a woman to whom Buckingham is already attracted. Once the wedding takes place, Bertha will announce that Bianca and the Barnard family has been disgraced through marriage to the grandson of a smuggler and murderer. However, her planned revenge is much more elaborate and was concocted years before. Bertha had switched her baby with that of Barnard shortly after their births with the assistance of her African-American servant Dolores. So, in marrying Bianca, Buckingham would actually be marrying his own sister. Bertha is so close to seeing her long-cherished plan come to fruition that she is poorly equipped to react effectively when Dolores reappears and threatens to kill her if she does not pay a bribe, the resources for which she does not possess. However, Dolores is primarily motivated by a sense of justice and actively thwarts Bertha in ways calculated to bring her before the authorities. At the same time, Buckingham, who had to go into hiding after being falsely accused of knifing Robert Barnard's son Benedict, is trying to find out who actually committed the violence and in observing his Bertha eventually learns the truth. Although New Orleans is referenced throughout, the city has little presence in the narrative that ends with Bertha brought to justice, Barnard freed of the morally corrupt Benedict (who he had only barely tolerated because he thought the reprobate was his son), and Buckingham (who is shown to be possessed of sterling qualities) restored to the bosom of his true family. Even though Dolores, an African-American, plays the key role in bringing Bertha to justice, she is not presented as an admirable character, but as driven by an almost animalistic sense of revenge.

381. Pretorius (Kouts), Hertha. *Tallien's Children.* New York: Appleton-Century-Crofts, 1961. 344pp.

This family novel directly deals with issues of Cajun identity by telling the story of Henry Tallien's children. The widowed Tallien lives in a historic house on Esplanade in the French Quarter in traditional Cajun fashion and tries to hold onto to his youngest daughter, Persis, a student at the University of New Orleans. However, her older siblings, Jean and Honorine, feel obligated to broaden her world, while unconsciously justifying and, perhaps, re-making their own past decisions. Jean and Honorine are both worldly and have remade themselves entirely, abandoning their accents and their social set to live in the North. To them, Henry Tallien is a dangerous, limiting influence on Persis. After graduating from Tulane and serving in World War II, Jean has become a well-known New York City reporter. He is a vocal anti-segregationist, whereas Henry adheres to traditional prejudices concerning race. Honorine is the wife of a wealthy society figure and lives as a Long Island matron. Despite their apparent assurance and eagerness to advise and mentor Persis, both Jean and Honorine have serious conflicts in their personal lives. As the novel unfolds the issue becomes whether anything can be salvaged from the Cajun perspective that is free from racism and relevant to 1960s America, so that Henry's children can value him and their heritage.

382. Prose, Francine. *Marie Laveau.* New York: Putnam / Berkley, 1977. 342pp.

Prose uses elements of the Marie Laveau (c. 1801–1881) legend to create a narrative that celebrates the Voodoo priestess as a symbol of liberation for African-Americans and women. For instance, the Roman Catholic Church taught the sinfulness of women by using the story of Adam and Eve. Here Laveau is the priestess of the snake as a symbol of the source of power that transformed Adam and Eve from children to adults. Traditionally women's heads were to be covered, but in this account Laveau celebrates the hair of women as the locus of strength over men and, by becoming an accomplished hairdresser, she aids her female clients in their power relationships with men. A person of mixed race, Laveau transcends race, but also affirms non-white cultures through the dancing and drumming she inspires, which are so transgressive in their power that Caucasian listeners are alternately transfixed by the sound and sight or fearful, identifying in the drumming the very essence of social revolt. Although the novel concludes with an account of Laveau's death, various heroines are identified as her reincarnation, among them Rosa Parks and Zora Neale Hurston. Prose grounds her narrative with historical elements like mentions of well-known yellow fever epidemics, Father Antoine, quadroon balls, and the Battle of New Orleans.

383. Pugh, Eliza Lofton (Phillips). *Not a Hero.* New Orleans: Blelock, 1867. 131pp.

This romance novel is mostly set in New Orleans, although physical setting is of minor importance in the narrative that is mostly concerned with the nature of romantic love and marital fidelity. When Rachel Grant fell in love with Stanley Powers, she felt a need to confess her infidelity to her husband, even though she was more unfaithful in thought than in deed, and Powers was leaving New Orleans for San Francisco. Nonetheless, her husband Philip banished Rachel from his house and forbade any contact with their infant daughter Judith. Fifteen years later Rachel seeks a rapprochement, which Philip partially grants under the pretense of accepting her into his household as a governess for Judith, with the assumed identity of Mrs. Harleigh. Judith, at the age of fifteen, is on the verge of entering society and the socially isolated Philip relies upon Hillory and Elinor Grey, artist Nevil Brent, and portraitist Janet Somers for assistance in her debut. In the meantime, Stanley Powers returns to New Orleans, a wealthy lawyer, and breaks into

Grant's circle through Janet Somers, who has fallen in love with him. The manipulative Powers toys with Somers, but knows he will only marry to advance his social position. When he meets Judith and Philip Grant he believes Rachel to be dead, and remembering Philip's cruelty to her, destroys Philip by introducing him to drink and gambling. Even after Judith is told of Powers' role in her father's death, she falls in love with him. Rachel, still in the guise of Mrs. Harleigh, pledges financial support for Judith, who would otherwise have been thrown on the street, due to Philip's debts. At this point, Rachel is still in love with Powers, as are Somers and Judith. However, Powers has found a socially advantageous match in Hillory Grey's sister Isabel. When she is killed in a steamboat accident shortly after their marriage, Powers lets Judith comfort him and she is only freed of her infatuation when she hears the revelation that Rachel is her mother and that she had been ruined by her love for Powers. Fortunately, before Powers can destroy any more women, he enlists as the Civil War breaks out, vainly dreaming of battlefield triumphs, only to be immediately killed. While the novel is mostly set in New Orleans, the book only occasionally describes the city or social events, rarely abandoning its theme of the proper relations between men and women, married or otherwise.

384. Radford, Ruby Lorraine. *Marie of Old New Orleans.* Illustrated by Harold E. Snyder. Philadelphia: Penn, 1931. 271pp.

This work of juvenile historical fiction recounts events surrounding the British attack on New Orleans, from the perspective of Marie Feuillert, the daughter of a physician who immigrated to America from France with his parents. The family sugar plantation enables Dr. Feuillert to devote all his time to medicine, without regard for money. He is often paid in furs and when Marie's older brother Pierre decides to study medicine in Paris, his father plans on sending furs with him to cover his costs. Marie finds a way to make a contribution as well after her warning saves a French frigate from shipwreck on a sand bar. The ship's Captain Dauphine and his son, Victor, who is Pierre's age, present Marie with solid gold bracelets. She sells the jewelry and buys Pierre a doctor's instrument case. However, not long after Pierre and Dr. Feuillert's furs sail on Captain Dauphin's frigate, Marie hears rumors that pirates have captured the ship. Dr. Feuillert has no means to pursue inquiries as the city prepares for British attack, and shortly afterwards Marie, her mother, and most of the household slaves are sent to the Feuillert sugar plantation. When she learns through family slaves that Pierre and Victor Dauphine are prisoners on a British ship, she goes to her father, with the help of neighboring backwoodsmen, who smuggle her into New Orleans under Andrew Jackson's martial law. When she discovers her father is on the front helping the wounded she gets Jackson's pledge of aid, but he also indicates it may be weeks in coming. So, she gets slaves to disguise her as a wounded Redcoat soldier and arms herself with acid from her father's dispensary. During their escape, Pierre, Victor, Marie, and their accomplices take refuge on a shipwreck in the bayou only to discover wounded Antoine Fernandez whom Marie nurses back to health. She later discovers he was one of the pirates who robbed Captain Dauphine's ship and he remorsefully returns Dr. Feuillert's furs. The Feuillerts reunite on their sugar plantation by the end of the novel. The book's description of New Orleans focuses mainly on piracy and the British attack. However, the author conveys a sense of daily life, sugar plantation activities, and raises some of the issues a girl faced growing up in a sexist society.

385. Reeser, Edwin Isherwood. *Pushmataha.* New York: Exposition, 1954. 169pp.

This work of historical fiction transpires on a single night, January 7, 1815, on the eve of the Battle of New Orleans when Pushmataha (c. 1760–1824), a Choctaw chief important in earlier campaigns, is supposedly persuaded to continue to fight on the side of the Americans. The meetings transpire at an inn, requisitioned as Pushmataha's headquarters and owned by French immigrant André (no last name is given), who serves as a first-person narrator. André's eighteen-year-old daughter Joan has the romantic notion that she is the reincarnation of Joan of Arc and when she hears her father's inn has been requisitioned she believes that her destiny to save New Orleans is about to be fulfilled. Pushmataha's Prime Minister, Harken, a visionary, his wives, and several braves are the first to arrive and Harken immediately recognizes a fellow spirit in Joan. Strengthened by Harken in her sense of mission, when Pushmataha's wives appear, they and Joan decide that she should also marry Pushmataha. When the chief arrives later that night, he doubts that Joan would be satisfied in accepting the traditional, servile role of squaw. Against these discussions of matrimony, the British officers appear to offer Pushmataha all the land west of the Mississippi if he will withdraw his large force of braves from New Orleans. Oddly (since she saw herself as the heroine of New Orleans) Joan encourages him to accept. However, when Andrew Jackson (1767–1845) appears, the chief is reminded of the alliances he has made with the Americans. By the end of the novel, Joan is dressed in Indian garb and accompanying Harken to the land of peace in the West to which he had dreamed a white woman would lead him. Since the entire action of the novel is confined to André's inn, it includes little physical description of the city. However, the work relates aspects of New Orleans' history up to 1815 and explores the symbolic nature of the city. André relates why he and other Frenchmen immigrated to the city and their emotions concerning the Louisiana Purchase.

386. Reymond, Dalton S(haffer). *Earthbound.* Chicago: Ziff-Davis, 1948. 381pp.

Although most of this novel is set on Cypriere Plantation, sixteen miles outside of New Orleans, the city is integral to the plot and to the lives of the main characters. When plantation owner Thomas Baxter dies fighting a flood, his will reveals that he divided the plantation between his son Eric and daughter Clare, and left all of his liquid assets to his wife Ellen. To his oldest son and namesake he leaves nothing, but forgives debts amounting to seventy-five thousand dollars. Irate at the settlement, Thomas pledges to revenge himself on his brother and through the rest of the novel uses political manipulation to prevent the Levee Board from carrying through on his father's anti-flooding plan, which Eric has made his mission. Into the midst of their enmity comes Linda Bassoom, the daughter of shanty boat dwellers, who literally washes ashore at Cypriere. Her beauty entrances Eric and he eventually marries her, but she is untamable and craves the excitement of New Orleans, making excuses to be constantly traveling there. Even after she gives birth to a son, she takes no satisfaction in home life. Intent upon attending the Comus Ball, she goes on her own when an emergency prevents Eric from escorting her, and when Eric is free to search for her, he finds her drunk and with his brother Thomas. He promptly exiles her from Cypriere, but she begins spending money in New Orleans on his credit until his lawyer advises that there are few options that can prevent her from ruining him. As floods begin to threaten New Orleans and Cypriere, Linda discovers that Thomas is having an affair and has sent men to dynamite Eric's levee, causing her to begin a dramatic ride to warn him. The novel makes clear the life and death consequences of politically motivated decisions concerning the Mississippi. New Orleans settings include the Hotel Royal and the French Opera House.

387. Rice, Anne. *The Feast of All Saints.* New York: Simon and Schuster, 1979. 571pp.

The novel focuses on free people of color at a particular point in time, the 1840s, when it was becoming more difficult for mixed-race people to live the affluent, independent lives they had previously led in New Orleans. Marcel and Marie are the children of wealthy plantation owner Philippe Ferronaire and his placée Cecile Ste. Marie. Although Marie and Marcel are strikingly attractive, only Marie can pass as white, even though Marcel has blonde hair. Both children grow up privileged, however, and just as Marcel anticipates leaving to study in Paris at the École Normale, Ferronaire apprentices him to an African-American undertaker. Marcel flees, leaving New Orleans to live with his aunt among Creole planters on the Cane River. Not long afterwards, Ferronaire dies in debt and Cecile and Marie are thrown upon their own meager resources. As a result, Marie cannot pursue her love match with Richard Lermontant and must become the placée of a wealthy man in order to help her mother and Marcel and ensure that he can escape to Paris to live without fear of being captured and sold into slavery. Before Marie can find a white protector she is kidnapped and raped by five men. When Marcel returns in secrecy to New Orleans he finds out about Marie's rape and discovers that Lermontant has been locked in the family's attic to keep him from taking revenge on the rapists and being executed for the murders. In a bizarre twist, Marcel also discovers that Vincent Dazincourt, the brother of Ferronaire's wife, has decided that the rape was an offence against his family, since the rapists knew that Marie was the daughter of Ferronaire's placée. In addition to describing daily life in nineteenth-century New Orleans, the novel includes discussions within the mixed race community that present strategies for dealing with societal racism, many of which emphasize distinctions based on skin color and legal status.

388. Rice, Anne. *Interview with the Vampire: A Novel.* New York: Knopf, 1976. 371pp.

In this debut novel Rice establishes vampire characters she uses in other books and depicts New Orleans in the eighteenth, nineteenth, and early-twentieth centuries as a backdrop for the vampire Louis's narration given to a young reporter of the two hundred years of his life. Turned into a vampire by Lestat to provide companionship, Louis never fully accepts his new identity, putting him at odds with Lestat and other vampires. Prior to meeting Lestat in 1791, Louis is an indigo plantation owner bereft over the death of his brother. For a time he and Lestat live on the plantation, but when the slaves begin to identify Lestat with a string of deaths, they are forced to flee to New Orleans where they establish a household. The novel describes social events, public spaces, and the city's identity as a port subject to contagious diseases. As Louis wearies of having Lestat as his only social outlet, Lestat turns an orphaned girl, Claudia, into a vampire and for a time Louis is preoccupied with creating a home for Claudia. However, as she psychologically matures into adulthood and realizes that she will forever be trapped inside a child's body, Claudia seethes with resentment and eventually gets Louis' assistance in revenging herself on Lestat. After this, she and Louis leave New Orleans for Egypt and France, where most of the remainder of the novel transpires, until late in the book when Louis returns to New Orleans. The book was adapted for a film of the same name released by The Geffen Film Company in 1994 starring Tom Cruise, Brad Pitt, and Kirsten Dunst.

389. Riordan, Robert. *The Lady and the Pirate.* Milwaukee, Wisc.: Bruce, 1957. 182pp.

In this work for young people, the focus is once again on the Battle of New Orleans, but principal characters (Lafitte, Claiborne, Jackson, et al.) take second stage to fictional young people, even though historical figures and events are accurately portrayed to provide readers with a useful history lesson. Sixteen-year-old Paul Belleterre is smitten with Ursuline Convent girl Nicki Fleurette. However, like most of her classmates, Fleurette comes from an affluent Creole family with well-defined ideas about a suitable husband, and Belleterre, a Baratarian pirate, falls well off the rubric. Even though Belleterre convinces Fleurette that his piratical activities are a form of warfare between the countries providing letters of marque, and not outright criminality, her family remains unconvinced. Not until the Battle of New Orleans and the public acknowledgement that the pirates acted patriotically and played a crucial role in protecting the city, is Belleterre officially accepted as a suitor. In addition to providing a good deal of historical information about events leading up the battle, the author relates some of the history of the Ursuline Convent, particularly in connection with the casket girls (women brought from France to be married).

390. Ripley, Clements. *Mississippi Belle.* New York: D. Appleton-Century, 1942. 307pp.

A significant portion of this historical romance novel, about life along the Mississippi River in the 1830s and 1840s, is set in New Orleans. Boston native Caitlyn Ryan is orphaned at fifteen but she is the heiress to an estate of more than twenty thousand dollars. Schooled by nuns and without any relatives, Ryan naively falls in love with Harvard College student Beuchley Preswald. Soon after their marriage they head South to follow through on Preswald's scheme to make a fortune in cotton by using Irish immigrant labor. However, Preswald falls prey to riverboat gambler Jim Blake and, after losing his own money and that of Ryan, commits suicide. A fellow passenger,

Dan Bedford, with whom Ryan had become acquainted and begun to love, is prepared to step in and take Ryan to his family's Memphis plantation to eventually marry her. However, an interloper thwarts him and Ryan is left to deal with Blake, who offers her a partnership in the New Orleans gambling house he wants to start. Pregnant, with no husband, family, or money, Ryan agrees. Subsequently, she gives birth to a son, James. Even though the gambling house does a large business, in part due to Caitlyn's vocal performances as Kate Ryan, the unsettled economy and the upheavals in the currency markets and banking industry prevent significant financial success. When Dan Bedford reappears she decides to go to Memphis as the respectable Widow Preswald in hopes of winning Bedford and creating a respectable life for James. Matters are complicated by Bedford's decision to run for state assembly as a Jacksonian Democrat and by the jealousy of another woman with designs on Bedford. Counter-intrigues and several duels ensue. New Orleans in the novel is a center for vice, and the characters in this book find it difficult to win fortunes in such a lawless, politically insecure environment. The novel includes a good deal of information about political issues of the 1830s and 1840s.

391. Robert, Paul J(ones). *Grande Terre: An Historical Romance of Older Creole Days.* Washington D.C.: Congressional, 1930. 210pp.

Even though the title of this work would lead the reader to believe the book was set outside of New Orleans, that is not the case. Covering the period between the Louisiana Purchase and the Battle of New Orleans, the novel begins with Jean Lafitte (c.1776–c.1823) announcing his capture of the island of Grand Terre, which he will use as a base of operations to sell to Acadians in remote swamp areas, as well as to residents of New Orleans. The early part of the book recounts the alliances he builds with various Francophone families who resent the Americans who have recently come to power. By the War of 1812, many of these same families have become proud Americans and as a Committee of Safety and Defense, petition Lafitte to fight with General Jackson. The novel ends with the aftermath of the battle and the acknowledgement of the contributions of Lafitte and the Baratarians. In addition to telling some of the history of Lafitte and his men, the novel is concerned with describing the history and culture of Francophone people around New Orleans.

392. Roberts, Charles Blanton. *Edmond Peyré.* New York: Fleming H. Revell, 1936. 206pp.

This romance novel, almost exclusively set in New Orleans, spans the years 1883 to 1919 and tells how a man and woman find true love through an extramarital relationship, while describing the life of their son. Civil War hero and sugar plantation owner Cassius Langdon has been in a loveless marriage to Maude, née Humphreys, for more than a decade. Their son, Sydney, born in the first year of their union, has become Maude's excuse for refusing to divorce, although her attachment to society life and the disfavor with which divorcées are treated are also factors. To advance in society she gets Langdon to occupy their 1820s New Orleans mansion as their primary residence. Langdon takes advantage of city life to build his library and falls in love with bookshop proprietress Julie Duret. The novel leaps ahead fourteen years so readers do not know how Duret overcame her distaste for having a relationship with a married man, or how the couple navigated their personal and social life. Their son, Edmond Peyré, resides in the household of a respectable New Orleans couple and has been told he is an orphan with Langdon his guardian and Julie his aunt. During a chance encounter with Sidney Langdon he introduces himself as Langdon's ward and when Sidney finds out the truth from his mother, he eagerly tells Peyré that he is illegitimate. Shamed by his illegitimacy, Peyré runs away, adopts the name Bertrand Roubillard, and gets a job as a purser's assistant on a steamer bound for France. Determined to establish his own identity in Paris before returning to New Orleans, through twenty-one hard years Peyré establishes himself as a journalist and serves heroically on the battlefield in World War I. He returns to New Orleans in March 1919 to find his family landscape considerably altered. After the death of Mrs. Langdon, Peyré's father and mother married and moved to Langdon's sugar plantation on Bayou

Barberousse. Furthermore, Sydney caused some unspecified scandal that got him disinherited by Langdon, after which he supposedly died. In fact, he is the mysterious figure lurking around the swamps and "Negro quarter" of the sugar plantation, and, under an assumed identity, is pursuing Clarisse, the woman in whom Peyré is also interested. Their rivalry ends in a dramatic confrontation in the bayou. The novel violates social conventions by treating an adulterous affair as true love and a bastard as noble and heroic, in contrast to an evil, legitimate child. Despite the romantic focus, or perhaps as a means of enhancing the novel's sentiment, New Orleans is lovingly described, particularly the French Quarter's architecture and life at the Hotel des Voyageurs where long-term European guests, Northerners, and plantation owners mingle. African-Americans appear as beloved servants, who, though freed during the Civil War, maintain family loyalties to continue in servile positions.

393. Roberts, Marjorie. *Webs in the Sky.* New York: Wilfred Funk, 1940. 299pp.

Don Sterling leaves his affluent life and abandons his career plans to become a civil engineer after the death of his best friend in a plane crash. Don had been flying the two-seater aircraft and parachuted to safety before he had made certain that his friend was out of the airplane. The key figure in his transition to the life of a common laborer is Jim Anderson, whom he meets in a bar on the same day that a jury found Sterling innocent of his friend's death. That day was momentous for Anderson as well, because his best friend had plummeted to his death from the bridge on which the two of them were employed in construction. Having been unable to get a job in the midst of the Great Depression and having been living off a nearly depleted trust fund, Sterling accepts Anderson's offer of help in getting a job on a New Orleans bridge project. Although they later live and work in San Francisco, the fifty-page section set in New Orleans provides readers with a good idea of the French Quarter during the 1930s and of the divertissements of laborers. The description of the summer heat and the few escapes, mostly swimming in Lake Pontchartrain and riding on riverboats, is particularly evocative.

394. Roberts, Walter Adolphe. *Brave Mardi Gras: A New Orleans Novel of the '60s.* Indianapolis: Bobbs-Merrill, 1946. 318pp.

In this historical romance that begins in January 1861 and continues through June 1865, the protagonist is well positioned to observe the social conflicts brought by the Civil War and occupation of New Orleans. Blaise Lamotte, the well-connected scion of a plantation family with their principal residence on the estate of Basseterre, just outside New Orleans, and a town residence on Royal Street, is a member of the new Krewe of Artemis. Although preoccupied with Mardi Gras planning, he is cognizant of the krewe's secret focus on persuading holdouts to join the Confederacy once Louisiana votes for secession. For Lamotte and his friends, who are mostly Creole, secession is an opportunity to cast off Yankees and return New Orleans to control by Francophone peoples with a shared heritage. Lamotte's secessionist leanings complicate his personal life, when he falls in love with Gwendolyn Lewis, whose family is politically divided. Her one brother, Philip, is a member of the Krewe of Artemis with Lamotte, but her father David and her brother Hugh, her strict chaperone, are ardent Unionists. As the story progresses the environments in which men socialize and discuss politics (the Boston Club and the Chess, Checkers, and Whist Club, as well as expensive brothels) are fully described. Men can only socialize with women in the family circle, an impossibility when there is family opposition. The Krewe of Artemis Mardi Gras ball gives Lamotte an opportunity to reveal his feelings to Gwendolyn, who welcomes his attentions before scandalizing her family when she strikes Hugh for protesting the playing of Dixie and the unfurling of Confederate flags. Once Mardi Gras is over, Hugh and David Lewis join the Union Army and Philip Lewis aids Lamotte's engagement to Gwendolyn before Lamotte joins the Orleans Guards. He later returns to New Orleans to utilize the Krewe of Artemis to ferret out Union spies. Later, with the fall of the city imminent, Lamotte moves to a hotel and registers as a French citizen, exempting himself from Butler's persecution of Confederate loyalists. Even though

Hugh thwarts Lamotte and Gwendolyn's elopement, slightly before the end of the war, they are reunited and marry, returning to Basseterre and Reconstruction New Orleans to prepare for the first post-war Mardi Gras. The novel provides a good picture of social life in New Orleans immediately prior to and during the Civil War

395. Roberts, Walter Adolphe. *Creole Dusk: A New Orleans Novel of the '80s.* Indianapolis: Bobbs-Merrill, 1948. 325pp.

This post-Reconstruction novel begins in 1884 with the opening of the Cotton Exposition and ends in 1888 with the general election. Protagonist, Dr. Yvon Olivier, a physician who lives and works in Royal Street, is a subtle observer of the social scene. Active in politics, well connected socially, and privy to family secrets, his native social milieu is that of other long-settled Creoles struggling economically in the aftermath of the Civil War. One of his cousins, Camille Lamotte, is continuously throwing himself into improbable schemes to recover his family's fortune, including buying expensive lottery tickets and selling Panama Canal bonds on commission. Declining fortunes have been accompanied by social displacement brought about by an influx of Yankees whose businesses, both legitimate and disreputable (gambling parlors, bars, and brothels), have brought dramatic physical change to the city. Those Creole families with insufficient means to leave the French Quarter are also subjected to an influx of Italian immigrants as family homes are converted into apartments and boarding houses. Olivier is a cousin of Blaise Lamotte, a character this novel shares with *Brave Mardi Gras.* Blaise, now in his late forties, has lost Basseterre Plantation and his wife Gwendolyn is dead. In straitened circumstances, he must devote all of his energy to his legal practice to support an extended family circle of widows and orphans. In a quandary over the meaning of his cultural heritage (whether it is still meaningful or recoverable), Olivier must choose between two women with whom he is in love—Dora Booth, a distant relative and member of his cultural milieu, whose family resettled in Baltimore just before the War—and Rachele Capello, an Italian opera singer. With Booth he shares a familiar culture heritage while Capello appeals to his interest in art and European culture. His relationship with Capello has the added spice of intrigue since his family considers her a disreputable match. Under the pretext of conducting scientific research, he follows her to Panama where she is resting between opera seasons. Seeking a financial backer for a future tour, she befriends Alfredo Pardo, who challenges Olivier to a duel, which he loses. By the time he returns to New Orleans, his mother has decided to support his romance with Booth and the two eventually marry. While a significant portion of the novel is set in Panama, where Olivier nobly fights a yellow fever epidemic, the novel is mostly occupied with descriptions of New Orleans social life that for Creoles like Olivier focuses on literary societies, opera, and politics. The entire Olivier family gathers for the 1888 election and takes satisfaction that it is the first in decades that is not corrupt (in New Orleans).

396. Roberts, Walter Adolphe. *Royal Street: A Novel of Old New Orleans.* Indianapolis: Bobbs-Merrill, 1944. 324pp.

In this historical romance novel, a young man devoted to Gallic culture and to the mission of extending its influence in an enlarged Louisiana Territory, must deal with the fact that his mercantile family is not considered socially acceptable by the family of the woman he loves, even though they are wealthier. Victor Olivier's parents and grandparents were immigrants who were displaced from Santo Domingo by the slave revolt there and arrived in New Orleans in 1809. Victor's father, Charles Olivier, decided not to establish a plantation, the way in which his family had traditionally made a living, but establishes himself as an exchange agent selling sugar abroad and operating an import/export business. Although his decision was economically savvy and enabled him to quickly recover the family's lost wealth, he is regarded as belonging to a lower social rank than the planters. However, his sons live as gentlemen, are sent to Paris to be educated, and are aided by Charles in establishing businesses. The protagonist of the story, Victor Olivier, is thirty-two-years-old when the novel starts in 1842. He earns a more-than-adequate income from his business with little effort and spends his time with other Creole gentlemen of fashion. Although he does not plan to marry until he is thirty-five, he has had one long-term lover, an octoroon mistress named Rosalie, whom he kept in a house on Rampart Street until she died five years before. His current love interest, Claudette "Cherie" Lamotte, could become his wife if her parents' objection to his social rank can be overcome. Madame Lamotte, who spends part of every year in Paris, is particularly focused on social status. In addition to Lamotte, Victor's other passion is preserving New Orleans' Gallic culture and extending the same to an enlarged Louisiana Territory. He is disturbed by Anglo-Americans in New Orleans and has joined Société Gauloise to win political positions for Francophones. He forwards the idea of securing Gallic culture in Louisiana by extending the territory to include other French-speaking areas, and for this purpose returns to Santo Domingo to provide Louisiana aid to French planters rebelling against the Haitian government. While there he reconnects with relatives and helps his cousin Teresa move to New Orleans. Although he behaved heroically in Santo Domingo in a cause the Lamottes' support, their opinion of him does not change until he fights a duel of honor. The novel details social, cultural, and political life in New Orleans in the 1840s, focusing on French-speaking Americans with a fierce devotion to maintaining their culture. Numerous historical figures appear in the course of the book.

397. Robinson, J(ohn) H(ovey). *White Rover, or, The Lovely Maid of Louisiana: A Romance of the Wild Forest*. New York: Samuel French, 1851. 100pp.

Set in 1720s New Orleans when the village was under the control of Governor Bienville (1680–1767), this romantic adventure novel focuses on Helen Lerowe, an orphan who grew up as Bienville's ward, and the orphan Henri Delcroix. The ward of Father Davion as a boy, Delcroix earned the respect of the Natchez and Chickasaw, by whom he is known as White Rover. Even though the two grew up in sibling friendship, they are unrelated and secretly in love. Delcroix has a rival for Helen in Captain Lesage, who has earned Bienville's respect. Lesage hires frontiersman Pierre Moran to kill Delcroix, but the two become allies, along with Onalaska, a chieftain who had been plotting to eliminate French settlement along the Mississippi. Then, Lesage falsely accuses Delcroix of fomenting the Indian uprising and supplies false evidence and lying witnesses that convince Bienville, who sentences Delcroix to death. Before the sentence can be carried out, Moran and Onalaska rescue Delcroix and aid him in getting evidence against Lesage. In the meantime, Helen rejects Lesage and he engineers the kidnapping by Comanches of her and her friend Adelaide Riddle, making Delcroix and Moran look like the culprits. By the end of the novel Lesage is finally shown to be a villain and Delcroix is shown to be a nobleman and heir to a significant fortune. Adelaide's father meets Delcroix and Moran, discovers they were not involved in the plot, and the three of them pursue the trail along with Onalaska. The novel describes physical conditions in New Orleans during the 1720s and presents some of the most important historic figures, as well as attitudes toward Native Americans.

398. Rogér, Katherine Harvey. *Always the River*. New Orleans: Pelican, 1957. 243pp.

At the beginning of this gothic romance, in 1878, seventeen-year-old orphan Mary de Traville is reunited with the family of her New Orleans uncle Paul de Traville, that also includes his son Paul, second wife Madame d'Autin and her son Ovide. Paul de Traville senior had lived on a plantation and had a happy life with his first wife, but she was drowned in a Mississippi River flood, leading him to forever despise the river and even try to shield himself from views of it. His second wife's first marriage had also ended tragically after the death of her husband and all but one of her children from yellow fever. She sold the plantation and slaves she inherited and moved into the Garden District, subsequently marrying Traville, although even at the time of their marriage, Mrs. Traville was an invalid (not due to rheumatism as was popularly claimed, but alcoholism). When Mary arrives at the Travilles, Paul junior immediately falls in love with her, but she has been warned against marriages between cousins by Creole girls attracted to Paul. Mary tries to enjoy a friendship with Ovide, but Madame d'Autin jealously thinks she is trying to alienate Ovide from her. After a yellow fever epidemic kills Paul senior and Ovide becomes more fearful of what Madame de Traville might do to Mary, Paul and Mary move out of the Garden District into the ancestral Traville house on Royal Street. Although Paul thwarts a plot to sell Mary into white slavery, she still resists marriage and is about to enter a convent until she realizes she cannot bear to part from Paul and the two marry and live in New York City, where he becomes rich and famous, although they never have any children. The novel details Mardi Gras, Creole debutante society, and Madame d'Autin's Voodoo practice.

399. Root, Corwin. *An American, Sir.* New York: E.P. Dutton, 1940. 383pp.

In yet another account of events surrounding the Battle of New Orleans, the protagonist, Jeremy Peabody of Boston, falls in love with Marilyn Hastings of New Orleans while she visits relatives. After she eventually leaves for home, Jeremy follows, even though he has no money. The bulk of the book is devoted to his trip. In approximately the final ninety pages of the novel he arrives in New Orleans to find the British poised to attack and must maneuver through their lines. He is unable to convince General Jackson that he is not British, but escapes captivity as the battle begins and finds American troops from Boston who let him fight alongside them. One of these men is Marilyn Hastings' relative and after he is wounded, he is taken to the Hastings residence, where Marilyn nurses him. By the end of the novel they are betrothed. The book provides a great deal of information about the political and economic issues surrounding the War of 1812 and an extended account of the Battle of New Orleans.

400. Ross, Clinton. *Chalmette: The History of the Adventures & Love Affairs of Captain Robe before & during the Battle of New Orleans.* Philadelphia: J.B. Lippincott, 1898. 264pp.

Christopher "Kit" Robe was raised by an uncle on the family estate Westmore in Virginia where both of his parents had died in 1791. In 1814, after study at West Point, Robe is traveling south to New Orleans to join Jackson's forces. His uncle gives him a letter of introduction to Jean Lafitte (c.1776–c.1823). He acknowledges to Robe the crimes that built Lafitte's fortune, but notes that Lafitte has become a powerful man and one of New Orleans' greatest financiers. When Robe arrives in the city he befriends Raoul Deschamps, a young man his age, who becomes his guide to New Orleans. Soon afterwards, Baratarian pirates capture Robe and he is surprised to learn that his Virginia girlfriend, Sally Maurice, has become Lafitte's ward and is pleased that she is able to get him released. She divides her time between Lafitte and her aunt who is a nun at the Ursuline Convent. When Jackson eventually arrives in New Orleans, Sally plays the crucial role in persuading Lafitte to join the American side. Much of this work of historical fiction is set outside New Orleans, but there are descriptions of the city, the battle, and the feting of Jackson.

401. Ross, William Edward Daniel [Marilyn Ross, pseud.]. *Delta Flame.* New York: Popular Library, 1978. 448pp.

This historical novel set in 1827 uses English actress Ellen Price as a foil to expose the evils of slavery and the abuse of women in nineteenth century New Orleans. She, her sister Mary, and father Winston are classically trained British actors hired by James Cranston to open the new St. Clare Theater in New Orleans and they sail from Boston to take up their job. On the journey they are exposed to Americans and meet wealthy plantation owner Phillip Baudier, who is immediately attracted to Ellen, even though he is older than her father. They also become acquainted with journalist Bob Shea, who occasionally writes abolitionist articles, in addition to covering the theater. The Prices immediately win an audience in New Orleans, despite the fact that Winston, still mourning the death of his wife, is drinking too much. Their stage success earns invitations to social events by prominent society figures. When Ellen gets invitations from Baudier, she would prefer to reject them, but because he is an investor in the St. Clare Theater, Cranston encourages Ellen to accept them, even when she must go unchaperoned to his huge plantation, Rothby, miles outside of the city. Her uneasiness about Baudier is confirmed by a "mulatto" she befriends named

Harry Drew, who says Baudier and his family are cruel to slaves and takes her to the slave market to witness Baudier purchasing a young woman who, Drew implies, will become his sex slave. During one of her visits to Rothby, Ellen is horrified to discover that Baudier owns more than two hundred and fifty slaves. However, when her father dies suddenly, financial circumstances propel her to accept Baudier's marriage proposal. In residence on the plantation, Ellen witnesses the plantation slaves' sexual subjugation to Baudier and his relatives. When Baudier dies, Ellen runs away from the plantation so that her son can be raised in St. Louis away from slave culture. The novel makes a pretense of exploring antebellum slave culture but it is written from the perspective of 1970s America, and is mostly concerned with issues of race and feminism. New Orleans settings are shallowly described.

402. Ryan, Marah Ellis. *A Flower of France: A Story of Old Louisiana.* Chicago: Rand, McNally, 1893. 327pp.

Mostly set in the New Orleans of the 1790s when Louisiana is under Spanish rule and many French exiles are arriving in the colony, this tale of love and Voodoo traces the aftermath of a murder. In 1768, Gaston de Noyens is killed and the new Spanish governor, Don Diego Zanalta, falsely accuses Basil de Bayarde of the crime. He is exiled to the Mexican mines, leaving the woman he has been courting, Felice Henriette St. Malo, to mourn his absence and her evil slave Zizi to exalt. St. Malo collapses into a state declared to be lunacy and is taken to a remote plantation where she dies after giving birth to Bayarde's child. Eighteen years later Zizi has taken the name Venda and earned a reputation as a Voodoo priestess. Even though the colony continues to have a strong French presence, Spaniards have influenced the architecture and Zanalta has firmly established his rule. However, the most influential host in New Orleans is the fabulously wealthy Victor Lamont, who promotes French culture in society. Lamont and Zanalta become rivals for the hand of convent girl, Denise, who was a foundling at the nuns' gates eighteen years before. They also become rivals in financial matters. By the end of the novel Zanalta has been driven out of Louisiana and Lamont is revealed to be the returned Basil de Bayarde, who Zanalta had plotted against to get the Bayarde lands, just as he had ordered Gaston de Noyens' murder in order to gain control of his property. Denise turns out to be the daughter of Felice Henriette St. Malo. Furthermore, St. Malo became a nun and, as Sister Andrea, has been living in the same convent as Denise, although she had never realized the identity of the infant who Venda brought to the convent. She is proved to have been the wife of Bayarde when she bore Denise, his child. The happiness of the reunited family is complete when Bayarde is proved to be innocent of killing le Noyens and the faithful Venda reveals that she killed the French nobleman who had found her in Africa and loved her as a princess, but who made her a slave once they arrived in Louisiana. The novel introduces historical facts about political control of Louisiana, traces a continuing enmity between the French and Spanish in the colony, and touches on issues of race and gender, while presenting the character of Zizi/Venda as a strong, feared person of color who earns respect for her faithfulness to her master.

403. Sargent, Epes. *Peculiar: A Tale of the Great Transition.* New York: Carleton, 1864. 500pp.

This abolitionist novel also reveals the plight of nineteenth-century women whose husbands gained control of all the assets they brought to a marriage. New York businessman, Charlton (only referred to by surname), takes advantage of the law to gain the Berwick family fortune. He marries the widow of Henry Berwick, one of the victims of a steamboat explosion. To further secure the fortune, he testifies in court that Henry Berwick's infant daughter, Clara, had died in the accident. However, he actually had Clara kidnapped and sold into slavery in New Orleans to Carbury Ratcliff, who epitomizes all the evils of a slaveholder. Initially, Ratcliff sees Clara as a clever investment because she will be highly valued for her white skin once she reaches adulthood. For this reason, he has her educated and raised in his household. As she matures, he realizes she will be a beauty and decides to marry her. When she resists, he uses all the forms of coercion in his power, including threatening to mate her to one of his African-American slaves. Clara becomes familiar with a number of enslaved African-Americans, and their plight and mistreatment become important to the narrative (one of these slaves is named "Peculiar Institution" giving the book its title). Through a lawyer, William Vance, Clara learns her real identity, but when she tries to force her liberation, Ratcliff incarcerates her in his house telling everyone she is insane. The fall of New Orleans brings freedom for Clara and incarceration for Ratcliff, a debtor, who had invested everything in slaves. When Clara comes into her inheritance, she gives part of her wealth to fund a school in New Orleans for the children of freed slaves, although she immediately returns to New York City and the ancestral home of her family to devote herself to the Union cause. After the Battle of Gettysburg she goes there to minister to the wounded and purchases farms to shelter the injured. The novelist uses the New Orleans setting to present the evils of slavery, treating the city as the center of slave culture.

404. Schachner, Nathan. *By the Dim Lamps.* New York: Frederick A. Stokes, 1941. 577pp.

In this historical romance novel, the author comprehensively recounts the history of the South from the election of 1860 to the White League Riot of 1874. He uses a large number of characters to tell his story, but the main protagonist is Hugh Flint, a Princeton-educated man whose work with his father Stephen has taught him valuable lessons of economics in the firm of Flint & Sons, Commission Merchants and Sugar Factors from offices on Poydras Street. As the war approaches, he trains as a soldier and enlists in the Confederate Army, but, shocked at the abandonment of New Orleans to the Union Army, disobeys orders and returns to the city, trying to protect the goods in his father's offices so that plantation owners will not be ruined. He has an emotional interest in one plantation, Moon Hill, for he is in love with Sally Wailes, the daughter of its owner. The novel relates many human aspects of the occupation of New Orleans and of the war on the home front through Wailes' experiences. Flint lives with his father in their house on Prytania Street and secretly trades cotton and sugar to corrupt Yankees to get supplies needed by the Confederates in their war effort. In addition to describing wartime New Orleans, a significant portion of the book is devoted to postwar developments and the impact of Reconstruction carpetbaggers on the city. Throughout, the plight of African-Americans is presented through the character of Quash, who has a vision of creating a "Black Empire" in the post-Civil War South. The book presents the history of New Orleans in great detail from a number of viewpoints over a crucial fifteen-year period.

405. Schertz, Helen Pitkin. *An Angel by Brevet: A Story of Modern New Orleans.* Philadelphia: J.B. Lippincott, 1904. 384pp.

The forward of this book makes clear that the author's goal is to expose the deleterious effects of witchcraft and Voodoo as practiced by African-Americans. She is confident that in the future, Northern civilization will destroy Voodoo by bringing skyscrapers to replace the bayou gathering places of practitioners and by leveling ancient French Quarter houses, like that of Marie Laveau. However, she is also concerned about the plight of her contemporaries held powerless by drugs and forced to participate in outlawed "voudouism and warlockry." The novel is set in a traditional Creole household on Bourbon Street, where Madame la Marquese de Marigny, a woman who came of age before the Civil War, presides. Her husband and all of her children are dead, except for Madame Ernestine Livaudais, who has two unmarried children, Angelique and Carmelite, living with her. Carmelite has just been engaged to Numa Delery, a good match. Her somewhat older sister, twenty-two-year-old Angelique, is increasingly concerned about her spinsterhood and although she considers her suitor, the Episcopalian Rev. Dr. Martin Paradise, wise and spiritually insightful, she does not consider him a good match since she is a Catholic. She has tried all the traditional prayers to various saints to no avail and begins participating in the Voodoo practice of her African-American servants. Under the guidance of Victorine, her mammy, and Toussine, her mixed-race hairdresser, Angelique tries to win Numa Delery away from Carmelite through

Voodoo. The book includes lengthy descriptions of Voodoo practice. After Carmelite begins to suffer migraines following a hostile Voodoo priestess' curse, Angelique fears her Voodoo practices are unleashing evil. She nurses Carmelite and finds a Voodoo priest to perform a spell-breaking ritual. In confessing her transgressions to Dr. Paradise, she realizes how much he loves her and the two become engaged. The novel gives some sense of a traditional Creole household of the 1880s, while conveying a wealth of biased information about Voodoo practice, popular superstitions, traditional tales, songs, and poems.

406. Seifert, Shirley. *Those Who Go Against the Current.* Philadelphia: J.B. Lippincott, 1943. 612pp.

   This fictionalized account of the life of Manuel de Lisa (1772–1820) covers the 1780s to 1820 and presents the impact of the changing political control of Louisiana on New Orleans. Both of Manuel's parents were born in Spain to aristocratic families and initially object to a business career for Manuel. However, his pre-teenage successes as a trader eventually outweigh their objections. Some of his earliest business coups stem from investments in rebuilding New Orleans after the destruction of about eight hundred buildings in the 1788 fire. He also quickly realizes that the Mississippi will eventually be controlled by the Americans and makes business alliances with individuals along the river. Manuel is one of the earliest traders at what would become St. Louis and he is instrumental to the founding of the city. Although much of the novel is set in frontier settlements along the Mississippi, Manuel frequently returns to New Orleans where he has an office managed by his ne'er-do-well brother, Jaoquin (sic), and his visits give Seifert the opportunity to catalog the major changes to the city over the time period. Numerous historical figures people the novel.

407. Seley, Stephen. *Baxter Bernstein: A Hero of Sorts.* New York: Charles Scribner's Sons, 1949. 239pp.

   The eponymous, self-absorbed protagonist experiences the world as though he were a character in a novel and he is preoccupied with internal monologues referencing great works of literature from which he quotes extensively. Mostly set during World War II in Mexico, a significant portion of the work transpires in New Orleans. Weighed down by ennui and a life of inaction, Bernstein travels to the Crescent City in November 1941 to break his routine. He is surprised to learn that his great love, Fortune Riley, is living there. To his dismay, she is married to another man, Fredo Orviedo, and is selling pralines in a shop. The two eventually have a boozy encounter at Hennessey's that ends with Fortune deciding to do nothing that would endanger her marriage. In despair, Bernstein continues his evening at a whorehouse, getting even more intoxicated, and finally picking up an African-American prostitute. Afterwards, he witnesses her being strangled to death in a racist attack and takes no action to prevent it or detain the murderer. After another exchange with Fortune she agrees to run away with him, and he leaves with the understanding that they will meet in Texas. Even though Bernstein stays at the St. Charles Hotel, during much of the eighty-five pages in which he is in New Orleans he is on the streets and in the bars of the French Quarter, about which the novel conveys a good sense of the people, sounds, and the accents and slang terms of daily conversation.

408. Sharkey, Emma Augusta Brown [Mrs. E. Burke Collins, pseud.]. *Mam'selle: A Modern Heathen.* Philadelphia: William J. Benners, Jr., 1895. 246pp.

   Growing up in the Louisiana swamps, Mam'selle is raised by grandparents who are mostly concerned with how much work they can get out of her. Her parents are never mentioned and she has no idea whether they are alive or even who they were. Her only solace is a single-volume collection of Shakespeare's plays given to her by a failed priest. Her life is transformed as a sixteen-year-old by her friendship with Alaric Brandon, a New Orleans society figure and cultured playwright, who accidentally meets her and realizes her potential as an actress. He pays her grandparents to board in their home and tutor Mam'selle. When business necessitates his return to the city, Brandon leaves Mam'selle a library of books. When her grandfather burns them she runs away to New Orleans and Brandon. Although Brandon's fiancée, Althea Marsden, immediately scorns Mam'selle, Althea's sister Valerie (née Marsden) Wright takes her into her affluent home. Valerie's interest in the girl partly stems from her suspicion that based on her appearance and mannerisms, she is the daughter of the great actor, Lawrence Dorne. As Brandon introduces her to New Orleans, her beauty and forthrightness interest some writers and a bishop, but also inspire Althea Marsden's jealousy since she believes the girl is in love with Brandon. When Mam'selle rejects the advances of wealthy Sebastian Orme, she makes another enemy. During the five years she is in boarding school at a famous theatrical conservatory she is safe from her enemies. Her first post-school role in New Orleans propels her to stardom and Orme, even more insistent that she marries him, threatens to reveal a terrible secret about her protector, Valerie Wright. When Mam'selle approaches Wright about the matter, she learns that the woman is her mother. Wright had secretly married Lawrence Dorne due to her own mother's opposition. When Dorne died shortly after the wedding, Wright found she was pregnant and her mother arranged for Wright to give birth in rural Louisiana and then claimed that Mam'selle had been stillborn. She destroyed all proofs of Wright's marriage to Dorne and forced her to marry wealthy Stephen Wright. Mam'selle helps Wright leave her husband and New Orleans, while she leaves the stage to return to her hometown. Brandon is so moved by her self-sacrificing nature that he throws over the selfish Althea and seeks out Mam'selle for his bride. Although the work is mostly set in New Orleans, physical setting is not very important in this novel, but it does give some description of the theater community in the city. The major theme is the helplessness of women in a society filled with ruthless men.

409. Shore, William. *The Witch of Spring.* Pelligrini and Cudahy, 1950. 348pp.

This novel introduces a wealthy Northerner into 1835 New Orleans to highlight the evils of slave culture and race-based social castes. Kirkpatric is the offspring of David Kirkpatric, a physician, and Amelia Van Horst, the only child of Willem Van Horst, a wealthy New York City shipbuilder and merchant. Kirkpatric's mother died when he was eight, but his father and grandfather raised him with a love focused on what was best for him. So, when as a young man, he rejected his father's profession and the opportunity to take over his grandfather's business in order to study painting, they supported his decision and even travelled abroad with him as he pursued his art instruction. When they died within a short time of each other, his servant and companion, the hunchbacked African-American Reheul, encouraged him to get away from the familiarities of New York for the exotic New Orleans, where his father's best friend, Doctor Carlysle, resides. Kirkpatric is quickly accepted into the highest circles of New Orleans society. His initial entrée is aided by a friendship he develops with Antony Saint-Marc, a wealthy, young, Creole plantation owner. Kirkpatric is admired for his physical attractiveness, wealth, and abilities as an artist. He rents a house, hires servants, and begins exploring the culture of New Orleans. Early on, he is forced to accept a challenge and when he knowledgeably and precisely duels his opponent, a much-disliked bully, he wins further admiration in New Orleans society. Before long, Saint-Marc's fiancée, Rojean D'Avigny, has let him know that she is in love with him, dismissing Kirkpatric's concern about hurting Saint-Marc, by informing him that their engagement was a loveless match, arranged by their families. Saint-Marc takes Kirkpatric to a quadroon ball, during the course of which Dr. Carlysle explains how quadroon women have no choice but to become the mistresses of wealthy New Orleans men since they are too refined to marry African-American men and cannot marry a white man due to miscegenation laws. Kirkpatric comes to admire and chastely love Laurolea, Saint-Marc's mistress. He does eventually form an attachment to a woman without a relationship to Saint-Marc—Twila Lavelle. However, the woman is a young widow and Kirkpatric has been warned against her because of her past that involves the practice of Voodoo. During the course of the novel he discovers the ways in which slave culture has poisoned all of the women with whom he comes into contact. However, after helping thwart a slave uprising, he finds he is still in love with Twila Lavelle and promises to marry her if she will leave for New York City. Although Kirkpatric finds aspects of New Orleans beautiful and fascinating, in the end he decides he wants nothing to do with Southern slave culture and leaves the city in disgust. The novel is most concerned with racial prejudice, but does relate aspects of New Orleans culture and history and references many actual locations and businesses.

410. Sinclair, Harold. *Journey Home.* Garden City, N.Y.: Doubleday, Doran, 1936. 290pp.

James David Hall, the first-person narrator of this Depression-era novel, travels from New York to Chicago, New Orleans and Fort Worth in the course of the narrative. Only roughly fifty pages are set in New Orleans, but they evoke important aspects of the city during the time period. Born in 1900, Hall has briefly experienced life as a married man in New York City, working as an accountant in a brokerage firm. When he loses both his wife and his job in the wake of the 1929 stock market crash, he sets off for New Orleans, inspired solely by a railroad poster. However, his journey is circuitous and entails much adventure, particularly in Chicago where he works as a bootlegger for a time. When he finally arrives in the Crescent City, he easily finds a room in a pleasant boarding house off Royal Street, but can only get a job unloading banana boats. His spare-time activity of browsing second-hand book shops leads to a temporary job managing such an establishment, through which he meets Anthony Cardas, an importer, who hires Hall as a sympathetic acquaintance, who happens to have accounting skills. Hall soon discovers that Cardas will import anything, including stolen diamonds, dates, olive oil, and heroin. He quickly settles into the routine and his only qualms about the job are inspired by his new girlfriend, Eve Caraway, an art student who anticipates a return to the Midwest, marriage to Hall, and securing him an accounting job in her father's factory. When Hall finds Cardas dead in his office one morning, he decides to flee town and break up with Caraway, who he has decided he does not love. The novel depicts aspects of economic conditions in New Orleans, job opportunities, boarding house life, as well as touching on the large underground economy in the port city.

411. Smith, Annie Laura [Catherine Von Scyler, pseud.]. *Rosine: The Story of a Fair Young Girl.* New York: Broadway, 1903. 132pp.

The wealth and attractiveness of thirty-four-year-old Rupert St. Claire make him one of New Orleans' most eligible bachelors and heiress Alice Wendever secretly decides that she must marry him. By the time she announces herself, however, St. Claire has become engaged to Florrie Meadows, a beautiful but poor girl. Vowing revenge, Wendever adopts a disguise and gets the St. Claires to hire her as "Mrs. Burgess," a nurse to their infant daughter Rosine. Burgess/Wendever arouses no suspicion during the two years she serves the family, but then suddenly abducts Rosine. St. Claire offers a large reward and hires private detectives to no avail. Fifteen years pass during which Rosine lives as a member of the New York City Mudge family, doted on by her stepbrother Chip. When Chip stops a runaway carriage, the vehicle happens to be carrying St. Claire and his wife. In gratitude, St. Claire offers Mudge a job and he goes to New Orleans with them. In the meantime, Burgess/Wendever, who is now known as Mrs. Campbell, retrieves Rosine from the Mudges, declaring that she is her daughter Rena Campbell. She now heightens her revenge by forcing Rosine/Rena to become the mistress of a married physician. Meanwhile, Chip cannot forget his sister and as he talks about her, St. Claire begins to think that she may be his missing daughter and eventually that Chip may be Rosine's twin brother who was said to be dead at birth. Rosine is recovered in New York City and Alice Wendever meets a terrible end when she dies in a self-inflicted conflagration. Although much of the novel transpires in New Orleans, the city receives little description.

412. Smith, Minette Graham. *Maid of New Orleans*. New York: Vantage, 1954. 121pp.

This author's paean to the aristocrats of the South (in the tradition of "the Lost Cause"), is populated by incredibly noble, long-suffering characters. Caroline DeLarand, of a long-distinguished and wealthy family, is sixteen when her parents die and she takes responsibility for maintaining the ancestral DeLarand house for her older brothers, Robert and Daniel. With war approaching both brothers marry quickly; Daniel and his wife continuing to live with Caroline and Robert buying a cottage near the tobacco export company he establishes. Daniel's wife soon gives birth to Alice DeLarand, but dies within a year and when Daniel dies on the battlefield his deathbed wish is that eighteen-year-old Caroline cares for Alice. Due to this responsibility, Caroline rejects the proposal of her childhood sweetheart, Jack Holzac. By this point New Orleans has fallen and the suddenly impoverished Caroline has only Confederate currency and a house stripped of all valuables by Union troops. Her responsibilities increase when her sister-in-law Louise dies and her brother Robert and niece Biddy move in. Holzac remains devoted and helps financially, but is soon missing in a ship explosion. A decade has passed by the end of the novel. Alice and Biddy are engaged, Robert's tobacco firm has burgeoned and thirty-year-old Caroline has resigned herself to being single and dedicating herself to charity work. However, when she attends the Comus Ball a masked knight changes her future. Throughout the novel, the protagonists are concerned with vengeful "free niggers" and their radical Republican supporters, as well as the lack of reliable laborers, since former slaves refuse to work. Even the family servants who remain with the family are negligent in their duties and cause two disasters by their inattention.

413. Smith, Richard Penn. *Lafitte, or the Baratarian Chief: A Tale Founded on Facts*. Auburn, N.Y.: Free, 1828. 106pp.

In this tale Lafitte is an American and the book explains how he turned into a pirate. Lafitte entered adulthood as a promising business clerk named Mortimer Wilson under the tutelage of his wealthy Manhattan merchant uncle. When his uncle decided to open offices in Charleston he put Wilson in charge. Although Wilson was immediately successful, he succumbed to yellow fever and was nursed back to health by Mary Mornton with whom he fell in love. However, the well connected, but nasty George Hanson pursues her as well. On the night that Mornton chooses Wilson as her true love, Hanson attacks Wilson and is accidentally killed. Mornton's father urges Wilson to flee on one of his own merchant ships, which is captured by pirates and Wilson is forced into the life of a sailor aboard a privateer. When he is finally able to return to Charleston, Mary Mornton is dead and the embittered Wilson becomes a fierce pirate, taking the name Jean Lafitte. In the tale's dramatic climax Lafitte is vital to the British defeat at New Orleans and receives his pardon. Shortly after the battle, one of Mary Mornton's best friends visits New Orleans and Lafitte is immediately smitten. Although New Orleans is mentioned frequently, the city receives little description and this book is included mostly for its early publication date and as yet another account of Lafitte and the Battle of New Orleans.

414. Snelling, Laurence. *The Return of Lance Tennis*. New York: Holt, Rinehart and Winston, 1965. 189pp.

Graduate student Norton Wilkins had hoped that he could prolong his student life indefinitely, but his wife, Athelia, née Hogg, stops supporting him out of frustration over his lack of initiative. She insists that they move to Nashville and he gets a job in her uncle's real estate firm if he is not going to finish his thesis. Ryker, Wilkins' thesis advisor loses patience around the same time after Wilkins repeatedly cancels classes he is to teach to earn his fellowship stipend. When Ryker gives Wilkins a deadline for submitting a thesis draft, he leaves for New Orleans where Ryker's wife, with whom Wilkins is infatuated, has gone for the summer. After forging Ryker's signature to get his stipend, Wilkins hitchhikes to New Orleans where he infiltrates a circle of young novelists and poets, using the sobriquet Lance Tennis. He is soon a houseguest of literary patron Wilder Carruthers, a not-unattractive young woman whose allures are enhanced by her income from her

Texan oil millionaire father. Although Wilkins has no real literary skill, he submits a plagiarized version of an obscure play to the competition Ryker's wife is coordinating and the arty house-wives and businessmen of New Orleans think it wonderful. He uses this success to convince Car-ruthers to become his patron and move to Mexico with him. The novel focuses on Wilkins' adept-ness in evading people and responsibilities, including Ryker (who has also employed a private detective) and Athelia (joined by her father Judge Hogg), while pursuing both Mrs. Ryker and Wilder Carruthers. In the end, Carruthers' wealth eases him out of all commitments and entangle-ments and, by the end of the novel, he is established with Carruthers in Saint Martin, Mexico, where he has actually been able to complete several novels about his previous adventures. Wil-kins' New Orleans is filled with many poseurs and the literary/art scene is dominated by talentless eccentrics who are tourist attractions, bringing business to bars that sponsor readings and to the French Quarter in general where tourists arrive by the busload to see bohemian characters. The novel mentions well-known addresses, restaurants, hotels, and watering places, while providing little physical description.

415. Snelling, Laurence. *The Temptation of Archer Watson*. New York: Norton, 1974. 240pp.

This social satire focuses on the impact of 1970s Texas oil money on Louisiana politics and New Orleans society. As an instructor at the socially prestigious New Orleans Tennis Club, Wat-son is accustomed to dealing with the wives and children of New Orleans' most prominent men and even though he does not respect them, he has become accustomed to understanding them and finding ways to enjoy low-risk sexual exploits with their women. When Texas millionaires begin joining the club, they are impatient with the unbusiness-like traditions in place. One of the mil-lionaires, Olin McKeene, is dissatisfied with New Orleans in general and is taking over New Or-leans businesses in a bid to control Louisiana politics and impose his vision of an industrialized New Orleans metropolitan area that will become the Ruhr Valley of the Americas. Watson thinks himself above all of these matters, gliding through life with enough free drinks and sexual liaisons to occupy his extensive free time (he has arranged to work only twenty hours a week). Then he is caught having sex with the sixteen-year-old daughter of Fred Moseley, McKeene's second-in-command. Watson is shocked to learn that Moseley arranged for Watson to be caught in flagrante delicto in order to blackmail him to convince two college professor friends to play a role in McKeene's political machinations. A state-funded college campus is the scene of much of the po-litical maneuvering and the novel raises issues of free speech, tenure, and manipulation of the me-dia. The book articulates racist positions, aspects of identity politics and 1970s youth culture. De-scriptions of New Orleans are focused on status politics among the upper classes with little to evoke the physical environment.

416. Sparkia, Roy Bernard [Mitchell Caine, pseud.]. *Creole Surgeon.* Greenwich, Conn.: Fawcett Books, 1977. 446pp.

Paul Abbott was adopted by a physician who found him alive in 1831, in the midst of slaugh-tered members of a wagon train in Missouri. Abbott trained in his adopted father's profession, even going to Edinburgh, Scotland, to study. Just as he was about to get his degree, he was falsely implicated in a scandal over a cadaver acquired for dissection. Abbott fled and, working as a ship's surgeon, he ends up in New Orleans where, for the first time in his life, he finds a commu-nity that embraces him—the Creoles. Because he is a newcomer, the people explain to him (and the reader) the history of New Orleans and aspects of the culture, particularly as it relates to people of mixed race. As the Civil War is about to start, Abbott will clearly side with the Union since he is sympathetic to the plight of slaves, has a Creole for a wife, and a quadroon as a lover.

417. Sparling, (Edward) Earl. *Under the Levee.* New York: Charles Scribner's Sons, 1925. 290pp.

All of these rather sensational stories are set in New Orleans' seediest neighborhoods and often deal with ethnicity-based animosities among Italians, Irish, and South Americans. Typical occupations, in addition to thief, include barmaid, dockworker, boxer, shrimp runner, and a street vendor of snowball ices. Joining this mix are several bohemian artists who fare just as badly as their menially employed fellows, for most of the stories include at least one death from murder or suicide. The book presents the life of bars, docks, and the streets in the 1920s, capturing aspects of social history.

418. Spencer, Elizabeth. *The Snare.* New York: McGraw-Hill, 1972. 407pp.

Set in 1960s New Orleans, this novel purports to display, through the experiences of Julia Garrett, the corruption just beneath the surface of New Orleans society. As an orphaned six-year-old, Garrett was sent to live with her maternal aunt, Isabel Devigny. Isabel and her husband Maurice live in the Audubon Place mansion of Henri Devigny, Maurice's father, who had grown up in Iberville but longed for the life of a New Orleans gentleman. He was thrilled to be accepted into the innermost social circles, becoming a member of gentlemen's clubs, benefiting handsomely from social connections in business deals before realizing too late that his new acquaintances sometimes employed violent intimidation, sometimes violent. Julia loved Henri and his vision of a grandly social New Orleans that had more to do with the late-nineteenth century than the city in which she lived. Even as a girl, however, she suspected some mysterious underside when she witnessed Henri fly into a rage and later grieve over the corpse of a "mulatto" woman. She came to realize that even Maurice, the image of lawyerly probity and restraint, was in the employ of a company engaged in less-than-honorable business practices and often legitimized their activities through misrepresentation. By the time she graduates, cum laude, from Tulane, Julia has the opportunity to marry a classmate from a wealthy Baton Rouge family but, convinced that strength comes from the ability to live at the margins of social acceptability, instead works as a nude model for an art class, couriers illicit goods around New Orleans, and lives in a rundown Amelia Street house. A series of events that extend over roughly eight years bring her into contact with a murderer and causes her to fall in love with a jazz musician and bear his child out of wedlock. By the end of the novel she has begun working on a doctorate and has established a balance between the world of apparent respectability and the margins of society. New Orleans in the novel is filled with corruption at all levels, including the police department and most respectable social circles. An additional theme is the relative independence of women in a newly sexually liberated era.

419. Sperry, Armstrong (Wells). *Black Falcon: A Story of Piracy and Old New Orleans.* Illustrated by Armstrong Sperry. Philadelphia: J.C. Winston, 1949. 218pp.

The eponymous Black Falcon is Jean Lafitte (c.1776–c.1823) and this work of historical fiction is yet another retelling of the role of the buccaneer and his men in the defense of New Orleans. In 1814, sixteen-year-old Wade Thayer and his loyal freedman, Christian, are taken prisoners by the British after they capture the blockade-running ship of Thayer's indigo-planter father, who is killed in the encounter. After a week of confinement, Christian engineers their escape. They encounter Dominique You and are soon the guests of Jean Lafitte. The novel makes a careful explanation of why Lafitte and his men cannot really be considered criminals, since they sail under letters of marque from Cartagena, in rebelling Colombia, which is trying to throw off Spanish rule and is encouraging attacks on Spanish ships. After witnessing Lafitte's rejection of a lucrative alliance with the British, Wade becomes an emissary to Governor Claiborne, since his father had been a friend of the Governor. Claiborne reads Lafitte's letter with distrust and shortly afterwards destroys his bayou base. When Andrew Jackson (1767–1845) arrives, Lafitte shows up to make his own case that Jackson accepts, based on the armaments and men Lafitte can provide. A rather detailed account follows of preparations for war and troop actions in December 1814 and early January of 1815. Wade, who was gravely wounded in battle and saved by Christian, misses the victory celebrations, but Lafitte gives him the medal he was awarded in absentia. He is also reunited with his girlfriend from the plantation neighboring his father's and will clearly return to his plantation married and ready to restore the land from the floodwaters brought by a broken levee. Yet another in a series of books for young adults that relate the history of the Battle of New Orleans, this work is similar in articulating the conflicting loyalties in New Orleans, rationalizing Lafitte's piracy, and presenting him as a patriot. The book is different in presenting Christian, a heroic, free African-American character, although the book is not without racism.

420. Sprague, William Cyrus. *Boy Courier of Napoleon: A Story of the Louisiana Purchase.* Illustrated by A.B. Shute. Boston: Lee and Shepard, 1904. 331pp.

While most of this work of historical fiction is not set in New Orleans, a significant portion describes the city at the point of its transfer from Spain to France. Pierre Barré lived in France from his birth. His father went to Louisiana to establish himself with the plan to send for Pierre and his mother after preparing a home for them. Before that could happen, Pierre's mother died and Pierre responded to the call Napoleon Bonaparte (1769–1821) made for soldiers. The young Pierre joins the army as a drummer boy, comes to the attention of Napoleon for his bravery, is eventually made a valet to the First Consul, and is later sent as Napoleon's courier to New Orleans to announce Louisiana's transfer from Spain to France. Several adventures occur, including capture by Pierre-Dominique Toussaint L'Ouverture (1746–1803), shipwreck, and aid from the pirates of Barataria, including the brothers Lafitte. All of this delays Pierre for more than a year. When he finally arrives in New Orleans he is surprised to learn that many Louisianans oppose Napoleon for countenancing the overthrow of the Roman Catholic Church and consider him a despot who would abrogate the freedoms they had known under Spanish rule. Over approximately sixty pages Pierre stays in or near New Orleans on a sugar plantation and is there when he learns that Napoleon Bonaparte has sold Louisiana to the United States. He is eventually reunited with his frontiersman father and becomes an enthusiastic supporter of United States. Pierre meets a number of historical figures, including those important to the history of New Orleans, such as: Julien de Lallande Poydras (1746–1824) and Étienne de Boré (1741–1820).

421. Stahls, Charles Gilbert. *Grand Bouquet.* Los Angeles: Watling, 1951. 328pp.

In the first few years after World War II, Peter Gardner and Paul Dunphy return to New Orleans to resume civilian life. Each of them is serious about a woman. Gardner dates Talma Temple, a schoolteacher, and Dunphy dates Sandra Kane, a woman whose beauty has always made life easy for her. Gardner works as a reporter and is writing a novel. Dunphy, an engineer who was a fighter pilot, anticipates a job in commercial aviation. Gardner is soon involved in broadcast journalism and Temple follows him into the world of radio. Before Dunphy is fully separated from military service he dies tragically. Kane, accustomed to having a man to look out for her, alienates Gardner from Temple and they become the ones who marry. Temple continues in broadcasting and develops her own popular radio show, while Gardner becomes a well-known radio columnist and begins traveling extensively. Kane seizes an opportunity to move to Hollywood, becomes an actress, and insists on a divorce, leaving Gardner free to pursue his original love, Talma Temple, to whom he returns in New Orleans. The novel is of most interest for capturing the conversations and activities of people in their early thirties who dine out, go to popular clubs, and experience the frustrations and triumphs of careers in New Orleans.

422. Statham, Frances Patton. *The Flame of New Orleans.* Greenwich, Conn.: Fawcett, 1977. 447pp.

This historical romance novel covers the Civil War and Reconstruction eras and is mostly set in New Orleans. After the protagonist, Aimee Saint-Moreau, is orphaned and impoverished by the death of her gambler father, she and her brother Etienne are sent to live with their grandparents in New Orleans. Arriving just before the Civil War, Etienne enlists in the Confederate Army and is killed at Shiloh. Shortly afterwards, Aimee's grandmother dies and when New Orleans falls to the Union, Aimee's grandfather is imprisoned and dies in captivity. When the impoverished Aimee's house is requisitioned for the use of Major Bryan Garrard, she tries to maintain her social position through haughty behavior that offends Garrard, who eventually insults her honor. Remorseful over his behavior, he redeems himself and proposes, with the intervention of a Catholic priest. After the marriage, Aimee falls in love with him and bears his child, but not before there are lengthy, complex plot twists, involving her continued allegiance to the Confederacy. After marrying Aimee, Garrard sends her to the country plantation of a relative and she becomes a Confederate courier when she visits the unwitting Garrard in the city. When she is caught, her husband defends her and eventually gets her released to house arrest. However, after he is ordered elsewhere, she is imprisoned outside of New Orleans and the couple must struggle to be reunited. After the war they decide to begin married life in earnest in New Orleans and the novel describes the early carpetbagger period in the city. Throughout the book, national political issues are a focus as Garrard explains current events to his wife. Even though direct descriptions of New Orleans are superficial, the experiences of Aimee and her family touch on the impact of the Civil War and Reconstruction on city residents.

423. St. Cyr, Sylvester. *The Saint and Sinners*. New York: Vantage, 1972. 158pp.

An African-American man who joined the New Orleans police force in 1958 and was assigned to the undercover narcotics unit wrote this fictionalized autobiography. The book is of great interest as a first-hand account of street life in the city during the late 1950s, particularly as segregation and racism is addressed. The main character, "Saint," is married and interacts with his wife and family members as well as co-workers on his undercover jobs as a substitute teacher, YMCA employee, and trampoline performer at charity events. From these interactions we get a sense of middle-class African-American culture in the city. Saint's father was a member of Louis Armstrong's Hot Five jazz band and, in first-person narrative, Saint relates the past history of some neighborhoods, based on his father's reminiscences. The book sometimes mentions actual news stories from 1958, and on one occasion Saint is introduced to John Howard Griffin (1920–1980), the author of *Black Like Me* (Houghton Mifflin, 1961). However, the book is mostly set in dive bars where crime and drug abuse are prevalent. Large sections of the book are expository, conveying the meaning of street slang, details about drug culture, and about gay and lesbian culture of the time period.

424. Stephens, Ann Sophia. *Myra, the Child of Adoption.* New York: Beadle and Adams, 1860. 120pp.

In this novel, loosely based on the life of Myra Clark Gaines (1804–1885), Myra's mother, Zulima, was tricked as a very young woman into marrying a man named De Grainges, only to find that he already had a wife. She fled and fell under the protection of a wealthy banker and businessman named Gaines and, after they fell in love, secretly married. However, they could not marry openly since she had never sought any legal resolution of her tie to De Grainges. So, she maintained the identity of a single woman and lived in the plantation house of one of Gaines' friends a few miles outside New Orleans. When they had a daughter named Myra, Gaines arranged for the baby to be raised by a foster family. He promised Zulima that after De Grainges was brought to justice and he and Zulima could live openly as husband and wife, Myra would be retrieved. Unfortunately, Gaines trusted some of his employees with his secret. They helped De Grainges escape from prison and destroyed a will Gaines wrote that named Zulima and Myra as his sole beneficiaries, so that De Grainges could gain control of his assets upon his death. Although most of the novel is set in New Orleans, the city receives almost no description.

425. Stoddard, William Osborn. *The Errand Boy of Andrew Jackson: A War Story of 1814.* Illustrated by Will Crawford. Boston: Lothrop, Lee and Shepard, 1902. 327pp.

This account of the Battle of New Orleans for young people has sixteen-year-old Daniel Martin of Tennessee as a protagonist and presents a very different version of Lafitte's negotiations with Andrew Jackson (1767–1845). Martin's patriotic family immediately realize the implication when word comes of Napoleon Bonaparte's surrender: the British will send more troops to the United States, so the Martins are proud to send their son, Daniel, along with their farmhand, Black Sam, a French-speaking free man of color, familiar with New Orleans, as his companion to the city. When Dan reaches the forces mustering around Jackson, he wins a marksman competition and he is appointed orderly to Captain Hutton. Hutton's mission is to travel to Barataria and present an offer from Jackson. Black Sam remains with Dan and is joined by Seminole Chief Ki-a-wok, a valuable guide to the swamplands, who is fascinated by Sam's skin color. In this version of negotiations with Lafitte, Hutton reaches the buccaneer before any British representatives, and Lafitte accepts the guarantee that he and his pirates will be given amnesty if they close their illegal operations at Grand Terre and fight with Jackson. They are even offered the opportunity to empty their warehouses of stolen goods. Lafitte has accepted Jackson's offer before the British approach him. Stoddard claims the pirate accepts because he is on the side of the United States, but also because he can more easily negotiate with Jackson, than with his long-time enemy Governor Claiborne. The author spends a good deal of time describing strategy and fortifications, but does not really describe New Orleans, except for battle scenes.

426. Stone, Elisabet M. *Murder at the Mardi Gras.* New York: Sheridan House, 1947. 244pp.

This murder mystery/romance features a female journalist as protagonist. Margaret Slone is a reporter for the Phipps Syndicate, but spends most of her time on rewrites until Ash Wednesday, 1934—the first Mardi Gras after the end of Prohibition—when almost every reporter in the city is out drinking. She is finally given a story, even though it seems mundane: interviewing Gaston Villiere, the owner of Le Coq d'Or, about the end of Prohibition. However, while at Villiere's restaurant, she observes a double date nearly end in murder when two women get into a confrontation that climaxes in one of them almost getting stabbed with a steak knife. A short time later she is assigned to cover the apparent suicide of Donald Edward Barnett, a jockey, and realizes he was a member of the foursome at the restaurant. Shortly afterwards his date from the restaurant is found garroted behind an Italian market and police reporter Tommy Morrow becomes Slone's partner in investigating the murders. For a time it seems that the odd relationship between Barnett and two women is crucial evidence. He was married to New Orleanean Bette Marshall and, without divorcing her, moved to New York City and became the common-law husband of French-Canadian Annette "Nita" Jeans. Then, Barnett returned to New Orleans and allowed Marshall to socialize with him and Jeans without Jeans ever knowing of the marriage. Slone eventually solves the case when she realizes it is connected to an earlier murder. The novel touches on journalist work culture, women in the workforce, and the effects of Prohibition on New Orleans. In addition, the book conveys negative ethnic stereotypes for "Latins," describing French and Italian people as overtly emotional and given to certain forms of murderous violence. Finally, the novel describes new modest apartments as an innovative form of rental for New Orleanans.

427. Stone, Elisabet M. *Poison, Poker and Pistols.* New York: Sheridan House, 1946. 254pp.

Although many aspects of this murder mystery are stereotypical of the genre, the portrayals of women in the workplace and of a womanizer, surfaces cultural attitudes toward gender roles after World War II. Even though city reporter Margaret Slone is acquainted with murder victim Ned McGowan, she is emotionless in pursuing a scoop on the story. Her cool appraisal of the corpse reflects her tough-girl identity in the mold of noir versions of journalists, as do her forthright conversations and no-nonsense attitudes toward burly policemen. The description of the victim as "a male chippy, a sensualist" reveals social mores concerning extramarital sex, for McGowan is villainized for dating women until he had sex with them and then breaking off contact. A promising young heart specialist, McGowan researched poisons with the help of his "oriental" nurse Miss Lili Cheng. After only a brief conversation with Cheng, Slone concludes that she was an "office wife," working evening hours in McGowan's research laboratory after spending the day in his examination suite. Slone happened on the death scene while the murderer was still lurking and although she was quickly bashed over the head with a poker, the experience gives her the evidence that will eventually aid her to solve the case. The New Orleans of the novel is somewhat inter-changeable with the major cities of other crime novels, with newspaper offices dominated by loud, fast-talking editors, and police stations with rather thick-witted detectives who happen to be Irish. However, New Orleans locales are specific and Slone's living situation is definitely "Southern." She resides in a large family house with her mother and older brother that takes up a city block and constitutes the family's only remnant of antebellum wealth. The expenses of the household that keep her and her brother, a pilot, barely ahead of bill collectors, includes the care and feeding of "a motley assembly of Negro dependents whose ancestors had been slaves of Mother's family." The racism and ethnic prejudices of the author are expressed directly and indirectly through the odd responses servants and hotel employees give the police and Slone.

428. Stone, Michael [name legally changed from Oberia Scott]. *And Tomorrow.* New York: Sovereign House, 1938. 349pp.

In this 1920s society novel, nineteen-year-old Geraldine "Jerry" Brock is forced to leave the Southern Ladies' Institute after the death of her mother, and say farewell forever to her beautiful family home in Glendale, a small town near Alexandria, Louisiana. Her father, Wallingford Brock, a banker, made a series of unfortunate investments before his death and only his long record of service and the kindness of his business associates had prevented them from foreclosing on Brock's mother. Fleeing emotional and physical dependence upon the kindness of Glendale residents, Brock relocates to New Orleans to find a job. Through school friends, she has contacts in the city, but they are affluent and even staying as a guest in their households is expensive, due to the cost of appropriate clothing and lunches at the Roosevelt Hotel. So, she moves into a rented room in a respectable house in the shabby French Quarter. Her first job at a small department store owned by two Jewish men ends disastrously when they make inappropriate advances. In this context Brock's exposure to anti-Semitism becomes obvious and the predominant theme of the novel, an analysis of ways of being Jewish while integrating into respectable American society, begins. Brock starts dating Ray Jamieson, a well-connected socialite, and a short time later gets a job in a newly opened branch of Lane's Department store, working directly for the manager, Morris Freedman. She works hard, advances quickly, and begins socializing with Freedman and his wife Sylvia. The couple is in their mid-thirties and she finds their company more appealing than Jamieson's circle. The Freedmans, Reformed Jews, are cultured, read and discuss poetry, and encourage Brock to learn conversational French. Among Jamieson's friends, women are merely ornaments and most activities focus on slightly drunken young men making a spectacle of themselves on yachts, in ballrooms, or on football fields. Various social events of each set are described in detail and much verbiage is devoted to the ways in which the Freedmans, whose Jewishness places them in the lowest social class in the estimation of Americans of the time, are superior in Brock's esteem. Hal Miller, a wealthy friend and business associate of the Freedmans, arrives in New Orleans shortly after Jerry's twenty-first birthday, (which is extravagantly feted at the Roosevelt Hotel). He and Brock are soon dating and when Miller reveals that he is from an Orthodox Jewish family, Brock is unfazed, in part because Miller blends in so easily into any social setting. As their romance deepens, she is ready to marry him and convert to Judaism, but he maintains that such a marriage would never be accepted by his family. Instead, Miller takes Brock to New York City and creates a life for the two of them in a penthouse apartment in the East Seventies. The rest of the novel presents secular Jewish life in 1920s New York. When Miller dies unexpectedly, Brock's inheritance makes her a wealthy woman, but she loses all interest in life until she meets a WASP physician who takes a romantic interest in her. Approximately eighty pages of the novel are set in New Orleans and it is rich in details that convey a good sense of upper-class social life in the 1920s and the prejudices and assumptions it contained.

429. Stone, Robert. *A Hall of Mirrors*. Boston: Houghton Mifflin, 1966. 409pp.

The experiences of two young people in 1960s New Orleans provides the foil the author uses to explore the disillusionment of the post-World War II generation, the incipient youth culture, and a burgeoning right-wing political movement, bolstered by religious fanaticism. In lean economic times, Rheinhardt and Geraldine arrive separately in New Orleans as their last hope for finding jobs, and meet while working in a soap factory owned by the right-wing Matthew T. Bingamon. The many businesses Bingamon operates further his mission to reform the United States by a revival of patriotism and protection of the country's Anglo-Saxon patrimony, which in the South means subjugating African-Americans even further. He is also building a media empire to support his mission and Rheinhardt is soon tapped to rewrite newswire stories for the WUSA radio station, to fuel hysteria that the United States is threatened by Communists, foreigners, and people of color. Geraldine and Rheinhardt begin living together in French Quarter accommodations occupied by other young people in their twenties, many of whom indulge in drug use and premarital sex, and all of whom are members of the element Bingamon so despises. One apartment dweller, Morgan Rainey, a Harvard-educated Southerner, has long experience working for social service organizations and is committed to racial equality and the redistribution of wealth to aid the poor. When he realizes that the social welfare survey for which he was hired is actually being used to intimidate informants, his investigation leads him to Calvin Minnow, a politician funded by Bingamon, who is building a huge political base campaigning against social entitlement programs. He also uncovers a plan to use a large public rally to incite violence against African-Americans and confronts Rheinhardt for being a pawn to such an evil campaign. The dramatic rally includes a corrupt Christian evangelist, Rheinhardt as announcer, Minnow, Hollywood stars, and Bingamon behind the scenes. When the organized violence Bingamon had funded is pre-empted by a bomb, Rheinhardt and Geraldine are left to extricate themselves from the fallout. Stone's account of 1960s New Orleans emphasizes the bleak poverty of some residents, the dangers of the city for women, the rising numbers of disaffected youth, and the social powder keg created by increasingly polarized right-wing and left-wing elements.

430. Stuart, (Mary) (Routh) Ruth McEnery. *George Washington Jones: A Christmas Gift that Went A-Begging.* Illustrated by Edward Potthast. Philadelphia: Henry Altemus, 1903. 147pp.

Through the eponymous George Washington Jones, Stuart espouses the notion, familiar from other Southern works, that the only happy African-American is one who has a master. A short time after the death of his grandfather, Jones (a pre-adolescent, African-American boy), decides on Christmas Day that the best gift he could get would be a blonde-haired young woman to serve. He also hopes that she will play the harp since his grandfather reminisced about his first task as a slave, which was to fan a young lady as she practiced her music. Jones ties his most valuable possessions in a bundle, attires himself in Sunday clothing and heads for Prytania Street, the locale in which the mistress of his imagination is most likely to reside. By dusk he has been rejected and sometimes laughed at for proposing to make of himself a Christmas gift. Fortunately, he sits on a bench outside a humble cottage that is the home of an African-American washerwoman, Sarah Elvira Sparrow, whose own boy had died at around Jones' age. She takes him in and tells him of a house where he can work for an elderly woman who needs a boy who she will dress in livery to brush away flies, find her eyeglasses, and bring her the calling cards of ladies on a silver tray. Once Jones gets the job his obedience, sincerity, and sentimentality comfort the lady who gives him his own white iron bed in a room next to hers and allows him to be one of her footmen when she goes on drives. One of Jones' prized possessions is a photograph of his grandfather fanning his lady and when Jones' mistress sees it she identifies the image as a study done for a painting of her mother, who died young and whose faithful servant was given his freedom. Jones and his lady are very moved to realize that he has found his home and the woman eventually retains Sarah as her onsite washerwoman, establishing her in a cabin where Jones can live with her and enjoy her motherly influence. While the story conveys little about the physical setting of New Orleans, the work provides insights into the legacy of slave culture decades after the Civil War.

431. Stuart, (Mary) (Routh) Ruth McEnery. *A Golden Wedding, and Other Tales.* New York: Harper and Brothers, 1893. 366pp.

Although only two of the short stories in this volume are set in New Orleans, this book is included since the text is unusual for capturing the life of freed people of color after the Civil War. In the title story two reserved, elderly African-Americans, who live on opposite sides of a cabin divided down the center by a partition wall, marry amidst a great deal of traditional celebration in their New Orleans community. The other New Orleans story, "Camelia Riccardo," focuses on the rivalrous courtship of an Italian fruit seller in the French Market by a Sicilian and a French man and details aspects of daily life in the market, as well as touching on attitudes toward immigrant groups. The rest of the stories deal with African-Americans in rural areas, particularly on plantations.

432. Stuart, (Mary) (Routh) Ruth McEnery. *The Story of Babette: A Little Creole Girl.* New York: Harper and Brothers, 1894. 209pp.

When a girl disappears during Mardi Gras, decades pass before she is reunited with her family. To protect toddler Babette Le Charmant during the Civil War her family sends her to live with her grandmother and be nursed by the retired mammy of many Le Charmants, Tante Angèle. After she is separated from Angèle by a Mardi Gras crowd, the grieving mammy dies and is honored by the Le Charmants with a beautiful funeral and burial in St. Louis Cemetery. When it becomes clear the missing girl will never return, the Le Charmants go into mourning and leave on a thirteen-year sojourn in France. In the meantime, Babette lives with a gypsy family who kidnapped her in hopes of a reward, before they become too frightened of prosecution to return her. When Babette gets a fever in 1872, she is left at the house of Bondurante, a well-to-do physician. Bondurante and his wife had lost their children to yellow fever nineteen years before and been in mourning ever since, and even though they realize from her clothing that Babette had been kidnapped from a wealthy family, they do not pursue her origins, but adopt her as their own. Babette eventually hears the story of how she came to the household and refuses to inherit the Bondurante fortune upon their death, since she believes she may have been the offspring of an Italian fisherman and unworthy of such distinction. She nobly finds work as a governess. However, in a bizarre coincidence, the job is with the returned Le Charmants. While in their employ, she gets a fever and in her delirium uses names that the Le Charmants recognize. They also discover the bundle containing her christening dress and realize that she is their lost Babette. She goes on to have her debut in 1885 and later marries a physician. This maudlin tale demonstrates the prevalence of fever and the way in which upper-class households could become isolated islands within the city.

433. Summerton, Winter [pseud.]. *Will He Find Her?: A Romance of New York and New Orleans.* New York: Derby and Jackson, 1860. 491pp.

In this gothic romance, Hugh Stanford attempts to discover what happened to his friend Gordon Clarke and his daughter, Mary Gifford Clarke, both of whom disappeared in New Orleans in 1865. Stanford, a successful architect, is also a philosopher and amateur psychologist. At the outbreak of the Civil War, Clarke left the United States and gave Stanford twenty thousand dollars to invest in Chicago real estate, with the stipulation that the real estate would be turned over to Clarke or his daughter should either return within twenty-five years. If no claim is made in that time, Stanford gets to keep the land. As 1886 approaches, Stanford is eager to find either of the Clarkes and believes that applying the new "occult science," will be successful. He hires lawyer George Denfield to accompany him and they assemble evidence against the young doctor and his wife whom Stanford suspects of being murderers. In New Orleans Stanford presents letters of introduction to Emile du Valcourt and Dr. Hypolite Meissonier, a "magnetiseur." Although in

Denfield's estimation the sensitives, mesmerists, and hypnotists that Stanford wants to consult are villains, he tags along to protect his client. However, Stanford eventually convinces Denfield of the validity of his investigations when his consultants are able to handle a sample of Clarke's hair and the last letter he wrote and supply credible leads to his murderers. In the course of his investigations Stanford falls in love with Ninette du Valcourt, thinking that she is Emile du Valcourt's daughter. When she is later revealed to be adopted, and suspected of having African-American ancestry, the book goes into great detail about miscegenation and the determinative influence of "black blood." A surprise conclusion reveals Ninette's true identity, makes it possible for Stanford to marry her, and reveals the whereabouts of Mary Gifford Clarke. An appendix presents a dialogue between Stanford and Denfield concerning the race problem in which Stanford contends all humans are equal and Denfield that Africans are of a lower order.

434. Sumner, Albert W. *The Sea Lark, or, The Quadroone of Louisiana: A Thrilling Tale of the Land and Sea*. Boston: F. Gleason, 1850. 100pp.

French nobleman Count Jerome Bouvé comes into his estate after his father fell out of favor with the king and died of despair. Punished for his father's transgressions, his title, lands, and wealth are confiscated and he has only enough to purchase a schooner, the *Sea Lark* of the title, that he uses as a slave ship to quickly make money, which he shares with his brother Louis Bouvé. Soon disgusted with the slave trade, he obtains letters of marque during the War of 1812 and preys on British ships. With a small fortune he is able to buy a plantation near Vicksburg where he installs his mother, Madame Bouvé, and which he soon makes a great success. When Louis visits him there, he falls in love with Lucille, his mother's quadroon personal attendant and pet. Disturbed by the romance's effect on the slave population, Jerome takes Louis abroad. Without anyone knowing, Lucille is actually pregnant with Louis' daughter. She is able to have the baby secretly, naming her Pauline, and giving her to the plantation agent to raise in New Orleans. Pauline leaves school at sixteen to become a schoolmistress, saves all her money and, through the plantation agent, secretly arranges to purchase Lucille's freedom. In the meantime, Francois Rouillet courts Pauline. However, he is a villain and just as he is having her kidnapped when she is eighteen, she is rescued by Henri May, a Harvard-educated young man reading law. May and Rouillet duel and Rouillet is killed. Soon afterwards May goes to Covington on legal business and is set upon by highwaymen. Left for dead, he is nursed back to health by the highwayman's daughter, fifteen-year-old Eugenie, and falls in love. He rescues her and installs her in a New Orleans hotel, but before too long, the highwayman appears. To May's astonishment, the man is Francois Rouillet, who had faked his death in the duel. Rouillet kills his disobedient daughter in May's presence but gets May convicted of the crime. However, after Rouillet is wounded in another duel, he makes a confession that frees May, who returns to Pauline, only to be revealed to be Jerome Bouvé's son, Henri. He explains to Lucille's satisfaction, if not the reader's, his assumed identity and vows to marry Pauline (his first cousin). However, Jerome and his mother adamantly refuse to acknowledge the match, insisting that he follow through with an arranged marriage to Emily Winslow, the daughter and only heir of the owner of the plantation adjacent to the Jerome's. Emily, however, is in love with someone else and Henri aids in their elopement. Having thwarted his parents, Henri's wedding to Pauline is briefly delayed when he returns to New Orleans to find Rouillet once again forcing himself on Pauline, only this time Rouillet also meets Lucille, who realizes he is actually Louis Bouvé. The villain promptly (and definitively) dies after realizing that he had been forcing himself on his own daughter (of whose existence he had not previously known). Cut off by his elders, Henri builds up a successful law practice and Jerome sells off his plantation for a fortune and returns to France where his title and estates are restored. A deathbed reconciliation with his father leads to Henri's accession to the title and estates with his mixed-race wife at his side and Lucille the quadroon treated as Madame Bouvet's sister. While the novel is remarkable for the number of coincidences, dramatic incidents, and concealed identities, it is of greater interest for its treatment of the issue of mixed-race people, which is perhaps why the author chose to set much of the narrative in New Orleans.

435. Swann, Francis. *Royal Street.* New York: Lancer, 1966. 174pp.

When Melissa Jane Robinson's unconventional father, George, dies in 1817 in Doughty, Illinois, she is left an orphan under the care of Caleb Pettibone, the crooked administrator of her father's estate. Demonstrating a surprising amount of courage and independent thinking (the result of her father's tutelage), she decides to escape down the Mississippi to New Orleans and her only living relative, her Aunt Emily, about whom she knows practically nothing except her place of employment, Fran's Place on Royal Street. After several river adventures, she is fortunate to meet Jonathan Wish, a worldly traveler, who treats her like a lady. He gets her to Fran's Place, which turns out to be a famous gambling parlor, and soon learns that her aunt is actually the proprietress under the assumed name Fran Hyde. Hyde was cheated out of a fortune by the family of an elderly wealthy New Yorker she had befriended (and from whom she had learned to be a gambler), and, parlaying a small stake into a fortune through a series of adventures, she ended up in New Orleans to open a grand, and immediately successful, gambling parlor. Immediately identifying in Melissa some of her own qualities, Fran turns her into Kate Hyde and prepares her to take over the business. Suddenly Melissa has independence, suitors and a level of affluence she has never before experienced. Unfortunately, she also has an enemy who is trying to kill her. At first she believes the man to be Dominique Chauvet, whose managerial role she is beginning to usurp. However, with the aid of Jonathan Wish (who turns out to be associated with Jean Lafitte), she helps uncover an elaborate plot involving the French planter's son, Armand Le Freniere, and his fellow conspirators, many of whom are Lafitte's former pirates, dissatisfied with the life of law-abiding citizens. They are stealing Navy ships and armaments to outfit an expedition to free Napoleon Bonaparte (1769–1821) and bring him to Louisiana, in order to foment a revolution in the colony and make him King. While the novel introduces details about New Orleans life and history in the early nineteenth century, it probably tells readers more about the rise of swashbuckling female heroines in the popular literature of the 1960s.

436. Sweet, George Elliot. *The Petroleum Saga.* Los Angeles: Science, 1969. 230pp.

This volume consists of a three-act play, *A Simple Case of Economics*, and a novel, entitled *Sand Line Sam* (pp. 61–210). Although only part of the novel is set in New Orleans, the city is the major focus in this account of a millionaire's efforts to end the power of the Mafia. Edward Machris' wealth stems from his Delta Oil Corporation and he spends it to set up a private library on the history of crime, hire criminologists, and kidnap key organized crime figures and detain them for questioning. The events recorded transpire in 1968 and focus on the New Orleans Mafia Council, whose fifteen members Machris has kidnapped and held in a secret facility in the Mississippi Delta, until they agree to divulge all they know about crime. With the exception of the Hotel Monteleone and some streets of the French Quarter, the novel devotes little space to physical description of New Orleans, focusing instead on Machris' corporate offices, boats, aircraft, female secretaries, and fortress-like detention centers. While the novel is hardly unique in identifying New Orleans as a center for organized crime, the protagonist's intellectual approach to attacking crime that does not rely on violent confrontation, but instead, on information gathering, is unusual. The lists of names of those involved in organized crime are enough to rid the New Orleans of the Mafia. The novel is also unusual in presenting beautiful blonde women as accomplished scientists who freely fulfill the sexual expectations of men.

437. Tabony, Annie Heller. *Eulalie.* Cynthiana, Ky.: Hobson, 1944. 304pp.

Although much of this romance novel is set in Plaquemines Parish in a tiny village named St. Sophie, New Orleans is a major focus. Taking place between 1925 and 1928, the story begins soon after Eulalie Wintere's graduation from Esplanade High School in New Orleans. She left behind friends in the city and has one suitor, Oscar Barton, who continues to influence her even though she has ostensibly returned to St. Sophie in expectation of a marriage proposal from her childhood sweetheart and neighbor, Malcolm Gleason. Eulalie's mother, Miriam, opposes the match even though she likes Malcolm, because the young man has become a farmer like his father and Miriam's own husband, Jules. Miriam knows the sacrifices of a farm wife and wanted more for her daughter. The young couple postpones their wedding, not because of parental opposition, but because they want to have a house to move into. After Malcolm uses all his savings for the construction of a cottage he begins finishing the exterior and slowly acquiring furnishings. Before he can finish, the farmers of Plaquemines Parish are informed by government officials that to protect New Orleans from flooding a dyke will be opened that will inundate their land. With no recourse, within a few days the farm families must pack and leave. While Eulalie and her family resign themselves to circumstances and try to see God's will in the apparent reversal, Malcolm displeases Eulalie by his complaints and, when he misinterprets a gesture of comfort on her part, a rift opens that Miriam wishes to encourage. She thinks good may come of a separation and before Malcolm and Eulalie can reconcile, the Winteres have relocated to temporary housing with relatives in New Orleans. Malcolm and his family go to Macon where his brother lives. In New Orleans, Eulalie begins socializing with her high school crowd, most of whom are newlyweds and, with a feeling of inevitability, begins seeing wealthy Oscar Barton once again. Because he went so reluctantly, everyone is surprised at Malcolm's immediate adaptation and success in Macon, working in his brother's real estate office and being pursued by the young socialite Rosalind Webster, a connection he knows will be good for business. Even though he is open about his engagement to Eulalie, Rosalind continues her pursuit and news accounts of social events make it seem that Rosalind and Malcolm are linked romantically. In New Orleans, Eulalie hears reports of Malcolm's friendship with Rosalind and a series of miscommunications seem to be leading to a permanent rift between the lovers from St. Sophie. However, during a trip to New Orleans engineered by Rosalind, to once and for all free Malcolm from Eulalie, she realizes how much the two are still in love, and instead brings about a reconciliation. The novel includes accounts of New Orleans social life and spends a good deal of time describing an extramarital affair and its consequences. Throughout the book religious values are upheld and when Malcolm and Eulalie reconcile they return to St. Sophie and a rural lifestyle that even Eulalie's mother has come to realize is to be valued far above a life of affluence in the city.

438. Tait, Dorothy [Ann Fairbairn, pseud.]. *Five Smooth Stones.* New York: Crown, 1966. 756pp.

In racially segregated 1930s New Orleans, David Champlin's life could have gone much as those of previous generations of free people of color and he would have become a dockworker or domestic. However, his grandparents, L'il Joe and Geneva Champlin, had lost their son to race-motivated mob violence and a horrible death. Although they consider education dangerous for dividing man from God and inciting racial hatred, they are gradually persuaded by Danish history professor Bjarne Knudsen to let him undertake David's education when he proves intellectually capable. After a college course in the Midwest he goes on to Harvard Law School and Oxford. Beginning a legal career, he is offered a diplomatic position by the U.S. government and must decide between an international career and a return to New Orleans to fight for racial equality. He returns to the South, crushing the hopes of his grandparents and the pride of the African-American community, and begins the dangerous struggle that angers many of the people he is hoping to help. While much of the novel is set outside of the South and deals with the prejudice that David confronts in the North and elsewhere, as well as his own internal debates and transformations, the first one hundred pages of the book and subsequent sections are set in the city and depict the racial divisions and frightening racial violence of New Orleans in the 1940s and 1950s.

439. Tallant, Robert. *Angel in the Wardrobe*. Garden City, N.Y.: Doubleday, 1948. 271pp.

This domestic novel focuses on Mattie Lou Wycliff's family during the social season (October through Mardi Gras) of her granddaughter Betty's debutante year. Mattie Lou, a member of the first generation of Wycliffs born after the Civil War, is dedicated to preserving her family's notable history extending back more than six generations. Rather eccentrically, she believes the family's guardian angel is present in an heirloom eighteenth century wardrobe and spends part of each day praying there. She rues her contemporary social environment in which, as she notes, "the wrong people" have the money. Generations of inherited wealth ended with her father, who one day realized that all he had left was the Wycliff Garden District mansion. Mattie Lou, who married a third cousin to preserve the family name, is distressed by the choices of her own children. Her eldest, the twins Amelia and Sylvester, are now well past middle age. Neither has married and Sylvester has been jailed several times for public indecency because of his distressing tendency to press up against young girls in crowded public places. Through the course of the novel he descends into mental illness as paranoia begins to shape his life. While Sylvester has spent his life trying to repress his impulses his twin sister broke away from her mother to follow hers, living a bohemian life in the French Quarter, painting and having lesbian affairs with her models. Mattie Lou's other daughters, Elizabeth and Constance, both are married. Although Constance married a wealthy businessman, she never had children and has continued to behave like a petulant child to the occasional disgust of her emotionally distant husband. Elizabeth married a man outside her social circle, John Duncan, and the union produced Betty, but ended in divorce as Duncan became frustrated with Elizabeth's obedience to convention (his second wife is fashionable and sociable, even to the extent of no longer wanting to live in the Garden District, but in a Lake Pontchartrain house). In this milieu, Betty, who has graduated from Newcomb College, an education paid for with funds Mattie Lou raised by selling off the family library, begins to emerge into adulthood and rebels against the wishes of both her mother and Mattie Lou. For she has fallen in love with Joe Bivona, the son of Italian immigrants, who is finishing his architecture degree on the G.I. bill, after military service in World War II. Not only does he have no family background, but he is also from that element of society Mattie Lou so despises, a striver who is trying to become a self-made man. She concedes with a shudder that he may become rich some day, while refusing to be introduced, and continuing to present young men with the right background to Betty as she continues to pray to her guardian angel. One of her prayers is answered when, after another debutante breaks her leg, Betty is named to the court of a Mardi Gras ball. For a while it also looks like a rift has developed between Betty and Joe, but that is only temporary. Mattie Lou's own daughter the takes up with a man, a decade older than her, and from an ancient Creole family so traditional that they would never even acknowledge planter families like the Wycliffs, who came to Louisiana as part of the American immigration after the Louisiana Purchase. Tallant richly describes social events, food, and clothing, while articulating several different worldviews that motivate his various characters. The novel is also of interest for touching on race issues, centered on the treatment of African-American servants, and on the use of mood-enhancing drugs, including alcohol, but also Phenobarbital and Benzedrine. Prejudice against Italian-Americans is openly expressed.

440. Tallant, Robert. *Love and Mrs. Candy*. Garden City, N.Y.: Doubleday, 1953. 287pp.

One of a series of novels presenting boarding-house owner Mrs. Eustacia Candy and her social network, this book presents a wide variety of personalities and yet is confined by the boundaries of Candy's neighborhood. Mrs. Candy is proud that she has rarely traveled outside her immediate environs (that appear to be Metairie). For her, the trip downtown by bus to the large stores on Canal Street is a major undertaking and especially so in this novel when her sole object is purchasing Christmas gifts. Mrs. Candy is in her second marriage. Her husband is Henry Petit, who works in a cannery for frogs' legs. Mrs. Candy's first husband used a modest inheritance to purchase the large house on Lemon Street that Mrs. Candy started operating as a boarding house once she was widowed. Her tenants include Steve Wilson, who barely holds onto a low-level, white-collar job, while betting everything he earns on horse races; the aging Philandra Fazende, whose entire social persona is based on pretensions stemming from her self-described success as a movie actress and her tragic family life; and a retired civil servant, Mr. Nocca, who spends his evenings peering through windows to watch people carrying on with their daily lives. The dramatic tensions that unsettle Mrs. Candy's boarding house as Christmas approaches include Wilson's love affair with Emelda Davenport, who expects a wedding ring and the promise of a home from the impoverished gambler; and adjustments to two new tenants, Mr. Gleason and Noonie Belle Thibodeaux. Mr. Gleason uses his typewriter hour after hour, asks many intrusive questions, and gives flowers and chocolates to Mrs. Candy, inspiring Henry's jealousy. Thibodeaux, who is in her early twenties, is the daughter of nearby neighbors, who flees her home to escape the constant, drunken fights of her parents over their three unmarried daughters. Once Thibodeaux confesses her love for Johnny Kogo, a young man from the neighborhood employed as a Coca-Cola delivery driver, Mrs. Candy is determined to bring the two together without engendering the wrath of the couple's parents who oppose the match. The novel captures the conversational style and slang of Mrs. Candy's social milieu, as well as conveying a sense of boarding house life in a working-class 1950s neighborhood.

441. Tallant, Robert. *Mr. Preen's Salon.* New York: Doubleday, 1949. 271pp.

After the death of his second wife, Oliver Preen bought a house with five apartments in the French Quarter. His "salon" mostly consists of his tenants and their friends, as well as one of his female admirers, Molly Sands, a murder mystery writer. His other admirer, Lily Arnez, has the advantage of living in the apartment above his own. Other tenants include a gay male couple, Lanny Pavanik and William Townsend "Baby" Curtis, Bud Flanagan (whose apartment is frequented by his lover Rita d'Esprit, a sometime prostitute), and insurance man/novelist Fred Dailey. Dailey, the youngest of Preen's tenants, is thwarted in his romance with Mildred Luster by her mother, Lura, and, since Preen is an old friend of Lura's, he tries to sway her. Mostly, however, he keeps out of the personal affairs of his tenants, even though he is constantly serving them drinks and sandwiches in his courtyard, to the irritation of his African-American houseman Clifford, who resents being kept after hours and away from his wife. To Preen's surprise, at the advanced age of fifty-three, he is preoccupied with avoiding romantic entanglements. His friend, social worker Carlotta "Lotta" Nip (a character in other of Tallant's New Orleans novels as well), decides to foster a relationship between Preen and Sands. Nip claims to be in a passionate affair with her young hanger-on, Leon Leon, but none of her acquaintances believe her since Leon is so obviously homosexual. As with other Tallant novels, the many barroom and restaurant conversations, as well as the minor characters (like stripper Cherry Blossom Morel, Banjo Annie, and con-man Count de Rasputin), provide insight into a segment of New Orleans culture.

442. Tallant, Robert. *Mrs. Candy Strikes It Rich.* Garden City, N.Y.: Doubleday, 1954. 253pp.

Part of the Mrs. Candy series, in this volume Eustacia Candy enters New Orleans society after oil is found on her husband's land in Bogalusa. She closes her boarding house on Cairo Street and transforms the place to fit her image of a private residence appropriate to her new social status, begins wearing diamond necklaces and rings day and night, and travels by chauffeur-driven Cadillac. However, once she sets her sites on entering society, she needs a house in the Garden District and buys Wycliff Manor from impoverished society lady Mattie Lou Wycliff. To furnish the house she hires Mr. Leon Leon, who takes her from one French Quarter antiques shop to another, introducing her to a parade of eccentrics, including his colleague Mrs. Lotta Nip who begins advising Mrs. Candy on her appearance, dress, and home entertaining. After a disastrous first party in her new house about which her neighbors complain, she hires a social secretary, Mrs. Clapp, and focuses on becoming a Mardi Gras queen, even though it means establishing a new krewe, the Krewe of Circe, for women. By the end of the book the Candys have decided to give up high society and return to Cairo Street.

443. Tallant, Robert. *The Pirate Lafitte and the Battle of New Orleans.* Illustrated by John Chase. New York: Random House, 1951. 186pp.

In this book for children, Tallant makes less effort to fictionalize his account than other authors, preferring to expand a generally historical account by adding physical descriptions, and illustrations. To introduce the Lafittes, he uses an imagined 1809 visit to New Orleans by fictional creation Esau Glasscock and his plantation-owning father who looks to Lafitte to supply six new slaves. Tallant does not address the morality of selling or owning slaves, simply stating that slaveholding was a part of the culture of the time period (although noting that the importation of slaves had been outlawed). Esau does not become a fully realized character, however, and the rest of the book uses legendary accounts of Lafitte's appearances in New Orleans after Governor Claiborne targeted him for prosecution, (at a masked ball, and, under an assumed name, as an overnight guest in the household of Mrs. Claiborne) to enliven the history. The work also uses Lafitte's disobedient camp followers, like Gambi, who attacked a few American ships as a foil, to demonstrate Lafitte's claims that he was primarily a merchant who helped the people of New Orleans during the British embargo and that he was not a pirate, because he only attacked Spanish ships. Tallant is also fairer to Governor Claiborne than some works for children, indicating why Claiborne needed to be concerned about the security of the mouth of the Mississippi River. The other main character in this depiction is John Randolph Grymes (1786–1854), Lafitte's friend and lawyer. The narrative gives a detailed account of the Battle of New Orleans and the military action's historical importance and continues through Jean Lafitte's abandonment of Grand Terre for Galveston.

444. Tallant, Robert. *Southern Territory.* Garden City, N.Y.: Doubleday, 1951. 250pp.

This novel about traveling salesmen is set in a number of cities in addition to New Orleans, as it follows the characters—office supply salesman Bill Henderson; Johnny Mallory, who works for a publisher; brewery supply representative Henry Steele; and hat salesman Doak Miller. The New Orleans section mentions a number of bars, restaurants and hotels as the salesmen try to avoid the temptations of the French Quarter and the temptresses who make their living from traveling salesmen and conventioneers.

445. Tallant, Robert. *The Voodoo Queen: A Novel.* New York: Putnam, 1956. 314pp.

Following Tallant's compilation of fact and legend about Marie Laveau (c. 1801–1881) in his book *Voodoo in New Orleans* (New York: Macmillan, 1946), he produced this work of historical fiction that begins when Laveau is twenty-five-years-old and her mother, Marguerite, is facing her final illness. Laveau finally feels free to marry a carpenter from Santo Domingo named Jacques Paris. Even though Paris disapproves of Voodoo, Laveau is friends with renowned practitioner Marie Saloppe, countering Paris' objections by pointing out that she embraces Catholicism and only those aspects of Voodoo that convey the cultural wisdom of African people. She begins using gris-gris when she is pregnant and even allows Saloppe to present her as a Voodoo queen at a St. John's Day ceremony. However, when her baby dies she blames Saloppe. In her own Voodoo practice she will only do good and rejects those aspects used for evil. Her new mentor, Madame Laclotte, teaches her hairdressing, for which she is soon in demand. To Paris' increasing opposition Laveau is also sought out as a Voodoo queen and he abandons her. However, she eventually marries Charles Glapion, the ship's captain who brings word of Paris' death, bearing him fifteen children and enjoying his support for her Voodoo practice. Laveau had a long life and the book illustrates the good she brought for people of all races, through Voodoo practice, and nursing people through childbirth and yellow fever epidemics. She must deal with charlatan rivals and civil authorities that ban gatherings of blacks, particularly as the Civil War approaches. The final section of the novel deals with Laveau's succession. Although one daughter lives more freely, another daughter tries to establish herself as Laveau's successor without being chosen. However, after Laveau is falsely accused of murdering her long-time rival, her daughter Marie Philome takes actions that prove her ability to carry on Laveau's work. While focused on Laveau's biography and the history of Voodoo practice, the book does provide details of New Orleans social history, particularly in respect to African-American life.

446. Thompson, John B(urton). *Love and the Wicked City.* New York: Arco, 1951. 182pp.

In this erotic novel young Texas oil heiress Favra McMullin dedicates herself to experiencing bohemian life in the French Quarter and pursuing premarital sexual pleasures. McMullin is purported to be searching for romantic love, but her adventures seem unlikely to lead to long-term relationships. They include a visit to a sex show, several lesbian encounters, the oral attentions of a gay man, sexual intercourse in a public venue, and sexual relations with a father and each of his twin sons (on separate occasions). McMullin lives two blocks from the French Quarter and breakfasts there on beignets, often in the company of two fifty-plus, penurious individuals she knows as the "Professor" and Alice. After Alice reveals that the Professor, who never recognizes her, is her first love, McMullin secretly becomes their financial patroness. Each grew up in affluent families, but their youthful affair, that ended in Alice's pregnancy, led to social disgrace and disinheritance. Although Alice was forced onto the streets of New Orleans, the Professor was an expatriate who only returned after his parents died. McMullin disdains the social conventions that destroyed the lives of Alice and the Professor and when she realizes that Arden Drake, a City Park tennis partner, lives in a repressed household, she undertakes her sexual awakening and that of her brother. McMullin is later surprised to learn new sexual techniques from Elton Chance, a millionaire contractor she meets on the Algiers's ferry, and from T'ling her Chinese/African-American maid. While the novel's celebration of social freedoms for women may have appealed to female readers, the book seems to have been written for men and, although McMullin successfully exposes and punishes a man who behaves with violence toward women, she will clearly be content to be dominated by a man in a sexual or romantic relationship. The New Orleans of the novel is mostly that of the French Quarter and the city is clearly equated with sexual freedom and exploration. Settings include the ateliers of painters and sculptors who are friends of McMullin.

447. Thompson, (John) Edward. *Listen for the Laughter.* Philadelphia: Macrae-Smith, 1942. 328pp.

Only approximately eighty pages of this novel, set in the first decades of the twentieth century, transpire in New Orleans. The book is included here for the evocative power with which it describes daily life in the city. Jonathan Slocum of Pine Bluff, Arkansas, falls into despair after his wife Amanda dies in childbirth and, through financial reverses, he loses his drugstore. However, with his daughter Roxana to support, he begins peddling tonics of his own concoction, spending most of the year traveling with from small town to small town with his African-American servant Abner. His life is transformed on a semi-annual trip to New Orleans for tonic ingredients. Thinking he has seen a former lover, he pursues her in a downpour and is struck by a postal truck. Philippe Laurent, the proprietor of the French Quarter's Le Agneau Blanc, rescues him and the two become friends. During World War I Slocum buys up mules and hogs cheaply in remote rural areas, gets them to New Orleans, and Laurent sells them at great profit to the U.S. government. Within two years they are rich; just in time for Slocum and his daughter to relocate to New Orleans so that she can attend Tulane University. The two reside in a French Quarter house on Dauphine Street, the tenants of a Frenchwoman who studied art in Paris. With the advent of Prohibition, Slocum and Laurent form a new partnership to smuggle alcohol from Cuba. One of the young men involved, Jeff Random, accidentally gets introduced to Roxana and they fall in love. Only after a near disaster reveals the depth of their love does Slocum approve, but by the end of the novel they are living together as a family in Pine Bluff with a newly born baby. Although only a section of the novel is set in New Orleans, the author captures early twentieth-century life in the city.

448. Thompson, Maurice. *The King of Honey Island.* New York: Robert Bonner's Sons, 1893. 343pp.

Although set immediately before and after the Battle of New Orleans, this novel does not feature Lafitte, but a band of irredeemable brigands based on Honey Island in Bay Saint Louis. Led by Pierre Rameau, these highwaymen steal from people living in or passing through frontier areas outside New Orleans. Rameau has set up a network to fence the stolen goods in the city through a social club known as the Chats-Huants (screech owls). As the British threat rises, wealthy planters and more humble farmers gather in New Orleans to await the arrival of Andrew Jackson and his troops. In this setting, Rameau assumes the identity of Colonel Philip Loring so that he might enter respectable society, with the unwitting assistance of Jules Vernon, who introduces Loring to society through balls and dinners at his grand townhouse, Chateau d'Or. Much of the narrative is devoted to Vernon learning the truth about Loring, who is not only a brigand and a fence, but also a despoiler of women and a British spy. In this account, like others, Jackson is a divisive figure, scorned by cultivated French and Spanish society and political leaders and resented as a crude Anglo-American. Vernon plays a crucial role by getting working-class men and Creole society figures to side with the Americans. After raising a militia company to defend the city, Vernon sends his wife and daughter to the safety of his Bay Saint Louis plantation, only for them to fall captives to Loring, requiring a dramatic rescue. If the reader is to gather anything from this confusing narrative in which Loring and other characters have multiple identities, it is that Louisiana, and New Orleans in particular, attracted people with a wide range of personal histories—some noble, some criminal—but the Battle of New Orleans helped good men, like Vernon, to realize their loyalty to the United States and become patriots. While Vernon had previously indulged pirates and fencers of stolen goods, after the British defeat he helps put an end to such activity, and even the momentarily celebrated Lafitte must move out of the territory.

449. Thornton, Marcellus Eugene. *The Lady of New Orlean: A Novel of the Present.* New York: Abbey, 1901. 330pp.

In this novel New Orleans is nothing like the gracious city of old families who appreciate art and culture, celebrated in so many other books. The author presents a city filled with immigrants from a wide range of countries who behave and speak in risible fashion. Alpha Millyard, the descendant of an Anglo-American Virginian family, is subjected to repeated indignities at their hands for the unlikely transgression of forcing his attentions on Bertha Rosenstin (sic), a beautiful Jewish woman of Polish descent supplied with a significant allowance by her shop-owning father, Morritz. Millyard, whose father was killed at Gettysburg and whose family lost their wealth during and immediately after the Civil War, read law and was admitted to the bar at an unusually young age. Recently arrived in New Orleans, he is fortunate that Judge Cotton is an old family friend; when Millyard is repeatedly arrested on trumped-up charges, the judge uses his influence to get him out. Millyard's enemies include an old legal associate, Galen Dalgal, from Hickory, North Carolina, who wants to alienate Millyard's girlfriend, Lucilla Helms, so that she will marry him instead. There is also Honoré Villeguine, a New Orleans bank owner, who wants to marry Bertha Rosenstin and is offended that she has inexplicably fallen in love with Millyard, upon slight and impersonal acquaintance. Rosenstin's outraged father is poorly educated and only able to react to Millyard with vituperation. Bertha Rosenstin's plan is to entrap Millyard into marriage by orchestrating their discovery in an intimate setting. Fortunately, after repeated imprisonments, false charges, and the resulting damaging gossip, Rittea de Ampbert, a beautiful young woman reputed to be the wealthiest female in Louisiana, takes on Millyard's defense. She helps thwart Bertha, and she and Millyard fall in love and marry. Only after several years of domestic life in Paris do they return to the United States. In New York society they are confronted by the revelation that Ampbert is mixed-race. Millyard is relatively unconcerned, but after ascertaining Rosenstin is dead, they relocate to New Orleans as a more accepting social climate than New York. Millyard even declares the city far superior to Paris.

450. Tinker, Edward Larocque. *Toucoutou*. New York: Dodd, Mead, 1928. 312pp.

This novel about the legal implications of mixed-race identity also addresses the special help-lessness of mixed-race mistresses of white men. The octoroon, Claricine Sevrisol, had been the mistress of a man named Bujac in Santo Domingo and fled the country with him during slave up-risings in 1809, first to Cuba, and then to New Orleans. Nearly destitute when he arrived in Loui-siana, Bujac worked as a dancing instructor and met and married the wealthy daughter of a wine merchant, leading to an estrangement from Claricine. However, when a French-speaking Swiss lodge brother of his died, Bujac took in his two children, establishing Claricine in a house to care for them. When Bujac dies of yellow fever, the boy is of age, but Anastasie (nicknamed Toucoutou) is still a girl. Claricine tries to get the Ursuline nuns to accept her as a charity student, but she is expelled at fourteen for her uncontrollable temper. Toucoutou is thrilled when Creole Placide Taquin courts her, although the romance is almost derailed by accusations that the bride is African-American. However, Claricine provides a Swiss baptismal certificate and the wedding hastily follows. The rest of the novel traces the ways in which rumors about Anastasie have an insidious influence on her life. Her husband's love and affluence are no protection and Claricine must repeatedly testify as to Anastasie's origins. When the tenant of a house Taquin had given Anastasie stops paying rent Taqin sues him on behalf of Anastasie and the plaintiff countersues saying that Anastasie, as a free woman of color, could not sue him. The court decides in her favor with testimony from Claricine. However, Anastasie banishes Claricine for fear that the association with a black will cause her trouble again, and in a fit of drunkenness, Claricine revenges her hurt by claiming that she is Anastasie's mother. When Anastasie's identity becomes an issue in a later court case, Claricine is dead and cannot be forced to recant her drunken statements. However, the testimony of her many auditors weigh heavily in court and the judge rules Anastasie's baptismal certificate is a fake. The ruling effectively nullifies Anastasie's wedding and she and Taquin eventually flee to Cuba.

451. Tinker, Frances and Edward Larocque Tinker. *Widows Only: The Sixties*. New York: D. Ap-pleton, 1931. 164pp.

Although there are many references to New Orleans in this volume, the work is mostly set at Le Cheniere, the country house of the Beaudines, which is primarily occupied by widows and their female friends. The household could only be revived if young Antoinette Beaudine, who is fin-ishing school at the Ursuline Convent, marries well. The young Karl Link, who does not at first seem an appropriate suitor, even though he is wealthy, proves himself when the family endures the tragic death of one of the last males in their circle on the wreck of the Evening Star paddle-wheeler in 1866. However, before Link and Beaudine can marry, he is killed on a steamboat as well. He leaves his entire fortune to found a home for impoverished widows in the American sec-tion of New Orleans and it is there that Antoinette Beaudine is depicted as living as the elderly matron at the end of the novel, the Beaudine family mansion long gone. The novel presents the social dislocation and plight of women in New Orleans after the decimation of the male population during the Civil War.

452. Tinker, Frances and Edward Larocque Tinker. *Strife: The Seventies*. New York: D. Appleton, 1931. 185pp.

Through the story of the Labatut and Duplantier families this novel deals with the period of Reconstruction and carpetbaggers. Jacques Labatut came from Paris as a young man and is cul-tured in a way that "Popo" Duplantier is not. However, he is forced into conventionality by his wife Marilisse, the schoolgirl friend of Popo's wife Artemise. The Duplantiers are an old planta-tion family and Popo is virulently opposed to all the changes around him, particularly African-Americans in positions of authority, and he is a strong supporter of the White League, while his wife is socially liberal. In many ways the and cultivated Artemise would have been the more appropriate wife for Jacques, but everyone in the foursome plays the roles fate dealt them and behave honorably. The Labatuts and Duplantiers socialize and have children at similar ages and both families have houses in New Orleans (although the Duplantiers spend a good deal of their time on their plantation). The novel focuses on the armed conflict between the White Leaguers and the New Orleans police in September 1874 when the true feelings within the couples emerge.

453. Tinker, Frances and Edward Larocque Tinker. *Closed Shutters: The Eighties.* New York: D. Appleton, 1931. 104pp.

Elderly African-American Emma lives within a few blocks of the shuttered Ledoux cottage on Annunciation Street. One day she meets twelve-year-old Alys Ledoux and learns that Madame Ledoux, the widow of a Judge, who supported herself and two daughters with fine embroidery, can no longer see well enough for such work and now she and her girls sew coarse overalls for little money. Concerned that they are starving, Emma makes the Ledouxs her charity through gifts to Alys that include food and small sums of money. However, Emma cannot overcome the family's pride and the illness that eventually destroys them.

454. Tinker, Frances and Edward Larocque Tinker. *Mardi Gras Masks: The Nineties.* New York: D. Appleton, 1931. 148pp.

When Amédée "Dee" Roudon cannot marry his beloved Septima Sejour because of a grudge his father bears her family, he engineers a Mardi Gras prank to wrest consent from the stubborn man. The grudge began when Septima's father was on a ball committee from which Monsieur Roudon asked for an invitation on behalf of a relative. The committee responded by asking about genealogy that, by extension, questioned Roudon's origins. After Amédée gets a young woman to entice his elder to a private champagne lunch and threatens to reveal his embarrassing pleas for physical contact if he does not accept his son's chosen bride, the engagement can proceed. A great deal of this book is devoted to detailed descriptions of Mardi Gras and to "Creole" family life.

455. Tomlinson, Everett T(itsworth). *The Boys with Old Hickory.* Illustrated by A. Burnham Shute. Boston: Lee and Shepard, 1898. 352pp.

In this novel for young adults, a group of men in their late teens and early twenties who have been on other Jackson campaigns, come together to aid the general in defending New Orleans. However, much of the novel records their adventures elsewhere. Andrew and David Field and Elijah and Henry Spicer are on Lake Ontario at the beginning of the story and Tom and Jerry Hunter of Alabama are near Mobile. In this account, even before Jackson gets to New Orleans, he is negotiating with Jean Lafitte and he makes the Hunters his couriers. No one claims that Lafitte is anything but an outlaw, but he is sympathetic with the Americans and sends a message by his trusted slave Israel to apprise Jackson of British movements. Another pirate, Pierre Rameau, does not think Lafitte should be supporting the Americans and he repeatedly intercepts Tom and Jerry Hunter and later captures the Field brothers once they arrive in New Orleans. The book differs markedly from other historical novels in its perspective on the battle and the subplot involving Pierre Rameau and his supporters conveys a sense that there was not uniform support for the Americans.

456. Toole, John Kennedy. *A Confederacy of Dunces.* Baton Rouge, La.: Louisiana State University, 1980. 338pp.

Ignatius Reilly, the protagonist of this well-known and much-written about novel, has avoided getting a job until events force him to engage with the world on a new level as a thirty-year-old. A medievalist, at odds with twentieth-century American culture, his only "occupation" consists of his work on a lengthy, written diatribe against his age. Living at home with his mother, Reilly took many years to complete his education at Tulane, suffering from a self-diagnosed digestive condition that is probably brought on by the unhealthy ways in which he satisfies his gargantuan appetite. The only social contact he has maintained outside his home is with Myrna Minkoff, a left-wing Brooklynite he met in college and with whom he has maintained a correspondence. Reilly's world is forever changed when an overzealous policeman, Patrolman Mancuso, decides he is a suspicious loiterer as he waits on Canal Street for his mother. When Reilly causes a scene, Mancuso is forced to retreat, taking an elderly man who defends Reilly into custody. Roundly criticized by his chief, Mancuso reappears throughout the novel in miserable undercover assignments, mostly involving entrapping homosexuals. However, he takes an interest in Reilly's mother and sets up social activities involving his own mother that draw Mrs. Reilly out into the world, leaving Reilly to fend more for himself. With the dawning hope of liberation from being Reilly's domestic servant, Mrs. Reilly begins to insist that he get a job, but is shocked when he actually secures a position as file clerk at Levy Pants, a company he happens upon in response to a newspaper advertisement. Immediately realizing that the poorly-managed, oddly-staffed firm is the perfect setting for him, he works there long enough to wreak havoc that could bring the historic company to an end. His actions are not discovered until after he has left the firm to operate a mobile hot dog stand, through which he gets entangled again with the hyper-vigilant Mancuso, who realizes that the hot dog stand is a temporary stash for drugs being distributed on school playgrounds. Pursued by the police and the owner of Levy Pants, Reilly is rescued at the end of the novel by Minkoff, and he heads off to Brooklyn, an environment with which he is more in tune. The book is filled with descriptions of bars and public spaces, as well as the "typical" characters who inhabit them. Their quirkiness sometimes rivals even Reilly's eccentricities, giving a good feel for the French Quarter in the 1970s and its mix of impoverished residents and affluent conference attendees and tourists. The Reillys live on Constantinople Street and the neighborhood receives some description.

457. Townsend, Mary Ashley. *The Brother Clerks: A Tale of New Orleans.* New York: Derby and Jackson, 1857. 417pp.

Two well-born young men are forced to work as lowly clerks for a mean-spirited New Orleans merchant in this novel that addresses the plight of low-paid white-collar workers. When the father of Arthur and Gulian Pratt dies suddenly their mother must sell the Pratt estate on the Hudson River and most of their possessions to pay creditors and the boys must look for work. Twenty-year-old Arthur was trained in business by his father, although his fourteen-year-old brother Gulian was too young to benefit from such tutelage. Believing New Orleans to offer even more opportunity than nearby Manhattan, the boys are able to secure a position through correspondence with Mr. Delancey, the owner and proprietor of a large dry goods store on Chartres Street. Accustomed to the life of affluent gentlemen, they are shocked by the demeaning treatment they receive from Delancey, who considers them lowlier than his household slaves. Living in the store attic and with scant free time, the Pratts have few social outlets. When they try to attend the Episcopal Church and sit in Delancey's pew, he rudely turns them away and, rather than sit with the impoverished in the balcony, Arthur insists they leave. Their religious practice remains important to them and they read the Bible aloud to each other, joined by Delancey's slave, Jeff, who is assigned to sleep inside the store's front door. Over time Arthur is befriended by fellow clerk Charles Quirk and through him, meets Clinton, a fixture among the "b'hoys" of the city who live a rough and tumble life centered on bars and brothels. Although Arthur holds himself slightly aloof from many of their activities, he tastes alcohol for the first time and comes to crave strong drink and the excitement of the streets. Gulian continues his steadfast devotion to his job and Bible reading and earns the sympathy of the head clerk Bernard Wilkins (also a Northerner), who introduces him to Blanche Duverne, a recently impoverished girl from a wealthy Creole family who supports herself and ailing grandfather with fine embroidery. Gulian is immediately smitten. Wilkins' own love affairs are a great secret, for early in his career in New Orleans he had met Minny, a quadroon in Delancey's household. Not realizing Minny's social status, he married her, although when he discovered that doing so was illegal, he ended his romantic connection with her. In the meantime he had met and fallen in love with Della, Delancey's daughter. Delancey had already disinherited his only son for marrying a woman beneath his class, so Wilkins and Della carry on their affair via love letters carried by Minny, Della's personal servant. Della never discovers that Minny had been Wilkins' lover, but she is shocked by another revelation: Minny is her sister, the child of Delancey and one of his slaves. A series of dramatic incidents transpire (the near rape of Blanche by Clinton and some of his b'hoys, including Arthur; a store break-in that leads to the imprisonment of Clinton and the revelation that he is Delancey's estranged son; Arthur being declared dead from cholera, only to revive from a coma on the death cart carrying him with other paupers to the cemetery; and the elopement of Wilkins and Della) before the sentimental denouement brings rewards for the righteous. The faithful slaves Jeff (who kills himself after Delancey holds him responsible for the store break-in) and Minny (who is murdered by Wilkins while he drunkenly forces himself on her while she is watching his and Della's children) are given grand public funerals and cemetery monuments. Gulian is made head clerk and his Christian influence over Delancey deepens to the point that the merchant rues his purposeless life and offers to treat Gulian as his son and heir. Gulian refuses and encourages Delancey to revise his will in favor of Della and Clinton, immediately after which the reformed merchant is struck by a bolt of lightning, allowing the financially distressed heirs to come into their inheritances. At almost the same time, a crippled dwarf, whom Gulian had made his charity, even while living on a pittance, dies bequeathing Gulian a fortune large enough to make respectable his marriage proposal to Blanche, who has in the meantime returned to her former social status after her adoption by wealthy society lady Mrs. Belmont. By the end of the novel the married couple is living in Gulian's reclaimed family home on the banks of the Hudson with a redeemed Arthur and their mother. While the novel resembles tales of mercantile life set in New York City, several elements make the narrative distinct to New Orleans, including the importance of funerary culture, descriptions of the foggy and dangerous nighttime streets, and the centrality of slave culture and mixed-race identity to the plot.

458. Tracey, Francis and Henri Romani. *The Sensational Tragedy in the New Orleans Parish Prison: Startling Confession of Henri Romani, the King of the Mafia, Whose Beautiful but Heartless Wife, Nina, Was at the Bottom of the Assassination of Chief of Police David C. Hennessy.* Philadelphia: Barclay, 1891. 96pp.

This book is narrated in the voice of Henri Romani, king of the Mafia, who died of yellow fever in 1887. This is the story of his betrayal and a series of violent events. Left a wealthy man upon the death of his father, Romani mostly lived in the company of his best friend George Farrell, until he met and married a beautiful sixteen-year-old named Nina. She was the daughter of a ruined planter who subsisted on winnings from the gaming tables. Farrell and Nina soon put a plot in place to make it seem as though Romani had died of yellow fever, leaving him to really die in his tomb. He awakens in time to break out and, as he does, he finds a coffin filled with treasure and soon afterwards witnesses Farrell and Nina gloating. Realizing that the Mafia figure Esposito hid the treasure, Romani steals it and leaves the city in disguise. He plants a story in the press that the wealthy Edouard Olivia is returning to the city after many years and then assumes that identity to be taken up by New Orleans society. Farrell is an artist manqué, who Romani indulged by purchasing his art. Soon after Romani/Olivia returns, he claims to be a friend of Romani. Farrell must leave for the West Coast to nurse his father. He comes back a month later to find that Romani, in the guise of Olivia, has married Nina. During a confrontation, Romani reveals that he knows of Farrell's treachery and kills him with Mafia-acquired weapons. Later he takes Nina to the tomb to punish her and get her to confess. A block falls from the ceiling and crushes her. To this tale is appended an account of the Mafia in New Orleans that includes a list of the murders their members committed from 1855–1881.

459. Tressner, William B. *Queens of the Quarter.* San Diego, Calif.: Publishers Export, 1968. 151pp.

An erotic novel that includes extended descriptions of gay sex, this book surveys a number of homosexual types and at times expounds positive ideas about sex in general and gay sex in particular, even while condemning some aspects of gay life. Nineteen-year-old Jim Parker is living at home in Metairie. He is a star junior college football player, dating attractive Sue Ellen Jackson until she destroys his life. While they are at summer camp Jackson discovers Parker is having an affair with another boy and writes his parents. His father abandons the family and his mother Martha's life becomes so unbearable that she moves them to New Orleans' French Quarter where she gets a job as a waitress and Parker as a busboy, while also enrolling in the city's junior college. His anonymous life in New Orleans is destroyed when former classmate Jerry Alison enrolls at the same college. Although Parker is friendly at first, Alison soon becomes sexually aggressive and later gets other boys to physically intimidate Parker into providing oral sex to a whole series of his fellow students, forcing Parker to drop out of school. Fortunately, Danny Wellman, a new busboy at the restaurant, who is slightly older and very attractive in a macho way, soon afterwards befriends him. After Parker's mother is accidentally killed, Wellman moves in to help with the rent. Wellman has recently embraced his bisexuality and their friendship takes on a sexual dimension that Parker interprets as love and Wellman as physical release. Melvin Carlyle, a private school teacher who is slightly older and from a wealthy family, becomes their mentor after he decides to get an apartment in New Orleans and devote himself to writing. He espouses theories of sexual development and introduces them to older men who live a gay life that includes frequenting bars, pursuing casual sexual encounters, and sometimes appearing in public in drag. Both Wellman and Parker are disgusted by these "queens of the quarter" who see them as sexual prey. Their friendship, which is increasingly imperiled by Parker's expectations of romance, begins to falter after Wellman forces Parker to participate when an older woman hires him for sex and she wants him to provide a second man. The final break comes when Parker arrives at their apartment to find Wellman having sex with a young woman in their shared bed. Unable to pay the rent on his own, Parker takes up homosexual prostitution and comes to a bad end, friendless and destitute. The novel portrays New Orleans as a town to which people of all sexual orientations come for encounters and the French Quarter as populated by large numbers of openly homosexual men.

460. Trollope, Frances Milton. *The Barnabys in America, or, Adventures of the Widow Wedded.* Paris: Baudry's European Library, 1843. 362pp.

This lesser-known work by the author of *Domestic Manners of the Americans* is partly set in New Orleans. Even though the book is a satire on American greed, the protagonists, the Barnabys, an English couple, travel to the United States in an attempt to improve their troubled finances. Told that New Orleans is a place of great financial opportunity, they make the city their first destination and Mrs. Barnaby immediately attracts the warm interests of natives by announcing that she is writing a pro-slavery book. Employing this and other misrepresentations about their identities, the Barnabys find various means to take financial advantage of their hosts before hastily departing for the North where they mine a Quaker abolitionist network and eventually depart for Britain, their coffers enriched by one hundred thousand dollars. The New Orleans section is preoccupied with regional and national chauvinism and a catalog of the signifiers of social status. Beyond highly specific references to local flora and weather, little description is specific to the city. Boarding house life is detailed to some extent, but the nature of socializing (teas and dinners) seems general to nineteenth-century culture.

461. Trollope, Frances Milton. *The Life and Adventures of Jonathan Jefferson Whitlaw, or, Scenes on the Mississippi.* London: Richard Bentley, 1836. 3 vols.: 327pp., 331pp., 348pp.

Jonathan Jefferson Whitlaw is born in the Deep South to an avaricious father who came from the North to make his fortune. Father and son operate a store selling supplies to riverboats until

Whitlaw meets Captain Dart, a plantation owner, who hires him as his confidential clerk, exposing him to plantation culture and raising his aspirations to become a slave holder and planter. The bulk of the narrative is devoted to his rise and the ways in which his increase in power and wealth enable him to subjugate women to his will. He is only thwarted by one of his slaves, an elderly woman, Old Juno, to whom he attributes supernatural powers. She prevents him from forcing himself on one of his young, mixed-race slave girls named Phebe (sic). Later, when he is courting a New Orleans woman named Selina Croft, Old Juno reveals that Croft is her great-granddaughter, preventing a marriage and so horrifying Croft that the young woman commits suicide. As with other plantation novels, the action inevitably transpires in New Orleans, the center for banking and trade, as well as much social life. While in most of these novels the city's treatment is inconsequential, here Trollope's masterful observation provides insight into the city's antebellum social life, as she explores the hypocrisy practiced toward miscegenation and satirizes the competition for wealth and social status in a supposedly classless society.

462. Turner, James H(enry), (Jr.). *One Fine Spring.* New Orleans: Pelican, 1951. 195pp.

During spring 1948, twenty-six-year-old David Paxton vacations at a resort between Biloxi and Gulfport called the Edgewater Park, in a vacation area for affluent people from New Orleans and various places in Mississippi. Paxton is a socially connected young man who studied at the College of William and Mary and just graduated from Princeton. Through mutual friends and family members he gets to know George Fenton who has just purchased an Italianate stone villa near the resort. Fenton is slightly notorious for his impending marriage to a wealthy woman thirty years older than him. Paxton's friend Mary soon tells him that she is having an affair with Fenton. She is married to Charles Thomas, a college friend of Paxton. In their mid thirties, the couple has several children but Paxton is not surprised by Mary's revelation. He knows that Charles has for years had a French Quarter mistress named Suzette Fleur, who has been told that Charles has an ill mother and can only spend a limited amount of time in New Orleans. Mary and Fenton rendezvous in New Orleans, dining in the French Quarter and spending time onboard *The Orion*, Fenton's luxurious yacht that he keeps docked in a nondescript area and not in the Yacht Club. The affair only ends when revelations force Fenton to flee. Fenton was a desk clerk at the Peabody in Memphis when he met a woman who got him involved in drug smuggling, which finances his extravagant life. He escapes the country before prosecution. Like novels about nineteenth-century plantation life, here New Orleans is a center for urban social life that includes pieds-á-terre, where one spends time with one's lover and one's friends look away when they see you with some inappropriate person.

463. Van der Veer, (John) Stewart [a.k.a., Stewart Vanderveer]. *Death for the Lady.* New York: Phoenix, 1939. 256pp.

When Allen Starke's childhood friend, Paul Cloud, becomes a murder suspect, Starke tries to solve the crime out of loyalty and also out of a hope that he can get a "scoop" and transition to journalism from his unsuccessful career as a promoter of a new brand of Kentucky bourbon. A native of Louisville, Kentucky, where his employer, Bluegrass Distilling, is based, Starke arrives in mid-1930s New Orleans knowing no one except the members of the Cloud family (Jeff, Lulie, and their three children Amber, Jane and Paul) who had been neighbors of Starke's family. The affluent Clouds reside in a Garden District mansion at 1399 Jackson Avenue. Starke lives on Royal Street in a boarding house maintained as an outpost of France by proprietress Madame Bertonnier, where he has gotten to know fellow boarder Mike Odell. Odell is a forty-something newspaper cartoonist with whom he goes to French Quarter bars, restaurants, and burlesque houses, including The Gayety of Dauphine Street, where Paul Cloud is also a habitué, as he is having an affair with Norma Goold, one of the dancers. The night that Cloud bows to family pressure and becomes engaged to a society woman, he takes Starke with him to Goold's elegant Jackson Square apartment where he plans to break up with her. Instead, he finds Goold stabbed to death on her bed. As Starke pursues various leads in the French Quarter, Mardi Gras events form a backdrop. Since Goold was Italian-American, Starke interacts with people in that community, some of whom are connected to organized crime. Through introductions to the upper-class Creole men the Cloud girls are dating, he also has contact with that community. As a result, the novel captures several aspects of 1930s New Orleans social life.

464. Van Epps, Margaret T. *Nancy Pembroke in New Orleans.* New York: A.L. Burt, 1930. 248pp.

This is one of a series of books featuring Nancy Pembroke and her great friend Jeanette Grant. Here the duo travels to New Orleans to visit Pembroke's uncle, Dr. John Donovan, a physician at City Hospital. From the title one might expect the work to be entirely set in New Orleans, but that is not the case. The girls travel to New Orleans to meet Donovan's new bride when junior year in college is delayed by a small pox outbreak. They travel by train to Buffalo and then Chicago to meet up with the Panama Limited for an express trip to New Orleans. The girls' time in the city is primarily taken up with typical excursions (Audubon Park, the French Quarter, St. Roch's Cemetery, the mansions along St. Charles Avenue, the French Market), and meals at Galatoire's and La Louisiane (which still has its cages of canaries). However the book is of more interest for the social details. The Donovans live in a mixed-race neighborhood and the girls are fascinated by the behavior of the African-Americans they observe. Their hosts have an African-American maid who is a source of great amusement. Unlike true Southerners, the Donovans do not support Jim Crow laws, but they note that they must tolerate them in the same way that they tolerate the other surprising aspects of New Orleans culture that stem from Roman Catholicism. Dr. Donovan causes great scandal at his hospital when he treats visiting African-American physicians exactly as he would his Caucasian colleagues. However, both he and his wife treat the African-Americans with whom they come into contact, in alternately paternalistic and patronizing fashion. Other social details of interest to contemporary readers concern domestic matters like ice deliveries, the purchase of fruits and vegetables from street vendors, and the uses to which the space under raised houses is put.

465. Veillon, Lee. *Hart.* New York: Harper and Row, 1974. 168pp.

In this novel concerning 1970s life on the streets of the French Quarter, the protagonist is a hump-backed orphan boy named Hart. Although he has a social support network no one in it has the stability or maturity to take the boy in and care for him. Rena, a prostitute at Madam Bess's, provides him with a place to bathe and gives him the very sweet cafe au lait he loves, while her lover is a friendly male presence. Hart gets money by selling street finds to an antiques dealer he calls Candyman, much to that individual's irritation. Candyman is mixed race. While many novels discuss the implications of being mixed race in the nineteenth century, sometimes presenting the French Quarter as a place of broader acceptance, this is one of the few novels with a twentieth-century character who reflects upon the racism he has experienced from both whites and blacks. Exiled from both worlds, Candyman decided to become educated and acquire a broader perspective by spending his time reading great philosophers and writers. While finding books for Hart he comes across journals that reawaken long buried emotions attached to a male lover who committed suicide. Overcome by his loneliness, Candyman kills himself, unsettling Hart's life and making his search for his father a more immediate need. His aid is Lord Emery, an alcoholic who, by being tall and elegant, still lives up to aspects of the name "Lord" that his parents gave him. With no sense of control over his life, however, he has embraced gambling and is constantly looking for signs and talismans to aid his luck. The hunchbacked boy seems like such a talisman and he aids Hart by presenting him to the Voodoo lady Ruth Ellen, whom Hart involves in his search for his father. The novel includes a trip to Audubon Park, several cockfights and Candyman's jazz funeral. By the end of the novel Hart has decided that his search for his father is leading him to St. Martinville. The book provides useful insights about street life in the French Quarter in the 1970s, although Hart's is the main narrative voice. As a narrator, his perspective is of course skewed by the fact that he is a child and may also have a developmental disability that clouds his thinking.

466. Vidal, [Eugene] [Luther] Gore [Katherine Everard, pseud.] *A Star's Progress.* New York: Dutton, 1950. 252pp.

In this fictional biography of entertainer Graziella Serrano, the young Mexican immigrant gets her start in New Orleans. Born into an impoverished circus family, her father is a renowned lion tamer and accepts a job offer with a circus based in New Orleans, partly to help his pregnant, unmarried daughter Rosita avoid social censure. By the time Graziella is fourteen, her older brother has a job driving a truck to Baton Rouge, her older sister is married and two younger siblings have died. Graziella and her mother are mostly left alone in a riverfront boarding house room with other Spanish-speaking immigrants while the circus is on the road. During the Great Depression, Graziella, who is given the stage name Grace, begins dancing in a Bourbon Street club where owner George Wilson seduces her. At first no one in her family knows about her job and they are puzzled about why she is so tired and unmotivated in school. Then her brother discovers her secret. He warns her about her skimpy costume and the club's clientele, but Grace persists with her shows. By the time her father is able to confront her, she has met Jason Carter, a wealthy older man who had been married to a Mexican woman who died young. Carter thinks Grace looks just like his deceased wife and offers to marry her and make her a star. Unable to bear living with her impoverished family just to finish school, Grace leaves town with Carter for California and, when she returns to New Orleans as a twenty-four-year-old, she is a movie star. Her father is dead, but her mother and brother come to the premiere she is in town to promote, after which they all go to George Wilson's to celebrate her success. She returns to New Orleans one final time, when she is embroiled in scandal, as World War II is about to start.

467. Vinton, Iris. *We Were There with Jean Lafitte at New Orleans.* Illustrated by Robert Glaubke. New York: Grosset and Dunlap, 1957. 182pp.

In this work of historical fiction for youngsters, Barnaby Winn, a Salem native, is a ship's boy on the U.S.S. Charleston, sailing on a mission to destroy the pirate stronghold at Barataria. Along with his shipmates, he is convinced of the righteousness of his mission. Word reaches the ship that Lafitte (c.1776–c.1823) has pledged support to the United States and sent letters to Governor Claiborne, revealing the British attempt to enlist Lafitte's support. Everyone on the Charleston is convinced the letters are Lafitte's ploy to avoid the attack on Barataria. The Charleston approaches Grand Terre along with six other ships. During a fusillade of cannon fire from the pirates, Winn is knocked overboard. To escape danger he stows away in a boat that turns out to be the vessel on which Lafitte and his closest associates are fleeing. Among the people onboard are Monsieur Picot, a planter associate of Lafitte's, and his daughter Suzanne, who is of an age with Winn. The stowaway is soon discovered and held in a friendly manner on the Picot plantation to prevent him giving information about Lafitte's whereabouts. From Lafitte and Picot, Winn gets a better understanding of Barataria and comes to admire Lafitte. Once Lafitte goes into hiding in the bayous, Winn and the Picots travel to New Orleans where Winn reunites with his shipmates. Unlike other tales of this sort, Winn is not directly involved in meetings between Lafitte and Jackson, but has been convinced that Lafitte and his men are crucial to the defense of New Orleans. The book is also unlike other accounts in dedicating more than half the narrative to naval actions preceding the Battle of New Orleans, during which Suzanne saves Winn. The novel treats the battle as the end of an era for Lafitte, as the blockade is broken and ships can once again serve the Crescent City. He pledges to find a "wild, free place" and heads for the Texas coast.

468. Waldo, James Curtis [Tim Linkinwater, pseud.]. *Mardi Gras: A Tale of Ante Bellum Times.* New Orleans: P.F. Gogarty, 1871. 131pp.

Like many nineteenth-century novels, this book involves kidnapping, mistaken identity, and a villain's remorse. Percy MacVain, a successful Irish businessman, had known Cecelia Mary Christie in Ireland and had never gotten over her rejection. She is the wife of George Macourty, a commission merchant with a large, attractive Uptown house who makes his money on importing liquor and foreign goods. MacVain has Cecelia's baby kidnapped at a Mardi Gras parade. With no intention of returning the infant, he sets up a household and assigns an old family servant, Sarah Murrey, to care for her. Two years pass and by the time MacVain discovers Murrey has died he does not know what happened to the baby. He employs a private detective and even seeks the aid of a fortune-teller. Years pass and a girl named Cecelia appears, whom MacVain believes to be the kidnapped girl after seeing her but once. For a time Cecelia even lives in the Macourtys' house, before abruptly leaving New Orleans. MacVain continues unsuccessfully to seek the true kidnapped girl and bequeaths a large amount of his fortune to her. The real Cecelia is finally reunited with her family after she and Philip Cumming fall in love. Cumming is a friend of the Macourtys and introduces Cecilia to them. They soon realize she is their missing daughter and celebrate her marriage to Cumming in great style. Throughout the novel the Roman Catholic Church is defended and the Irish Diaspora rued. An additional theme is the nobility of birth and the good character that is dependent upon family. The novel is confusing for including many subplots and minor characters and at various times it is set in New York City and Boston. Descriptions of private clubs and Mardi Gras, Christmas, and New Years' celebrations are included.

469. Walker, Mary Alexander. *To Catch a Zombi.* New York: Atheneum, 1979. 193pp.

This novel for children, set in the years 1784 and 1785, presents free people of color as industrious, attractive, and independent. Protagonist, fifteen-year-old Vance, spent the first part of his life in Santo Domingo. He lives with his mother and younger brother in a community of free people of color in Louisiana bayou country. His mother's lover, Randall, was a slave on a nearby plantation and taught Vance how to fish and catch snakes, so that he has been able to save money. When Randall follows through on his plan to escape and live in the North, he leaves enough money with Vance's mother to pay the transportation costs for her and their sons. However, she gives it all to Voodoo priest Dr. Ducasse, when he claims that Randall has been recaptured and requires a ritual of protection to be performed. Vance despairs over his mother's naivety and later takes steps to expose Ducasse. With Randall gone, Vance supports his family by foraging for food and capturing snakes to sell for Voodoo rituals. In search of snakes, Vance travels further from home than usual and, after an injury, is taken in by Madame LaGrue, a free woman of color and Voodoo priestess who seems to be modeled on Madame Laveau (c. 1801–1881). She helps Vance recover with the help of Dr. Broussard and, to repay them, he does chores for LaGrue and hunts for Broussard. Broussard lives in New Orleans and Vance gradually becomes the physician's assistant. In the city he is surprised to find that one of his childhood friends from the bayou, Melinda, is studying with the nuns of the Ursuline Convent and being trained by an elderly midwife. Over the next year, he learns how to spell his name, accumulates hundreds of dollars selling game to householders and restaurants, befriends some young people his age, learns about aspects of New Orleans culture, and falls in love with beautiful quadroon Querelle. However, Vance learns that a girl with whom he had once been in love is in trouble and he rushes back to the bayou with unexpected results. By the end of the book it is clear that Vance will unite with Melinda and help their bayou community with knowledge of medical practice learned in New Orleans. The novel is more concerned with evoking an emotional response in readers than conveying sound historical information and, unlike other works in this bibliography, entirely dismisses Voodoo practice.

470. Wall, Evans. *Ask for Therese*. New York: Rio, 1952. 128pp.

Like several other novels about New Orleans prostitutes, this book portrays a streetwalker protagonist as an independent businesswoman. Distinctively, however, the heroine here provides inadvertent social benefits that could lead the reader to believe sex workers serve a far-reaching social good. Therese LeDuc grew up outside a small bayou town, the daughter of harsh parents ready to beat her senseless for her own good. By the time she is repeating eighth grade for the second time she is sixteen-years-old (having been held back in other grades as well), and has attained a surprisingly mature body. A resentful spinster school teacher gets her expelled and when her only friend, David Robichaux, the son of a well-to-do local accountant, comforts her late into the night and pledges his love, LeDuc's parents confront her with charges of wantonness and she is forced to run away to New Orleans. Almost immediately, she is picked up by Madam Collett and, six years later, has become one of the city's most skilled prostitutes. The reader is treated to her encounters with ten clients, over the course of one evening. Carey Tadell, a civil engineer who has just accepted a South American job, has avoided marriage to pursue his career and finds Therese the temporary release he needs to continue to single-mindedly pursue his career goals. Ramon Lamana is about to behave foolishly over the marriage of his true love to his brother, but meets Therese instead. Wealthy Walter Garis gives vent to his sexual desires so that he can remain married to his socially respectable, sexless wife and return home to his children. To an army captain she gives reassurance that he has only engaged in homosexuality in the absence of available women and she gives an innocent college boy his first sexual experience. When Dave Robichaux unexpectedly happens upon her, her life as a social utility is almost brought to an end. Robichaux has cherished his love for her, ignoring a hometown girl who would make him an excellent wife, in the hope that Therese will return. Over the past six years he has patiently built up a business and established significant financial security. Within a few hours of meeting Therese, he has successfully proposed to her and they marry. Fortunately for both of them, he finds her address while she sleeps and thinking to help her, he goes there only to learn the truth about her. She remains unaffected when she finds the note he leaves to announce his intention to divorce her and returns to Madam Collett to prepare for another evening of male company.

471. Wall, Evans. *Lovers Cry for the Moon*. New York: Macaulay, 1935. 258pp.

In the late 1920s, Dorothy Ingram moves from Tampa to New Orleans with her successful husband John, a real estate developer. Although she was born in the city, she moved away as a toddler and John's enthusiasm does little to inspire her. Their new home has been carefully designed by acclaimed local interior decorator, Octavia Sherrell, and readied by servants, but Dorothy can think of nothing but the contrast between the mansion on Exposition Boulevard, with a view of Audubon Park that she finds suffocating, and the beach house she left behind in Florida. John quickly introduces Dorothy to his social set, but she is scandalized by all the unconventional relationships. When automobile dealer Ricky Harned and his wife Myrtis are not at society events, they spend their time apart, Myrtis with male admirers and Ricky with secretaries and dancers. Landscape designer Leigh Sherrell and his wife, Octavia, not only pursue separate love affairs, but they also maintain separate residences, visiting each other only occasionally. Dennis Martel, the owner of a trucking company, remains faithful to his wife, Helen, who is hospitalized with a muscular disorder, but mostly because his lover, Ozelle Macey, rejects his notion of divorcing Helen. Other characters have no interest in even the pretense of an exclusive relationship. Margaret Atherton, a very successful automobile dealer, prides herself in exercising male privilege, including a string of lovers. Her male counterpart is the novelist Lynn Tarleton, who also avoids commitment, but mostly because he seeks out experiences on which to base his fiction. As years pass and the Depression approaches, all of these relationships undergo crises. The only ones that survive are marriages in which at least one partner is committed to fidelity. The New Orleans of the novel is filled with romantic possibilities for characters that possess upper-class affluence and inhabit exquisitely furnished apartments and houses with an abundance of servants. Automobile culture has an overwhelming presence in the novel, with men and women taking pride in their cars and relishing the freedom and privacy they enable. The book includes a number of descriptions of Audubon Park, Mardi Gras, nightclubs, and restaurants, as well as private residences, including an apartment in the Pontalba Buildings.

472. Waller, Leslie. *Blood and Dreams.* New York: Putnam, 1980. 344pp.

This bodice-ripping historical romance uses the dramatic economic growth and political corruption in late nineteenth-century New Orleans as a backdrop, to add titillating images of wealth and power. A number of families, some dynastic, and others with dynastic ambitions, are all linked through marriage by the end of the novel. By the 1870s Irish immigrant Neil Blood has assembled a network of businesses to feed the sensual needs of New Orleans men, including bars, restaurants, and brothels. The quality of his establishments attracts men of wealth as secret investors and politicians as patrons, giving Blood a corrupt influence that he builds into considerable power, controlling mayors, congressmen, and even the governor. He raised his daughter, Kate, to be innocent and pure with the help of a convent school. However, with her mother dead, she early took on responsibility for four younger siblings, including the incorrigible Ned. Starting at sixteen, her father employed her aptitude for business and accounting, since he can find no one else so trustworthy. Through a chance encounter, Kate meets Edmund Crozat, the scion of a wealthy Creole banking family. The two are immediately smitten, but to the obvious impediments of such a match is added the fact that Crozat has a mixed-race mistress. Ned Blood also makes an unlikely alliance, given the openly expressed hatred between the English and Irish, when he chooses Kate Badger, daughter of Alexander Badger, a British textile agent who had come to New Orleans and, with the aid of Neil Blood (who of course further enriched himself via inside information on cotton transactions), made a fortune through crooked means. Linked by marriage, these families are poised to build a great oil fortune, for the prescient Crozat bought up oil land in Louisiana in the 1880s, long before crude oil was valuable and before anyone even realized the extent of petroleum resources in the state. The novel details the political skullduggery, the financial shell games, and the twisted sexual practices that give some men and women power over others. In the way of such novels, to provide a façade of respectability for the book, aspects of social, cultural, and political history are covered and the injustices of social inequality based on race, ethnicity, gender, and social status are touched upon.

473. Walworth, Jeannette H(adermann). *True to Herself.* New York: A.L. Burt, 1888. 311pp.

This morality tale set in upper-class New Orleans teases out the effects of one woman's crime. When Emily Ballantyne was left alone with her dying father-in-law she prevented him from changing a harsh codicil in his will that punished his son Everard. She later uses the codicil to force her husband, Everard's brother Frederic, to eject the young man from his Esplanade mansion and prevent him from benefiting from his father's estate. The codicil was to go into effect when the will was executed, but, as executor, Frederic tried to give Everard a chance, by taking him into his household and finding him a job in the cotton exchange firm of family friend, Leslie Davenport. After three years, even though Everard is diligent during the workday, he still drinks and gambles. Everard's only defenders are his mother, who has also been living in the Frederic Ballantyne household, and Emily's young unmarried sister, Theresa Gordon, who Emily fears may love Everard. While Emily claims Everard's redemption to be her only concern, her lawyer, Phillips, knows that Emily also re-wrote the codicil so that Everard's forfeited money would go to Frederic and, eventually, their son Emile. Phillips, a social climber, blackmails Emily by threatening to reveal her treachery if she does not get her sister Theresa to marry his son Josiah Phillips. Unfortunately, Josiah is socially inept and thick-witted and although Emily tries to force a betrothal, Theresa resists and eventually flees New Orleans. Her true love is Leslie Davenport but much of the plot is devoted to untangling the status of his first marriage. By the end of the novel Everard has redeemed himself to some extent by marrying an orphaned plantation heiress and taking on the responsibilities of a family man. Furthermore, Emily's transgression is revealed in such a way that she is able to avoid public ridicule. The social settings in which the novel's action transpire—an upper-class boarding house; Esplanade Street mansion; private clubs; dining rooms; and ballrooms—are detailed to an extent that the novel conveys a good sense of late nineteenth-century social life in New Orleans.

474. Ward, William. *The Murderer of New Orleans: A Story of Hypnotism, Passion, and Crime.* Cleveland, Ohio: Buckeye, 1907. 212pp.

In solving the mystery of criminal lawyer Frank Legarde's murder, investigators eventually conclude that the murderer was hypnotized. Throughout the case, Louis Lanfer, a Creole lawyer, is bizarrely eager to aid the police. He had been a friend of Legarde's and of Mrs. Legarde, who, as Ida Von Alstine, the daughter of one of Louisiana's wealthiest families, had been dating his brother Bertrand. Until, that is, Lanfer persuaded Bertrand to give up his work as a civil engineer for sheep ranching in Australia. When he returns, his school friend Frank Legarde has married Von Alstine. After the marriage, Louis Lanfer insinuates himself into the Legarde household and puts into place an elaborate plot to have Bertrand murder Legarde, seemingly as a calculated revenge. In 1882, Lanfer has Bertrand rent and furnish a Chartres Street house under an assumed name and lure Legarde there with the promise of a large legal fee. Even the brilliant Lanfer makes several mistakes however, particularly when he starts an affair with the widow Legarde. The police become suspicious, but his fille de joie, Laura Larue, becomes jealous and eventually destroys him. In the end Legarde's abilities as a hypnotist are revealed. Although set in New Orleans with references to locations there, the novel is mostly concerned with presenting hypnotism and its power, describing police methods, and with referencing legal procedures.

475. Warren, Robert Penn. *Band of Angels.* New York: Random House, 1955. 375pp.

Like other New Orleans novels that plumb the issue of racial prejudice, this book's protagonist is a person of mixed race. Amantha Starr grows to early adulthood as the beloved daughter of Aaron Pendleton Starr. Even though her mother is dead, Amantha lives in comfortable circumstances on a farm near Danville, Kentucky, and is sent to school in the abolitionist hotbed of Oberlin, Ohio, when she is a little more than nine-years-old. Since her father is still a slaveholder, abolitionist rhetoric is much rehearsed on Starr. Although she is convinced, when she tries the rhetoric on her father, he is unfazed. As a young adult she rushes back to Kentucky in 1859 for her father's funeral, only to arrive just as the ceremony is concluding and the sheriff is enabling Starr's creditor, Cy Marmaduke, to claim the deceased's entire estate, including Amantha. To her shock, she learns that she is Starr's daughter by a slave. She is taken to Lexington where she is sold to a slave trader, to be resold in New Orleans. There she is purchased by wealthy Hamish Bond and begins life in a residence just outside the city. She is forced to define her own identity as an enslaved person, for she has freedom within the house and eventually comes and goes in the city, but when Bond makes arrangements for her freedom in Cincinnati, she returns to him instead. The two begin a relationship that ends with the occupation of New Orleans. With the arrival of Union troops, Starr is forced to reevaluate her identity and eventually marries Union officer Tobias Sears. Her self-identity is complicated by her contact with one of Bond's most trusted slaves who has become a Union soldier and she is tragically involved in the 1866 New Orleans "riot" and its aftermath, only to be reunited with Sears who accepts her mixed race and the two leave the South for St. Louis. The New Orleans of the novel is mostly used to symbolize the center of slave-based society.

476. Wassermann, Moses. *Judah Touro: A Biographical Romance.* Translated from the German by Harriet W. Mayer. New York: Bloch, 1923. 275pp.

As the subtitle indicates, this fictional account of Judah Touro (1775–1854) emphasizes the man's romantic life by focusing on a thwarted love affair. Born in Newport, Rhode Island, to a

Sephardic Jewish immigrant family, Touro was apprenticed to his uncle Moses Hayes, a prominent Boston merchant. By the time he was in his early twenties, Hayes was entrusting Touro with getting valuable shipments through pirate-infested waters and Touro was ready to begin adult married life. His true love happened to be his cousin, Catherine Hayes, whose family stopped the courtship, causing Touro to move to New Orleans in 1803, where he suffered a near-fatal wound during the Battle of New Orleans. He helped found a Jewish congregation and funded charities both within and outside the Jewish community. Much of this novel deals with Touro's life prior to moving to New Orleans, but approximately one hundred pages are set in the city. The author had no direct knowledge of New Orleans and based his descriptions on what he was told by a relative who had lived there for decades. The book repeatedly emphasizes that Touro was a committed patriot whose charitable interests extended to Christians as well as Jews.

477. Watkins, Glen. *Hotel Wife.* New York: Knickerbocker, 1943. 126pp.

When Jim Randall and Anne Browne meet in a New Orleans USO Club during World War II, each had just been jilted by lovers they expected to marry. Randall, an Alabama gas station owner, received a "Dear John" letter while in basic training for the U.S. Air Force, announcing his fiancée Susan's impending marriage to a defense plant owner. Browne was so certain of marrying Dick Mason that she had sex with him and was shocked when he broke off their relationship before shipping out for an overseas army posting. Pregnant with Mason's baby, she arrives at the USO looking for a man to marry and deceive into believing that Mason's baby is his. Randall proves the perfect mark. After a chaste first encounter, they begin a correspondence and by the time they meet again she has arranged for Randall to stay at her apartment house, letting him know that she had to convince the landlady that he was her fiancé. The two decide to marry immediately and consummate their relationship. The rest of the novel is set in Alabama and outside New York City, where the plot revolves around how the lovers who jilted them, dissatisfied with their choices, try to break up Randall and Browne's marriage; as well as how the two genuinely fall in love and deal with the revelation of the identity of the father of Browne's baby. Although New Orleans receives little physical description, the city is portrayed as a typical port city where transient military men encounter many available women. New Orleans is also a place where women can live independently with jobs and their own rooms or apartments, even though they must cope with prying landladies and co-workers. Throughout the novel it is deemed natural for men to express their sexuality but women who have sex outside of a relationship focused on marriage are vilified.

478. Waugh, Alec. *The Golden Ripple.* New York: Farrar and Rinehart, 1933. 306pp.

As the financial exuberance of the first half of 1929 begins to subside into the Great Depression, people in London, New York City, and New Orleans are affected by the lackadaisical attitude of the manager of an oil wildcatting expedition in Santa Marta, Colombia. The owner of the prospective Santa Marta oil field, John Shirley, resides in New Orleans. A World War I veteran, the disaffected Shirley decides not to resume his legal practice, but to live off a modest trust provided by his wealthy family. He buys an apartment in the Pontalba Buildings facing St. Ann Street and adjusts his clothing, food, and entertainment to live within his income. Although he still associates with his upper-class set, he also forms a network of artist friends in the French Quarter and eats many of his meals at his parents' Garden District mansion, rather than at restaurants or private clubs. When Shirley signs with an oil-prospecting firm, the significant payments change his perspective and he slows down his pursuit of artist's model Marian Corelli, the daughter of Italian immigrant delicatessen proprietors, to court Julia Maine, the daughter of his life-long friend, Hugh Maine, who had inherited his father's business and become one of New Orleans's civic and social leaders. Because Julia has such a significant private income, he would never have dated her, were it not for the prospect of oil money. Once the two of them are engaged, Shirley invests his oil money in the stock market and is fascinated by the rapid increase in his paper assets. Within a few weeks of the stock market crash, the oil prospecting syndicate ends the prospecting. When Shirley inquires about his investments he realizes that his broker wrongly invested his trust fund assets and he is wiped out. He is soon made to feel what being married to Julia without an independent income will be like and ends the engagement to go off to live on the land in Santa Marta, the only asset not caught up in his financial collapse. For his mate he chooses Marian Corelli. The novel's deeply analytic perspective provides a rich picture of several social circles in New Orleans in the late 1920s (upper-class society, working-class immigrants, bohemian artists, and businessmen). Of particular interest are upper-class perspectives on members of lower social orders and immigrants.

479. Webber, Everett and Olga Webber. *Rampart Street.* New York: E.P. Dutton, 1948. 318pp.

In this historical romance/adventure novel, New Englander John Carrick holds fast to unpopular convictions, making dangerous enemies in New Orleans in the early decades of the nineteenth century. Carrick, the son of a merchant, was expelled from Harvard College for tarring and feathering slave catchers. His outraged father cut him off, forcing him to take to the sea in a menial position. Some years have passed and although he now owns a ship, he still behaves imprudently. After fending off a pirate attack, he straps the culprits' bodies onto the prow of his ship, even though one of them is the aristocratic Raoul Galvez. Arriving in New Orleans with his ship thus adorned, Carrick happens upon the sale of Raphaelle d'Arendel as a slave—an unfair punishment by a vengeful mistress that is legal since d'Arendel has a tiny percentage of African-American blood, even though she is, to all appearances, white. Carrick purchases d'Arendel after physically attacking auction personnel, earning Governor Claiborne's enmity for defying authority. He then elopes with the dead Galvez' fiancée, Elizabeth d'Ivre. Since the powerful madam, Simone de Tourneau, is in love with Carrick and incensed that he would never even consider her as a bride because of her profession, she vows to get revenge. Carrick's only reliable allies throughout the book are Jean Lafitte (even though Carrick despises privateers) and his banker, Lafenbaugh. While the book is preoccupied with Carrick's romances and social transgressions, some of the historical context is incorporated into the plot, including the British embargo; letters of marque from Cartagena; the Battle of New Orleans; the social status of women; the treatment of mixed-race people; conflicts among the French, Spanish, and Americans; and aspects of the Southern economic system.

480. Wellman, Manly Wade. *Flag on the Levee.* Illustrated by William Ferguson. New York: Ives Washburn, 1955. 209pp.

In yet another novel about the effect of the Battle of New Orleans to unite the city's divided ethnic loyalties, friendship develops between two young men who begin as enemies and become allies in getting Lafitte to join the American cause. Ben Parker, a recent college graduate, arrives in New Orleans in 1811 to work in his Uncle Frank Parker's shipping firm and is immediately confronted with hostility based on his American appearance. When loafers dunk him in the Mississippi without realizing his inability to swim, Casimir Beaumont retrieves him and he ends up as a boarder in the house of Beaumont's father. Beaumont quickly acclimates Parker, taking him to his tailor, teaching him to fence, and to swim in Lake Pontchartrain. However, Parker rejects the New Orleans fashion of considering Jean Lafitte (c.1776–c.1823) an honorable businessman, until Lafitte makes Parker his emissary to Governor Claiborne to report a Spanish assassination plot as a first step to capturing New Orleans. Instead, he and Beaumont prevent the attack by driving off the conspirators and wounding one of them. Later, during Mardi Gras, Parker and Beaumont follow an escaped conspirator to a meeting that includes some powerful New Orleans citizens, all of them engaged in planning a final attempt to bring war between Spain and the United States. Their presence discovered, Beaumont and Parker are taken hostage, but Lafitte and his men have secretly followed them and soon the plot is effectively quelled. Lafitte, still Claiborne's enemy, charges the young men to tell Claiborne that they alone prevented the plot. The novel ends with Claiborne's announcement of the U.S. declaration of war against Britain and with commissions for Parker and Beaumont as militia lieutenants under General Wilkinson.

481. Wellman, Paul Iselin. *The Iron Mistress.* Garden City, N.Y.: Doubleday, 1951. 404pp.

This work of historical fiction begins in 1817, with James Bowie's (1796–1836) arrival in New Orleans, a youth from Bayou Boeuf in Rapides Parish, whose life in the bayous has left him with manners that are a constant affront to the refined Creoles of the city. However, he immediately befriends John James Audubon (1785–1851), who becomes his guide to city life as he tries to find the merchant to whom he and his brothers wish to sell timber. Audubon finds in Bowie a knowledgeable and appreciative audience for the accuracy of his artwork. Through Audubon he soon acquires another guide to Creole culture in Narcisse de Bornay. With Bornay's help, Bowie has some social success at a ball and at a famous gambling house, but Bornay's attentions to a girl offend one of her suitors, the famous duelist Henri Contrecourt, who picks a fight with Bornay and kills him. Bowie, however, avenges his friend in a second duel in which he is able to use his skills as a frontiersman to kill the duelist. Without the support of Bornay, Bowie's tentative social network unravels and he must leave New Orleans. In the roughly eighty pages set in New Orleans this novel focuses on the tensions between Creole and American culture and the code duello. The author introduces a number of historic personages in addition to Bowie and Audubon, including John Randolph Grymes, and Dominique You. The book was made into a movie with the same title (Warner Brothers, 1952).

482. Wells, Charlie. *Let the Night Cry.* New York: Abelard, 1953. 287pp.

In this noir detective novel, Bill Fox returns to New Orleans for revenge. He had run a small French Quarter bar and used the proceeds to pay his sister Elaine's medical bills from a tuberculosis hospital. When the police falsely arrest him for operating a drug drop through his bar, one of gangster Frank Thomas' men offers him twenty thousand dollars and payment of Elaine's medical expenses if he will not fight the charge. He agrees, only to discover that Thomas faked the payments and he goes to jail with nothing in return. Released after eight years, he immediately heads to New Orleans, where he is soon approached by Roger Sanson, who says he has enough evidence against Frank Thomas to convict him, but he needs Fox's assistance. Fox agrees to help Sanson, in part because he needs an ally, and in part because of Sanson's beautiful niece Judy Garrett. After killing several of Thomas' men when they attack him, Fox accumulates other allies, only to realize after Sanson is killed, that he has made some false friends and a number of people are concealing their identities, including some who are drug dealers in competition with Thomas. In this novel, New Orleans is filled with bars, drug dealers, and corrupt policemen.

483. Welty, Eudora. *The Optimist's Daughter.* New York: Random House, 1972. 180pp.

This novel focuses on a clash of cultures and family allegiances, with a significant portion set in New Orleans, which is represented as a center of medical expertise. Seventy-one-year-old Judge McKelva travels from his life-long home in Mount Salus, Mississippi, for an operation on his eyes. Fay, his second wife, accompanies him. She grew up poor in Texas and has none of the cultural refinement of the judge or his family and is resented by his daughter Laurel, who immediately flies from Chicago after hearing of her father's hospitalization and tries to control his care and, when he dies unexpectedly, his funeral. Although an important segment of the book is set in New Orleans, the novel is not terribly concerned with the city and keeps a narrow focus on the judge's hospital stay.

484. Wharton, Edward Clifton. *The War of the Bachelors: A Story of the Crescent City, at the Period of the Franco-German War.* New Orleans: The Author, 1882. 406pp.

In 1870 New Orleans, three men modeling quite different approaches to male social conduct, are written about by a New Orleans reporter, and garner both supporters and detractors. Two of the men had held sway over society gossip for some time. The one who has spent the longest time in the public eye, General John Jonathan Urwins, is a social conservative and rigid observer of traditional codes of behavior. He is still a great favorite of older ladies who thinks he has much to teach middle-aged men about politeness. His competitor for attention, Corporal William Linton, appeared in society as a young man and had unmarried ladies aflutter. He is a veritable renaissance man, helpful to everyone, affluent, a donor to charities and supporter of art and literature. However, he has lost appeal in some circles for mysteriously remaining a bachelor. The Corporal is unvaryingly polite toward the General and even tries to get him to be his mentor. Mr. Prensyll, a society reporter, records encounters between the two and his coverage establishes cliques. When Mr. Prensyll, who prefers the company of frivolous young dandies, finds that such men vaunt Corporal Linton as their hero because of his less-affected behavior, he stirs up controversy by forming them into a club—The D'Orsay Coterie—and getting them to elect a newcomer, Albert Ferdinand Dashleigh, as their president. Dashleigh is a striking example of "Young America." He left college at eighteen with plenty of money from a guardian, and traveled extensively over a two year time period to experience life. The war of the bachelors begins, fueled by Mr. Prensyll's nudgings and public commentary. What follows is a densely written text filled with high drawing room drama. To interpret the book thoroughly one needs to know a great deal about the major figures in New Orleans society and much about nineteenth-century social and cultural history.

485. Wharton, George M(ichael) [Stahl, pseud.]. *The New Orleans Sketch Book.* Illustrated by Felix Octavius Carr Darley. Philadelphia: T.B. Peterson, 1843. 202pp.

Although the contents of this book of short stories may actually have originated as newspaper sketches and adheres fairly closely to their author's observations of people in public places in New Orleans, the accounts are heavily flavored by the author's attitudes and commentary, as well as the tall-tale tradition in which they partake. Few landmarks are described. Instead, the focus is on street life, businesses, and current fads. Charity Hospital is described, but the focus is on the diseases commonly suffered by city residents, and the frequent mentions of the blind and deaf throughout the work remind the reader of how common these afflictions were at the time, as were digestive disorders that are treated humorously here. While it is no surprise that cemeteries and restaurants are a consistent focus, the book also includes descriptions of German beer gardens, fruiterers, and florists. Nineteenth-century fads that play a part in the stories include phrenology, public displays of microscopy, the craft of sentimental hairwork, and séances. Although Italians and Irish are mentioned, the stories almost entirely exclude African-Americans.

486. White, Charles William [Max White, pseud.]. *The Man Who Carved Women from Wood.* New York: Harper, 1949. 304pp.

What starts off as a descriptive work about the personalities drawn to rent in a French Quarter complex in the mid-1940s ends as a murder mystery. Geneva Howard, a former opera singer, who finally gave up her career at age sixty, purchased two New Orleans houses side by side to rent out apartments to the right sort of people, with the idea that they will become a social outlet. The main property is a large residence with converted garçonnières and slave quarters and the smaller adjoining property connects through the inner courtyard of each house. Although her affluence means she can be particular about renters, when she receives a flurry of inquiries within a single twenty-four hour period, she simply fills her apartments indiscriminately. Among her tenants are a fifty-year-old physician who has decided to take some time off to write a book; his buxom young secretary, who he has installed in the apartment next to his; an oil man and his petit bourgeois wife, who affects a social distinction she will never achieve; a young Creole couple; and the elegant, asocial proprietress of a French Quarter perfumery. Howard's most intriguing tenants are Maria Weber and the Malin brothers. Weber has recently been released from a mental institution and claims to have her mother living with her, although no one sees the mother, who supposedly arrives in a custom trunk, since in 1910 she decided that her looks were gone and she no longer wished to be seen. The Malins, Oleg and Elia, moved to New Orleans to be near their mother, a Roumanian countess who operates a boarding stables near City Park and who, despite her elevated social status, enhanced by decades of society life in Manhattan, smokes cigars and gambles far into the night with her stable hands and horse trainers. Both of the Malin brothers are Harvard educated. Oleg is a sometime deckhand who sculpts and Elia is a trained physician who is a connoisseur of oriental rugs, who has left his wife to aid his brother in his current sculpture. The close focus of the novel on personalities means that there is little general description of New Orleans. However, the book does give a good sense of life in a French Quarter apartment during the time period and food is lovingly described, some of it eaten at famous restaurants. Issues of race are touched on through African-American character Leontine, who is treated with respect, even though she is also the butt of humor.

487. Whiteside, Muriel McCullen. *Mizpah, or, Drifting Away.* St. Louis, Mo.: A.R. Fleming, 1885. 142pp.

Although this temperance novel has various settings, New Orleans is crucial to the plot. Madeline Marshal is the daughter of a wealthy lawyer, Colonel Marshal, who married late in life to a much younger woman, Alien (sic) Cosgrove, and constructed a mansion named Hazelkirke five miles from New Orleans. When Madeline was six and her brother Bertie four, Alien died. Even though the Colonel lived on until Bertie and Madeline were young adults, Madeline always felt protective toward her younger brother, to the extent that when Malcolm Cosgrove proposed to her, she rejected him, indicating that she would make a home for Bertie until he married. Only a short time passes before a yellow fever epidemic originating in New Orleans strikes Hazelkirke and kills Bertie in 1867. Soon afterwards Madeline accepts Malcolm's renewed proposal, even though her father warned her against this suitor because of hereditary alcoholism. For a time Malcolm builds his medical practice and cherishes home life that soon includes the infant Alien Dolores Cosgrove. Eventually, however, he begins drinking and gambling. Unable to control himself, he pays off all his debts, establishes a sizable bank account for Madeline, and leaves before he brings ruin to his family (he eventually ends up in London). When he departs in the middle of the night he leaves a letter behind for Madeline, along with a bracelet engraved with the word "Mizpah" to remind Madeline of a biblical verse invoking God's protection. Although Madeline could simply live at Hazelkirke and raise her daughter, she is driven to redeem Malcolm and, after making arrangements for the care of her baby, leaves to begin searching for him. Several years pass and she supports herself through acting with a traveling stage company. Strangely, she never finds Malcolm until each of them unwittingly returns to New Orleans in 1877. Malcolm, who has been redeemed by being forced to care for an orphan, is shocked when he sees Madeline on stage. When he seeks her after the performance at her hotel, The Southern, the structure is burning and he is able to save her. The two return to Hazelkirke to resume their life together. The only settings important to the novel, in addition to Hazelkirke, are those in New Orleans, which include a gambling parlor, the Olympic Theatre, and The Southern Hotel.

488. Whitman, (Vivian) Willson. *Contradance: A Puritan's Progress in New Orleans.* Indianapolis: Bobbs-Merrill, 1930. 350pp.

This fictionalized biography of John McDonogh (1779–1850) begins with the twenty-one-year-old merchant's first appearance in New Orleans, details the reasons why he thought it important to establish a branch of his father's business in the port, and spells out the factors that made him successful (his willingness to learn Spanish and French, his efforts to establish himself in society since business is conducted in drawing rooms in Spanish and French culture, and his Northern business sense). Although McDonogh is a Puritan, prayerful and hard working, who is not given to distraction, he becomes infatuated with Micaela de Almonester (1795–1874). When his courtship leads to scenes with his competitors that he considers undignified, he withdraws and she marries a Pontalba (becoming the famous builder of the Pontalba Buildings). He then courts a woman with his own Scots cultural background, Elizabeth Johnson. However, events connected to the Battle of New Orleans strengthen her commitment to Catholicism (he is, of course, a Protestant) and she enters a convent while he is away on a business trip. Since he had established his city house on Chartres Street as the place to which he would bring his bride, he sells the house and contents and moves to his plantation to live more frugally. An attempt to bring his brother into his life and business fails when the young man has no work ethic and dies of fever, but not before producing Inez, a daughter from a quadroon. Race comes up repeatedly in the novel and McDonogh eventually helps fund a colony in Liberia. The book ends with a tally of his philanthropies. The big historical events are the Battle of New Orleans and the arrival of the first steamboats down the Mississippi.

489. Whitney, Phyllis A(yame). *Creole Holiday.* Philadelphia: Westminster, 1959. 206pp.

This 1950s romance novel for adolescents tells the story of a young woman in the 1890s discovering her place in the world, after thinking through whether rebellion against adult authority and striving for a non-traditional social role are right for her. Soon after Lauré Beaudine's mother died, her father, stage actor Jules Beaudine, sent the seven-year-old to live with her maternal aunt Judith Allen. As an eighteen-year-old, Lauré could no longer contain her resentment over her aunt's strictness and, discovering her father was in town, brazened her way backstage for a confrontation. Shocked at Lauré's new maturity, Jules includes her on a trip to his hometown, New Orleans, to visit his friends Celeste and Foster Drummond, who reside in a Garden District mansion on St. Charles Avenue. Secretly, Jules hopes for a rapprochement with his mother, now that his father, who had disinherited Jules over his choice of profession, was dead. Lauré quickly befriends the Drummonds and their children, eight-year-old Jessamyn and twenty-year-old Cole. All of the Drummonds guide Lauré in learning New Orleans' history and culture and, over time, Cole becomes her confidante. Much of the New Orleans content is devoted to describing social events (particularly those related to Mardi Gras) and detailing expectations for how a "lady" is to behave in a variety of social settings. While Lauré thinks she is justified in expressing anger in public or mimicking her grandmother, she finds no one to support her and when she begins to actually think about her choice of acting as a career and not simply to assert her right to become an actress against opposition by authority figures, she realizes that tradition and parental authority can be positives. Whitney presents a nostalgic vision of well brought-up young people in 1890s New Orleans and admirable adults whose social conventions are beneficial for their adherents.

490. Whittington, Harry [Ashley Carter, pseud.]. *Scandal of Falconhurst.* New York: Fawcett / Gold Medal Books, 1980. 446pp.

In this bodice-ripper about mixed-race people living in New Orleans around the time of the Civil War, the eponymous Scandal is so white in appearance that, with the help of Julien-Jacques Gischairn, she becomes the star debutante of 1861 and marries into a wealthy white family. Born in 1844, on Falconhurst Plantation in Alabama, she is the daughter of the plantation owner's quadroon mistress, Ellen, and Herman "Brass Door" Hengst, a handsome "mustee" (octoroon) on the plantation who is the son of one of New Orleans most celebrated quadroons and a German cotton broker. While Scandal is still an infant, the plantation owner manumits Ellen, and gives her a farm in order to get her off the plantation. Ellen is repeatedly subjected to racial violence. When Hengst, who is about to marry and move to Europe, comes to take Scandal with him he finds the house burned and everyone tells him that Ellen and the infant Scandal were killed in the arson. The story resumes in 1860. Scandal was actually rescued and raised in squalid conditions by whites who denigrated her for her mixed race. In order to get to New Orleans, she employs a ruse on a traveler and the man is forced to become her protector. He is soon imprisoned, however, and Scandal must find another sponsor. Fortunately, she catches the eye of wealthy Julien-Jacques Gischairn, who decides to amuse himself by re-making her into the belle of New Orleans. In cruel fashion he has her tutored to behave like a lady, while remaining preoccupied with his harem of effeminate gay black slaves. She is finally presented to society in 1861 as Ellen, a relative of Gischairn, and he takes great pleasure in watching the most eligible and wealthy young men flock to her. Later, even General Butler insists on audiences with her and eventually insists that she be his mistress. His insistence and an outbreak of yellow fever make Ellen/Scandal desperate to leave New Orleans, but Butler will not issue an exit visa until Ellen/Scandal has sex with him. Fortunately, plantation owner Alex Vigneaux takes her to his plantation. However, the dowager of the plantation wants Alex married before she dies and offers Ellen/Scandal twenty thousand dollars per year. With no alternatives, she accepts the dowager's offer. Alex turns out to be homosexual and, after his mother's death, she gets the marriage annulled. The novel deals with issues concerning mixed-race people and describes occupied New Orleans. Throughout the novel homosexual references are presented as though they would titillate readers (even Hengst has to submit to an evil homosexual white man). The portrayal of Butler as a womanizer is a novelty.

491. Whyte, J. H. *New Orleans in 1950: Being a Story of the Carnival City, from the Pen of a Descendant of Herodotus, Possessing the Gift of Prescience.* New Orleans: A.W. Hyatt, 1899. 167pp.

This futurist work, set in 1951, reveals the concerns (whether serious or satirical) of New Orleans residents at the turn of the century. The main subjects are sewers, geography (New Orleans is presented as the center of the United States subsequent to the annexation of South American into the Union), the social status of African-Americans (the influx of white Americans after the Spanish-American war redressed the imbalance in the population and African-Americans are no longer in the majority of the population), water supply, air conditioning, and transportation (air ships are in regular use in 1951).

492. Wibberley, Leonard (Patrick) (O'Connor). *The Last Battle.* New York: Farrar, Straus and Giroux, 1976. 197pp.

Most of this work of historical fiction is set at sea in the West Indies; however, approximately the last thirty pages describe the Battle of New Orleans and the book's title conveys the significance of the military action as the final end to the conflict with Britain. Two brothers from Salem, Massachusetts—Manley and Peter Treegate—are serving on the U.S.S. Wild Duck, Manley as captain and his younger brother as midshipman. The brothers' personalities are in dramatic contrast as Manley is an authoritarian and Peter, although a skilled seaman, has a more relaxed attitude toward naval discipline. Inevitably, Peter is a favorite of the crew and resented by his older brother. When they capture the British schooner Athena, the brothers separate and Peter and "Captain" Gubu, an African-American and former pirate, supervise repairs on the Athena to enable her to sail to New Orleans to be sold as a military prize. Soon afterwards Peter discovers that the Athena was to become part of the British convoy preparing to attack New Orleans. When the Athena does arrive, she plays a role in defending New Orleans. Although the novel provides little description of the city, the book is unusual for presenting an account of the naval battle in 1814 and assessing the cultural importance of the Battle of New Orleans for definitively ending the British threat so that Americans could focus their attention on Westward expansion.

493. Widmer, Mary Lou. *Night Jasmine.* New York: Dell, 1980. 479pp.

This historical romance novel addresses the prejudice faced by Italian-Americans around the turn of the twentieth century in New Orleans. Protagonist Katie Raspanti is the oldest sibling in a family of five, living in a modest apartment on Julia Street that is one of three carved out of the service wing of a row house, all of which are occupied by Italian immigrants. In 1906, fourteen-year-old Raspanti spends all her time helping her mother cook and clean. She is uncomplaining, even when her father's violent temper flares up against her for no reason. However, soon after she witnesses her father having sex with the eighteen-year-old daughter of a neighbor, she leaves in revulsion to take a live-in position cooking for the family of John and Janet Eagan on St. Charles Avenue. The family includes Stephen, the oldest, about to graduate from Tulane University; nineteen-year-old Charlotte, who attends Newcomb College; and fifteen-year-old Warren, a student at Jesuit High School. The family tries to treat Katie with respect, but they and visitors are made uneasy by the fact that she is not the customary African-American domestic. When John

Eagan discovers that she is trying to teach herself to read, he assigns Warren to help her. However, when Stephen becomes romantically interested in her at seventeen, fearing repercussions, she regretfully leaves for another job. She takes a job as salesclerk at D.H. Holmes Department Store and it is there that Stephen appears to tell Katie his father has died, leaving everything to Janet Eagan, who disinherited him. The two marry and some time later are informed that John Eagan deeded a house to Stephen on Bayou St. John at 17 Moss Street. After success in selling electrification to businesses in New Orleans, Family friend, Thomas Edison, asks Stephen to work in his laboratory and he is killed in an accident. By the end of the novel in the early 1920s, all of Janet Eagan's children have rebelled against her: Stephen and Charlotte by marrying outside their social class and Warren by becoming a Hollywood actor. Janet is left alone in her St. Charles Street mansion while Katie flourishes, establishing a family and eventually marrying again to Stephen's brother, Warren. Most of the events in the novel are social events within the Eagan family and their circle, and include Charlotte's debutante ball, Mardi Gras parties, holiday celebrations, and a dinner for Theodore Roosevelt. The novel includes a great deal of information about the prejudices experienced by Italian-Americans and domestic life in upper-class households in the early twentieth century.

494. Wilburn, George T. *Sam Simple's First Trip to New Orleans.* Americus, Ga.: Hancock, Graham and Reilly, 1870. 106pp.

This humorous work was printed for sale on trains by the Parker Railway News Company and is preoccupied with the disconnect between Simple, a naïve Alabama mountain dweller, and the sophisticated residents of New Orleans. Simple's trip by stagecoach and riverboat takes some time, particularly since he is accused of theft and is separated from his luggage several times, and must recover the overfilled saddlebags that he carries in the absence of a horse (or more suitable bags). Fortunately for Simple, after surviving a steamboat boiler explosion, he is given a new suit of tailored clothes and is presented with a silver cup in recognition of his giving all his clothing to keep his fellow survivors warm. His stay at the St. Charles Hotel is paid in advance for a week and a news story describes his heroic behavior. The story prompts a letter from Kitty, a girl who claims they were schoolmates. She was lured to New Orleans and is living a virtual prisoner of an abusive man. Although Simple cannot remember her, he helps her escape after some farcical scenes in which he hides under the couple's bed. The two are separated immediately and Simple believes he has been the butt of some plot and leaves New Orleans to accept the invitation of one of the steamboat passengers to visit Baton Rouge. The New Orleans section of the book is only just over seventy pages, and provides little description of the city, focusing instead on the incongruity of Sam Simple in such an environment.

495. Wilkes-Hunter, Richard Albert [Diana Douglas, pseud.]. *New Orleans Nurse.* New York: New American Library, 1974. 157pp.

When Senator Colbert is diagnosed with multiple sclerosis he is sequestered in his beach house on Grand Isle, under the care of private nurse Melinda Fontane and physician Garth Woodward. When both of them had a hospital job they dated each other and their romantic feelings are re-awakened. However, Geoff Cromwell, a Harvard-educated lawyer who heads the Senator's staff, is also smitten with Fontane. A rivalry develops between the two men that keeps Fontane busy with dates at New Orleans restaurants during Mardi Gras season. In a final dramatic scene Fontane is taken hostage on traffic-jammed carnival streets. The novel provides details about Mardi Gras and New Orleans to create an exotic atmosphere for readers, but much of the book is set on waterways outside the city.

496. Wilkinson, Clement Penrose [Judge L.Q.C. Brown, pseud.]. *Kenneth Cameron.* Philadelphia: T.B. Peterson and Brothers, 1888. 349pp.

Set in the 1850s, New Orleans in this novel is both the center of social life for wealthy plantation families and a center of commerce and the legal profession, offering alternative professions for men uninterested in becoming planters. The sugar plantations on which the main characters live are seven hundred miles upriver from New Orleans. The Gastons live on Emerald Plantation and the Camerons on LaGrange Plantation. While Emerald prospers, LaGrange struggles and Kenneth Cameron, newly returned from college, knows that his father's investment in every new piece of equipment is what is keeping the plantation in debt. To avoid confrontation, Cameron sets up a legal practice in New Orleans. Just as the practice is beginning to prosper and he begins to hope that he will be able to establish himself financially and marry Hortense Gaston, his father dies and he is left with heavy debts. He is forced to return to give up his law practice and life in New Orleans, in order to return to the plantation and make it profitable. The book emphasizes the contrast between the uncertainties of sugar planting and living in rural areas and the desirable qualities of urban professional life.

497. Williams, Ben Ames. *The Unconquered.* Boston: Houghton Mifflin, 1953. 689pp.

One of a series of novels dealing with members of the Currain family over several generations, this work covers the years 1865 to 1874. Travis Currain returns from the Civil War prepared to return The Chimneys plantation in North Carolina to profitability, employing the agricultural and management skills through which he had originally transformed the place when he had received the farm from his father upon his marriage to Enid Albion. Unfortunately, his wife will be even less of a helpmate to him than she had been initially. Her need to be idolized by young men, that found fulfillment in Richmond while her husband Travis was away, is more suited to an urban environment. However, his daughter Lucy, now in her late teenage years, has become a sympathetic confidante. Unlike many of his fellow Confederate veterans, Travis is resigned to suffer redress from the Union government and willingly cooperates with the mandates of the Freedmen's Bureau in setting up mechanisms to employ the African-Americans who remain at The Chimneys. He is unprepared, however, for the betrayal of his older brother Tony, who finds a means to sell The Chimneys after the returned veteran has spent months restoring fields to cultivation and harvested the first tobacco crop. Tony, living in New Orleans with his quadroon mistress, Sapphira, has adopted the stance of a radical Republican, in part due to a sensitivity to racism inspired by Sapphira, but also out of a calculating sense of the possibilities of political and economic power as the South is taken over by Northerners. He sells The Chimneys to one of them. The sale energizes Travis to relocate to New Orleans and accept the managerial position his old comrade General James Longstreet (1821–1904) had offered him in a cottonseed oil production facility under construction, in which Travis had already invested a significant amount of money. While Enid is eager to leave plantation life for New Orleans, Lucy, who has become smitten with Union officer Lieutenant Donald Page, is reluctant until she learns that Page has been reassigned to the city. From their base in a rented mansion in the Garden District, the Currains' main challenge is not economic or social, but about protecting themselves from violence in the political upheavals and violent rioting of the Reconstruction era. The novel details the political factions, their often selfish motivations, and some of the best-known examples of overt violence. Based on a great deal of historical research, Williams dramatizes conflicting perspectives through diverse characters, including the Currains, their servants, Tony Currain's political allies, and Travis's son, Peter Currain, whose sadism finds expression in the white supremacist organization with which he allies himself.

498. Williams, Moses. *Shadows of a City Care Forgotten.* New York: Vantage, 1979. 206pp.

In this sensational novel, Nick Noko, a young lawyer and stepson of New Orleans judge Harold Finn, manages to continue to drink heavily and have random sexual encounters, while reforming himself socially and professionally in anticipation of proposing marriage to one of his former college classmates, Keal. Unlike Nick, Keal has always been focused on business, even if that business is prostitution. She has advanced from prostitute to the French Quarter's most power-ful madam. When a Keal prostitute is murdered and the undercover detective on the case gets shot, Judge Finn calls upon Nick to investigate. After several more murders it is obvious that illicit drugs are involved. Throughout the novel, elected and appointed officials in state and local gov-ernment are depicted as entirely corrupt in their public and private lives, involved in extramarital affairs, accepting bribes, and they are characterized as pawns of organized crime and international drug cartels. Most of the action transpires in the French Quarter, Garden District, and affluent neighborhoods around New Orleans; however, physical settings are shallowly described, the au-thor reserving his adjectives for the book's numerous sexual encounters. While seeming to disdain the oppression of women and racism, the book is filled with descriptions of women enslaved by their sexual passion who accept the physical violence perpetrated against them by men. Further-more, while most African-Americans are portrayed as victimized by whites, they also engage in criminal activity, including kidnapping, rape, and blackmail.

499. Williams, Wirt. *Ada Dallas*. New York: McGraw-Hill, 1959. 328pp.

One might think that a book in which a woman becomes governor of Louisiana would em-brace a positive view of women; however, the eponymous Ada uses her sexuality to manipulate men and her power to ignobly redress past slights. Appropriately for such a work, the entire narra-tive is told through the voices of three of the men most influenced by Ada: television writer Steve Jackson, who first met her when she was working her way through Newcomb College as a highly paid weekend prostitute; the Louisiana highway patrolman who does her bidding in the hope of winning her as a conquest; and, of course, her husband, Governor Dallas, the singing cowboy drawn into politics by a wealthy backer who saw an opportunity to create a pawn to do his bid-ding. Ada grew up in Irish Channel in a single-parent household with an alcoholic, abusive father who forced her to work as a B-girl as soon as she could wear enough make-up to look seventeen. Although she was rescued and given a job by the grocer father of a school friend, so that she could finish high school as a valedictorian, college was a distant goal financially. To expedite matters, she made enough money as a weekend prostitute to finish college in four years and graduate Phi Beta Kappa. Through a liaison with Steve Jackson, she gets a job at the television station where he works and she quickly manipulates herself into becoming a local personality. Using her position to meet powerful men, she is soon married to Governor Dallas. The rest of the novel details how she uses her power to punish the society women who will not accept her, as well as to establish a pub-lic image that could lead to even greater political power. However, her own inability to forget her past is an Achilles heel that proves fatal when she must prevent her prostitution from becoming public. New Orleans here is both a media hub and the home of the wealthy society people by whom Dallas wishes to be accepted. In addition to mentions of famous bars, restaurants and clubs, the book includes descriptions of modern office life and large-scale social events.

500. Williams, Wirt. *Love in a Windy Space*. New York: Reynal, 1957. 241pp.

In the form of a romance novel, Williams captures post-World War II cultural alienation against the backdrop of New Orleans' nightlife. Veteran Wilson Young Renley still has wartime flashbacks that reignite anxiety and he has carefully tailored his life to avoid commitment. Al-though he owns a public relations firm, it is housed in rented space in the Roosevelt Hotel, and he keeps the business artificially small so that he can manage it with little attention and only one sec-retary. His private life is expensive and he covers costs by billing multiple clients for the same "business" expenses (drinks, meals, hosted receptions, and even prostitutes are allowable in public relations work at the time). He lives in a Garden District apartment in an elegant mansion, has memberships at most of New Orleans' exclusive private gyms and men's clubs, and spends his days eating at the city's best restaurants and drinking in the most popular bars. His relationships with women are purely physical. Until, that is, Joan Beauchamp, a romantic interest from their school days at the University of Louisiana, comes back into his life. Twenty-eight-year-old Joan has been divorced and lives on her parents' cotton plantation in West Feliciana Parish. The reacquaintance of Renley and Beauchamp begins with a contest of wills over whether they will begin a sexual relationship (Renley's goal) or renew their romance (Beauchamp's hope). To their mutual surprise, they begin a romantic physical relationship that quickly leads to a marriage proposal. However, Beauchamp wants a church wedding and must wait until Episcopal Church authorities endorse the state-granted divorce. During the lengthy delay, Renley experiences what a marriage to Beauchamp would be like: she would make him jealous by using her free time socializing with men and he would become preoccupied with his work as his career matures. He rejects this future with dramatic consequences. The novel is filled with descriptions of nightlife and social activities pursued by affluent people in late-1940s New Orleans. Many of the city's famous restaurants are named and their menus described, while the characters also observe a prize fight, discuss the Junior League Fashion Show, go to men's-only bars and the Parisian Room jazz club, where men who wear sport coats without ties and women who wear sweaters without bras gather.

501. Winn, Mary Polk and Margaret Hannis. *The Law and the Letter: A Story of the Province of Louisiana.* Illustrated by George E. Hausman. New York: Neale, 1907. 184pp.

Most of the present in this novel is the period shortly before and after the Battle of New Orleans, but many of the characters have secrets in their past lives that are dramatically revealed after extensive flashbacks. At the center of the story is Cecilia, a foundling raised by Captain Jean and Madame Villiere after a mysterious, veiled, expensively-dressed female passenger on Jean Villiere's ship abandons her. In 1814 Cecilia is a beautiful and cultivated fifteen-year-old who, although officially pledged to the nuns of Ursuline Convent, has a secret arrangement to marry the Captain's nephew, Julian Villiere, after he establishes himself in his military career. Cecilia also has more recent and powerful champions besides her childhood playmate. These include the wealthy Gaston Poydras who has, in his mind, remained the subject of Louis XV through Spanish and American control of Louisiana and who still dresses as an eighteenth century courtier. Poydras believes Cecilia must be connected to nobility and gives her expensive jewelry. Cecilia's other notable champion is Madame McCarty, a fading society beauty with her own plantation. When Julian weds Cecilia, but never consummates the marriage, the Villieres get an annulment on the grounds that the underage Cecilia needed their consent. In the aftermath of the fiasco, Poydras settles a small fortune on Cecilia to give her some independence and Madame McCarty begins introducing her into society. She immediately attracts thirty-five-year-old Nathan Daille, a Northerner working in the South to promote his innovative sugar refining equipment, and Eugene La Grange, from a plantation family, recently returned from study in Paris. Cecilia is still reluctant to let Julian fade out of her life as a youthful mistake or forget the importance of the Villieres to her. She becomes preoccupied with their plight when Jean Villiere is imprisoned for inciting a slave revolt, Madame Villiere seeks refuge in Ursuline Convent, and Julian Villiere is accused of firing on a fellow officer in one of the early skirmishes before the Battle of New Orleans and he is sentenced to be executed. The misfortunes of the Villieres are revealed to have been brought about by the La Grange family, which is on the verge of bankruptcy, and a complex history emerges through the Comte de Choiseul, who turns out to be Cecilia's grandfather. In the course of his story he reveals that Cecilia is of mixed race and her options for living the rest of her life change. The novel touches on issues of gender and race while conveying aspects of New Orleans history in the early nineteenth century.

502. Wirt (Benson), Mildred A(ugustine). *The Shadow Stone.* New York: Cupples and Leon, 1937. 206pp.

In this book for young people, fourteen-year-old Carol Scott is drawn into a mystery when she is handed a box not meant for her during a Mardi Gras parade. The man who thrusts the box into her hands tells her that, "Identification for the House of Peacock Shutters is inside." Then another girl, wearing the same costume as her, appears and demands the box, claiming a mistake has been made. Carol is not certain and holds onto the box to find a beautifully carved green stone. Recognizing the stone's value, she goes to the House of Peacock Shutters in the hope of finding the stone's owner, only to discover two rather upset elderly women (Seenia and Sonia Mercier), awaiting their young niece. She later sees a newspaper story about the arrival of Angela Mercier in New Orleans to claim her inheritance and Carol and her brother Jack are soon deeply involved in a mystery involving the rescue of a kidnapped girl and the unmasking of an imposter. Carol still has time for the round of entertainments connected with Mardi Gras, including a party at the Glenwood Country Club. Although most of the mystery is set in New Orleans, it has relatively little New Orleans content.

503. Woodiwiss, Kathleen E(rin). *Ashes in the Wind.* New York: Avon Books, 1979. 665pp.

Much of this historical romance is set in Yankee-occupied New Orleans. The protagonist, seventeen-year-old Alaina MacGaren, had tried to hold onto her family's plantation near Cheneyville, Louisiana, after her mother's death, even though she was all alone since her father was dead and her brothers were away fighting for the Confederacy. Once the estate is controlled by the Union there are still many Confederate soldiers clandestinely passing through the area and MacGaren aids them. After she is unwittingly involved in the theft of a one hundred thousand dollar Union payroll, she disguises herself as a boy and heads downriver to New Orleans to her uncle, Angus Craighue, who was a prominent merchant before the war. Almost as soon as she arrives in New Orleans, MacGaren is saved from ruffians by Cole Latimer, a Union doctor from Minnesota, who later helps MacGaren reach her uncle's Garden District mansion and finds her a job in the hospital where he works. Continuing to fear capture, MacGaren maintains a male appearance and is forced to watch Angus Craighue's daughter Roberta flirt with Latimer and eventually marry him in a shotgun wedding, solely motivated by financial considerations and a plan to help her father revive his business through Latimer's connections. However, MacGaren, who repeatedly saves Latimer's life, is his true soul mate, if only she did not have to disguise herself as a male. Filled with dramatic plot reversals and incredible coincidences, the book conveys a sense of life in occupied New Orleans and the ways in which close contact may have ameliorated wartime hatreds for some Northerners and Southerners.

504. Woolfolk, Josiah Pitts [Jack Woodford, pseud.] and John Burton Thompson. *Desire in New Orleans.* Baltimore: Signature, 1952. 190pp.

In this mystery novel, Joe Fullilove has been residing in New Orleans for five years since serving in the Pacific during World War II. He is mystified when a beautiful woman, Mara Koeno from Honolulu, appears at a party and accuses him of being implicated in the beating death of her husband. Fullilove, a heavy drinker, remembers attending the party Koeno describes, but has a hard time understanding why she thinks him responsible since he simply beat up the man who subsequently beat up her husband. His houseboy, Luis Destrada, who was with him at the time, is of no assistance, although he does know that Fullilove received a package around the time that did not seem intended for him and has since been in a safe deposit box. The box contains very fine rubies. A connection in Honolulu recognizes Koeno as a smuggler who used U.S. enlisted men to unwittingly transport valuables and Fullilove and his colleagues, including Italian-American New Orleans Policeman Frank Pizzo, construct a plot to capture Koeno and her accomplices, one of whom is Luis Cartadas, who is supposedly with the Philippine consulate. New Orleans in the immediate aftermath of World War II is portrayed as a place filled with internationals, many from the South Pacific, who have turned the port city into a center for smuggling, often with the assistance of foreign diplomats and corrupt New Orleans politicians. The descriptions of the city are generally shallow and most often focus on Fullilove's irritation with drunks and tourist drivers as he rushes around the city in his powerful automobile.

505. Woolfolk, Josiah Pitts [Jack Woodford, pseud.] and Conrad Carter. *Nikki.* Baltimore: Signature, 1953, 183pp.

Cultural attitudes concerning female sexuality predominate in this novel about a young woman's travails. Twenty-four-year-old Nikki Lasage works as a typist in a personnel office in Baton Rouge. She hopes a year-long flirtation with her boss, Burt Welton, will lead to marriage, even though she is anxious over how straight-arrow Welton will react when he discovers she is no longer a virgin. After Welton finally proposes, the couple makes a celebratory engagement trip to New Orleans, accompanied by Nikki's housemate Donna Andrews, and Welton's work colleague, effeminate Billy Lofton. At the last minute Lofton invites Walter Roberts, a New Orleans resident and the heir to a fortune, to join the party. Roberts and Nikki had dated in the past, but Nikki never saw him after he tried to force himself on her. However, he seems to have reformed and after the rest of the party returns to Baton Rouge, she stays in New Orleans to complete her trousseau and she accepts a dinner invitation from Roberts. He lures her to his yacht where he drugs and rapes her. When she discovers she is pregnant, he provides the abortionist, but gets her to sign a statement while she is under anesthesia that she stole money from him and accepted other money from him in return for sex. Using this document Roberts forces her into prostitution and she disappears from Baton Rouge and Welton, leaving only a brief note for Andrews that she is going away. Several fortunate coincidences bring Billy Lofton, his artist friend Michelle Delacroix and Welton together in New Orleans, where they discover Nikki's plight and free her from Roberts' control with the aid of the police. The novel references bars, restaurants, and hotels mostly in New Orleans' French Quarter. While verging on the sexually graphic, the novel touches on issues of premarital sex, gender roles, and homosexuality.

506. Woolfolk, Josiah Pitts [Jack Woodford, pseud.] and Conrad Carter. *Tainted.* Baltimore, Md.: Signature, 1953. 182pp.

This novel displays bar culture in 1950s New Orleans and the ruses perpetrated to entrap women. After the death of her parents leaves twenty-four-year-old Gayle Brennon all alone in rural Mississippi she has little choice but to seek work in the city and makes her way to New Orleans. With her buxom figure her only qualification, she gets a job in one of Salvidore Martinez's Bourbon Street nightclubs. Although Brennon is at first dismayed when thirty-year-old hometown acquaintance Brad McVey, a now-famous author, comes into the bar, they soon commence a whirlwind romance that ends in a marriage proposal. When Brennon tries to quit her job, Martinez uses candid nude photographs of her to force her to entertain Cuban Alfonso Torres. Torres is opening a Cuban brothel specializing in American girls and wants Martinez to supply them. Before long, McVey must use all his cunning to rescue Brennon from a gangster hideout. The novel presents the notorious aspects of New Orleans French Quarter life underlying the bar culture there.

507. Woolrich, Cornell (George) (Hopley-) [William Irish, pseud.]. *Waltz into Darkness.* New York: Penguin, 1947. 310pp.

In this romantic suspense novel set in 1880s New Orleans, Louis Durand marries a woman he has known only through correspondence as Julia Russell (she is really Bonnie Castle). Fifteen years have passed since Durand's fiancée died on the night before the wedding. Loneliness and romantic notions lead him to disrupt his life for a woman that he realizes, after they marry, has concealed her real identity and personality. Exhilarated by her sexuality and beauty and wanting to believe he is in love, Durand ignores the danger signs until too late. Shortly, he is far along on a downward spiral that leads from complicity in a crime to murder and the destruction of his reputation and loss of his fortune. Woolrich's plot is dependent upon a culture in which well-mannered women in beautiful gowns are above reproach. More interested in a time period than an actual place, he makes few efforts to depict New Orleans, even though that is where the novel is set.

508. Yates, Dorothy. *The Family Tree: A Novel.* New York: Farrar, Straus and Giroux, 1967. 184pp.

During the few days surrounding the arrival of a baby the members of an extended family confront a long-buried truth. The baby is Roland Parrington's son, his seventh child, and enhances his status as his father André's favorite since his older brothers, Edward and Duke, never had children. André, who made a fortune and has for decades been aware of his legacy, is proud the family name will go forward, although he is discontented that none of his grandchildren resemble him. The birth causes his wife Mathilde to reflect on her life and regret how thwarted it has been. She married André for the wrong reasons. Then, when he reached forty, he decided to stop having sex to preserve his vigor and prolong his life. Mathilde, who was in her early thirties at the time, had difficulties suppressing her sexuality and had an affair with Jean-Pierre Balmain. Soon after she ended the affair, she discovered she was pregnant and forced André to have sex with her again. Then, the secret affair of her sister-in-law Henriette and Balmain is revealed and they marry. Henriette gives birth to a premature Etienne around the same time that Mathilde has Roland. Everyone ignores the fact that both babies look like Balmain and that he plays delightedly with Roland while ignoring Etienne. Several years later, when Henriette discovers Balmain is having an affair, they separate and André installs her and Etienne in a house next to his own near Audubon Park. The birth of André's grandchild has its impact on Henriette as well as Mathilde, as she reflects on her thirty-four-year-old, unmarried Etienne's life and decides to strike out against André and Henriette's apparent familial bliss. Set in Uptown New Orleans in the 1950s, the larger city has little impact on the sheltered lives of the characters who live within domestic confines, where they are cared for by African-American servants, chauffeured to social events in private houses and only go out occasionally to club events, the opera, or New Orleans' best restaurants. Through the plights of Mathilde and Henriette, the novel deals with the limited choices and lack of independence for women in the early twentieth century.

509. Yerby, Frank. *Captain Rebel.* New York: Dial, 1956. 343pp.

This historical romance is almost exclusively set during the Civil War and traces the adventures of rakish Tyler Meredith, the son of a plantation owner and member of New Orleans society, and his transformation into a charitable Christian prepared to defy his cultural milieu and build schools for African-Americans after the Civil War. Meredith's wartime service was devoted to getting war supplies through the blockade to aid the Confederacy; however, he also enriched himself by transporting consumer goods. After the fall of New Orleans, Yankee General Benjamin Butler unsuccessfully tries to prosecute him for blockade running, while he carries on a longstanding romance with Valerie Forrestal, resisting the social propriety of marriage, and secretly has an affair with Lauriel, a mixed-race beauty. Meredith's feelings for Lauriel lead him to reject his inherited notions of race and slavery. While introducing historical characters and incidents, the romance novel is preoccupied with descriptions of Meredith's courageous adventures on the high seas and his bold defiance of authority

510. Yerby, Frank. *The Foxes of Harrow.* New York: Dial, 1946. 534pp.

Stephen Fox arrives in New Orleans on a flatboat of swine in 1821, having been put off a steamboat onto a sandbar after being accused of cheating at cards. Within three years he owns Harrow, a plantation with a grand house, and has married the most desirable and wealthiest of New Orleans' Creole debutantes, Odalie Arceneaux. Fox had fled Ireland after winning a fabulous pearl from an aristocrat in a card game and he pawns the pearl to get a stake that he increases through gambling. He invests the capital to start a business with Tom Warren, buying flatboats and their contents at low prices and auctioning the goods for huge profits. Soon after entering New Orleans, Fox befriends André LeBlanc, who becomes his guide to the city and Creole culture. Fox has an impeccable command of French, developed while living in Paris, but is still treated badly as an American. When Fox falls in love with Odalie Arceneaux, he manages to impress her father,

Pierre Arceneaux, by letting the old man win at cards. However, Arceneaux insists Fox will never be respected until he becomes a planter. When Fox succeeds in creating Harrow plantation, constructing an impressive residence with furnishings from many parts of Europe, he wins over New Orleans society and Odalie consents to marriage. The match proves unfortunate, but after years with a quadroon mistress, named Desiree, on Rampart Street, Fox gets a second chance at love and finally marries his soul mate. The novel ends shortly after the Civil War, a conflict that brought a great crisis at Harrow due to mixed allegiances. While the narrative is preoccupied with Fox's dynastic ambitions and centers on Harrow, the first eighty pages are exclusively set in New Orleans and the narrative conveys a sense of daily life in the city, describing food, clothing, and domestic life. Common themes include the social dominance of Creoles and the hatred of Americans. The text has a tendency toward stereotyping (all Creole men are gamblers; Americans have a skill for business) and in general slavery is treated as a necessary evil and that good slaves become devoted to their masters and take pride in serving them.

511. Yerby, Frank. *The Girl from Storyville: A Victorian Novel.* New York: Dial, 1972. 476pp.

In a preface Yerby explains why he subtitles this a Victorian novel, but his attitude toward female sexuality reflects the time period in which he was writing, not his 1895 to 1903 setting. Heroine Fannie Turner demonstrates a frankness about sexual matters and a disregard for social convention that makes her stepmother, Martha, accuse her of being irredeemably corrupt. Martha reminds Fannie's father, New Orleans police detective Bill Turner, of his first wife, Maebelle, a woman he divorced when he found she was having an affair (she has since become the most famous madam on the Barbary Coast). The ensuing four hundred plus pages continue to explore the idea of genetics versus environment, or perhaps just the author's view of female sexuality. Led astray at fifteen by a rich man's son, Fannie is subsequently gang-raped and fears she is at fault due to her genetics. When respectable and loving Philippe Sompayac comes forward as a protector and suitor, she repeatedly rejects him for fear of corrupting him. The event-filled plot includes a series of other suitors and Fanny's struggle with tuberculosis before she resolves the conflicts in her life by making a dramatic decision. A significant portion of the novel is set in New York City, Italy, and the Louisiana countryside, but most of the work is set in New Orleans. The very existence of Storyville and the implied double-standard of insisting on the purity of women while granting men opportunities to be openly sexual outside of marriage is a focus of much of the narrative.

512. Yerby, Frank. *The Serpent and the Staff.* New York: Dial, 1958. 377pp.

Born in 1870, Duncan Childers grew up in poverty in New Orleans' Irish Channel. His mother, Gabrielle Aubert, came from a prominent Creole family that traced its history to the earliest settlers of Louisiana. When she revealed her pregnancy to her lover, nouveau riche James Childers, of Caneville-Sainte Marie, he claimed her "French" morals led him to disbelieve his paternity. Shunned by her own family, Aubert moved to New Orleans' poorest neighborhood and eventually married Johann Bruder, a man much her senior, who exhausted the small income he earned as a musician to support her and her son. By the time Duncan is fifteen his situation is turning desperate after the death of his mother and stepfather, and he has never had any contact with James Childers. Fortunately, Minna von Sturck Bouvoir comes to his rescue. Her daughter had married James Childers. They had a son together, but Childers made life miserable and, after all three died of yellow fever, the widowed Bouvoir finds Duncan and takes him back to Caneville-Sainte Marie to devote the few remaining years of her life to his education. Bullied for his illegitimacy, his only true friend was an African-American boy named Mose Johnson. After severely beating one of Mose's persecutors, Childers was forced to return to New Orleans and work in the import/export office of his stepfather's brother, eventually saving enough money, with the addition of a small inheritance, to complete medical school in Vienna. When he returns to New Orleans he marries Hester Vance, the daughter of a wealthy resident of Caneville-Sainte Marie, and works in a private hospital patronized by the city's wealthiest families. By age thirty-three Childers is getting attention for introducing the latest surgical techniques. Although he is pleased to be earning an attractive salary, since he never wants to experience the bite of poverty again, he is also concerned about the inequity of medical care and starts a free clinic beside the expensive hospital where he works. In addition, he helps Mose Johnson start a medical practice in Caneville-Sainte Marie. Shortly afterwards, when he decides not to renew his contract with the hospital and moves back to Caneville-Sainte Marie to help the rural poor, disaster follows as long-standing discord with his wife leads to a final estrangement and the spectacle of an educated black man fuels murderous racist attacks on African-American residents by the local white population. The New Orleans section of the novel conveys a sense of life in the city in the late-nineteenth century, and illustrates the economic difficulties of single women, and the effects of poverty.

513. Yerby, Frank. *The Vixens: A Novel.* New York: Dial, 1947. 347pp.

A significant portion of this book that tells the story of carpetbaggers, Knights of the White Camellia, and Scalawags in the form of a historical romance, is set in New Orleans, the city at the center of political power and money. The action focuses on the conflict between Laird Fournois and Hugh Duncan. Fournois grew up on his family's plantation, Plaisance, near Colfax, Louisiana. However, his criticism of the treatment of slaves brought a definitive rift with his father and forced him North to his mother's family, the MacAllisters. Having fought for the Union, at the end of the war he was left ill in the prisoner-or-war camp in Andersonville, Georgia and made his way back to Louisiana with difficulty. Despite his situation, he is optimistic about the future and believes that he can get the votes of African-Americans in his home parish to win political office and help the South recover, while rebuilding the family fortune (after the death of family members, he is the heir to Plaisance). He does not take into account men like Hugh Duncan, who inherited a fifteen thousand acre plantation from an uncle. Initially, Laird Fournois believes the inexperienced Hugh will never be able to get his land into production quickly enough to pay the taxes. However, he also does not take into account Duncan's political cunning and more accurate vision of the defeated South. While Fournois cultivates the respect of African-Americans in order to build an alliance with them, Duncan cultivates the race hatred of whites as a surer road to power. By coincidence, in 1866, both men are in love with sixteen-year-old Denise Lascals. However, even though Lascals is only interested in Fournois, he believes their age difference is unbridgeable and he begins to court Duncan's cousin, Sabrina McHugh. Only a few days after the wedding Fournois realizes that Sabrina is insane and should never have children. He focuses on reclaiming Plaisance and eventually wins election to the legislature. However, he finds the political landscape, filled with openly corrupt figures controlled by Duncan and men like him, intolerable. The rest of the novel details the ways in which Duncan manipulates co-conspirators to control and openly murder African-Americans. His scheming also brings him the hand of Denise Lascals and nearly kills Fournois on several occasions. Near the end of the novel, shortly after the Colfax Massacre of 1873, Fournois is found surrounded by a destroyed plantation, with his plantation workers dead or headed to the North. With his wife Sabrina dead, he rescues Denise from Duncan's New Orleans mansion and as the novel closes they are headed for a life outside the South. The New Orleans content is very detailed in the instances in which actual historical events are recounted.

514. Yoseloff, Martin. *Lily and the Sergeant.* New York: Funk and Wagnalls, 1957. 250pp.

Taking place in New Orleans in the years 1946 and 1947, this novel presents a city shaped by military use of the port and the presence of Camp Gumper. Through the characters of Sergeant Harold Paulsen and Lillian "Lily" Forbes the author presents life in a military camp and the motivations, opportunities, and dangers of life in New Orleans for women in the time period. In the military since 1936, thirty-five-year-old Paulsen is suddenly in the midst of an army decreasing to post-war levels, with most soldiers returning to civilian life. An orphan, raised by a remote uncle, he has never really had a family life. His life is transformed after he stops a knife fight over

Forbes. Arriving in New Orleans from a small town in Minnesota with her girlfriend, Forbes has been forced to give up her dream of opening a glamorous dress shop. When her girlfriend elopes, Forbes is eager for married life and lets Paulsen spend most of his free time with her, going to clubs, restaurants, hotel dances, and having dinners in her apartment at 210 Bienville. Paulsen even begins studying for a high school equivalency examination in anticipation of leaving the army. Paulsen is only a safety option for Forbes, however, and when she meets a dress shop model the two begin planning a move to New York City. Distressed by the uncertainties of civilian life, Paulsen quickly drops his plans to leave the military and asks for a transfer to Hawaii, where he anticipates serving out the rest of his career with ease. The New Orleans of the novel is a wide-open city where enlisted personnel are wary of being robbed and single women in bars are considered easy sexual prey for the right price. However, as peace returns, the local government is imposing major crackdowns, just as opportunities for women in the workforce are dwindling. Issues of race are touched upon since Camp Gumper is segregated and Paulsen only sees civilian African-Americans in menial service jobs. Although the novel does not include much physical description, major restaurants and bars are named, and social settings are well described.

# Biographies

Abaunza, Virginia (1909–1998)

Born in St. Martinville, La. and educated at the Academy of the Sacred Heart in Grand Coteau, La., Abaunza was the author of the one novel for which she is included here. An auto-biographical work about her own divorce, the book was considered innovative for presenting the emotional impact of divorce on children, at a time when divorce was still unusual and a taboo subject. She moved to New Orleans around 1938 and lived there for the rest of her life. (*Times-Picayune*, 8 April 1998).

Ackland, William Hayes (September 6, 1855–February 16, 1940)

Born William Hayes Acklen in Nashville, Tenn., Ackland later changed the spelling of his name to that used by his English ancestors. His father, Joseph Alexander Smith Acklen, a hero of the Mexican-American War, had married a wealthy young widow, Adelicia Hayes Franklin, a relative of President Rutherford B. Hayes and Ackland benefited from significant affluence all his life. A graduate of the University of Nashville (BA) and Vanderbilt University (LLB), he was dedicated to society life, traveling to Europe each year and seasonally from Ormond, Fla., to Washington, D.C., to Lake Mohonk, N.Y., and to York Harbor, Me. The author of three volumes of poetry and the novel for which he is included here, Ackland was an art collector who willed his estate to found an art museum which today exists at the University of North Carolina, Chapel Hill as the Ackland Art Museum.
(*Biography of William Hayes Ackland*, http://ackland.org/about/history/biography-of-william-hayes-ackland/, accessed 3 October 2013).

Algren, Nelson (March 28, 1909–May 9, 1981)

Algren is most closely identified with Chicago for his works of fiction and non-fiction dealing with the city. Born in Detroit, the only son of a machinist, Algren grew up in a working-class neighborhood of Chicago. He graduated from the University of Illinois at Chicago with a journalism degree in 1931. In the Depression-era economy he found few jobs. He lived in New Orleans for a time working as a door-to-door salesman and in Texas working as a gas station attendant. These experiences informed his later work, as did a term in prison for vagrancy and a second term for stealing a typewriter. After hitchhiking back to Chicago, he published his first novel in 1935, based on his time in Texas. Algren's following books, published between 1942 and 1949, including novels and volumes of short stories, established his career. He served as a medical corpsman in the U.S. Army from 1942 to 1945 and began traveling in Europe and South and Central America in 1947, sometimes in the company of Simone de Beauvoir, the French novelist. His book about drug addiction, *The Man with a Golden Arm*, published in 1949, won the national Book Award and brought him international celebrity. He moved to the East Coast in 1974 when he got an assignment from *Esquire* magazine to cover the retrial of boxer Rubin "Hurricane" Carter. Algren continued to publish, mostly short stories and works of non-fiction (including travel writing) until his 1981 death in Sag Harbor, New York.
(*Contemporary Authors Online*, Detroit: Gale, 2007, accessed 14 July 2013).

Allen, Hervey (December 8, 1889–December 28, 1949)

Although his father was an inventor known for his automatic blast furnace stoker, from an early age Allen, a life-long patriot, was enthusiastic about military service. In 1909 he enrolled in the U.S. Naval Academy, but a sports injury forced him to end his study there. After returning to his native Pittsburgh, he enrolled at Pittsburgh University where he majored in economics, graduating with honors in 1915. As a member of the National Guard of Pennsylvania, Allen was sent to patrol the border between Texas and Mexico in 1916 and in 1917 to France, where he later enlisted in the U.S. Army as a first lieutenant. He served most significantly in the Marne and Meuse-Argonne campaigns. Returning to the United States as a twenty-nine year old, Allen studied at Harvard before taking a teaching job at a high school in Charleston, S. C. Earlier he had published a volume of poetry based on his experiences in Texas and in 1921 he published a second collection after founding the Poetry Society of South Carolina with his friend DuBose Heyward. In 1925 he taught at Columbia University and the following year at Vassar College. During this period he published *Israfel*, a well-received biography of Edgar Allan Poe. In 1927 Allen took a sabbatical on a Bermuda plantation, occupying himself by reading and study that laid the groundwork for his best-known work, the historical novel *Anthony Adverse*. Published in 1933, the one-thousand-page work was an immediate best seller that became a model for historical fiction and brought the financial security that Allen enjoyed for the rest of his life. Later novels with Civil War and World War I settings did not meet with the same success and he was never able to finish his five-part Colonial American novel cycle.
(*Contemporary Authors Online*, Detroit: Gale, 2007, accessed 14 July 2013).

Altsheler, Joseph A[lexander] (1862–1919)

The author of ninety-five books, mostly for boys, Altsheler was born in Three Springs, Ky., near Louisville, where his father's German immigrant family operated a store. After study at Liberty College (Glasgow, Ky.) and Vanderbilt University (Nashville, Tenn.), he began his work life in 1885 as a journalist with the *Courier-Journal* in Louisville, Ky. and later joined the New York *World* in 1892 where he remained until his death. Most of his forty-eight novels are works of historical fiction that fall within six series, the most popular of which, The Young Trailers, deals with the pioneer era in the Ohio River Valley. Many of his books have conventional plots incorporating romance that leads to marriage and were intended for a general audience. He also published a large number of short stories in major national magazines.
(*Dictionary of American Biography*, vol. 1, s.v. "Joseph Alexander Althsheler").

A Man o' the Town, *see* James, Samuel Humphreys

Amoss, Berthe (September 26, 1925–)

A writer and illustrator of children's books, Amoss was born to lawyer Sumter Davis and his wife Berthe (Lathrop) Marks in New Orleans. She attended Newcomb College and received a bachelor's and a master's degree from Tulane University. The author of twenty-four picture books, four young-adult novels, and three how-to books, Amoss taught children's literature at Tulane and was president of Cocodrie Press for which she designed a number of calendars sold in art museums and other cultural institutions.
(Book jacket copy).

Annandale, Barbara, *see* Bowden, Jean

Ansell, Jack (November 21, 1925–September 20, 1976)

Best known as a novelist who wrote about Southern Jews enmeshed in battles over integration, Ansell was born in Monroe, La., attended Louisiana State University (1942–43) and graduated from the University of Missouri (BA, 1948; MA, 1950). After jobs in his hometown with the

local newspaper and radio station, Ansell relocated to New York City in 1959 and became a writer at ABC Television Network in 1962. He was promoted several times, rising to assistant to the president by the time he left the network in 1975. With the exception of his first novel, which was published in 1960, Ansell's six other novels were published between 1971 and 1975.
(*New York Times*, 22 September 1976)

Antrobus (Robinson), Suzanne (?–?)
    Born in New Orleans, Antrobus grew up in Chicago and Detroit. Her father John Antrobus (1831–1907) was an artist who painted the first official portrait of Ulysses Grant. She married Albert A. Robinson and wintered in New Orleans most of her life. She was the author of the one novel for which she is included here.
(Lucian Knight, ed., *A Biographical Dictionary of Southern Authors*, s.v. "Antrobus, Suzanne").

Arguedas, Janet Wogan [Anne Labranche, pseud.]
    The author, who was best known as a poet who wrote in the Creole dialect under the pen name Anne Labranche, was the wife of Gustave J. Arguedas, Peru's consul general to Guatemala. The author of the one novel for which she is here included, Arguedas also wrote the essay on race in the WPA New Orleans city guide published in 1938. (*Augustin and Wogan Families Papers*, Louisiana Research Collection, Howard-Tilton Memorial Library, Tulane University).

Arnold, Margot, *see* Cook, Petronelle Marguerite Mary

A.S.M., *see* McNeill, Nevada

Aswell, James (Benjamin), (Jr.) (April 27, 1906–February 23, 1955)
    Best known as a syndicated columnist and social commentator, Aswell was born in Baton Rouge, La., but also lived in Washington, D.C. as a child since his father (also James Aswell) was a U.S. Congressman from 1913–31. He attended the University of Virginia (1924–27) and was a congressional candidate in 1931 after his father's death. Although an outspoken political commentator calling for reform in a Louisiana controlled by Huey P. Long, he was the author of many short stories published in magazines and newspapers, as well as a collection of poems, several collections of short stories, and three novels. Residents of Natchitoches did not appreciate Aswell's satirical take on their town in his thinly fictionalized Rivermark, where much of his fiction was set, and had a habit of burning his literary output in public. After his death they burned his papers, as well.
(*Encyclopedia of Louisiana History*, http://www.lahistory.org/site18.php, accessed 3 October 2013).

Augustin, George (February 22, 1866–February 15, 1935)
    The author was born into a notable New Orleans family, resident in the city since the mid-eighteenth century whose ancestral home, the Augustin mansion, was located at the corner of Esplanade Avenue and St. Claude Street. The son of Judge James D. and Micaela (Fortier) Augustin, after an education in New Orleans schools, Augustin got involved in the city's literary culture, writing verse and newspaper articles and eventually owning the weekly New Orleans newspaper, *The Creole Fireside*.
(Book jacket copy).

Baker, Julie Keim Wetherill (July 15, 1858–July 25, 1931)
    A poet and writer of fiction, Baker was published in *The Atlantic Monthly*, *The Century*, and *The Critic*, and *Lippincott's Magazine*. The wife of Marion A. Baker, editor of the New Orleans *Times-Democrat*, she often published as Julie K. Wetherill.

Ball, Zachary, *see* Masters, Kelly Ray

Banks, (Algernon) Polan (July 21, 1906–1984)
    A native of Norfolk, Va., Banks served in World War II in the rank of captain as the chief of the U.S. War Department's stage and screen section. His first wife, Amalie Baruch, was the niece of financier Bernard Baruch.

Barker, Lillian
    The author of six romance novels mostly published in the 1920s and 1930s, Barker took a good deal of interest in the Dionne Quintuplets, authoring four books about the sisters.

Barron, Ann Forman [Annabel Erwin, pseud.] (July 26, 1917–March 30, 1998)
    Born into an affluent Oakdale, La. family, Barron's husband was a Texas realtor. She lived most of her adult life in Texas and took a great deal of interest in the state's folklore as a writer. She was the author of numerous periodical articles and nine books.

Bartlett, Napier (1836–1877)
    During the Civil War, Bartlett served with Louisiana's Washington Artillery and published an account of his experiences as *A Soldier's Story of the War* (New Orleans: Clark and Hoferline, 1874).

Basso, (Joseph) Hamilton (September 5, 1904–May 13, 1964)
    A native of New Orleans, Basso studied law at the University of Tulane, but left before finishing his degree to become a full-time writer and moved to New York City. After setbacks he returned to New Orleans and got jobs as a reporter while writing novels and a biography of General P. G. T. Beauregard. After his first novel met with mild success, Basso returned to New York City in the 1940s and by 1943 had become associate editor at *The New Yorker*, a position he held until his death while continuing to publish criticism, novels, and short stories.
(Joseph R. Millichap, *Hamilton Basso*, Boston, Mass., Twayne, 1979).

Bay, Gabriel (?–?)
    No information available.

Beach, Rex (Ellingwood) (September 1, 1877–December 7, 1949)
    The author of more than thirty books, Beach's adventure novels achieved wide popularity and several were made into plays and movies. Born in Atwood, Mich., Beach's affluent family moved to Florida in 1884 and he began studies at Rollins College before moving to Chicago to study at Kent College of Law and work in his brother's legal practice. He was on the silver-medal winning U.S. Olympic Water Polo Team in 1904 and when the Klondike Gold Rush began, went to Alaska. Unsuccessful as a gold prospector, he returned to Florida and published his first novel based on his prospecting experiences. That book launched a lucrative writing career and Beach invested money in Florida land, eventually owning twelve thousand acres around Sebring and Indiantown on which he ranched and raised tender crops like celery and gladiolas for Northern markets, earning a second fortune. After the death of his wife and a long struggle with throat cancer, Beach committed suicide when he was seventy-one.
(*Internet Movie Database*, http://www.imdb.com/name/nm0063492/bio?ref_=nm_ov_bio_sm, accessed, 5 August 2013).

Beaumont, Pierre, *see* Ferrall, Robert J.

Bedford-Jones, Henry (April 29, 1887–May 6, 1949)

A Canadian, Bedford-Jones was the son of a clergyman and decided early in life to make his living as a writer. He left college after two semesters and moved to the United States, where from 1912 onwards his prolific output dominated pulp magazines. He eventually wrote more than ninety novels and more than one thousand shorter works for the mass-market, usually in the science fiction and fantasy genres, although he also wrote historical adventure novels that demonstrate a facility for historical research.

(*H. Bedford-Jones Collection*, Harry Ransom Humanities Research Center, University of Texas at Austin, http://www.lib.utexas.edu/taro/uthrc/00876/hrc-00876.html, accessed, 5 August 2013).

Bell, Sallie Lee (?–May, 1970)

A Christian novelist, Bell was a life-long resident of New Orleans, although her extensive travels are apparent in the more than thirty-five novels she authored. Bell was the daughter of physicians and her husband was a doctor as well.

Berry, Erick, *see* Best, Allena Champlin

Best, Allena Champlin [Erick Berry, pseud.] (January 4, 1892–February 1974)

Children's book illustrator and author Best, was born in Bedford, Mass. and educated at the Pennsylvania Academy of Fine Arts and art schools in New York City and Paris. Best specialized in books that introduced foreign, particularly non-European, cultures, to American children. However, she also wrote U.S. historical fiction set in the Colonial and Revolutionary War eras. Throughout her career of almost fifty years she used the pseudonym Erick Berry and occasionally collaborated with Herbert Best, her husband and fellow author, and illustrated the books of other children's writers.

(*Contemporary Authors Online*, Detroit: Gale, 2003, accessed 5 August 2013).

Biery, William (October 14, 1933–?)

A native of New Orleans and graduate of Louisiana State University (BA, 1957), Biery served in the U.S. Marine Corps (1952–55) during the Korean Conflict. Subsequently, he worked as a disc jockey and newscaster at WDSU (New Orleans) and later as a writer and producer at WWL-TV (New Orleans). He moved to New York City in 1963 and worked as a news correspondent for Granada Television (London, U.K.) and as a writer, producer, and announcer for WPIX-TV (New York, N.Y.).

(*Contemporary Authors Online*, Detroit: Gale, 2001, accessed 5 August 2013).

Blake, Christopher Stanislas (March 10, 1921–?)

Born in Brooklyn, Blake began his education at Columbia University before serving in the U.S. Army during World War II. After his honorable discharge, he spent six years in Paris where he befriended Gertrude Stein and Alice B. Toklas. He then moved to New Orleans to finish his education at Loyola University. He eventually worked as a restaurateur while continuing to write and publish as he had done throughout the war. For a time he owned the restaurant Christopher Blake's, and although he claimed to have only had cooking lessons from Alice B. Toklas, received favorable reviews for his cooking.

(*Tank Destroyer*, http://tinyurl.com/keou94n, accessed 6 August 2013).

Blake, Gladys

Blake authored ten books published between 1926 and 1935. No additional information available.

Blake, Jennifer, *see* Maxwell, Patricia

Blassingame, Wyatt (February 6, 1909–January 8, 1985)

The author of hundreds of national magazine articles, as well as more than fifty-four works of non-fiction and fiction for children, Blassingame was born in Demopolis, Ala. and lived most of his life in Florida. He attended Howard College and graduated from the University of Alabama (AB, 1930), subsequently completing graduate study at New York University. He served in the U.S. Navy during World War II and received the Bronze Star. Although he taught as an instructor at Florida Southern College (Lakeland, Fla.) for six years, Blassingame has worked exclusively as a writer for most of his adult life.

(*Contemporary Authors Online*, Detroit: Gale, 2003, accessed 5 August 2013).

Bontemps, Arna(ud) Wendell (October 13, 1902–June 4, 1973)

Best known as a poet and contributor to the Harlem Renaissance, Bontemps was born in Alexandria, La., but moved with his family to the Watts section of Los Angeles when he was three years old. After graduating from Pacific Union College in 1923, he moved to New York City to teach at Harlem Academy. He later completed a master's degree in library science (University of Chicago, 1943) and was employed as head librarian at Fisk University (Nashville, Tenn.), working there for twenty-five years. After his retirement he worked at the University of Illinois, Chicago Circle and at Yale University as the curator of the James Weldon Johnson Collection. Through his work as a librarian and bibliographer he created important African-American research collections. The author of twenty-five books, Bontemps wrote several non-fiction works for children.

(Kirkland C. Jones, *Renaissance Man from Louisiana: A Biography of Arna Wendell Bontemps*, Westport, Conn.: Greenwood, 1992).

Bouchon, Henry L. (?–?)

No information available.

Bouvet, Marguerite (February 14, 1865–May 27, 1915)

A linguist and children's author, Bouvet was born in New Orleans, the daughter of Jean François Bouvet (d. 1870) and Adelphine Bertrand Bouvet. Both of her parents had distinguished backgrounds—her father descended from Comte de Bouvet d'Asti and her mother was the daughter of a cavalry officer of Charles X. However, the family fortune was lost in the Civil War and when her father died while she was still a small child, Bouvet was sent to Lyons, France to live with her father's family for seven years. She returned to New Orleans to attend Loquet-Leroy Female Institute and graduated from St. Mary's College in Knoxville, Ill. in 1885. Although she taught French for a time, she eventually devoted herself to writing books for young people. Except for the book for which she is included here, most of her works have a European setting.

(*Dictionary of American Biography*, vol. 1, s.v. "Marie Marguerite Bouvet").

Bowden, Jean [Barbara Annandale, pseud.] (October 16, 1925–)

A romance novelist who published under a number of pen names, Bowden was born in Edinburgh, Scotland, but lived most of her life in London, England. An editorial assistant at a series of publishers in the 1950s (Panther Books, Four Square Books, Armada Books), she was a feature writer at *Woman's Mirror* magazine (1962–64) and assistant fiction editor at *Woman's Own* (1964–71) before becoming editorial consultant at Mills and Boon starting in 1971. She published her first novel in 1958 and was still publishing in 2009, more than eighty-two books later.

(*Contemporary Authors Online*, Detroit: Gale, 2011, accessed 1 October 2013).

Braddon, M(ary) E(lizabeth) (October 4, 1835–February 4, 1915)

An English author, Braddon started writing in her early twenties when her father abandoned her mother. She met with almost immediate success in the potboiler genre. Within a few years of her writing debut, she was living as the mistress of John Maxwell, a magazine publisher whose

wife was in a mental institution. The couple resided together for fourteen years and had five children before the death of Mrs. Maxwell made legal recognition of their union possible. Braddon's forte was the sensation novel, a genre that combined illicit passion with crime and mystery. While her early work was considered mildly scandalous, by the end of the nineteenth century such books had become the norm. While tastes changed she openly and successfully wrote for profit over the span of her fifty-five year career, publishing in magazines for the barely literate as well as authoring novels in the respectable three-volume format. Her *Lady Audley's Secret* (London: Tinsley, 1862) was one of the century's best-selling books. By the end of her career she had authored more than seventy novels and lived to see her son, W.B. Maxwell, far along in his career as a successful novelist.
(*Contemporary Authors Online*, Detroit: Gale, 2007, accessed 5 August 2013).

Bradford, Roark (August 21, 1896–November 13, 1949)
    Raised on a plantation worked by African-American sharecroppers, Roark authored short stories and novels that reflected the stereotypical depictions of African-Americans that were popular with audience of his day. Roark portrayed his dialect-speaking characters, as fun loving, but simple-minded and in need of white guidance. The subject matter of his work is often folklore or Bible stories translated into the setting of rural Southern culture. In addition to his writing, Roark worked as a reporter for several major newspapers, including the *Times-Picayune* (New Orleans) and served in the U.S. Army Reserve during World War I and the U.S. Navy Reserve during World War II.
(*Contemporary Authors Online*, Detroit: Gale, 2007, accessed 5 August 2013).

Brandon, Winnie (?–?)
    No information available.

Braun, Matthew (November 15, 1932–?)
    The descendant of Western pioneers, Braun grew up in rural Oklahoma and became known as an author of Western historical fiction. Educated at Florida State University (BA, 1955), Braun served in the military for two years before commencing a career as a journalist and writer. He has published more than forty novels.
(*Contemporary Authors Online*, Detroit: Gale, 2007, accessed 10 August 2013).

Breslin, Howard (December 23, 1912–May 30, 1964)
    A life-long New Yorker, whose Irish immigrant parents met while working at The Waldorf-Astoria, Breslin graduated from Manhattan College (Riverdale, Bronx, N.Y.) in 1936 and hoped to get a job as a journalist. When nothing materialized, he started working as a writer for radio programs and achieved significant financial success by 1946, when he gave up his position to become a writer. One of his first published short stories was adapted into a movie directed by John Sturges and starring Spencer Tracy (*Bad Day at Black Rock*, Metro-Goldwyn-Mayer, 1955). By the time of his early death he had published twelve novels.
(*New York Times*, 31 May 1964).

Bristow, Gwen (September 16, 1903–August 16, 1980)
    Born in Marion, S.C., Bristow graduated from her hometown's Judson College (AB, 1924) and attended Columbia University School of Journalism. She married author Bruce Manning in 1929 and collaborated with him on several murder mysteries. Her own work mostly fit into the genre of historical romance and often deals with issues of Southern history and culture.

Bromfield, Louis (December 27, 1896–March 18, 1956)

A native of Mansfield, Ohio, where he grew up on a farm, Bromfield studied at Cornell Agricultural College (1914–15) and Columbia University (1916) before serving in the American Field Service during World War I. Returning to New York, he worked as a reporter before publishing his first novel, *The Green Bay Tree* (New York: Frederick A. Stokes) in 1924. He followed the well-received book with *Early Autumn* (New York: Frederick A. Stokes) in 1926, which won the Pulitzer Prize the following year. He went on to publish a total of thirty books, all of which were best sellers and several of which were adapted for the screen. Between 1925 and 1938 Bromfield, his wife, and children lived in Paris, coming to know the key figures of the expatriate community, including Edith Wharton, Sinclair Lewis, and Gertrude Stein, and befriending many prominent writers and artists visiting the city. He returned to the United States and to his hometown where he established the thousand-acre Malabar Farm, dedicating himself to exploring organic means of agricultural production. An enthusiastic host, he entertained friends from his Paris days, and Hollywood figures such as Humphrey Bogart and Lauren Bacall.
(Ivan Scott, *Louis Bromfield, Novelist and Agrarian Reformer*, New York: Edwin Mellen, 1998).

Brown, Beth (1900?–1975?)

The author of more than twenty books of fiction and non-fiction, Brown was known for taking unusual jobs (burlesque show stripper, carnival show dancer, nightclub checkroom girl) as background research for her novels. In a job unrelated to book research, she worked as a scriptwriter for Metro-Goldwyn-Mayer and Paramount Pictures.

Brown, Joe David (May 12, 1915–April 22, 1976)

A native of Birmingham, Ala., Brown was the son of a newspaper publisher and, after attending the University of Alabama, he worked on newspapers in Alabama and Missouri and as a feature writer at the *New York Daily News* from 1939–46. His journalism career was interrupted by service in the U.S. Army in World War II, during which he was one of the first men to parachute into Normandy in preparation for D-Day, earning the Purple Heart and Croix de Guerre with Palm (France). After the war, Brown worked for *Time* and *Life* as a foreign correspondent in London, Moscow, New Delhi, and Paris. He published his first novel in 1946 and eventually published five more. His first book, *Stars in My Crown* (New York: Morrow, 1946) was made into a movie, as were two more, the last of which was *Addie Pray* (New York: Simon and Schuster, 1971), released as *Paper Moon* starring Ryan and Tatum O'Neal (Paramount, 1973).
(*Contemporary Authors Online*, Detroit: Gale, 2007, accessed 5 August 2013).

Bryan, Jack Yeaman (September 24, 1907–May 15, 1988)

The author of one novel, Bryan had a career in government service that spanned more than twenty years. Born in Peoria, Ill., he studied at the University of Chicago and graduated from the University of Arizona (BA, 1932; MA, 1933), later earning a doctorate at the University of Iowa (PhD, 1939). His government jobs mostly entailed work as a public information officer or as a cultural affairs officer. He worked at embassies in Cairo, Egypt; Manila, Philippines; Teheran, Iran; and Karachi, Pakistan.

Buckner, Alice Morris (?–1918)

Born Mississippi Morris, the daughter of Colonel E.W. Morris, owner of Bending Willow Plantation in Madison Parish, La., Buckner was the wife of Confederate Captain Richard L. Buckner, a New Orleans cotton merchant. She moved from Shreveport, La. to New Orleans in the 1860s.
(Sarah Wadsworth and Wayne A. Wiegand, *Right Here I See My Own Books*, University of Massachusetts, 2012).

Buntline, Ned, *see* Judson, Edward Zane Carroll

Burroughs, William S(eward) [William Lee, pseud.] (February 5, 1914–August 2, 1997)

Best known as a member of the Beat circle of writers that included Alan Ginsberg and Jack Kerouac, Burroughs was born in St. Louis, Mo., a grandson of the inventor of the Burroughs adding machine and reputedly a direct descendant of Robert E. Lee. He was educated at Harvard College (AB, 1936) and began studying medicine in Vienna before the outbreak of World War II. Living in New York City, after an initial period of working in an advertising agency, he embraced an alternative lifestyle focused on sexual exploration and ingesting mind-altering drugs, while supporting himself via odd jobs. He began writing and became a member of Ginsberg and Kerouac's circle in the mid-1940s through his relationship with Joan Vollmer, a friend of Kerouac whom he married in 1946. He was forced to leave New York City because of increasing police harassment stemming from his morphine addiction and settled in Texas for a time where he grew cotton and marijuana, a crop that drew attention from law enforcement officials, after which he moved to Algiers, La. After a police raid that could have led to prosecution on charges of illegal substance possession, as well as weapons charges, Burroughs fled to Mexico City with his wife. The couple found easy access to drugs and Burroughs pursued esoteric academic interests (Aztec culture and Mayan codices) at Mexico City College. The sojourn ended dramatically in 1951 when Burroughs accidentally shot Vollmer to death. After he was released without charges, he left Mexico and traveled extensively over the following years, living in South America, Paris, London, New York City, and Tangiers. His first published work was an account of his drug use entitled *Confessions of an Unredeemed Drug Addict* (New York: Ace Books, 1951). Burroughs continued to re-work the novel, eventually publishing the book as *Junky* (New York: Penguin, 1971). Cured of his addiction to morphine in the late 1950s, Burroughs published *The Naked Lunch* in 1959 (Paris: Olympia). Although the merits of the experimental novel that employed his "cut-up" method were debated, the work became a best seller and established Burroughs. As a result of notoriety brought by the obscenity trial over the book, subsequent books that spoke openly of drug abuse and sexuality, and his public appearances, Burroughs attracted a following among members of subsequent counter-culture movements in the 1970s and 1980s. Burroughs returned to live in the United States full-time in 1973, settling in Lawrence, Kan.
(Graham Caveney, *Gentleman Junkie: The Life and Legacy of William S. Burroughs*, Boston: Little, Brown, 1998).

Butterworth, W(illiam) E(dmund), (III) (November 10, 1929–?)

Born in Newark, N.J., Butterworth served in the U.S. Army (1946–47) and as a Korean Conflict combat correspondent (1951–53). Under ten pen names he has published more than one hundred books, both fiction and non-fiction. He is best known for his military adventure novels, many written in popular series that cover decades of American military history.
(Dave Mote, ed., *Contemporary Popular Writers*, Detroit: St. James, 1997, s.v. "William Edmund Butterworth, III").

Cable, George Washington (October 12, 1844–January 31, 1925)

Cable was a New Orleans native whose parents' wealthy slaveholding families had arrived in the area shortly after the Louisiana Purchase—his father's from Virginia and his mother's from New England (with a heritage back to the early colonial period). Cable served in the Confederate Army during the Civil War and quickly became the sole financial support of his mother's household and an extensive network of relatives after the war devastated his family's resources. Although he published works of short fiction in popular magazines, he did not have a significant income until he published the story collection *Old Creole Days* (New York: Charles Scribner's Sons, 1879), and shortly afterwards the novel *The Grandissimes* (New York: Charles Scribner's Sons, 1880). His skill in capturing New Orleans and Louisiana plantation life won him a Northern audience in the era of the local color movement. However, his open criticism of aspects of Southern life, including mistreatment of African-Americans, garnered hostility in the South and he moved to Northampton, Mass. in 1889, subsequently publishing attacks on racism and founding a network of reading groups called Home Culture Clubs that studied Southern social problems. (Arlin Turner, *George W. Cable*, Durham, N.C.: Duke, 1956).

Cain, James M(allahan) (July 1, 1892–October 27, 1977)
    After more than a decade of work as a journalist, Cain moved to Hollywood, Calif. to work as a scriptwriter and soon published *The Postman Always Rings Twice* (New York: Knopf, 1934), which, along with three other novels, including *Mildred Pierce* (New York: Knopf, 1941), sold widely and were made into movies. Cain, the son of college president James William Cain, was born in Annapolis, Md. Between 1917 and 1923 he worked as a reporter for several Baltimore newspapers before teaching journalism for a year and later moving to New York City where he was an editorial writer for *The New York World* (1924–31). He was later managing editor of *The New Yorker,* working for roughly a year. Lured to Hollywood in 1931 after one of his short stories was made into a movie, Cain resumed earlier efforts to produce a novel and found his voice using a first person narrator speaking in California vernacular who was devoid of everyday moral considerations. By the early 1940s Cain had experienced almost a decade of success in Hollywood and as a novelist, and began to focus his attention on advocating for an organization to protect authors' rights. In the time period, his ideas were critiqued as an attempt to control the free agency of writers. Returning to his native Maryland in 1947, Cain continued to write, eventually authoring nine more novels, only three of which were published in his lifetime and none of which matched the success of his earlier work.
(Roy Hoopes, *Cain*, New York: Holt, Rinehart and Winston, 1982).

Caine, Mitchell, *see* Sparkia, Roy Bernard

Caldwell, Barry (c. 1910–?)
    The author was a romance novelist primarily active in the 1930s. No additional information available.

Carb, David (1885–1952)
    Born in Mississippi, Carb grew up in Fort Worth, Tex., graduated from Harvard College, and built a career in the New York theater world. Early on he acted in productions of the Provincetown Playhouse in several works by Eugene O'Neill. He wrote plays of his own between 1912 and 1934 and sometimes collaborated with Edith Barnard Delano. His only novel is the fictionalized biography of his grandmother, Babette Carb, for which he is included here.

Carpenter, Edward Childs (December 13, 1872–June 28, 1950)
    A Philadelphia native and journalist, Carpenter wrote more than fourteen plays in the period 1903 to 1932, more than ten of which were produced in New York. He served as the president of both the Dramatists Guild and the Society of American Dramatists and Composers.
(Gerald Bordman and Thomas S. Hischak, *The Oxford Comapnion to American Theatre*, 2004, s.v. "Edward Childs Carpenter").

Carr, John Dickson (November 30, 1906–February 27, 1977)
    Known as one of the most important American writers of mystery fiction, Carr was born in Uniontown, Penn., the son of Wooda (sic) Nicholas Carr, a lawyer, newspaper editor, postmaster, and one term U.S. Congressman. A 1928 graduate of Haverford College (Penn.), Carr published his first mystery in 1932 and went on to write more than seventy works under several pseudonyms. He created three memorable detective characters—Henri Bencolin, Dr. Gideon Fell, and Sir

Henry Merrivale—writing a series of novels featuring each. From 1930 until his death he also wrote radio scripts for the British Broadcasting Corporation, and was chosen by the descendants of Sir Arthur Conan Doyle to be his official biographer. Writing initially in an era when "hard-boiled" detective fiction was popular, Carr's work went against the trend, focusing on puzzle solving over action-laden plots. Carr was also known for his contributions to the development of the historical mystery genre, taking great care to accurately represent historical settings.
(Douglas G. Greene, *John Dickson Carr: The Man Who Explained Miracles*, New York: Otto Penzler, 1995).

Carter, Ashley, *see* Whittington, Harry

Carter, Conrad (c. 1910–1980)
    A co-author with Jack Woodford of many sexually provocative paperback books, Carter also wrote short plays and was most active in the 1930s through 1950s.

Carter, John Henton (1832–March 2, 1910)
    Initially known on the Mississippi River as a pastry chef on steamboats prior to the Civil War, after the war Carter became a popular journalist (under the pen name Commodore Rolling Pin) and went on to write a series of books, including memoirs, poems, and novels, some of which were inspired by his riverboat days and others by the trans-Mississippi West. Born in Marietta, Ohio, after more than twenty years working on the river he mostly resided in St. Louis. During his lifetime, he was best known for his annual that celebrated the Mississippi with folklore, humor, and short fiction under the title *Commodore Rollingpin's Almanac*.
(Lee Ann Sandweiss, *Seeking St. Louis: Voices from a River City, 1670–2000*, St. Louis: Missouri Historical Society Press, 2000).

Cash, Charles E. (?–?)
    No information available.

Catling, Patrick Skene (February 14, 1925–?)
    The author of more than fourteen books for adults and children, Catling was born in London, England and began working for the *Baltimore* (Md.) *Sun* in 1947, and was also a journalist for the *Manchester* (U.K.) *Guardian*, *Newsweeek*, and *Punch*.
(*Contemporary Authors Online*, Detroit: Gale, 2003, accessed 14 August 2013).

Chaber, M.E., *see* Crossen, Kendell Foster

Chapman, John Stanton Higham [Maristan Chapman, joint pseud. with Mary Ilsley Chapman] (May 21, 1891–October 13, 1972)
    Using the pseudonym Maristan Chapman, John Stanton Higham Chapman and his wife Mary Ilsley Chapman co-authored more than thirty books, mostly mystery and adventure books for children. John Chapman was born in England where he was educated and trained as an aeronautical engineer. He immigrated to the United States in 1917 and became a full-time writer after 1928.
(*Contemporary Authors Online*, Detroit: Gale, 1998, accessed 14 August 2013).

Chapman, Maristan, *see* Chapman, John Stanton Higham and Mary Ilsley Chapman.

Chapman, Mary Ilsley [Maristan Chapman, joint pseud. with John Stanton Higham Chapman] (1895–January 26, 1978)
    Wife of John Stanton Higham Chapman (see above) with whom she wrote more than thirty books for children under the pseudonym Maristan Chapman, Mary Chapman was born in Chatta-

nooga, Tenn. and met her husband in England where she was working as a secretary during World War I.
(*Maristan Chapman Papers, 1841–1977*, Special Collections and University Archives, University of Oregon Libraries).

## Charnley, Mitchell V. (April 9, 1898–February 16, 1991)

Born in Goshen, Ind. Charnley was educated at Williams College and the University of Washington's School of Journalism. For a few years in the early 1920s he worked as a reporter in Honolulu and later Detroit before joining *American Boy* magazine as assistant managing editor (1923–30). For the rest of his career, Charnley was a journalism professor, mainly at the University of Minneapolis. He wrote several books for boys, mostly biographical, and his non-fiction book, *Reporting* (New York: Holt, 1959), became a key text in teaching journalism. Several of his students went on to national prominence and credited his influence.
(*Minneapolis Star Tribune*, 17 February 1991).

## Chastain, Madye Lee (December 15, 1908–December 1, 1989)

An illustrator and author of children's books, Chastain was born in Texarkana, Tex. and moved with her family to Atlanta, Ga. after high school, where she attended Oglethorpe University and the Art School of the High Museum. She later moved with her parents to New York City and studied art at the Grand Central Art School and Columbia University. In the 1930s she married artist Henry Kurt Stoessel and, after giving birth to a daughter, became interested in children's books. She authored seventeen books and illustrated the work of other authors.
(*Madye Lee Chastain Papers*, Special Collections and University Archives, University of Oregon).

## Chaze, (Lewis) Elliott (November 15, 1915–November 11, 1990)

Known for his noir classic *Black Wings Has My Angel* (New York: Fawcett, 1953), Chaze was born in Mamu, La. and graduated from Bolton High School in Alexandria, La. He attended Washington and Lee College, and Tulane University, and graduated in 1937 with a degree in journalism from Oklahoma University. His first job as a journalist was as a news editor in the New Orleans Associated Press office. He served in the U.S. Army during World War II and was part of the Army of Occupation in Japan. Returning to civilian life, he worked as a news editor in the Denver office of the Associated Press (1945–51) before going to the *Hattiesburg* (Miss.) *American* where he was a reporter (1951–70) and city editor (1970–81). The author of nine novels, Chaze also published articles in magazines, including *Life*, *The New Yorker*, and *Collier's*.
(James B. Lloyd, ed., *Lives of Mississippi Authors, 1817–1967*, Oxford, Miss.: University of Mississippi, 2009, s.v. "Elliott Chaze").

## Chesnutt, Charles W(addell) (June 20, 1858–November 15, 1932)

Widely studied and written about, Chesnutt has attracted interest as a free person of color born in the North who could have "passed" as a white person, but chose to live as an African-American and devote his writing career to the unpopular topics of miscegenation and racial hatred. Chesnutt's parents were free people in Fayetteville, N.C. before the Civil War, who escaped increasing racism and resettled in Cleveland, Ohio, where Chesnutt was born. After the war the family returned to Fayetteville where Chesnutt's father operated a marginally successful grocery business and Chesnutt was forced to leave the Freedman's Bureau school at fourteen to help support the family. Fortunately the school's principal created a teacher-pupil position that allowed Chesnutt to continue his studies and contribute to his family's support. After becoming a full-time teacher and school principal, Chesnutt moved North where he held jobs as a stenographer, journalist, and railway clerk in New York City and Cleveland. He eventually studied law and passed the Ohio Bar in 1887. Declining offers to become George Washington Cable's secretary, or accept

support to move to Europe and start a law practice, Chesnutt established a court reporting business in Cleveland in 1890 that he combined with writing articles and novels. During his lifetime he published six books. Although his early work was well received, as he more fully explored the issues of racism and the treatment of mixed-race people, the critics turned against him.
(*Dictionary of Literary Biography*, vol. 12, s.v. "Chesnutt, Charles W.").

Chidsey, Donald Barr (May 14, 1902–March 17, 1981)

Chidsey, best known for historical fiction set during the American Revolution, was born in Elizabeth, N.J. He began his career as a journalist when he was seventeen, working for *The Elizabeth* (N.J.) *Daily Journal*. By 1928 he devoted himself to a writing career, publishing detective fiction and adventure stories in pulp magazines. His adventurous youth was filled with work on tramp steamers and odd jobs in exotic places, including the South Seas. In World War II, Chidsey was stationed in North Africa. In the 1950s and 1960s he published several adventure novels that reflected his experiences. However, the books for which he became known, biographies and historical fiction, predominated. By the end of his career he had published more than fifty titles.
(*New York Times*, 26 March 1981).

Child, Lydia Maria (February 11, 1802–October 20, 1880)

A writer of great influence in the period of the 1820s through 1860s, Child was a persistent advocate for the rights of people of color. Born Lydia Maria Francis in Medford, Mass., she was relatively young when her remaining parent, her mother, died. Educated in the house of her brother, she was still residing with him when she published her first novel, *Hobomok, a Tale of Early Times* (Boston: Cummings, Hilliard, 1824). Although released under a pseudonym, the attention the book received quickly led to Child's exposure as author. In the next decade she published a children's book, an advice book, a historical work for children, and biographical works. She married lawyer David Lee Child in the mid-1820s, but he was improvident, a factor, perhaps, in her voluminous output. The two had a shared interest in the antislavery movement and, starting in the 1830s, Child began writing about the treatment of African-Americans. Her *An Appeal in Favor of That Class of Americans Called Africans* (Boston: Allen and Ticknor, 1833), is considered the first scholarly work about slavery by an American. Even though the book was attacked, Child went on to write other antislavery books and novels. Although known by scholars for her life and writings, she is more widely known for a verse: "Over the River and through the Wood."
(*Contemporary Authors Online*, Detroit: Gale, 2013, accessed 14 August 2013).

Chipman, William Pendleton (1854–February 28, 1937)

An author of books for boys, Pendleton was a Baptist minister who was born in Mystic, Conn. and served churches in Walton and Pawling, N.Y.
(*New York Times*, 1 March 1937).

Chopin, Kate (February 8, 1850–August 22, 1904)

A native of St. Louis, Chopin's imagination was influenced by her grandmother, Athénaïse Charleville, who had grown up in the Deep South and told her tales of the Louisiana Territory during French control. Since her father, Thomas O'Flaherty, was an affluent Irish-American businessman and her mother, Eliza Faris, a popular figure in the French community in St. Louis, Chopin had an upper-middle class childhood that culminated with a debutante year. In 1870 she married cotton broker Oscar Chopin of New Orleans, a city she had visited before and found congenial. Within the first decade of her marriage she had given birth to six children and experienced the collapse of her husband's business. The family moved to Cloutierville, La. in Natchitoches Parish in 1879 so that Chopin could manage some small plantations and a general store. When Chopin died in 1882, he left his wife with huge debts and she was soon forced to sell the Louisiana properties and move back to St. Louis to live with her mother. When her mother died in 1885,

Chopin's finances were again precarious and the family physician Dr. Frederick Kolbenheyer recommended the therapeutic value of writing. By the early 1890s Chopin was publishing in literary magazines and newspapers, finding an audience for stories set in Louisiana during a time when the local color movement was burgeoning. Chopin quickly broke the boundaries of such writing by focusing on psychologically realistic portrayals of women that dealt with sexual passion and extramarital affairs without moral judgments. Negative criticism and poor sales did not deter her, but she died at an early age before the audience she may have attracted somewhat later in the century emerged.
(*Dictionary of Literary Biography*, vol. 12, s.v. "Chopin, Kate").

### Churchill, Winston (November 10, 1871–March 12, 1947)
Son of wealthy importer Edward Spalding Churchill of St. Louis, Churchill spent most of his childhood in boarding school and graduated from the U.S. Naval Academy in 1894. He married in 1895 to Mabel Harlakenden Hall, heiress to an iron fortune, and the couple settled in New Hampshire. His first novel *The Celebrity: An Episode*, a satirical novel was published by Macmillan in 1898 and was immediately popular, selling more than a million copies and establishing him as a literary celebrity. His next book *Richard Carvel* (New York: Macmillan, 1899) established his career as a writer of popular historical fiction. He went on to publish fourteen more books. In the early twentieth century he was involved in politics, serving as a Republican in the New Hampshire legislature, but became frustrated when he did not win a race for governor and wrote a novel about political corruption. His later work increasingly censured immoral behavior and this turn from historical fiction to an airing of theological and moral questions won a small readership. For a time, however, Churchill was a literary celebrity and his *Richard Carvel* sold more than one million copies.
(*Encyclopedia of World Biography*, s.v. "Churchill, Winston").

### Clack, Marie Louise (1835?–?)
A native of New Orleans, born Marie Louise Thompson, Clack was from an affluent background and in 1849 married Franklin Hulse Clack (1828–64), a graduate of Yale College and a successful lawyer. He was a Confederate Lieutenant-Colonel in the Consolidated Crescent Regiment and died of wounds received at the Battle of Mansfield. In financial straits after the war, Clack wrote the book for which she is included here, as well as *General Lee and Santa Claus* (New York: Blelock, 1866). She wed Marcus Richardson of New Orleans in 1870.
(W.L. Fleming, et al., *The South in the Building of the Nation: Southern Biography*, Richmond, Va.: Southern Historical Publication Society, 1909, s.v. "Clack, Marie Louise").

### Clark, Ellery H(arding) (1874–1949)
Born in West Roxbury, Mass., Clark graduated from Harvard College (AB, 1896) and Harvard Law School (JD, 1899). He was a member of the U.S. Olympic team in 1896, winning gold medals in the high and broad jump competitions. A coach and English teacher at Browne and Nichols School (Cambridge, Mass.) from 1918–28, he practiced law afterwards. He was the secretary of the Massachusetts Humane Society for forty years (1909–49) and the author of several novels and works of non-fiction.
(*New York Times*, 26 July 1949).

### Claymore, Tod, *see* Clevely, Hugh

### Cleaver, Anastasia N. [Natasha Peters, pseud.] (1948–?)
A graduate of Tulane University (MA, 1972), Cleaver writes erotic historical romance novels

under the pseudonym of Natasha Peters and lives outside Philadelphia with her husband Frederick Clinton Cleaver.
(Aruna Vasudevan, ed., *Twentieth-Century Romance and Historical Writers*, 3rd ed., Chicago: St. James, 1994, s.v. "Cleaver, Anastasia N.").

Clevely, Hugh [Tod Claymore, pseud.] (1898–1964)
    An Englishman, Clevely was born in Bristol, raised by his vicar uncle, and trained as a pilot. Enlisted in the Royal Air Force during World War II, he ended the war as a Wing Commander. Clevely's writing career dates to the 1930s, during which he was a major contributor to *The Thriller*, a newspaper that published adventure, detective, and mystery stories. He published more than twenty novels under his own name, most of which featured serial characters such as John Martinson, "the Gang-Smasher," and Inspector Williams of Scotland Yard. Under the pseudonym Tod Claymore he published another nine mysteries featuring the author as narrator. Near the end of his career he joined the two hundred authors that contributed to the Sexton Blake series published by the Amalgamated Press, completing nine novels published between 1952 and 1955.

Cline, C(harles) Terry, Jr. (July 14, 1935–May 21, 2013)
    Known for horror and suspense novels, Cline was born in Birmingham, Ala., but his family moved often. His father managed a migratory labor camp in 1941 on Lake Okeechobee and his interest in animals was fueled by his experiences there. Although he had an early interest in writing, in his youth he served in the U.S. Army and later was the director of the Land Alive Foundation, that brought exotic animals into schools for educational programs. In his twenties he married author Linda Street and began writing advertising copy and scripts for radio and television, as well as working as a disc jockey and announcer. He published his first novel when he was forty. He remarried to writer Judith Richards several years after the breakup of his first marriage of eighteen years. In 1978 Richards published a novel about Cline's youth on the everglades around Lake Okeechobee, entitled *Summer Lightning* (New York: St. Martin's, 1978). Cline wrote ten books and fostered the growth of a literary community in Fairhope, Ala. through a bookstore he owned and readings in which he participated.
(Alabama Center for the Book, *Literary Landscape*, http://alabamaliterarymap.lib.ua.edu/author?AuthorID=148, accessed 14 August 2013).

Cobb, Joseph B(eckham) (April 11, 1819–September, 1858)
    Cobb published two books of fiction and one non-fiction volume in the 1850s. His most popular work, *Mississippi Sketches* (Philadelphia, Penn.: A. Hart, 1851) was modeled on other compilations of humorous short works popular at the time. Born near Lexington, Ga., the son of a U.S. Senator, Cobb studied at the University of Georgia before marrying and moving to Noxubee County, Miss. where he was successful as a planter and politician in the 1840s. However, his strongly held Unionist position in which he endorsed slavery, but affirmed the federal government's right to limit its spread, made him unpopular in the late-antebellum period. His non-fiction book *Leisure Labors* (New York: D. Appleton, 1858) contains the Whig essays he published as editor of *Whig* (Columbus, Ga.), as well as other work he contributed to newspapers.
(James B. Lloyd, ed., *Lives of Mississippi Writers, 1878–1967*, Jackson: University of Mississippi, 1981, s.v. "Cobb, Joseph B.").

Cohen, Alfred J. [Alan Dale, pseud.] (May 14, 1861–May 21,1928)
    Born in Birmingham, England, Cohen graduated from King Edward's School in that city and studied drama for three years in Paris. He arrived in New York City in 1887 and began work as a journalist at the New York *Evening World*. He soon made a name for himself as a drama critic to be feared. He was later  drama critic  at the New York *Evening Journal* (1895–1915) and the New

York *American* (1915–28). He was the author of nine novels published between 1885 and 1902. (*New York Times*, 22 May 1928).

Collier, Julia (1888?–May 19, 1979)

An author of books and short stories for children, Collier was active in the Louisiana Pen Women's Association. Born in Converse, La., she lived most of her life in Mansfield, La. (http://files.usgwarchives.net/la/sabine/obits/c/c4600025.txt, accessed 14 August 2013).

Collins, E. Burke, Mrs., *see* Sharkey, Emma Augusta Brown

Comfort, Mildred Houghton (December 11, 1886–February, 1976)

Born Mildred Houghton Bergemann in Winona, Minn., Comfort was the wife of lawyer Hollis Murdock Comfort (1885–1937). A graduate of Carleton College (Northfield, Minn.) (BS, 1908), Comfort taught school for six years in towns located in Minnesota and South Dakota and began writing books for children in 1932. Over a career spanning over forty years she published thirty-five books, including several biographies, some works of historical fiction, and a number of adventure stories.
(*Contemporary Authors Online*, Detroit: Gale, 2001, accessed 4 October 2013).

Conaway, James (April 15, 1941–?)

Known for the novel for which he is included here and the movie version (*The Big Easy*, Kings Road Entertainment, 1986) starring Dennis Quaid and Ellen Barkin, Conaway has had a long career as a journalist and author of fiction and non-fiction. Born in Memphis, Tenn., he attended the University of North Carolina and graduated from Southwestern University at Memphis (BA, 1963). After graduate study at Stanford University, he worked as a reporter for the *Times-Picayune*, the *Daily American* (Rome, Italy), *Washington* (D.C.) *Post*, and editor for *Harper's Bazaar*. At the *Post* he served as wine critic and has written two non-fiction books about Napa Valley, published articles on wine and the wine industry, and in 2013 published a novel featuring a wine critic (*Nose*, New York: Thomas Dunne, 2013).
(*Contemporary Authors Online*, Detroit: Gale, 2008, accessed 14 August 2013).

Converse, Florence (1871–1967)

Born in New Orleans and a graduate of Wellesley College (AB, 1893), Converse worked on the editorial staff of *The Churchman* from 1900–1908 before joining the staff of *Atlantic Monthly*. The author of twenty books, including novels, poems, and a history of Wellesley, Converse has garnered recent interest for her lesbian relationship with Vida Dutton Scudder.
(Lillian Faderman, *Odd Girls and Twilight Lovers: A History of Lesbian Life in Twentieth-Century America*, Penguin, 1991, 23).

Conway, Theresa (June 8, 1951–?)

Over a period of more than twenty years Conway has published romance novels, including several historical romances. Born in St. Louis, Mo., she attended St. Louis Community College and worked as a secretary before devoting herself to raising a family and writing.
(*Contemporary Authors Online*, Detroit: Gale, 2007, accessed 15 August 2013).

Cook, Ella Booker (1886–1974?)

An author of romance novels, mostly set in Mississippi, Cook was born in Attala County in that state. She moved with her husband to Houston, Tex. and was most active in the 1940s and 1950s.
(James B. Lloyd, ed., *Lives of Mississippi Authors, 1817–1967*, Jackson: University of Mississippi, 1981, s.v. "Cook, Ella Booker").

Cook, Petronelle Marguerite Mary [Margot Arnold, pseud.] (May 16, 1925–?)

Known for her detective mystery fiction, Cook was born in Plymouth, England. Educated at Oxford University, she received a BA with a Diploma in Prehistoric Archaeology and Anthropology in 1947, and an MA in 1950. For much of her life she has lived in Hyannis, Mass. Most of her fiction is part of either the Dr. Penny Spring series, featuring a female Oxford anthropologist, or the Sir Toby Glendower series, featuring a male Oxford archeologist.

(*Contemporary Authors Online*, Detroit: Gale, 2001, accessed 15 August 2013).

Cooke, Grace MacGowan (1863–1944)

The member of a literary family, most of Cooke's work was set in Appalachia, an area in which she lived almost from the time she was an infant, until 1906. Her father was for thirty years the editor of *The Chattanooga* (Tenn.) *Times.*

(Engelhardt, Elizabeth S.D., *The Tangled Roots of Feminism, Environmentalism, and Appalachian Literature*, Athens, Ohio: Ohio University Press, 2003, 136–144)

Cooley, Stoughton (April 23, 1861–1934)

The author was named for his father, a Mississippi steamboat captain, based in Ohio and, later, in Savanna, Ill., where Cooley was born. A journalist, he lived most of his life in Chicago, Ill.

Cooper, Parley J. (June 8, 1937–?)

The son of a lumberman, Cooper was born in Glendale, Ore. and, after study at Santa Monica City College and the University of Hawaii, graduated from the University of California, Berkeley, in 1963. After a few years working at *Diplomat* magazine and as business manager to David L. Wolper Productions, Cooper devoted himself to writing full-time, publishing mostly with Ace and Pocket Books. He is the author of more than twenty titles under his own name and eight pseudonyms.

(*Contemporary Authors Online*, Detroit: Gale, 2001, accessed 21 August 2013).

Corrington, John William (October 28, 1932–November 24, 1988)

Known as a writer about the South and most respected for his poetry and short stories, Corrington was born in Memphis, Tenn. and grew up in Shreveport, La. He graduated from Centenary College (BA, 1956), Rice University (MA, 1960) and the University of Sussex (PhD, 1964) and began his career as a college professor at Louisiana State University and Loyola (New Orleans) University before getting his law degree at Tulane University (JD, 1975). Throughout his writing career he also practiced law and co-authored work with his wife Joyce Hooper, including television screenplays as head writers for "Search for Tomorrow" and "Texas." The author of four volumes of poetry, two books of short stories, and five novels, Corrington was a long-time resident of New Orleans.

(*Dictionary of Literary Biography*, vol. 244, fourth series, 2001, s.v. "John William Corrington").

Costain, Thomas B(ertram) (May 8, 1885–October 8, 1965)

Born in Brantford, Ontario, Costain started working as an editor after graduation from high school, eventually serving on several Canadian publications, including *Maclean's*, before moving to Philadelphia to become chief associate editor of the *Saturday Evening Post* for almost fifteen years. He was later an editor at Twentieth Century-Fox and at Doubleday. Known for books of history and works of historical fiction, Costain wrote eleven novels, four histories, two biographies and several books for children.

(*Dictionary of Literary Biography*, vol. 9, s.v. "Costain, Thomas Bertram").

Cowdrey, A(lbert) E(dward) (December 8, 1933–?)

Best known as an author of fantasy and science fiction, Cowdrey was born in New Orleans and educated at Tulane University (BA, 1956) and Johns Hopkins University (MA, 1957). After several years of teaching history as a lecturer at Tulane and Louisiana State University, Cowdrey began writing full-time, including as Chief of the Special History Branch of the U.S. Army.
(*Contemporary Authors Online*, Detroit: Gale, 2002, accessed 20 August 2013).

Cox, George D. (?–1896)

A long time resident of Philadelphia, for many years Cox was the drama editor for *The Philadelphia Inquirer*. He also wrote bestselling books for Philadelphia publisher T. B. Peterson, some of which were translations of French classics by Alexandre Dumas and Emile Zola, but most of which used such works as the basis for adulterated versions that expanded on salacious plot elements.
(*New York Times*, 18 April 1903).

Coxe, George Harmon (April 23, 1901–January 30, 1984)

Born in Olean, New York and educated at Purdue University (1919–20) and Cornell University (1920–21), Coxe worked as a reporter and advertising salesperson, before a two year writer stint at Metro-Goldwyn-Mayer (1936–38) and a career writing mystery novels full time, eventually publishing more than sixty books. His detective novels featured Flash Casey, newspaper photographer; Kent Murdock, a socially sophisticated photographer; and medical examiner Paul Standish.
(Jay P. Pederson and Taryn Benbow-Pfalzgraf, eds., *St. James Guide to Crime and Mystery Writers*, 4th ed., Detroit: St. James, 1996, s.v. "Coxe, George Harmon").

Craddock, Irving (?–?)

No information available.

Crane, Frances (October 27, 1890–November 6, 1981)

Born Frances Kirkwood into an affluent Lawrenceville, Ill. family that included a number of physicians, Crane was a Phi Beta Kappa graduate of the University of Illinois at Urbana. She married a wealthy advertising executive, Ned Crane, and became a regular contributor to *The New Yorker* magazine, as well as writing gently satirical novels about English life from the viewpoint of an American abroad, based on her own extended residence there. In the 1930s she was living in Germany, but was expelled from the country for her protests over the arrests of her Jewish housekeeper and the woman's son. No longer married to Crane and with a college-age daughter to support, she relocated to New Mexico and began writing mystery novels, eventually publishing more than thirty, twenty-six of which had husband and wife team Jean and Pat Abbott as their main characters. The Abbotts remained popular fictional characters for two decades and were featured in several radio programs.
(*Contemporary Authors Online*, Detroit: Gale, 2006, accessed 21 August 2013).

Creole, pen name of Massena, Agnese M.C.

No information available.

Crossen, Kendell Foster [M.E. Chaber, Clay Richards, pseuds.] (July 25, 1910–November 29, 1981)

A native of Albany, Ohio, Crossen attended Rio Grande (Ohio) College and worked as editor of *Detective Fiction Weekly*, as an insurance claims investigator, and as a Work Projects Administration writer before embarking on a writing career in 1940. His detective fiction was mostly written as volumes within series, his most popular being the books he authored as M.E. Chaber, with New York insurance investigator Milo March as the protagonist. He used six pen names and created other insurance investigator detectives, as well as the pulp and comic book hero, Green Lama, a crime-fighting Buddhist with super hero powers summoned up through a Tibetan mantra. (Jay P. Pederson and Taryn Benbow-Pfalzgraf, eds., *St. James Guide to Crime and Mystery Writers, 4th ed.*, Detroit: St. James, 1996).

Curtis, Alice Turner (fl.1913–1937)

Born in Sullivan, Me. and a resident of Boston for most of her life, Curtis was the wife of Irving Curtis and wrote a series of popular children's books featuring "The Little Maid."

Cushman, Jerome (1914–?)

A librarian and author of children's books, Cushman was a graduate of Park (Parkville, Mo.) College (now University) (AB, 1940) and Louisiana State University (BS, library science, 1941). He served in the U.S. Army Engineer Corps during World War II and worked in public libraries in Jefferson City, Mo. and Salina, Kan. and as head librarian at New Orleans Public Library (1961–65).

(*Contemporary Authors Online*, Detroit: Gale, 2012, accessed 20 August 2013).

Daniels, Dorothy Smith (July 1, 1915–December 3, 2001)

Born in Connecticut and a graduate of Central Connecticut State College, Daniels married writer Norman A. Daniels on October 7, 1937. While living in New York City in the 1950s, she began writing short stories. However, not until 1961, after a move to California, did she find her genre by authoring doctor-nurse novels published by Paperback Library. The books sold well and the publishing firm suggested she follow a shift in reader tastes and write Gothic romance novels, which she did, going on to publish more than one hundred and forty books by the end of her career.

(*Dorothy Smith Daniels Collection*, Browne Popular Culture Library, Bowling Green State University http://www2.bgsu.edu/colleges/library/pcl/page69010.html, accessed 21 August 2013).

Davis, M(ollie) E(velyn) M(oore) (April 12, 1844–January 1, 1909)

An editor of *The Picayune* (New Orleans) (now *Times-Picayune*), Davis was born in Talladega, Ala. and moved with her family to Texas in 1855, living in several rural areas until an 1867 move to Galveston. Her poems had been published in newspapers since the time she was sixteen and she published a book of poetry in 1867 (*Minding the Gap*, Houston, Texas: Cushing and Graves) that attracted statewide interest. In 1874 she married Thomas E. Davis and when he became a reporter at the *Times* (New Orleans) the couple began a very active life that eventually led Davis to host a literary salon. She became editor of *The Picayune* in 1889 and continued to publish poetry, as well as novels and children's books set in Texas and New Orleans.

(*Handbook of Texas Online*, http://www.tshaonline.org/handbook/online/articles/fda44, accessed 21 August 2013).

Decoin, Didier (March 13, 1945–?)

The son of filmmaker Henri Decoin, the author published his first novel at twenty-one and by the time he was in his early forties had established a distinguished reputation in France that did not entirely transfer to the United States when several of his novels were published in English. In 1977 he won the Prix Goncourt and has published more than thirty books while working as a journalist and writing scripts for film and television.

(*Contemporary Authors Online*, Detroit: Gale, 2005, accessed 21 August 2013).

De Forest, John William (March 31, 1826–July 17, 1906)
    Known as an early literary realist, De Forest is best remembered for his novel *Miss Ravenel's Conversion from Secession to Loyalty* (New York: Harper, 1867). The son of affluent manufacturer John Hancock De Forest, De Forest attended Yale University, traveled extensively in the Near East and Europe, and had completed an important history of Connecticut Indians before he was twenty-five. During the Civil War, he organized a New Haven, Conn., company of Union volunteers that served in Louisiana and the Shenandoah Valley. Discharged for health reasons at the end of 1864, De Forest was commissioned a captain in the Veteran Reserve Corps and stationed in Washington, where he finished *Miss Ravenel's Conversion*.
(*Dictionary of Literary Biography*, vol. 12, s.v. "De Forest, John William").

De Jourlet, Marie, *see* Little, Paul H(ugo)

DeLavigne, Jeanne (?–1962)
    A New Orleans native, DeLavigne is best known for her collection of ghost stories included here.

Delmar, Viña (January 29, 1903–January 19, 1990)
    Born Alvina Croter in New York City, Delmar had a series of jobs, many of them in a Harlem theater where she engaged in both office work and as an usher before publishing her first novel, *Bad Girl* (New York: Literary Guild of America, 1928). The novel, which included premarital sex and pregnancy, was a best seller and attracted Hollywood (released under the same title by Fox in 1931). From then until the 1950s Delmar wrote or adapted roughly twenty plays for the movies, often with the editorial assistance of her husband Eugene Delmar. She published novels up until the late 1970s.
(Lesley Henderson, ed., *Twentieth-Century Romance and Historical Writers*, 3rd ed., Detroit: St. James, 1994, s.v. "Delmar, Viña").

Demarest, Donald (c.1910–?)
    Demarest mostly grew up in the Philippines with extended visits to New Orleans to visit his mother's family. He was educated in England and was a pilot in the U.S. Navy. The book for which he is included here was his only novel.
(*New York Times*, 21 March 1954).

Denbo, Anna Margaret (?–?)
    No information available.

Devereux, Mary (?–February 9, 1914)
    A daughter of General J.H. Devereux, the author was born in Marblehead, Mass. where her ancestors had settled in 1636. As an infant she moved with her family to Tennessee where she lived until the outbreak of the Civil War. As an adult she lived in Boston, Chicago, Cleveland, and New York City, but always summered in Marblehead. She published poetry and stories in newspapers and magazines as well as writing five novels.
(*New York Times*, 28 June 1902).

Dickson, Harris (July 21, 1868–March 17, 1946)
    The author of ten novels that appealed to popular notions of Southerners and African-Americans, Dickson was born in Yazoo City, Miss. and grew up in Vicksburg, Meridian, and Jackson, Miss. In his late adolescence Dickson learned shorthand and later founded a court-reporting firm. He followed up on this exposure to the legal profession by studying law at the University of Virginia. He completed his studies at Columbian (now George Washington) University when he

served in Washington, D.C. as secretary to a congressman from his home district. In the slow early years of his law practice in Vicksburg he passed the time writing and published his first novel, *The Black Wolf's Breed* (Indianapolis, Ind: Bowen-Merrill) in 1899. In 1905 he became a Vicksburg Municipal Court judge, while continuing to write and publish in national magazines. Dickson's most popular stories featured "Old Reliable," an African-American with humorous actions and sayings. During World War I, Dickson was in France as a war correspondent for Collier's and in the 1930s was a technical advisor for the Works Projects Administration.
(*Dickson (Harris) Papers, 1889–1943*, Mississippi Department of Archives and History).

Dorsey, Anna Hanson (1815–December 26, 1896)
A daughter of Rev. William McKenney, a chaplain in the U.S. Navy, Dorsey traced descent from a number of Maryland families prominent since the Colonial period. In 1837 she married Owen Dorsey, a Baltimore judge and several years later converted to Roman Catholicism. Over the next fifty years she published more than forty novels, as well as essays, poems, and plays, many of which had to do with the joys of religious conversion. She was honored by Pope Leo XIII and the University of Notre Dame (Ind.) awarded her the Laetare Medal in recognition of her writing.
(Charles Heberman, ed., *Catholic Encyclopedia*, New York: Robert Appleton, 1913, s.v. "Dorsey, Anna Hanson").

Douglas, Amanda Minnie (July 14, 1831–July 18, 1916)
Douglas was born in New York City and received her education at the City Institute; however her family moved to Newark, N.J. in 1853, and she spent the rest of her life there. Prior to the appearance of her first book in 1866, she published a number of short stories in the *Saturday Evening Post*, *New York Ledger*, and the *Lady's Friend*. From *In Trust* (Boston: Lee & Shepard, 1866), her first book, until *Red House Children Growing Up* (Boston: Lothrop, Lee, and Shepard, 1916), she published at least one book annually. *Larry* (Boston: Lee & Shepard, 1893) received the *Youth's Companion* Prize for best young people's fiction. Most of her works were for young adults. She published three extensive series: the Kathie Series, the Little Girl Series, and the Helen Grant Series. Even though her characters sometimes travel, Douglas's works celebrate the virtue of family life and all the traditional virtues with which it is associated.
(Stanley Kunitz and Howard Haycraft, eds., *American Authors, 1600–1900*, New York: H.W. Wilson, 1938, s.v. "Douglas, Amanda Minnie").

Douglas, Diana, *see* Wilkes-Hunter, Richard Albert

Dresser, Davis [Brett Halliday, pseud.] (July 31, 1904–February 4, 1977)
Known for the creation of detective character Mike Shayne, who appeared in works by Dresser from 1939 through the 1960s, and in works by other authors through the mid-1980s, Dresser wrote over seventy mystery, romance, and western novels. His work appeared under his own name, as well as the pseudonyms Asa Baker, Matthew Blood, Sylvia Carson, Kathryn Culver, Don Davis, Peter Field, Brett Halliday, Anthony Scott, Jerome Shard, Christopher Shayne, Peter Shelley, Eliot Storm, and Hal Debrett (a joint pseudonym with his first wife, Kathleen Rollins). Born in Chicago, Dresser grew up on his family's ranch near Monahans, Tex. At fourteen he misrepresented his age and joined the U.S. Army to serve on the Rio Grande border patrol. After two years his true age was discovered and he was discharged. Dresser finished high school and later attended Tri-State College (now University) in Angola, Ind., preparing to become a civil engineer, a profession in which he engaged for several years before his writing found an audience. The popularity of Dresser's Shayne extended to movies (twelve "B" films featured him), radio plays, and a 1960s television series. In 1956 Dresser and Leo Margulies founded the *Michael Shayne Mystery*

*Magazine* (later *Mike Shayne Mystery Magazine*) that was published until 1985. Dresser was a founding member of the Mystery Writers of America.
(*Dictionary of Literary Biography*, vol. 226, s.v. "Dresser, Davis").

Dugan, James (?–?)
   No information available.

Duke, Mary Kerr (?–?)
   No information available.

Dunbar-Nelson, Alice Moore (July 19, 1875–September 18, 1935)
   Born in modest circumstances in New Orleans, Dunbar-Nelson was an African-American who, even though she was able to pass as white, spent most of her life educating blacks and advocating for the rights of African-Americans. She graduated from a teacher-training program at Straight College (now Dillard University) in New Orleans in 1892 and published a book of essays, poetry, and stories in 1895 entitled *Violets and Other Tales* (Boston: Monthly Review). After moving with her family to Medford, Mass. in 1896, she began teaching in Brooklyn and later helped found the White Rose Home for Girls in Harlem. She married Paul Laurence Dunbar in 1898 and relocated to Washington, D.C. After the two separated, she moved to Wilmington, Del. and taught at the Howard High School. After Dunbar's death in 1906, Dunbar-Nelson briefly married a fellow teacher, and later wed a final time, in 1916, to journalist Robert J. Nelson, with whom she published the *Wilmington* (Del.) *Advocate*. Her political activities in the 1920s on behalf of women's and civil rights led to her dismissal from Howard High School. Subsequently, she founded and directed the Industrial School for Colored Girls (Marshalltown, Del.), 1924–28. As executive secretary of the American Inter-Racial Peace Committee, a unit of the American Friends Service Committee, she organized the National Negro Music Festival in 1929. Dunbar-Nelson has attracted renewed interest in recent years after the discovery of her diary, which provided confirmation of her lesbian relationships.
(Colin A. Palmer, ed., *Encyclopedia of African-American Culture and History*, 2nd ed., Vol. 2, Detroit: Macmillan Reference, 2006, s.v. "Dunbar-Nelson, Alice").

Dupuy, Eliza A(nn) (1814–December 29, 1880)
   The author of over twenty novels, Dupuy was a very popular mid-nineteenth century writer. She proudly traced descent from one of the oldest Huguenot families in America through her ancestor Colonel Bartholomew Dupuy, who settled on the James River in 1685. Born in Petersburg, Va. into an affluent family her father was a merchant and ship owner and the family relocated to Norfolk as his business grew. There, he experienced several reversals of fortune and the Dupuys were forced to resettle, nearly bankrupt, on the Kentucky frontier. Her family's economic situation inspired Dupuy to publish a novel at the age of fourteen to augment her father's income. Upon the death of her father, she worked as a governess in Natchez, Miss. and became part of a literary circle that included Joseph Holt Ingraham. With the support and advice of her new friends she began publishing in national magazines beginning in the late 1830s and was publishing novels with the firm Childs and Peterson by the 1840s. Although her novels were set in the South, Dupuy avoided taking sides in the slavery debate. Instead, she described Southern life and built plots around heroines, usually at the mercy of weak, irresponsible men, who nonetheless embraced their passions. On the eve of the Civil War, Dupuy relocated to Flemingsburg, Ky., close enough to Cincinnati that she was able to get stories across the Mason-Dixon Line and continue publishing in Northern magazines. After the war she had a lucrative contract with the *New York Ledger* for serials that were later published as novels. By the 1870s and 1880s, Dupuy's fiction was attacked by reformers for immorality, although she continued to publish until her death.
(*Dictionary of Literary Biography*, vol. 248, s.v. "Eliza Ann Dupuy").

Duralde, H. Eduardo (?–?)
  No information available.

Eads, William J. (?–?)
  No information available.

Easterling, Narena (Brooks) (December 12, 1890–September 26, 1957)
  Born in Zanesville, Ohio, Easterling attended Columbia University and lived most of her adult life in Jackson, Miss. She published her first novel, *Broken Lights* in 1929 (Boston: Four Seas) and over her career published five more books, the last one in 1952.
  (James B. Lloyd, ed., *Lives of Mississippi Authors, 1817–1967*, Jackson: University Mississippi, 1981, s.v. "Easterling, Narena Brooks").

Eberhart, Mignon Good (July 6, 1899–October 6, 1996)
  Born and educated in Nebraska, in 1923 Eberhart married civil engineer Alanson C. Eberhart, whose career proved influential in two ways. First, she traveled a great deal, accompanying her husband on business trips and she wrote as a distraction. Second, many of her romantic, male protagonists are civil engineers. Although she authored several novels and a number of short stories, Eberhart is best known for her mysteries that provide all of the clues needed for the reader to uncover the solution. She wrote more than sixty books during her fifty-year career.
  (Robin W. Winks and Maureen Corrigan, eds., *Mystery and Suspense Writers: The Literature of Crime, Detection, and Espionage*, New York: Charles Scribner's Sons, 1998, s.v. "Eberhart, Mignon Good").

Ebeyer, Pierre Paul (1893–October 10, 1966)
  A Cajun-American born in New Orleans whose family had a long connection to Louisiana, Ebeyer was best known for a self-published book asserting that Napoleon Bonaparte escaped from St. Helena in 1819 and lived in Europe for another sixteen years. Ebeyer lived the final years of his life in Chackbay, La.
  (*Times-Picayune*, 12 October 1966).

Edmunds, (Thomas) Murrell (March 23, 1898–August 15, 1981)
  Between 1923 and 1977 Edmunds published seventeen books, including poems, plays, short stories, and nine novels. He began writing in an era when Jim Crow laws were becoming more punitive and throughout his career advocated for the civil rights of all Americans. Born into a socially prominent family in Halifax, Va., Edmunds was educated at the University of Virginia, receiving his bachelor of laws degree in 1921. After a year of teaching in a private school, he was a deputy clerk of courts and entered private practice after his admission to the bar. When Edmunds gave up his legal career in 1926 for the life of a writer, he moved to New Orleans, where he lived until his death. In recent years, Edmunds has been rediscovered as a homosexual writer.
  (*Encyclopedia of Virginia*, Virginia Foundation for the Humanities, 2012, s.v. "Murrell Edmunds," (by Clifton W. Potter, Jr.), www.encyclopediavirginia.org, accessed 23 August 2013).

Elliott, Maud Howe (November 9, 1854–March 19, 1948)
  The daughter of two distinguished Bostonians, Samuel Gridley Howe (the founder of the Perkins Institute for the Blind) and Julia Ward Howe (abolitionist, social activist, and poet), Elliott recounted her childhood amongst distinguished intellectuals and writers in an autobiography *Three Generations* (Boston: Little, Brown, 1923). She also wrote several novels and was a newspaper correspondent. With her sister Laura E. Richards she wrote a biography of their mother that won

the first Pulitzer Prize for Biography (1917) ever awarded. She was the wife of artist John Elliott (1850–1925).
(Ann Commire and Deborah Klezmer, eds., *Women in World History: A Biographical Encyclopedia*, Waterford, Conn.: Yorkin, 1999–2002, vol. 5, s.v. "Maud Howe Elliott").

Ellis, Julie (February 21, 1933–February 2006)
    Born in Columbus, Ga., after a period working as an off-Broadway actress and playwright, Ellis began writing novels full-time, producing more than 150 family sagas and suspense and romance novels under her own name and pseudonyms. She is best known for historical romances, with her typical book being five-hundred pages long. Many of her novels are set in the first half of the twentieth century.
(Lesley Henderson, ed., *Twentieth-Century Romance and Historical Writers*, 3rd ed., London: St. James, 1994, s.v. "Ellis, Julie").

Ely, Mary S. (?–?)
    No information available.

Emery, Anne (September 1, 1907–July 4, 1987)
    A teacher in the Evanston, Ill. public schools and an author of more than thirty-six books for children, Emery was born in Fargo, N.D. She graduated from Northwestern University (BA, 1928) and completed a certificate at the University of Grenoble, France (1929). She was a wife and mother of five children and was living in Menlo Park, Calif. at the time of her death.
(*Contemporary Authors Online*, Detroit: Gale, 2008, accessed 23 August 2013).

Erskine, John (October 5, 1879–June 2, 1951)
    The author of more than fifty books, Erskine was an English professor at Columbia University for twenty-eight years and the president of the Julliard School of Music for nine years. Born in New York City, he completed a bachelor's degree (1900), master's degree (1901), and doctorate (1903) at Columbia University. In 1929 he finished a doctor of laws degree at the same institution. A talented pianist, he resumed study mid-life and performed as a soloist with the New York Symphony Orchestra and the Baltimore Civic Orchestra. Erskine wrote on a number of subjects. His fiction tended to be retellings of legends or sequels to classic works. In later life he wrote several fictionalized biographies, biographies, and four volumes of autobiography.
(*Dictionary of Literary Biography*, vol. 9, s.v. "Erskine, John").

Escoffier, Lillian Ann DuRocher (1895–c.1996)
    The author of two books, Escoffier was also known as a painter and ragtime pianist.
(*Times-Picayune*, 2 November 1996).

Erwin, Annabel, *see* Barron, Ann Forman

Evans, Lawton Bryan (October 27, 1862–April 6, 1934)
    A native of Lumpkin, Ga., Evans resided in Georgia all his life. A graduate of Emory College (AB, 1880; AM, 1881), he was superintendent of schools for Augusta, Ga. for most of his career and for many years a popular Chautauqua circuit lecturer. Evans was the author of numerous books for children, many retellings of classics and collections of stories, as well as books intended for use in the classroom.
(*National Cyclopaedia of American Biography*, vol. 13, s.v. "Evans, Lawton Bryan").

Everard, Katherine, *see* Vidal, Gore

Eyster, Nellie Blessing (1836–1922)

Temperance movement campaigner Eyster was the maternal grandmother of Paul Elder, Sr., the founder of the San Francisco bookseller and publisher Paul Elder and Company. She moved to California in the mid-1870s and published in national magazines. Her grandson published several of her books.

(http://paulelder.org, accessed 24 August 2003).

Fair, A. A., *see* Gardner, Earl Stanley

Fairbairn, Ann, *see* Tait, Dorothy

Faulkner, William (September 25, 1897–July 6, 1962)

Widely considered one of the twentieth century's finest writers, Faulkner was born in New Albany, Miss. and lived most of his life in Oxford, Miss. His native region was the basis for his fictional Yoknapatawpha County, dominated by a burgeoning "red-neck" culture represented by families like the fictional Snopes. Faulkner dropped out of high school, later became a cadet in training in the Royal Air Force of Canada during World War I by misrepresenting his birthdate and birthplace and re-spelling his family name (actually Falkner). He returned to his home state to attend the University of Mississippi for a few semesters and began publishing short stories and poetry and working on a novel. With the help of a friend, he published his first book, a volume of poetry titled *The Marble Faun* (Boston: Four Seas) in 1924. In 1925, he moved to New Orleans and became a member of a literary circle that included Sherwood Anderson, and revolved around a literary magazine titled *The Double Dealer* which published some work by Faulkner and other emerging writers who would go on to fame. Although Faulkner lived in New Orleans for a relatively brief time, he wrote a number of sketches about the city for magazines and newspapers, as well as the novel for which he is included here. Faulkner's writing career included work as a Hollywood scriptwriter, as well as the publication of fiction in national magazines. The books for which he garnered attention (winning the Nobel Prize, a Pulitzer Prize, and the National Book Award) often received poor reviews and sold poorly. Except for limited international travel and sojourns in Hollywood, he lived almost entirely in Oxford, Miss. in the antebellum house he had purchased and renamed Rowan Oak. Toward the end of his life he was writer-in-residence at the University of Virginia and willed his papers to the institution.

(*Dictionary of Literary Biography*, vol. 330, s.v. "Faulkner, William").

Feibleman, James K(ern) (July 13, 1904–September 14, 1987)

Born into a well-established New Orleans family that owned several businesses including a department store, Feibleman was educated at the Horace Mann School, the University of Virginia, and privately in Europe. He began working in family businesses in 1925 and became vice-president and general manager of James K. Feibleman Realty in 1930, a position in which he would continue until 1954. In 1943 he began teaching at Tulane University as an assistant professor of English and went on to become a distinguished philosophy professor, holding the W.R. Irby Professor of Philosophy chair. He retired and was named professor emeritus in 1975. Feibleman is best known for his presentations of philosophy for the general reader.

(*American National Biography*, vol. 7, s.v. "Feibleman, James K.").

Feibleman, Peter S. (1930–?)

A novelist and screenwriter, Feibleman was born in New York City, but raised in New Orleans. He was educated at the Carnegie Institute of Technology and Columbia University where he studied acting. In the 1940s he was a radio actor and in the 1950s a stage actor in Spain. He published his first novel in 1958 (*A Place Without Twilight*, Cleveland: World) and went on to publish five more books.

**Ferber, Edna (August 15, 1885–April 17, 1968)**

The daughter of unsuccessful, small-town merchant Jacob Charles Ferber, a Hungarian immigrant, Ferber spent most of her childhood and young adulthood in Appleton, Wis. after a number of moves. Unable to attend college due to family finances, Ferber held several jobs as a reporter before she began to sell short stories. She published her first novel in 1911 and for more than fifty years published novels, volumes of short stories, and plays that were well-received by the public but rejected by critics. Ferber lived in Chicago for a few years after her father's death in 1909, but primarily resided in New York City after 1912.
(*New York Times*, 17 April 1968).

**Ferrall, Robert J. [Pierre Beaumont, pseud.] (?–?)**

No information available.

**Finley (Witte), Glenna (June 12, 1925–?)**

An author of romance novels, mostly for the Signet Books Division of New American Library, Witte was born in Puyallup, Wash., the daughter of John Ford and Gladys Finley, and graduated from Stanford University (BA, 1945). She lived in New York City in the 1940s, working for National Broadcasting Company as a producer (1945–47); Time, Inc. as a staff member for *Life* (magazine) (1947), and as a film librarian for "March of Time" (1948–50). She married corporate executive Donald Macleod Witte in 1951 and afterwards worked as a freelance writer.
(*Contemporary Authors Online*, Detroit: Gale, 2001, accessed 1 October 2013).

**Fisher, Steve (August 29, 1912–March 27, 1980)**

An author of pulp fiction who later found success as a screenwriter for movies and television, Fisher grew up in the greater Los Angeles metropolitan area, the son of an actress. Schooled in a military academy, Fisher ran away from home at the age of sixteen to join the U.S. Navy and served on a submarine. He began writing about his adventures and when he left the service in 1932 moved to New York City to become a writer. After several years of poverty, Fisher's work was accepted for pulp magazines and he eventually introduced the hard-boiled detective character Sheridan Doome, leading to a series of pulp fiction novels. With steady income from his writing, Fisher was eventually able to move back to Los Angeles. In the 1940s and 1950s he wrote screenplays, which became his main source of income once the market for pulp fiction disappeared. By the 1970s he had found a new career writing for television, authoring scripts for some of the most popular series of the day.
(*Dictionary of Literary Biography*, vol. 226, s.v. "Fisher, Steve").

**Fleming, Rudd (November 1, 1908–October 22, 1991)**

Known as a translator of Greek classics and a professor of literature and creative writing at the University of Maryland for more than thirty-five years, Fleming was born in Bloomington, Ill. and was educated at Washington University, Illinois Wesleyan University, the Sorbonne, the University of Chicago, and Cornell University, from which he received a doctorate in comparative literature. Fleming began his teaching career at Newcomb College, where he taught from 1934 to 1943. He served in Navy intelligence during World War II. In 1949 Fleming collaborated with Ezra Pound in translating Euripides' *Electra* (published by Princeton). Later, Fleming translated Sophocles' *Seven Against Thebes*.
(*The Washington* [D.C.] *Post*, 24 October 1991).

**Fortmayer, Aenida V. Gonzales (December 23, 1918–March 22, 2006)**

A life-long resident of Louisiana, Fortmayer was a member of the Women's Army Air Corps during World War II, attaining the rank of sergeant of the 1500th Army Air Force Base Unit. She married Theodore J. Fortmayer, Jr. She and her sister, both widowed, achieved regional fame late

in life as the characters named the "Boomtown Girls" promoting the Boomtown Casino in Harvey, La. on billboards and in television commercials.
(http://files.usgwarchives.net/la/orleans/obits/2006/2006-03.txt, accessed 28 August 2013).

Foster, John T(homas) (July 19, 1925–?)
    Born in Chicago, Foster attended the University of Wisconsin for a year before active duty in the U.S. Naval Reserve in the Pacific 1943–46. After the war he completed a bachelor's degree at Florida Southern College in Lakeland, Fla. (1950). A journalist, Foster worked for papers in Lakeland, Fla.; Wilmington, N.C.; and Deer Park, N.Y. He was a staff writer and assistant editor on the *Dixie Roto* (New Orleans) from 1955–66. In later life he was assistant to the director for public relations at Long Island University (1968–70) and a technical writer at the New York Ocean Science Laboratory in Montauk, N.Y. (1970–75). Most of his fourteen books are either adult non-fiction or fictional works for children.

Gardner, Erle Stanley [A.A. Fair, pseud.] (July 17, 1889–March 11, 1970)
    Although he was born in Malden, Mass., Gardner's father was a mining engineer and his youth was spent in remote parts of California, Oregon, and the Klondike Territory. The family eventually settled in Oroville, Calif. and Gardner finished school at Palo Alto High School. He was briefly enrolled at Valparaiso (Ind.) University, but was expelled for fighting and for a time boxed and organized boxing competitions. While working in law offices as a typist he studied law and was admitted to the California Bar in 1911. For roughly the next twenty years he practiced law and gained a reputation as a litigator for his knowledge of the law and his ability to effectively employ the theatrical aspects of court trials for the benefit of his clients, often impoverished or disenfranchised members of ethnic minorities. In 1948 he founded the Court of Last Resort, a nationwide organization of attorneys who took on difficult defenses. He began writing short fiction for pulp magazines in the 1920s, experimenting with several genres before the publication of his first Perry Mason novel, featuring a tenacious defense attorney who was a skilled detective with superb courtroom abilities. He quickly received a proposal for a series featuring Mason and began publishing books that attracted a huge audience. His lifetime sales topped two hundred million, making him the best-selling American author of all time. In addition, several of his novels were filmed as movies and popular radio and television series featured Perry Mason.
(*New York Times*, 12 March 1970).

Garfield, Dick (?–?)
    No information available.

Gayarré, Charles (January 9, 1805–February 11, 1895)
    Considered Louisiana's most important historian, Gayarré was the grandson of Etienne de Boré, the first successful granulated sugar producer in Louisiana, and was born at Boré plantation which was later incorporated into Audubon Park. After completing his education at the College of Orleans, Gayarré studied law in Philadelphia, returning to join the Louisiana bar in 1829. He was elected to his first term in the state legislature in 1830 and was frequently a member of that body before the Civil War, over time serving as attorney general and secretary of state. During his time in the latter office, he devoted a good deal of effort to improving the state library. Between 1830 and 1866 he wrote the histories for which he is known, as well as several novels. Although he supported the Confederacy, investing all of his significant family fortune in Confederate bonds, he unsuccessfully navigated the shoals of politics and by the end of the war no longer had any support for public office. His fortune lost, he devoted himself to earning a modest living from writing dramas and romances.
(*Dictionary of Literary Biography*, vol. 30, s.v. "Gayarré, Charles").

Genois, Renald H(enry) (October 16, 1918–October 27, 1991)
    No additional information available.

Gerson, Noel Bertram [Carter A. Vaughan, pseud.] (November 6, 1914–November 20, 1988)
    An author of popular fiction under his own name and eleven pseudonyms, Gerson was born in Chicago and educated at the University of Chicago (AB, 1934; MA, 1935). During World War II he served in U.S. Army Military Intelligence. He began work as a journalist at the *Chicago Herald-Examiner* in 1931, but broadcast journalism soon became his focus and he served as the executive of WGN-Radio (Chicago) from 1936–41 and was a scriptwriter for national radio and television networks from 1936–51. He began writing full-time after the publication of his second novel in 1951, specializing in biographies, historical novels, westerns, and books for children, producing more than one hundred titles.
(*Contemporary Authors Online*, Detroit: Gale, 2001, accessed 27 August 2013).

Gibbs, George (March 8, 1870–October 10, 1942)
    A native of New Orleans, Gibbs was educated at the U.S. Naval Academy, but opted for an art career, studying at the Corcoran School of Art in Washington, D.C., and at the New York Art Students' League. His continued interest in military history influenced his choice of subjects and he completed several paintings depicting historic naval battles. In the period 1901–19 he had an active career as a book illustrator. He was also the author of more than forty novels, mostly mysteries and romances, for many of which he provided illustrations. He was active over a forty-year period from 1900–41.
(*Contemporary Authors Online*, Detroit: Gale, 2003, accessed 28 August 2013).

Grau, Shirley Ann (July 8, 1929–?)
    A New Orleans native and graduate of the Ursuline Academy and Newcomb College (BA, 1942), Grau is the wife of James K. Feibleman, another author included in this volume. The couple married in 1955, the same year that Grau published her first book, a collection of short stories entitled *The Black Prince* (New York: Knopf). The work received a good deal of positive critical attention; her first novel, *The Hard Blue Sky* (New York: Knopf, 1958), published a few years later, garnered more mixed reviews. Grau has gone on to publish five additional novels and two more volumes of short stories, earning her a reputation as a Southern writer, continuing in the local color tradition with a focus on character studies.
(Taryn Benbow-Pfalzgraf, ed., *American Women Writers: A Critical Reference Guide from Colonial Times to the Present*, vol. 2, 2nd ed., Detroit: St. James, 2000, s.v. "Grau, Shirley Ann").

Gray, Charles Wright, *see* Grayson, Charles (Wright)

Grayson, Charles (Wright) (August 15, 1903–May 4, 1973)
    Son of Lucien Gray, as an adult Grayson legally changed his name. A screenwriter, short story anthologist, and novelist, Grayson graduated from the University of California, Los Angeles (BA, 1926) and subsequently studied at the Sorbonne and Harvard University. He published seven novels, but was best known for his more than twenty screenplays that included *The Barbarian and the Geisha* (Twentieth-Century Fox, 1958) and *Battle Hymn* (Universal International Pictures, 1957).
(*New York Times*, 9 May 1973).

Greene, Frances Nimmo (April 5, 1867–December 9, 1937)
    Daughter of Methodist clergyman Thomas Finley Greene, the author was born in Tuscaloosa, Ala. and after attending Tuscaloosa Female College became principal of Lafayette School, a public grammar school in Montgomery. She later taught in Birmingham at the Athenaeum, an all-

girl's private school. Between 1901 and 1920 she published a series of books for children and novels for adults. Several of the novels were made into movies and as she grew older she focused on writing plays and was active in the Birmingham Little Theater. She was director of the Southern Play Bureau of the Federal Theater Project in the years before her death.
(Alabama Humanities Foundation, *Encyclopedia of Alabama*, http://www.encyclopediaofalabama. org/face/Article.jsp?id=h-2361, accessed 28 August 2013).

Grethe, James (March 22, 1935–)
A native of New Orleans, Grethe graduated from Louisiana State University (BA, 1954) and completed a year of graduate work in engineering before serving in the U.S. Air Force from 1955 to 1963, stationed in Madison, Wisc. and for four years in Germany. After working as an aerospace engineer for the Chrysler Corporation in New Orleans from 1963 to 1969, he helped found Sally Beauty Company in the city, which was later sold to Alberto-Culver Corporation in the early 1970s when Grethe moved to Atlanta and engaged in a period of entrepreneurial activity, founding, establishing, and selling small companies. Since 2006, he has lived on Amelia Island, Fla. Grethe began writing in college, completing an unpublished novel, continued writing in the Air Force, and wrote the novel for which he is included here while building the Sally Beauty Company. In recent years, he has published a spy novel and a volume of gory re-writes of traditional nursery rhymes with the print-on-demand publisher, Trafford, based in Bloomington, Ind.
(James Grethe, email message to James A. Kaser, October 21, 2013).

Grice, Julia (May 28, 1940–)
Historical romance author Grice was born in Battle Creek, Mich., and educated at Albion College (BA, 1962).
(*Contemporary Authors Online*, Detroit: Gale, 2001, accessed 28 August 2013).

Gross, Josiah (January 9, 1862–March 26, 1928)
A New Orleans attorney who specialized in pension law, often on behalf of widows, Gross was born in Drake, Mo., the son of a physician who had been a military surgeon during the Civil War. Gross obtained a bachelors degree from Columbia (Mo.) University and taught school for several years before enrolling at Tulane University from which he received a bachelor of laws degree. He later received a master of laws degree from Loyola University in New Orleans. He was admitted to National Pension Law practice in 1908 and admitted to practice before the Supreme Court of the United States in 1912. In 1892, he married Caroline Zilch, the daughter of a German immigrant brewer of New Orleans.
(William Richard Cutter, ed., *American Biography: A New Cyclopedia*, vol. 47, New York: Published under the direction of the American Historical Society, 1916, s.v. "Gross, Josiah").

Gunter, Archibald Clavering (October 25, 1847–February 24, 1907)
A popular playwright and novelist of the last decades of the nineteenth century, Gunter was born in Liverpool, England and emigrated with his parents when still a child. He grew up in California and graduated from the University of California, School of Mines. He worked as a civil engineer for Central Pacific Railroad and later had positions in the mining industry and as a stockbroker in San Francisco before moving to New York City in 1879. He was the founder and proprietor of Home Publishing Company, which issued his novels and published *Gunter's Magazine*, featuring short stories and work in serial format.
(*New York Times*, 26 February 1907).

Guyol, Louise Hubert (February 19, 1879–November 21, 1973)
Born in Baton Rouge, La., Guyol edited newspaper columns for the *Boston Evening Transcript* and was a contributing author to the *Atlantic Monthly* and *Americana* (later *Journal of the*

*American Historical Society*). She was the author of several novels, writing sometimes under the alias of Guy Hubert. Guyol was active in the animal rights movement as a delegate to the Louisiana State Society for the Prevention of Cruelty to Animals and to the American Humane Education Society.

(*Papers of Louise Guyol, 1881–1960*, Operational Archives Branch, Naval Historical Center, Washington Navy Yard, Washington, D.C., http://www.history.navy.mil/ar/golf/guyol_l.htm, accessed 5 September 2013).

Hagen, Annunciata (July 22, 1888–February 7, 1983)
     Born in Tailors Creek, Ohio, Hagen entered St. Benedict's Convent in St. Joseph, Minn. in 1905 and made her perpetual vows July 11, 1909. She taught music for fifty-eight years in Minnesota schools. The book for which she is included here was her only novel.
(*St. Cloud* [Minn.] *Times*, 8 February 1983).

Hailey, Arthur (April 5, 1920–November 24, 2004)
     Canadian writer Hailey is known for creating meticulously researched suspense novels that sold millions of copies and were usually adapted for television or film. Born in Luton, England, Hailey enlisted in the Royal Air Force during World War II and began publishing short fiction during his military service. He immigrated to Canada after the war, settling in Toronto where he worked in editorial positions for a trade publication until he sold a screenplay to Canadian Broadcasting Corp., which led to jobs writing for television networks. After 1959 he began writing novels full-time.
(*New York Times*, 26 November 2004).

Hale, Edward Everett, Sr. (April 3, 1822–June 10, 1909)
     The author of hundreds of literary works, including biographies, essays, novels, sermons, and travel books, Hale was a scion of one of Boston's most prominent families, a graduate of Harvard University (AB, 1839; AM, 1842; STD, 1879) and an ordained Unitarian minister.
(*Dictionary of Literary Biography*, vol. 74, s.v. "Hale, Edward Everett").

Hales, Carol (1916–?)
     No information available.

Hall, Georgette Brockman (November 24, 1915–?)
     The daughter of engineer Thomas Harry Brockman and his schoolteacher wife Gertrude, Hall was born in New Orleans, but lived most of her life in Bay St. Louis, Miss. She was the wife of college professor Norman Bernard Hall (married 1938). A graduate of Tulane University (BA, 1937), she was an English teacher in Bay St. Louis public schools from 1948–62. She began working as a librarian in St. Bernard Parish public schools in Chalmette, La. in 1962 and received a master's degree in library science from George Peabody College for Teachers in 1966. She was active in a number of greater New Orleans clubs. Both of her novels are included here.
(James B. Lloyd, ed., *Lives of Mississippi Authors, 1817–1967*, Jackson: University of Mississippi, 1981, s.v. "Hall, Georgette Brockman").

Hallbing, Kjell [Louis Masterson, pseud.] (November 5, 1934–May 6, 2004)
     Norwegian author Hallbing is best known for his series of books featuring Morgan Kane, a Texas Ranger. Between 1966 and 1978 he published eighty-three Kane books that sold twenty million copies worldwide. Before writing full time he was a bank clerk. Hallbing authored more than twenty other books outside of the Kane series that were still mostly westerns. He was born in Bærum, Norway and died in Tønsberg, Norway.

Halliday, Brett, *see* Dresser, Davis

Hallman, Ruth (June 30, 1929–?)
    Children's author Hallman was born in Hertford, N.C., the daughter of school superintendent Edgar E. Bundy and his wife Mattie (née Reid). A 1951 graduate of Winthrop College (BA), she married Robert E. Hallman, an advisory engineer in 1952. Although periodically a schoolteacher, Hallman mostly worked as an executive secretary and volunteer with literacy programs.
(*Contemporary Authors Online*, Detroit: Gale, 2001, accessed 28 August 2013).

Hamilton, Harry (1896–?)
    No information available.

Hammond, Hilda Phelps (1890–October 20, 1951)
    A New Orleans native, Hammond was the daughter of Ashton Phelps, the first president of the board of the *Times-Picayune*. A graduate of Newcomb College, where she was president of the class of 1909, Hammond earned a master's degree in English from Tulane University. During World War I she chaired the Woman's Committee of the Council of National Defense. In 1917 she married Arthur Hammond, an attorney with the New Orleans Dock Board. The Phelps family controlled the *Times-Picayune* during Huey P. Long's rise to power and often took editorial stances in opposition to him. As one form of retribution, he saw that Arthur Hammond was fired from his state position in 1930, a serious economic reversal. Hilda Phelps Hammond organized a group of New Orleans society women to call for Long's removal from the U.S. Senate. Although she gained a national public forum, nothing came of the effort, however many of the women Hammond brought together went on to found the League of Women Voters, the Independent Women's Organization, and other political organizations. Hammond wrote about her anti-Long campaign (*Let Freedom Ring*, New York: Farrar and Rinehart, 1936), although she was mainly an author of books for children.
(David Johnson, ed., *KnowLA Encyclopedia of Louisiana*, Louisiana Endowment for the Humanities, s.v. "Hilda Phelps Hammond," http://www.knowla.org/entry/863/, accessed 28 August 2013).

Hancock, Frances Dean, *see* Judson, Jeanne

Hancock, H(arrie) Irving (January 16, 1868–March 12, 1922)
    A trained chemist and working journalist who wrote more than fifty books for boys, Hancock was born in Massachusetts, but spent most of his adult life in New York State. He was a reporter for the *Boston Globe* from 1885–90 and served as a war correspondent in Cuba and the Philippines during the Spanish-American War. He wrote several books based on his war experiences, as well as volumes on physical fitness, etiquette, the history of West Point, and jiu-jitsu. However, he mostly wrote for boys in a number of series under various pseudonyms. His best-known work is a multi-volume futurist account of the invasion of the United States by Germany. In addition to his writing career, in 1908 he founded the Ferguson-Hancock Laboratories with Prof. George A Ferguson.
(*Encyclopedia of Science Fiction*, s.v. "Irving H. Hancock," http://www.sf-encyclopedia.com/entry/hancock_h_irving, accessed 28 August 2013).

Handl, Irene (December 27, 1902?–November 29, 1987)
    British character actress Handl was born in Maida Vale, London to a Viennese banker father and aristocratic French mother. At age thirty-six she trained as an actress and made her London stage debut in 1937. She went on to appear in more than one-hundred films in supporting roles,

often as landladies, servants, mothers, or grandmothers. She also appeared in guest cameos on a number of television series. She was the author of two novels.
(*New York Times*, 30 Nov 1987).

Hannis, Margaret (?–?)
    No information available.

Harrington, Dare (?–?)
    No information available.

Harris, Thomas (April 11, 1940–?)
    Best known for novels that became screenplays for major films starring Jodi Foster and Anthony Hopkins, Harris was born in Jackson, Tenn. and grew up in Rich, Miss. A graduate of Baylor University (BA, English, 1964), he was a reporter for the *Waco* (Tex.) *Tribune-Herald* before moving to New York City in 1968, where he worked for the Associated Press until 1974. The author of five books, all of which have been made into movies, Harris is best known for his trilogy of works featuring a cannibalistic serial killer, Hannibal Lector.
(David Pringle, ed., *St. James Guide to Horror, Ghost, and Gothic Writers*, Detroit: St. James, 1998, s.v. "Harris, Thomas").

Harrison, Edith Ogden (November 16, 1861–May 22, 1955)
    Born on her mother's plantation in Thibodaux Lafourche Parish, La., Harrison spent most of her childhood in New Orleans (her family summered at Bay St. Louis). She was the daughter of Judge Robert Nash Ogden of the Louisiana Court of Appeals. A children's book author and wife of Carter Harrison, Jr., five term mayor of Chicago, Harrison published the first of fifteen books for children in 1902. Family friend L. Frank Baum began working with her on dramatizations with the idea of establishing a children's theatre in Chicago, although the project did not come to fruition.
(Mrs. Carter H. Harrison, *Strange to Say—Recollections of Persons and Events in New Orleans and Chicago*, Chicago: A. Kroch, 1949, 188).

Harrison, James Albert (August 21, 1848–January 31, 1911)
    A distinguished scholar of Romance and Germanic Languages who played an important role in higher education in the South after the Civil War, Harrison was born in Pass Christian, Miss., but grew up in New Orleans. Harrison was the son of Jilson Payne Harrison, an influential lawyer and planter and had distinguished ancestry in both his mother and father's family. He began his education at the University of Virginia, which he attended from 1866–68 and then continued his studies in German universities through 1871. Returning to the South when a new emphasis was being placed on modern languages and literatures over classical studies, Harrison quickly built his academic reputation, first as Professor of Modern Language at Randolph Macon College (1871–76). In 1876 he became Professor of English and Modern Languages at Washington and Lee University. He left in 1895 for his alma mater, the University of Virginia, to serve as Professor of Romance and Germanic Languages and in 1897 was named Head of the School of Teutonic Languages. Most of his literary output consisted of essays and academic studies.
(James B. Lloyd, ed. *Lives of Mississippi Authors, 1817–1967*, Jackson: University of Mississippi, 1981, s.v. "Harrison, James Albert").

Harrison, William (1933–?)
    No information available.

Hay, Corinne (?–?)
   No information available.

Hedden, Worth Tuttle (January 10, 1896–September 14, 1985)
   An advocate for the rights of minorities and women, Hedden was born in Raleigh, N.C., the daughter of a Protestant minister. She graduated from Trinity College (now Duke University) in 1916 and moved to New York City to attend Columbia University School of Journalism (1917–18). During this time she was an assistant to Socialist leader Norman Thomas and the following year to author/educator Walter B. Pitken. In 1919 she married Walter Page Hedden a one-time director of port development for the Port Authority of New York City, who later became an independent consultant on port development with cities around the world. Hedden was the author of three novels and a memoir and was a contributor to short story anthologies and an author of stories and articles for national magazines, including *American Scholar*, *Atlantic*, *Harper's*, *New Republic*, *New York Times*, *New York Herald Tribune*, *Saturday Review*, and *World Tomorrow*.
(*New York Times*, 21 September 1985).

Heinz, W(ilfred) C(harles) (Richard Hooker, joint pseud. with Richard Hornberger) (January 11, 1915–February 27, 2008)
   Best known as a sports journalist, Heinz was a forerunner of the New Journalism that combined traditional reporting with the style of fiction. He was born in Mount Vernon, N.Y., graduated from Middlebury College (Vt.) (AB, 1937), and began his career at *The Sun* (New York) in 1937 as a copy boy. From 1943 to the end of World War II he was a correspondent in the European theater and when he returned to New York he joined *The Sun's* sports department, writing feature stories and athlete profiles, mostly about boxers. When *The Sun* ceased publication he became a freelance writer, mostly publishing sports stories in magazines, but also beginning to write books. In addition to novels featuring sports figures, he aided Vince Lombardi with a memoir and collaborated with H. Richard Hornberger to write *M.A.S.H.* (New York: Morrow, 1968) under the joint pseudonym Richard Hooker.
(*New York Times*, 28 February 2008).

Hicks, John (Kenneth) (May 19, 1918–?)
   Broadcaster, photographer, and writer for film, radio, and television, Hicks was born in Kansas City, Mo. and studied at the University of Texas (1936–40). Before serving in the U.S. Army Special Services (1943–45) he was a radio broadcaster in Austin and Fort Worth and a program manager at KTBC, Austin from 1942-43. His wife, Regina (Cassidy), was also an author and he collaborated with her on several books.
(*Contemporary Authors Online*, Detroit: Gale, 2002, accessed 28 August 2013).

Higginbotham, (Prieur) Jay (July 16, 1937–?)
   Born in Pascagoula, Miss. and a graduate of the University of Mississippi (BA, 1960), Higginbotham undertook graduate study at Hunter College of the City University of New York and American University before working as an assistant clerk in the Mississippi State House of Representatives (1955–61). He taught in the Mobile, Ala. Public Schools from 1962 to1973 and in 1973 became the head of the local history department at the Mobile Public Library. In 1983 he was the founding director of the Mobile Municipal Archives, becoming director emeritus in 2001. The author of four well-regarded history books about Mobile and its vicinity, published between 1966 and 1977, Higginbotham also published a memoir of his 1966 trip on the Trans-Siberian Railway in 1966 that was part of a journey around the world, during which he visited forty-two countries. An advocate of international understanding, he partnered with poet Yevgeny Yevtushenko in 1986

to create a sister city relationship between Mobile and the Russian city of Rostov. He has also advocated for improved relations with Cuba and worked with the Red Cross.
(James B. Lloyd, ed., *Lives of Mississippi Authors, 1817–1967*, Jackson: University of Mississippi, 1981, s.v. "Higginbotham, Prieur Jay").

Hills, Alfred C. (?–?)
    Hills was a journalist who was employed by the *New York Evening Post* before the Civil War. During the war he was a Lieutenant-Colonel in the Fourth Louisiana Native Guards, a Union regiment formed of African-Americans commanded by white officers. A Civil War correspondent, for much of the war he was based in New Orleans and associated with newspapers that had been confiscated by the Union Army, including the *Daily Delta*, (renamed *The Era*), and the *New Orleans True Delta*.
(*Times-Picayune*, 25 March 1865).

Hilton, Alice Howard (?–?)
    Although born in the South, Hilton, a journalist and writer, mostly lived in New York City and San Francisco. She was active in the American Author's Guild and the Women's Press Club.
(*Times-Picayune*, 22 April 1897).

Hoerner, Aline (?–?)
    No information available.

Holcombe, William H(enry) (May 29, 1825–November 28, 1893)
    A homeopathic surgeon and Swedenborgian, Holcombe was born in Lynchburg, Va., the son of physician William James Holcombe. The senior Holcombe was an abolitionist and Methodist minister who freed his slaves and moved his family to Indiana to extricate them from the influence of slave culture. His son studied study at the College of William and Mary and the University of Virginia, and began traditional medical practice in Cincinnati, Ohio, before an epidemic of Asiatic cholera interested him in homeopathy. He relocated to Natchez, Miss. in 1852, where he went into partnership with a Dr. Davis and they were subsequently appointed physicians and surgeons to the Mississippi State Hospital. Holcombe joined the Confederate cause and after the war moved to New Orleans where he lived for the rest of his life.
(*William H. Holcombe Diary and Autobiography*, Southern Historical Collection, The Wilson Library, University of North Carolina, Chapel Hill, http://www2.lib.unc.edu/mss/inv/h/Holcombe, William_H.html, accessed, 28 August 2013).

Holland, Rupert Sargent (October 18, 1878–May 3, 1952)
    Born in Louisville, Ky., Holland lived most of his life in Philadelphia where his father was first a chemistry professor and then the dean of Jefferson Medical College. Holland was a 1900 graduate of Harvard College, where he was active on *The Crimson, Lampoon*, and *Advocate*. In 1903, he received his law degree from the University of Pennsylvania and established a law office, eventually becoming the head of the Legal Aid society of Philadelphia. Beginning in 1913, he devoted himself full-time to writing, eventually publishing more than fifty books for children.
(*New York Times*, 5 May 1952).

Homes, Mary Sophia Shaw [Millie Mayfield, pseud.] (c.1830–1872)
    Born Sophia Shaw in Frederick County, Md., she moved as a child to New Orleans with her mother and siblings after the death of her father Thomas Shaw. She was briefly married to Norman Rodgers, who died in his youth. In 1864 she married New Orleans blacksmith Luther Homes (1814–1881). She had begun writing articles, essays, and poems for *The Daily Crescent* (New

Orleans) in 1857 and later wrote for the *True Delta* (New Orleans), as well. She published two novels and a book of poetry.
(Homes Family Genealogy Notes, http://www.werelate.org/wiki/Person:Mary_Shaw_%2833%29, accessed 28 August 2013).

Hooker, Richard [joint pseudonym], *see* Heinz, W(ilfred) C(harles) and Richard Hornberger

Hornberger, Richard [Richard Hooker, joint pseud. with W(ilfred) C(harles) Heinz] (c. 1923–November 4, 1997)
      Born in Trenton, N.J., Hornberger lived most of his life in Maine, where he had an active medical practice in Waterville for many years. He served as a U.S. Army doctor in Korea with the 8055th Mobile Army Surgical Hospital (MASH) and wrote three novels based on his experiences using the pseudonym Richard Hooker. The characters he created were used in additional novels, co-authored with W(ilfred) C(harles) Heinz under the same Richard Hooker pseudonymn. A film version of his first novel *MASH* (Morrow, 1968) was directed by Robert Altman with a screenplay by Ring Lardner, Jr., starring Donald Sutherland and Elliott Gould (Twentieth Century Fox, 1970). A television series, M*A*S*H, aired on CBS from 1972–1982.
(*New York Times*, 7 November 1997).

Houston, Margaret Bell (1876–June 22, 1966)
      The author was born at Cedar Bayou, Tex., the daughter of Sam Houston, Jr. (son of Sam Houston). She began writing poetry as a child and after studying at St Mary's College (Dallas, Tex.), the American Academy of Dramatic Arts, and Columbia University, her first book of poetry appeared in 1907. She published two more volumes of poetry and one of her poems won the annual award of the Poetry Society of America. Houston also wrote fiction and between 1914 and 1958 published thirteen novels. Her poetry, serials, and short stories appeared in nationwide magazines and newspapers for over fifty years.
(William E. Bard, "Houston, Margaret Bell," *Handbook of Texas Online*, http://tshaonline.org/handbook/online/articles/fho71, accessed 28 August 2013).

Huff, Lawrence (?–?)
      No information available.

Huff, T(om) E(lmer) [Jennifer Wilde, pseud.] (January 8, 1938–January 16, 1990)
      The author of best-selling gothic and historical romance novels, Huff was born in Tarrant County, Tex. and graduated from Texas Wesleyan College in 1960. His first career was as a teacher at R.L. Paschal High School in Fort Worth, Tex. He published his first gothic romance novel in 1968 as Edwina Marlow, one of several pseudonyms he employed as market demands changed. Starting in 1976, he transitioned to writing erotic historical romance novels, and from then on mostly published under the name Jennifer Wilde. In all, he wrote more than twenty-three novels. His books have reached the *New York Times* paperback bestseller list and one of his titles sold more than 2.5 million copies.
(*Contemporary Authors Online*, Detroit: Gale, 2002, accessed 29 August 2013).

Imbert, Dennis I(gnatius) (February 1, 1869–May 19, 1947)
      Born in Caracas, Venezuela, the son of a prosperous mixed-race merchant, Imbert arrived in the United States around 1895 and settled in California in 1896. He married Alta Royer, a white woman from Missouri, and pursued a career as a hotel manager. The couple had one daughter. They subsequently separated and Imbert relocated to New Orleans where he worked as a book-

keeper and clerk. In the final years of his life he was employed by the Venus Mutual Benevolent Society Community Center. His longest residence in the city was at 929 Barracks Street.
("The Stranger Within Our Gates," http://www.creolegen.org/2013/05/06/the-stranger-within-our-gates-dennis-i-imbert/, accessed 12 December 2013).

Ingraham, Joseph Holt (January 26, 1809–December 18, 1860)
        The grandson of a shipbuilder and merchant, Ingraham was born in Portland, Me. and traveled to Buenos Aires as a sailor on one of his grandfather's ships before he was seventeen. Although it was later claimed that he attended Bowdoin College and subsequently Yale University, no record substantiates his attendance. He relocated to the South in 1830, settling in Natchez, Miss., and taught at Jefferson College (Washington, Miss.). He published his first book in 1835. Over the next ten years he published a number of serial novels in newspapers, some of which were later gathered as books. In the 1840s he married Mary Brooks, the daughter of a wealthy planter and a cousin of Phillips Brooks, and moved to Nashville, Tenn. in 1849, establishing a female seminary. His brother, the Rev. J.P.T. Ingraham, was in Nashville as the rector of Christ's Church and later Ingraham became a deacon in Trinity Episcopal Church in Natchez. In 1852 Ingraham was ordained an Episcopal priest in St. Andrews Church in Jackson, Miss. and later served as a rector in Mobile, Ala.; Aberdeen, Miss.; and Riverside, Tenn. He took up his final appointment at Holly Springs, Miss. in 1858. His increasing focus on religion and theology influenced his writing and in the 1850s and 1860s he primarily published Bible stories in popularized novel format.
(James Grant Wilson and John Fiske, eds., *Appleton's Cyclopedia of American Biography*, vol. 3, New York: D. Appleton, 1889-90, s.v. "Ingraham, Joseph Holt").

Ingraham, Colonel Prentiss (December 28, 1843–August 16, 1904)
        The son of Joseph Holt Ingraham, included above, Ingraham was born in Natchez, Miss. and educated at St. Timothy's Military Academy (Catonsville, Md.) and Jefferson College (Washington, Miss.). He was attending Mobile (Ala.) Medical College at the outbreak of the Civil War when he enlisted in the Confederate Army. After the war he became a mercenary soldier, fighting with Juárez against the French in Mexico; for Austria on General Hoffmann's staff in the Battle of Sadowa in the Austro-Prussian War; against the Turks in Crete; in the Khedive's army in Egypt; and as a ship's captain in the Cuban Revolution against Spain. When he returned to the United States he located himself on the Western frontier and worked as a scout. In this way, he became friends with Buffalo Bill Cody and eventually worked to publicize Buffalo Bill's Wild West Show and write dime novels featuring Buffalo Bill. He had begun writing adventure novels in 1869 and developed several series in addition to Buffalo Bill, including the Buck Taylor series, Merle Monte series, and Dick Doom series. He used nine pseudonyms and supposedly produced six hundred novels, mostly westerns and tales of piracy, before his death at the Beauvoir Confederate Home in Biloxi, Miss.
(George Perkins, et al., *Benet's Readers' Encyclopedia of American Literature*, N.Y.: Harper Collins, 1991, s.v. "Ingraham, Colonel Prentiss").

Irish, William, *see* Woolrich, Cornell [George] [Hopley-]

Isham, Frederic Stewart (March 29, 1865–September 6, 1922)
        The author of short stories, plays, and eighteen novels, several of which were made into movies, Isham was born in Detroit, Mich. and began his career as a reporter with the *Detroit Free Press*. His stories were printed in *Harper's Monthly* and *The Popular Magazine* and most of his novels were published by Bobbs-Merrill. He had several plays produced in New York that had long runs and his novel *Nothing But the Truth* (Indianapolis, Ind.: Bobbs-Merrill, 1914) filmed

originally in 1920 (Holmes Productions), was made into movies a total of six times; twelve of his other novels were also made into films.
(*New York Times*, 9 September 1922).


Jackson, Charles Tenney (October 15, 1874–1955)

Born in St. Louis, Mo., Jackson was the son of a military officer and was raised in a series of forts until he was orphaned. He was sent to live with an aunt and uncle in the Nebraska Territory around 1879 when he was eight years old, an experience he recorded in a memoir (*Buffalo Wallow*. Indianapolis, Ind.: Bobbs-Merrill, 1953). An adventurous young man, he fought in the Spanish-American War and later explored the Mississippi Delta by pirogue around 1913. He worked as a newspaperman in Chicago and San Francisco and was eventually an editor of the *Modesto* (Calif.) *News*. The author of more than ten novels, four of his works were made into movies between 1917 and 1927.
(Kevin Starr, *Golden Dreams: California in an Age of Abundance, 1950–1963*, New York: Oxford University Press, 2009).


Jacobs, Howard (June 23, 1908–April 30, 1985)

A reporter for the *Times-Picayune*, Jacobs was born in Lake Charles, La. and lived most of his life in New Orleans. He started working at the *Times-Picayune* in 1938 as a reporter and features writer and in 1948 initiated "Remoulade," a popular column depicting Acadian life and culture that he wrote for more than twenty-five years. He was also a correspondent for *Newsweek* from 1952–74. He was an active member of the New Orleans Press Club of which he was a sometime president and from which he received more than thirty-five awards.
(*Contemporary Authors Online*, Detroit: Gale, 2001, s.v. "Jacobs, Howard").


Jahncke, Carol Saunders (July 21, 1929–January 1, 2008)

The author of three books, Jahncke was born in Covington, La., where she lived most of her life. She was an owner of small-businesses including a bookstore and was an enthusiastic promoter of Covington.


James, Samuel Humphreys [A Man o' the Town, pseud.] (December 12, 1857–?)

A Louisiana planter, James was born at Cottage Oaks Plantation in Madison Parish (La.), the son of Dr. D.H. and Susan Edith (Barnes) James. Descended from a long-settled Virginia family, James studied in that state at Emory and Henry College (1872–76) and Roanoke College (1876–78). He also studied in Germany at Heidelberg University (1878–79) and the University of Berlin (1879–80) before continuing study in the United States at the University of Virginia (1880–81; 1882–83). He received his bachelor of law degree from Tulane University in 1884 and for the rest of his life owned and managed a plantation at Mound in Madison Parish, La. He was the author of two novels.
(Rossiter Johnson and John Howard Brown, eds., *Twentieth Century Biographical Dictionary of Notable Americans*, Boston: Biographical Society, 1904, s.v. "James, Samuel Humphreys").


Jamison, C(ecilia) V(iets) Dakin Hamilton (1837–April 11, 1909)

The daughter of Viets Orlando and Elizabeth Bruce Dakin, Jamison enjoyed an affluent childhood and was educated at private schools in Boston, New York, and Paris. She was an accomplished portraitist and shortly after her first marriage to George Hamilton circa 1860, she relocated to study art in Rome for three years. There she met Henry Wadsworth Longfellow, who edited a manuscript for her first novel and helped her get the work published. Her second marriage in 1878, to New Orleans lawyer Samuel Jamison, took her to the South where most of her books are set, earning her the reputation of a local-color writer. She was a major figure in New Orleans literary culture and frequented the literary salon of Mollie Moore Davis (see above). In the 1870s and

1880s she was a contributor to national magazines and wrote several novels. However, she is best known for books for children published in the 1880s and 1890s.
(*Dictionary of American Biography*, vol. 5, s.v. "Jamison, Cecilia Viets Dakin Hamilton").

Janas, Frankie-Lee [Salliee O'Brien, pseud.] (November 19, 1908–February 15, 2002)
    Born in Appleton, Mo., Janas was a prolific author of romance novels under the pseudonyms Marie Eyre, Francesca Greer, Stuart Jason, and Salliee O'Brien. She majored in rhetoric and writing at the University of Texas and began publishing short stories and writing for a radio show shortly after her marriage to Thurlow Weed. She relocated to Hollywood, Calif. in 1948 and divorced soon afterwards. She was later married to Leroy Zelley (d. 1958) and Eugene Janas, a reporter for the *Fort Lauderdale* (Fla.) *News* (d. 1998). She wrote several series, one of which deals with Cajun migration from Canada to Louisiana and another that deals with antebellum African-American life in the South.
(*Sun-Sentinel* [Ft. Lauderdale, Fla.], 22 February 2002).

Janssen, Milton W. (April 4, 1928–July 9, 1990)
    The author was a life-long resident of New Orleans.

Johnson, Barbara Ferry (July 7, 1923–May 30, 1989)
    An author of six romance novels, Johnson was born in Grosse Pointe, Mich. and graduated from Northwestern University (BS, 1945) and Clemson University (MA, 1964). She edited *American Lumberman* (Chicago, Ill.) from 1945–48 and after marrying educator William David Johnson in 1947 devoted herself to being a homemaker and mother. Later, she was an associate professor of English at Columbia (S.C.) College (1964–89).
(*Contemporary Authors Online*, Detroit: Gale, 2003, s.v. "Barbara F(erry) Johnson").

Jones, Alice Ilgenfritz (January 9, 1846–March 5, 1906)
    Born in Shanesville, Ohio, Ilgenfritz moved with her family to Clarksville, Iowa where her father was a furniture dealer and later the mayor. She was educated at Evansville (Wis.) Seminary and published her first novel in 1879. A romance entitled *High-Water-Mark* (New York: J.B. Lippincott), the book is considered the first novel with an Iowa setting (Clarence A. Andrews, *A Literary History of Iowa*, Iowa City: Iowa University Press, 1972). In the early 1880s Ilgenfritz was a contributor of short stories and travel essays to *Lippincott's Monthly Magazine*. She married in 1884 to widower Hiram Edgar Jones, a furniture dealer, and did not publish her next writings until the 1890s. Although she lived most of her life in Cedar Rapids, Iowa, as an adult she often spent winters in Jennings, La. and several of her novels and short stories are set in Louisiana.
(Carol A. Kolmerten, introduction to *Alice Ilgenfritz Jones and Ella Merchant, Unveiling a Parallel*, Syracuse, N.Y.: Syracuse University Press, 1991).

Joseph, Robert F(arras) (November 30, 1935–?)
    Born in Philadelphia, Farras received his bachelor's degree from the University of Pennsylvania and completed additional graduate study at the University of California, Los Angeles; Trinity University in San Antonio, Tex.; and Hahnemann Medical College (MD). After service as a military surgeon at Chu Lai hospital in Vietnam, Joseph worked as a physician specializing in adolescent medicine at University of Southern California Health Center in Los Angeles. In addition to writing seven novels, Joseph authored plays, screenplays, and television scripts.
(*Bryant Collection of Physician Writers*, Ehrman Medical Library, New York University).

Judge L.Q.C. Brown, *see* Wilkinson, Clement Penrose

Judson, Clara Ingram (May 4, 1879–May 24, 1960)

The author of more than seventy-nine books for children, Judson began her writing career when she realized the need for newspaper content for children. Within six weeks of her appearance in her hometown newspaper in Richmond, Ind., she was publishing a nationally-syndicated column, "Bedtime Tales." Soon afterwards, in 1915, she published her first book. Born in Logansport, Ind., Judson grew up in Indianapolis and was a school teacher. After marrying James M. Judson, she lived in Richmond, Ind.; Chicago; and Evanston, Ill. Beginning in World War I, Judson began a public speaking career addressing domestic topics. In addition to her lectures, for many years she broadcast a weekly radio program in the Chicago area.
(*Chicago Tribune*, 11 November 1956).

Judson, Edward Zane Carroll [Ned Buntline, pseud.] (March 20, c.1823–July 16, 1886)

After an adventurous youth as a sailor, soldier, and scout, Judson engaged in an influential career as a newspaper publisher and author of more than four-hundred dime novels. Born near Stamford, N.Y., the son of a lawyer, Judson ran away to sea when he was twelve, after his family moved to Philadelphia. After a few years as a cabin boy, he played a key role in a rescue in New York's East River and was commissioned as a midshipman in 1838. He later fought in the Seminole War and in the Civil War. He published his first story in 1838 and started several newspapers and story papers in the 1840s before his great success with *Ned Buntline's Own*, which he started in Nashville, Tenn. in 1845. After a scandalous love affair, duel, and murder trial, Judson relocated to New York City. An advocate of nativism and temperance (despite his frequent public drunkenness), Judson was a leading member of the Know Nothing movement and was convicted several times of instigating riots. Judson became aware of William Cody on a speaking tour through Nebraska and in 1869 began publishing stories about the Indian Scout that established "Buffalo Bill" as an internationally known figure. He later wrote a best-selling fictionalized account of Cody's life that was turned into a play in 1872. His own play about Cody, *Scouts of the Prairie*, opened the same year and starred Cody playing himself. Buntline received a significant income from his story papers and dime novels and built an estate, Eagle's Nest, in Stamford, N.Y., where he spent the last years of his life.
(Jay Monaghan, *The Great Rascal: The Life and Times of Ned Buntline*, Boston: Little, Brown, 1952).

Judson, Jeanne (Frances Dean Hancock, pseud.] (September 5, 1888–January 9, 1981)

A reporter, editor, and prolific romance novelist, Judson was born in St. Louis, Mo. and began working in a newspaper office at fifteen. After a peripatetic youth during which she lived in Chicago, Detroit, and San Francisco, as well as smaller towns and cities, she worked in New York as an editor for *Smart Set* magazine starting in 1910. She published a number of novels as magazine serials and books from the late 1910s to the early 1920s. However, she returned her focus to editing and reporting until she began writing romance novels in 1953, producing more than seventy, mostly for Avalon. Judson was married to writer Gordon Stiles (d. 1930).
(Exhibition catalog, *The Greenwich Village Bookshop Door: A Portal to Bohemia, 1920–1925*, Harry Ransom Center, The University of Texas at Austin).

Kane, Frank (July 19, 1912–November 29, 1968)

A scriptwriter for radio and television who wrote a popular series of detective mysteries, Kane was born in Brooklyn, N.Y. and completed a bachelor of sciences degree at the College of the City of New York (now City College/CUNY) and studied law at St. John's University (Jamaica, N.Y.). He worked as a reporter (1935–40) and as public relations director for the Conference of Alcoholic Beverage Industries (1942–46), subsequently becoming a freelance writer, radio and television scriptwriter, and president of Frank Kane Corporation. He developed the hard-boiled

private detective character Johnny Liddell, featuring him in twenty-nine adventures. The books achieved great popularity over twenty years with sales of over five million copies.
(Jay Pederson and Taryn Benbow-Pfalzgraf, eds., *St. James Guide to Crime and Mystery Writers*, 4th ed., Detroit: St. James, 1996).

Kane, Harnett T(homas) (1910–September 4, 1984)
A New Orleans native, Kane was the author of twenty-six books of fiction and non-fiction dealing with the South. He also wrote book reviews and travel articles for *Saturday Review*, *Reader's Digest*, *The New York Times*, and *National Geographic*. He was a native of New Orleans and a 1931 graduate of Tulane University.
(*New York Times*, 14 September 1984).

Keating, Lawrence A. [H.C. Thomas, pseud.] (January 21, 1903–June16, 1966)
An author under his own name and pseudonyms, including John Keith Bassett, Keating wrote westerns, mysteries, and books for boys. He was educated at Marquette University (PhB in journalism, 1926) and was a freelance writer from 1932 until his death, producing over thirty books. He was also a writing instructor at Northwestern University (1941–60) and later at Marquette University and the University of Wisconsin.
(*Contemporary Authors Online*, Detroit: Gale, 2002, accessed 31 July 2013).

Keeler, Harry Stephen (November 3, 1890–January 22, 1967)
The author of over seventy novels, Keeler was born and grew up in Chicago in his widowed mother's boarding house for thespians. A graduate of Armour Institute (now Illinois Institute of Technology) with a degree in electrical engineering, he began publishing serialized novels in magazines in 1914 and published his first book in 1924. Almost all of Keeler's works are mysteries and he is known for inventing the form known as the "webwork novel," in which hundreds of seemingly unrelated events prove to be interlinked. Perhaps because of his use of this literary form Keeler wrote some of the longest mystery novels ever published, including one with over seven hundred pages. Starting in the 1930s and throughout the 1940s and 1950s, Keeler published novels in series. The length of his novels and their challenging narrative devices left Keeler with few readers by the 1950s, although he continued to write until his death.
(*Contemporary Authors Online*, Detroit: Gale, 2005, accessed 14 August 2009).

Keene, Carolyn [house pseudonym, *see also* Wirt (Benson), Mildred A(ugustine)]
A creation of the Stratemeyer syndicate, publisher of young adult book series, the fictional Carolyn Keene is listed as the author of the Nancy Drew books included here. The first book to feature the girl detective was published in 1930 and hundreds of the novels have been written by various, anonymous authors since then under the house pseudonym.

Keller, Martha Carolyne, *see* Miller, Martha Carolyne Keller

Kelly, Regina Zimmerman (January 4, 1898–April 9, 1986)
Although she was born and raised in New Orleans, Kelly graduated from the University of Chicago (PhB, 1920) with a degree in education and took courses in journalism at Northwestern University. She began teaching high school history at Chicago's Austin High School immediately after college graduation and lived and worked on Chicago's North Side for the rest of her life. Kelly is known for her well-researched works of historical fiction for young adults and a particular interest in Midwestern history.
(*Contemporary Authors Online*, Detroit: Gale, 2001, accessed 12 March 2009).

Kent, Madeleine Fabiola (1910–?)

A native of Montreal, Kent mostly wrote detective stories and articles for magazines. She was the wife of William Espinosa, a member of the Cuban diplomatic corps and the couple lived in New Orleans for a time where she became interested in Jean Lafitte, researching his life in primary documents there and elsewhere.
(*The Montreal Gazette*, 12 December 1955).

Keyes, Frances Parkinson (July 21, 1885–July 3, 1970)

Keyes' girlhood was spent on Beacon Street during the winter social season and during the rest of the year at a family house in Newbury, Vt. and traveling in the United States and abroad. She was educated in fashionable private schools and completed her education with studies in Geneva and Berlin. In 1903, at age eighteen, she married Henry Wilder Keyes, a man from her social circle, who became governor of New Hampshire and served in the U.S. Senate from 1919 to 1937. Keyes was a great social success in Washington during the 1920s and 1930s, and she wrote about her experiences in *Letters from a Senator's Wife* (New York: D. Appleton, 1924) and *Capital Kaleidoscope* (Harper, 1937). She published her first novel, *The Old Gray Homestead* (Boston: Houghton Mifflin), in 1919 and in 1923 became a contributing editor for *Good Housekeeping Magazine*, eventually authoring a monthly column describing her travels. She continued to publish books until a few years before her death, completing more than fifty, among them several titles that sold over a million copies. Keyes wrote many of her books while wintering in New Orleans at 1113 Chartres Street in the house now known as the Beauregard-Keyes house for the author who made certain the structure was transferred to a foundation and preserved; and for Confederate General Pierre Gustave Toutant Beauregard, who lived there from 1866–68 while president of the New Orleans, Jackson, and Great Northern Railroad. Keyes resided in the house seasonally as a renter from 1944 until her death.
(*New York Times*, 4 July 1970).

King, Charles (October 12, 1844–March 18, 1933)

A soldier for seventy years who rose to the rank of general, King wrote sixty novels (most are set on the western frontier) that had the sentimentalized plots of other popular, nineteenth-century fiction. King's novels were informed by his own experiences and featured accurate details about life on the frontier. King studied at Columbia College (now University) where his grandfather was president, interrupting his class work to enlist in the Union Army during the Civil War. He attended West Point (1862–65) and was posted to the West during the 1874 Apache campaign in Arizona and against the Sioux in 1876. Although an arm wound forced his retirement from the U.S. Army in 1879, at which time he began his writing career, King was commissioned as a general at the time of the Spanish-American War in 1898 and was posted to the Philippines. His writing found a broad audience. King's books tell us a great deal about frontier conditions and military service in the 1870s through 1890s and near the end of his career begins to reflect the realist movement that was becoming popular.
(*Dictionary of Literary Biography*, vol. 186, s.v. "King, Charles").

King, Grace Elizabeth (November 29, 1852–January 14, 1932)

A daughter of prominent New Orleans parents who lost their money as a result of the Civil War, in her fiction King portrayed contemporary people in similar situations. King's father, William Woodson King was a planter, lawyer and state legislator before the war. She was educated privately at home and finished her education at the Institut St. Louis in New Orleans. A short time afterwards she attended the Institut Cenas (New Orleans) and earned membership in the Pan-Gnostic literary society organized by Julia Ward Howe. Through this and other groups, King became a part of literary culture in New Orleans, although her choice of fictional subjects did not win her a wide audience. During summers in Hartford, Conn., she became friends with Charles

Dudley Warner and through him with Samuel Clemens and members of his family. Beginning in the 1890s King shifted her focus away from fiction to history following her mentor Charles Gayarré, writing about New Orleans and Louisiana and eventually received an honorary doctor of letters degree from Tulane University.
(Robert Bush, *Grace King*, Baton Rouge: Louisiana State University Press, 1983).

Knapp, George L. (April 6, 1872–?)
     A journalist born in Dover, Minn., Knapp is known for opinion pieces that celebrated progress (even at the expense of the environment) and for several works of science fiction, including *Face of Air* (New York: John Lane, 1912). Most of his books are for boys and are fictionalized biographies or descriptions of historic places.

Knight, Gladys (?–?)
     No information available.

Knipe, Alden Arthur (June 1870–May 22, 1950)
     An accomplished football player and coach, Knipe trained as a physician and wrote more than thirty books for children, mostly co-authored with his wife Emilie Benson Knipe. Born in Philadelphia, Knipe studied at Haverford College (Penn.) and received his MD from the University of Pennsylvania in 1894. A member of the football team, he made a historic touchdown against Yale that ended their record for zero touchdowns by opposing teams, and was named an All-American. He moved to Iowa City, Iowa and became Professor of Physical Training at the University there in 1897, eventually becoming Director of Physical Training and the coach for four athletic teams. He began writing in 1902 and after his marriage to Emilie Benson, resigned his appointment at the University of Iowa, and moved back to the East Coast, where he and his wife produced books over a forty year period.
(*New York Times*, 24 May 1950).

Knipe, Emilie Benson (June 12, 1867–October 25, 1958)
     Wife of Alden Arthur Knipe with whom she co-authored more than thirty books for children, Knipe studied at the Chicago Academy of Fine Arts in 1915 and began her career as an illustrator for children's magazines. She illustrated several of her husband's stories before they became a writing team.
(*New York Times*, 26 October 1958).

Knoblock, K(enneth) T(homas) (1898–1946)
     No information available.

La Farge, Oliver (December 9, 1901–August 2, 1963)
     Born in affluent circumstances in New York City, La Farge attended Groton and Harvard University (BA, 1924; MA, 1929) and became a nationally known expert of Native American culture. He taught at Tulane University (1926–28) and was a research fellow at Columbia University (1931–33) and later a teacher there. He held a number of positions with governmental and non-governmental commissions and organizations dealing with Native American matters and much of his fiction deals with Native Americans. During World War II he served in the U.S. Army Air Force (1942–45) and became a decorated lieutenant colonel. He wrote a number of non-fiction works in history and the social sciences in addition to fiction.
(*Dictionary of Literary Biography*, vol. 9, s.v. "La Farge, Oliver").

Laing, Sallie Wear (April 7, 1857–November 26, 1940)
An author of children's stories and novels, Laing was born in Brenham, Tex. and lived in Shreveport, La.

Labranche, Anne, *see* Arguedas, Janet Wogan

Laird, Marion Murdoch (Lind) (May 27, 1875–1965)
Born in Baltimore, Md., Laird was the wife of the Rev. William Henry Laird, DD, a minister of the Episcopal Church in America.

L'Amour, Louis (March 22, 1908–June 10, 1988)
The self-educated author of more than one-hundred novels, four-hundred short stories, and sixty-five television scripts L'Amour attracted a huge audience with meticulously researched writing that reflected his personal experiences and that of family members and friends. Born in Jamestown, N. Dak., L'Amour's family had been pioneers who fought in the Sioux Indian Wars and in the Civil War. As a young man he had jobs on ranches through which he befriended by White men who had been orphaned and raised as Indians. He gained broad personal experience by working as a boxer, elephant handler, fruit picker, longshoreman, lumberjack, and miner. Although he published a volume of poetry when he was in his thirties, he did not begin writing novels until he was in his forties, but soon had a contract from Bantam Books to write three novels per year. By the time of his death more than two hundred million copies of his books were in print. He was awarded both the Congressional Gold Medal and the Presidential Medal of Freedom and received a National Book Award.
(*New York Times*, 13 Jun 1988).

Lane, Frederick A. (?–?)
No information available.

LaScola, Ray(mond) (May 11 1915–April 4, 1994)
Born in New Orleans, LaScola studied at the New Orleans Conservatory of Music (1929–39) and received his bachelor's degree from Louisiana State University (1937). He was a professional pianist from 1927–41, but after graduating from the Louisiana State University Medical Center in 1941, he completed internships, residencies and graduate study in pediatric medicine. He began a private practice as a pediatrician in Los Angeles, Calif., in 1945. He authored several medical books and in addition to the novel for which he is included here, wrote a number of television scripts. In later life he became an expert clinical hypnotist. In 1980 LaScola was charged with murdering Georgia Thera, who had adopted him, even though he was sixty-three at the time, with the agreement that he would inherit the Thera estate if he would promise to care for Georgia's husband Ariya Dhamma Thera, who was suffering from dementia and living in a nursing home. After Georgia Thera died and LaScola was the one to sign the death certificate and have her body cremated, he was suspected of overdosing her with insulin. The murder charge was dropped, but the adoption was voided and LaScola subsequently returned to live the final years of his life in New Orleans.
(*Los Angeles Times*, 23 August 1985).

Lattimore, Eleanor Frances (June 30, 1904–May 12, 1986)
A daughter of academic David Lattimore, Professor of Comparative Literature and Sociology at Dartmouth University, the author was born in China and studied at the California School of Arts and Crafts (1920–22) and in New York at the Art Students League and the Grand Central School of Art (1924). She married Robert Armstrong Andrews, a freelance writer and designer in 1934.

Lattimore published her first book for children in 1931 and continued to write and illustrate children's stories until her death more than fifty years later.
(Laura Standley Berger, ed., *Twentieth-Century Children's Writers*, 4th ed., Detroit: St. James, 1995, s.v. "Lattimore, Eleanor Frances").

Lawrance, William V(icars) (November 8, 1834–January 5, 1905)
    A poet and novelist, Lawrance was an Ohio lawyer. Born in Greene County, Ohio, he studied at Antioch College (1856–58) and read law in Xenia, Ohio. He was admitted to the Ohio bar in 1860 and enlisted in the Twelfth Ohio Volunteer Infantry in 1861. At the end of the war practiced law in Waverly, Ohio (1865–68), before relocating to Chillicothe, Ohio, his residence for the rest of his life.
(William Coyle, ed., *Ohio Authors and Their Books*, Cleveland, Ohio: World, 1962).

Lea, Fanny Heaslip (October 30, 1884–January 13, 1955)
    Lea was a New Orleans native and daughter of newspaperman James J. Lea, who was long employed by *The Daily States* (New Orleans). She attended Newcomb College (BA, 1904) and undertook graduate study in English at Tulane University (1904–06) before starting a journalism career, publishing feature articles in New Orleans papers from 1906–11. During this same period she was beginning to get stories published in national magazines. She continued to write and publish during her marriage to academic, Hamilton P. Agee, while living in Honolulu. After her 1926 divorce from Agee, Lea moved to New York City and went on to publish more than one hundred essays, stories, and poems in addition to nineteen novels. At the time of her death her final volume of poetry was in galleys and was published posthumously.
(*New York Times*, 14 January 1955).

LeBlanc, Doris Kent (1896–1975)
    Although she grew up in Kentwood, La., the town named for her grandfather, she was educated at Newcomb College (AB, 1917) and was a long time resident of New Orleans. For many years she was a reporter and feature writer for the *Times-Picayune* and later wrote feature articles for national magazines.
(*Times-Picayune*, 12 January 1975).

Lee, William, *see* Burroughs, William

Le May, Alan (June 3, 1899–April 27, 1964)
    Known as an author of Western novels, as well as for magazine serials, LeMay also wrote screenplays and was a director and producer of movies. Born in Indianapolis, Ind., he attended Stetson University in 1916, but interrupted his studies to serve in World War I as a Second Lieutenant in the U.S. Army. He graduated from the University of Chicago (BPhil, 1922) before starting his writing career as a journalist. He published his first novel, *Painted Ponies* (New York: George H. Doran) in 1927. Two of his novels *The Searchers* (New York: Harper, 1954) and *The Unforgiven* (New York: Harper, 1957) established an enduring reputation when they were adapted for film. John Ford directed *The Searchers* (Warner Brothers, 1956), starring John Wayne. *The Unforgiven* (James Productions, 1960) was directed by John Huston and starred Burt Lancaster and Audrey Hepburn.
(James Vinson, ed., *Twentieth-Century Western Writers*, Detroit: Gale, 1982, s.v. "LeMay, Alan").

Le Moine, Weston J. (?–?)
    No information available.

Linfield, Mary Barrow (?–?)

Born on Poplar Stand Plantation in West Feliciana Parish near St. Francisville, La., land that had been in her family since the seventeenth century, Linfield was a high school teacher. She completed graduate study at the University of Chicago and Tulane University and settled in New Orleans in 1928, working as a stenographer during the day and writing at night. She was the author of three novels.
(*Times-Picayune*, 20 March 1935).

Linkinwater, Tim, *see* Waldo, James Curtis

Lipscomb, Marie Lauve (March 12, 1883–January 26, 1972)

No information available.

Little, Paul H(ugo) [Marie De Jourlet, pseud.] (February 5, 1915–June 22, 1987)

The author of more than seven hundred novels, Little was a Chicago native and lived there for most of his life. The son of Israel Isaac Litwinsky, a linen merchant, Little attended the University of Chicago (1932) and graduated from Northwestern University (BS, 1937). After working in advertising in Chicago (1944–58), Little got a job as sales manager and announcer with KHIP-FM Radio in San Francisco (1959–61). He returned to Chicago for an account executive job with Chicago Car Advertising (1962–64) and afterwards was a full-time writer. Except for the 1937 novel for which he is included here, he wrote all of his many books after 1964. Publishing under many pseudonyms, Little's work mostly falls into three genres: historical, pornographic, and romance.
(*Chicago Tribune*, 24 June 1987).

Llewellyn, Michael [Maggie Lyons, pseud.] (May 6, 1944–?)

Born in Fountain City, Tenn. and a cousin of James Agee, Llewellyn lived in New York's Greenwich Village for twenty years while working as a copywriter and writing part-time. He found his niche in the 1970s writing historical romance novels under a pseudonym and moved to New Orleans' French Quarter, a setting he used for several of his books.
(Author webpage, http://michael-llewellyn.net/about-michael/, accessed 6 September 2013).

Lockwood, Myna (1888–1987)

An author and illustrator of books for children, Lockwood produced more than sixteen books from the 1940s to the 1970s.

Long, Amelia Reynolds (November 25, 1904–March 26, 1978)

An author of more than thirty-five mystery and science fiction books under various pseudonyms, Long was born in Columbia, Penn., but lived most of her life in Harrisburg. She was a graduate of the University of Pennsylvania (AB, 1931) and had a number of science fiction stories published in pulp magazines in the 1930s. In the 1940s she turned to mystery novels and published most of her books in the 1940s, sometimes as a co-author with William L. Crawford under the joint pen name Peter Reynolds. Later she worked as an editor at Stackpole Books in Philadelphia and as a curator at the William Penn Museum in Harrisburg. In the last decades of her life she devoted herself to poetry, publishing several volumes and serving as an anthologist and editor for others.
(http://amelialong.tripod.com, accessed 6 September 2013).

Lyons, Maggie, *see* Llewellyn, Michael

**MacDonald, Edwina Levin (May 10, 1898–April 17, 1946)**
Little is known about MacDonald. She was born in Campti, La. and was the author of three novels published in the 1920s and 1930s, as well as stories printed in pulp magazines. Her son, Jackson Clifford MacDonald brought a lawsuit on her behalf against Daphne du Maurier claiming that the famous British author had substantially borrowed from some of MacDonald's short stories in writing *Rebecca*. MacDonald died before the case her son brought was dismissed.
(*MacDonald v. Du Maurier*, 75 F.Supp 655, S.D. New York 1948).

**MacDonald, John D(ann) (July 24, 1916–December 28, 1986)**
The creator of the Travis McGee detective mystery series, MacDonald wrote books in several genres other than mystery-detection, including adventure-suspense, science fiction, and manners and morals. Born in Sharon, Penn., he grew up in Utica, N.Y. and attended the Utica Free Academy. He graduated with business degrees from Syracuse University (1938) and Harvard Business School (MBA, 1939). He began work in the insurance industry but, after serving in the U.S. Army in World War II, devoted himself to writing for pulp magazines, eventually publishing more than sixty novels while mostly living in Sarasota, Fla. and traveling widely, especially by cruise ship.
(Robin W. Winks and Maureen Corrigan, eds., *Mystery and Suspense Writers: The Literature of Crime, Detection, and Espionage*, New York: Scribners, 1998, s.v. "MacDonald, John W.").

**Madere, Hubert (November 7, 1897–September 27, 1962)**
All that is known about Madere is that he was a long-time resident of St. Charles Parish, Louisiana and held the office of registrar of voters.

**Mally, Emma Louise (January 18, 1908–1977)**
Born in Dallas, Tex. and educated at Barnard College (BA, 1930) and Columbia University (graduate study), Mally was active in the Socialist movement.
(*Contemporary Authors Online*, Detroit: Gale, 2001, s.v. "Mally, Emma Louise").

**Manning, Bruce (July 15, 1900–August 3, 1965)**
A co-author with his wife, Gwen Bristow, of several mystery novels, Manning is best known as an author of screenplays. His longest contract was with Universal (1936–42) and through the course of his career between 1934 and 1957 he received writing credits on thirty-seven films.
(*New York Times*, 7 August 1965).

**Margulies, Leo (June 22, 1900–December 26, 1975)**
An editor and publisher of pulp magazines and science fiction paperbacks, Margulies was born in Brooklyn, N.Y. and grew up in Norwalk, Conn. He commenced study at Columbia University, but left college to work for the Munsey pulp magazine chain in the early 1930s. He later worked for Ned Pine's Thrilling Publications, editing *Thrilling Wonder Stories* starting in 1936 and over time was editing forty-six different titles. A war correspondent during World War II, when he returned to civilian life he began publishing science fiction paperbacks under his own Popular Paperback Library imprint. In 1953, he began *Fantastic Universe* science fiction magazine and also that year, *The Saint Detective Magazine*, with Leslie Charteris, and in 1956 began *Mike Shayne's Mystery Magazine*, which he continued to edit until his death.
(Peter Nicholls, ed., *Science Fiction Encyclopedia*, London: Roxby Press, 1979, s.v. "Margulies, Leo").

**Marko, Samuel (?–?)**
No information available.

Marshe, Richard [pseud.] (1886–?)
   No information available.

Martin, Aylwin Lee (?–?)
   No information available.

Martin, Fleming (?–?)
   A native of Burlington, Tex., Martin attended Nixon-Clay School of Business in Austin, San Antonio College, and Saint Mary's (San Antonio) University. He served with an anti-aircraft battalion in World War II and participated in the invasion of North Africa from Oran to the Libyan Desert. After a career in the Federal Civil Service, he retired to South Texas to indulge his love of hunting. The book for which he is included here is his only published work.
   (Book jacket copy).

Martin, Valerie (March 14, 1948–?)
   Although she was born in Sedalia, Mo., Martin grew up in New Orleans and attended the University of New Orleans (BA, 1970). She completed a graduate degree at the University of Massachusetts (MFA, 1974) and taught at several academic institutions, including the University of Alabama, University of Massachusetts at Amherst, Mount Holyoke College, New Mexico State University and the University of New Orleans. Although she has published short fiction and short story collections, Martin is known for her four novels, several of which are set in New Orleans.
   (Taryn Benbow-Pfalzgraf, ed., *American Women Writers: A Critical Reference Guide from Colonial Times to the Present*, 2nd ed., vol. 3. Detroit: St. James, 2000).

Martinez, Raymond J(oseph) (October 17, 1889–January 1, 1982)
   The son of a sugar planter, Martinez was born in West Baton Rouge, La. and attended Louisiana State University (1907). For many years he was an editor, first of the commercial and industrial pages of the *New Orleans States* (1920–24), then of *The Rice Journal* (New Orleans, La.) from 1924–41. After wartime service in the U.S. Maritime Commission, he devoted himself to writing full-time. He had previously established Hope Publications and printed three plays and a novel between 1916 and 1935. In addition to fiction, Martinez published regional titles, including cookbooks and natural history.
   (*Contemporary Authors Online*, Detroit: Gale, 2001, accessed 15 October 2013).

Mason, F(rancis) van Wyck (November 11, 1901–August 28, 1978)
   Born into a historic and socially prominent Boston family, Mason spent part of his childhood abroad, mostly in Paris, where his grandfather was U.S. Consul. In his late teens, he volunteered as an ambulance driver in World War I and by the end of the war, when he was only seventeen, he was a lieutenant in the U.S. Army. He graduated from Harvard University (SB, 1924) and started an antiques-importing business that afforded him the opportunity to travel extensively, even after his father lost his money. In 1928 he began publishing short fiction in pulp magazines and in 1930 introduced the character Captain Hugh North, an army intelligence detective, who was the hero in a long series of mystery and intrigue novels that he continued until 1968. He is best known, however, for his works of historical fiction which he began publishing in 1938 and continued to the end of his life. In World War II, he was Chief Historian on General Eisenhower's staff. In the 1950s he began writing historical fiction for juveniles.
   (*New York Times*, 6 November 1978).

Massena, Agnese M.C. [Creole, pseud.] (?–?)
   No information available.

**Massicot, Norita (Newman) [Norita, pseud.] (December 29, 1887–May 17,1972)**
   The author of historical fiction based on her own family, Massicot was born Norita Diane Newman in New Orleans and married Andrew Alphonse Massicot in 1909. Massicot and her husband were French Creoles and the author was descended from U.S. Army Captain Francis Newman (1786–1851), the commander of Fort Petit Coquilles during the Battle of New Orleans and Manuela Marie Solís (1794–1868), whose family played an important role in introducing the sugar cane industry to Louisiana.
(Jerry Gandolfo, email message to Jeffrey Coogan, August 20, 2013).

**Masters, Kelly Ray [Zachary Ball, pseud.] (June 16, 1897–July 4, 1987)**
   Best known as the author of more than fifteen adventure books for boys, Masters was born in the Blackjack Hills west of Princeton, Mo. He left school after sixth grade to help support his family and, after a series of factory jobs and work as a bellhop, he joined a small theatrical company touring a circuit through rural Missouri. Over the next twenty-five years he worked with a series of similar companies throughout the Midwest, a livelihood that ended with World War II gasoline rationing. After his marriage in 1931, Masters began a settled life in Austin, Tex., delivering newspapers and submitting short stories to pulp magazines, using a pseudonym based on his admiration for Zachary Scott and Lucille Ball. For a time he co-authored works with Frankie-Lee Janas (see entry above) under the joint pseudonym Saliee O'Brien. After the publication of two novels for adults, he began writing children's books and wrote a series of books featuring Joe Panther, a Seminole Indian boy. This character was featured in a motion picture, *Joe Panther* (Stewart H. Beveridge Productions) in 1976. In the mid-1960s he developed a non-profit, Joe Panther Enterprises, to supply audio recordings of Ball reading his works in order to encourage reading in young children.
(*The Zachary Ball Papers*, de Grummond Children's Literature Collection, University of Southern Mississippi Libraries).

**Masterson, Louis, *see* Hallbing, Kjell**

**Matschat, Cecile Hulse (1895–March 4, 1976)**
   An illustrator and botanist who wrote seven books on horticulture and eight works of historical fiction, the author was born in upstate New York, a descendant of early Dutch settlers. Educated in private schools, she studied art at the Pratt Institute and in Paris. As the wife of engineer Louis Matschat, she traveled to remote areas in South America, an opportunity that led to a travel memoir and a series of orchid paintings and botanical illustrations. She also traveled for extended periods in the Okefenokee Swamp, leading to her best known botanical works. Her art work was featured in solo exhibitions and she lectured widely. Matschat's published work was the basis for her election to the Explorer's Club.
(*New York Times*, 10 Mar 1976).

**Matthews, Clayton Hartley (October 24, 1918–March 25, 2004)**
   The author of more than thirty-five books, Matthews began his career writing short stories for pulp magazines, like *Mike Shayne Mystery Magazine*, in the 1950s. He began writing erotic paperback novels in the 1960s, as well as occasional mysteries. After wedding second wife Patricia "Patty Brisco" Matthews (1972–2004), a fellow writer, he collaborated with her on mystery and romance novels.

**Matthews, Harold (?–?)**
   No information available.

Maxwell, Patricia [Jennifer Blake, Maxine Patrick, pseud.] (March 9, 1942–?)

Born in Winn Parish, La., Maxwell was a fifteen-year-old bride and had two children by age nineteen. She began writing as a hobby and published her first book, a mystery, in 1970. Known for works of historical romance, she has published more than fifty titles, many under her pseudonym, Jennifer Blake.

(*Contemporary Authors Online*, Detroit: Gale, 2012, accessed 10 October 2013).

Mayfield, Millie, *see* Homes, Mary Sophia Shaw

May, Margery Land (January 14, 1897–May 13, 1932)

The daughter of Louisiana Supreme Court Justice Alfred Land, May was born in New Orleans. She began publishing short stories in national magazines in 1911 and lived most of her adult life in Shreveport, La. as the wife of attorney James Martin Foster. After some of her stories and a novel were adapted for the screen, she was employed as a screenwriter by The Selznick Motion Picture Company. She committed suicide at a young age after the death of her husband.

(*Margery Land May Collection*, Special Collections, Louisiana State University).

McCormick, William Bennett (January 22, 1870–November 26, 1930)

No information available.

McCurtin, Peter (October 15, 1929–January 27, 1997)

A prolific author of paperback action novels in the 1970s and 1980s, mostly hard-boiled Westerns, McCurtin immigrated from Ireland when he was in his twenties and lived most of his life in New York City and Ogunquit, Me.

McHale, Larry (?–?)

No information available.

McKeag, Ernest Lionel [Roland Vane, pseud.] (September 19, 1896–1974)

A prolific author of pulp fiction, McKeag was born in Newcastle-upon-Tyne and trained as a sailor, serving in the Royal Navy (1915–19) and receiving his Master Mariner's Certificate in 1919. He began his writing career as a journalist, quickly specializing in story papers for juveniles. In addition to editing, he contributed stories and published his first novel for boys in 1923 and continued to publish paperback fiction for forty years. Much of his work was for children, but as early as the 1920s he was occasionally writing sensational adult fiction featuring prostitutes and seamy aspects of urban life. He served in the Royal Navy during World War II (1939–43) and advanced to the rank of lieutenant.

(*Contemporary Authors Online*, Detroit: Gale, 2001, accessed 9 September 2013).

McKinney, Annie Booth (1855–1926)

Born in Natchez, McKinney was the wife of newspaper publisher and public official Samuel McKinney, and the couple lived in Knoxville, Tenn. A frequent contributor to national magazines in the late nineteenth and early twentieth century, McKinney was a member of Knoxville's Ossoli Club, a women's literary society founded in 1885, and the publisher of *Chilhowee Echo*, a Knoxville women's newspaper that began publication in 1899.

(William Rule, et al., *Standard History of Knoxville, Tenn.*, Chicago: Lewis, 1900, 526).

McNeill, Nevada [A.S.M., pseud.] (?–?)

No information available.

Merwin, Sam (April 28, 1910–January 13, 1996)
    An editor and author of science fiction and mystery books, Merwin was born in Plainfield, N.J., graduated from Princeton (BA, 1931), and completed further study at the Boston Museum School of Fine Arts. He began his writing career as a journalist and worked for the *Boston Evening American* and *The Philadelphia Inquirer* as New York City Bureau Chief. After 1936 he held a series of editing jobs at Dell, Standard Magazine Group, King Size Publications, Renown Publications, and Brandon House. He started publishing his own fiction in 1940 and had mysteries and works of science fiction published in pulp magazines, as well as more than twenty books.
(*Contemporary Authors Online*, Detroit: Gale, 2002, accessed 10 October 2013).

Michaels, Irene (?–?)
    No information available.

Miller, Martha Carolyne Keller (also known as Martha Carolyne Keller) (?–?)
    No information available.

Minnigerode, Meade (June 19, 1887–October 27, 1967)
    Minnegerode's historical fiction dealt with French and American history and focused on personalities. Although his parents were Americans, he was born in London, educated at Harrow, and did not begin living in the United States until he was nineteen and a student at Yale University (BA). His first writing success was as a co-author with George S. Pomeroy of the lyrics for Yale's "Whiffenpoof Song." Except for early career starts in shipping and publishing and service with the Red Cross and on the United States Shipping Board in France during World War I, Minnigerode spent his entire adult life as a freelance author, producing more than one hundred volumes of fiction, non-fiction, and anthologies.
(William Jeremiah Burke, et al., *American Authors and Books: 1640 to the Present Day*, 3rd rev. ed., New York: Crown, 1972, s.v. "Minnigerode, Meade").

Mitchell, Carl (?–?)
    No information available.

Moon, Ilanon (February 20, 1900–July 6, 1980)
    The author of four books, including memoirs, fiction, and plays, spent most of his life in Texas.

Moore, John Trotwood (August 26, 1858–May 10, 1929)
    A native of Alabama, Moore is best known for his writing set in Tennessee and for his role in building historical collections at the State Library of Tennessee. The son of lawyer John Moore, the author was born in Marion, Ala. and educated at Howard College (now Samford University, Birmingham, Ala.) Although he studied law and passed the bar examination, he never practiced, but after teaching for several years, moved to his wife's hometown of Columbia, Tenn. where he farmed and bred horses. His first writing was about horses and hunting dogs, but he was soon publishing local color writing with African-American characters. He began writing novels and from 1905–1910 published *Trotwood's Monthly* (later *Taylor-Trotwood Magazine*), a miscellany of agricultural writing, fiction, and history. As Moore's career progressed he became interested in Andrew Jackson, collected primary sources, and wrote a fictionalized biography. Appointed Tennessee State Librarian in 1919, Moore convinced the Tennessee Historical Society to merge its collections with the State Library and undertook a number of successful campaigns to develop the library's collection of historical documents.
(*John Trotwood Moore Papers*, Tennessee State Library and Archives, http://www.tn.gov/tsla/history/manuscripts/findingaids/178.pdf, accessed 24 March 2014).

Morrow, Susan (?–?)
    No information available.

Murphy, Edward F(rancis) (July 21, 1892–August 2, 1967)
    A native of Salem, Mass. and a Roman Catholic priest, Murphy was a member of the Society of St. Joseph of the Sacred Heart for the Conversion of Colored People in America. He entered the society in 1907 and completed most of his education at St. Mary's Seminary in Baltimore, Md., receiving his BA, MA, and STB. After his ordination in 1917 he completed graduate study at The Catholic University of America. For twenty-seven years he was chaplain and chair of the philosophy department at Xavier University, an institution founded in New Orleans by Katherine Drexel in 1915 to provide higher education to African-Americans. Murphy was the author of several popular books that used Biblical figures as the subjects of novels.
(J. Murphy, ed., *Philosophical Studies*, vol. 8-11, Wash. D.C.: Catholic University of America, 1915).

Murray, John (1886–?)
    No information available.

Neubauer, William Arthur [Norma Newcomb, pseud.] (April 1, 1916–November 25, 1982)
    An author of romance novels for young adults and adults, as well as pornographic fiction, Neubauer was born in Maspeth, N.Y., but lived most of his life in California. He began writing professionally in 1935, and between 1944 and 1967 was publishing more than ten books per year with the Gramercy and Arcadia publishing houses. He used at least nine pseudonyms and is estimated to have written more than two hundred and forty books.
(*Contemporary Authors Online*, Detroit: Gale, 2001, accessed 10 October 2013).

Neugass, James (January 29, 1905–September 7, 1949)
    Born into an affluent Jewish family in New Orleans, Neugass began writing poetry at seventeen. He attended Harvard University, Yale University, University of Michigan, and Balliol College, Oxford University, although he never completed a degree. Working a series of jobs in New York City, he became politically engaged with the Communist Party and, as a thirty-two-year-old went to Spain to aid the Republicans, eventually becoming an ambulance driver with the Abraham Lincoln Brigade. A contributor to national magazines, he published one novel, for which he is included here. He prepared the journals of his experiences in Spain to be published as a memoir (rediscovered and issued in 2008).
(*New York Times*, 10 September 1949).

Newcomb, Norma, *see* Neubauer, William Arthur

Nixon, Joan Lowery (February 3, 1927–June 28, 2003)
    An award-winning author of books for children and young adults, Nixon was born in Los Angeles, Calif. and grew up in Hollywood. A graduate of the University of Southern California (BA, 1947), she taught kindergarten for several years before marrying and moving with her petroleum engineer husband to Midland, Tex. Over the course of her career she authored more than 150 books, many of them mysteries for young adults; however, she also wrote historical novels in the series "Orphan Train" and "Young Americans." Among the many awards she received were a record for Edgar Allen Poe Awards.
(Joyce Nakamura, ed., *Something About the Author Autobiography Series*, vol. 9, Detroit: Gale, 1990, s.v. "Nixon, Joan Lowery").

Nunez, Nemours Henry, Jr. (December 3, 1897–April 1968)
   A life-long resident of New Orleans, Nunez graduated from Tulane University in 1918.

O'Brien, Salliee, *see* Janas, Frankie-Lee

O'Connor, Florence J. (?–?)
   A Louisiana native of Irish-American descent, O'Connor wrote poems for Southern news-papers before the Civil War, spent the war years in Paris, married and in later life was known as Mrs. Florence J. Willard.
(Mary T. Tardy, ed., *The Living Female Writers of the South*, Philadelphia: Claxton, Remsen, and Haffelfinger, 1872, s.v. "O'Connor, Florence J.").

O'Donnell, Mary King, (March 2, 1909–1990)
   The daughter of an oil driller, O'Donnell was born near Angleton, Tex. and attended the University of Texas. She lived in New Orleans during the 1930s and married fellow novelist Edwin P. O'Donnell. She won a Houghton Mifflin literary fellowship to write her first novel set in the Texas oil fields. After her husband's death, O'Donnell moved to San Francisco in 1943. She subsequently married journalist and radio news commentator Michael Quin and after his death in 1947 moved to Olema outside San Francisco and married Steven Charter, an agricultural engineer, in 1951.
(Lou Halsell Rodenberger, introduction to *Quincie Bolliver,* Lubbock, Tex.: Texas Tech University Press, 2001).

O'Hara, Edith C(ecilia) (?–?)
   No information available.

Olivier, Robert L(ouis) (October 25, 1903–November 1986)
   Born in Grand Coteau, La., Olivier was a graduate of Loyola (University (BA, 1925) and had a long career as a school teacher and administrator. A historic preservationist, Olivier restored Arlington Plantation outside Franklin, La.
(*Contemporary Authors Online*, Gale, 2001, accessed 10 October 2013).

Olmstead, Florence (?–?)
   No information available

Ondaatje, Michael (September 12, 1943–?)
   Although he has lived most of his life in Canada, Ondaatje was born in Ceylon, Sri Lanka and spent his childhood in England, where he studied at Dulwich College. He relocated to Canada in 1962 and graduated from the University of Toronto (BA, 1965) and Queen's University (Kingston, Can.) (MA, 1967). Best-known as a novelist, due in part to the success of the film version of his Booker Prize-winning book *The English Patient* (Picador, 1992), Ondaatje is an equally accomplished poet.
(*Dictionary of Literary Biography*, vol. 323, s.v. "Michael Ondaatje").

Onstott, Kyle (January 12, 1887–June 3, 1966)
   An author of pulp fiction, the best-known of which dealt with issues of race, Onstott was born in Du Quoin, Ill. and an expert dog breeder and competitor. He was licensed as a judge by the American Kennel Club in 1921. Onstott's writing career peaked with his Falconhurst series, his

torical romances that focused on slave culture that, in addition to presenting interracial sexual relationships, traced the emotional and psychological effects on master and slave.
(James Vinson, ed. *Twentieth-Century Romance and Gothic Writers*, Detroit: Gale, 1982, s.v. "Onstott, Kyle").

Osborn, Pete H. (August 16, 1913–March 10, 1995)
    The author was a resident of New Orleans; no additional information available.

Otis, G.H. (?–?)
    No information available.

Oursler, (Charles) Fulton (January 22, 1893–May 24, 1952)
    An author of popular detective novels, often under the pen name Anthony Abbott, Oursler was born in Baltimore, the son of a transit worker, and left school at fourteen to help with his family's finances. He became a reporter with the *Baltimore American* at seventeen and a few years later started editorial work with magazines. He had a long career with Bernarr Macfadden publications that included a decade as editor of *Liberty Magazine* (1931–42) and the position of vice-president and editorial director of Macfadden Publications. Oursler went on to become a senior editor at *Reader's Digest*. Both his second wife, Grace Perkins, and a son by his first marriage, Will Oursler, were writers and in later life were Oursler's co-authors, as he began writing popularized versions of biblical stories and inspirational biographies of Roman Catholics, such as Father Flanagan, the founder of Boy's Town. His *The Greatest Story Ever Told* (New York: Doubleday, 1949) was made into a movie with the same title starring Charlton Heston (MGM, 1965) and Oursler had writer credits on ten other films. He was the author of thirty-two books and several plays.
(*New York Times*, 25 May 1952).

Parker, Walter (c.1874–July 17, 1950)
    A reporter who arrived in New Orleans at the age of nineteen, Parker was for many years a leading advocate for port and waterway development. He was prominent in both the Louisiana Boat Owners Association and the New Orleans Association of Commerce. He led a nationwide campaign for an inner harbor and navigation canal at New Orleans that dramatically increased port traffic. He also headed a successful campaign to protect Bayou St. John from over-development. He lived in The Sanctuary, a house built in 1798 at 924 Moss Street in Bayou St. John and the nearby Dumaine Street Bridge is named for him.
(New Orleans *Times-Picayune*, 18 July 1950).

Patrick, Maxine, *see* Maxwell, Patricia

Peacocke, James S. (?–?)
    A physician and resident of Bolivar County, Miss., the novel about antebellum plantation life for which he is included here was Peacocke's only known book and went through at least six editions under various titles.
(James B. Lloyd, ed., *Lives of Mississippi Authors, 1817–1967*, Jackson: University of Mississippi, 1981, s.v. "Peacocke, James S.").

Peck, William H(enry) (December 30, 1830–February 4, 1892)
    Although his family was one of the first to settle on Florida's Indian River, Peck spent most of his boyhood in schools elsewhere and attended Harvard College, receiving his bachelor's degree in 1853. In 1854 he married Mona Blake Kenny, granddaughter of Sir Thomas Blake of Menbough Castle, County Galway, Ireland. Between 1854 and 1860 he held several positions in

New Orleans public schools and at the University of Louisiana and during the Civil War was president at the Masonic Female College (Greenville, Ga.) and later the Collinsworth Institute (Talbotton, Ga.). In 1861 he established *The Georgia Weekly*, based in Atlanta and continued the publication through the war years, selling and moving to New Orleans in 1866 to devote himself to writing. In 1868 he relocated to New York City, where he lived in Harlem and was a major contributor to the *New York Ledger*, reportedly having an annual contract for the then-remarkable sum of ten-thousand dollars. The author of more than seventy-five books, Peck, moved to Atlanta in 1875 and purchased a hundred acres of orange grove in 1886 at Courtney along the Indian River in Florida, as well as a residence in Cocoa, Fla.
(*Report of the Harvard College Class of 1853*, Cambridge, Mass.: Harvard University, 1913).

Peddie, Jon (?–?)
    No information available.

Pendleton, Don (December 12, 1927–October 23, 1995)
    Pendleton had no formal education, but he wrote more than eighty books and is credited with introducing the action-adventure genre. Born in Little Rock, Ark., he lied about his age to enlist in the U.S. Navy in 1941, as a fourteen-year-old. In 1957, he enrolled in a mail order writing course and published a book before he completed the program. Although he began writing full-time when he was forty, producing a few mysteries and science fiction books each year, his breakthrough came when he wrote the first book featuring Mack Boland, "The Executioner," who battled the Mafia.
(*New York Times*, 28 October 1995).

Percy, Walker (May 28, 1916–May 10, 1990)
    Born in Birmingham, Ala., Percy's father committed suicide when he was eleven and his mother died in an automobile accident when he was thirteen. Along with his two brothers, he was adopted by his paternal cousin, writer William Alexander Walker, a resident of Greenville, Miss., who was well-connected in social and literary circles and friends with William Faulkner. After completing a pre-medical major in chemistry at the University of North Carolina (BA, 1937) and his MD at Columbia University College of Physicians and Surgeons (1941), Percy began his internship at New York's Bellevue Hospital with the intention of becoming a psychiatrist. However, he contracted pulmonary tuberculosis and, after several years of invalidism, decided to begin writing in preference to a medical career, a step enabled by the independence an inheritance provided. In 1946 he converted to Roman Catholicism, married, and subsequently established a family and wrote several novels, while publishing criticism and philosophical essays. He published his first book in 1961 and went on to publish a total of six novels and two works of non-fiction. He lived most of his adult life in Covington, La.
(*New York Times*, 11 May 1990).

Perkins, Kenneth (?–?)
    No information available.

Perko, Margaret (Snyder) (?–?)
    Born in Thorp, Wis. the daughter of Levi "Lee" and Eleanor (David) Snyder), Perko graduated from the University of Wisconsin-Madison (BA, 1942; MA, 1945). She married geologist Albert Perko in 1945 and lived with him in Venezuela. She is the author of one novel based upon this experience.

Perry, Stella G(eorge) S(tern) (December 8, 1877–November 7, 1956)
   An author of more than fifteen books and a contributor of poetry, stories, and articles to magazines, Perry was born in New Orleans and attended Newcomb College. She graduated from Barnard College of Columbia University in 1898, where she was one of four founding members of Alpha Omicron Pi, a national sorority. After working in advertising with the John Wanamaker Department Store, she founded her own advertising agency. She was the wife of George Hough Perry (married 1906) and lived in New Jersey, New York, and San Francisco. Perry was heavily involved in child welfare organizations and particularly active in advocating for legislation to control child labor and to protect working women.
(John William Leonard, ed., *Women's Who's Who of America, 1914–15*, New York: American Commonwealth, 1915, s.v. "Perry, Stella G. S.").

Peters, Natasha, *see* Cleaver, Anastasia N.

Pinkerton , Myron (?–?)
   No information available.

Pretorius (Kouts), Hertha (September 7, 1922–June 1, 1973)
   Born in New Orleans, the daughter of Harold Frederick and Isla (Hall) Pretorius, Kouts graduated from Louisiana State University (BA, 1942) and married Herbert John Cecil Kouts in 1942. She was the author of the one book for which she is included here.
(*Contemporary Authors Online*, Detroit: Gale, 2002, accessed 10 October 2013).

Prose, Francine (April 1, 1947–?)
   An author of twelve novels, numerous short stories, and books for children, Prose was born in Brooklyn, N.Y., the daughter of two physicians. She attended Radcliffe College (BA, 1968) and Harvard University (MA, 1969) and has taught creative writing at Harvard University (1971–72), the University of Arizona (1982–84), and Warren Wilson College in Swannanoa, N.C. (1984–present). In addition to her fiction which is known for incorporating allegorical, fanciful, or magical elements, Prose has earned a reputation as a skilled non-fiction writer for her journalism, literary criticism, and non-fiction books.
(*Dictionary of Literary Biography*, vol. 234, Gale, 2001, s.v. "Prose, Francine").

Pugh, Eliza Lofton (Phillips) (1841–July 24, 1889)
   A native of Louisiana, Pugh lived most of her life on plantations. Educated privately and at Miss Hull's Seminary in New Orleans, Pugh married the William W. Pugh, Jr. of Lyn's Hope Plantation in Assumption Parish, Louisiana when she was seventeen. Pugh's husband was president or chairman of several businesses, including a railroad, and politically active, serving in the Louisiana House of Representatives from 1852–58. She began writing and contributing short pieces to the *New Orleans Times* and national newspapers and magazines under the nom de plume "Arria" and published her first novel when she was twenty-six.
(Ida Raymond, *Southland Writers: Biographical and Critical Sketches of the Living Female Writers of the South*, Philadelphia: Claxton, Remsen, and Haffelfinger, 1870, 294).

Radford, Ruby Lorraine (December 7, 1891–July 19, 1971)
   Daughter of a city fireman in Augusta, Ga., Radford completed a teacher's training course and taught in the Augusta public schools from 1912–20, then completed graduate coursework at Columbia University in 1921 and began working as a freelance writer, publishing magazine fiction and books for children and young adults. She was a co-founder of the Augusta Authors Club in

1928 and a member of several literary and artistic clubs in Augusta, as well as the president of the Augusta Theosophical Society.
(*Atlanta* [Ga.] *Constitution*, 21 July 1971).

Reeser, Edwin Isherwood (July 29, 1900–September 5, 1976)
    A member of the Princeton class of 1922, Reeser worked as a reporter for several years at the New York *American*, before attending Yale University's School of Drama. He wrote radio scripts and worked in public relations before moving to Tulsa, Okla., and working in the oil royalty business. He went on to become a full-time writer. Reeser's campaign for governor of Oklahoma in 1934 attracted nationwide attention when he highlighted the evils of the political patronage system. He was the author of one novel for which he is included here.
(*Princeton Alumni Weekly*, vol. 78, 12 September, 1977).

Reymond, Dalton S(haffer) (October 11, 1896–January 23, 1978)
    After teaching as a college professor at Louisiana State University, Reymond worked in Hollywood as a set designer and technical adviser on films set in the South. He wrote the story for the movie *Song of the South* (Disney, 1946), a film that was widely criticized for racist portrayals of African-Americans.
(*Internet Movie Database*, http://www.imdb.com/name/nm0721468/bio, accessed, 1 October 2013).

Rice, Anne (October 4, 1941–?)
    Best-selling novelist Rice is a New Orleans native, the daughter of Howard Allen O'Brien, a postal worker. She grew up in the Irish Channel neighborhood until the death of her alcoholic mother, when Rice was fourteen, prompted her father to relocate his family to Texas where Rice finished school. She studied at Texas Women's University and graduated from San Francisco State University (BA, political science, 1964; MA, creative writing, 1971) and undertook additional study at the University of California, Berkeley. The wife of poet Stan Rice (1942–2002), she is known for a series of novels featuring vampires and another featuring witches. She has also written historical fiction and many of her works use New Orleans as a setting.
(*Dictionary of Literary Biography*, vol. 292, s.v. "Rice, Anne").

Richards, Clay, *see* Crossen, Kendell Foster

Riordan, Robert (?–?)
    No information available.

Ripley, Clements (August 26, 1892–July 22, 1954)
    A native of Tacoma, Wash., Ripley served in World War I, attaining the rank of captain in the 14th Field Artillery Regiment. In 1919, while stationed at Camp Jackson (Columbia, S.C.), he met Katherine Ball, the daughter of journalist W. W. Ball. The two married and had a long career as writers, often co-authoring works credited to Clements Ripley. Ripley contributed stories and serialized novels to pulp and national magazines, including *Adventure*, *Collier's*, *Redbook*, and *The Saturday Evening Post*. Several of his novels were made into movies and he co-authored some screenplays, as well. From the 1930s through the 1940s, Ripley had a series of contracts with Hollywood studios, some of which paid him $1,000 per week. His short story, "A Lady Comes to Town" was purchased by Metro-Goldwin-Mayer in 1934 for $30,000, up to that time the highest amount paid for a short story by a movie studio.
(*Clements and Katharine Ball Ripley Papers*, 1909–1996, South Caroliniana Library, University of South Carolina, http://library.sc.edu/socar/uscs/1998/ripley98.html, accessed 24 March 2014).

Robert, Paul J(ones) (?–?)
    No information available.


Roberts, Charles Blanton (January 1, 1874–February 9, 1939)
    A native of Blount County, Tenn., Roberts was secretary to Alexander A. Arthur, the founder of Middlesboro, Ky. Afterward, he lived in New York City for more than thirty-five years as the employee of a law firm, a journalist, and the author of several books. In later life he returned to the suburbs of Knoxville in Blount, Co. Tenn.
*(Charles Blanton Roberts Papers, 1881–1938*, Special Collections, The Filson Historical Society, Louisville, Ky., http://kdl.kyvl.org/catalog/xt7tht2g806q, accessed 24 March 2014).


Roberts, Marjorie (?–?)
    No information available.


Roberts, Walter Adolphe (October 15, 1886–September 14, 1962)
    A major figure in Jamaica's self-government movement, Roberts, the son of a clergyman, was born in Kingston in 1886. He migrated to the United States in 1904 at the age of eighteen, but had worked for roughly two years prior to this as a reporter for the *Daily Gleaner* (Kingston, Ja.). He continued to work as a journalist in New York City and was a war correspondent for the *Brooklyn Daily Eagle* from 1914–16. Later the editor of *Ainslee's Magazine* and *American Parade*, Roberts also published poetry, novels, and historical works. In 1936 he founded the Jamaica Progressive League, an association of Jamaican expatriates dedicated to self-government for their home country. The president of numerous Jamaican organizations, including the Jamaica Historical Society and the Poetry League of Jamaica, Queen Elizabeth II bestowed the title of Officer of the Most Excellent Order of the British Empire on him in 1961.
*(The* [Kingston, Jamaica] *Gleaner*, 31 Jul, 2011).


Robinson, J(ohn) H(ovey) (December 1820–February 18, 1867)
    Born in Sebec, Me., Robinson studied medicine at Bowdoin and Harvard Colleges without receiving any degrees and began a medical practice in Leicester, Mass. in 1848, later relocating to Worcester, Mass. He published a number of stories and serialized novels in the New York Mercury and Gleason's Pictorial and other story newspapers. After his death, his fiction was republished in book form by the publishing firm of Beadles and Adams.
(Albert Johannsen, *The House of Beadle and Adams Online*, Northern Illinois University, http://www.ulib.niu.edu/badndp/robinson_john.html, accessed 23 September 2013).


Rogér, Katherine Harvey (December 29, 1886–February 22, 1977)
    The member of two notable Louisiana families, the Harveys and the Destrehans, Rogér was the daughter of Horace Hale Harvey, who entered history as "Father of Inland Waterways." Earlier members of the family as far back as the 1720s were also important in the development of waterways in Louisiana. Rogér was born in Harvey, La. and later resided in Covington. She was the author of one novel, several family histories, and numerous magazine and newspaper articles.
(Katherine Harvey Rogér, *Memom's Diary*, Louisiana: Jeanie Marsolan Bazer, 2009).


Romani, Henri (?–?)
    No information available.


Root, Corwin (d. 1940?)
    A journalist and news editor for the *Toledo* (Ohio) *Blade*, Root was the author of one novel for which he is included here.
*(Toledo* [Ohio] *Blade*, 15 September, 1944)

Ross, Clinton (1861–March 26, 1920)

Born in Binghamton, N.Y., Ross was educated at Phillips Andover Academy and worked as a journalist before dedicating himself to writing historical fiction, mostly concerned with the American Revolution. He was living in Oswego, N.Y. at the time of his death.
(William Stewart Wallace, *A Dictionary of North American Authors Deceased Before 1950*, Toronto: Ryerson, 1968, s.v. "Ross, Clinton").

Ross, Marilyn, *see* Ross, William Edward Daniel

Ross, William Edward Daniel [Marilyn Ross, pseud.] (November 16, 1912–November 1, 1995)

Born in New Brunswick, Canada, Ross studied at Provincetown Theatre School (New York, N.Y.) in 1934 and took courses at Columbia University, the University of Chicago, the University of Michigan, and the University of Oklahoma. He was a traveling actor and actor manager with his own company (1930–48) and a film distributor for companies including Paramount and Monogram (1948–57). The author of more than three hundred gothic thrillers, nurse romances, and westerns, mostly under female pseudonyms, Ross is perhaps best known for his contributions to the Dark Shadows series.
(*W.E. Dan Ross Papers*, Howard Gotlieb Archival Research Center, Boston University).

Rutherford, Jacques (?–?)

No information available.

Ryan, Marah Ellis (February 27, 1866–July 11, 1934)

In her life time Ryan was regarded as an expert on Native American culture. Born in Butler County, Pa., early in adulthood she was an actress and published poetry. She married Samuel Erwin Ryan (1834–?) an Irish actor and comedian in 1883. In 1909 she moved to Arizona to live among the Navajo people and learn their culture. Between 1889 and 1924 she published nineteen novels.
(*New York Times*, 12 July 1934).

Sargent, Epes (September 27, 1813–December 30, 1880)

The son of a ship master, Sargent was born in Gloucester, Mass., but grew up in Roxbury, Mass., attending Boston Latin School (1823–29) and Harvard College. He held a series of editing positions in Boston and under the combined pseudonym Peter Parley collaborated with Samuel Goodrich to produce biographical fiction about America's founding fathers. In the 1830s he wrote several plays, including his great success, *Velasco*, in 1837. Written for English actress, Ellen Tree, the work was performed in several cities in the United States and in London. About the same time, Sargent wrote a poem that was set to music as the enduringly popular "A Life on the Ocean Wave," later the official march of the U.S. Merchant Marine Academy. He moved to New York City in 1839 and edited newspapers and magazines, including the *New York Mirror* and *The New World*. During this period he published his own magazine, a biography of Henry Clay, a collection of poems, and a novel. His writing and social life in New York placed him in the Knickerbocker Group of writers. Returning to Boston in 1847 as the editor of *The Boston Evening Transcript*, in the 1850s he published a series of books for Boston public schools that achieved national distribution. Beginning in the 1860s Sargent became a spiritualist and hosted séances and wrote several books on the topic. He was at work on his authoritative *Harper's Cyclopaedia of British and American Poets* at the time of his death; the book was published the following year (New York: Harper and Brothers, 1881).
(Francis Henry Underwood, *The Builders of American Literature: Biographical Sketches of American Born Authors Previous to 1826*, Boston: Lee and Shepard, 1893, 199–201).

Schachner, Nathan (January 16, 1895–October 2, 1955)

Born in New York and a graduate of City College (BS, 1915), Schachner worked as a chemist while earning his law degree from New York University (JD, 1919). A founder of the American Rocket Society, during World War I he served in the U.S. Army Chemical Warfare Division and after returning to civilian life worked as an attorney. He ended his legal practice in 1936 to write and went on to publish science fiction, historical fiction, and biographies. From 1945–51 he was a public relations and editorial consultant to the American Jewish Committee.
(*New York Times*, 3 October 1955).

Schertz, Helen Pitkin (August 8, 1877–December 26, 1945)

A New Orleans native and daughter of John Robert Graham Pitken and Helen Fearing Fuller, her father was Minister to the Argentine Republic. Schertz was privately educated and attended Newcomb College. She married German immigrant Christian Schertz in 1909, the owner of a chain of drugstores. Schertz was an organist, harpist, and amateur actress, and a charter member of Le Petit Théâtre du Vieux Carré. For a time she was a staff writer for the *New Orleans-Times Democrat*. She was devoted to women's suffrage and historic preservation. The owner of the residence known as the Spanish Custom House at 1300 Moss Street, she founded Spring Fiesta at her home in 1937. She was the author of collections of stories about New Orleans and several fictional works set there. She was an avid club woman and leader in philanthropic associations.
(John William Leonard, ed., *Women's Who's Who of America, 1914–15*, New York: American Commonwealth, 1915, s.v. "Schertz, Helen Pitkin").

Scott, Oberia, *see* Stone, Michael

Seifert, Shirley (May 22, 1888–September 1, 1971)

Known for the careful research on which her historical fiction was based, Seifert often chose to dramatize important figures, such as Ulysses S. Grant, Jefferson Davis, and George Rogers Clark. However, she also told the stories of now-forgotten Americans, focusing in all of her work on Kentucky and Missouri. She was born in St. Peters, Mo., and graduated from Washington University in St. Louis with majors in classical and modern languages. After working for a time as a teacher, she took courses in journalism and began writing. She published her first short story in 1919.
(*New York Times*, 4 September 1971).

Seley, Stephen (1915–May 8, 1982)

The author of three books published between 1945 and 1969, Seley was born in Brooklyn and grew up in South Orange and Newark, N.J. and Liberty, N.Y. He moved to Ibiza, Spain in 1957 and resided there until his death.
(*Stephen Seley Papers, 1953–79*, Kroch Library, Division of Rare and Manuscript Collections, Cornell University).

Sharkey, Emma Augusta Brown [Mrs. E. Burke Collins, pseud.] (1858–May 6, 1902)

The prolific author of serial novels for story newspapers and magazines as well as dime novels, Sharkey was born in Rochester, N.Y. and raised with her three sisters by her father after her mother's death when Sharkey was eight. She married disabled Union Army veteran Emmett Burke Collins when she was nineteen, with whom she had one son who died in infancy. After a failed bid for re-election as Justice of the Peace, Emmett relocated with Sharkey to Ponchatoula, La. in 1871 to an area where his father had purchased a plantation. He died from an accidental shooting in 1872. After her husband's death, Sharkey began publishing stories mostly with Louisiana settings in newspapers such as the *New York Clipper* and the New Orleans' *Times-Picayune*. She married James F. Skelton in 1879 and the couple divided their time between Tangipahoa, La. and a house

in New Orleans. Her second husband died in 1881 and during the next decade Sharkey's output increased dramatically and she was published in national publications. She relocated to Hendersonville, N.C. in 1898 and lived there for the rest of her life.
(Thomas William Herringshaw, ed., *Herringshaw's National Library of American Biography*, Chicago: American, 1909-14, s.v. "Sharkey, Emma Augusta Brown").

**Shore, William (February 4, 1919–June, 1974)**
    Born in Wyoming, Shore was a librarian who served as director of the Lake County (Ill.) Library District from 1961–64.

**Sinclair, Harold (May 8, 1907–May 24, 1966)**
    The author of nine novels, Sinclair was born in Chicago but grew up in Bloomington, Ind. with a maternal aunt and uncle, after his railroad fireman father abandoned his mother. Even after publishing his first novel and receiving a Guggenheim fellowship to work on a second, Sinclair was forced to support himself and his family (he married in 1933 and had six children with his wife Ethel Moran) with a series of jobs, including machine operator. His most successful book was *The Horse Soldiers* (New York: Harper, 1956), a Civil War novel that was made into a movie of the same title and directed by John Huston and starred John Wayne (Mirisch Corporation, 1959). Sinclair took an avid interest in Dixieland jazz, taught himself the trumpet, and for a time had his own band. The novel for which he is included here focuses on jazz.
(*Harold Sinclair Collection*, McLean County [Ind.] Museum of History).

**Smith, Annie Laura [Catherine Von Scyler, pseud.] (1873–?)**
    No information available.

**Smith, Minette Graham (1888–December 6, 1955)**
    The daughter of a Baptist minister, the author was born in Meridian, Miss. and graduated from Blue Mountain College. She was the wife of Methodist minister Reverend Gobe Smith and devoted herself to aiding him in his pastorates.
(*Florence* (S.C.) *Morning News*, 3 April 1955).

**Smith, Richard Penn (March 13, 1799–August 12, 1854)**
    A native of Philadelphia and life-long resident of the city, Smith studied law with William Rawle, but after the success of a newspaper column he entitled "The Plagiarist" he bought a small newspaper named *The Aurora* which he published and edited from 1822–27. After the production of his first play in 1828 he turned his focus to the theater and sold his newspaper. From 1828–36 he wrote thirteen plays and two novels. His most successful work was also his most scandalous. Several journals by Davy Crockett had previously been published, but in 1836, Smith claimed to have discovered Crockett's final journal, carried from the Alamo by a Mexican general. The work he published was actually fiction written by Smith.
(Everett Augustus Duyckinck and George L. Duyckinck, eds., *Cyclopaedia of American Literature*, vol. 2, New York: C. Scribner, 1856, s.v. "Richard Penn Smith").

**Snelling, Laurence (?–?)**

**Sparkia, Roy Bernard [Mitchell Caine, pseud.] (October 31, 1914–November 6, 1992)**
    Best known as the designer and creator of the Empire State Building's illuminated panels depicting the Seven Wonders of the World, the author was born in Owosso, Mich. He studied at the Art Students League in New York City before serving as a staff sergeant in the U.S. Army during World War II in Europe. After the end of the war, Sparkia attended the University of Shrivenham (1945–46), Columbia University (1947–48) and New York University (1950–51).

The technique he used for creating the Empire State panels that involved hardened resin was considered innovative and led to a number of commissions. He was the author of fourteen novels published between 1954 and 1981.
(*Contemporary Authors Online*, Detroit: Gale, 2009, accessed 14 October 2013).

Sparling, (Edward) Earl (November 23, 1897–February 15, 1951)
    Born in Little Rock, Ark., Sparling was a New York journalist who wrote several books about notable members of the American Stock Exchange. He studied at Tulane University and served in the coast artillery during World War I. He then began a career as a journalist, writing for *The New Orleans Item* before relocating to New York City to work for *The World* (later *The New York World-Telegram*) for which he worked the rest of his life. He published widely in national magazines and was the author of one novel for which he is included here.
(*New York Times*, 16 February 1951).

Spencer, Elizabeth (July 19, 1921–?)
    The author was born in Carrollton, Miss. into a family that had lived in the area for generations. She graduated from Belhaven College in Jackson, Miss. (BA, 1942) and completed a master's degree at Vanderbilt University (1943). She taught at the college level before a Guggenheim Fellowship took her to Italy where she met and married Englishman John Rusher, subsequently moving with him to Canada where she lived from 1961 to 1986. She returned that year to the United States and a faculty position at the University of North Carolina, Chapel Hill, from which she retired in 1992. The author of nine novels, Spencer is noted for her short stories, many of which have been published in seven collections. Her novel *The Light in the Piazza* (New York: McGraw-Hill, 1960) was made into a movie starring Olivia de Havilland and Yvette Mimieux in 1962 (Metro-Goldwyn-Mayer) and a musical version (lyrics and music by Adam Guettel) opened in New York City in 2005 and went on to win six Tony Awards in 2006.
(*Contemporary Authors*, vol. 65, New Revision Series, Detroit: Gale, 1998).

Sperry, Armstrong (Wells) (November 7, 1897–April 26, 1976)
    The great-grandson of sea captain Sereno Armstrong (1811–1894), Sperry was inspired by the sailing tradition in his family, even though his father was a New Haven, Conn. businessman. He attended Stamford Preparatory School (1908–15), the Art Students League (1915–1918) and Yale School of Art (1918) before his draft to serve in World War I. Shortly after returning to civilian life he traveled around the South Pacific (1920–21) and in 1924 and 1925 was part of an ethnological expedition for the Bishop Museum of Honolulu, traveling to remote islands. Although he returned to New York City, married, and settled in New Haven, Conn., the trips became the basis for a series of paintings and illustrations (he was the illustrator for the first edition of *Tarzan and the Lost Empire*), and for his own illustrated children's books, published in the 1930s set in the South Seas. After an extended stay in Santa Fe, N. Mex., he wrote several books set in the Southwest. He is best known for *Call It Courage* (New York: MacMillan, 1940), a Newberry Medal Award Winner that remains in print.
(*Armstrong Wells Sperry Papers*, de Grummond Children's Literature Collection, The University of Southern Mississippi).

Sprague, William Cyrus (1860–1922)
    A publisher known for pioneering instruction through correspondence courses, Sprague was born in Malta, Ohio and graduated from Denison College (now University, Granville, Ohio) (BA, 1881). After graduating from Cincinnati Law School (1883) and being admitted to the bar, he was president of Sprague Publishing Company, the Sprague Correspondence School of Journalism, and the Sprague Correspondence School of Law, all in Cincinnati. He subsequently relocated to

Chicago and edited several publications of interest to lawyers, as well as publishing at least five works of historical fiction for boys.
(William Raimond Baird, *Biographical Records of Members of the Beta Theta Pi*, New York: Beta, 1914, s.v. "Sprague, William Cyrus").

Stahl, *see* Wharton, George M(ichael)

Stahls, Charles Gilbert (July 25, 1905–August 7, 1971)
   Born in Tennessee, Stahls graduated from Northwestern State College in Natchitoches, La. and subsequently lived in Shreveport and New Orleans. During World War II he was a fighter pilot with the U.S. Air Force in North Africa and Italy. In the final decades of his life he lived in California and is buried in Forest Lawn Memorial Park (Hollywood Hills), Los Angeles, Calif.

Statham, Frances Patton (January 26, 1931–?)
   A lyric coloratura soprano who concertized internationally, Statham published more than a dozen romance novels. Born in Catawba, S.C., she graduated from Winthrop College (Rock Hill, S.C.) (BS, 1951) and after marriage and children completed graduate study at the University of Georgia (MFA, 1970). In addition to singing, teaching choral music, and writing, Statham has an extensive record of service with community and charitable organizations, earning her a place in the *International Who's Who of Community Service*.
(*Contemporary Authors Online*, Detroit: Gale, 2002, accessed 10 October 2013).

St. Cyr, Sylvester (May 29, 1931–January 3, 2002)
   A native of New Orleans and the son of jazz musician Johnnie St. Cyr, a member of Louis Armstrong's band, the author was a paratrooper in the U.S. Army during the Korean Conflict and later a member of the New Orleans Police Department. His experiences as a policeman form the basis for his only novel, for which he is included here.
(Book jacket copy).

Stephens, Ann Sophia (March 30, 1810–August 20, 1886)
   Considered one of the United States' most significant female writers during her lifetime, Stephens was a highly prolific author of popular fiction and domestic advice books, as well as an editor of several popular magazines. Born Ann Sophia Winterbotham in Humphreysville (now Seymour), Conn., the author married printer Edward Stephens in 1831. The couple relocated to Portland, Me., where they founded the *Portland Magazine* for women and Stephens began writing stories for national magazines and newspapers that often featured Native American characters. After several serialized novels, she published her first book in 1839 and went on to publish over forty more. She is noted for writing the first novel published by Beadle and Adams, a firm that would have such an enormous impact on nineteenth-century readers. After the couple moved to New York City in 1837, Stephens added to her literary activities editorship of national magazines such as *Ladies' Companion*, *Peterson's Magazine*, and *Frank Leslie's Lady's Gazette*. She and her husband also became hosts of a well-attended literary salon through which they befriended major writers. Although her novels are not read today, current scholars have noted Stephens as the first example of a literary businesswoman who made savvy decisions to establish a career as a well-paid author and editor.
(*Dictionary of Literary Biography*, vol. 250, Detroit: Gale, 2002).

Stoddard, William Osborn (September 24, 1835–August 29, 1925)
   An early supporter of Abraham Lincoln who went on to serve as a secretary in the White House, Stoddard was born in Homer, N.Y., and graduated from the University of Rochester (BA, 1858). He relocated to Illinois to work as a journalist, becoming editor and proprietor of the *Cen-*

*tral Illinois Gazette* in Champaign. After Lincoln's election, Stoddard was made an assistant to John Hay and John Nicolay. He was later appointed U.S. Marshall for Arkansas (1864–65) but resigned on health grounds and moved to New York City where he had a long career on Wall Street. He later innovated textiles for the automobile industry and invented the artificial leather known as Duratex, subsequently establishing a factory in Newark, N.J. to manufacture textiles. A prolific author, mostly for boys, Stoddard published more than one hundred books between 1869 and his death.
(*Dictionary of American Biography*, vol. 9, pt. 2 New York: Scribners' Sons, 1964, s.v. "Stoddard, William Osborn").

Stone, Elisabet M. (?–?)
    No information available.

Stone, Michael [legally changed from Oberia Scott] (1912–May 12, 1965)
    A native of Louisiana and a New Orleans debutante, Scott married Herbert J. Freezer, a New York businessman. Freezer invested in real estate and backed Broadway shows, including a revival of Mae West in *Diamond Lil* and a Michael Todd production of *Star and Garter*. The couple divorced in the 1950s and went through legal wrangles over property, including the Park Avenue apartment which Scott (who legally changed her name to Michael Stone) eventually sold to Zsa Zsa Gabor. Her first novel, *And Tomorrow* (Sovereign House, 1938) dealt with the challenges of a Jewish-Christian marriage. She was a professional lecturer living in Beverly Hills, Calif. at the time of her death.
(*New York Times*, 14 May 1965).

Stone, Robert (?–?)
    No information available.

Stuart, (Mary) (Routh) Ruth McEnery (February 19, 1852–May 16, 1917)
    An author of local color writing that was widely popular in the late nineteenth century, Stuart was born Mary Routh McEnerny in Marksville, La., where her father served as mayor. Her family had significant land holdings in Louisiana and was prominent in state politics. By 1860, Stuart's family was living in New Orleans where her father was employed in the U.S. Customs House and Stuart attended school. As a young woman she taught at the Loquet-LeRoy Institute and married a businessman and landholder from Washington, Ark., named Alfred Ogden Stuart. After his death in 1883, Stuart returned to New Orleans and began earning her own living by publishing short fiction. Her works set in fictional Simkinsville, Ark. won her a national audience and enabled her to move to New York City. Between 1888 and 1917 she published over seventy-five stories in national magazines such as *Harper's Bazaar*, *Century Magazine*, and *Lippincott's*.
(Nancy A. Williams and Jeannie Whaym, eds., *Arkansas Biography: A Collection of Notable Lives*, Fayetteville: University of Arkansas, 2000, s.v. "Stuart, Ruth McEnerny").

Summerton, Winter [pseud.] (?–?)
    No information available.

Sumner, Albert W. (?–?)
    No information available.

Swann, Francis (July 16, 1913–August 27, 1983)
    Born in Annapolis, Md., Swann attended Princeton University (1931) and Johns Hopkins University (1932–33). An actor, musician, and stage director in his youth, Swann wrote several

plays that were mostly produced in the 1940s and 1950s. He later wrote motion picture scripts. In the 1960s and 1970s he published eleven novels, mostly with Lancer Books.
(*Contemporary Authors Online*, Detroit: Gale, 2003, accessed 10 October 2013).

Sweet, George Elliot (September 26, 1904–January 30, 1997)
   A geophysicist and Shakespeare denier, Sweet was born in Denver, Colo., and graduated from the University of Oklahoma (BS, 1927; MS, 1928). He undertook additional study at Harvard University (1940–41) and was in the U.S. Naval Reserve (1942–45). He founded Sweet Geophysical Company in 1940 in Malibu, Calif. and the firm discovered several oil fields, most notably in Alabama. Most of Sweet's books deal with the oil industry or present his theory that Shakespeare did not author the works attributed to him.
(*Contemporary Authors Online*, Detroit: Gale, 2003, accessed 10 October 2013).

Tabony, Annie Heller (c. 1883–March 5, 1965)
   The wife of William H. Tabony of Pointe á la Hache, Plaquemines Parish, La., Tabony was very active in the Methodist Church.
(*Times-Picayune*, 26 April 1960).

Tait, Dorothy [Ann Fairbairn, pseud.] (c.1902–February 8, 1972)
   A native of Cambridge, Mass. and a graduate of the Leland Powers School in Boston, Tait was secretive about her personal life. Although she was twice married and divorced, the names of her husbands are unknown. Among the few known facts are her residence in New Orleans for a number of years as a young woman and that she lived in Rio de Janeiro for two and a half years. In addition to working as a newspaper reporter and a news editor, she had jobs with radio and television stations in California, where she was living in Monterey at the time of her death. She had also handled the tours of George Lewis and his band for ten years, an experience on which her novel (for which she is included here) and her biography of Lewis are based.
(*New York Times*, 11 February 1972).

Tallant, Robert (April 20, 1909–April 1, 1957)
   A New Orleans native, Tallant's friendship with Lyle Saxon inspired his writing career that began with an appointment as an editor on the Louisiana Writers' Project of the Works Project Administration. In this position Tallant completed the folklore compilation entitled *Gumbo Ya-Ya*. Between 1946 and his death he wrote eight novels and six non-fiction books, as well as a number of shorter works mostly with New Orleans settings, earning him the unofficial title of "novelist-laureate" of New Orleans.
(*Robert Tallant Papers, 1938–1957*, Manuscripts Collection, Louisiana Division, New Orleans Public Library)

Thomas, H.C., *see* Keating, Lawrence A.

Thompson, John B(urton) (1913–?)
   No information available.

Thompson, (John) Edward (1910–?)
   No information available.

Thompson, Maurice (?–?)
   No information available.

Thornton, Marcellus Eugene (?–?)
No information available.


Tinker, Edward Larocque (September 12, 1881–July 6, 1968)
A New Yorker with a significant inherited income, Tinker took as his second wife New Orleanean Frances McKee, and made Louisiana a focus of research. Born in New York and educated at the Browning School, Tinker graduated from Columbia University (AB, 1902) and got his law degree from New York Law School (1905). Although he was admitted to the New York bar and worked as a lawyer for the Legal Aid Society, in private practice, and for the El Paso and Southwestern Railroad, by 1913 he devoted himself to his many avocations and intellectual projects, engaging only in officer positions with his family's bank and realty company. Although his interests were fairly broad, Louisiana and New Orleans were a consistent focus. His doctoral dissertation at the Sorbonne (1932) was on written and spoken French in nineteenth-century Louisiana. He later published a bibliography of Louisiana newspapers and magazines; a study on Creole dialects; and collected the writings of Lafcadio Hearn. He co-authored the works of historical fiction for which he is here included with his wife.
(Perkins, et al., *Benet's Encyclopedia of American Literature*, New York: HarperCollins, 1991, s.v. "Tinker, Edward Larocque").


Tinker, Frances (July 4, 1886–December 16, 1958)
Born in Vicksburg, Miss., the daughter of Federal Judge James Martin McKee, Tinker grew up in New Orleans and married Omenzo Colby Ford Dodge, a naval officer. The couple resided in Washington, D.C. and were active in society. After her divorce from Dodge, Tinker married Edward Larocque Tinker in 1919. The couple resided in New Orleans, Washington, D.C., and New York City and were active in society. Tinker was a co-author of historical fiction with her husband and, after he founded the Tinker National Bank on Long Island, she was listed as an officer. After her death, her husband established The Tinker Foundation in her memory, devoted to promoting better understanding among the peoples of the United States, Latin America, Spain, and Portugal.
(*New York Times*, 18 December 1958).


Tomlinson, Everett T(itsworth) (May 5, 1859–October 31, 1931)
Born in Shiloh, Md., Tomlinson graduated from Williams College (AB, 1879) and Colgate University (PhD, 1888). He was the head of several schools prior to 1888 when he was called to the pastorate of Central Baptist Church in Elizabeth, N.J., where he served for twenty-three years. During this time period he began writing books for boys, and his work became so popular that he resigned his position to devote himself to writing. However, he continued in leadership roles with the American Baptist Education Board and the American Baptist Mission Home Society. He also successfully led the Ministers and Missionaries' Benefit Board of the Northern Baptist Convention in establishing a pension system for the Baptist Church of America.
(*New York Times*, 31 October 1931).


Toole, John Kennedy (December 17, 1937–March 26, 1969)
A native of the Uptown neighborhood of New Orleans, Toole was the son of an automobile salesman whose early deafness forced his mother to contribute to the family finances with music and elocution lessons. He graduated from Tulane University (BA, 1958) and Columbia University on a Woodrow Wilson Fellowship (MA, 1959). After a period teaching at Southwestern Louisiana Institute (now University of Louisiana, Lafayette), Toole accepted a doctoral fellowship at Columbia during which he taught at Hunter College. When he resigned the fellowship in 1961, he was drafted and served two years at the U.S. Army Training Center at Fort Buchanan, Puerto Rico. After his honorable discharge in 1963 he began teaching at Dominican College in New Orleans and spent a considerable amount of his time in the French Quarter, while still living with his

parents. After a mental breakdown, he committed suicide outside Biloxi, Miss., unsuccessful in getting published the novel in which he had such faith (and for which he is included here). In 1976 his mother convinced Walker Percy, then teaching at Tulane University, to read the novel and he became the work's advocate, seeing it to publication. Toole was posthumously awarded the Pulitzer Prize for fiction for the book in 1981.
(Cory MacLauchlin, *Butterfly in the Typewriter*, Boston: Da Capo, 2012).

Townsend, Mary Ashley (1836–June 7, 1901)
    Born Mary Ashley Van Voorhis in New York City, after her marriage in 1853 she relocated with her husband to New Orleans. Under the pen name "Xariffa," she submitted essays and articles to the New Orleans *Delta*, *Crescent*, and *Picayune*. She was also known for her novels and poetry.
(Perkins, et al., *Benet's Reader's Encyclopedia of American Literature*, vol. 1, New York: HarperCollins, 1991, s.v., "Townsend, Mary Ashley").

Tracey, Francis (?–?)
    No information available.

Tressner, William B. (?–?)
    No information available.

Trollope, Frances Milton (March 10, 1779–October 6, 1863)
    Born into modest circumstances in Heckfield, England, the daughter of a clergyman, Trollope's marriage did not materially improve her circumstances and the more than one hundred books she published during her lifetime were partly written out of financial need. In an age when women had little independence, Trollope managed to travel widely, leaving her husband in England and voyaging with her sons. She first journeyed to the United States with three of her children to join her friend Frances Wright's utopian community, Nashoba, located in Tennessee. When the community failed, she was thrown upon her own resources and began writing her observations of Cincinnatians. This became the germ of her first book, *Domestic Manners of the Americans* (London: Whitaker, Treacher, 1832) and established a kind of franchise of such accounts that focused on people rather than sights, and was followed with accounts of travel in Belgium, Germany, France, Austria, Bavaria, and Italy. She later wrote novels, and is known for using them to advance the rights of individuals such as children, factory workers and African-American slaves. She relocated permanently to Florence, Italy in 1838. Two of her sons went on to become writers, most notably her fourth son, Anthony Trollope.
(*Dictionary of Literary Biography*, vol. 166, Detroit: Gale, 1996, s.v. "Trollope, Frances").

Turner, James H(enry), (Jr.) (1933–?)
    Born in Hattiesburg, Miss., Turner graduated from Princeton University and is the author of one novel for which he is included here.
(James B. Lloyd, ed., *Lives of Mississippi Authors*, 1817–1967, Jackson: University of Mississippi, 1981, s.v. "Turner, James H.").

Vane, Roland, *see* McKeag, Ernest Lionel

Van Epps, Margaret T. (?–?)
    No information available.

Vaughan, Carter A., *see* Gerson, Noel Bertram

Van der Veer, (John) Stewart [also known as Stewart Vanderveer] (June 27, 1893–December 27, 1966)

Born in Frankfort, Ky., Vanderveer relocated to New Orleans as a young man when his family moved to the city. He served in the local Washington Artillery in order to join the Pershing Expedition to Mexico and in World War I was an ambulance driver on the Italian Front as part of the American Red Cross. He later worked as a journalist for the New Orleans *Times-Picayune* and founded his own advertising firm in Birmingham, Ala. in 1924. He began writing short fiction and published his first novel in 1939. He published two additional novels, but unable to transition to writing full-time, continued in the advertising business, until retiring to his farm outside Birmingham when he wrote an unpublished memoir.

(*John Stewart Van der Veer Papers*, Birmingham (Ala.) Public Library).

Veillon, Lee (October 2, 1942–?)

Born in Church Point, La., Veillon graduated from Our Lady of the Lake College (Baton Rouge) (BA, 1966) and University of Southwestern Louisiana (now University of Louisiana, Lafayette) (MA, 1970). A Roman Catholic nun for seven years (Sisters of Divine Providence, 1958–65), she later worked as a teacher in public schools and as an English instructor at the college level. In addition to novels, she wrote several plays.

(*Contemporary Authors Online*, Detroit: Gale, accessed 30 September 2013).

Vidal, (Eugene) (Luther) Gore [Katherine Everard, pseud.] (October 3, 1925–July 31, 2012)

The author of twenty-five novels, two memoirs, plays, screen plays, and television dramas, Vidal's personality and provocative opinions made him one of the most visible literary figures in twentieth-century American culture. Born at West Point, N.Y., where his father was a flying instructor (he would found three airlines, one of which would become T.W.A. and serve as director of the Bureau of Air Commerce in the Roosevelt administration), Gore began a life of social privilege and direct connection to political power. His mother, Nina Gore, was the daughter of Oklahoma senator Thomas P. Gore and, after divorcing Vidal's father, she married Hugh D. Auchincloss, who was also the stepfather of Jacqueline Kennedy Onassis. Educated at St. Albans School and Philips Exeter Academy, Vidal enlisted in the Army upon graduation and wrote his first novel based on his experiences. Published in 1946, the book attracted broad attention. After several more books, Vidal published a novel that directly dealt with homosexuality and, although a bestseller, drew the animosity of some publications and reviewers, causing Vidal to publish under pseudonyms for a period of years, even as he was becoming a public figure by running for political office, hosting radio and television programs, and engaging in political commentary. After the success of *Myra Breckinridge* (Boston: Little, Brown, 1968) a book that dealt with sexual reassignment surgery and homosexuality, Vidal published a series of historical novels and secured an enduring reputation for his essays on American culture and politics. Near the end of his life he was honored for lifetime achievement by the National Book Awards.

(*New York Times*, 2 August 2012).

Vinton, Iris (March 3, 1905–February 6, 1988)

An author of biographies, novels, and plays for children, Vinton was born in West Point, Miss., but lived most of her adult life in New York City. A graduate of Incarnate Word College (San Antonio, Tex.) (AB, 1928) she was a school teacher before working as editor for *You and Your Child* magazine. She was the director of publications for the Boys' Clubs of America for twenty years (1944–64) and published more than twenty books.

(*New York Times*, 9 February 1988).

Von Scyler, Catherine, *see* Smith, Annie Laura

Waldo, James Curtis [Tim Linkinwater, pseud.] (December 10, 1835–August 28, 1901)

Born in Meredosia, Ill., the son of James Elliott Waldo, his father had taught in New Orleans for several years before relocating to take advantage of his family's land grants in Illinois, when President Tyler named him a Custom House Officer in Louisiana. He became a member of the import firm, Miller, Harris and Waldo in 1849. After an education in public schools, Waldo began working at his father's firm. He also worked for a time in a mercantile firm in New York City, but returned South to fight in the Confederate Army. His support for the Southern Cause continued after the war and he was active as a journalist and editorialist. One of the founders of the White League, he was later very active in New Orleans Mardi Gras organizations and was one of the founders of the Carnival Court.

(Alcee Fortier, ed., *Louisiana: Comprising Sketches of Parishes, Towns, Events, Institutions and Persons*, Madison, Wisc.: Century Historical Association, 1914, vol. 3, 584-5).

Walker, Mary Alexander (September 24, 1927–August 28, 2009)

An author of children's books, Walker was born in Beaumont, Tex., and graduated from Lamar Technological College (Beaumont, Tex.) (AA, 1947), Texas Woman's University (Denton, Tex.) (BA, 1950), and San Francisco State University (MA, 1981). The wife of physician Tom Ross Walker, the author taught in public schools in Arkansas, Iowa, Ohio, Texas, and Washington from 1947–68. She later taught courses as an instructor at the college level about writing children's literature.

(*Contemporary Authors Online*, Detroit: Gale, accessed 30 September 2013).

Wall, Evans (November 16, 1886–June 10, 1963)

Born on his family's cotton plantation, Richland, Wall attended Soule Commercial College (New Orleans), Tulane Law School, and Louisiana State University. He held many types of jobs, including automobile salesman, deputy sheriff, steamboat deckhand, and wheat harvester, however he lived extended periods of his life in relative isolation at Richland Plantation and in the swamps of Louisiana. From 1929 to 1953 Wall published short stories and novels, mostly set in the South.

(*Evans Spencer Wall, Jr. Papers*, Special Collections, Lousiana State University).

Waller, Leslie (April 1, 1923–March 29, 2007)

Born in Chicago and a graduate of Hyde Park High School, Waller became a police reporter after high school before attending Wilson Junior College. A volunteer with the U.S. Army Air Corps during World War II, he began publishing novels in the early 1940s. At the end of the war, he attended the University of Chicago and later worked in New York City as an advertising account executive. One of his organized crime novels made it to the *New York Times* bestsellers list, and several of his books were produced as movies, including *Dog Day Afternoon* (directed by Sidney Lumet and starring Al Pacino; Warner Brothers, 1975), *Close Encounters of the Third Kind* (directed by Steven Spielberg and starring Richard Dreyfuss; Columbia Pictures, 1977), and *Hide in Plain Sight* (directed by and starring James Caan; Metro-Goldwin-Mayer, 1980).

(*Internet Movie Database*, http://www.imdb.com/name/nm0909063/, accessed 12 December 2013).

Walworth, Jeannette H(adermann) (February 22, 1837–February 4, 1918)

Although she was born in Philadelphia, Walworth moved as a child to Washington, Miss. where her father was a faculty member at Jefferson College. She became governess to a plantation family in Louisiana when she was sixteen and lived with them through the Civil War. Afterwards, she moved to New Orleans and published in newspapers but, unable to support herself, went to live with her sister and began writing novels. Within a few years of publishing her first book in 1870 she married Major Douglas Walworth of Natchez, Miss. The couple lived on the Walworth plantation in Arkansas; in Memphis, Tenn.; and for a few years in New York City, before returning to Natchez in 1889 where Major Walworth was editor of the *Natchez Democrat*. After his death in 1915, Walworth relocated to live in the home of relatives in New Orleans until her death. From 1870 to 1900 Walworth wrote and published twenty-eight books.

(James B. Lloyd, ed., *Lives of Mississippi Authors*, 1817–1967. Jackson: University of Mississippi, 1981, s.v. "Walworth, Jeannette Hadermann").

Ward, William (?–?)
No information available.

Warren, Robert Penn (April 24, 1905–September 15, 1989)

Considered one of America's most notable twentieth-century authors, Warren was born in the small town of Guthrie, Ky., near the Tennessee border. A precocious student, he graduated high school at fifteen and earned degrees at Vanderbilt University, Yale, and Oxford (on a Rhodes Fellowship) by the time he was twenty-three years old. He then began the career of a writer and English professor that he was to pursue for the rest of his life. A poet, as well as a novelist, he was the Poet Laureate (1944–45) and won Pulitzer Prizes for both his poetry and fiction. While a professor at Louisiana State University (1933–42) he became a close observer of the administration of Governor Huey Long, the inspiration for his best known novel, *All the King's Men* (New York: Harcourt, Brace, 1946).

(*Dictionary of Literary Biography*, vol. 152, s.v. "Warren, Robert Penn").

Wassermann, Moses (July 15, 1811–October 18, 1892)

Born in Ansbach, Bavaria, Wasserman was educated at the universities of Würzburg and Tübingen, from which he received his doctorate in 1832. From 1837–73 he was the rabbi of Möhringen and from 1873 until his death the rabbi of Stuttgart. Wassermann had no connection with the United States and wrote no other fiction except for the fictional biography on Judah Touro for which he is included here.

(Albert M. Friedenberg, "Moses Wasserman," *American Jewish Historical Quarterly*, vol. 20, 1911, 152–154).

Watkins, Glen (?–?)
No information available.

Waugh, Alec (July 8, 1898–September 3, 1981)

An English author from a literary family that included his father, well-known critic and publisher Arthur Waugh, and his brother Evelyn, who would become a famous novelist, Waugh was born in Hampstead, England and educated at Sherborne school, from which he was expelled after a series of inappropriate romantic friendships. While serving with the Dorset Regiment in World War I, Waugh authored his first novel drawing upon his school experiences. Although the book was considered scandalous, sales were substantial and the title was reprinted sixteen times. From then until his death Waugh wrote approximately sixty books, including novels, story collections, memoirs, travel books, and non-fiction. A bon vivant who traveled extensively throughout his life while pursuing numerous love affairs, Waugh lived in the United States for extended periods of time and visited New Orleans repeatedly, setting the novel for which he is included here in that city.

(*Dictionary of Literary Biography*, vol. 191, s.v. "Waugh, Alec").

Webber, Everett (August 30, 1909–?)

A scholar of utopian communities as well as a novelist, Webber was born in Charleston, Miss. and graduated from the College of the Ozarks (Point Lookout, Mo.) (AB, 1931) and the University

of Missouri (AM, 1933). He was a teacher of English and journalism at Northwestern State University (1956–75) and lived in Natchitoches, La. after his retirement.
(James B. Lloyd, ed., *Lives of Mississippi Authors*, Jackson: University of Mississippi, 1981, s.v. "Webber, Everett").

Webber, Olga (1910–1974)
    Wife and co-author with Everett Webber.

Wellman, Manly Wade (May 21, 1903–April 5, 1986)
    Best known for his short science fiction published in the 1930s through 1950s, Wellman also wrote novels, thirty-five mysteries and works of historical fiction for young adults, and more than a dozen history books. Born in what is now the country of Angola, where his father was working as a medical officer, Wellman was educated at the Municipal University of Wichita (now Wichita State University) (AB, 1926) and Columbia University (BLitt, 1927). Although he lived in New York City in the 1930s to be near publishers of science fiction, he spent most of his adult life in North Carolina, where he was considered a major figure among state writers. He also taught creative writing at Elon College and the University of North Carolina.
(Noelle Watson and Paul E. Schellinger, eds., *Twentieth Century Science Fiction Writers*, St. Martin's, 1991, s.v. "Wellman, Manly Wade").

Wellman, Paul Iselin (October 14, 1898–September 16, 1966)
    A brother of Manly Wade Wellman, the author was born in Enid, Okla., but spent much of his childhood in Angola where his father was a medical officer in mission hospitals. A graduate of Fairmont College (now Wichita State University) (AB, 1918), Wellman was a journalist with Wichita and Kansas City newspapers for twenty-five years. Subsequently, he was a screenwriter for Warner Brothers (1944, 1946) and Metro-Goldwyn-Mayer (1945–46), a freelance writer (1946–66), and partner in a cattle ranch. As a teenager, Wellman worked on cattle drives and visited the major cattle towns, experiences which informed his historical fiction and works of popular history about the West. He was the author of more than thirty books of juvenile and adult fiction and adult non-fiction. Seven of his books were adapted for the movies and he authored several screenplays.
(Geoffrey Sadler, ed., *Twentieth-Century Western Writers*, 2nd ed., Chicago: St. James, 1991, s.v. "Wellman, Paul Iselin").

Wells, Charlie (August 2, 1923–October 10, 2004)
    A native of Greenwood, Miss., Wells studied at Georgia Institute of Technology, Tulane University, and graduated from Mississippi State University (BA, 1943). Wells served in the U.S. Army during World War II. For most of his adult life, Wells worked as a draftsman. He was the author of one hardback and one paperback noir mystery. He was personally acquainted with Mickey Spillane, who helped him revise his books for publication.
(James B. Lloyd, ed. *Lives of Mississippi Authors, 1817–1967*, Jackson: University of Mississippi, 1981, s.v. "Wells, Charlie").

Welty, Eudora (April 13, 1909–July 23, 2001)
    One of the most revered writers in the United States during the twentieth century, Welty wrote short stories and novels set in the South. A life-long resident of Jackson, Miss., Welty attended Mississippi State College for Women (now Mississippi University for Women) (1926–27), graduated from the University of Wisconsin (BA, 1929) and took graduate coursework at Columbia University Graduate School of Business (1930–31). After working for several newspapers and small radio stations, Welty was the publicity agent for the Mississippi state office of the Works Progress Administration before working full-time as a writer. Her short stories were published

widely and printed in collections; she also wrote six novels. A winner of the O. Henry Award, she also received a Pulitzer Prize for Fiction, the National Institute of Arts and Letters Gold Medal, and the Presidential Medal of Freedom. After her death, her home was named a National Historic Landmark and opened as a public museum.
(Carolyn J. Brown, *A Daring Life: A Biography of Eudora Welty*, Jackson: University Press of Mississippi, 2012).

Wharton, Edward Clifton (November 18, 1827–June 13, 1891)
A journalist and New Orleans resident, Wharton was educated at Jefferson College in St. James Parish, La., and was a colonel in the Confederate Army, serving in the Trans-Mississippi Department. He wrote and produced plays in addition to the novel for which he is included here.
(*Edward Clifton Wharton Family Papers*, Louisiana and Lower Mississippi Collection, Louisiana State University Libraries)

Wharton, George M(ichael) [Stahl, pseud.] (July 10, 1825–August 28, 1853)
Born near the current Tuscumbia, Ala., Wharton attended West Point Academy (1841–43) and graduated from New York University Medical School (1847). After practicing medicine for a few years in his hometown he joined the staff of the *Weekly Delta* (New Orleans) in 1852 on the basis of humorous sketches he had published in Southern newspapers that were collected in a book in 1851. His sketches for the *Delta* were also collected as a book in 1853 some months before his death from yellow fever.
(Frederick Jonas Dreyfus, "Life and Works of George Michael Wharton, MD," *Tennessee Historical Quarterly*, vol. 6, no. 4, December 1947, 4–24).

White, Charles William [Max White, pseud.] (1906–?)
Active from the 1930s to 1950s, White resided in New York's Greenwich Village, Paris, and Spain and was member of a circle that included well-known writers and artists. Alice Neel painted his portrait twice and he worked with Alice B. Toklas on her autobiography (a failed project). He published six novels, mostly works of fictional biography about great artists (Francisco Goya, Charles Baudelaire, and William Blake).
(Catalog Record, [*Painting of Max White*], 1935 by Alice Neel).

White, Max, *see* White, Charles William.

Whiteside, Muriel McCullen (?–?)
No information available.

Whitman, (Vivian) Willson (1874–1957)
Nothing could be found about the author who wrote a biography on David Lilienthal and histories of the Tennessee Valley Authority and the Federal Theatre Project and was a frequent contributor to *The Nation*. The novel for which she is included here is her only known work of fiction.

Whitney, Phyllis A(yame) (September 9, 1903–February 8, 2008)
The daughter of an American shipping line representative, Whitney's youth was spent in China, Japan, and the Philippines. After the death of her father, she moved back to the United States in 1918 with her mother, who was terminally ill with cancer. Following her mother's death two years later, Whitney lived with an aunt in Chicago and graduated from McKinley High School there in 1924. Although she wanted to attend college, she was not able to afford the costs and worked at the Chicago Public Library and in bookstores. After publishing her first book for children, she worked as a children's book editor at the *Chicago Sun* (1942–1946) and subsequently at

the *Philadelphia Inquirer*. Starting in 1947 she was a freelance writer, publishing more than seventy-five books of juvenile fiction, adult romantic suspense, and mysteries. She traveled frequently throughout her life and was known for the care with which she established the physical settings of her novels based on direct observations.
(Martin Seymour-Smith and Andrew C. Kimmens, eds., *World Authors, 1900–1950*, New York: H. W. Wilson, 1996, s.v. "Whitney, Phyllis Ayame").

Whittington, Harry [Ashley Carter, pseud.] (February 4, 1915–June 11, 1989)
    A prolific author of soft cover original fiction, between 1951 and 1963 he published eighty-five books, mostly pseudonymous Westerns and crime novels. Born in Ocala, Fla., he was educated in public schools and took extension and night courses in a wide range of subjects. He served in the U.S. Navy during World War II and was stationed at Pearl Harbor (1945–46). After a series of editing and copywriting jobs in the 1930s and 1940s, he was a freelance writer for most of his career. In addition to novels, he wrote screenplays and television scripts and published more than one-hundred short stories, mostly in national magazines for men.
(Geoff Sadler, ed., *Twentieth-Century Western Writers*, 2nd ed., St. James Press, 1991, s.v. "Whittington, Harry").

Whyte, J.H. (?–?)
    No information available.

Wibberley, Leonard [Patrick] [O'Connor] (April 9, 1915–November 22, 1983)
    Born in Dublin, Ireland, Wibberley attended public schools and had started working at sixteen as a newspaper copy boy before the disruption brought about by the Great Depression forced him into a series of modest jobs, including ditch digger and dishwasher. He arrived in the United States in 1943 and worked in shipyards before getting newspaper jobs. In 1950, he began working for the *Los Angeles Times*. He published his first book in 1952 and went on to write more than one-hundred more, including a significant body of work for juveniles and young adults. He is perhaps best known for his "Mouse" trilogy of satires that featured the fictional Duchy of Grand Fenwick. Two books in the trilogy were made into movies.
(*Contemporary Authors Online*, Detroit: Gale, 2007, accessed 1 October 2013).

Widmer, Mary Lou (1926–?)
    A native of New Orleans, and descendant of a soldier who fought with General Jackson in defense of the city, Widmer graduated from Loyola University (AB, 1944) at the age of eighteen through an accelerated degree program. She did not begin writing novels until after she had raised a family and worked as a schoolteacher. Her first book, for which she is included here, was published in 1980 and she has gone on to write twelve more novels, mostly works of historical fiction.
(*Author Page, Willow Moon Publishing*,
    http://www.willowmoonpublishing.com/marylouwidmer.html, accessed 1 October 2013).

Wilburn, George T. (?–?)
    No information available.

Wilde, Jennifer, *see* Huff, T(om) E(lmer)

Wilkes-Hunter, Richard Albert [Diana Douglas, pseud.] (March 14, 1906–January 20, 1991)
    An Australian writer who authored more than 110 paperback novels under various pseudonyms between 1948 and 1964, Wilkes-Hunter began his writing career as a journalist working for the *Sydney* (Australia) *Daily Guardian* (1926–30). When the newspaper closed he worked jobs ranging from truck driver to ranch hand, while writing hundreds of short stories for story papers

and magazines in a number of English-speaking countries. In the 1940s and 1950s he edited several publications before devoting himself to writing full time, starting in 1954.
(*Contemporary Authors Online*, Detroit: Gale, 2002, accessed 1 October 2013).

Wilkinson, Clement Penrose [Judge L.Q.C. Brown, pseud.] (November 21, 1850–January 31, 1917)
    No information available.

Williams, Ben Ames (March 7, 1889–February 4, 1953)
    The author of more than two-hundred short stories and forty novels, Williams was one of America's best known writers in the 1930s and 1940s. The grandson of a Welsh immigrant who had settled in Ohio, Williams was born in Macon, Miss. but grew up in Jackson, Ohio where his father, Daniel Webster Williams, owned and operated a newspaper. Williams learned many aspects of printing working for his father before attending Dartmouth College (AB, 1910). For a time Williams was a reporter with the *Boston* (Mass.) *American* and published in pulp magazines before the steady acceptance of his short stories by the *Saturday Evening Post* emboldened him to begin writing full time in 1917. Over his career the *Saturday Evening Post* printed 135 of his short stories. He began summering in Maine in 1918 and eventually many of his short stories were set in the imaginary village of Fraternity, Me. As the magazine industry changed over the 1930s, Williams transitioned from short stories to longer fiction and in the last thirteen years of his life focused on writing novels.
(*Dictionary of Literary Biography*, vol. 102, s.v. "Williams, Ben Ames").

Williams, Moses (?–?)
    No information available.

Williams, Wirt (August 21, 1921–June 29, 1986)
    A reporter for Louisiana newspapers in the 1940s, beginning in 1953 Wirt was a professor of English at California State College at Los Angeles and published six novels. Born in Goodman, Miss., Wirt graduated from Mississippi Delta State College (Cleveland, Miss.) (BA, 1940), Louisiana State University (MA, 1941), and the State University of Iowa (PhD, 1953). During World War II he served in U.S. Navy. Before the war he was a reporter for the *Shreveport* (La.) *Times* (1941–42) and afterwards worked for the *New Orleans Item* (1946–49). After completing his doctorate, he began a thirty-three year career as a college professor. His novel *Ada Dallas* was filmed as Ada (Metro-Goldwyn-Mayer, 1961).
(James Vinson, ed., *Contemporary Novelists*, 3rd ed., New York: St. Martin's, 1982, s.v. "Wirt, Williams").

Winn, Mary Polk (?–?)
    No information available.

Wirt (Benson), Mildred A(ugustine) (July 10, 1905–May 28, 2002)
    Benson grew up on a farm near Ladora, Iowa and, at the age of fourteen, sold her first story to *St. Nicholas* magazine. She studied journalism at the University of Iowa, becoming the program's first female graduate in 1927. When she married Asa A. Wirt in 1928, she moved with him first to Cleveland and then Toledo, Ohio. While still in graduate school, she began writing for the Edward Stratemeyer Syndicate, initially as a ghostwriter for the Ruth Fielding series. She went on to write, under the author name of Carolyn Keene, twenty-three of the first thirty of the Nancy Drew books published by the syndicate. She also wrote under four other pseudonyms for the Syndicate. Beginning in 1944, she was a columnist for the *Toledo (Ohio) Blade.* By the end of her writing career

she had produced more than one hundred novels in addition to her many news articles and columns, and was officially recognized as the original author for the Nancy Drew books.
(Laurie Collier and Joyce Nakamura, eds., *Major Authors and Illustrators for Children and Young Adults*, 2nd ed., Detroit: Gale, 1993, s.v. "Benson, Mildred Augustine Wirt").

Woodford, Jack, *see* Woolfolk, Josiah Pitts

Woodiwiss, Kathleen E[rin] (June 3, 1939–July 6, 2007)
    Born Kathleen Erin Hogg in Alexandria, La., the daughter of a disabled veteran who died when she was a child, she was raised in a single-parent household of eight children. Woodiwiss married U.S. Air Force Lieutenant Ross Eugene Woodiwiss when she was seventeen and lived with him in Japan, Topeka, Kan., and rural Minnesota. She had difficulty placing her first novel, a six hundred page work of historical fiction that included frank descriptions of sex, until she approached Avon books and a new subgenre of historical romance was born when it was finally published in 1972. Woodiwiss' novels are lengthy, include exotic settings on several continents, and feature plots in which the relationship between the hero and heroine gradually develops with repeated sexual encounters. The length of her books and the care she took in writing limited her output to eleven novels, however her books have sold a total of thirty-six million copies and one of her books was on the *New York Times* bestseller list for over a year. Although she lived much of her adult life in Minnesota, she returned to Louisiana in her final decade.
(Lesley Henderson, ed., *Twentieth-Century Romance and Historical Writers*, Chicago: St. James, 1990, 2nd ed., s.v. "Woodiwiss, Kathleen").

Woolfolk, Josiah Pitts [Jack Woodford, pseud.] (March 25, 1894–May 16, 1971)
    An author of pulp fiction and how-to books on writing who published under several pseudonyms, Woolfolk also wrote for the motion picture industry. He grew up in Chicago, living with an affluent grandmother while his father worked as a physician in private practice in Sioux City, Iowa (his mother died when he was quite young). Although his father returned to Chicago to teach at Rush Medical College, he died when Woolfolk was still a boy. Woolfolk began publishing in story magazines in the 1920s and during his main period of productivity, from the 1930s to 1953, published sixty novels. Because Woolfolk's writing was often sexually suggestive, he was persecuted by authorities and citizen's groups dedicated to "moral purity." In response, he founded his own publishing house, Woodford Press, in 1946, although the books he published were often banned and seized by police. He was eventually sentenced to a year in prison for mail fraud as part of this persecution. The bookstore owners that sold his novels were sometimes sentenced to prison as well. From the early 1930s until 1951 he lived in Hollywood and worked as a scriptwriter, although most of his writing for movies is uncredited. His only child, daughter Louella Woolfolk, wrote as Louella Woodford. She suffered from schizophrenia and was eventually institutionalized. Woolfolk's finances were kept drained by the costs of her hospitalization and he was eventually bankrupted. Woolfolk was institutionalized with delusional paranoia in 1962 and spent the last decade of his life hospitalized in the Eastern State Hospital (Williamsburg, Va.), the same facility as his daughter. Woolfolk's books on writing are still highly regarded and have been praised by Piers Anthony, Ray Bradbury, and Robert Heinlein.
(*Washington Post*, 19 May 1971).

Woolrich, Cornell [George] [Hopley-] [William Irish, pseud.] (December 4, 1903–September 25, 1968)
    An influential author of suspense and hard-boiled detective fiction novels that have been credited with inspiring French film noir, Woolrich was a native New Yorker and lived most of his life there. His father, a civil engineer, separated from his mother when Woolrich was a youngster and he spent a number of years with his father in South America and Mexico before returning to New

York City to live with his mother at age twelve. Woolrich attended Columbia University (1921–25) but left without taking a degree after the publication of his first book in 1926. His second novel, published in 1927, won a prize from National Pictures and he moved to Los Angeles in 1928 to work on a screenplay of the book. After a brief marriage that reputedly ended due to Woolrich's promiscuous homosexuality, he moved back to New York City in 1931, living with his mother in a residential hotel until her death in 1957. Despite a troubled personal life that included alcoholism and an inability to build lasting personal relationships, Woolrich published more than forty novels, as well as numerous short stories, several of which were adapted for movies. One of these was *Rear Window*, adapted into a movie of the same name directed by Alfred Hitchcock and starring James Stewart (Paramount, 1954). The Francois Truffaut film *The Bride Wore Black* (Dino de Laurentis, 1968) was based on the novel of the same title (Simon and Schuster, 1940) (*Dictionary of Literary Biography*, vol. 226, Detroit: Gale, 2000, s.v. "Woolrich, Cornell").

Yates, Dorothy (1929–?)
    No information available.

Yerby, Frank (September 5, 1916–November 29, 1991)
    Born in Augusta, Ga., a person of mixed race who was treated as an African-American, Yerby published thirty-three books between 1946 and 1985 that sold over fifty-five million copies. A graduate of Paine College (Augusta, Ga.) (AB, 1937) and Fisk University (Nashville, Tenn.) (MA, 1938) he began a career as a teacher in historically African-American colleges, before rejecting segregated education and engaging in defense-related factory work during World War II. His first writings were short stories that dealt with race issues, but he soon focused on mainstream historical fiction featuring Anglo-Saxon protagonists. He was criticized for this throughout his career and received mostly critical notices from reviewers, despite his broad readership. He left the United States in 1955 to reside in Madrid, Spain and in France for extended periods. Three of his books were adapted as films, all under their original titles, The Foxes of Harrow, starring Rex Harrison and Maureen O'Hara (Twentieth Century Fox, 1947); The Golden Hawk, starring Sterling Hayden and Rhonda Fleming (Esskay Pictures, 1952); and The Saracen Blade, starring Ricardo Montalban (Columbia Pictures, 1954).
(*Dictionary of Literary Biography*, vol. 76, "Yerby, Frank").

Yoseloff, Martin (July 26, 1919–March 27, 1997)
    The author of nine novels published over a forty year career, Yoseloff was born in Sioux City, Iowa and graduated from the University of Iowa (BA, 1941). He served in the U.S. Army during World War II and after a time working in New York City as an editorial assistant in publishing firms, was a teacher at the Drake Business School in Manhattan for more than forty-six years and a novelist.
(*Contemporary Authors Online*, Gale, 2000, accessed 2 October 2013).

# Appendix A
# Works First Published after 1980

Abbott, Jeff. *Panic*. London, U.K.: Time Warner Books, 2006. 370pp.

Abbott, Tony. *Bayou Dogs*. New York: Scholastic, 2009. 117pp.

Abbott, Tony and Alex Eckman-Lawn. *City of the Dead*. New York: Scholastic, 2009. 134pp.

Abel, Kenneth. *The Burying Field*. New York: G.P. Putnam's Sons, 2002. 291pp.

—. *Cold Steel Rain*. New York: G.P. Putnam's Sons, 2000. 386pp.

—. *Down in the Flood*. New York: Minotaur Books, 2009. 346pp.

Adamov, Bob. *Promised Land*. Cuyahoga Falls, Ohio: Packard Island, 2006. 268pp.

Adams, Pepper. *That Old Black Magic*. New York: Silhouette Books, 1992. 189pp.

Adcock, Thomas Larry. *Thrown-Away Child: A Neil Hockaday Mystery*. New York: Pocket Books, 1996. 340pp.

Adeline, L. Marie. *S.E.C.R.E.T.: A Novel*. New York: Broadway Books, 2013. 271pp.

Agnello, Frank J. *The Contadino*. Houston, Tex.: Royal Hill, 2008. 472pp.

Agresti, Aimee. *Infatuate*. Boston: Houghton Mifflin Harcourt, 2013. 407pp.

Albert, Michele. *Getting Her Man*. New York: Avon Books, 2002. 378pp.

—. *Off Limits*. New York: Avon Books, 2003. 375pp.

Alexander, Lacey. *French Quarter*. Hudson, Ohio: Ellora's Cave, 2004. 204pp.

Alexander, R.G. *Tempt Me*. New York: Heat, 2011. 260pp.

Alfonsi, Alice. *Eternal Vows*. New York: Jove Books, 1997. 355pp.

Alison, Jane. *The Marriage of the Sea*. New York: Farrar, Straus, Giroux, 2003. 262pp.

Allan, Christa. *Love Finds You in New Orleans, Louisiana*. Minneapolis: Summerside, 2012. 318pp.

Allen, Danice. *Arms of a Stranger*. New York: Avon Books, 1995. 374pp.

Allen, R.E. *Ozzy on the Outside*. New York: Delacorte Press, 1989. 196pp.

Allende, Isabel. *Island Beneath the Sea*. Translated by Margaret Sayers Peden. New York: Harper Collins, 2010. 457pp.

Alsobrook, Rosalyn. *Beyond Forever*. New York: Kensington, 1995. 398pp.

Amoss, Berthe. *Secret Lives*. New York: Dell, 1988. 180pp.

Andersen, Susan. *Be My Baby*. New York: Avon Books, 1999. 372pp.

Anderson, Celia. *Love, Ocean: A Novel*. Little Rock, Ark.: Tempie Rene, 2009. 138pp.

Andrews, V(irginia) C(leo). *All That Glitters*. New York: Pocket Books, 1995. 344pp.

—. *Hidden Jewel*. New York: Pocket Books, 1995. 373pp.

—. *Pearl in the Mist*. New York: Pocket Books, 1994. 374pp.

—. *Ruby*. New York: Pocket Books, 1993. 428pp.

—. *Tarnished Gold*. New York: Pocket Books, 1996. 314pp.

—. *Twisted Roots*. New York: Pocket Books, 2002. 389pp.

Antieau, Kim. *Ruby's Imagine*. Boston: Houghton Mifflin, 2008. 201pp.

Archer, Jane. *Bayou Passion*. New York: Zebra Books, 1991. 447pp.

Arnold, Judith. *In the Dark*. New York: Harlequin Books 2006. 248pp.

—. *Legacy of Secrets*. New York: Harlequin Books, 1998. 248pp.

—. *Married to the Man*. New York: Harlequin Books, 1996. 298pp.

Arnold, Margot. *Death of a Voodoo Doll*. Woodstock, Vt.: Foul Play Press, 1989. 220pp.

Asfar, Dan. *Ghost Stories of Louisiana*. Edmonton, Alb.: Lone Pine, 2007. 206pp.

Ashley, Diane and Aaron McCarver. *Camellia*. Uhrichsville, Ohio: Barbour, 2012. 313pp.

Asprin, Robert. *Dragons Wild*. New York: Ace Books, 2008. 360pp.

Asprin, Robert and Jodi Lynn Nye. *Dragons Deal*. New York: Ace Books, 2010. 385pp.

Asprin, Robert, Quinn Fawcett, and Teresa Patterson. *No Quarter*. College Station, Tex.: Dark Star Books, 2009. 288pp.

Atkins, Ace. *Crossroad Blues: A Nick Travers Mystery*. New York: St. Martin's Press, 1998. 226pp.

—. *Dirty South*. New York: William Morrow, 2003. 291pp.

August, Anita. *Gut Bucket Blues: A Novel*. El Paso, Tex.: Stanley, 2007. 267pp.

Austin, Dee. *Reckless Heart*. New York: Pocket Books, 1985. 180pp.

Azod, Shara. *Remy Goes to Therapy*. Tacoma, Wash.: Cacoethes, 2008. 131pp.

—. *Thierry's Angel*. Tacoma, Wash.: Cacoethes, 2007. 208pp.

Bahr, Howard. *Pelican Road: A Novel*. San Francisco: MacAdam Cage, 2008. 299pp.

Bailey, Frankie Y. *You Should Have Died on Monday*. Johnson City, Tenn.: Silver Dagger Mysteries, 2007. 219pp.

Bain, Donald. *Murder in a Minor Key: A Novel*. New York: Signet Mystery, 2001. 263pp.

Baker, Mark Ballard. *Da Queen A'Sleep: A Story of Waking and Sleeping in New Orleans*. Victoria, B.C.: Trafford, 2006. 299pp.

Baker, S.H. *Death of a Dancer*. Austin, Tex.: Zumaya Enigma, 2009. 244pp.

Banks, L.A. *Left for Undead*. New York: St. Martin's Paperbacks, 2010. 288pp.

—. *Never Cry Werewolf*. New York: St. Martin's Paperbacks, 2010. 323pp.

Barbieri, Elaine. *Midnight Rogue*. New York: Kensington, 1995. 384pp.

Barnes, Linda. *Cities of the Dead*. New York: St. Martin's Press, 1986. 184pp.

Barr, Nevada. *13 1/2*. New York: Vanguard, 2009. 311pp.

—. *Burn: An Anna Pigeon Novel*. New York: Minotaur Books, 2010. 378pp.

Barrett, Jean. *Private Investigations*. Richmond, Va.: Silhouette Books, 2003. 251pp.

Bart, Aubrey. *The Bluesiana Snake Festival: A Novel*. Berkeley, Calif.: Counterpoint, 2010. 180pp.

Barton, Fredrick. *Black and White on the Rocks: (with Extreme Prejudice)*. New Orleans: Univ. of New Orleans Press, 2013. 388pp.

—. *Courting Pandemonium: A Novel*. Atlanta: Peachtree, 1986. 350pp.

—. *The El Cholo Feeling Passes*. Atlanta: Peachtree, 1985. 461pp.

—. *A House Divided: A Novel*. New Orleans: University of New Orleans Press, 2003. 352pp.

Barton, Fredrick. *With Extreme Prejudice: A Novel.* New York: Villard Books, 1993. 368pp.

Basham, A.C. Red [C. Boy, pseud.]. *Chandler's Destiny.* Coral Springs, Fla.: Llumina, 2005. 127pp.

Batonne, Eva. *Resurrection Diva.* Austin Tex.: Zumaya Enigma, 2008. 311pp.

Battle, Lois. *Storyville.* New York: Viking, 1993. 435pp.

Baxter, Mary Lynn. *Without You.* Don Mills, Ont.: Mira Books, 2004. 377pp.

Bazán, Nicolás G. *Una Vida: A Fable of Music and the Mind.* Chandler, Ariz.: Five Star Publications, 2009. 218pp.

Beaumont, Charles and John Tomerlin. *Run from the Hunter.* Illustrated by J.K. Potter. Lakewood, Colo.: Centipede, 2012. 192pp.

Beckman, Patti. *Lousiana Lady.* New York: Silhouette Books, 1981. 189pp.

Becnel, Rexanne. *Old Boyfriends.* Don Mills, Ont.: Harlequin Books, 2005. 298pp.

Bellestri, Joseph. *The Sins of the Father.* New York: Carlton, 1981. 142pp.

Bellingeri, Chelsea. *Wicked Betrayal.* N.p.: Chelsea Bellingeri, 2012. 278pp.

Benedict, Barbara. *Always.* New York: Kensington, 1995. 411pp.

Benoit, Remy. *Loving.* Liverpool, U.K.: Pharaoh Press / Remy Benoit, 2003. 272pp.

Bens, Jeff W. *Albert, Himself.* Harrison, N.Y.: Delphinium Books, 2001. 180pp.

Berkowitz, Alan B. and Allen K. Kinchen. *The Jazz Girls and the Flyboy: A Jewish Saga of WWII and Israel, Tragedy, Revenge, Love and Redemption.* Charleston S.C.: CreateSpace, 2010. 421pp.

Bessette, Alicia. *Scrumpy Delight for Polly Pinch.* Millers Point, Australia: Pier 9, 2010. 311pp.

Bicos, Olga. *Risky Games.* New York: Kensington, 2002. 342pp.

—. *Wrapped in Wishes.* New York: Kensington, 1996. 429pp.

Biggs, Cheryl. *Devil of a Chance.* New York: Bantam Books, 1996. 212pp.

—. *Hearts Deceived.* New York: Kensington, 1994. 400pp.

Billerbeck, Kristin. *A Billion Reasons Why.* Nashville, Tenn.: Thomas Nelson, 2011. 311pp.

Black, Brandon and Christopher Wong, eds. *New Orleans by Gaslight.* New Orleans: Black Tome Books, 2013. 232pp.

Black, Clever. *The Holland Family Saga. Part One, They Don't Mind Dying.* N.p.: Clever Black Books, 2012. 372pp.

Black, Nikita, Allyson James, and Sheri Whitefeather. *Wedding Favors.* New York: Heat, 2010. 309pp.

Blackstock, Terri. *Line of Duty.* Grand Rapids, Mich.: Zondervan, 2003. 381pp.

Blackwell, Elise. *The Unnatural History of Cypress Parish.* Denver, Colo.: Unbridled Books, 2007. 210pp.

Blair, Cynthia. *The Jelly Bean Scheme.* New York: Fawcett / Juniper, 1990. 122pp.

Blake, Daniel. *City of Sins.* London, U.K.: Harper Collins, 2011. 468pp.

Blake, James Carlos. *A World of Thieves: A Novel.* New York: William Morrow, 2002. 295pp.

Blake, Toni. *In Your Wildest Dreams.* New York: Warner Books, 2005. 421pp.

Blakely, Mike. *Moon Medicine.* New York: Forge, 2001. 414pp.

Blume, Lesley M.M. *Tennyson.* New York: Alfred A. Knopf, 2008. 288pp.

Boll, Andrea. *The Parade Goes on without You.* New Orleans: NOLA Fugees Press, 2009. 152pp.

Bonansinga, Jay R. *Twisted.* New York: Kensington, 2006. 351pp.

Bonin, William O. *House on Arabella Street.* N.p.: William O. Bonin, 2011. 412pp.

Born, James O. *Burn Zone.* New York: G.P. Putnam's Sons, 2008. 310pp.

Bosworth, Sheila. *Almost Innocent.* New York: Simon and Schuster, 1984. 268pp.

—. *Slow Poison: A Novel.* New York: Alfred A. Knopf, 1992. 321pp.

Bowie, J.P. *A Deadly Deception: A Nick Fallon Investigation.* Albion, N.Y.: MLR Press, 292pp.

Bowker, Richard. *Replica.* Toronto, Ont.: Harlequin Books, 1986. 300pp.

Boyden, Amanda. *Babylon Rolling.* New York: Pantheon Books, 2008. 307pp.

Bradley, Eden, Sydney Croft, and Stephanie Tyler. *Hot Nights, Dark Desires.* New York: Bantam Books, 2008. 336pp.

Bradley, Jean Burr. *Shamrock Green.* Edmonton, Alb.: Commonwealth Publications, 1995. 454pp.

Bradley, John Ed. *My Juliet.* New York: Doubleday, 2000. 260pp.

—. *Restoration: A Novel.* New York: Doubleday, 2003. 308pp.

Bradman, Tony and Martin Chatterton. *Voodoo Child*. London, U.K.: Egmont, 2004. 85pp.

Brady, Jacklyn. *Arsenic and Old Cake*. New York: Berkley Prime Crime, 2012. 299pp.

—. *Cake on a Hot Tin Roof*. New York: Berkley Prime Crime, 2012. 297pp.

—. *The Cakes of Wrath*. New York: Berkley Prime Crime, 2013. 295pp.

—. *A Sheetcake Named Desire*. New York: Berkley Prime Crime, 2011. 296pp.

Branley, Bill. *Sea Changes: A Novel*. Bainbridge Island, Wash.: One Sock Press, 2006. 241pp.

Brant, Kylie. *Close to the Edge*. New York: Silhouette Books, 2005. 250pp.

—. *Truth or Lies*. New York: Silhouette Books, 2003. 250pp.

Brashear, Jean. *Love Is Lovelier*. New York: Harlequin Books, 2006. 245pp.

Braxton-Barshon, Brenna. *Through All Eternity*. New York: Harper Collins, 1992. 374pp.

Breaux, Jerry. *Kinfolks*. New York: Vantage, 1992. 347pp.

Breaux, Magdalene. *Imaginary Playmate*. Fairburn, Ga.: Breaux Books, 2002. 326pp.

Brewer, James D. *No Bottom*. New York: Walker, 1994. 249pp.

—. *No Justice*. New York: Walker, 1996. 246pp.

—. *No Remorse*. New York: Walker, 1997. 263pp.

—. *No Virtue*. New York: Walker, 1995. 232pp.

Brezenoff, Steven. *The Zombie That Visited New Orleans*. Illustrated by C.B. Canga. Mankato, Minn.: Stone Arch, 2010. 80pp.

Brickell, Claude. *The Napoleon Connection: A Novel*. New York: Bricbooks, 2008. 254pp.

Brite, Poppy Z. *Antediluvian Tales*. Burton, Mich.: Subterranean, 2007. 116pp.

—. *The Devil You Know*. Burton, Mich.: Subterranean, 2003. 198pp.

—. *Drawing Blood*. New York: Delacorte Press, 1993. 373pp.

—. *Exquisite Corpse*. New York: Simon and Schuster, 1996. 240pp.

—.*The Lazarus Heart*. New York: Harper Prism, 1998. 213pp.

—. *Liquor: A Novel*. New York: Three Rivers, 2004. 339pp.

—. *Lost Souls*. London, U.K.: Penguin Books, 1994. 359pp.

Brite, Poppy Z. *Prime: A Novel.* New York: Three Rivers, 2005. 283pp.

—. *Second Line: Two Short Novels of Love and Cooking in New Orleans.* Easthampton, Mass.: Small Beer, 2009. 259pp.

—. *Soul Kitchen: A Novel.* New York: Three Rivers, 2006. 276pp.

—. *The Value of X.* Burton, Mich.: Subterranean, 2003. 183pp.

Brown, Dave. *Pinkerton Partners.* Jefferson, Colo.: Golden Feather, 2001. 239pp.

Brown, John Gregory. *Decorations in a Ruined Cemetery.* Boston: Houghton Mifflin, 1994. 244pp.

—. *The Wrecked, Blessed Body of Shelton Lafleur.* Boston: Houghton Mifflin, 1996. 257pp.

Brown, Sandra. *Fat Tuesday.* New York: Warner Books, 1997. 454pp.

—. *French Silk.* New York: Warner Books, 1992. 403pp.

—. *Sunny Chandler's Return.* New York: Bantam Books, 1987. 183pp.

Brownworth, Victoria A. *Day of the Dead.* Midway, Fla.: Spinsters Ink, 2009. 170pp.

Bruhns, Nina. *Sweet Revenge.* New York: Silhouette Books, 2002. 249pp.

Brunner, John. *The Great Steamboat Race.* New York: Ballantine Books, 1983. 568pp.

Buck, Carole. *Peachy's Proposal.* New York: Silhouette Books, 1996. 186pp.

Buckey, Sarah Masters. *The Haunted Opera: A Marie-Grace Mystery.* Illustrated by Sergio Giovine. Middleton, Wis.: American Girl, 2013. 184pp.

—. *Marie-Grace and the Orphans.* Illustrated by Christine Kornacki and Cindy Rosenheim. Middleton, Wis: American Girl, 2011. 91pp.

—. *Marie-Grace Makes a Difference.* Illustrated by Christine Kornacki and Cindy Rosenheim. Middleton, Wis.: American Girl, 2011. 88pp.

—. *Meet Marie-Grace.* Illustrated by Christine Kornacki and Cindy Rosenheim. Middleton Wis.: American Girl, 2011. 105pp.

—. *The Smuggler's Treasure.* Middelton, Wis.: Pleasant, 1999. 163pp.

Bulot, Blaise. *Dark Waters.* Boston: Croker Sack Books, 1993. 117pp.

. *Starr Lyte.* Boston: Croker Sack Books, 1996. 159pp.

Burke, James Lee. *Black Cherry Blues.* New York: Avon Books, 1990. 326pp.

Burke, James Lee. *Burning Angel: A Novel*. New York: Hyperion Books, 1995. 340pp.

—. *Cadillac Jukebox: A Dave Robicheaux Novel*. New York: Hyperion Books, 1996. 297pp.

—. *Creole Belle*. New York: Simon and Schuster, 2012. 528pp.

—. *Dixie City Jam*. New York: Hyperion Books, 1994. 367pp.

—. *Glass Rainbow*. New York: Simon and Schuster, 2010. 433pp.

—. *Heaven's Prisoners*. New York: Pocket Books, 1989. 274pp.

—. *In the Electric Mist with Confederate Dead*. New York: Hyperion Books, 1993. 344pp.

—. *Jolie Blon's Bounce*. New York: Pocket Star Books, 2002. 449pp.

—. *Last Car to Elysian Fields*. London, U.K.: Phoenix, 2003. 369pp.

—. *Light of the World*. New York: Simon and Schuster, 2013. 548pp.

—. *The Lost Get-back Boogie: A Novel*. Baton Rouge: Louisiana State University Press, 1986. 241pp.

—. *A Morning for Flamingos*. New York: Avon Books, 1990. 319pp.

—. *The Neon Rain*. New York: Henry Holt, 1987. 248pp.

—. *Pegasus Descending*. London, U.K.: Orion Books, 2006. 356pp.

—. *A Stained White Radiance*. New York: Hyperion Books, 1992. 305pp.

—. *Sunset Limited*. New York: Doubleday, 1998. 309pp.

—. *Swan Peak*. London, U.K.: Phoenix, 2009. 476pp.

—. *The Tin Roof Blowdown: A Novel*. New York: Simon and Schuster, 2007. 373pp.

Burnes, Caroline. *A Christmas Kiss*. New York: Harlequin Books, 1996. 249pp.

—. *Familiar Obsession*. New York: Harlequin Books, 2000. 250pp.

Burns, Jillian. *Relentless Seduction*. Don Mills, Ont.: Harlequin Books Blaze, 2013. 218pp.

Burton, Jaci. *Riding on Instinct*. New York: Heat, 2009. 296pp.

Burton, Milton T. *The Devil's Odds: A Mystery*. New York: Minotaur, 2012. 257pp.

Busbee, Shirlee. *Love Be Mine*. New York: Warner Books, 1998. 403pp.

Butler, Robert Olen. *A Small Hotel*. New York: Grove Press, 2011. 256pp.

Byerrum, Ellen. *Raiders of the Lost Corset: A Crime of Fashion Mystery*. New York: Signet, 2006. 282pp.

Callahan, James P. and T. Stanley Bradley. *Blue Dog Saloon: A Tale of Old New Orleans*. Edmonton, Alb.: Commonwealth, 1997. 516pp.

Callahan, Kathryn. *Gilded Greed: A Story of Corruption, Revenge and Desire in Old New Orleans*. Indianapolis, Ind.: Dog Ear, 2011. 419pp.

Cambridge, Terrie Barney. *And the Rain Came Down*. N.p.: Terrie Cambridge, 2012. 315pp.

Cameron, Stella. *French Quarter*. New York: Kensington, 1998. 371pp.

—. *A Grave Mistake*. Don Mills, Ont.: Mira Books, 2005. 536pp.

—. *Now You See Him*. Don Mills, Ont.: Mira Books, 2004. 348pp.

—. *Out of Body: A Court of Angels Novel*. Don Mills, Ont.: Mira Books, 2010. 392pp.

—. *Out of Mind: A Court of Angels Novel*. New York: Kensington, 2010. 394pp.

—. *Out of Sight: A Court of Angels Novel*. Don Mills, Ontario: Mira Books, 2010. 394pp.

Campbell, R. Wright. *Fat Tuesday*. New Haven, Conn.: Ticknor and Fields, 1983. 372pp.

Canfield, Sandra. *The Loving*. New York: Harper Paperbacks, 1992. 370pp.

Cannon, C.W. *Soul Resin*. Tallahassee, Fla.: FC2, 2002. 304pp.

Carlisle, Amanda. *Southland*. New York: Pinnacle, 1982. 437pp.

Carlisle, Jo. *Desire after Dark*. New York: Heat, 2012. 273pp.

—. *Temptation at Twilight*. New York: New American Libraries, 2011. 292pp.

Carroll, Jay. *Napoleon Banks: A Historical Novel*. Washington, D.C.: Jay Carroll, 2004. 284pp.

Cast, P(hyllis) C(hristine) and Kristin Cast. *Lenobia's Vow*. New York: St. Martin's Griffin, 2012. 147pp.

Castillo, Holli. *Gumbo Justice*. Taylorville, Ill.: Oak Tree Press, 2009. 237pp.

Castillo, Linda. *Jambalaya Justice*. Springfield, Ill.: Oak Tree Press, 2011. 241pp.

—. *Remember the Night*. New York: Silhouette Books, 2003. 248pp.

—. *A Whisper in the Dark*. New York: Berkley, 2006. 340pp.

Castle, Marie. *Hell's Belle: Dark Mirror Agency*. Tallahassee, Fla.: Bella Books, 2013. 281pp.

Castro, Joy. *Hell or High Water*. New York: St. Martin's Press, 2012. 340pp.

Cawood, Chris. *The Year of the Beast*. Kingston, Tenn.: Magnolia Hill Press, 1996. 312pp.

Chastain, Sandra. *Sunshine and Satin*. New York: Harlequin Books, 2000. 288pp.

Child, Maureen. *Bourbon Street Blues*. New York: Harlequin Books, 2006. 250pp.

Childs, Laura. *Bound for Murder*. New York: Berkley Prime Crime, 2004. 238pp.

—. *Death by Design*. New York: Berkley Prime Crime, 2006. 469pp.

—. *Death Swatch*. New York: Berkley Prime Crime, 2008. 303pp.

—. *Fiber and Brimstone*. New York: Berkley Prime Crime, 2010. 322pp.

—. *Frill Kill*. New York: Berkley Prime Crime, 2007. 273pp.

—. *Keepsake Crimes*. New York: Berkley Prime Crime, 2003. 244pp.

—. *Motif for Murder*. New York: Berkley Prime Crime, 2006. 275pp.

—. *Photo Finished*. New York: Berkley Prime Crime, 2004. 260pp.

—. *Postcards from the Dead*. New York: Berkley Prime Crime, 2012. 323pp.

—. *Skeleton Letters*. New York: Berkley Prime Crime, 2011. 336pp.

—. *Tragic Magic*. New York: Berkley Prime Crime, 2009. 307pp.

Childs, Laura and Diana Orgain. *Gilt Trip*. New York: Berkley Prime Crime, 2013. 307pp.

Chris D. *Shallow Water*. N.p.: Poison Fang Books, 2013. 167pp.

Christopher, Nicholas. *Tiger Rag: A Novel*. New York: Dial Press, 2013. 266pp.

Clark, Beverly. *Beyond the Rapture*. Columbus, Miss.: Genesis Press, 2005. 225pp.

Clark, Mindy Starns. *Under the Cajun Moon*. Eugene, Ore.: Harvest House, 2009. 332pp.

Clarke, Stephen. *Merde Happens*. New York: Bloomsbury, 2008. 369pp.

Clausen, Lowen. *River*. St. Paul, Neb.: Silo Press, 2008. 277p.

Coalson, Jonathan S. *Land Tumbling Backwards*. N.p.: Antediluvian Press, 2011. 276pp.

Codrescu, Andrei. *Messiah: A Novel*. New York: Simon and Schuster, 1999. 366pp.

Colbert, James. *All I Have Is Blue*. New York: Atheneum, 1992. 280pp.

Colbert, James. *No Special Hurry*. Boston: Houghton Mifflin, 1988. 204pp.

—. *Skinny Man*. New York: Atheneum, 1991. 212pp.

Cole, Henry. *A Nest for Celeste: A Story About Art, Inspiration, and the Meaning of Home*. New York: Katherine Tegen Books, 2010. 342pp.

Cole, Kresley. *Dark Needs at Night's Edge*. New York: Pocket Books, 2008. 368pp.

Coleman, Evelyn. *The Necklace: A Cecile Mystery*. Illustrated by Sergio Giovine. Middleton, Wis.: American Girl, 2012. 165pp.

Colley, Barbara. *Death Tidies Up*. New York: Kensington, 2003. 247pp.

—. *Dusted to Death*. New York: Kensington, 2010. 276pp.

—. *Maid for Murder*. New York: Kensington, 2002. 286pp.

—. *Married to the Mop*. New York: Kensington, 2006. 245pp.

—. *Polished Off*. New York: Kensington, 2004. 283pp.

—. *Scrub-a-Dub Dead*. New York: Kensington, 2007. 245pp.

—. *Wash and Die*. New York: Kensington, 2008. 249pp.

—. *Wiped Out*. New York: Kensington, 2005. 259pp.

Collins, Laurel. *Magic Nights*. New York: Diamond Books, 1991. 261pp.

Compton, Ralph. *Sixguns and Double Eagles*. New York: Signet, 1998. 347pp.

Conaway, J.C. *A Pale Moon Rising*. New York: Dell, 1982. 281pp.

—. *The River of Time*. New York: Dell, 1982. 477pp.

Coner, Kenyetta. *The Mockingbirds: A Maxine Michaels Mystery*. Washington, D.C.: 52 Weeks, 1998. 242pp.

Connolly, Vivian. *Moonlight and Magnolias*. New York: Berkley, 1984. 183pp.

Connor, John David. *Contagion*. New York: Diamond Books, 1992. 250pp.

Conrad, Ellie. *Let the Romance Begin*. Birmingham, Ala.: 2Life Publications, 2001. 153pp.

Conwell, Kent. *The Crystal Skull Murders*. New York: Avalon Books, 2008. 250pp.

—. *Death in the French Quarter*. New York: Avalon Books, 2008. 214pp.

—. *The Diamonds of Ghost Bayou*. New York: Avalon Books, 2011. 186pp.

Conwell, Kent. *The Gambling Man*. New York: Avalon Books, 2003. 184pp.

—. *The Puzzle of Piri Reis*. New York: Avalon Books, 2009. 266pp.

Cookson, Janet. *Quest of the Heart*. Leicester, U.K.: Linford, 1999. 208pp.

Cooley, Nicole. *Judy Garland, Ginger Love*. New York: Regan Books, 1998. 290pp.

Copeland, Sheila. *Princess Sister*. Washington D.C.: Black Entertainment Television, 2002. 295pp.

Corley, Donald. *Double Murder in New Orleans*. Baltimore: AmErica House, 2002. 158pp.

Corrington, John William. *The Southern Reporter: Stories*. Baton Rouge: Louisiana State University, 1981. 192pp.

Corrington, John William and Joyce Corrington. *A Civil Death*. New York: Viking, 1987. 207pp.

—. *The Collected Stories of John William Corrington*. Columbia: University of Missouri Press, 1990. 515pp.

—. *A Project Named Desire*. New York: Viking, 1987. 207pp.

—. *So Small a Carnival*. Baton Rouge: Louisiana State University Press, 1981. 191pp.

—. *The White Zone*. New York: Viking, 1990. 180pp.

Cote, Lyn. *The Desires of Her Heart*. New York: Harper Collins, 2009. 301pp.

—. *Echoes of Mercy: A Novel*. Nashville, Tenn.: Broadman and Holman, 2000. 245pp.

Cotter, Bill. *Fever Chart*. San Francisco: McSweeney's Books, 2009. 305pp.

Cox, Greg Abrams Jeffrey. *Two of a Kind? An Original Novel*. New York: Simon Spotlight Entertainment, 2005. 356pp.

Craft, Francine. *The Black Pearl*. New York: Kensington, 1996. 347pp.

Cresswell, Jasmine. *Contract: Paternity*. New York: Harlequin Books, 1997. 248pp.

Crews, Harry. *Dream State: Stories*. Jackson: Univ. of Mississippi, 1995. 189pp.

—. *The Knockout Artist*. New York: Harper and Row, 1988. 269pp.

—. *The Not Yet*. New Orleans: Univ. of New Orleans, 2012. 274pp.

Crook, Elizabeth. *Promised Lands: A Novel of the Texas Rebellion*. Dallas: Southern Methodist Univ., 1995. 517pp.

Cunningham, Mary. *Curse of the Bayou*. Laurel, Md.: Echelon, 2007. 157pp.

Currier, Jameson. *The Wolf at the Door*. New York: Chelsea Station Editions, 273pp.

Curtis, Jack. *Blood to Burn*. New York: Pocket Books, 1992. 185pp.

Dahlen, K.J. *No One to Hear you Scream*. New York: Avalon Books, 2010. 184pp.

Dailey, Janet. *Masquerade: A Novel*. Boston: Little, Brown, 1990. 326pp.

—. *Wildcatter's Woman*. New York: Silhouette Books, 1982. 186pp.

Dalby, Rob. *God of the Door: A Novel*. Covington, La.: Palmetto Lodge Press, 1993. 254pp.

Dale, Ruth Jean. *Family Secrets*. New York: Harlequin Books, 1999. 299pp.

Dalton, Margot. *French Twist*. New York: Harlequin Books, 1998. 248pp.

Dancer, Rex. *Bad Girl Blues*. New York: Simon and Schuster, 1994. 301pp.

—. *Postcard from Hell*. New York: Simon and Schuster, 1995. 297pp.

Dane, Lauren. *Thrice United*. Akron, Ohio: Ellora's Cave, 2007. 233pp.

—. *Vengeance Due*. Akron, Ohio: Ellora's Cave, 2007. 192pp.

Daniel, Megan. *All the Time We Need*. New York City: Love Spell, 1993. 388pp.

Danielewski, Mark Z. *Only Revolutions*. New York: Pantheon Books, 2006. 360pp.

Daniell, Rosemary. *The Hurricane Season*. New York: William Morrow, 1992. 363pp.

Daniels, Kayla. *Heiress Apparent*. New York: Silhouette Books, 1993. 252pp.

Danos, Paul. *The Cajun West Bank: Stories of the Flow of Cajun Culture*. West Hartford, Vt.: Full Circle, 2012. unpaged.

D'Aquila, Ignatius. *Remembering Dixie: A Novel*. New Orleans: Hot August Nights, 1997. 375pp.

Daudert, Charles. *The Temptation of St. Rosalie: Portrait of a Black Slave Owner*. Kalamazoo: Hansa-Hewlett, 1999. 379pp.

Davis, Alan. *Alone with the Owl: Stories*. Minneapolis: New Rivers Press, 2000. 139pp.

Davis, Don. *The Gris-Gris Man*. Atlanta: Turner, 1997. 320pp.

Davis, J. Madison. *Red Knight: A Novel*. New York: Walker, 1992. 232pp.

—. *White Rook: A Novel*. New York: Walker, 1989. 268pp.

Davis, Rod. *Corina's Way: A Novel*. Montgomery, Ala.: New South Books, 2003. 264pp.

Davis, Rod. *South, America: A Novel*. Montgomery: New South Books, 2013. unpaged.

Davis, Russell Greenberg Martin Harry. *Mardi Gras Madness: Stories of Murder and Mayhem in New Orleans*. Nashville, Tenn.: Cumberland House, 2000. 400pp.

De Jarnette, Harriette. *The Passion Stone*. New York: Book Margins, 1984. 378pp.

De Noux, O'Neil. *Battle Kiss*. New Orleans: Big Kiss, 2011. 571pp.

—. *The Big Kiss*. New York: Kensington, 1990. 320pp.

—. *The Big Show*. New Orleans: Pontalba, 1998. 349pp.

—. *Blue Orleans*. New York: Zebra Books, 1991. 319pp.

—. *City of Secrets*. New Orleans: Big Kiss, 2013. 207pp.

—. *Crescent City Kills*. New York: Kensington, 1992. 286pp.

—. *Enamored: A Crime Novel*. New Orleans: Big Kiss, 2012. 215pp.

—. *Grim Reaper*. New York: Kensington, 1988. 300pp.

—. *John Raven Beau*. New Orleans.: Big Kiss, 2010. 273pp.

—. *LaStanza: New Orleans Police Stories*. New Orleans: Autumn Books, 1999. 273pp.

—. *Mistik: A Superhero Novel*. New Orleans: Big Kiss, 2012. 158pp.

—. *New Orleans Confidential*. Rockville, Md.: Pointblank, 2006. 212pp.

—. *New Orleans Homicide*. New Orleans: Big Kiss, 2013. 355pp.

—. *New Orleans Irresistible: Erotic Mystery Fiction*. New Orleans: Big Kiss, 2011. 215pp.

—. *New Orleans Prime Evil: 10 Crime Stories*. New Orleans: Big Kiss, 2011. 237pp.

Dearman, Jewel E. *Ola: The Courtesan's Daughter: A Novel*. Dallas, Tex.: Darklove, 2002. 352pp.

DeLeon, Jana. *The Accused*. Don Mills, Ont.: Harlequin Books, 2013. 219pp.

—. *The Betrayed*. Don Mills, Ont.: Harlequin Books, 2013. 218pp.

—. *Showdown in Mudbug*. New York: Love Spell, 291pp.

Delk, Karen Jones. *Emerald Queen*. London, U.K.: Diamond Books, 1994. 433pp.

Dennis, Mike. *The Take*. London, Tex.: L and L Dreamspell, 175pp.

Dennis, Roberta. *Between the Lines*. New York: Silhouette Books, 1983. 186pp.

DeNorré, Rochel. *A Woman of New Orleans*. Wayne, Penn.: Banbury Books, 1983. 294pp.

Destefano, Merrie. *Afterlife: The Resurrection Chronicles*. New York: EOS, 322pp.

DeStefano, Paul. *Necessary Evil*. Pittsburgh: Dorrance, 2000. 235pp.

Deveraux, Jude. *The Awakening*. New York: Pocket Books, 1988. 249pp.

Devlin, Delilah. *Darkness Burning*. New York: Avon Books, 2009. 294pp.

—. *Into the Darkness*. New York: Avon Books, 2007. 307pp.

—. *Seduced by Darkness*. New York: Avon Books, 2008. 294pp.

Dickinson, Stephanie. *Waking Water*. New York: Rain Mountain, 2012. unpaged.

—. *Kate and Ruth: A Novel*. Grand Rapids, Mich.: Zondervan, 1999. 304pp.

—. *They Shall See God*. Wheaton, Ill.: Tyndale House, 2002. 439pp.

Diket, A.L. Rex *is Dead: The Mardi Gras Murder: A Novel.* Gretna, La: Her, 1982. 136pp.

Dixon, Franklin W. [pseud.] *Frame-Up*. New York: Pocket Books, 1995. 152pp.

—. *The Voodoo Plot*. New York: Pocket Books, 1982. 177pp.

Dobie, Ann B. *Something in Common: Contemporary Louisiana Stories*. Baton Rouge: Louisiana State Univ. Press, 1991. 303pp.

Dodd, Christina. *Thigh High*. New York: Signet, 2007. 400pp.

Dodson, Burt. *A River of Change*. Charlotte, N.C.: Dodson Books, 2003. 613pp.

Domingue, Ronlyn. *The Mercy of Thin Air: A Novel*. New York: Atria Books, 2005. 310pp.

Dominick, Anna. *Soapstone: Savonarola in New Orleans*. Anchorage, Ky.: Tympanum Press, 1990. 132pp.

Donachie, David. *The Scent of Betrayal*. London, U.K.: Pan, 1997. 489pp.

Donaldson, D.J. *Blood on the Bayou.* New York: St. Martin's Press, 1991. 216pp.

—. *Cajun Nights.* New York: St. Martin's Press, 1998. 234pp.

. *Louisiana Fever: An Andy Broussard/Kit Franklin Mystery*. New York: St. Martin's Press, 1996. 278pp.

—. *New Orleans Requiem*. New York: St. Martin's Press, 1994. 227pp.

Donaldson, D.J. *No Mardi Gras for the Dead.* New York: St. Martin's Press, 1992. 229pp.

—. *Sleeping with the Crawfish: An Andy Broussard/Kit Franklyn Mystery.* New York: St. Martin's Press, 1997. 260pp.

Donati, Sara. *Queen of Swords.* New York: Bantam Books, 2006. 564pp.

Downs, Tim. *First the Dead.* Nashville, Tenn.: Thomas Nelson, 2007. 363pp.

Dozois, Gardner R. *Dying for It: More Erotic Tales of Unearthly Love.* New York: Harper Prism, 1997. 331pp.

Dreyer, Eileen. *Sinners and Saints.* New York: St. Martin's Press, 2005. 372pp.

DuBay, Sandra. *By Love Beguiled.* New York: Dorchester, 1986. 479pp.

Duberstein, Larry. *Eccentric Circles.* Sag Harbor, N.Y.: Permanent Press, 1992. 191pp.

Dubus, Elizabeth Nell. *Cajun: A Novel.* New York: G.P. Putnam's Sons / Seaview, 1983. 342pp.

—. *To Love and to Dream.* New York: G.P. Putnam's Sons , 1986. 342pp.

—. *Twilight of the Dawn.* New York: St. Martin's Press, 1989. 443pp.

Dufresne, John. *Louisiana Light and Power.* New York: W.W. Norton, 1994. 306pp.

Dunbar, Anthony P. *City of Beads.* New York: G.P. Putnam's Sons, 1995. 225pp.

—. *The Crime Czar.* New York: Dell, 1998. 230pp.

—. *Crooked Man.* New York: G.P. Putnam's Sons, 1994. 224pp.

—. *Lucky Man.* New York: Dell, 1999. 227pp.

—. *Shelter from the Storm.* New York: G.P. Putnam's Sons, 1997. 226pp.

—. *Trick Question.* New York: G.P. Putnam's Sons, 1996. 230pp.

Dunbar, Sophie. *A Bad Hair Day.* Angel Fire, N. Mex.: Intrigue Press, 1998. 298pp.

—. *Behind Eclaire's Doors.* New York: St. Martin's Press, 1993. 213pp.

—. *Shiveree.* Angel Fire, N. Mex.: Intrigue Press, 1999. 304pp.

Duncan, Jenna-Lynne. *Hurricane.* Salem, N.H.: Divertir, 2011. 199pp.

DuPre, Gabrielle. *Forget Me Not.* New York: Charter Books, 1985. 444pp.

Dureau, Lorena. *Iron Lace.* New York: Pocket Books, 1983. 309pp.

Dureau, Lorena. *The Last Casquette Girl.* New York: Pinnacle, 1981. 276pp.

Early, Joan. *Fireflies.* Columbus, Miss.: Genesis Press, 2009. 327pp.

Eddy, Paul. *Flint.* New York: G.P. Putnam's Sons, 2000. 338pp.

Eden, Cynthia. *Angel in Chains.* New York: Brava / Kensington, 2012. 335pp.

—. *Avenging Angel.* New York: Brava / Kensington, 2013. 345pp.

—. *Die for Me: A Novel of the Valentine Killer.* Las Vegas: Montlake Romance, 2013. 347pp.

Edwards, Louis. *N: A Romantic Mystery.* New York: Dutton, 1997. 228pp.

Eggers, Dave. *Zeitoun.* New York: Vintage Books, 2010. 337pp.

Elias, Amelia. *Chosen.* Warner Robins, Ga.: Samhain, 2008. 300pp.

Ellis, Laurie. *Shadow Dances.* San Jose, Calif.: Writers' Club Press, 2000. 225pp.

Ellis, Wesley. *Lone Star and the Ghost Pirates.* New York: Berkley, 1984. 180pp.

Elliston, Susan. *Laffite's Lady: An Epic Adventure.* Orlando, Fla.: FirstPublish.com, 1998. 602pp.

Ellory, Roger Jon. *A Quiet Vendetta.* New York: Overlook Press, 2005. 454pp.

Elsley, Judy. *Heart of the Matter: Autobiographical and Biographical Essays.* Ogden, Utah: Weber State Univ., 2006. unpaged.

Emery, Lynn. *Tell Me Something Good.* New York: Harper Torch, 2002. 375pp.

Engler, Robert Klein. *American Shadow: Three Novellas and Other Stories.* Baltimore, Md.: AmErica House, 2002. 244pp.

Enoch. *Fifth Ward Soldier.* Houston: Appropriate, 2006. 292pp.

Estopinal, Stephen V. *Escape to New Orleans: A Novel from the Demelilla Chronicles.* Gonzales, La.: Libros Isleños, 2012. 449pp.

—. *Incident at Blood River: A Novel from the Demelilla Chronicles.* Durham, Conn.: Strategic Book Group, 2011. 355pp.

—. *El Tigre De Nueva Orleáns (The Tiger of New Orleans): A Novel from the Demelilla Chronicles.* Durham, Conn.: Eloquent, 2010. 256pp.

Evans, Mary Anna. *Floodgates.* Scottsdale, Ariz.: Poisoned Pen Press, 2009. 256pp.

Evans, Tabor. *Longarm and the Voodoo Queen.* New York: Jove Books, 1997. 182pp.

Everett, Peter. *Bellocq's Women.* London, U.K.: Jonathan Cape, 2000. 249pp.

Evey, Ethel L. *Stowaway to Texas*. Houston, Tex.: Larksdale, 1982. 201pp.

Ewen, Pamela Binnings. *Chasing the Wind: A Novel*. Nashville, Tenn.: BandH, 2012. 343pp.

—. *Dancing on Glass*. Nasville, Tenn.: BandH, 2011. 371pp.

Fairbanks, Nancy. *Crime Brûlée*. New York: Berkley Prime Crime, 2001. 274pp.

Farmer, Ben. *Evangeline*. New York: Overlook Press, 413pp.

Fawcett, Quinn. *Honor Among Spies*. New York: Forge Book, 2003. 352pp.

Feather, Jane. *Reckless Seduction*. New York: Kensington, 1987. 446pp.

Feehan, Christine. *Dark Magic*. New York: Avon Books, 2000. 358pp.

—. *Leopard's Prey*. London, U.K.: Piatkus, 2012. 366pp.

—. *Night Game*. Waterville, Me.: Thorndike Press, 2006. 613pp.

Fennelly, Tony. *1-900-Dead*. New York: St. Martin's Press, 1997. 214pp.

—. *The Closet Hanging*. New York: Carroll and Graf, 1987. 216pp.

—. *Don't Blame the Snake*. Dallas, Tex.: Top Publications, 2000. 260pp.

—. *Glory Hole Murders*. New York: Carroll and Graf, 1985. 204pp.

—. *The Hippie in the Wall*. New York: St. Martin's Press, 1994. 229pp.

—. *Murder with a Twist*. New York: Carroll and Graf, 1991. 422pp.

Fenton, Thomas. *Dominion*. Illustrated by Jamal Igle and Steven Cummings. Hollywood, Calif.: Humanoids, 2011. 144pp.

Ferrarella, Marie. *The Setup*. Don Mills, Ont.: Harlequin Books, 2006. 248pp.

Ferris, Jean. *Weather the Storm*. New York: Avon Books, 1996. 164pp.

Fichter, George S. *First Steamboat Down the Mississippi*. Illustrated by Joe Boddy. Gretna, La.: Pelican, 1989. 112pp.

Finch, Carol. *Once Upon a Midnight Moon*. New York: Kensington, 1997. 352pp.

Fincher, Murray C. *The Big Uneasy: Terror Strikes Mardi Gras*. Victoria, B.C.: Trafford, 2002. 266pp.

Fleet, Susan. *Absolution: A Novel*. N.p.: Susan Fleet, 2008. 263pp.

Flint, Eric. *1812: The Rivers of War*. New York: Del Rey / Ballantine Books, 2005. 534pp.

Foley, Louise Munro. *The Mardi Gras Mystery*. Illustrated by Ron Wing. New York: Bantam Books, 1987. 118pp.

Fontenot, Ken. *For Mr. Raindrinker: A Novel*. College Station, Tex.: Slough Press, 229pp.

Forbes, Colin. *The Savage Gorge*. London, U.K.: Simon and Schuster, 2006. 278pp.

Forrest, Elizabeth. *Killjoy*. New York: Daw Books, 1996. 458pp.

Forrester, Sandra. *Dust from Old Bones*. New York: William Morrow, 1999. 164pp.

Foster, B.J. *Bayou Shadows*. Houston, Tex.: Crescent House, 2000. 267pp.

Foster, Ken. *The Kind I'm Likely to Get: A Collection*. New York: Quill, 1999. 193pp.

Fox, Andrew. *Bride of the Fat White Vampire: A Novel*. New York: Del Rey / Ballantine Books, 2004. 429pp.

—. *Fat White Vampire Blues*. New York: Ballantine Books, 2003. 334pp.

Fox, F(rank) G. *Funky Butt Blues*. New Orleans: St. Expedite Press, 1994. 213pp.

Fox, Jimmy. *Lineages and Lies: A Nick Herald Genealogical Mystery*. New York: Writers Advantage, 2002. 275pp.

Fox, Paula. *The God of Nightmares*. San Francisco: North Point Press, 1990. 225pp.

—. *The Slave Dancer*. New York: Dell, 1991. 152pp.

Fredrick, Stephen A. *Cassandra's Crossing: A William Langdon Novel*. Charleston, S.C.: Stephen A. Fredrick, 2011. 492pp.

—. *Fortunate Son: A William Langdon Novel*. Charleston, S.C.: Stephen A. Fredrick, 2012. 693pp.

Frieden, André C. *Tranquility Denied*. Chicago: Avendia, 2006. 394pp.

—. *The Serpent's Game*. Chicago: Avendia, 2013. 455pp.

Friedmann, Patty. *Eleanor Rushing*. Washington, D.C.: Counterpoint, 1999. 275pp.

—. *A Little Bit Ruined: A Novel*. Emeryville, Calif.: Shoemaker and Hoard. 2007. 247pp.

—. *No Takebacks: A Novel*. Philadelphia: Tiny Satchel Press, 2012. 146pp.

—. *Odds*. Washington, D.C.: Counterpoint, 2000. 249pp.

—. *Second Hand Smoke*. Washington, D.C.: Counterpoint, 2002. 292pp.

Friedmann, Patty. *Side Effects: A New Orleans Love Story.* Emeryville, Calif.: Shoemaker and Hoard, 2005. 298pp.

—. *Taken Away.* Philadelphia: Tiny Satchel, 2010. 413pp.

Frost, Jeaniene. *One Grave at a Time.* New York: Avon Books. 2011. 358pp.

Fullerty, Matt. *The Knight of New Orleans: The Pride and the Sorrow of Paul Morphy.* N.p.: Parkgate Press, 2011. 556pp.

Fulmer, David. *Chasing the Devil's Tail.* Scottsdale, Ariz.: Poisoned Pen Press, 2001. 320pp.

—. *Jass.* Orlando, Fla.: Harcourt, 2005. 334pp.

—. *Lost River.* Boston: Houghton Mifflin Harcourt, 2009. 317pp.

—. *Rampart Street.* Orlando, Fla.: Harcourt, 2005. 336pp.

Funderburk, Robert. *Tenderness and Fire.* Minneapolis: Bethany House, 1997. 287pp.

Gaffrey, Arlette. *Behind the Columns.* Denver: Outskirts Press, 339pp.

—. *A World of His Own: In the Land of the Creoles.* Denver: Outskirts Press, 2007. 388pp.

Gaiter, Leonce. *Bourbon Street.* New York: Carroll and Graf: 2005. 169pp.

Gallagher, Patricia. *Echoes and Embers.* New York: Avon Books, 1983. 309pp.

Gallo, Louis. *Breakneck: A Katrina Fugue.* Radford, Va.: Orphic Press, 2010. 227pp.

—. *The Night I Shot Herbert Marcuse's Eyeball.* Radford, Va.: Orphic Press, 268pp.

—. *The Yeast of Revelation: Stories.* Radford, Va.: Orphic Press. 244pp.

Garwood, Ellen. *Come to Me, Megan.* Alexandria, Va.: Cameron Press, 1984. 184pp.

Garwood, Julie. *Mercy.* Leicester, U.K.: Thorpe, 2004. 632pp.

Gaskell, Whitney. *Testing Kate.* New York: Bantam Books, 2006. 321pp.

Gaus, Laura Sheerin. *Simon: Irish Boy Encounters New Orleans.* Illustrated by Katherine Harman Harding. San Jose, Calif.: Writers Club Press, 2001. 96pp.

Gauthier, Ronald M. *Crescent City Countdown: A Novel.* New Orleans: JoJo Press, 2007. 298pp.

—. *Hard Time on the Bayou: A Novel.* New Orleans: JoJo Press, 2005. 200pp.

—. *Prey for Me: A Novel.* New Orleans: JoJo Press, 2005. 211pp.

Gautreaux, Tim. *The Missing.* New York: Vintage, 2009. 375pp.

Gengler, Cindy. *Fallen Angels: Rafe's Heart.* Milwaukee, Wis.: Gardenia Press, 2002. 354pp.

George, Alex. *A Good American.* New York: G.P. Putnam's Sons, 2012. 387pp.

Gerbig, Jody. *Unmasked.* Newcastle, Ont.: I Publish Press, 2008. 232pp.

Gibson, Rachel. *Blue by You.* New York: Avon Books, 2013. 133pp.

Gideon, Nancy. *Bound by Moonlight.* New York: Pocket Books, 2011. 335pp.

—. *Captured by Moonlight.* New York: Pocket Books, 2010. 353pp.

—. *Chased by Moonlight.* New York: Simon and Schuster, 2010. 371pp.

—. *Hunter of Shadows.* New York: Pocket Books, 2011. 383pp.

—. *Masked by Moonlight.* New York: Pocket Books, 2010. 375pp.

—. *Midnight Crusader.* Hickory Corners, Mich.: ImaJinn Books, 2002. 255pp.

—. *Midnight Enchantment.* Hickory Corners, Mich.: ImaJinn Books, 1999. 276pp.

—. *Midnight Masquerade.* Hickory Corners, Mich.: ImaJinn Books, 2001. 269pp.

Gifford, Barry. *Arise and Walk: A Novel.* New York: Hyperion Books, 1994. 156pp.

—. *Baby Cat-Face: A Novel.* New York: Harcourt Brace, 1995. 171pp.

—. *Memories from a Sinking Ship.* New York: Seven Stories Press, 2009. 270pp.

Gilchrist, Ellen. *The Annunciation.* Boston: Little, Brown, 1983. 353pp.

—. *The Courts of Love: Stories.* Boston: Little, Brown, 1996. 288pp.

—. *In the Land of Dreamy Dreams: Short Fiction.* Boston: Little, Brown, 1981. 167pp.

—. *Nora Jane: A Life in Stories.* Boston: Back Bay Books / Little, Brown, 2005. 420pp.

—. *Starcarbon: A Meditation on Love: A Novel.* Boston: Little, Brown, 1994. 306pp.

—. *Victory over Japan: A Book of Stories.* Boston: Little, Brown, 1984. 277pp.

Gilliam, Richard, Martin H. Greenberg, and Thomas R. Hanlon, eds. *South from Midnight.* New Orleans: Southern Fried, 1994. 427pp.

Gilroy, Herbert. *Didn't Look Back: A Novel.* South Beach, Ore.: Herbert Gilroy, 2009. 172pp.

Girardi, Robert. *Madeleine's Ghost.* New York: Delacorte Press, 1995. 356pp.

Goethe, Ann. *Midnight Lemonade.* New York: Delacorte Press, 1993. 278pp.

Gold, Kristi. *Damage Control*. New York: Harlequin Books, 2006. 250pp.

Golden, Christopher and Tim Lebbon. *The Map of Moments: A Novel of the Hidden Cities*. New York: Bantam Books, 2009. 354pp.

Good, Phillip. *I Love You Maggie*. N.p.: Zanybooks, 2007. 211pp.

Goodnight, Linda. *A Touch of Grace*. New York: Steeple Hill Books, 2007. 247pp.

Goonan, Kathleen Ann. *Crescent City Rhapsody*. London, U.K.: Millennium, 2000. 564pp.

Goudeau, Renée. *Once Upon a Place*. N.p.: Swamp Iris, 346pp.

Graham, C.S. *The Archangel Project*. New York: Harper Collins, 2008. 374pp.

Graham, Heather. *Blood Red*. Don Mills, Ont.: Mira Books, 2007. 347pp.

—. *Deadly Gift*. Don Mills, Ont.: Mira Books, 2008. 395pp.

—. *Ghost Walk*. Don Mills, Ont.: Mira Books, 2005. 393pp.

—. *Heart of Evil*. Don Mills, Ont.: Mira Books. 376pp.

—. *The Keepers*. Toronto, Ont.: Harlequin Books, 2010. 283pp.

—. *Kiss of Darkness*. Don Mills, Ont.: Mira Books, 2006. 395pp.

—. *Let the Dead Sleep*. Don Mills, Ont.: Mira Books, 2013. 331pp.

—. *Phantom Evil*. Don Mills, Ont.: Mira Books, 2011. 360pp.

—. *Sacred Evil*. Don Mills, Ont.: Mira Books, 2011. 371pp.

Graham, Heather [Shannon Drake, pseud.]. *Beneath a Blood Red Moon*. New York: Kensington, 1999. 383pp.

—. *Deep Midnight*. New York: Kensington, 2001. 478pp.

—. *When Darkness Falls*. New York: Kensington, 2000. 428pp.

Gran, Sara. *Claire Dewitt and the City of the Dead*. Boston: Houghton Mifflin Harcourt, 2011. 273pp.

Grant, James L. *Pedestrian Wolves*. Holicong, Penn.: Prime Books, 2004. 231pp.

Greenberg, Martin Harry Davis Russell. *Mardi Gras Madness: Tales of Terror and Mayhem in New Orleans*. Nashville, Tenn.: Cumberland House, 2000. 239pp.

Greenough, Malcolm W. and Lily Violett. *Dear Lily: A Love Story*. Dublin, N.H.: Yankee Books, 1987. 239pp.

Gregory, Todd. *Need*. New York: Kensington, 2012. 276pp.

Grimsley, Jim. *Boulevard: A Novel*. Chapel Hill, N.C.: Algonquin Books, 2002. 292pp.

Grisham, John. *The Client*. New York: Doubleday, 1993. 421pp.

—. *The Pelican Brief*. New York: Island Books, 1992. 436pp.

Grue, Lee Meitzen. *Goodbye Silver, Silver Cloud*. Austin, Tex.: Plain View Press, 1994. 124pp.

Grumley, Michael. *Life Drawing: A Novel*. New York: Grove Weidenfeld, 1991. 156pp.

Guillory, Lloyd J. *Summary Justice: A Story of Revenge*. Bethel, Conn.: Rutledge Books, 1996. 163pp.

Guzmán, Lila and Rick Guzmán. *Lorenzo and the Turncoat*. Houston, Tex.: Piñata Books, 2006. 183pp.

Hague, Nora. *Letters from an Age of Reason*. New York: William Morrow, 2001. 648pp.

Haines, Carolyn. *Hallowed Bones*. New York: Delacorte Press, 2004. 338pp.

—. *Ham Bones*. New York: Kensington, 2008. 304pp.

Hall, Carolyn. *Keys to Daniel's House*. New York: Silhouette Books, 1982. 250pp.

Hall, Jessica. *Heat of the Moment*. New York: New American Library, 2004. 294pp.

—. *Into the Fire*. New York: Onyx, 2004. 298pp.

Halston, Carole. *The Pride of St. Charles Avenue*. New York: Silhouette Books, 1993. 250pp.

Hambly, Barbara. *Days of the Dead*. New York: Random House, 2004. 571pp.

—. *Dead and Buried*. Sutton, U.K.: Severn House, 2010. 250pp.

—. *Dead Water*. New York: Bantam Books, 2004. 297pp.

—. *Die Upon a Kiss*. New York: Bantam Books, 2001. 333pp.

—. *Fever Season*. New York: Bantam Books, 1998. 321pp.

—. *A Free Man of Color*. New York: Bantam Books, 1997. 311pp.

—. *Good Man Friday*. Sutton, U.K.: Severn House, 2013. 250pp.

—. *Graveyard Dust*. New York: Bantam Books, 1999. 315pp.

—. *Ran Away: A Benjamin January Novel*. Sutton, U.K.: Severn House, 2011. 252pp.

Hambly, Barbara. *Sold Down the River*. New York: Bantam Books, 1999. 409pp.

—. *Wet Grave*. New York: Bantam Books, 2002. 288pp.

Hambright, Jan. *Keeping Watch*. New York: Harlequin Books, 2010. 216pp.

Hamilton, Phyllis. *Cypress Whisperings*. Columbus, Miss.: Indigo, 2000. 268pp.

—. *A Lark on the Wing*. Columbus, Miss.: Genesis Press, 2003. 291pp.

Handeland, Lori. *Crescent Moon*. New York: St. Martin's Press, 2006. 338pp.

—. *Rising Moon*. New York: St. Martin's Press, 2006. 338pp.

—. *Thunder Moon*. New York: St. Martin's Press, 2008. 339pp.

Hanover, M.L.N. *Darker Angels*. New York: Pocket Books, 2009. 360pp.

Harper, M.A. *The Year of Past Things: A New Orleans Ghost Story*. Athens, Ga.: Hill Street Press, 2003. 256pp.

Harris, Charlaine. *All Together Dead*. New York: Ace Books, 2008. 342pp.

—. *Definitely Dead*. New York: Ace Books, 2006. 324pp.

—. *From Dead to Worse*. New York: Ace Books, 2008. 359pp.

Harris, Darryl. *The Gathering: A Historical Novel Based on a True Story*. Idaho Falls: Harris, 2004. 455pp.

Harte, Bryce. *Creed's War*. New York: Berkley, 1991. 265pp.

Hawk, Rhodi. *The Tangled Bridge*. New York: Tor, 2012. 528pp.

—. *A Twisted Ladder*. New York: Forge, 2009. 540pp.

Hawke, Ethan. *Ash Wednesday: A Novel*. New York: Alfred A. Knopf, 2002. 221pp.

Hawthorne, Rachel. *Labor of Love*. New York: Harper Collins, 2008. 298pp.

Hayden, Channing. *Magdalenes*. San Jose, Calif.: Writers Club Press, 1998. 454pp.

Haymaker, Lafayette. *Nola 46: Twelve Stories from the End of World War II*. New Albany, Ohio: Mainesburg Press, 1995. 211pp.

Haynes, Darleen. *Dark Face of Light: A Novel*. Coral Springs, Fla.: Llumina Press, 2003. 284pp.

Hebert, Charles. *Swimming to Atlantis*. New Orleans: Autumn Books, 1997. 279pp.

Hecht, Daniel. *City of Masks*. New York: Bloomsbury, 2002. 438pp.

Heck, Peter J. *A Connecticut Yankee in Criminal Court: A Mark Twain Mystery*. New York: Berkeley Prime Crime, 1996. 311pp.

—. *The Guilty Abroad: A Mark Twain Mystery*. New York: Berkeley Prime Crime, 1999. 306pp.

Hegwood, Martin. *Big Easy Backroad*. New York: St. Martin's Press, 1999. 247pp.

Heinan, T.R. *L'immortalité: Madame Lalaurie and the Voodoo Queen*. Tucson: Nonius, 2012. 126pp.

Helms, Richard W. *Joker Poker*. San Jose, Calif.: Writer's Showcase, 2000. 243pp.

—. *Juicy Watusi*. Weddington, N.C.: Back Alley Books, 2002. 297pp.

—. *Voodoo That You Do*. Weddington, N.C.: Back Alley Books, 2001. 325pp.

—. *Wet Debt: A Pat Gallegher Mystery*.Weddington, N.C.: Back Alley Books, 2003. 254pp.

Helton, Venita. *Pirate's Prize*. New York: Harper Collins, 1994. 343pp.

—. *Sapphire*. New York: Harper Collins, 1993. 372pp.

Henderson, T.T. *Too Much Hennessy*. Loma Linda, Calif.: Parker, 2007. 252pp.

Henley, Patricia. *In the River Sweet*. New York: Pantheon Books, 2002. 291pp.

Henricksen, Bruce. *After the Floods: A Novel*. Duluth, Minn.: Lost Hills Books, 2008. 212pp.

Herlong, M.H. *Buddy*. New York: Viking, 2012. 296pp.

Herren, Greg. *Bourbon Street Blues*. New York: Kensington, 2003. 264pp.

—. *Jackson Square Jazz*. New York: Kensington, 2004. 296pp.

—. *Mardi Gras Mambo*. New York: Kensington, 2006. 289pp.

—. *Murder in the Garden District: A Chanse Macleod Mystery*. Los Angeles: Alyson Books, 2009. 256pp.

—. *Murder in the Irish Channel*. Valley Falls, N.Y.: Bold Strokes Books. 234pp.

—. *Murder in the Rue Chartres: A Chanse Macleod Mystery*. New York: Alyson Books, 2007. 258pp.

—. *Murder in the Rue Dauphine*. Los Angeles: Alyson Books, 2002. 227pp.

—. *Murder in the Rue St. Ann: A Chanse Macleod Mystery*. Los Angeles: Alyson Books, 2004. 262pp.

Herren, Greg. *Murder in the Rue Ursulines: A Chanse Macleod Mystery*. Los Angeles: Alyson Books, 2008. 228pp.

—. *Vieux Carré Voodoo*. Valley Falls, N.Y.: Enfield, 230pp.

—. *Who Dat Whodunnit*. Valley Falls, N.Y.: Bold Strokes Books. 231pp.

Herries, Anne. *My Lady, My Love*. Sutton, U.K.: Severn House, 2005. 220pp.

Herrmann, Phyllis. *Golden Promise*. New York: Kensington, 1994. 400pp.

Herron, Rita. *Say You Love Me*. Don Mills, Ontario: Harlequin Books, 2007. 378pp.

Herschler, Mildred Barger. *The Walk into Morning*. New York: Tor, 1993. 318pp.

Hewat, Alan V. *Lady's Time*. New York: Love Spell Books, 1997. 338pp.

Hicks, Robert. *A Separate Country*. New York: Grand Central, 2009. 424pp.

Hill, Donna. *Interlude*. Columbus, Miss.: Genesis Press, 1999. 185pp.

—. *Temptation*. Washington, D.C.: Kimani, 2008. 312pp.

Hill, Elizabeth Starr. *The Banjo Player*. New York: Viking, 1993. 197pp.

Hill, Sandra. *Frankly My Dear*. New York: Leisure Books, 1996. 358pp.

—. *Sweeter Savage Love*. New York: Love Spell Books, 1997. 394pp.

Hillyer, Cindy. *Fireworks*. New York: Kensington, 1999. 253pp.

Hingle, Metsy. *The Baby Bonus*. Toronto, Ont.: Silhouette Books, 2000. 186pp.

—. *Behind the Mask*. Don Mills, Ont.: Mira Books, 2002. 379pp.

—. *Black Silk*. Don Mills, Ont.: Mira Books, 2006. 377pp.

—. *Navy Seal Dad*. New York: Silhouette Books, 2002. 187pp.

—. *Surrender*. New York: Silhouette Books, 1996. 186pp.

—. *The Wager*. Don Mills, Ont.: Mira Books, 2001. 379pp.

—. *What the Millionaire Wants*. New York: Silhouette Books, 2008. 185pp.

Hix, Martha. *Destiny's Magic*. New York: Kensington, 1996. 315pp.

—. *Magnolia Nights*. New York: Kensington, 1988. 448pp.

Hoag, Tami. *The Restless Heart*. Waterville, Me.: Thorndike Press, 2009. 275pp.

Hoag, Tami. *A Thin Dark Line*. New York: Bantam Books, 1997. 496pp.

Hobbs, Peter. *I Could Ride All Day in My Cool Blue Train*. London, U.K.: Faber and Faber, 2006. 258pp.

Hodge, Brian. *The Darker Saints*. New York: Dell, 1993. 414pp.

Hogan, Ray. *Guns of Freedom: A Western Duo*. Unity, Me.: Five Star, 1999. 287pp.

Hoh, Diana. *Spring Fever*. New York: Scholastic, 1987. 281pp.

Hohenstein, Traci. *Cut and Run: A Rachel Scott Adventure*. Las Vegas, Nev.: Thomas and Mercer, 2013. 194pp.

Holden, Christine. *A Hitch in Time*. New York: Jove Books, 2000. 322pp.

—. *A Time for Us*. New York: Jove Books, 1998. 353pp.

Holder, Nancy. *Daughter of the Blood*. New York: Silhouette Books, 2006. 299pp.

Holder, Nancy and Debbie Viguié. *Crusade*. New York: Simon and Schuster, 470pp.

Hollis, John. *The Four-Minute Ambush*. Houston, Tex.: Halcyon Press, 2001. 285pp.

Holt, Conrad G. *Arizona Law*. Leicester, U.K.: Thorpe, 2005. 280pp.

Holt, Kimberly Willis. *Piper Reed, the Great Gypsy*. Illustrated by Christine Davenier. New York: Henry Holt, 2008. 152pp.

Honeycutt, Leo. *Over the Edge: A Novel*. Gonzales, La.: Chef John Folse, 1999. 250pp.

Horn, Dara. *All Other Nights: A Novel*. New York: W.W. Norton, 2009. 363pp.

Horsman, Jennifer. *With One Look*. New York: Avon Books, 1994. 409pp.

Houston, Sterling. *Le Griffon: A True Tale of Supernatural Love*. San Antonio, Tex.: Pecan Grove Press, 1999. 105pp.

Howard, Clark. *Crowded Lives and Other Stories of Desperation and Danger*. Unity, Me.: Five Star, 2000. 220pp.

Howard, Linda. *Kill and Tell*. New York: Pocket Books, 1998. 305pp.

Hubbard, Norma. *The Archbishop's Daughter*. Panama City, Fla.: Wimberley Books, 1992. 729pp.

—. *The Haunting of Willowwynn*. Panama City, Fla.: Wimberley Books, 1996. 300pp.

Huckaby, Darrell. *Need Four*. Covington, Ga.: Southland Press, 2003. 271pp.

Huckaby, Darrell. *Need Two*. St. Simons Island, Ga.: St. Simons Press, 1995. 293pp.

Hudson, Janis Reams. *Remember My Heart*. New York: Pinnacle / Kensington, 1995. 347pp.

Hudson-Smith, Linda. *Fields of Fire*. New York: Kimani Press, 2007. 310pp.

Hughes, Faye. *Gotta Have It*. New York: Bantam Books, 1995. 228pp.

Hunt, B.B. *Samantha Stone and the Mermaid's Quest*. Hollywood, Calif.: Hollywood Books, 2007. 147pp.

Hunter, Faith. *Blood Cross: A Jane Yellowrock Novel*. New York: Roc, 2010. 321pp.

—. *Death's Rival: A Jane Yellowrock Novel*. New York: Roc, 2012. 324pp.

—. *Mercy Blade: A Jane Yellowrock Novel*. New York: Roc, 2011. 305pp.

—. *Skinwalker: A Jane Yellowrock Novel*. New York: Roc, 2009. 320pp.

Hunter, Gwen. *False Truths*. New York: Pocket Star Books, 1995. 376pp.

Hunter, Seth. *The Tide of War*. Ithaca, N.Y.: McBooks Press, 2009. 318pp.

Hunter, Travis. *At the Crossroads*. New York: Dafina Books, 2010. 231pp.

Hustmyre, Chuck. *The Axman of New Orleans: A Novel (Based on a True Story)*. Donaldsonville, La.: Margaret Media, 2013. 280pp.

—. *House of the Rising Sun*. Bend, Ore.: Salvo Press, 2004. 252pp.

—. *A Killer Like Me*. New York: Dorchester, 2011. 349pp.

Iles, Greg. *Blood Memory*. New York: Scribner, 2005. 496pp.

—. *Dead Sleep*. New York: G.P. Putnam's Sons, 2001. 372pp.

—. *Mortal Fear*. New York: Dutton, 1997. 564pp.

Inman, Sarah K. *Finishing Skills*. Livingston, Ala.: Livingston Press, 2005. 232pp.

—. *The Least Resistance*. New Orleans: NOLAFugees Press, 108pp.

Inness-Brown, Elizabeth. *Burning Marguerite*. New York: Alfred A. Knopf, 2002. 237pp.

Isom, Johnathan. *Ambition! Be Careful What You Ask For*. Memphis, Tenn.: M2N, 2005. 260pp.

Jac, Cherlyn. *Night's Immortal Touch*. New York: Kensington, 1995. 348pp.

—. *Shadows in Time*. New York: Windsor, 1994. 431pp.

Jackson, Lisa. *Absolute Fear*. New York: Kensington, 2007. 404pp.

—. *Cold Blooded*. New York: Kensington, 2002. 463pp.

—. *Devious*. New York: Kensington, 2011. 439pp.

—. *Hot Blooded*. New York: Kensington, 2001. 464pp.

—. *Lost Souls.* New York: Kensington, 2008. 403pp.

—. *Malice*. New York: Kensington, 2009. 424pp.

—. *Shiver*. New York: Kensington, 2001. 512pp.

Jackson, Melanie. *The Courier*. New York: Love Spell, 2004. 322pp.

Jackson, Rhodesia. *Pecan Candy and Huck-a-Bucks.* New Orleans: Orgena Enterprises, 1993. 428pp.

—. *Three Times Sweeter: Love, Home and Family*. New Orleans: Orgena Enterprises, 2000. 371pp.

Jakes, T.D. *On the Seventh Day: A Novel*. New York: Atria Books, 2012. 316pp.

Jakubowski, Maxim. *On Tenderness Express*. London, U.K.: Do-Not Press, 2000. 211pp.

James, B.J. *The Saint of Bourbon Street*. New York: Silhouette Books, 1995. 185pp.

James, Ellie. *Broken Illusions: A Midnight Dragonfly Novel*. New York: St. Martin's Griffin, 2012. 339pp.

—. *Fragile Darkness*. New York: St. Martin's Griffin, 2012. 337pp.

—. *Shattered Dreams: A Midnight Dragonfly Novel*. New York: St. Martin's Griffin, 2011. 342pp.

Jancar, Drago. *Mocking Desire.* Translated from the Slovenian by Michael Biggins. Evanston, Ill.: Northwestern Univ. Press, 1998. 267pp.

Jarman, Mark Anthony. *New Orleans Is Sinking*. Ottawa, Ont.: Oberon Press, 1998. 121pp.

Jarrett, Norma L. *Sweet Magnolia: A Novel*. New York: Harlem Moon / Broadway Books, 2006. 336pp.

Jeffries, J.M. *Blood Lust*. Columbus, Miss.: Genesis Press, 2005. 241pp.

Jenkin, Len. *N Judah*. Los Angeles.: Green Integer, 2006. 312pp.

Jenkins, Beverly. *Through the Storm*. New York: Avon Books, 1998. 371pp.

Jensen, Jane. *Sins of the Fathers*. New York: Penguin Books, 1997. 402pp.

Jernigan, Brenda. *The Duke's Lady*. New York: Kensington, 1999. 348pp.

Johnson, Barb. *More of This World or Maybe Another*. New York: Harper Perennial, 2009. 188pp.

Johnson, Charles Richard. *Middle Passage*. New York: Atheneum, 1990. 209pp.

Johnson, Dedra. *Sandrine's Letter to Tomorrow*. Brooklyn, N.Y.: Ig, 2007. 212pp.

Johnson, Keith Lee. *Little Black Girl Lost*. Dix Hills, N.Y.: Urban Books, 2005. 371pp.

—. *Little Black Girl Lost 2*. New York: Urban Books, 2006. 372pp.

—. *Little Black Girl Lost 3*. Deer Park, N.Y.: Urban Books, 2006. 294pp.

—. *Little Black Girl Lost 4: The Diary of Josephine Baptiste*. West Babylon, N.Y.: Urban Books, 2009. 245pp.

—. *Little Black Girl Lost 5: The Diary of Josephine Baptiste:Lauren's Story*. West Babylon, N.Y.: Urban Books, 2010. 370pp.

Johnson, Shirley Jean. *New Orleans Style*. San Jose, Calif.: Writers Club Press, 2001. 179pp.

Johnson, Suzanne. *Sentinels of New Orleans*. New York: Tor Books, 2013. 352pp.

—. *Elysian Fields*. London, U.K.: Headline, 2013. 377pp.

—. *Royal Street*. New York: Tor, 2012. 336pp.

—. *River Road*. New York: Tor, 2012. 332pp.

Jones, Bruce T. *The Lost Reflection: Unleashing the Darkest Legend of New Orleans*. New York: Koehler Books, 2012. 253pp.

Jones, Daniel H. *St. Jude's Secret*. Lincoln, Neb.: Writer's Showcase, 2000. 238pp.

Jones, LaTonya. *Southern Discomfort*. Charleston, S.C.: Plenary, 2010. 315pp.

Jones, Moon, Brenda Ray, and Tim Lattie. *Moon Jones' Bighead and Cornrow: Trouble in New Orleans*. New Haven, Conn.: Solmar, 2006. 149pp.

Jones, Patricia. *The Color of Family: A Novel*. New York: Avon Books, 2004. 374pp.

Jones, Pauline Baird. *Do Wah Diddy Die*. Amherst Junction, Wis.: Hard Shell Word Factory, 2001. 219pp.

Jones, Ward R. *The Southerner and the Serpent*. New York: Vantage, 1998. 252pp.

Jordan-Mims, Christal. *Under the Cherry Moon*. Columbus, Miss.: Genesis, 2006. 254pp.

Kadlecek, Jo. *A Quarter after Tuesday*. Colorado Springs: Nav, 2007. 295pp.

Kafka, Paul. *Love Enter*. Boston: Houghton Mifflin, 1993. 326pp.

Kane and Abel. *Eyes of a Killer; Behind Enemy Lines*. New York: St. Martin's Griffin, 1999. 150pp.

Kane, Dixie. *Dreaming of You*. New York: Kensington, 2002. 317pp.

Kane, Mallory. *Bulletproof Billionaire*. New York: Harlequin Books, 2004. 250pp.

—. *Death of a Beauty Queen*. Don Mills, Ont.: Harlequin Books, 2012. 283pp.

—. *Dirty Little Secrets*. Don Mills, Ont.: Harlequin Books, 2013. 284pp.

—. *Double-Edged Detective*. New York: Harlequin Books, 283pp.

—. *Star Witness*. Don Mills, Ont.: Harlequin Books, 2013. 216pp.

Karwoski, Gail. *When Hurricane Katrina Hit Home*. Illustrated by Julia Marshall. Charleston, S.C.: History Press, 2013. 189pp.

Kasapo, Mary M. *The Case of the Will Contest*. Nottingham, U.K.: Vola, 1996. 171pp.

Katrovas, Richard. *Mystic Pig: A Novel of New Orleans*. New York: Smallmouth Press, 2001. 295pp.

Kay, Sharon. *Legacies*. San Jose, Calif.: Writer's Showcase, 2002. 183pp.

Keaton, Kelly. *A Beautiful Evil*. New York: Simon and Schuster, 2012. 287pp.

—. *Darkness Becomes Her*. New York: Simon and Schuster, 2011. 273pp.

—. *The Wicked Within*. New York: Simon and Schuster, 2013. 280pp.

Keene, Carolyn. *The Ghost of Blackwood Hall*. New York: Grosset and Dunlap, 1986. 178pp.

—. *The Haunted Showboat*. New York: Grosset and Dunlap, 1981. 184pp.

—. *The Mardi Gras Mystery*. New York: Pocket Books, 1988. 153pp.

—. *Nightmare in New Orleans*. New York: Pocket Books, 1997. 214 pp.

Keene, Carolyn and Franklin W. Dixon. *Bonfire Masquerade*. New York: Aladdin, 2011. 164pp.

Kelley, William. *A Servant of Slaves: The Life of Henriette Delille: A Novel*. New York: Crossroad, 2003. 223pp.

Kent, Alison. *Goes Down Easy*. New York: Harlequin Books, 2006. 251pp.

Kenyon, Sherrilyn. *Infamous*. New York: St. Martin's Press, 2012. 468pp.

Kenyon, Sherrilyn. *Infinity*. New York: St. Martin's Press, 2010. 464pp.

—. *Invincible*. New York: St. Martin's Press. 2011, 420pp.

—. *Kiss of the Night*. New York: St. Martin's Press, 2004. 376pp.

—. *Night Embrace*. New York: St. Martin's Press, 2003. 408pp.

—. *Night Play*. New York: St. Martin's Press, 2004. 371pp.

—. *Night Pleasures: A Dark-Hunter Novel*. New York: St. Martin's Press, 2002. 324pp.

—. *No Mercy*. New York: St. Martin's Press, 2010. 343pp.

—. *Seize the Night: A Dark-Hunter Novel*. New York: St. Martin's Press, 2005. 289pp.

Kenyon, Sherrilyn and Dianna Love. *Phantom in the Night*. New York: Pocket Books, 2008. 404pp.

Kidd, Rob. *City of Gold*. Illustrated by Jean-Paul Orpinas. New York: Disney Press, 2007. 122pp.

Kiernan, Caitlin R. *To Charles Fort, with Love*. Burton, Mich.: Subterranean Press, 2005. 270pp.

Kihn, Greg. *Mojo Hand*. New York: Forge, 1999. 255pp.

King, Gabriel. *The Golden Cat*. New York: Ballantine Books, 1999. 350pp.

King, Peter. *Roux the Day: A Gourmet Detective Mystery*. New York: St. Martin's Press, 2002. 231pp.

Kingsley, Kate. *Ransom of the Heart*. New York: Harlequin Books, 1991. 300pp.

—. *Season of Storms*. New York: Harlequin Books, 1991. 300pp.

Kiraly, Marie. *Leanna*. New York: Berkley Books, 1996. 341pp.

Kirkland, Elithe Hamilton. *The Edge of Disrepute*. Bryan, Tex.: Shearer, 1984. 377pp.

Kirkwood, M.A. *Claire Ange: A Novel*. San Francisco: Spirit Star Press, 2012. 282pp.

Kirsch, J. Allen. *The Big Uzi*. San Jose, Calif.: Writers Club Press, 2001. 233pp.

Klein, Victor. *New Orleans Ghosts*. Chapel Hill, N.C.: Lycanthrope Press, 1993. 126pp.

Kleypas, Lisa. *Only in Your Arms*. New York: Avon Books, 1992. 426pp.

—. *When Strangers Marry*. New York: Avon Books, 2002. 390pp.

Kline, Jonathan. *The Wisdom of Ashes*. New Orleans: Lavender Ink, 2013. 100pp.

Komarnicki, Todd. *Free.* New York: Doubleday, 1993. 273pp.

Koontz, Dean R. *Dead and Alive.* New York: Bantam Books, 2009. 352pp.

Koontz, Dean R. and Edward Gorman. *City of Night.* New York: Bantam Books, 2005. 455pp.

Koontz, Dean R. and Kevin J. Anderson. *Prodigal Son.* New York: Bantam Books, 2005. 469pp.

Kovacs, Ed. *Burnt Black: A Cliff St. James Novel.* New York: Minotaur Books, 2013. 278pp.

—. *Good Junk: A Cliff St. James Novel.* New York: Minotaur Books, 2012. 325pp.

—. *Storm Damage.* New York: Minotaur Books, 2011. 307pp.

Krieger, Helen. *In the Land of What is Now.* Lexington, Ky.: Hatchery Media, 2010. 165pp.

Kuzneski, Chris. *The Plantation.* San Jose, Calif.: Writers Showcase, 2000. 426pp.

Lacy, Al and JoAnna Lacy. *Pillow of Stone.* Sisters, Ore.: Multnomah Publishers, 1998. 301pp.

Ladd, Linda. *Mostly Murder.* New York: Kensington, 2013. 344pp.

LaFaver, R.S. *Uzema, the Belle of New Orleans.* N.p.: Roy S. LaFaver, 2005. 466pp.

LaFlaur, Mark Gregory. *Elysian Fields.* Kew Gardens, N.Y.: Mid-City Books, 2013. 399pp.

Lagasse, Mary Helen. *The Fifth Sun: A Novel.* Willimantic, Conn.: Curbstone Press, 2004. 337pp.

LaGrande, Edward. *Saints in the Shadows.* Baton Rouge, La.: VAAPR, 1984. 216pp.

Lakeman, Thomas. *Broken Wing.* New York: Minotaur Books, 2009. 308pp.

Lambdin, Dewey. *The Captain's Vengeance: An Alan Lewrie Naval Adventure.* New York: Thomas Dunne Books, 2004. 336pp.

Lande, Nathaniel. *The Life and Times of Homer Sincere: Whose Amazing Adventures Are Documented by His True and Trusted Friend, Rigby Canfield: An American Novel.* New York: Overlook Press, 2010. 366pp.

Landis, Jill Marie. *Day Dreamer.* New York: Jove Books, 1996. 399pp.

—. *Just Once.* New York: Jove Books, 1997. 336pp.

Lane, Micheal. *The Wisdom of Yawdy Rum.* Andover, Minn.: Expert, 2007. 194pp.

Lang, Kimberly. *The Downfall of a Good Girl.* Don Mills, Ont.: Harlequin Books, 2013. 216pp.

Langello, Kip. *The Clinic.* New York: Pocket Star Books, 1997. 282pp.

LaPlante, Linda. *Cold Blood.* New York: Macmillan, 1996. 453pp.

Lawhon, Margaret. *The Poydras Project*. Baton Rouge: Two Ones, 2003. 220pp.

Lawrence, Katherine A. *Drop of Blood*. Lexington, Ky.: Clark, 2010. 156pp.

Lawson, John. *If Pigs Could Fly*. Boston: Houghton Mifflin, 1989. 135pp.

Lawson, Rhonda M. *Putting It Back Together*. New York: Urban, 2009. 292pp.

Lawson, Shandy. *The Loop*. New York: Hyperion Books, 2013. 198pp.

Lazo, Irete. *The Accidental Santera*. New York: Thomas Dunne Books, 2008. 318pp.

Leganski, Rita. *The Silence of Bonaventure Arrow: A Novel*. New York: Harper Collins, 2012. 378pp.

Legg, John. *Flintlock Trail*. New York: Harper Collins, 1997. 245pp.

Leigh, Jo. *One Wicked Night*. New York: Harlequin Books, 1998. 217pp.

Lemann, Nancy. *The Fiery Pantheon*. New York: Scribner, 1998. 255pp.

—. *Lives of the Saints: A Novel*. New York: Alfred A. Knopf, 1985. 143pp.

—. *Sportsman's Paradise*. New York: Alfred A. Knopf, 1992. 225pp.

Lennon, David. *Echoes: A Novel*. Newtonville, Mass.: Blue Spike, 2010. 355pp.

—. *The Quarter Boys: A Novel*. Newtonville, Mass.: Blue Spike, 239pp.

—. *Reckoning: A Novel*. Newtonville, Mass.: Blue Spike, 2012. 311pp.

—. *Fierce: A Novel*. Newtonville, Mass.: Blue Spike, 2013. 305pp.

—. *Second Chance: A Novel*. Newtonville, Mass.: Blue Spike, 2011. 299.

Leonard, Elmore. *Bandits*. New York: Arbor House, 1987. 345pp.

Leslie, Lynn. *Street of Dreams*. New York: Harlequin Books, 1990. 250pp.

Leto, Julie Elizabeth. *New Orleans Nights*. New York: Harlequin Books, 2006. 383pp.

—. *Too Wild to Hold*. New York: Harlequin Books, 2011. 217pp.

Lewis, Jennifer. *The Heir's Scandalous Affair*. New York: Silhouette Books, 2009. 187pp.

Lewis, Marilyn Jaye. *In the Secret Hours*. New Milford, Conn.: Magic Carpet Books, 2003. 254pp.

Lilly, DeVaughn M. *The Magnificent Life of Gravvy Brown: The Last Great American Story*. Cleveland, Ohio: Intelligent, 2012. 344pp.

Link, Gail. *There Never Was a Time*. New York: Love Spell, 1995. 438pp.

Linko, G.J. *Indigo*. New York: Random House, 2013. 293pp.

Llewellyn, Michael. *Creole Son*. Healdsburg, Calif.: Water Street Press, 2012. 415pp.

—. *Twelfth Night*. New York: Kensington, 1997. 372pp.

Llewellyn, Michael [Maggie Lyons, pseud.]. *Tempted*. New York: Zebra Books, 1999. 253pp.

Llewellyn, Michael [Michael LaCroix, pseud.]. *Alex in Wonderland*. New York: Southern Tier Editions / Harrington Press, 2006. 268pp.

—. *Through with the Looking Glass; The Continuing Adventures of Alex in Wonderland*. New York: Southern Tier Editions / Harrington Press, 2007. 276pp.

Lochte, Dick. *Blue Bayou*. New York: Simon and Schuster, 1992. 302pp.

—. *The Neon Smile: A Novel*. New York: Simon and Schuster, 1995. 332pp.

Lockwood, Tressie. *Wolf on the Bayou*. Charlotte, N.C.: Amira Press, 2010. 141pp.

Logan, Anne. *That Old Devil Moon*. New York: Harlequin Books, 1996. 298pp.

London, Jeanie. *One-Night Man*. New York: Harlequin Books, 2002. 250pp.

Long, Loren and Phil Bildner. *Blastin' the Blues*. New York: Simon and Schuster, 2010. 434pp.

—. *Home of the Brave*. New York: Simon and Schuster, 316pp.

Longo, Joe and Jarret Lofstead, eds. *Life in the Wake: Fiction from Post-Katrina New Orleans*. New Orleans: NOLA Fugees, 2007. 275pp.

Longstreet, Stephen. *Delilah's Fortune*. New York: Pinnacle, 1984. 304pp.

Loré, Joe. *Yeah, This Is New Orleans: Ware Yat, Vince!* San Jose, Calif.: Writers Club Press, 2002. 213pp.

Love, Kathy. *Any Way You Want It*. New York: Brava / Kensington, 2008. 286pp.

—. *I Want You to Want Me*. New York: Brava / Kensington, 2008. 312pp.

Lummis, David. *The Coffee Shop Chronicles of New Orleans. Part 1*. New Orleans: River House, 2012. 325pp.

—. *The Coffee Shop Chronicles of New Orleans. Part 2, the Last Beaucoeur*. New Orleans: River House, 2012. 353pp.

Lutz, John. *The Right to Sing the Blues*. New York: St. Martin's Press, 1986. 175pp.

Lykins, Jenny. *Echoes of Tomorrow*. New York: Jove Books, 1997. 345pp.

Lyons, David. *Blood Game: A Jock Boucher Thriller*. New York: Emily Bestler Books / Atria, 2013. 410pp.

Macdonald, Anne-Therese. *A Short Time in Luxembourg*. Round Lake Park, Ill.: Gardenia Press, 2004. 334pp.

MacNeill, Alastair. *Counterplot*. London, U.K.: Orion Books, 1999. 250pp.

Macomber, Debbie and Maura Seger. *Christmas Treasures*. New York: Harlequin Books, 1992. 477pp.

Madden, David. *The New Orleans of Possibilities: Stories*. Baton Rouge: Louisiana State Univ. Press, 1982. 115pp.

Madison, Cliff. *The Gafferty Momentum*. Talisheek, La.: Ron Barthet, 2007. 138pp.

Madl, Linda. *Bayou Rose*. New York: Kensington, 1996. 382pp.

Madyme X. *Picking Blackberries*. Baton Rouge: House of Songhay, 2006. unpaged.

Maiman, Jaye. *Old Black Magic: The 6th Robin Miller Mystery*. Tallahassee, Fla.: Naiad Press, 1997. 257pp.

Maistros, Louis. *The Sound of Building Coffins*. New Milford, Conn.: Toby Press, 2009. 358pp.

Manhein, Mary H. *Floating Souls: The Canal Murders: A Novel*. Donaldsonville, La.: Margaret Media. 164pp.

Mann, Catherine. *Honorable Intentions*. Don Mills, Ont.: Harlequin Books, 2012. 186pp.

March, Stephen. *Catbird: A Novel*. Sag Harbor, N.Y.: Permanent Press, 2006. 201pp.

Marlowe, Shaughn. *Under the Lion's Paw*. Alamogordo, N. Mex.: Shaughn Marlowe, 2010. 369pp.

Marmell, Ari and C.A. Suleiman. *City of the Damned: New Orleans*. Stone Mountain, Ga.: White Wolf, 2005. 144pp.

Marsh, Carole. *The Mystery on the Mighty Mississippi*. Peachtree City, Ga.: Gallopade, 1996. 146pp.

Martin, David Lozell. *Pelikan: Love, Redemption and Felony Theft: A Novel of the French Quarter*. New York: Simon and Schuster, 1999. 314pp.

Martin, Deborah. *Creole Nights*. New York: Leisure Books, 1992. 394pp.

Martin, George R.R. *Fevre Dream*. New York: Poseidon, 1982. 350pp.

Martin, George R.R., ed. *Busted Flush: A Wild Cards Mosaic Novel*. New York: Tor, 2009. 447pp.

Martin, Valerie. *The Consolation of Nature*. Boston: Houghton Miffllin, 1988. 147pp.

—. *The Great Divorce*. New York: Nan A. Talese, 1994. 340pp.

—. *Property*. London, U.K.: Abacus, 2003. 212pp.

—. *A Recent Martyr*. Boston: Houghton Mifflin, 1987. 204pp.

—. *Set in Motion*. New York: Washington Square Press, 1991. 209pp.

Mask, Ken. *Murder at the Butt: A Novel*. Los Angeles: Milligan Books, 2003. 233pp.

Mason, Connie. *Pirate*. New York: Leisure Books, 1998. 395pp.

Massie, Timothy W. *Death by the Drop*. Charleston: S.C.: Book Surge, 2008. 289pp.

Masson, Sophie. *Malvolio's Revenge*. London, U.K.: Hodder Children's Books, 2005. 329pp.

Mathews, Jean Holbrook. *Escape to Zion*. American Fork, Utah: Covenant Communications, 2010. 294pp.

Maughon, Robert Mickey. *New Orleans ER*. Kodak, Tenn.: Cinnamon Moon, 1996. 315pp.

Maveety, Nancy. *The Stagnant Pool: Scholars Below Sea Level*. New Orleans: Univ. Press of the South, 2000. 386pp.

Maxwell, Patricia [Jennifer Blake, pseud.]. *Challenge to Honor*. Don Mills, Ont.: Mira Books, 2005. 410pp.

—. *Dawn Encounter*. Don Mills, Ont.: Mira Books, 2006. 409pp.

—. *Embrace and Conquer*. New York: Severn House, 1992. 320pp.

—. *Louisiana Dawn*. New York: Fawcett Columbine, 1993. 328pp.

—. *Love and Smoke: A Novel*. New York: Fawcett Columbine, 1989. 389pp.

—. *Prisoner of Desire*. New York: Fawcett Columbine, 1986. 393pp.

—. *Rogue's Salute*. Don Mills, Ont.: Mira Books, 2007. 505pp.

—. *Spanish Serenade*. New York: Fawcett Columbine, 1990. 405pp.

—. *The Storm and the Splendor*. New York: Ballantine Books, 1985. 446pp.

—. *Tigress*. New York: Fawcett Gold Medal, 1996. 372pp.

Maxwell, Patricia [Jennifer Blake, pseud.]. *Triumph in Arms*. Don Mills, Ont.: Mira Books, 2010. 373pp.

—. *Wildest Dreams*. New York: Fawcett Columbine, 1992. 341pp.

Mayer, Robert. *Danse Macabre*. Camarillo, Calif.: Combustoica, 2011. 229pp.

McCade, Jillian. *New Orleans Nocturne: A Novel*. New York: St. Crispin's Press, 2002. 246pp.

McCall, Virginia. *To Love a Pirate*. New York, Harlequin Books, 1993. 298pp.

McCarthy, Erin. *Fallen*. New York: Jove Books, 2008. 309pp.

—. *My Immortal*. New York: Jove Books, 2007. 311pp.

McCarthy, Erin and Kathy Love. *The Fangover*. New York: Berkley, 2012. 298pp.

McCloskey, Walter. *Risking Elizabeth*. New York: Simon and Schuster, 1997. 302pp.

McDaniel, Sylvia. *The Price of Moonlight*. New York: Kensington, 2002. 315pp.

—. *Starlight Surrender*. New York: Kensington, 2004. 336pp.

—. *Sunlight on Josephine Street*. New York: Kensington, 2002. 316pp.

McEntire, Myra. *Infinityglass*. New York: Egmont, 2013. 293pp.

McGaughey, Neil. *Otherwise Known as Murder: A Mystery Introducing Stokes Moran*. New York: Scribner, 1994. 215pp.

McGehee, Nicole. *No More Lonely Nights: A Novel*. Boston: Little, Brown, 1995. 465pp.

McGlothin, Victor. *The Secrets of Newberry*. Waterville, Me.: Thorndike Press, 2010. 547pp.

McKade, Mackenzie. *Six Feet Under*. Dotham, Ala.: Samhain, 2006. 228pp.

McKinney, Meagan. *A Man to Slay Dragons*. New York: Kensington, 1996. 368pp.

—. *Moonlight Becomes Her*. New York: Kensington, 2001. 314pp.

—. *My Wicked Enchantress*. Unity, Me.: Five Star, 1997. 353pp.

McKinney, T.D. *Dancing in the Dark*. Indian Hill, Colo.: Amber Quill Press, 2004. 172pp.

McMahon, Barbara. *Bachelor's Baby Promise*. New York: Silhouette Books, 2000. 250pp.

McMurtry, Ken. *Zombie Penpal*. Illlustrated by Louie Wes and Newton Keith. Waitsfield, Vt.: Chooseco, 2011. 123pp.

McMurtry, Larry. *Folly and Glory: A Novel*. New York: Simon and Schuster, 2004. 236pp.

Meader, Stephen W. *Longshanks*. Little Rock, Ark.: Southern Skies, 2006. 243pp.

Melman, Peter Charles. *Landsman: A Novel*. New York: Counterpoint Press, 2007. 323pp.

Meyer, L.A. *Mississippi Jack: Being an Account of the Further Waterborne Adventures of Jacky Faber, Midshipman, Fine Lady, and the Lily of the West*. Orlando: Harcourt, 2007. 611pp.

Michaels, Fern. *Listen to Your Heart*. New York: Kensington, 2000. 214pp.

Michaels, Monette and Janet Ferran. *Blind-Sided*. Cincinnati, Ohio: Mundania Press, 2003. 270pp.

Michalik, James E. *Superhero Surtain: Future President of the United States Combats Katrina*. Illustrated by Scott Smith. Florence, S.C.: Castle Keep, 2010. 115pp.

Mickelbury, Penny. *One Must Wait*. New York: Simon and Schuster, 1998. 252pp.

Midkiff, D.K. *New Orleans Besieged*. Donaldsonville, La: Margaret Media, 2011. 325pp.

Milan, Angel. *Anna's Child*. New York: Silhouette Books, 1985. 187pp.

Miles, Cassie. *A New Year's Conviction*. New York: Harlequin Books, 1997. 251pp.

Miller, Carlos Ledson. *French Quarter Danny*. Livonia, Mich.: Bebob, 2010. 314pp.

Miller, Corey [C. Murder, pseud.]. *Death around the Corner: A Novel*. New York: Vibe Street Lit / Kensington, 2007. 276pp.

Miller, John and Genevieve Anderson, eds. *New Orleans Stories: Great Writers on the City*. San Francisco: Chronicle Books, 1992. 217pp.

Miller, John R. *Upside Down*. New York: Bantam Books, 2005. 337pp.

Miller, Judith. *Morning Sky*. Minneapolis: Bethany House, 2006. 379pp.

Miller, W. Maureen. *The French*. Wayne, Penn.: Banbury, 1983. 518pp.

Minton, Mary. *Dark Waters*. Sutton, U.K.: Severn House, 1995. 312pp.

Mize, B. Ray. *A Kill Line*. Kenner, La.: Bald Cypress Press, 2002. 200pp.

—. *Shadow of the Great Owl*. Austin, Tex.: Turn Key Press, 2004. 210pp.

Molina, Michael Otieno. *The Second Line*. New Orleans: MC Books, 2007. Unpaged.

Monroe, Mary. *Mama Ruby*. New York: Kensington, 2011. 406pp.

Montecino, Marcel. *Big Time*. New York: William Morrow, 1990. 493pp.

Montgomery, Ramsey. *Outlaw Gulch*. Illustrated by Ron Wing. New York: Bantam Books, 1987. 116pp.

Montgomery, Selena. *Never Tell*. New York: St. Martin's Press, 2004. 342pp.

Moore, Heather. *Surrender to Love*. New York: Kensington, 1996. 317pp.

Moores, Amanda. *Dream Palace*. New York: Carroll and Graf, 1994. 276pp.

Morris, Gilbert. *And Then There Were Two*. Wheaton, Ill.: Crossway Books, 2000. 285pp.

—. *Deadly Deception*. Tarrytown, N.Y.: Fleming H. Revell, 1992. 320pp.

—. *Four of a Kind*. Wheaton, Ill.: Crossway Books, 2001. 264pp.

—. *Then There Were Two*. Wheaton, Ill.: Crossway Books, 2000. 285pp.

Morris, Gilbert and Lynn Morris. *The Alchemy*. Nashville, Tenn.: West Bow Press, 2004. 259pp.

—. *The Exiles*. Nashville, Tenn.: West Bow Press, 2003. 267pp.

—. *The Immortelles*. Waterville, Me.: Thorndike Press, 2007. 439pp.

—. *Secret Place of Thunder*. Unity, Me.: Five Star, 1998. 423pp.

—. *The Tapestry*. Nashville, Tenn.: West Bow Press, 2005. 240pp.

—. *Toward the Sunrising*. Minneapolis: Bethany House, 1996. 368pp.

Morris, Paula. *Queen of Beauty*. Auckland, N.Z.: Penguin Books, 2002. 310pp.

—. *Ruined: A Novel*. New York: Point, 2009. 309pp.

—. *Unbroken: A Ruined Novel*. New York: Point, 2013. 291pp.

Morris, Taylor. *All the Clouds'll Roll Away. Vol. 1, Book 1, New Orleans. Book 2, Flight*. Jaffrey, N.H.: Gap Mountain Press, 2008. 436pp.

—. *All the Clouds'll Roll Away. Vol. 2, Book 3, Dreams to Life*. Jaffrey, N.H.: Gap Mountain Press, 2009. 368pp.

Morrison, Constance C. *Claudette of the Vieux Carré: The Adventures of a Homeless Cat in the French Quarter*. Illustrated by Thomas R. Morrison. Salt Lake City, Utah: Northwest, 1996. 101pp.

Moss, Robert. *Fire Along the Sky: Being the Adventures of Captain Shane Hardacre in the New World*. Albany, N.Y.: Excelsior Editions, 1995. 375pp.

Mowry, Jess. *Voodu Dawgz*. Port Orchard, Wash.: Blue Works, 2007. 253pp.

Muldrow, Diane. *Recipe for Trouble*. Illustrated by Barbara Pollak. New York: Grosset and Dunlap, 2003. 154pp.

Murray, C.J. *The Legend of Story Cazaunoux: A New Orleans Novel*. Atlanta: Vanimair, 1998. 265pp.

Myers, Walter Dean. *The Journal of Biddy Owens, the Negro Leagues*. New York: Scholastic, 2001. 141pp.

Myles, Jill. *Succubi Like It Hot*. New York: Pocket Star Books, 338pp.

Nance, Kathleen. *Phoenix Unrisen*. New York: Love Spell, 2007. 357pp.

—. *The Warrior*. New York: Love Spell, 2001. 395pp.

Nazworth, Lenora H. *Carly's Song*. New York City: Love Spell, 1996. 391pp.

Neate, Patrick. *Twelve Bar Blues*. New York: Grove Press, 2001. 400pp.

Neihart, Ben. *Burning Girl*. New York: Rob Weisbach Books, 1999. 245pp.

—. *Hey, Joe: A Novel*. New York: Simon and Schuster, 1996. 200pp.

Neil, Barbara. *A History of Silence: A Novel*. New York: Nan A. Talese, 1998. 334pp.

Nelson, Rick. *Bound by Blood*. New York: Thomas Dunne Books, 2008. 293pp.

Nero, Clarence. *Cheekie: A Child out of the Desire: A Novel*. Tulsa, Okla.: Council Oak Books, 1998. 276pp.

—. *Three Sides to Every Story: A Novel*. New York: Harlem Moon, 2006. 332pp.

—. *Too Much of a Good Thing Ain't Bad*. New York: Broadway Books, 2009. 235pp.

Newman, Holly. *A Lady Follows*. New York: Forge, 1999. 382pp.

Nicaud, Edgar. *Tremble and Ennui: A Novel*. New Orleans: Coat Pocket Press, 2005. 192pp.

Nicholas, Deborah. *Night Vision*. New York: Dell, 1993. 342pp.

—. *Shattered Reflections*. New York: Zebra Books, 1996. 413pp.

Nicholson, Eliza Jane Poitevent. *A Dead Life or the Nobelman's [Sic] Heir*. Picayune, Miss.: Donald C. Wicks, 2007. 112pp.

Nielsen, Virginia. *To Love a Pirate*. New York: Harlequin Books, 1993. 285pp.

Nipper, Clara. *Kiss of Noir*. New York: Bold Strokes Books, 2010. 229pp.

Nolan, James. *Higher Ground: A Novel*. Lafayette, La: Univ. of Louisiana at Lafayette Press, 2011. 271pp.

—. *Perpetual Care: Stories*. Lookout Mountain, Tenn.: Jefferson Press, 2008. 239pp.

Nolan, Jazz. *Girlfriends. Bk. 2, Creole Magic.* New York: Ibooks, 2003. 266pp.

Nordan, Frances. *The Marsh Vampire and Other Horrors.* New Orleans: California Concepts, 1994. 144pp.

—. *Night Magic.* Lucama, N.C.: California Concepts, 1990. 187pp.

North, Hailey. *Bedroom Eyes.* New York: Avon Books, 1998. 377pp.

—. *Opposites Attract.* New York: Avon Books, 2003. 375pp.

—. *Perfect Match.* New York: Avon Books, 2000. 373pp.

Nye, Jody Lynn. *Robert Asprin's Dragons Run.* New York: Ace, 2013. 406pp.

O'Day-Flannery, Constance. *Timeless Passion.* New York: Kensington, 1986. 495pp.

O'Brien, Sallie. *The Creole.* New York: Bantam Books, 1983. 295pp.

Offill, Jenny. *Last Things.* New York: Farrar, Straus and Giroux, 1999. 263pp.

Olson, John B. *Powers: A Novel.* Nashville, Tenn.: B and H, 2009. 392pp.

O'Neal, Reagan. *The Fallon Pride.* New York: Forge, 1996. 373pp.

O'Neill, Robin. *Wish You Were Here: New Orleans.* New York: Berkley Books, 1996. 211pp.

Orloff, Curt. *Keys to the V-Door.* New York: Rockhouse Press, 2002. 392pp.

Orloff, Erica. *Diary of a Blues Goddess.* Don Mills, Ont.: Red Dress Ink, 2003. 296pp.

Orwig, Sara. *New Orleans.* New York: Penguin Books, 1993. 411pp.

Osborne, Mary Pope. *A Good Night for Ghosts.* Illustrated by Sal Murdocca. New York: Random House, 2009. 112pp.

Otfinoski, Steven. *Carnival of Terror.* Illustrated by Dick Smolinski. Middletown, Conn.: Weekly Reader Books, 1986. 118pp.

Owen, Wanda. *Forever my Fancy.* New York: Kensington, 1997. 381pp.

—. *Louisiana Lovesong.* New York: Kensington, 1993. 248pp.

Pace, Laurel. *Blood Ties.* New York: Harlequin Books, 1993. 248pp.

Pace, Miriam. *Delta Desire.* New York: Kensington, 1982. 398pp.

—. *New Orleans.* New York: Kensington, 1981. 560pp.

Paige, Laurie. *The Unknown Woman.* New York: Harlequin Books, 2006. 248pp.

Painter, Kristen L. *Bad Blood*. New York: Orbit, 2011. 448pp.

Palmer, Diana. *After the Music*. Don Mills, Ont.: Mira Books, 1986. 251pp.

Palmer, Karen. *All Saints*. New York: Soho Press, 1997. 260pp.

Paolini, Nicole. *Swamp Gas*. New York: Thomas Dunne Books, 2000. 295pp.

Pappano, Marilyn. *Convincing Jamey*. New York: Silhouette Books, 1998. 248pp.

—. *Knight Errant*. New York: Silhouette Books, 1998. 250pp.

—. *A Man like Smith*. New York: Silhouette Books, 1995. 251pp.

Parker, Daniel. *Magic at the Crossroads.* New York: Harper Collins, 1996. 196pp.

Parker, F.M. *The Assassins*. New York: New American Library, 1989. 247pp.

—. *Distant Thunder*. New York: Kensington, 1999. 382pp.

—. *A Score to Settle*. New York: Kensington, 1999. 254pp.

Parkhurst, Carolyn. *The Dogs of Babel*. Boston: Little, Brown, 2003. 264pp.

Parkin, Bernadette. *Nate's Lady.* New York: Avon Books, 1981. 346pp.

Parry, Owen. *The Rebels of Babylon: A Novel*. New York: William Morrow, 2005. 309pp.

Patrick, Denise Lewis. *Cécile's Gift.* Illustrated by Christine Kornacki and Cindy Rosenheim. Middleton, Wis.: American Girl, 2011. 85pp.

—. *Meet Cécile*. Illustrated by Christine Kornacki and Cindy Rosenheim. Middleton, Wis.: American Girl, 2011.109pp.

—. *Troubles for Cécile*. Illustrated by Christine Kornacki and Cindy Rosenheim. Middleton, Wis.: American Girl, 2011. 94pp.

Patten, Lewis B. *Trail to Vicksburg: Golden Magnet*. Thorndike, Me.: Thorndike Press, 1997. 248pp.

Patterson, James. *Violets Are Blue: A Novel*. Boston: Little, Brown, 2001. 393pp.

Payne, Charlotte. *Lord of the River.* New York: Bantam Books, 1982. 345pp.

Pearse, Lesley. *Belle*. New York: Penguin Books, 2011. 588p.

Peart, Janc. *The House of Haunted Dreams*. New York: Diamond, 1992. 234pp.

Peck, Richard. *The River Between Us*. New York: Dial Books, 2003. 164pp.

Pellicane, Patricia. *Nights of Passion*. New York: Kensington, 1994. 446pp.

Pemberton, Margaret. *Undying Love*. Sutton, U.K.: Severn House, 1999. 191pp.

Pendleton, Don. *Blood Harvest*. New York: Worldwide Library, 1993. 219pp.

—. *Shadow Hunt*. New York: Worldwide Library, 2011. 188pp.

Pennington, Sharon Cupp. *Hoodoo Money*. Columbia, Md.: Draumr, 2008. 292pp.

Percy, Walker. *The Thanatos Syndrome*. New York: Farrar, Straus and Giroux, 1987. 372p.

Perelman, Helen. *Tiana: The Grand Opening*. Illustrated by David Courtland. New York: Disney Press, 2010. 87pp.

Perly, Susan. *Love Street: A Novel*. Erin, Ont.: Porcupine's Quill, 2001. 195pp.

Perrin, Kayla. *The Delta Sisters*. New York: St. Martin's Press, 2004. 357pp.

Perronne, Michael Holloway. *Falling into Me*. Los Angeles: Chances Press, 2007. 136pp.

Perry, Andre M. *The Garden Path: The Miseducation of a City*. New Orleans: Univ. of New Orleans Press, 2010. 266pp.

Pete, Eric. *Gets No Love*. New York: New American Library, 2004. 269pp.

Peters, Ray. *The Lafitte Case: A (sic) Historical Mystery*. Aurora, Colo.: Write Way, 1997. 247pp.

Phillippi, Dennis. *A Quarter Triangle*. Memphis, Tenn.: SV2, 2004. 237pp.

Phillips, Marti. *The Last Pirate: An American Historical Novel*. Ormond Beach, Fl.: Southern Star, 1999. 236pp.

Phillips, Patricia Anne. *No Turning Back*. New York: Dafina, 2008. 350pp.

Phoenix, Adrian. *Black Dust Mambo*. New York: Pocket Books, 2010. 368pp.

—. *In the Blood*. New York: Pocket Books, 2009. 389pp.

—. *A Rush of Wings*. New York: Pocket Books, 2008. 404pp.

Piazza, Tom. *City of Refuge: A Novel*. New York: Harper Collins, 2008. 403pp.

Piñeiro, Caridad. *The Perfect Mix*. New York: Kensington, 2001. 256pp.

Plain, Belva. *Crescent City: A Novel*. New York: Delacorte Press, 1984. 429pp.

Potter, Patricia. *Cold Target*. New York: Berkley Books, 2004. 425pp.

Powell, Charlotte. *The Black Hour*. Petrie Queensland, Australia: Livewire, 2004. 337pp.

Powell, Charlotte. *Lipstick Traces*. Petrie Queensland, Australia: Livewire, 2004. 311pp.

Powell, Cynthia. *Hero for Hire*. New York: Bantam Books, 1997. 213pp.

Pozzessere, Heather Graham. *Down in New Orleans*. New York: Kensington, 1996. 384pp.

Praefke, R.S. *Eternity's Missing Children*. Madison, Wis.: Intrigue Books, 2009. 263pp.

Priest, Cherie. *Ganymede*. New York: Tor, 2011. 349pp.

Proctor, Candice E. *Midnight Confessions*. New York: Ballantine Books, 2002. 409pp.

Pronzini, Bill. *Masques*. New York City: Leisure Books, 1999. 269pp.

Proulx, E. Annie. *Accordion Crimes*. New York: Scribner, 2003. 431pp.

Pruitt, L.M. *Shades of Gray*. Sterling, Va.: Red Hot, 2011. 263pp.

Randell, Kimberly. *In the Midnight Hour*. New York: Jove Books / Berkley Books, 1999. 310pp.

Randisi, Robert J. Matthews Christine. *The Masks of Auntie Laveau: A Gil and Claire Hunt Mystery*. New York: Thomas Dunne Books / St. Martin's Press, 2002. 247pp.

Raphael, Morris. *Halo for a Devil*. New Iberia, La.: M. Raphael Books, 1989. 117pp.

Reaves, Michael. *Voodoo Child*. New York: Tor, 1998. 350pp.

Receveur, Betty Layman. *Molly Gallagher*. New York: Ballantine Books, 1982. 462pp.

Redmann, Jean. *The Intersection of Law and Desire*. New York: W.W. Norton, 1995. 333pp.

—. *Death by the Riverside*. Norwich, Vt.: New Victoria Publishers, 1990. 243pp.

—. *Death of a Dying Man*. Valley Falls, N.Y.: Bold Strokes, 2009. 281pp.

—. *Deaths of Jocasta*. Norwich, Vt.: New Victoria, 1992. 279pp.

—. *Ill Will*. Valley Falls, N.Y.: Bold Strokes Books, 2012. 307pp.

—. *The Intersection of Law and Desire*. New York: W.W. Norton, 1995. 333pp.

—. *Lost Daughters*. New York: W.W. Norton, 1999. 319pp.

—. *Water Mark*. Valley Falls, N.Y.: Bold Strokes, 2010. 281pp.

—. *The Shoal of Time*. New York: Bold Strokes, 2013. 261pp.

Reece, Robert. *Alaskan Gold*. New York: Berkley Books, 1998. 297pp.

Reed, Ishmael. *Shrovetide in Old New Orleans*. New York: Atheneum, 1989. 292pp.

Reeser, Jason Phillip. *Cities of the Dead: A Collection of Short Stories*. Westlake, La.: Saint James Infirmary Books, 2012. 201pp.

Reizenstein, Ludwig von. *The Mysteries of New Orleans*. Baltimore: Johns Hopkins Univ. Press, 2002. 559pp.

Remick, Mary Kay. *Searching for Blanche: A Novel*. Hollywood, Ala.: Pen Oak Press, 1998. 310pp.

—. *The Spirit in Washington Square: A Novel*. Hollywood, Ala.: Pen Oak Press, 2004. 297pp.

Reynolds, Fleur. *The House in New Orleans*. London, U.K.: Black Lace, 1994. 265pp.

Rhodes, Jewell Parker. *Hurricane*. New York: Washington Square Press, 2011. 277pp.

—. *Ninth Ward*. Boston: Little, Brown, 217pp.

—. *Voodoo Dreams: A Novel of Marie Laveau*. New York: St. Martin's Press, 1993. 436pp.

—. *Voodoo Season*. New York: Washington Square Press, 2005. 277pp.

—. *Yellow Moon*. New York: Atria Books, 2008. 293pp.

Rice, Anne. *The Feast of All Saints*. New York: Ballantine Books, 1986. 640pp.

—. *Interview with the Vampire: The First Book of the Vampire Chronicles*. New York: Alfred A. Knopf, 1990. 274pp.

—. *Lasher: A Novel*. New York: Alfred A. Knopf, 1988. 577pp.

—. *Merrick*. New York: Alfred A. Knopf, 2000. 307pp.

—. *Pandora: New Tales of the Vampires*. New York: Alfred A. Knopf, 1998. 353pp.

—. *The Tale of the Body Thief*. New York: Alfred A. Knopf, 1992. 430pp.

—. *Taltos*. New York: Ballantine Books, 1995. 563pp.

—. *The Vampire Armand*. New York: Alfred A. Knopf, 1998. 387pp.

—. *The Vampire Lestat*. New York: Alfred A. Knopf, 1985. 481pp.

—. *Violin*. New York: Alfred A. Knopf, 1997. 289pp.

—. *The Witching Hour: A Novel*. New York: Alfred A. Knopf, 1990. 965pp.

Rice, Anne. [Anne Rampling, pseud.]. *Exit to Eden*. New York: Avon Books, 2007. 377pp.

Rice, Christopher. *A Density of Souls*. New York: Hyperion Books, 2000. 307pp.

Rice, Christopher. *The Heavens Rise*. New York: Gallery Books, 2013. 321pp.

Richards, Emilie. *Iron Lace*. Don Mills, Ont.: Mira Books, 1996. 472pp.

—. *Lady of the Night*. New York: Silhouette Books, 1986. 251pp.

—. *Rising Tides*. Don Mills, Ont.: Mira Books, 1997. 475pp.

—. *Runaway*. New York: Silhouette Books, 1990. 253pp.

—. *The Unmasking*. Toronto, Ont.: Harlequin Books, 1985. 303pp.

Richards, Penny. *Desires and Deceptions*. New York: Harlequin Books, 1998. 248pp.

Richie, Nicole. *Priceless: A Novel*. New York: Atria Books, 291pp.

Riley, Eugenia. *The Great Baby Caper*. New York: Dorchester, 2001. 395pp.

Ringo, John. *Princess of Wands*. Riverdale, N.Y.: Baen Ebooks, 2006. 323pp.

Ripley, Alexandra. *New Orleans Legacy*. New York: Macmillan, 1987. 435pp.

Robards, Karen. *Bait*. New York: G.P. Putnam's Sons, 2004. 372pp.

—. *Hunted*. New York: Gallery Books, 2013. 375pp.

Robbins, David. *New Orleans Run*. New York: Leisure Books, 1991. 190pp.

Robbins, Tom. *Jitterbug Perfume*. New York: Bantam Books, 1984. 342pp.

Roberts, J.R. *New Orleans Fire*. New York: Ace Charter, 1982. 214pp.

Roberts, Jack Stacey Daniel. *Bad Idea: The Anthology*. London, U.K.: Portico, 2008. 239pp.

Roberts, Nora. *Honest Illusions*. New York: G.P. Putnam's Sons, 1992. 383pp.

—. *The Macgregors: Alan, Grant*. New York: Silhouette Books, 1999. 498pp.

—. *The Macgregors: Daniel and Ian*. New York: Silhouette Books, 2006. 411pp.

—. *Midnight Bayou*. New York: G.P. Putnam's Sons, 2001. 352pp.

—. *Partners*. New York: Silhouette Books, 1985. 251pp.

Roberts, Sally-Ann. *Angel Vision*. Gretna, La.: Pelican, 2002. 271pp.

Robinet, Harriette. *The Twins, the Pirates, and the Battle of New Orleans*. New York: Atheneum, 1997. 138pp.

Robinson, Diana Gates. *The Rogue and the Lily*. New York: Kensington, 1993. 444pp.

Robison, Mary. *One D.O.A., One on the Way: A Novel.* Berkeley, Calif.: Counterpoint, 2009. 166pp.

Rochelle, Larry. *Bourbon and Bliss: A Palmer Morel Mystery.* Burnaby, B.C.: Zumaya Publications, 2002. 213pp.

Rochon, Farrah. *Deliver Me.* New York: Dorchester, 2007. 340pp.

Rody, Savoy. *Dead End Bayou.* West Conshohocken, Penn.: Infinity, 2005. 163pp.

Rogers, Evelyn. *A Love So Wild.* New York: Kensington, 1991. 448pp.

Rogers, Moira. *Crossroads.* Macon, Ga.: Samhain, 2010. 266pp.

—. *Crux.* Macon, Ga.: Samhain, 2010, 253pp.

—. *Impulse.* Cincinnati, Ohio: Samhain, 2013. 254pp.

Rose, Emily. *Bargained into Her Boss's Bed.* New York: Silhouette Books, 2009. 185pp.

Rose, Lloyd. *The City of the Dead.* London, U.K.: British Broadcasting Corporation, 2001. 278pp.

Rose, Rex. *Toast: A Novel.* Berkeley, Calif.: Creative Arts Book Company, 2002. 181pp.

Rosemoor, Patricia. *Saving Grace.* New York: Harlequin Books, 2010. 215pp.

Rosnau, Wendy. *The Right Side of the Law.* New York: Silhouette Books, 2001. 251pp.

Ross, Dana Fuller. *Mississippi!* New York: Bantam Books, 1985. 334pp.

Ross, JoAnn. *Michael: The Defender.* New York: Harlequin Books, 1997. 219pp.

—. *No Safe Place.* New York: Pocket Books, 2007. 383pp.

—. *Out of the Blue.* New York: Pocket Books, 2002. 263pp.

—. *Private Passions.* New York: Harlequin Books, 1995. 219pp.

—. *Roarke: The Adventurer.* New York: Harlequin Books, 1997. 216pp.

—. *Shayne: The Pretender.* New York: Harlequin Books, 1997. 214pp.

Rossi, Jeri Cain. *Red Wine Moan.* San Francisco: Manic D Press, 2000. 138pp.

Rotenberg, David. *The Shanghai Murders: Of Love and Ivory.* New York: St. Martin's Press, 1998. 307pp.

Roux, Abigail. *Touch and Geaux.* Hillsborough, N.J.: Riptide, 2013. 288pp.

Rowe, Myra. *Cypress Moon.* New York: Warner Books, 1990. 346pp.

Roy, Ron. *The Zombie Zone*. Illustrated by John Steven Gurney. New York: Random House, 2005. 84pp.

Ruffin, Paul. *Pompeii Man*. Hammond, La.: Louisiana Literature Press, 2001. 313pp.

Rupprecht, Olivia. *Bad Boy of New Orleans*. New York: Bantam Books, 1990. 180pp.

Russell, Josh. *My Bright Midnight*. Baton Rouge: Louisiana State Univ. Press, 2010. 138pp.

—. *Yellow Jack*. New York: W.W. Norton, 1999. 250pp.

Ryan, Marie-Nicole. *Holding Her Own*. Macon, Ga.: Samhain, 2009. 305pp.

Ryan, Nan. *The Countess Misbehaves*. Don Mills, Ont.: Mira Books, 2000. 377pp.

Sallis, James. *Black Hornet*. New York: Carroll and Graf, 1994. 150pp.

—. *Bluebottle: A Lew Griffin Novel*. New York: Walker, 1999. 161pp.

—. *Eye of the Cricket: A Lew Griffin Novel*. New York: Walker, 1997. 190pp.

—. *Ghost of a Flea*. Harpenden: No Exit, 2001. 224pp.

—. *The Long-Legged Fly*. New York: Avon Books, 1994. 184pp.

—. *Moth*. New York: Carroll and Graf Publishers, 1993. 205pp.

Samiloglu, Erin. *Disconnection*. Palm Beach, Fla.: Medallion Press, 2005. 368pp.

Sands, Charlene. *Do Not Disturb Until Christmas*. New York: Silhouette Books, 2008. 185pp.

Sashi, Jeané. *The J Spot*. N.p.: DonJea, 2012. 147pp.

Saux, Jack. *Clueless in New Orleans*. Mandeville, La: Arthur Hardy Enterprises, 2011. 152pp.

Savic, Sally. *Elysian Fields: A Novel*. New York: Scribner, 1988. 149pp.

Sawyer, Cheryl. *Siren*. New York: Signet, 2005. 520pp.

Sawyer, Meryl. *Closer Than She Thinks*. New York: Kensington, 2001. 415pp.

Schiefelbein, Michael E. *Vampire Maker*. New York: St. Martin's Press, 2009. 228pp.

Schilling, Vivian. *Sacred Prey*. Sherman Oaks, Calif.: Truman Press, 1994. 245pp.

Schlegel, Jorgen Ulrik. *The Luger*. Independence, Mo.: International Univ. Press, 1989. 208pp.

Schuler, Candace. *Easy Lovin'*. New York: Harlequin Books, 1991. 220pp.

Scott, Joanna C. *Cassandra, Lost*. New York: St. Martin's Press, 2004. 321pp.

Scott, Laura Ellen. *Death Wishing*. Brooklyn, N.Y.: Ig, 2011. 285pp.

Seabrooke, Brenda. *The Vampire in My Bathtub*. New York: Holiday House, 1999. 150pp.

Semerad, Sandy. *Mardi Gravestone*. Richmond, Ky.: Wings ePress, 2004. 291pp.

Senauth, Frank. *Hurricane Katrina*. Denver: Outskirts Press, 2007. 148pp.

—. *Hurricane Katrina, Part Two: The Fantastic Adventures of the Scott's (sic) Family*. Denver: Outskirts Press, 2007. 120pp.

Sepetys, Ruta. *Out of the Easy*. New York: Philomel Books, 2013. 346pp.

Shaik, Fatima. *The Mayor of New Orleans: Just Talking Jazz*. Berkeley, Calif.: Creative Arts, 1987. 143pp.

Shankman, Sarah. *Now Let's Talk of Graves*. New York: Pocket Books, 1990. 309pp.

Sharenow, Rob. *My Mother the Cheerleader: A Novel*. New York: Laura Geringer Books, 2007. 288pp.

Sharp, Alex. *Driver: Nemesis; a Story from the Driver Game Series*. London, U.K.: Corgi, 2010. 389pp.

Sharp, Zoë. *Die Easy*. New York: Pegasus Books, 2012. 398pp.

Sharpe, Jon. *Louisiana Gold Race*. New York: Signet, 1993. 172pp.

Shattuck, Sim. *Krew of Hecate*. Cumming, Ga.: Dream Catcher, 2006. 310pp.

Shaw, Linda. *Fire at Dawn*. New York: Silhouette Books, 1987. 251pp.

Sheldon, Sidney. *If Tomorrow Comes*. New York: William Morrow, 1985. 416pp.

Sheridan, Barbara. *Silver Rain*. New York: Jove Books, 2000. 302pp.

Sherman, Richard A. *Return to Mardi Gras*. Fort Lauderdale: Key Largo, 2000. 505pp.

Shoemaker, Bill. *Stalking Horse*. New York: Fawcett Columbine, 1994. 311pp.

Shuman, Malcolm. *The Caesar Clue*. New York: St. Martin's, 1990. 216pp.

—. *Deep Kill*. New York: St. Martin's Press, 1991. 199pp.

—. *The Last Man to Die: A Micah Dunn Mystery*. New York: St. Martin's Press, 1992. 214pp.

—. *The Maya Stone Murders*. New York: St. Martin's Press, 1989. 246pp.

Shuman, Malcolm. [M.S. Karl, pseud.]. *Killer Ink*. New York: Dodd Mead, 1988. 246pp.

Shurr, Lynn. *Goals for a Sinner.* Adams Basin, N.Y.: Wild Rose Press, 2009. 220pp.

—. *Wish for a Sinner.* London, Tex.: L and L Dreamspell, 2010. 321pp.

Shurtz. *Mojos.* Longmont, Colo.: Southpaw Press, 2000. 146pp.

Sidwell, Adam Glendon. *Evertaster. Course of Legends.* Los Angeles: Future House, 2012. 298pp.

Siler, Danielle. *Secrets on Tobacco Road.* N.p.: Rising Storm, 2012. 245pp.

Simmons, William Mark. *Dead Easy.* Riverdale, N.Y.: Baen Ebooks, 2007. 371pp.

Skinner, Robert E. *Blood to Drink: A Wesley Farrel Novel.* Scottsdale: Ariz.: Poisoned Pen Press, 2001. 251pp.

—. *Cat-Eyed Trouble.* New York: Kensington, 1997. 248pp.

—. *Daddy's Gone a-Hunting.* Scottsdale, Ariz.: Poisoned Pen Press, 1999. 306pp.

—. *Pale Shadow: A Wesley Farrell Novel.* Scottsdale, Ariz.: Poisoned Pen Press, 2001. 226pp.

—. *The Righteous Cut: A Wesley Farrell Novel.* Scottsdale, Ariz.: Poisoned Pen Press, 2002. 253pp.

—. *Skin Deep, Blood Red.* New York: Kensington, 1997. 247pp.

Sledge, L.D. *Dawn's Revenge.* Lexington, Ky.: Appaloosa Press, 1998. 308pp.

Smart, Alexa. *Masquerade.* New York: Windsor, 1994. 508pp.

Smith, Anthony Neil. *The Drummer: A Novel.* Brooklyn, N.Y.: Two Dollar Radio Movement, 2006. 226pp.

Smith, Bobbi. *Wanton Splendor.* New York: Love Spell, 2002. 447pp.

Smith, Craig. *Ladystinger.* New York: Crown, 1992. 232pp.

Smith, Debra June. *Yankees on the Doorstep: The Story of Sarah Morgan.* Gretna, La.: Pelican, 2001. 176pp.

Smith, Florence B. *Separated by Hate.* Independence, Mo.: Blue and Grey Book Shoppe, 1998. 371pp.

Smith, Julie. *The Axeman's Jazz.* New York: St. Martin's Press, 1991. 341pp.

—. *Boneyard Blues.* London, U.K.: Robert Hale, 2004. 240pp.

—. *Crescent City Kill: A Skip Langdon Novel.* New York: Fawcett Columbine, 1997. 326pp.

—. *82 Desire.* Rockland, Mass.: New York: Fawcett Columbine, 1998. 309pp.

Smith, Julie. *House of Blues: A Skip Langdon Novel*. New York: Fawcett Columbine, 1995. 343pp.

—. *Jazz Funeral: A Skip Langdon Novel*. New York: Fawcett Columbine, 1993. 365pp.

—. *The Kindness of Strangers: A Skip Langdon Novel*. New York: Fawcett Columbine, 1996. 338pp.

—. *Louisiana Bigshot*. New York: Forge, 2002. 303pp.

—. *Louisiana Hotshot*. New York: Forge, 2001. 335pp.

—. *Louisiana Lament*. New York: Forge, 2004. 301pp.

—. *Mean Woman Blues*. New York: Forge, 2003. 304pp.

—. *New Orleans Beat: A Skip Langdon Novel*. New York: Fawcett Columbine, 1994. 359pp.

—. *New Orleans Mourning*. New York: St. Martin's Press, 1990. 376pp.

—. *New Orleans Noir*. New York: Akashic Books, 2007. 281pp.

—. *P.I. On a Hot Tin Roof*. New York: Forge, 2005. 304pp.

Smith, L.J. *The Asylum*. Harper Collins, 2012. 221pp.

—. *The Craving*. New York: Harper Collins, 2011. 234pp.

—. *Stefan's Diaries 2: Bloodlust*. New York: Harper Collins, 2011. 225pp.

Smith, Mary-Ann Tirone. *The Port of Missing Men*. New York: William Morrow, 1989. 216pp.

Smith, Sherri L. *Orleans*. New York: G.P. Putnam's Sons, 2013. 324pp.

—. *Sparrow*. New York: Delacorte Press, 2006. 184pp.

Sokoloff, Alexandra. *The Shifters*. Toronto, Ont.: Harlequin Books, 2010. 281pp.

Sommerfield, Sylvie F. *Catalina's Caresses*. New York: Kensington, 1987. 496pp.

Speart, Jessica. *Gator Aide*. New York: Avon Books, 1997. 299pp.

Speir, Jerry and Wade Schlindler. *Help! Murder! Police!: A Novel*. New Orleans: Crescent City Press, 1989. 440pp.

Spencer, Elizabeth. *The Snare*. Jackson: Univ. Press of Mississippi, 1993. 407pp.

Spindler, Erica. *Bone Cold*. Don Mills, Ont.: Mira Books, 2001. 506pp.

—. *Forbidden Fruit*. Don Mills, Ont.: Mira Books, 1996. 504pp.

Spindler, Erica. *Killer Takes All*. Don Mills, Ont.: Mira Books, 2005. 376pp.

—. *Last Known Victim*. Don Mills, Ont.: Mira Books, 2007. 443pp.

—. *Watch Me Die*. New York: St. Martin's Press, 2011. 341pp.

Staecker, Del. *Chocolate Soup*. Brule, Wisc.: Cable, 2010. 282pp.

Stanford, Sondra. *Magnolia Moon*. New York: Silhouette Books, 1982. 250pp.

Starr, Pamela Leigh. *Storm*. Columbus, Miss.: Genesis Press, 2008. 246pp.

Stayton, Jeff. *Silent Comedians*. New York: Context Books, 2004. Unpaged.

Stennett, Jane. *There Is No Such Thing as a Literary Agent: A New Orleans Mystery*. Boonsboro, Md.: Hilliard and Harris, 2006. 184pp.

Stevens, Amanda. *The Whispering Room*. Don Mills, Ont.: Mira Books, 2009. 378pp.

Stewardson, Dawn. *The Valentine Hostage*. New York: Harlequin Books, 1997. 248pp.

Stewart, Whitney. *Jammin' on the Avenue*. New York: Four Corners, 2001. 151pp.

St. George, Margaret. *For the Love of Beau*. New York: Harlequin Books, 1997. 249pp.

Stine, R.L. *House of Whispers*. New York: Pocket Books, 1996. 149pp.

Stone, Robert. *A Hall of Mirrors*. Boston: Houghton Mifflin, 1981. 409pp.

Story, Rosalyn. *Wading Home*. Chicago: Bolden Books, 2010. 306pp.

Strahan, Jerry E. *Managing Ignatius: The Lunacy of Lucky Dogs and Life in the Quarter*. Baton Rouge: Louisiana State Univ. Press, 1998. 237pp.

Straight, Susan. *A Million Nightingales*. New York: Pantheon Books, 2006. 340pp.

—. *Take One Candle Light a Room*. New York: Pantheon Books, 320pp.

Strickland, Denzil. *Swimmers in the Sea: Novel*. Winston-Salem, N.C.: Press 53, 2008. 312pp.

Sutcliffe, Katherine. *Bad Moon Rising*. New York: Jove Books, 2003. 340pp.

Sutherland, Peg, Roz Denny, and Ruth Jean Dale. *The Lyon Legacy*. New York: Harlequin Books, 1999. 296pp.

Suzanne, Jamie Pascal Francine. *Steven the Zombie*. New York: Bantam Books, 1994. 139pp.

Talley, Liz. *His Uptown Girl*. Don Mills, Ont.: Harlequin Books, 2013. 299pp.

Tan, Maureen. *A Perfect Cover*. New York: Silhouette Books, 2004. 295pp.

Tarashis, Lauren. *I Survived Hurricane Katrina, 2004*. Illustrated by Scott Dawson. New York: Scholastic, 2011. 95pp.

Tangerine, Tracey. *Buddy Zooka in the French Quarter and Beyond*. Seattle, Wash.: Chin Music Press, 195pp.

Taylor, Hiram Ed. *Secret Society of Saint Mystic*. Pittsburgh, Penn.: Rose Dog Books, 2009. 170pp.

Taylor, Mel. *The Mitt Man: A Novel*. New York: William Morrow, 1999. 372pp.

Taylor, Sybil H. *Friendly Betrayal*. New Orleans: NEAT Publications, 2000. 283pp.

Temple, Lou Jane. *Red Beans and Vice*. New York: St. Martin's Press, 2001. 273pp.

Tentler, Leslie. *Midnight Caller*. Don Mills, Ont.: Mira Books, 2011. 410pp.

Terry, J.A. *Macumba*. San Diego, Calif.: Aventine Press, 2004. 229pp.

Tervalon, Jervey. *Dead above Ground*. New York: Pocket Books, 2000. 226pp.

—. *Lita: A Novel*. New York: Atria Books, 2003. 211pp.

Thayer, James Stewart. *The Boxer and the Poet: Something of a Romance*. Baker City, Ore.: Black Lyon, 2008. 273pp.

Thomas, Lee. *The Dust of Wonderland*. New York: Alyson Books, 2007. 316pp.

Thomas, S.E. *Eclipse of the Son*. San Jose, Calif.: Writers Club Press, 2000. 261pp.

Thompson, Colleen. *Phantom of the French Quarter*. New York: Harlequin Books, 2011. 219pp.

Thompson, David. *Shadow Realms*. New York: Leisure Books, 2004. 193pp.

Thompson, E.V. *No Less Than the Journey*. London, U.K.: Robert Hale, 2008. 336pp.

Thompson, James M. *Dark Blood*. New York: Pinnacle Books, 2002. 352pp.

—. *Dark Moon Rising*. New York: Pinnacle Books, 2005. 320pp.

—. *Immortal Blood*. New York: Kensington, 2003. 314pp.

Thompson, Theresa D. *Dogs Gone Wild: After Hurricane Katrina*. Mustang, Okla.: Tate, 2008. 127pp.

Thornton, Carolyn. *Love is Surrender*. New York: Silhouette Books, 1982. 250pp.

Tidler, Charles. *Going to New Orleans*. Vancouver, B.C.: Anvil Press, 2004. 155pp.

Tiernan, Cate. *Balefire*. New York: Razorbill, 2011. 974pp.

Tiernan, Cate. *A Chalice of Wind*. New York: Razorbill, 2005. 250pp.

—. *A Circle of Ashes*. New York: Razorbill, 2005. 216pp.

—. *A Feather of Stone*. New York: Razorbill, 2005. 231pp.

—. *A Necklace of Water*. New York: Razorbill, 2006. 250pp.

Tierney, Ronald. *Glass Chameleon*. Sutton, U.K.: Severn House, 2006. 219pp.

Tisdale, Karen C. *Grave Error*. N.p.: Bookman, 2004. 123pp.

Titchener, Louise. *Déjà Vu*. New York: Kensington, 1996. 352pp.

Toldson, Achebe. *Black Sheep*. Baton Rouge: House of Songhay / Malcolm Generation, 2004. 260pp.

Toombs, Jane. *Creole Betrayal*. Indian Hills, Colo.: Amber Quill Press, 2009. 299pp.

Toth, Emily. *Daughters of New Orleans*. New York: Bantam Books, 1983. 424pp.

Trudell, Francis. *Terry Perry: A Novel of New Orleans Rivermen*. San Jose, Calif.: Writers Club Press, 2001. 302pp.

Tubb, Kristin O'Donnell. *The 13th Sign*. New York: Feiwel and Friends, 2013. 262pp.

Turner, Elizabeth. *Bayou Magic*. New York: Kensington, 1999. 415pp.

Turner, Frederick W. *Redemption*. Orlando, Fla.: Harcourt, 2006. 348 pp.

Turner, Louise Kreher. *Margaretha's Trunk*. Montgomery, Ala.: Court Street Press, 2004. 479pp.

Tyree, Omar. *Leslie: A Novel*. New York: Simon and Schuster, 2002. 385pp.

Valentine, Terri. *Louisiana Caress*. New York: Zebra Books, 1993. 447pp.

Vali, Ali. *Balance of Forces: Toujours Ici*. New York: Bold Strokes Books, 2011. 280pp.

—. *Calling the Dead*. New York: Bold Strokes, 2008. 325pp.

—. *Deal with the Devil*. New York: Bold Strokes Books, 2008. 355pp.

—. *The Devil Be Damned*. Valley Falls, N.Y.: Bold Strokes Books, 279pp.

—. *Second Season*. New York: Bold Strokes Books, 2007. 302pp.

VanRooy, Cynthia. *All That Glitters*. New York: Kensington, 1998. 173pp.

Vaughan, Robert. *Hawke: Vendetta Trail*. New York: Harper Torch, 2005. 242pp.

Vaughn, Evelyn. *Contact.* New York: Silhouette Books, 2005. 297pp.

Vaughn, Patricia. *Shadows on the Bayou.* New York: Pocket Books, 1998. 469pp.

Viehl, Lynn. *If Angels Burn: A Novel of the Darkyn.* New York: Signet, 2005. 295pp.

Vigorito, Tony. *Nine Kinds of Naked.* Orlando: Harcourt, 2008. 402pp.

Vinet, Lynette. *Midnight Flame.* New York: Kensington, 1988. 443pp.

Volponi, Paul. *Hurricane Song.* New York: Viking, 2008. 136pp.

Wainscott, Tina. *What She Doesn't Know.* New York: St. Martin's Press, 2004. 369pp.

Walker, Robert W. *Pure Instinct.* New York: Jove Books, 1995. 424pp.


Walker, William Sterling. *Desire: Tales of New Orleans.* New York: Chelsea Station Editions, 2010. 173pp.

—. *Odd Fellow's Rest.* Los Angeles: Alyson, 2010. 240pp.

Wall, P.Q. *The Marriage of Heaven and Hell.* N.p.: P.Q. Wall, 1996. 291pp.

Wall, Robert Emmett. *The Acadians: A Novel.* New York: Bantam Books, 1984. 404pp.

Ward, Amanda Eyre. *How to Be Lost.* New York: Ballantine Books, 2004. 305pp.

Ward, H.O. *Death by Unches.* Boonsboro, Md.: Hilliard and Harris, 2003. 203pp.

Ward, Toyi. *Par for the Curse.* Somerset, N.J.: Naphtali Books, 2008. 249pp.

Ware, Ciji. *Midnight on Julia Street.* New York: Fawcett Gold Medal, 1999. 470pp.

Warner, Gertrude Chandler. *The Mystery Bookstore.* Illustrated by Charles Tang. Morton Grove, Ill.: A. Whitman, 1995. 120pp.

Warren, Lynn. *The Discovery.* Surprise, Ariz.: Triskelion, 2004. 303pp.

Washburn, L.J. *Killer on a Hot Tin Roof.* New York: Kensington, 2010. 234pp.

Watson, K. Rhydell. *To Mardi Gras, Wit' Love.* Los Angeles: SheKen, 1997. 229pp.

Watson, Peter. *Capo.* London, U.K.: Richard Cohen Books, 1995. 437pp.

Wayne, Joanna. *All I Want for Christmas.* New York: Harlequin Books, 1998. 249pp.

—. *Behind the Mask.* Toronto, Ont.: Harlequin Books, 1995. 251pp.

Wayne, Joanna. *A Father's Duty*. New York: Harlequin Books, 2004. 249pp.

—. *The Gentleman's Club*. New York: Harlequin Books, 2005. 297pp.

—. *Mystic Isle*. New York: Harlequin Books, 2002. 251pp.

—. *Stranger, Seducer, Protector*. New York: Harlequin Books, 2011. 216pp.

Wayne, Joanna, Rita Herron, and Mallory Kane. *Cover Me*. Don Mills, Ont.: Harlequin Books, 2013. 284pp.

Weaver, Ingrid. *Unmasked*. Toronto, Ont.: Harlequin Books, 2006. 243pp.

Webb, Debra. *Man of Her Dreams*. New York: Harlequin Books, 2005. 314pp.

Webber, Jake. *Lafitte's Black Box (Bôite Noire)*. Coral Springs, Fla.: Llumina Press, 2009. 210pp.

Welch, Michael Patrick. *The Donkey Show*. Los Angeles: Equator Books, 2003. 282pp.

Wells, Jaye. *Green-Eyed Demon*. New York: Orbit, 2011. 389pp.

Wells, Rebecca. *The Crowning Glory of Calla Lily Ponder: A Novel*. New York: Harper Collins, 2009. 395pp.

Wells, Robin. *Ooh, La La!* New York: Dorchester, 2002. 366pp.

West, Joseph A. *The Convict Trail: A Ralph Compton Novel.* New York: New American Library, 2008. 295pp.

Westmoreland, Kent. *Baronne Street: A Burleigh Drummond Novel*. N.p.: Benjamin Alsmith and Daughter, 2010. 247pp.

Weyrich, Becky Lee. *Whispers in Time*. New York: Windsor, 1993. 476pp.

Wharton, Greg. *Of the Flesh: Dangerous New Fiction*. Chicago, Ill.: Suspect Thoughts Press, 2001. 264pp.

White, Elizabeth. *Crescent City Courtship*. New York: Steeple Hill, 2009. 273pp.

White, Stephen. *The Program: A Novel*. New York: Doubleday, 2001. 350pp.

Whiteside, Diane. *Bond of Fire*. New York: Penguin Books, 2008. 372pp.

Whitlock, Bache McEvers. *A New Orleans Love Story*. Huntington, W. Va.: University Editions, 1994. 197pp.

Widmer, Mary Lou. *Lace Curtain*. New York: Berkley Books, 1985. 392pp.

—. *Margaret, Friend of Orphans*. Gretna, La.: Pelican, 1996. 176pp.

Widmer, Mary Lou. *The View from Rampart Street*. Durham, Conn.: Eloquent Books, 495pp.

Wilde, Jennifer. *They Call Her Dana*. New York: Ballantine Books, 1989. 503pp.

Wilde, Lori. *Some Like It Hot*. Don Mills, Ont.: Harlequin Books, 2006. 251pp.

Wildeman, James Allen. *The Valedictorian of Summer School*. New Orleans: Univ. Press of the South, 2009. 191pp.

Wilding, Kay. *Stand by Me*. New York: Harlequin Books, 1991. 253pp.

Williams, John Alfred. *Clifford's Blues*. Minneapolis: Coffee House Press, 1998. 309pp.

Williamson, Penelope. *Mortal Sins*. New York: Warner Books, 2000. 416pp.

—. *Wages of Sin*. New York: Warner Books, 2003. 401pp.

Willoughby, Jack. *A Disposable Death*. Hong Kong: Niederhauser Anwendungen, 2011. 252pp.

Willoughby, Lee Davis. *The Creoles*. New York: Dell, 1982. 286pp.

Wilson, Gayle. *Never Let Her Go*. New York: Harlequin Books, 1998. 250pp.

—. *Victim*. Don Mills, Ont.: Mira Books, 2008. 361pp.

Wiltz, Chris. *A Diamond before You Die*. New York: Mysterious Press, 1987. 198pp.

—. *The Emerald Lizard*. New York: Dutton, 1991. 243pp.

—. *Glass House: A Novel*. Baton Rouge: Louisiana State Univ. Press, 1994. 189pp.

—. *The Killing Circle*. New York: Macmillan, 1981. 220pp.

Winegardner, Mark and Mario Puzo. *The Godfather's Revenge*. New York: Random House, 2004. 430pp.

Winn, Tracy. *Mrs. Somebody Somebody: Stories*. Dallas: Southern Methodist Univ. Press, 2009. 189pp.

Wisler, G. Clifton. *Buffalo Moon*. New York: Dutton, 1984. 105pp.

Wolff, Tracy. *Tease Me*. New York: Heat, 2010. 286pp.

—. *Tie Me Down*. New York: Heat, 2009. 309pp.

Womack, Steven. *Murphy's Fault: A Mystery*. New York: St. Martin's Press, 1990. 305pp.

—. *Smash Cut*. New York: St. Martin's Press, 1991. 293pp.

—. *The Software Bomb*. New York: St. Martin's Press, 1993. 282pp.

Wonk, Dalt. *French Quarter Fables*. New Orleans: Temperance Hall, 1993. Unpaged.

Wood, Sara. *Southern Passions*. New York: Harlequin Books, 1993. 188pp.

Woods, Brenda. *Saint Louis Armstrong Beach*. New York: Nancy Paulsen Books, 2011. 137pp.

Woodrell, Daniel. *Muscle for the Wing*. New York: Henry Holt, 1988. 168pp.

—. *The Ones You Do*. New York: Henry Holt, 1992. 212pp.

—. *Under the Bright Lights*. New York: Henry Holt, 1986. 182pp.

Woodrow, Marnie. *Spelling Mississippi: A Novel*. London, U.K.: Black Swan, 2002. 381pp.

Woodward, Angus. *Down at the End of the River: Stories*. Donaldsonville, La.: Margaret Media, 2008. 139pp.

Worth, Lenora. *The Diamond Secret*. New York: Love Inspired Books, 2012. 218pp.

—. *In Pursuit of a Princess*. New York: Love Inspired Books, 2013. 217pp.

—. *Lacey's Retreat*. New York: Steeple Hill Books, 2002. 250pp.

Wright, Jason F. *Recovering Charles: Novel*. Salt Lake City, Utah: Shadow Mountain, 2008. 284pp.

Y'Barbo, Kathleen. *Beloved Captive*. Uhrichsville, Ohio: Barbour, 2008. 318pp.

York, Rebecca. *In Search of the Dove*. New York: Harlequin Books, 1986. 248pp.

—. *Sudden Attraction*. New York: Harlequin Books, 2012. 284pp.

—. *Sudden Insight*. Toronto, Ont.: Harlequin Books, 2012. 282pp.

—. *Undercover Encounter*. New York: Harlequin Books, 2004. 249pp.

York, Rebecca, Ann Voss Peterson, and Patricia Rosemoor. *Boys in Blue*. Toronto, Ont.: Harlequin Books, 2003. 251pp.

York, Thomas. *Desireless*. Markham, Ont.: Viking, 1988. 292pp.

Young, Karen. *A Father's Heart*. New York: Harlequin Books, 1998. 299pp.

Zach, Cheryl. *Winds of Betrayal*. New York: Bantam Books, 1995. 246pp.

Zatarain, Mick. *Where's Murray Ross?* New York: Alarion, 1994. 271pp.

Zelinsky, Mary. *Something Very Wild*. Detroit, Mich.: Five Star Press, 2008. 283pp.

Zell, Michael Allen. *Errata*. New Orleans: Lavender Ink, 2012. 110pp.

Zigal, Thomas. *Many Rivers to Cross: A Novel*. Fort Worth, Tex.: Texas Christian Univ. Press, 2013. 393pp.

Zimmerman, Robert Lee. *Fair Warning*. New Orleans: Uxor Press, 2011. 279pp.

Zink, Michelle. *This Wicked Game*. New York: Dial Books, 2013. 350pp.

# Appendix B
# Annotated Works Listed
# Chronologically

## 1828–1890

413.  Smith, Richard Penn. *Lafitte, or the Baratarian Chief: A Tale Founded on Facts.* Auburn, N.Y.: Free Press, 1828. 106pp.

239.  Ingraham, Joseph Holt. *Lafitte: The Pirate of the Gulf.* New York: Harper, 1836. 2 vols.: 211pp., 216pp.

461.  Trollope, Frances Milton. *The Life and Adventures of Jonathan Jefferson Whitlaw, or, Scenes on the Mississippi.* London: Richard Bentley, 1836. 3 vols.: 327pp., 331pp., 348pp.

240.  Ingraham, Joseph Holt. *The Quadroone, or, St. Michael's Day.* London: Richard Bentley, 1840. 2 vols.: 244pp., 253pp.

460.  Trollope, Frances Milton. *The Barnabys in America, or, Adventures of the Widow Wedded.* Paris: Baudry's European Library, 1843. 362pp.

485.  Wharton, George M(ichael) [Stahl, pseud.]. *The New Orleans Sketch Book.* Illustrated by Felix Octavius Carr Darley. Philadelphia: T.B. Peterson, 1843. 202pp.

157.  Dupuy, Eliza A(nn). *Celeste: The Pirate's Daughter: A Tale of the Southwest.* New York: Ely and Robinson, 1845. 2 vols.: 195pp., 223pp.

434.  Sumner, Albert W. *The Sea Lark, or, The Quadroone of Louisiana: A Thrilling Tale of the Land and Sea.* Boston: F. Gleason, 1850. 100pp.

107.  Cobb, Joseph B(eckham). *The Creole, or, Siege of New Orleans: An Historical Romance: Founded on the Events of 1814–15.* Philadelphia: A. Hart, 1850. 131pp.

260.  Judson, Edward Zane Carroll [Ned Buntline, pseud.]. *The Mysteries and Miseries of New Orleans.* New York: Akarman and Ormsby, 1851. 104pp.

397.  Robinson, J(ohn) H(ovey). *White Rover, or, The Lovely Maid of Louisiana: A Romance of the Wild Forest.* New York: Samuel French, 1851. 100pp.

9.  Anonymous. *Fashion and Consequence, as Now Found in High Places and Low Places.* Louisville, Ky.: Author, 1855. 329pp.

10.     Anonymous. *James Wellard, Companion of John A. Murrell, the Great Western Land-Pirate.* Cincinnati, Ohio: The Author, 1855. 95pp.

368.    Peacocke, James S. *The Creole Orphans, or, Lights and Shadows of Southern Life: A Tale of Louisiana.* New York: Derby and Jackson, 1856. 365pp.

369.    Peacocke, James S. *The Orphan Girls: A Tale of Southern Life.* New York: Derby and Jackson, 1857, 365pp.

158.    Dupuy, Eliza A(nn). *The Planter's Daughter: A Tale of Louisiana.* New York: W.P. Fetridge, 1857. 416pp.

234.    Homes, Mary Sophia Shaw [Millie Mayfield, pseud.]. *Carrie Harrington, or, Scenes in New-Orleans: A Novel.* New York: A. Atchison, 1857. 354pp.

457.    Townsend, Mary Ashley. *The Brother Clerks: A Tale of New Orleans.* New York: Derby and Jackson, 1857. 417pp.

424.    Stephens, Ann Sophia. *Myra, the Child of Adoption.* New York: Beadle and Adams, 1860. 120pp.

433.    Summerton, Winter [pseud.]. *Will He Find Her?: A Romance of New York and New Orleans.* New York: Derby and Jackson, 1860. 491pp.

25.     Bartlett, Napier. *Clarimonde: A Tale of New Orleans Life, and of the Present War.* Richmond, Va.: M.A. Malsby, 1863. 79pp.

371.    Peck, William H(enry). *The Conspirators of New Orleans, or, the Night of the Battle.* Greenville, Ga.: Peck and Wells, 1863. 132pp.

228.    Hills, Alfred C. *MacPherson, the Great Confederate Philosopher and Southern Blower: A Record of his Philosophy, his Career as a Warrior, Traveler, Clergyman, Poet, and Newspaper Publisher, his Death, Resuscitation, and Subsequent Election to the Office of Governor of Louisiana.* New York: J. Miller, 1864. 209pp.

357.    O'Connor, Florence J. *The Heroine of the Confederacy, or, Truth and Justice.* London: Harrison, 1864. 432pp.

403.    Sargent, Epes. *Peculiar: A Tale of the Great Transition.* New York: Carleton, 1864. 500pp.

102.    Clack, Marie Louise. *Our Refugee Household.* New York: Blelock, 1866. 226pp.

97.     Child, Lydia Maria. *A Romance of the Republic.* Boston: Ticknor and Fields, 1867. 442pp.

137.    De Forest, John William. *Miss Ravenel's Conversion from Secession to Loyalty.* New York: Harper and Brothers, 1867. 521pp.

383.  Pugh, Eliza Lofton (Phillips). *Not a Hero*. New Orleans: Blelock, 1867. 131pp.

324.  Massena, Agnese M. C. [Creole, pseud.]. *Marie's Mistake: A Woman's History*. Boston: Pratt Brothers, 1868. 357pp.

26.  Bartlett, Napier. *Stories of the Crescent City*. New Orleans: Steel and Co.'s Times Job Print, 1869. 100pp.

52.  Braddon, M(ary) E(lizabeth). *The Octoroon, or, The Lily of Louisiana*. New York: R.M. DeWitt, 1869. 116pp.

175.  Eyster, Nellie Blessing. *Tom Harding and his Friends*. Philadelphia: Methodist Episcopal Book Rooms, 1869. 368pp.

494.  Wilburn, George T. *Sam Simple's First Trip to New Orleans*. Americus, Ga.: Hancock, Graham and Reilly, 1870. 106pp.

11.  Anonymous. *The Sisters of Orleans*. New York: G.P. Putnam and Sons, 1871. 341pp.

193.  Gayarré, Charles. *Fernando de Lemos*. New York: R.F. Fenno, 1871. 486pp.

468.  Waldo, James Curtis [Tim Linkinwater, pseud.]. *Mardi Gras: A Tale of Ante Bellum Times*. New Orleans: P.F. Gogarty, 1871. 131pp.

209.  Hale, Edward Everett, Sr. *Philip Nolan's Friends: A Story of the Change of Western Empire*. New York: Scribner, Armstrong, 1877. 395pp.

77.  Cable, George Washington. *Old Creole Days*. New York: Charles Scribner's Sons, 1879. 229pp.

154.  Dugan, James. *Dr. Dispachemquic: A Story of the Great Southern Plague of 1878*. New Orleans: Clark and Hofeline, 1879. 198pp.

73.  Cable, George Washington. *The Grandissimes: A Story of Creole Life*. New York: Charles Scribner's Sons, 1880. 448pp.

76.  Cable, George Washington. *Madame Delphine*. New York: Charles Scribner's Sons, 1881. 125pp.

484.  Wharton, Edward Clifton. *The War of the Bachelors: A Story of the Crescent City, at the Period of the Franco-German War*. New Orleans: The Author, 1882. 406pp.

342.  Miller, Martha Carolyne Keller. *The Fair Enchantress, or, How She Won Men's Hearts*. Philadelphia: T.B. Peterson, 1883. 260pp.

71.  Cable, George Washington. *Dr. Sevier*. Boston: J.R. Osgood, 1884. 473pp.

277.  King, Charles. *Kitty's Conquest*. Philadelphia: J.B. Lippincott, 1884. 302pp.

309.  Louisiana [pseud.]. *Blue and Gray, or, Two Oaths and Three Warnings*. New Orleans: L. Graham, 1885. 169pp.

487. Whiteside, Muriel McCullen. *Mizpah, or, Drifting Away.* St. Louis, Mo.: A.R. Fleming, 1885. 142pp.

108. Cohen, Alfred J. [Alan Dale, pseud.]. *Ned Bachman: The New Orleans Detective.* New York: J.S. Ogilvie, 1886. 134pp.

167. Elliott, Maud Howe. *Atalanta in the South: A Romance.* Boston: Roberts Brothers, 1886. 345pp.

380. Pinkerton, Myron. *A Woman's Revenge; or, The Creole's Crime.* The Pinkerton Detective Series. Chicago: Laird and Lee, 1887. 152pp.

66. Buckner, Alice Morris. *Towards the Gulf. A Romance of Louisiana.* New York: Harper and Brothers, 1887. 315pp.

149. Dorsey, Anna Hanson. *Warp and Woof.* Baltimore: John Murphy, 1887. 276pp.

69. Cable, George Washington. *Bonaventure: A Prose Pastoral of Acadian Louisiana.* New York: Charles Scribner's Sons, 1888. 314pp.

123. Cox, George D. *Run Down: A Psychological Novel.* Philadelphia: Peterson, 1888. 242pp.

222. Harrison, James Albert. *Autrefois Tales of Old New Orleans and Elsewhere.* New York: Cassell, 1888. 294pp.

280. King, Grace Elizabeth. *Monsieur Motte.* New York: A.C. Armstrong and Son, 1888. 327pp.

473. Walworth, Jeannette H(adermann). *True to Herself.* New York: A.L. Burt, 1888. 311pp.

496. Wilkinson, Clement Penrose [Judge L.Q.C. Brown, pseud.]. *Kenneth Cameron.* Philadelphia: T.B. Peterson and Brothers, 1888. 349pp.

247. James, Samuel Humphreys [A Man o' the Town, pseud.]. *A Woman of New Orleans.* The Author, 1889. 238pp.

372. Peck, William H(enry). *The Fortune-teller of New Orleans, or, The Two Lost Daughters.* New York: Street and Smith, 1889. 215pp.

79. Cable, George Washington. *Strange True Stories of Louisiana.* New York: Charles Scribner's Sons, 1889. 350pp.

232. Holcombe, William H(enry). *A Mystery of New Orleans: Solved by New Methods.* Philadelphia: J.B. Lippincott, 1890. 332pp.

370. Peacocke, James S. *The Two White Slaves Later, or, The Creole Orphans: A Tale of the Power of Virtue over Dishonor.* Philadelphia: Columbian, 1890, 365pp.

232.   Holcombe, William H(enry). *A Mystery of New Orleans: Solved by New Methods.* Philadelphia: J.B. Lippincott, 1890. 332pp.

# 1891–1920

19.    Augustin, George. *Romances of New Orleans.* New Orleans: L. Graham and Son, 1891. 214pp.

217.   Hancock, H(arrie) Irving. *Detective Johnson of New Orleans: A Tale of Love and Crime.* New York: J.S. Ogilvie, 1891. 247pp.

229.   Hilton, Alice Howard. *A Blonde Creole: A Story of New Orleans.* New York: J.S. Ogilvie, 1891. 270pp.

248.   Jamison, C(ecilia) V(iets) Dakin Hamilton. *Lady Jane.* New York: Century, 1891. 233pp.

458.   Tracey, Francis and Henri Romani. *The Sensational Tragedy in the New Orleans Parish Prison: Startling Confession of Henri Romani, the King of the Mafia, Whose Beautiful but Heartless Wife, Nina, Was at the Bottom of the Assassination of Chief of Police David C. Hennessy.* Philadelphia: Barclay, 1891. 96pp.

2.     Ackland, William Hayes. *Sterope: The Veiled Pleiad.* Washington, D.C.: Gibson Brothers, 1892. 300pp.

184.   Ferrall, Robert J. [Pierre Beaumont, pseud.]. *The Lanfer Case: A Tale of Hypnotic Passion.* Illustrated by Edward Mason. Chicago: Bow-Knot, 1892. 248pp.

282.   King, Grace Elizabeth. *Tales of a Time and Place.* New York: Harper and Brothers, 1892. 303pp.

278.   King, Grace Elizabeth. *Balcony Stories.* New York: Century, 1893. 245pp.

402.   Ryan, Marah Ellis. *A Flower of France: A Story of Old Louisiana.* Chicago: Rand, McNally, 1893. 327pp.

431.   Stuart, (Mary) (Routh) Ruth McEnery. *A Golden Wedding, and Other Tales.* New York: Harper and Brothers, 1893. 366pp.

448.   Thompson, Maurice. *The King of Honey Island.* New York: Robert Bonner's Sons, 1893. 343pp.

251.   Jamison, C(ecilia) V(iets) Dakin Hamilton. *Toinette's Philip.* New York: Century, 1894. 236pp.

432.   Stuart, (Mary) (Routh) Ruth McEnery. *The Story of Babette: A Little Creole Girl.* New York: Harper and Brothers, 1894. 209pp.

256.   Jones, Alice Ilgenfritz. *Beatrice of Bayou Têche.* Chicago: A.C. McClurg, 1895. 386pp.

340.    McNeill, Nevada [A.S.M., pseud.]. *The Yellow Rose of New Orleans: A Novel*. New York: G.W. Dillingham, 1895. 246pp.

408.    Sharkey, Emma Augusta Brown [Mrs. E. Burke Collins, pseud.]. *Mam'selle: A Modern Heathen*. Philadelphia: William J. Benners, Jr., 1895. 246pp.

89.     Cash, Charles E. *The Great Oriental and Trans-Continental Railroad*. Vicksburg, Miss.: Commercial Herald, 1896. 171pp.

249.    Jamison, C(ecilia) V(iets) Dakin Hamilton. *Seraph: The Little Violiniste*. Illustrated by Frank T. Merrill. Boston: W.A. Wilde, 1896. 298pp.

100.    Chopin, Kate. *A Night in Acadie*. Chicago: Way and Williams, 1897. 416pp.

113.    Converse, Florence. *Diana Victrix*. Boston: Houghton, Mifflin, 1897. 362pp.

205.    Gunter, Archibald Clavering. *Bob Covington: A Novel*. New York: Home Publishing Company, 1897. 313pp.

230.    Hilton, Alice Howard. *Paola Corletti: The Fair Italian*. London: James Henderson, 1897, 153pp.

6.      Altsheler, Joseph A(lexander). *A Herald of the West: An American Story of 1811–1815*. New York: D. Appleton, 1898. 359pp.

294.    Lawrance, William V(icars). *Defeated but Victor Still, or, Heirs of the Fonca Estate: A Story of the Mysteries of New Orleans, following the Civil War and Reconstruction*. New York: F. Tennyson Neely, 1898. 424pp.

400.    Ross, Clinton. *Chalmette: The History of the Adventures & Love Affairs of Captain Robe before & during the Battle of New Orleans*. Philadelphia: J.B. Lippincott, 1898. 264pp.

455.    Tomlinson, Everett T(itsworth). *The Boys with Old Hickory*. Illustrated by A. Burnham Shute. Boston: Lee and Shepard, 1898. 352pp.

80.     Cable, George Washington. *Strong Hearts*. New York: Charles Scribner's Sons, 1899. 214pp.

99.     Chopin, Kate. *The Awakening*. New York: H.S. Stone, 1899. 303pp.

156.    Dunbar-Nelson, Alice Moore. *The Goodness of St. Rocque and Other Stories*. New York: Dodd, Mead, 1899. 224pp.

491.    Whyte, J. H. *New Orleans in 1950: Being a Story of the Carnival City, from the Pen of a Descendant of Herodotus, Possessing the Gift of Prescience*. New Orleans: A.W. Hyatt, 1899. 167pp.

135.    Davis, M(ollie) E(velyn) M(oore). *The Queen's Garden*. New York: Houghton, Mifflin, 1900. 142pp.

13.    Antrobus (Robinson), Suzanne. *The King's Messenger.* New York: Harper and Brothers, 1901. 347pp.

117.    Cooke, Grace MacGowan and Annie Booth McKinney. *Mistress Joy: A Tale of Natchez in 1798.* New York: Century, 1901. 370pp.

150.    Douglas, Amanda Minnie. *A Little Girl in Old New Orleans.* New York: A.L. Burt, 1901. 325pp.

449.    Thornton, Marcellus Eugene. *The Lady of New Orleans; A Novel of the Present.* New York: Abbey, 1901. 330pp.

18.    Augustin, George. *The Haunted Bridal Chamber, a Romance of Old-Time New Orleans.* New Orleans: The Author, 1902. 249pp.

31.    Bay, Gabriel. *A Lord in His Fool-castle: A Novel; and Molly Anathema: A Tale.* New Orleans: Erstwhil (sic), 1902. 89pp.

145.    Devereux, Mary. *Lafitte of Louisiana.* Boston: Little, Brown, 1902. 427pp.

204.    Gross, Josiah. *Ondell and Dolee: A Story of Mysticism.* New York: Abbey, 1902. 260pp.

242.    Isham, Frederic Stewart. *The Strollers.* Illustrated by Harrison Fisher. Indianapolis: Bowen-Merrill, 1902. 499pp.

425.    Stoddard, William Osborn. *The Errand Boy of Andrew Jackson: A War Story of 1814.* Illustrated by Will Crawford. Boston: Lothrop, Lee and Shepard, 1902. 327pp.

88.    Carter, John Henton. *Mississippi Argonauts: A Tale of the South.* Illustrated by L. Berneker. New York: Dawn, 1903. 291pp.

132.    Davis, M(ollie) E(velyn) M(oore). *The Little Chevalier.* Illustrated by Henry Jarvis Peck. New York: Houghton Mifflin, 1903. 317pp.

250.    Jamison, C(ecilia) V(iets) Dakin Hamilton. *Thistledown.* New York: Century, 1903. 269pp.

411.    Smith, Annie Laura [Catherine Von Scyler, pseud.]. *Rosine: The Story of a Fair Young Girl.* New York: Broadway, 1903. 132pp.

430.    Stuart, (Mary) (Routh) Ruth McEnery. *George Washington Jones: A Christmas Gift that Went A-Begging.* Illustrated by Edward Potthast. Philadelphia: Henry Altemus, 1903. 147pp.

101.    Churchill, Winston. *The Crossing.* New York: Macmillan, 1904. 598pp.

405.    Schertz, Helen Pitkin. *An Angel by Brevet: A Story of Modern New Orleans.* Philadelphia: J.B. Lippincott, 1904. 384pp.

420.    Sprague, William Cyrus. *Boy Courier of Napoleon: A Story of the Louisiana Purchase.* Illustrated by A.B. Shute. Boston: Lee and Shepard, 1904. 331pp.

147.     Dickson, Harris. *Duke of Devil-May-Care.* Illustrated by H(arry) C. Edwards. New York: D. Appleton, 1905. 295pp.

148.     Dickson, Harris. *Gabrielle Transgressor.* Philadelphia: Lippincott, 1906. 374pp.

84.      Carpenter, Edward Childs. *The Code of Victor Jallot: A Romance of Old New Orleans.* Philadelphia: G.W. Jacobs, 1907. 334pp.

134.     Davis, M(ollie) E(velyn) M(oore). *The Price of Silence.* New York: Houghton Mifflin, 1907. 280pp.

474.     Ward, William. *The Murderer of New Orleans: A Story of Hypnotism, Passion, and Crime.* Cleveland, Ohio: Buckeye, 1907. 212pp.

501.     Winn, Mary Polk and Margaret Hannis. *The Law and the Letter: A Story of the Province of Louisiana.* Illustrated by George E. Hausman. New York: Neale, 1907. 184pp.

50.      Bouvet, Marguerite. *Clotilde.* Illustrated by Maginel Wright Enright. Chicago: A.C. McClurg, 1908. 216pp.

74.      Cable, George Washington. *Kincaid's Battery.* Illustrated by Alonzo Kimball. New York: Charles Scribner's Sons, 1908. 396pp.

133.     Davis, M(ollie) E(velyn) M(oore). *The Moons of Balbanca.* New York: Houghton Mifflin, 1908. 180pp.

5.       Altsheler, Joseph A(lexander). *The Free Rangers: A Story of Early Days Along the Mississippi.* New York: Appleton, 1909. 364pp.

78.      Cable, George Washington. *"Posson Jone" and Père Raphaël.* Illustrated by Stanley M. Arthurs. New York: Charles Scribner's Sons, 1909. 162pp.

201.     Greene, Frances Nimmo. *Into the Night: A Story of New Orleans.* New York: Grosset and Dunlap, 1909. 370pp.

20.      Baker, Julie Keim Wetherill. *The Wandering Joy.* New York: Broadway, 1910. 172pp.

98.      Chipman, William Pendleton. *The Boy Spies at the Battle of New Orleans: A Boys Story of the Greatest Battle of the War of 1812.* New York: A.L. Burt, 1910. 276pp.

118.     Cooley, Stoughton. *The Captain of the Amaryllis.* Illustrated by Leslie L. Benson. Boston: C.M. Clark, 1910. 416pp.

33.      Beach, Rex (Ellingwood). *The Net.* New York: Harper and Brothers, 1912. 332pp.

359.     O'Hara, Edith C(ecilia) and Mary S. Ely. *Confidences.* New Orleans: Press of Louisiana, 1912. 142pp.

379.     Perry, Stella G(eorge) S(tern). *Melindy.* New York: Moffat, Yard, 1912. 250pp.

155.    Duke, Mary Kerr. *The Mystery of Castlegreen: A Louisiana Romance.* New York: Broadway, 1913. 175pp.

32.     Beach, Rex (Ellingwood). *The Crimson Gardenia and Other Tales of Adventure.* Illustrated by Anton Otto Fischer and Charles Sarka. New York: Harper and Brothers, 1916. 377pp.

281.    King, Grace Elizabeth. *The Pleasant Ways of St. Médard.* New York: H. Holt, 1916. 338pp.

295.    Lea, Fanny Heaslip. *Chloe Malone.* Illustrated by F. Graham Cootes. Boston: Little, Brown, 1916. 292pp.

72.     Cable, George Washington. *The Flower of the Chapdelaines.* New York: Charles Scribner's Sons, 1918. 339pp.

75.     Cable, George Washington. *Lovers of Louisiana (To-Day).* New York: Charles Scribner's, 1918. 351pp.

125.    Craddock, Irving. *The Yazoo Mystery.* New York: Britton, 1919. 302pp.

299.    Le Moine, Weston J. *The Sacrifice: A True Story.* Illustrated by W.E. Greer, Jr. New Orleans: Cox, 1919. 212pp.

# 1921–1950

35.     Bedford-Jones, Henry. *The Mardi Gras Mystery.* Garden City, N.Y.: Doubleday, Page, 1921. 313pp.

95.     Chesnutt, Charles W(addell). *Paul Marchand.* Jackson, Miss.: University Press of Mississippi, 1998. 144pp. (Completed in 1921, but unpublished in the author's lifetime).

224.    Hay, Corinne. *Light and Shade 'Round Gulf and Bayou.* Illustrated by Julia Ann Mountfort. Boston: Roxburgh, 1921. 222pp.

288.    Laing, Sallie Wear. *Her Black Body.* Newark, N.J.: Essex Press, 1921. 324pp.

243.    Jackson, Charles Tenney. *Captain Sazarac.* New York: Grosset and Dunlap, 1922. 332pp.

361.    Olmstead, Florence. *Madame Valcour's Lodger.* New York: Charles Scribner's Sons, 1922. 261pp.

335.    May, Margery Land. *Such as Sit in Judgment.* London: Leonard Parsons, 1923. 287pp.

476.    Wassermann, Moses. *Judah Touro: A Biographical Romance.* Translated from the German by Harriet W. Mayer. New York: Bloch, 1923. 275pp.

266.    Keeler, Harry Stephen. *The Voice of the Seven Sparrows.* London: Hutchinson, 1924. 284pp.

279.    King, Grace Elizabeth. *La Dame de Sainte Hermine*. New York: Macmillan, 1924. 296pp.

311.    MacDonald, Edwina Levin. *A Lady of New Orleans*. New York: Macaulay, 1925. 314pp.

322.    Martinez, Raymond J(oseph). *In the Parish of St. John*. Thibodaux, La.: George A. Martin, 1925. 147pp.

336.    McCormick, William Bennett. *The Wanton: A Story of the Red Light*. Shreveport, La.: The Author, 1925. 495pp.

417.    Sparling, (Edward) Earl. *Under the Levee*. New York: Charles Scribner's Sons, 1925. 290pp.

21.     Banks, (Algernon) Polan. *Black Ivory*. New York: A.L. Burt, 1926. 305pp.

174.    Evans, Lawton Bryan. *The Pirate of Barataria*. Illustrated by Oliver Kemp. Springfield, Mass.: Milton-Bradley, 1926. 298pp.

346.    Moore, John Trotwood. *Hearts of Hickory: A Story of Andrew Jackson and the War of 1812*. Nashville, Tenn.: Cokesbury, 1926. 450pp.

177.    Faulkner, William. *Mosquitoes*. New York: Boni and Liveright, 1927. 349pp.

310.    MacDonald, Edwina Levin. *Blind Windows*. New York: Macaulay, 1927. 383pp.

343.    Minnigerode, Meade. *Cockades*. New York: G.P. Putnam's Sons, 1927. 374pp.

146.    Dickson, Harris. *Children of the River: A Romance of Old New Orleans*. New York: J.H. Sears, 1928. 326pp.

197.    Gibbs, George. *The Shores of Romance*. New York: D. Appleton, 1928. 292pp.

297.    Le May, Alan. *Old Father of Waters*. Garden City, N.Y.: Doubleday, Doran, 1928. 329pp.

450.    Tinker, Edward Larocque. *Toucoutou*. New York: Dodd, Mead, 1928. 312pp.

29.     Basso, (Joseph) Hamilton. *Relics and Angels*. New York: Macaulay, 1929. 286pp.

103.    Clark, Ellery H(arding). *The Strength of the Hills*. New York: Crowell, 1929. 350pp.

139.    DeLavigne, Jeanne and Jacques Rutherford. *Fox Fire*. New York: Duffield and Company, 1929. 411pp.

196.    Gibbs, George. *Isle of Illusion*. New York: J.H. Sears, 1929. 301pp.

206.    Guyol, Louise Hubert. *The Gallant Lallanes*. New York: Harper and Brothers, 1929. 251pp.

221.    Harrison, Edith Ogden. *Gray Moss.* Chicago: Ralph Fletcher Seymour, 1929. 205pp.

233.    Holland, Rupert Sargent. *Pirate of the Gulf.* Philadelphia: J.B. Lippincott, 1929. 270pp.

298.    Le May, Alan. *Pelican Coast.* Illustrated by George Illian. Garden City, N.Y.: Doubleday, Doran, 1929. 329pp.

301.    Linfield, Mary Barrow. *Young Woman in Love.* New York: Macaulay, 1929. 322pp.

318.    Martin, Aylwin Lee. *The Gambler.* New York: Thomas Y. Crowell, 1929. 350pp.

366.    Oursler, (Charles) Fulton. *The World's Delight.* New York: Harper and Brothers, 1929. 425pp.

55.     Brandon, Winnie. *Dixiana: A Romance of New Orleans.* New York: A.L. Burt, 1930. 253pp.

60.     Bristow, Gwen and Bruce Manning. *The Invisible Host.* New York: The Mystery League, 1930. 286pp.

63.     Brown, Beth. *For Men Only.* New York: Claude Kendall, 1930. 288pp.

96.     Chidsey, Donald Barr. *Pistols in the Morning.* New York: Day, 1930. 282pp.

129.    Curtis, Alice Turner. *A Little Maid of New Orleans.* Illustrated by Hattie Longstreet Price. Philadelphia: Penn, 1930. 224pp.

283.    Knapp, George L. *A Young Volunteer at New Orleans.* New York: Dodd, Mead, 1930. 271pp.

285.    Knipe, Emilie Benson and Alden Arthur Knipe. *The Treasure House.* Illustrated by Margaret Ayer. New York: Century, 1930. 300pp.

373.    Peddie, Jon. *The Crawfish Woman, and Other Stories.* New Orleans: Wetzel, 1930. 79pp.

391.    Robert, Paul J(ones). *Grande Terre: An Historical Romance of Older Creole Days.* Washington D.C.: Congressional Press, 1930. 210pp.

464.    Van Epps, Margaret T. *Nancy Pembroke in New Orleans.* New York: A.L. Burt, 1930. 248pp.

488.    Whitman, (Vivian) Willson. *Contradance: A Puritan's Progress in New Orleans.* Indianapolis: Bobbs-Merrill, 1930. 350pp.

48.     Bontemps, Arna(ud) Wendell. *God Sends Sunday.* New York: Harcourt, Brace, 1931. 199pp.

53.     Bradford, Roark. *John Henry.* Illustrated by J.J. Lankes. New York: Harper and Brothers, 1931. 225pp.

59.    Bristow, Gwen and Bruce Manning. *The Gutenberg Murders.* New York: Mystery League, 1931. 286pp.

83.    Carb, David. *Sunrise in the West.* New York: Brewer, Warren, and Putnam, 1931. 384pp.

235.   Houston, Margaret Bell. *Moon of Delight.* New York: Dodd, Mead, 1931. 282pp.

238.   Imbert, Dennis I(gnatius). *The Colored Gentleman: A Product of Modern Civilization.* New Orleans: Williams Printing Service, 1931. 86pp.

241.   Ingraham, Colonel Prentiss. *LaFitte's Lieutenant.* Cleveland, Ohio: Arthur Westbrook, 1931. 196pp.

284.   Knight, Gladys. *Binny's Women.* New York: Century, 1931. 310pp.

286.   Knoblock, K(enneth) T(homas). *There's Been Murder Done.* New York: Harper and Brothers, 1931. 337pp.

377.   Perkins, Kenneth. *Voodoo'd.* New York: Harper and Brothers, 1931. 289pp.

46.    Blake, Gladys. *Belinda in Old New Orleans.* New York: D. Appleton, 1932. 295pp.

61.    Bristow, Gwen and Bruce Manning. *The Mardi Gras Murders.* New York: Mystery League, 1932. 286pp.

4.     Allen, Hervey. *Anthony Adverse.* New York: Farrar and Rinehart, 1933. 1224pp.

23.    Barker, Lillian. *Cabaret Love.* New York: Grosset and Dunlap, 1933. 278pp.

200.   Grayson, Charles (Wright). *Original Sin.* New York: Alfred H. King, 1933. 254pp.

478.   Waugh, Alec. *The Golden Ripple.* New York: Farrar and Rinehart, 1933. 306pp.

27.    Basso, (Joseph) Hamilton. *Cinnamon Seed.* New York: Charles Scribner's Sons, 1934. 379pp.

54.    Bradford, Roark. *Let the Band Play Dixie.* New York: Harper and Brothers, 1934. 320pp.

92.    Charnley, Mitchell V. *The Buccaneer: The Story of Jean Lafitte; originally published as, Jean Lafitte, Gentleman Smuggler.* New York: Grosset and Dunlap, 1934. 240pp.

39.    Bell, Sallie Lee. *Marcel Armand: A Romance of Old Louisiana.* Illustrated by Harold Cue. Boston: L.C. Page, 1935. 343pp.

313.   Madere, Hubert. *Bachelor's Daughter.* Philadelphia: Dorrance, 1935. 259pp.

471.   Wall, Evans. *Lovers Cry for the Moon.* New York: Macaulay, 1935. 258pp.

82.    Caldwell, Barry. *Carnival Is for Lovers.* New York: Godwin, 1936. 291pp.

215.    Hamilton, Harry. *Banjo on My Knee.* Indianapolis, Ind.: Bobbs-Merrill, 1936. 320pp.

300.    Linfield, Mary Barrow. *Day of Victory.* Garden City, N.Y.: Doubleday, Doran, 1936. 239pp.

360.    Olivier, Robert L(ouis). *Pierre of the Teche.* New Orleans: Pelican, 1936. 236pp.

392.    Roberts, Charles Blanton. *Edmond Peyré.* New York: Fleming H. Revell, 1936. 206pp.

410.    Sinclair, Harold. *Journey Home.* Garden City, N.Y.: Doubleday, Doran, 1936. 290pp.

43.     Best, Allena Champlin [Erick Berry, pseud.]. *Homespun.* Illustrated by Harold Von Schmidt. New York: Junior Literary Guild and Lothrop, Lee and Shepard, 1937. 308pp.

502.    Wirt (Benson), Mildred A(ugustine). *The Shadow Stone.* New York: Cupples and Leon, 1937. 206pp.

162.    Easterling, Narena (Brooks). *Southern Moon.* New York: Gramercy Publishing, 1938. 253pp.

172.    Erskine, John. *The Start of the Road.* New York: Frederick A. Stokes, 1938. 344pp.

187.    Fleming, Rudd. *Cradled in Murder.* New York: Simon and Schuster / An Inner Sanctum Mystery, 1938. 293pp.

356.    Nunez, Nemours Henry, Jr. *Chien Negre: A Tale of Vaudoux.* Aurora, Mo.: Burney Brothers, 1938. 278pp.

428.    Stone, Michael [name legally changed from Oberia Scott]. *And Tomorrow.* New York: Sovereign House, 1938. 349pp.

28.     Basso, (Joseph) Hamilton. *Days before Lent.* New York: Charles Scribner's Sons, 1939. 371pp.

207.    Hagen, Annunciata. *The Unflinching M.D.* New York: Fortuny's, 1939. 262pp.

296.    LeBlanc, Doris Kent. *One Was Valiant.* New York: Arcadia House, 1939. 318pp.

367.    Parker, Walter. *New Orleans, The Hoe Doo Candle, and Other Stories* New Orleans: Rogers, 1939. 87pp.

463.    Van der Veer, (John) Stewart [a.k.a., Stewart Vanderveer]. *Death for the Lady.* New York: Phoenix, 1939. 256pp.

58.     Bristow, Gwen. *This Side of Glory.* New York: Thomas Y. Crowell, 1940. 400pp.

352.    Murray, John. *Son of the Bayou.* Notre Dame, Ind.: Ave Maria, 1940. 317pp.

393.    Roberts, Marjorie. *Webs in the Sky.* New York: Wilfred Funk, 1940. 299pp.

399.    Root, Corwin. *An American, Sir.* New York: E.P. Dutton, 1940. 383pp.

62. Bromfield, Louis. *Wild is the River.* New York: Harper and Brothers, 1941. 326pp.

183. Ferber, Edna. *Saratoga Trunk.* Garden City, N.Y.: Doubleday, Doran, 1941. 352pp.

404. Schachner, Nathan. *By the Dim Lamps.* New York: Frederick A. Stokes, 1941. 577pp.

30. Basso, (Joseph) Hamilton. *Sun in Capricorn.* New York: C. Scribner's Sons, 1942. 266pp.

161. Easterling, Narena (Brooks). *Peter and Anne.* New York: Gramercy Publishing, 1942. 256pp.

191. Gardner, Erle Stanley [A.A. Fair, pseud.]. *Owls Don't Blink.* New York: Grosset and Dunlap, 1942. 277pp.

273. Keyes, Frances Parkinson. *Crescent Carnival.* New York: J. Messner, 1942. 807pp.

287. La Farge, Oliver. *The Copper Pot.* Boston: Houghton, Mifflin, 1942. 295pp.

307. Lockwood, Myna. *Free River: A Story of Old New Orleans.* Illustrated by Myna Lockwood. New York: E.P. Dutton, 1942. 255pp.

308. Long, Amelia Reynolds. *Murder by Scripture.* New York: Phoenix Press, 1942. 254pp.

330. Matthews, Harold. *River-Bottom Boy.* New York: Thomas Y. Crowell, 1942. 354pp.

351. Murray, John. *Belle Esperance.* Notre Dame, Ind.: Ave Maria, 1942. 344pp.

390. Ripley, Clements. *Mississippi Belle.* New York: D. Appleton-Century, 1942. 307pp.

447. Thompson, (John) Edward. *Listen for the Laughter.* Philadelphia: Macrae-Smith, 1942. 328pp.

258. Judson, Clara Ingram. *Pierre's Lucky Pouch: They Came from France.* Illustrated by Lois Lenski. New York: Follett, 1943. 245pp.

259. Judson, Clara Ingram. *They Came from France.* Illustrated by Lois Lenski. Boston: Houghton, Mifflin, 1943. 245pp.

306. Lockwood, Myna. *Beckoning Star: A Story of Old Texas.* Illustrated by Myna Lockwood. New York: E.P. Dutton, 1943. 242pp.

328. Matschat, Cecile Hulse. *Murder at the Black Crook.* New York: Farrar and Rinehart, 1943. 250pp.

406. Seifert, Shirley. *Those Who Go Against the Current.* Philadelphia: J.B. Lippincott, 1943. 612pp.

477. Watkins, Glen. *Hotel Wife.* New York: Knickerbocker, 1943. 126pp.

47.    Blassingame, Wyatt. *John Smith Hears Death Walking.* New York: Bartholomew House, 1944. 190pp.

151.   Dresser, Davis [Brett Halliday, pseud.]. *Michael Shayne's Long Chance.* New York: Dodd, Mead, 1944. 218pp.

153.   Dresser, Davis [Brett Halliday, pseud.]. *Murder and the Married Virgin.* New York: Dodd, Mead, 1944. 179pp.

165.   Ebeyer, Pierre Paul. *Paramours of the Creoles.* New Orleans: Windmill Publishing, 1944. 178pp.

314.   Mally, Emma Louise. *The Mocking Bird is Singing.* New York: Holt, 1944. 394pp.

396.   Roberts, Walter Adolphe. *Royal Street: A Novel of Old New Orleans.* Indianapolis: Bobbs-Merrill, 1944. 324pp.

437.   Tabony, Annie Heller. *Eulalie.* Cynthiana, Ky.: Hobson, 1944. 304pp.

110.   Comfort, Mildred Houghton. *Search through Pirate's Alley.* Illustrated by Sari. New York: William Morrow, 1945. 200pp.

126.   Crane, Frances. *The Indigo Necklace.* New York: Random House, 1945. 238pp.

164.   Ebeyer, Pierre Paul. *Gems of the Vieux Carré.* New Orleans: Windmill Publishing, 1945. 348pp.

315.   Margulies, Leo and Sam Merwin. *The Flags were Three: A Novel of Old New Orleans.* New York: S. Curl, 1945. 283pp.

138.   DeLavigne, Jeanne. *Ghost Stories of Old New Orleans.* Illustrated by Charles Richards. New York: Rinehart, 1946. 374pp.

152.   Dresser, Davis [Brett Halliday, pseud.]. *Michael Shayne's Triple Mystery.* Chicago: Ziff-Davis, 1946. 225pp.

216.   Hammond, Hilda Phelps. *Pierre and Ninette in Old New Orleans.* Illustrated by Elizabeth Urquhart. New Orleans: Hauser, 1946. 80pp.

263.   Kane, Harnett T(homas). *New Orleans Woman: A Biographical Novel of Myra Clark Gaines.* Garden City, N.Y.: Doubleday, 1946. 344pp.

265.   Keating, Lawrence A. [H.C. Thomas, pseud.]. *A Boy Fighter with Andrew Jackson.* Illustrated by Henry E. Vallely. Racine, Wis.: Whitman, 1946. 249pp.

316.   Marko, Samuel. *To Struggle, to Laugh.* Boston: Chapman and Grimes, 1946. 236pp.

358.   O'Donnell, Mary King. *Those Other People.* Illustrated by F. Strobel. Boston: Houghton Mifflin, 1946. 338pp.

394.    Roberts, Walter Adolphe. *Brave Mardi Gras: A New Orleans Novel of the '60s.* Indianapolis: Bobbs-Merrill, 1946. 318pp.

427.    Stone, Elisabet M. *Poison, Poker and Pistols.* New York: Sheridan House, 1946. 254pp.

510.    Yerby, Frank. *The Foxes of Harrow.* New York: Dial, 1946. 534pp.

22.     Banks, (Algernon) Polan. *Carriage Entrance.* New York: G. P. Putnam's Sons, 1947. 280pp.

225.    Hedden, Worth Tuttle. *The Other Room.* New York: Crown, 1947. 274pp.

276.    Keyes, Frances Parkinson. *Once on Esplanade: A Cycle Between Two Creole Weddings.* New York: Dodd, Mead, 1947. 202pp.

350.    Murphy, Edward F(rancis). *Père Antoine.* Garden City, N.Y.: Doubleday, 1947. 304pp.

353.    Neubauer, William Arthur [Norma Newcomb, pseud.] *The Heart Story.* New York: Gramercy, 1947. 254pp.

426.    Stone, Elisabet M. *Murder at the Mardi Gras.* New York: Sheridan House, 1947. 244pp.

507.    Woolrich, Cornell (George) (Hopley-) [William Irish, pseud.]. *Waltz into Darkness.* New York: Penguin, 1947. 310pp.

513.    Yerby, Frank. *The Vixens: A Novel.* New York: Dial, 1947. 347pp.

16.     Aswell, James (Benjamin), (Jr.). *The Midsummer Fires: A Long Fiction.* New York: William Morrow, 1948. 311pp.

267.    Keene, Carolyn [house pseudonym]. *The Ghost of Blackwood Hall.* New York: Grosset and Dunlap, 1948. 216pp.

274.    Keyes, Frances Parkinson. *Dinner at Antoine's.* New York: J. Messner, 1948. 422pp.

386.    Reymond, Dalton S(haffer). *Earthbound.* Chicago: Ziff-Davis, 1948. 381pp.

395.    Roberts, Walter Adolphe. *Creole Dusk: A New Orleans Novel of the '80s.* Indianapolis: Bobbs-Merrill, 1948. 325pp.

439.    Tallant, Robert. *Angel in the Wardrobe.* Garden City, N.Y.: Doubleday, 1948. 271pp.

479.    Webber, Everett and Olga Webber. *Rampart Street.* New York: E.P. Dutton, 1948. 318pp.

121.    Costain, Thomas B(ertram). *High Towers.* Garden City, N.Y.: Doubleday, 1949. 403pp.

142.    Delmar, Viña. *New Orleans Lady.* New York: Avon, 1949. 189pp.

144.    Denbo, Anna Margaret. *A Romance of Old New Orleans*. New Orleans: Pelican, 1949. 331pp.

354.    Neugass, James. *Rain of Ashes*. New York: Harper and Brothers, 1949. 326pp.

407.    Seley, Stephen. *Baxter Bernstein: A Hero of Sorts*. New York: Charles Scribner's Sons, 1949. 239pp.

419.    Sperry, Armstrong (Wells). *Black Falcon: A Story of Piracy and Old New Orleans*. Illustrated by Armstrong Sperry. Philadelphia: J.C. Winston, 1949. 218pp.

441.    Tallant, Robert. *Mr. Preen's Salon*. New York: Doubleday, 1949. 271pp.

486.    White, Charles William [Max White, pseud.]. *The Man Who Carved Women from Wood*. New York: Harper, 1949. 304pp.

94.     Chaze, (Lewis) Elliott. *The Golden Tag: A Novel*. New York: Simon and Schuster, 1950. 279pp.

264.    Kane, Harnett T(homas). *Pathway to the Stars: A Novel Based on the Life of John McDonogh of New Orleans and Baltimore*. Garden City, N.Y.: Doubleday, 1950. 312pp.

293.    Lattimore, Eleanor Frances. *Christopher and His Turtle*. New York: William Morrow, 1950. 126pp.

409.    Shore, William. *The Witch of Spring*. Pelligrini and Cudahy, 1950. 348pp.

466.    Vidal, [Eugene] [Luther] Gore [Katherine Everard, pseud.] *A Star's Progress*. New York: Dutton, 1950. 252pp.

# 1951–1980

34.     Beach, Rex (Ellingwood). *Woman in Ambush*. New York: G.P. Putnam's Sons, 1951. 280pp.

93.     Chastain, Madye Lee. *Steamboat South*. New York: Harcourt, Brace, 1951. 233pp.

115.    Cook, Ella Booker. *A Magnolia for Joan*. New Orleans: Pelican, 1951. 246pp.

289.    Laird, Marion Murdoch (Lind). *Impounded Waters: A Novel of John McDonogh*. New Orleans: The Author, 1951. 114pp.

312.    MacDonald, John D(ann). *Murder for the Bride*. New York: Fawcett, 1951. 164pp.

323.    Mason, F(rancis) van Wyck. *Proud New Flags*. Philadelphia: Lippincott, 1951. 493pp.

339.    McKeag, Ernest Lionel [Roland Vane, pseud.]. *White Slaves of New Orleans*. Cleveland, Ohio: Kaywin, 1951. 128pp.

421.    Stahls, Charles Gilbert. *Grand Bouquet*. Los Angeles: Watling, 1951. 328pp.

443.    Tallant, Robert. *The Pirate Lafitte and the Battle of New Orleans*. Illustrated by John Chase. New York: Random House, 1951. 186pp.

444.    Tallant, Robert. *Southern Territory*. Garden City, N.Y.: Doubleday, 1951. 250pp.

446.    Thompson, John B(urton). *Love and the Wicked City*. New York: Arco, 1951. 182pp.

462.    Turner, James H(enry), (Jr.). *One Fine Spring*. New Orleans: Pelican, 1951. 195pp.

481.    Wellman, Paul Iselin. *The Iron Mistress*. Garden City, N.Y.: Doubleday, 1951. 404pp.

470.    Wall, Evans. *Ask for Therese*. New York: Rio, 1952. 128pp.

504.    Woolfolk, Josiah Pitts [Jack Woodford, pseud.] and John Burton Thompson. *Desire in New Orleans*. Baltimore: Signature, 1952. 190pp.

67.     Burroughs, William S(eward) [William Lee, pseud.]. *Junkie*. New York: Ace Books, 1953. 149pp.

91.     Chapman, John Stanton Higham and Mary Ilsley Chapman [Maristan Chapman, joint pseud.]. *Tennessee Hazard*. Philadelphia: J.B. Lippincott, 1953. 367pp.

176.    Faulkner, William. *Mirrors of Chartres Street*. Minneapolis, Minn.: Faulkner Studies, 1953. 93pp.

210.    Hales, Carol. *Wind Woman*. New York: Woodford. 1953. 288pp.

262.    Kane, Frank. *Poisons Unknown*. New York: Dell, 1953. 192pp.

365.    Otis, G.H. *Bourbon Street*. New York: Lion Books 1953. 160pp.

440.    Tallant, Robert. *Love and Mrs. Candy*. Garden City, N.Y.: Doubleday, 1953. 287pp.

482.    Wells, Charlie. *Let the Night Cry*. New York: Abelard, 1953. 287pp.

497.    Williams, Ben Ames. *The Unconquered*. Boston: Houghton Mifflin, 1953. 689pp.

505.    Woolfolk, Josiah Pitts [Jack Woodford, pseud.] and Conrad Carter. *Nikki*. Baltimore: Signature, 1953, 183pp.

506.    Woolfolk, Josiah Pitts [Jack Woodford, pseud.] and Conrad Carter. *Tainted*. Baltimore, Md.: Signature, 1953. 182pp.

143.    Demarest, Donald. *Fabulous Ancestor*. Philadelphia: Lippincott, 1954. 288pp.

173.    Escoffier, Lillian Ann DuRocher. *Heartbreak*. Ann Arbor, Mich.: Edwards Brothers, 1954. 282pp.

211.    Hall, Georgette Brockman. *House on Rampart Street*. New York, Vantage, 1954. 291pp.

291. Lane, Frederick A. *A Flag for Lafitte: Story for the Battle of New Orleans.* Illustrated by Leonard Vosburgh. New York: Aladdin Books, 1954. 191pp.

385. Reeser, Edwin Isherwood. *Pushmataha.* New York: Exposition Press, 1954. 169pp.

412. Smith, Minette Graham. *Maid of New Orleans.* New York: Vantage, 1954. 121pp.

442. Tallant, Robert. *Mrs. Candy Strikes It Rich.* Garden City, N.Y.: Doubleday, 1954. 253pp.

17. Aswell, James (Benjamin), (Jr.). *The Young and Hungry-Hearted.* New York: New American Library, 1955. 127pp.

105. Clevely, Hugh [Tod Claymore, pseud.]. *Appointment in New Orleans.* Baltimore, Md.: Penguin Books, 1955. 215pp.

244. Jackson, Charles Tenney. *New Orleans Adventure: A Story of the Last Romantic Flicker of Piracy-Privateering in the Gulf and New Orleans of the 1830s.* Philadelphia: Dorrance, 1955. 261pp.

271. Kent, Madeleine Fabiola. *The Corsair: A Biographical Novel of Jean Lafitte, Hero of the Battle of New Orleans.* Garden City, N.Y.: Doubleday, 1955. 299pp.

327. Masters, Kelly Ray [Zachary Ball, pseud.]. *Bar Pilot.* Illustrated by Arthur Shilstone. New York: Holiday House, 1955. 218pp.

349. Murphy, Edward F(rancis). *Bride for New Orleans.* Garden City, N.Y.: Hanover House, 1955. 313pp.

475. Warren, Robert Penn. *Band of Angels.* New York: Random House, 1955. 375pp.

480. Wellman, Manly Wade. *Flag on the Levee.* Illustrated by William Ferguson. New York: Ives Washburn, 1955. 209pp.

1. Abaunza, Virginia. *Sundays from Two to Six.* Indianapolis: Bobbs-Merrill, 1956. 222pp.

3. Algren, Nelson. *A Walk on the Wild Side.* New York: Farrar, Straus, and Cudahy, 1956. 346pp.

42. Bell, Sallie Lee. *Torchbearer.* Grand Rapids, Mich.: Zondervan, 1956. 185pp.

140. Delmar, Viña. *Beloved.* New York: Harcourt, Brace, 1956. 382pp.

188. Fortmayer, Aenida V. Gonzalez. *Came a Gentleman.* New York: Vantage, 1956. 287pp.

445. Tallant, Robert. *The Voodoo Queen: A Novel.* New York: Putnam, 1956. 314pp.

509. Yerby, Frank. *Captain Rebel.* New York: Dial, 1956. 343pp.

268. Keene, Carolyn [house pseudonym]. *The Haunted Showboat.* New York: Grosset and Dunlap, 1957. 184pp.

389. Riordan, Robert. *The Lady and the Pirate.* Milwaukee, Wisc.: Bruce, 1957. 182pp.

398. Rogér, Katherine Harvey. *Always the River.* New Orleans: Pelican, 1957. 243pp.

467. Vinton, Iris. *We Were There with Jean Lafitte at New Orleans.* Illustrated by Robert Glaubke. New York: Grosset and Dunlap, 1957. 182pp.

500. Williams, Wirt. *Love in a Windy Space.* New York: Reynal, 1957. 241pp.

514. Yoseloff, Martin. *Lily and the Sergeant.* New York: Funk and Wagnalls, 1957. 250pp.

38. Bell, Sallie Lee. *The Long Search.* Grand Rapids, Mich.: Zondervan, 1958. 194pp.

41. Bell, Sallie Lee. *The Silver Cord.* Grand Rapids, Mich.: Zondervan, 1958. 216pp.

127. Crossen, Kendell Foster [M.E. Chaber, pseud.]. *A Hearse of Another Color.* New York: Rinehart, 1958. 250pp.

178. Faulkner, William. *New Orleans Sketches.* Edited by Carvel Collins. New Brunswick, N.J.: Rutgers University, 1958. 223pp.

181. Feibleman, Peter S. *A Place Without Twilight.* Cleveland, Ohio: World, 1958. 382pp.

348. Murphy, Edward F(rancis). *Angel of the Delta.* New York: Hanover House, 1958. 311pp.

512. Yerby, Frank. *The Serpent and the Staff.* New York: Dial, 1958. 377pp.

37. Bell, Sallie Lee. *The Last Surrender.* Grand Rapids, Mich.: Zondervan, 1959. 183pp.

70. Cable, George Washington. *Creoles and Cajuns: Stories of Old Louisiana.* Edited by Arlin Turner. Garden City, N.Y.: Doubleday, 1959. 432pp.

302. Lipscomb, Marie Lauve. *The Lost Treasure.* Grand Rapids, Mich.: Zondervan, 1959. 118pp.

489. Whitney, Phyllis A(yame). *Creole Holiday.* Philadelphia: Westminster, 1959. 206pp.

499. Williams, Wirt. *Ada Dallas.* New York: McGraw-Hill, 1959. 328pp.

36. Bell, Sallie Lee. *The Hidden Treasure.* Grand Rapids, Mich.: Zondervan, 1960. 159pp.

124. Coxe, George Harmon. *One Way Out.* New York: Knopf, 1960. 214pp.

171. Emery, Anne. *A Spy in Old New Orleans.* Illustrated by Emil Weiss. New York: Rand McNally, 1960. 237pp.

231. Hoerner, Aline. *Song of the Bayou.* New York: Vantage, 1960. 135pp.

272.    Keyes, Frances Parkinson. *The Chess Players: A Novel of New Orleans and Paris.* New York: Farrar, Straus and Cudahy, 1960. 533pp.

128.    Crossen, Kendall Foster [Clay Richards, pseud.]. *The Marble Jungle.* New York: I. Obolensky, 1961. 183pp.

141.    Delmar, Viña. *The Big Family.* New York: Harcourt, Brace, 1961. 375pp.

199.    Grau, Shirley Ann. *The House on Coliseum Street.* New York: Knopf, 1961. 242pp.

292.    LaScola, Ray(mond). *The Creole.* New York: William Morrow, 1961. 311pp.

376.    Percy, Walker. *The Moviegoer.* New York: Knopf, 1961. 241pp.

381.    Pretorius (Kouts), Hertha. *Tallien's Children.* New York: Appleton-Century-Crofts, 1961. 344pp.

14.    Arguedas, Janet Wogan [Anne Labranche, pseud.]. *The Last Days of Oak Lane Plantation.* Illustrated by Warren J. Guthrie. New Orleans: Laborde and Sons, 1962. 136pp.

81.    Cain, James M(allahan). *Mignon.* New York: Dial Press, 1962. 246pp.

166.    Edmunds, (Thomas) Murrell. *Passionate Journey to Winter.* New York: T. Yoseloff, 1962. 156pp.

275.    Keyes, Frances Parkinson. *Madame Castel's Lodger.* New York: Farrar, Straus and Cudahy, 1962. 471pp.

325.    Massicot, Norita (Newman) [Norita, pseud.]. *The Beasts, the Sheep, and the Chariots.* Baton Rouge, La.: The Author, 1962. 88pp.

338.    McHale, Larry. *Dark Shadows.* Philadelphia: Dorrance, 1962. 269pp.

363.    Onstott, Kyle. *Drum.* New York: Dial Press, 1962. 502pp.

57.    Breslin, Howard. *Concert Grand.* New York: Dodd, Mead, 1963. 307pp.

65.    Bryan, Jack Yeaman. *Come to the Bower.* New York: Viking, 1963. 496pp.

253.    Janssen, Milton W. *Divided.* New York: Pageant, 1963. 141pp.

269.    Kelly, Regina Zimmerman. *New Orleans: Queen of the River.* Chicago: Reilly and Lee, 1963. 176pp.

326.    Massicot, Norita. *The Refugees.* Boston: Christopher, 1963. 223pp.

15.    Arguedas, Janet Wogan [Anne Labranche, pseud.]. *The Vow: Romance of Old New Orleans.* New Orleans: Laborde and Sons, 1964. 338pp.

261.    Judson, Jeanne [Frances Dean Hancock, pseud.]. *The Flowering Vine.* New York: Avalon Books, 1964. 192pp.

45.     Blake, Christopher Stanislas. *The Fair Fair Ladies of Chartres Street.* New Orleans: Beale Press, 1965. 189pp.

122.    Cowdrey, A(lbert) E(dward). *Elixir of Life: An Historical Novel of New Orleans.* Garden City, N.Y.: Doubleday, 1965. 270pp.

159.    Duralde, H. Eduardo. *Louisiana: A Tale of the Old South.* New York: Exposition, 1965. 304pp.

208.    Hailey, Arthur. *Hotel.* Garden City, N.Y.: Doubleday, 1965. 346pp.

218.    Handl, Irene. *The Sioux.* New York: New American Library, 1965. 308pp.

414.    Snelling, Laurence. *The Return of Lance Tennis.* New York: Holt, Rinehart and Winston, 1965. 189pp.

40.     Bell, Sallie Lee. *The Promise.* Grand Rapids, Mich.: Zondervan, 1966. 147pp.

109.    Collier, Julia. *Pirates of Barataria.* Illustrated by Judith Ann Lawrence. New York: Putnam, 1966. 158pp.

182.    Feibleman, Peter S. *Strangers and Graves.* New York: Atheneum, 1966. 351pp.

202.    Grethe, James. *Misses, Martyrs, Mayhem.* New York: Vantage, 1966. 172pp.

355.    Nixon, Joan Lowery. *Mystery of the Hidden Cockatoo.* Illustrated by Richard Lewis. New York: Criterion, 1966. 144pp.

429.    Stone, Robert. *A Hall of Mirrors.* Boston: Houghton Mifflin, 1966. 409pp.

435.    Swann, Francis. *Royal Street.* New York: Lancer, 1966. 174pp.

438.    Tait, Dorothy [Ann Fairbairn, pseud.]. *Five Smooth Stones.* New York: Crown, 1966. 756pp.

120.    Corrington, John William. *The Upper Hand.* New York: Putnam, 1967. 383pp.

190.    Foster, John T(homas). *Marco and the Tiger.* Illustrated by Lorence F. Bjorklund. New York: Dodd, Mead, 1967. 127pp.

270.    Kelly, Regina Zimmerman. *One Flag, One Land.* Illustrated by Wendy Kemp. Chicago: Reilly and Lee, 1967. 115pp.

319.    Martin, Fleming. *Despair in a Creole Garden.* New York: Vantage Press, 1967. 204pp.

344.    Mitchell, Carl. *Walk the Gay Night.* Van Nuys, Calif.: Triumph, 1967. 158pp.

347. Morrow, Susan. *The Insiders.* Garden City, N.Y.: Doubleday / Crime Club, 1967. 191pp.

508. Yates, Dorothy. *The Family Tree: A Novel.* New York: Farrar, Straus and Giroux, 1967. 184pp.

87. Carr, John Dickson. *Papa Lá-Bas.* New York: Harper and Row, 1968. 277pp.

195. Gerson, Noel Betram [Carter A. Vaughan, pseud.]. *The River Devils.* Garden City, N.Y.: Doubleday, 1968. 239pp.

459. Tressner, William B. *Queens of the Quarter.* San Diego, Calif.: Publishers Export, 1968. 151pp.

86. Carr, John Dickson. *The Ghosts' High Noon.* New York: Harper and Row, 1969. 255pp.

186. Fisher, Steve. *Saxon's Ghost.* Los Angeles: Sherbourne, 1969. 211pp.

189. Foster, John T(homas). *Marco and the Sleuth Hound.* Illustrated by Lorence F. Bjorklund. New York: Dodd, Mead, 1969. 153pp.

226. Hicks, John (Kenneth). *The Long Whip.* New York: David McKay, 1969. 344pp.

436. Sweet, George Elliot. *The Petroleum Saga.* Los Angeles: Science, 1969. 230pp.

111. Conaway, James. *The Big Easy.* Boston: Houghton, Mifflin, 1970. 216pp.

130. Cushman, Jerome. *Tom B. and the Joyful Noise.* Illustrated by Cal Massey. Philadelphia: Westminster, 1970. 110pp.

12. Ansell, Jack. *Jelly.* New York: Arbor House, 1971. 221pp.

64. Brown, Joe David. *Addie Pray.* New York: Simon and Schuster, 1971. 308pp.

85. Carr, John Dickson. *Deadly Hall.* New York: Harper and Row, 1971. 251pp.

136. Decoin, Didier. *Laurence: A Love Story.* Translated from the French by Helen Eustis. New York: Coward, McCann, and Geoghegan, 1971. 156pp.

179. Feibleman, James K(ern). *Great April.* New York: Horizon, 1971. 267pp.

198. Grau, Shirley Ann. *The Condor Passes.* New York: Knopf, 1971. 421pp.

194. Genois, Renald H(enry). *Forge of Destiny.* New York: Vantage, 1972. 337pp.

227. Higginbotham, (Prieur) Jay. *Brother Holyfield.* New York: Thomas-Hull, 1972. 377pp.

290. L'Amour, Louis. *Treasure Mountain.* New York: Bantam Books, 1972. 187pp.

418. Spencer, Elizabeth. *The Snare.* New York: McGraw-Hill, 1972. 407pp.

423.   St. Cyr, Sylvester. *The Saint and Sinners*. New York: Vantage, 1972. 158pp.

483.   Welty, Eudora. *The Optimist's Daughter*. New York: Random House, 1972. 180pp.

511.   Yerby, Frank. *The Girl from Storyville: A Victorian Novel*. New York: Dial, 1972. 476pp.

44.    Biery, William. *The House on Esplanade*. New York: Mason and Lipscomb, 1973. 216pp.

131.   Daniels, Dorothy Smith. *The Duncan Dynasty*. New York: Warner Paperback Library, 1973. 190pp.

192.   Garfield, Dick. *Mardi Gras Madness*. Chatsworth, Calif.: GX, 1973. 185pp.

245.   Jacobs, Howard. *Charlie the Mole and other Droll Souls*. Illustrated by Eldon Pletcher. Gretna, La.: Pelican, 1973. 152pp.

337.   McCurtin, Peter. *The Assassin; New Orleans Holocaust*. New York: Dell, Lorelei Publications, 1973. 191pp.

49.    Bouchon, Henry L. *Beyond Indecency: A Novel*. New Orleans: Roy L. Wilson Printing, 1974. 197pp.

169.   Ellis, Julie. *Kara*. New York: Dell books, 1974. 271pp.

185.   Finley (Witte), Glenna. *Love's Magic Spell*. New York: New American Library, 1974. 197pp.

219.   Harrington, Dare. *Fun Was Where You Found It*. Jericho, N.Y.: Exposition, 1974. 130pp.

331.   Maxwell, Patricia. *The Court of the Thorn Tree*. New York: Popular Library, 1974. 253pp.

374.   Pendleton, Don. *The Executioner: New Orleans Knockout*. New York: Pinnacle Books, 1974. 178pp.

415.   Snelling, Laurence. *The Temptation of Archer Watson*. New York: Norton, 1974. 240pp.

465.   Veillon, Lee. *Hart*. New York: Harper and Row, 1974. 168pp.

495.   Wilkes-Hunter, Richard Albert [Diana Douglas, pseud.]. *New Orleans Nurse*. New York: New American Library, 1974. 157pp.

68.    Butterworth, W(illiam) E(dmund), (III). *M\*A\*S\*H Goes to New Orleans*. Based on characters developed by W(ilfred) C(harles Heinz and Richard Hornberger under the joint pseudonym Richard Hooker. New York: Pocket Books, 1975. 189pp.

168.   Ellis, Julie. *Eden*. New York: Simon and Schuster, 1975. 350pp.

212.   Hall, Georgette Brockman. *The Sicilian*. Gretna, La.: Pelican, 1975. 264pp.

213.   Hallbing, Kjell [Louis Masterson, pseud.]. *New Orleans Gamble*. Translated from the Norwegian by Jeffrey M. Wallman. London: Corgi, 1975. 110pp.

220.   Harris, Thomas. *Black Sunday*. New York: Putnam, 1975. 318pp.

7.     Amoss, Berthe. *The Chalk Cross*. New York: Seabury Press, 1976. 150pp.

119.   Cooper, Parley J. *Dark Desires*. New York: Pocket Books, 1976. 312pp.

237.   Huff, T(om) E(lmer) [Jennifer Wilde, pseud.]. *Love's Tender Fury*. New York: Warner Brothers, 1976. 466pp.

246.   Jahncke, Carol Saunders. *Louisiana Visit*. Illustrated by Yvonne Voorthuysen. New York: Carlton, 1976. 94pp.

329.   Matthews, Clayton Hartley. *New Orleans: A Novel*. New York: Pocket Books, 1976. 223pp.

362.   Ondaatje, Michael. *Coming through Slaughter*. New York: Norton, 1976. 156pp.

388.   Rice, Anne. *Interview with the Vampire: A Novel*. New York: Knopf, 1976. 371pp.

492.   Wibberley, Leonard (Patrick) (O'Connor). *The Last Battle*. New York: Farrar, Straus and Giroux, 1976. 197pp.

104.   Cleaver, Anastasia N. [Natasha Peters, pseud.]. *Savage Surrender*. New York: Ace Books, 1977. 600pp.

114.   Conway, Theresa. *Gabrielle*. Greenwich, Conn.: Fawcett Books, 1977. 510pp.

160.   Eads, William J. *Listen to the Termites*. New York: Vantage, 1977. 582pp.

170.   Ellis, Julie. *Savage Oaks*. New York: Simon and Schuster, 1977. 345pp.

203.   Grice, Julia. *Lovefire*. New York: Avon Books, 1977. 373pp.

254.   Johnson, Barbara Ferry. *Delta Blood*. New York: Avon, 1977. 407pp.

257.   Joseph, Robert F(arras). *Odile*. New York: Ballantine, 1977. 437pp.

304.   Little, Paul H(ugo) [Marie De Jourlet, pseud.]. *Storm Over Windhaven*. Los Angeles: Pinnacle Books, 1977. 528pp.

332.   Maxwell, Patricia. *The Notorious Angel*. Greenwich, Conn.: Fawcett, 1977. 384pp.

333.   Maxwell, Patricia [Jennifer Blake, pseud.]. *Love's Wild Desire*. New York: Popular Library, 1977. 384pp.

345.   Moon, Ilanon. *Twilight on the River*. Austin, Tex.: Shoal Creek, 1977. 223pp.

375.    Percy, Walker. *Lancelot*. New York: Farrar, Straus and Giroux. 1977. 257pp.

382.    Prose, Francine. *Marie Laveau*. New York: Berkley, 1977. 342pp.

416.    Sparkia, Roy Bernard [Mitchell Caine, pseud.]. *Creole Surgeon*. Greenwich, Conn.: Fawcett / Gold Medal, 1977. 446pp.

422.    Statham, Frances Patton. *The Flame of New Orleans*. Greenwich, Conn.: Fawcett, 1977. 447pp.

51.     Bowden, Jean [Barbara Annandale, pseud.]. *The French Lady's Lover*. New York: Coward, McCann and Geoghegan, 1978. 288pp.

112.    Conaway, James. *World's End*. New York: William Morrow, 1978. 323pp.

214.    Hallman, Ruth. *Gimme Something, Mister!* Philadelphia: Westminster, 1978. 103pp.

223.    Harrison, William. *Pretty Baby*. New York: Bantam Books, 1978 184pp.

303.    Little, Paul H(ugo) [Marie De Jourlet, pseud.]. *Return to Windhaven*. Los Angeles: Pinnacle Books, 1978. 552pp.

321.    Martin, Valerie. *Set in Motion*. New York: Farrar, Straus and Giroux, 1978. 209pp.

334.    Maxwell, Patricia [Maxine Patrick, pseud.]. *Bayou Bride*. New York: New American Library, 1978. 171pp.

401.    Ross, William Edward Daniel [Marilyn Ross, pseud.]. *Delta Flame*. New York: Popular Library, 1978. 448pp.

8.      Amoss, Berthe. *Secret Lives*. Boston: Little, Brown, 1979. 180pp.

24.     Barron, Ann Forman [Annabel Erwin, pseud.]. *Aurielle*. New York: Warner, 1979. 461pp.

106.    Cline, C(harles) Terry, Jr. *Cross Current*. Garden City, N.Y.: Doubleday, 1979. 299pp.

116.    Cook, Petronelle Marguerite Mary [Margot Arnold, pseud.]. *Marie*. New York: Pocket Books, 1979. 486pp.

163.    Eberhart, Mignon Good. *The Bayou Road*. New York: Random House, 1979. 231pp.

236.    Huff, Lawrence. *Dome*. New York: Pocket Books, 1979. 296pp.

255.    Johnson, Barbara Ferry. *Homeward Winds the River*. New York: Avon Books, 1979. 471pp.

305.    Llewellyn, Michael [Maggie Lyons, pseud.]. *Bayou Passions*. New York: Jove/Harcourt, Brace, Jovanovich, 1979. 383pp.

320.   Martin, Valerie. *Alexandra.* New York: Farrar, Straus and Giroux, 1979. 179pp.

378.   Perko, Margaret (Snyder). *The Other Side of Silence.* New York: Leisure Books, 1979. 285pp.

387.   Rice, Anne. *The Feast of All Saints.* New York: Simon and Schuster, 1979. 571pp.

469.   Walker, Mary Alexander. *To Catch a Zombi.* New York: Atheneum, 1979. 193pp.

498.   Williams, Moses. *Shadows of a City Care Forgotten.* New York: Vantage, 1979. 206pp.

503.   Woodiwiss, Kathleen E(rin). *Ashes in the Wind.* New York: Avon, 1979. 665pp.

56.    Braun, Matthew. *The Stuart Women.* New York: Putnam, 1980. 362pp.

90.    Catling, Patrick Skene. *Jazz, Jazz, Jazz: A Novel.* London: Blond and Briggs, 1980. 320pp.

180.   Feibleman, Peter S. *Charlie Boy.* Boston: Little, Brown, 1980. 362pp.

252.   Janas, Frankie-Lee (Salliee O'Brien, pseud.]. *Black Ivory.* New York: Bantam Books, 1980. 354pp.

341.   Michaels, Irene. *Frenchman's Mistress.* New York: Dell, 1980. 432pp.

364.   Osborn, Pete H. *The Morals of a Tomcat.* Gretna, La.: Her, 1980. 185pp.

456.   Toole, John Kennedy. *A Confederacy of Dunces.* Baton Rouge, La.: Louisiana State University, 1980. 338pp.

472.   Waller, Leslie. *Blood and Dreams.* New York: Putnam, 1980. 344pp.

490.   Whittington, Harry [Ashley Carter, pseud.]. *Scandal of Falconhurst.* New York: Fawcett / Gold Medal, 1980. 446pp.

493.   Widmer, Mary Lou. *Night Jasmine.* New York: Dell, 1980. 479pp.

# Index

The numbers refer to entries, not page numbers.

# About the Author

**James A. Kaser**, professor and archivist at the College of Staten Island/CUNY, has worked as an archivist and special collections librarian since 1991. He is also the author of *The Chicago of Fiction: A Research Guide* (Lanham, Md.: The Scarecrow Press, 2011), *The Washington, D.C. of Fiction: A Research Guide* (Lanham, Md.: The Scarecrow Press, 2006) and *At the Bivouac of Memory: History, Politics, and the Battle of Chickamauga*. New York: Peter Lang, 1996. Kaser is a magna cum laude, Phi Beta Kappa, graduate of Kenyon College and earned a master's degree in library science from Kent State University and a master's degree and doctorate from Bowling Green State University in American culture studies.